Georgia Ballards

Compiled by

Lynne D. Miller
Email: LMiller603@aol.com

Revised July 2019

Books by Lynne D. Miller
Email: LMiller603@aol.com

Deer - Miller Lineage
The Maupin Family
Alabama - Louisiana - Mississippi Ballards
Arkansas Ballards
Georgia Ballards
Illinois Ballards
Indiana Ballards
Iowa Ballards
Kentucky Ballards
Owen County Kentucky Families
Massachusetts Ballards
Michigan, Wisconsin, Minnesota Ballards
Missouri Ballards
New Jersey, Connecticut, Rhode Island, Maryland, Maine, New Hamp. and Vermont Ballards
New York Ballards
Ohio and Pennsylvania
South Carolina Ballards
Tennessee Ballards
Texas Ballards
Bland Ballard Family
Curtis Ballard and Esther Gaines
Humphrey Gaines and Sarah Watts
John Ballard and Basheba
Larkin Ballard & Elizabeth Rebecca Gaines
Philip Ballard and Ann Nancy Johnson
Richard Ballard and & Ulsey Hubbard
Thomas Watts and Esther Stone
Thomas Ballard and Anne Thomas
William Ballard and Elizabeth Steppe
William and Philadelphia Ballard

VIRGINIA BOOKS

VA Wyatt - Ballard - Smith Family Descendants
Virginia Ballard Families
Early Virginia Families

NORTH CAROLINA BOOKS

Buncombe County NC Ballards
Lincoln County NC Ballards
North Carolina Ballards

Introduction

This book is a Work in Progress and subject to revision as new information becomes available. Corrections and additions are very much appreciated with supporting documentation.

I've attempted to use original spellings found on the legal documents. Census records will often show wrong spellings.

Lynne D. Miller

Table of Contents

Benjamin Ballard

Generation No. 1

1. BENJAMIN[4] BALLARD (JOHN[3], JOSEPH[2], JOHN[1]) was born 27 Feb 1742/43 in Princess Anne Co., VA, and died 16 Jun 1832 in Morgan Co., GA. He married KATHERINE HAMMOND Bet. 1778 - 1780 in Orangeburg Co., GA. She was born Abt. 1760 in Orangeburg Co., GA, and died 10 Jun 1844 in Madison Co., GA.

Notes for BENJAMIN BALLARD:
Source: Jan M. Ballard (72753.3121@compuserve.com), Janiece Keener (kenkeener@pdq.net), kaelmc@tenet.edu (Karen McClendon), Men of Mark in Georgia, The Baptist Biography by Balus Joseph Winzer Graham
* Karen McClendon found 9 pages of notes--written by the Honorable N. H. Ballard of Atlanta in 1928 while in Salt Lake. He (N H Ballard), mentions a German Protestant Settlement on Kemps Creek in Wilkes Co, GA, c1800. They had been part of the Londonderry Colony at Hard Labor Creek in the south portion of Abbeville District, S C, c1764-1768. Katherine's father was Abraham Herman, a name that was changed to Harmon, Hammon or Hammond. She had a sister named Susie who married 1) James Bently and 2) Robert Shaw. Abraham had a brother named John Herman. One of the brothers married Adeline Sibert, a daughter in another of these German families. A John Sibert founded St. George's Lutheran Church at Hard Labor Creek in S. C. Lincoln Co, GA is also mentioned.

* 1783 - Moved to Cam Creek, Wilkes Co., GA

* 1820 - Living in Morgan Co., GA - Ballard, Benjamin -
Free White Persons - Males - Under 10 - 1, Free White Persons - Males - 10 thru 15 - 1
Free White Persons - Males - 16 thru 25 -1, Free White Persons - Males - 26 thru 44 - 2
Free White Persons - Males - 45 and over - 1, Free White Persons - Fem - 26 thru 44 -1
Free White Persons - Females - 45 and over - 1, Slaves - Males - Under 14 - 2
Slaves - Males - 26 thru 44 -2, Slaves - Females - Under 14 - 3
Slaves - Females - 26 thru 44 - 3, Slaves - Females - 45 and over 1
Free White Persons - Under 16 - 2, Free White Persons - Over 25 - 5
Total Free White Persons, 8 Total Slaves 11 -
Total All Persons - White, Slaves, Colored, Other19

* 1830 - Living in Morgan Co., GA - Ballard, Benjamin -
Free White Persons - Males - 20 thru 29 - 1, Free White Persons - Males - 30 thru 39 - 1,
Free White Persons - Males - 80 thru 89 -1, Free White Persons - Females - 30 thru 39 1
Free White Persons - Females - 60 thru 69 -- 1, Slaves - Males - Under 10 - 5
Slaves - Males - 10 thru 23 - 1. Slaves - Males - 36 thru 54 - 1
Slaves - Females - Under 10 - 4. Slaves - Females - 10 thru 23 - 2
Slaves - Females - 24 thru 35 - 3, Slaves - Females - 36 thru 54 -1
Free White Persons - 20 thru 49 - 3,   Total Free White Persons - 5
Total Slaves17   Total - All Persons 22

Notes for KATHERINE HAMMOND:

Source: Charles Barham papers

Children of BENJAMIN BALLARD and KATHERINE HAMMOND are:

2.   i.   SILAS JOSEPH HARDY[5] BALLARD, b. 1781, of VA and NC; d. 1840, Montgomery Co., AL.
        ii.   JANE "JENNIE" BALLARD, b. 1783; m. JAMES WOODS, 25 Feb 1808, Wilkes Co., GA; b. Abt. 1780.
3.   iii. JOSHUA BALLARD, b. 1783, of Wilkes Morgan, Gwinnett and Campbell Co., GA; d. 13 Mar 1860, Campbell Co., GA.
        iv.   MARY BALLARD, b. Abt. 1784, GA; m. (1) WILLIAM BARFIELD, Sunny Side, Spalding Co, GA; m. (2) WASHINGTON GREENE.
4.   v.   JOHN BALLARD, b. 1790, Temple, Carroll Co, GA; d. 1874, GA.

5.	vi.	*JESSE BALLARD, b. 1796, GA; d. 1874, Morgan Co., GA.*
	vii.	*REBECCA BALLARD, b. 1796, GA.*
6.	viii.	*WILLIAM BALLARD, b. 1807, Morgan Co, GA; d. Aft. 1870.*
7.	ix.	*GEORGE WASHINGTON GREENE BALLARD, DR., b. 14 Nov 1810, GA; d. 21 Aug 1882, Madison Co., GA.*

Generation No. 2

2. *SILAS JOSEPH HARDY[5] BALLARD (BENJAMIN[4], JOHN[3], JOSEPH[2], JOHN[1]) was born 1781 in of VA and NC, and died 1840 in Montgomery Co., AL. He married TEMPERANCE "ANNE" TABITHA 1810. She was born 1785 in GA or SC, and died Abt. 1865.*

Notes for SILAS JOSEPH HARDY BALLARD:
Source: 1830-1850, Montgomery County Alabama Federal Census records, Jan M. Ballard (72753.3121@compuserve.com), The Andalusia Star News dated April 4, 1998 submitted by Jan Ballard, Libb (libb@alaweb.com), 1860 Covington County Alabama Federal Census Records
*NOTE - It is possible that there are two separate but incorrectly merged families listed in this grouping.

* YDNA results show that Benjamin Randall Ballard and Jonathan O Ballard descendants are not related to this family but carry the Herring YDNA. It's possible that Benjamin and Jonathan are his natural sons but their descendants are not related. Not knowing the complete story, I am including their branch for now.

Notes for TEMPERANCE "ANNE" TABITHA:
Source: 1850-1860 Covington County Alabama Federal Census Records
* 1850 - Living in Covington Co., AL - Ballard, Temperance 65 SC, Tabitha 32 NC, Ivins 29 farmer AL, Manda 10 AL
* 1860 - Living in Covington Co., AL - Ballard, Temperance 74 SC, Tabitha 46 (living next door to son Benjamin "Randall" Ballard

More About TEMPERANCE "ANNE" TABITHA:
Burial: Oakey Streak Methodist Church Cemetery

Children of SILAS BALLARD and TEMPERANCE TABITHA are:

8.	i.	*DAVID A.[6] BALLARD, b. 1805, GA; d. Aft. 1866.*
9.	ii.	*JOHN S. BALLARD, b. 1810, GA; d. Bef. Jul 1860, Montgomery Co., AL.*
10.	iii.	*BENJAMIN RANDALL BALLARD, b. 11 Apr 1811, NC; d. 15 Feb 1890, Oakey Streak, Covington Co., AL.*
11.	iv.	*MARY ANN BALLARD, b. Abt. 1812.*
12.	v.	*WILLIAM W. BALLARD, b. Bet. 1812 - 1813, GA; d. Aft. 1850.*
13.	vi.	*JONATHAN O. BALLARD, DR., b. 1813, SC; d. Abt. 1855, Crenshaw Co., AL.*
	vii.	*EVAN JOSHUA BALLARD, b. 1821, AL; d. Aft. 1850, moved to TX.*
14.	viii.	*TEMPERANCE TABITHA BALLARD, b. 22 Oct 1821, Conecuh Co., AL; d. 05 Mar 1898, Jun 13, 1897 AL.*
15.	ix.	*SILAS H. BALLARD, b. 22 Oct 1823, AL; d. 01 Jan 1906, TX.*
	x.	*PERMELIA ANN BALLARD, b. Abt. 1828; m. JOSEPH B. HEWES, 29 Mar 1845, Montgomery Co., AL; b. Abt. 1828.*

3. *JOSHUA[5] BALLARD (BENJAMIN[4], JOHN[3], JOSEPH[2], JOHN[1]) was born 1783 in of Wilkes Morgan, Gwinnett and Campbell Co., GA, and died 13 Mar 1860 in Campbell Co., GA. He married ELIZABETH "BETSEY" BRYANT 11 Feb 1812 in Morgan Co., GA, daughter of WILLIAM BRYANT and ELIZABETH BARNETT. She was born Abt. 1785 in GA, and died 17 Aug 1854 in Campbell Co., GA.*

Notes for JOSHUA BALLARD:
Source: 1850 Campbell County Georgia Federal Census Records, The Baptist Biography by Balus Joseph Winzer Graham

* 1850 - Living in Campbell Co., GA - Ballard, Joshua 67 farmer GA, Elizabeth 56 GA, Armstead 30 GA, Abram 27 GA, Obadiah 22 GA, Levi 22 GA, Polly Canady 22 GA, Amanda Blakely 11 GA, Lucretia Blackmon 6 GA

More About JOSHUA BALLARD:
Burial: Old Bryant Place, Rico, Campbell Co., GA

More About ELIZABETH "BETSEY" BRYANT:
Burial: Old Bryant Place, Rico, Campbell Co., GA

Children of JOSHUA BALLARD and ELIZABETH BRYANT are:

> i. ELIZABETH[6] BALLARD, b. Abt. 1813, GA; d. moved to Obion Co., TN; m. ANDREW GRIFFITH; b. Abt. 1810.
>
> *Notes for ANDREW GRIFFITH:*
> *Moved to Obion Co, TN*
>
> ii. GEORGE W. BALLARD, b. Abt. 1815, GA; d. 07 Feb 1850, Campbell Co., GA.
>
> *More About GEORGE W. BALLARD:*
> *Burial: Ballard Cemetery Campbell Co., GA*

16.	iii.	ELIJAH BALLARD, b. 1815, GA; d. 1883.
17.	iv.	ARMISTEAD BALLARD, b. 07 Aug 1819, GA; d. 13 Sep 1893.
18.	v.	MORTON BALLARD, b. 1821, GA; d. 02 Apr 1903, AR.
19.	vi.	OBEDIAH BALLARD, b. 1823, GA; d. 1894, Cleveland Co., AR.
	vii.	POLLY C. BALLARD, b. 1829, GA.
20.	viii.	ABRAHAM BALLARD, b. 1830, Gwinnett Co., GA; d. Aft. 1860, Civil War.
21.	ix.	LEVI BALLARD, b. 22 Nov 1833, Anniestown, Gwinnett Co., GA; d. 20 Mar 1921, Palmetto, Campbell Co., GA.

4. JOHN[5] BALLARD (BENJAMIN[4], JOHN[3], JOSEPH[2], JOHN[1]) *was born 1790 in Temple, Carroll Co, GA, and died 1874 in GA. He married MARY SCOTT REED 01 Jul 1819 in Putnam Co., GA. She was born 1804 in GA, and died Aft. 1870.*

Notes for JOHN BALLARD:
Source- Ballard-Ballord Bits pg 191 U-64, 1850-1870 Carroll County Federal Census Records
* 1850 - Living in Carroll Co., GA - Ballard, John 60 GA, Mary 46 GA, Wm. 20 GA, Catharine 17 GA, Sophronia 15 GA, Euphronius 13 GA
* 1860 - Living in Carroll Co., GA - Ballard, John 66 farmer GA, Mary 52 GA, Wm. W. 30 GA
* 1870 - Living in Carroll Co., GA - Ballard, John 79 GA, Mary 70 GA, William 36 GA

More About JOHN BALLARD:
Burial: Concord United Methodist Church Cemetery, Carrollton, Carroll Co., GA

Children of JOHN BALLARD and MARY REED are:

	i.	ADALINE[6] BALLARD, b. Abt. 1820; m. MR. DAVIS, TX.
	ii.	ELIZABETH "ELIZA SUE" ANN BALLARD, b. Abt. 1820; m. NOAH WHISENHUNT, 13 Sep 1840, Carroll Co., GA; b. Abt. 1814.
22.	iii.	AMANDA JANE BALLARD, b. Abt. 1822.
	iv.	LUCINDA A. "LOUISA" BALLARD, b. 18 Aug 1826, lived near Temple GA; d. 02 May 1923, Carroll Co., GA; m. ANDREW McCOLISTER, 15 Mar 1849, Carroll Co., GA; b. 24 Dec 1825; d. 14 Nov 1885, Carroll Co., GA.

Notes for LUCINDA A. "LOUISA" BALLARD:
Source: Carroll County Georgia Certificate of Death
* Death Certificate and Cemetery Records show McColister, not McAlister

More About LUCINDA A. "LOUISA" BALLARD:
Burial: Concord United Methodist Church Cemetery, Carrollton, Carroll Co., GA

Notes for ANDREW MCCOLISTER:
Source: Carroll County Georgia Wills
* His will names him as Andrew J. McCollister

More About ANDREW MCCOLISTER:
Burial: Concord United Methodist Church Cemetery, Carrollton, Carroll Co., GA

  v.   *FRANKLIN BALLARD, b. Abt. 1830, Civil War.*
  vi.   *TOM BALLARD, b. 1830, GA.*
  vii.   *WILLIAM W. BALLARD, b. 18 Apr 1830, GA; d. 16 Nov 1889.*

  More About WILLIAM W. BALLARD:
  Burial: County Line North Cemetery, Temple Carroll Co., GA

  viii.   *KATHERINE BALLARD, b. 1833, GA; d. Aft. 1850; m. JOHN C. MERRELL, 10 Feb 1859, Carroll Co., GA; b. Abt. 1833, of Cedartown Pole Co., GA.*
  ix.   *SOPHRONIA BALLARD, b. 1835, GA; d. Aft. 1850; m. WILLIAM MERRITT, Temple, GA; b. Abt. 1835.*
23.   x.   *EUPHRONIAS FRANKLIN BALLARD, b. 1837, GA; d. Aft. 1860.*

5.   *JESSE^5 BALLARD (BENJAMIN^4, JOHN^3, JOSEPH^2, JOHN^1) was born 1796 in GA, and died 1874 in Morgan Co., GA. He married (1) WINNIE BARFIELD Abt. 1821. She was born Abt. 1796, and died Bef. 1852. He married (2) NANCY FARROW 02 Feb 1852. She was born 09 Jun 1827 in GA, and died 09 Jul 1907.*

Notes for JESSE BALLARD:
Source: Ballard-Ballord Bits, 1860 - 1870 Morgan County Georgia Federal Census Records, Morgan County Georgia Wills pg 64, Land Records
* 1860 - Living in Morgan Co., GA - Ballard, Jesse 40 GA, Nancy 34 GA, Elizabeth 4 GA, Ida GA, Roan 1 GA
* 1867 - June 18 - Signed Oath book
* 1870 - Living in Morgan Co., GA - Ballard, Jesse 51 GA, Nancy 43 GA, Elizabeth 13 GA, Ida 12 GA, Roan 11 GA, George C 7 GA, Lenora 5 GA
* 1870 - Georgia - Morgan County - I - Jesse Ballard of the County of Morgan & State of Georgia being of Sound & disposing mind & memory but in feeble health & being desirous to Settle my worldly affairs, While I have Strenth (sic) So to do make & publish this my last Will & Testament hereby revoking all other Wills by me at any time heretofore made, my worldly Estate I dispose of as follows.
Item 1st - It is my Will & desire That all My Just debts be paid.
Item 2nd - It is My Will & desire; That all my Estate both real & personal remain in the possession of my beloved Wife for the Purpose of raising & Educating my five Minor children until the youngest child - Child shall arrive at the age of Twenty One Years or marriage - provided My Wife Should remain Single, in Case She Should marry it is My Will & desire That all of my Estate both real & personal Should be Sold & Equally divided among all my children & my grand children, The Children (sic repeat) The Children of my two deceased Sons Wm W Ballard & James Oliver Ballard to Each to have a childs parts.
Item 3rd - It is My Will & desire That My Executors hereinafter named after This my last Will & Testament is admitted & appraisement returned in Proper form they may not be required to Make annual returns of receipts & expenditures relying on My Wife to Manage my Estate to the best interest of herself & children.
Item 4th - I hereby Constitute & appoint my Son ? Mihon ? Ballard & My Wife Nancy Ballard My Executors to This My last Will & Testament. Signed Sealed & declared to be my last Will & Testament in the presence of William G Ballard, Joseph Nason, William Ballard 26th day of May 1870 Jesse Ballard (seal)

* 1873 - Morgan County Tax records - Jesse Ballard - 5 children under 18
* 1874 - At Chambers Feby 28 the 1874 - Before me in Person Came W. G Ballard & James Nason two of the Subscribing Witnesses to the Will in paper purporting to be the Last Will & Testament of Jesse Ballard, Who upon Oath Say that they Saw Jesse Ballard Sign & acknowledge The Within paper purporting to be the last Will & Testament in their presence & in the presence of the other Witness William Ballard & That all of the Witnesses in his presences & at his Special request Subscribed The Law proper as Witnesses & That the Said Jesse Ballard was at the time of Sound & disposing mind & memory, Sworn to & Subscribed, Washington G Ballard, Joseph Nason before me This day & date above Teste. W. Woods Ordinary

Notes for NANCY FARROW:
Source: 1880 Morgan County Georgia Federal Census Records
* 1880 - Living in Madison, Morgan Co., GA - Ballard, Nancy 53 widow GA, Elizabeth 24 GA, Ida 23 GA, Rowan W 21 RR conductor, George Colbert 18 farmer GA, Nora Lee 14 GA, Herman L 7 GA

More About NANCY FARROW:
Burial: Madison Historic Cemetery, Madison, Morgan Co., GA

Children of JESSE BALLARD and WINNIE BARFIELD are:
  i.   OLIVER[6] BALLARD.
  ii. WILSON BALLARD, b. Abt. 1823.

  Notes for WILSON BALLARD:
  In Civil War in Atlanta unit as a station master. DSP

24. iii. JAMES A. BALLARD, b. 1825; d. Bef. 1870.
     iv.   BENJAMIN BALLARD, b. 1827; d. 1860.
25. v.   WILLIAM W. BALLARD, b. 1829; d. Bef. 1860.
     vi.   JULIA BALLARD, b. 1834; m. JOHN C. GRIFFITH, 01 Sep 1852, Morgan Co., GA; b. of Spaulding Co., GA.
     vii. WASHINGTON G. BALLARD, b. 21 Apr 1836; d. 24 Jan 1857.

  More About WASHINGTON G. BALLARD:
  Burial: Madison Historic Cemetery, Madison, Morgan Co., GA

Children of JESSE BALLARD and NANCY FARROW are:
26. viii. ELIZABETH[6] BALLARD, b. 1856, GA; d. 1936.
     ix.   IDA BALLARD, b. 03 Apr 1857, GA; d. 19 Feb 1905; m. HUGH WEST; b. 27 Mar 1847; d. 07 Dec 1907.

  More About IDA BALLARD:
  Burial: Madison Historic Cemetery, Madison, Morgan Co., GA

  More About HUGH WEST:
  Burial: Madison Historic Cemetery, Madison, Morgan Co., GA

27. x.   ROAN B. BALLARD, b. 28 Feb 1860, lived in Waycross, Ware Co., GA; d. 16 Mar 1927, Ware Co., GA.
     xi.   GEORGE COLBERT BALLARD, b. 1862, GA; d. Aft. 1880.
28. xii. LENORA BALLARD, b. 07 Feb 1864, GA; d. 24 Apr 1946.
     xiii. HERMAN LEVERETTE BALLARD, b. 30 Apr 1873, GA; d. 11 Sep 1950.

  More About HERMAN LEVERETTE BALLARD:
  Burial: Madison Historic Cemetery, Madison, Morgan Co., GA

6. WILLIAM[5] BALLARD (BENJAMIN[4], JOHN[3], JOSEPH[2], JOHN[1]) was born 1807 in Morgan Co, GA, and died Aft. 1870. He married RUTHA A. SKIDMORE 10 Oct 1837 in Morgan Co., GA. She was born 1810 in GA, and died Aft. 1870.

Notes for WILLIAM BALLARD:
Source: 1850-1870 Morgan County Georgia Federal Census Records, Mary (MParker826@aol.com)
* William T. Ballard b. 1808 in GA CSA Army of N. VA 31st GA Regiment Co. D wounded at Chancellorsville
* 1850 - Living in Morgan Co., GA - Ballard, William 43 GA, Rutha A 40 GA, Henenetta A. 13 GA, Harriet Skidmore 15 GA, William B. Ballard 10, Albert D 8, Rutha L. 5 Georgianna 3
* 1860 - Living in Morgan Co., GA - Ballard, William 52 farmer GA, Rutha A. 47 GA, Albert 17 GA, Florine 14 GA, Georgianna 12, Osborn 9 GA
* 1870 - Living in Morgan Co., GA - (All these ages are way off. It's obvious the census taker didn't go to the house) Ballard, William 40 farmer GA, Rutha A. 35 GA, William T. 14, Florine 11 Osborn 7 GA

More About WILLIAM BALLARD:
Burial: Ballard Cemetery Morgan Co., GA

More About RUTHA A. SKIDMORE:
Burial: Ballard Cemetery Morgan Co., GA

Children of WILLIAM BALLARD and RUTHA SKIDMORE are:
	i.	HENRIETTA A[6] BALLARD, b. 1838, GA; d. Aft. 1870; m. J.T. CRAWFORD.
	ii.	HARRIETTA BALLARD, b. Abt. 1839, GA; d. Aft. 1860; m. MR SKIDORE.
	iii.	WILLIAM BALLARD, b. 1840, GA; d. Aft. 1870.
29.	iv.	ALBERT C. BALLARD, b. 1842, GA; d. Aft. 1900.
	v.	F. RUTHA BALLARD, b. 1845, GA; d. Aft. 1860; m. J. H. STOVALL; b. Abt. 1840.
	vi.	GEORGIANNA A. BALLARD, b. Bet. 1845 - 1848, GA; d. Aft. 1860; m. HARRIS NELSON.
30.	vii.	OSBORN S. BALLARD, b. 1850, GA; d. Aft. 1920.

7. GEORGE WASHINGTON GREENE[5] BALLARD, DR. (BENJAMIN[4], JOHN[3], JOSEPH[2], JOHN[1]) was born 14 Nov 1810 in GA, and died 21 Aug 1882 in Madison Co., GA. He married ELIZABETH TINSLEY POWELL 15 Dec 1846 in Morgan Co., GA, daughter of EVAN POWELL and HARRIETT UNDERWOOD. She was born 01 Nov 1826, and died 31 Jul 1882 in Madison Co., GA.

Notes for GEORGE WASHINGTON GREENE BALLARD, DR.:
Source: 1850-1880 Morgan County Georgia Federal Census Records

* 1846 - Georgia - Morgan County, To any Minister of the Gospel, Judge, Justice of the Inferior Court or Justice of the Pease; You are hereby authorized to join Washington G Ballard and miss Elizabeth T. Powell in the Holy State of Matrimony according to the Constitution and Law of the State; and for So doing this shall be your sufficient license: Givin Under My hand and Seal This Fourteenth day of December 1846. E. L. Witttich CCO
* 1847 - Georgia - Jasper County, I do hereby Certify that Washington G Ballard and Elizabeth T Powell were duly joined into the holy State of Matrimony by this Fifteenth day of December 1846/ Ernest l. Wittich M.G. Rendered January 27th 1847. E. L Wittich C.C.O.
* 1860 - Living in Morgan Co., GA - Washington G. 49 farmer GA, Elizabeth 33 GA, Charles 11 GA, Evon P. 10 GA, Adolphus 8 GA, Marion 6 GA, George H. 4 GA, Willie E. 3 GA, Jack P 1 GA
* 1870 - Living in Morgan Co., GA - Ballard, George W. 59 GA, Elizabeth 43 GA, Charles H. 21 Clerk GA, Evan F. 19 GA, Adolphus G. 17, Marion E. 15 GA, George W. 13 GA, Willy E. 12 GA, John. 10 GA, Anna C. 8 GA, B. Walter 7 GA, Bessy 3 GA
* 1880 - Living in Morgan Co., GA - Ballard, Washington 69 Retired Dentis (t) GA GA GA, Elizabeth 52 GA GA GA, Marion 28 GA farmer, George 24 GA, Willie 22 works on farm GA, Anna 18, Bessie 13

More About GEORGE WASHINGTON GREENE BALLARD, DR.:

Burial: Madison Historic Cemetery, Madison, Morgan Co., GA

More About ELIZABETH TINSLEY POWELL:
Burial: Madison Historic Cemetery, Madison, Morgan Co., GA

Children of GEORGE BALLARD and ELIZABETH POWELL are:

      i.   CHARLES HUDSON[6] BALLARD, b. 03 Mar 1849, GA; d. 19 May 1909, Duval Co., FL.

         More About CHARLES HUDSON BALLARD:
         Burial: Madison Historic Cemetery, Madison, Morgan Co., GA

31.   ii.   EVAN POWELL BALLARD, b. 13 Dec 1850, GA; d. 01 Jan 1899.
     iii. ANNA CORDELIA CAMAK BALLARD, b. 03 Nov 1860, GA; d. 12 Dec 1932, Madison Co,, GA.

         More About ANNA CORDELIA CAMAK BALLARD:
         Burial: Madison Historic Cemetery, Madison, Morgan Co., GA

     iv. ADOLPHUS GREENE BALLARD, b. 05 Jun 1852, GA; d. 04 Dec 1930.

         More About ADOLPHUS GREENE BALLARD:
         Burial: Madison Historic Cemetery, Madison, Morgan Co., GA

     v.   MARIAN ERNEST BALLARD, b. 28 Feb 1853, GA; d. 20 Dec 1928, Madison, Morgan Co., GA; m. PAULINE FOSTER, 18 Sep 1900, DeKalb Co., GA; b. 05 Aug 1870; d. 06 Jan 1932.

         Notes for MARIAN ERNEST BALLARD:
         Source: 1900 Morgan County Georgia Federal Census Record, Morgan County Georgia Local Registrar's Record of Death
         * 1900 - Living in Morgan Co., GA - Ballard, Marion - Feb 1854 56 farmer GA GA GA, George - brother - Mar 1856 - 44 wd GA, Willie nephew - Nov 1882 - 17 GA, Mabel niece - Oct 1884 - 17 GA, Lissy - niece - May 1888 - 12 GA, Earnice - nephew - Mar 1892 - 7 GA

         More About MARIAN ERNEST BALLARD:
         Burial: Madison Historic Cemetery, Madison, Morgan Co., GA

         Notes for PAULINE FOSTER:
         Source: 1930 Morgan County Georgia Federal Census Records
         * 1930 - Living in Madison, Morgan Co. GA - Ballard, Pauline 59 wd GA GA GA, Adolphus G - brother (actually his is her brother in law) 78 GA GA GA (Lenora Ballard Culpepper lives next door)

         More About PAULINE FOSTER:
         Burial: Madison Historic Cemetery, Madison, Morgan Co., GA

32.   vi. GEORGE HENRY BALLARD, b. 24 Mar 1856, GA; d. 03 Aug 1932, Monticello, Jasper Co, GA.
     vii. ELIZABETH "BESSY" TINSLEY BALLARD, b. 23 Mar 1867, GA; d. 23 Apr 1915; m. EVERT E. CLARK, DR., Jacksonville, Duval Co., FL; b. Abt. 1856; d. of Duval Co., FL.

         More About ELIZABETH "BESSY" TINSLEY BALLARD:
         Burial: Madison Historic Cemetery, Madison, Morgan Co., GA

33.   viii. WILLIAM "WILLIE" EDGAR BALLARD, b. 07 Jun 1857, GA; d. 30 Nov 1929, Monticello, Jasper Co., GA.
34.   ix. JOHN PORTER BALLARD, b. 1860, GA; d. Aft. 1870.
35.   x.   BENJAMIN WALTER BALLARD, b. 28 Jun 1863, Madison, GA; d. 26 Sep 1927, Atlanta, Fulton Co., GA.

Generation No. 3

8. DAVID A.[6] BALLARD (SILAS JOSEPH HARDY[5], BENJAMIN[4], JOHN[3], JOSEPH[2], JOHN[1]) *was born 1805 in GA, and died Aft. 1866. He married NANCY ANN SLAYTON 29 Aug 1831 in Morgan Co., GA. She was born Bet. 1813 - 1816 in GA, and died Aft. 1860.*

Notes for DAVID A. BALLARD:
Source: 1850 - 1860 Montgomery County Alabama Federal Census Records, 1866 Montgomery County Alabama State Census Records, Ron Head (ronhead@knology.net)

* 1850 - Living in Montgomery Co., AL - Ballard, David 45 GA, Nancy 34 GA, Wm. 15 GA, Cilus 12 AL, Rebecca 6 AL, Benj 3 AL, David 2 AL, Martha Ludlow 12 AL
* 1860 - Living in Montgomery Co., AL - Ballard, D.A. 54 overseer GA, N.A. 47 GA, Rebecca 17 GA, C.B. 15 AL, Joseph D. 9 AL, James 9 AL, W. H. 9 AL, MR H 6 AL
* 1866 - Living in Montgomery Co., AL - Ballard, David

Children of DAVID BALLARD and NANCY SLAYTON are:

- i. ELIZABETH[7] BALLARD, b. 1832; m. NATHAN HANKS, 22 Jan 1850, Montgomery Co., AL; b. Abt. 1830.
- ii. WILLIAM BALLARD, b. 1835, AL; d. Aft. 1850.
- iii. SILAS S. BALLARD, b. Bet. 1838 - 1844, AL; d. Aft. 1866; m. HARRIET S. DUCK, 16 May 1866, Montgomery Co., AL.
- iv. REBECCA BALLARD, b. Bet. 1842 - 1844, AL; d. Aft. 1860.
- v. BENJAMIN BALLARD, b. 1847, AL; d. Aft. 1850.
- vi. JOSEPH DAVID BALLARD, b. 1848, AL; d. Aft. 1860.
- vii. JAMES BALLARD, b. 1850, AL; d. Aft. 1860.
- viii. N. A. BALLARD, b. 1850.
- ix. M. A. H. BALLARD, b. 1853.

9. JOHN S.[6] BALLARD (SILAS JOSEPH HARDY[5], BENJAMIN[4], JOHN[3], JOSEPH[2], JOHN[1]) *was born 1810 in GA, and died Bef. Jul 1860 in Montgomery Co., AL. He married JANE ELIZABETH LEWIS 03 Jul 1833 in Montgomery Co., AL. She was born 29 Dec 1812 in Darlington Co., SC, and died 19 Aug 1881 in Montgomery Co., AL.*

Notes for JOHN S. BALLARD:
Source: Alice Ballard (bottleneck19@yahoo.com), 1850 Montgomery County Alabama Federal Census Records, Ron Head (ronhead@knology.net)

* 1850 - Living in Montgomery Co., AL - Ballard, John S. 40 farmer b. GA Jane E. 31 S.C., Elizabeth A. 14 AL; Jas. 12 AL; Mary A., 10 AL William 8 AL, Martha 6 AL; Permelia 4 AL, Zachariah 2 AL, Wesley Ludlow 23 - laborer.
* 1860 - Probate - Ballard, John S - Administrator's Notice of Final Settlement, in Estate of John S. Ballard, dec'd Administratrix Jane E Lord, Administrator. N. W. Lord. Probate Court, Aug 16, 1860 - Montgomery Weekly Mail, Montgomery, Ala, Sept. 7th 1860., p. 7 Co 2
(These were two different cards with similar information)
* 1860 - Probate - Ballard, John S. Estate of - Administrators' Notice of final settlement of John S. Ballard, dec'd. Aministratris;; Jane E. Lord, Administrator, M. W Lord. - Montgomery County Probate Court, Aug 16th, 1860. Montgomery Weekly Mail, Montgomery, Ala., Sept 7, 1860, p 7 c.2.

Notes for JANE ELIZABETH LEWIS:
Source: 1860 Montgomery County Alabama Federal Census Records

* 1860 - Living in Montgomery Co., AL - Lord, Malder 21, Jane E. 43, Pembia A. 13, Zachariah 12, Thomas E. 9, Sarah 7, Whitman 14
* 1880 - Living in Montgomery Co., AL - Lord, Jane E 60, Sarah 24, William Lewis 24

More About JANE ELIZABETH LEWIS:
Burial: Oakwood Cemetery, Montgomery Co., AL

Children of JOHN BALLARD and JANE LEWIS are:

      i.   ELIZABETH ANN "BETSEY"[7] BALLARD, b. 1834, AL; d. Aft. 1850; m. WESLEY W. LEDLOW, 05 Jun 1851, Montgomery AL; b. Abt. 1830.

      ii.   JOHN BALLARD, b. 1836, AL; d. Aft. 1850.

      iii.   JAMES BALLARD, b. 1838, AL; d. Aft. 1850.

      iv.   MARY ANN BALLARD, b. 1840, AL; d. Aft. 1850; m. HENRY J. BROWN, 15 Jul 1858, Montgomery Co., AL; b. 1835, AL; d. Aft. 1860.

         Notes for HENRY J. BROWN:
         Source: 1860 Montgomery County Alabama Federal Census Records
         * 1860 - Living in Montgomery Co., AL - Brown, Henry 25 Farmer AL, Mary A 21 AL, James 21 Farmer AL

      v.   WILLIAM BALLARD, b. 1842, AL; d. Aft. 1850.

      vi.   MARTHA BALLARD, b. 1844, AL; d. Aft. 1850; m. SAMUEL REVEL, 04 Aug 1859, Montgomery AL; b. Abt. 1840.

      vii.   PERMELIA BALLARD, b. 1846, AL; d. Aft. 1850.

36.   viii.   ZACHARIAH TAYLOR BALLARD, b. 02 Mar 1852, AL; d. 15 Oct 1932, Montgomery Co., AL.

      ix.   SARAH J. BALLARD, b. 1853, AL; d. Aft. 1880.

37.   x.   THOMAS EDWARD BALLARD, b. 24 Jan 1854, Montgomery Co., AL; d. 27 Jul 1939, Caldwell Co., TX.

      xi.   WHITMAN L. BALLARD, b. 1856, AL; d. Aft. 1880.

10. BENJAMIN RANDALL[6] BALLARD (SILAS JOSEPH HARDY[5], BENJAMIN[4], JOHN[3], JOSEPH[2], JOHN[1]) was born 11 Apr 1811 in NC, and died 15 Feb 1890 in Oakey Streak, Covington Co., AL. He married SARAH NANCY ANN JONES. She was born 19 Mar 1816 in GA, and died 13 Jan 1894 in Oakey Streak, Covington Co., AL.

Notes for BENJAMIN RANDALL BALLARD:
Source: Libb (libb@alaweb.com), 1860, 1870 Covington County Alabama Federal Census Records, The Anbalusia Star News dated April 4, 1998, Jan Ballard (72753.3121@compuserve.com), Joe Webb
* (Jan Ballard) When corresponding with Alabama Ballards, one of the descendants of your line wrote this when I asked about church affiliations: "He, Benjamin Randal Ballard, M.D. went to Alberton Methodist Church but never joined. Of course, he was a good supporter of the Church. In fact when they were getting new pews they ask me if I would like one even though I am Baptist because of my grandfather, I could not turn down a pew that had a board about one and one-half inches wide."
* 1860 - Living in Covington Co., AL - Ballard, Randal 49 NC, Nancy 45 GA, Joseph H 25 AL, Evans 20 AL, Jane 18 AL, Sarah Ann 16, Presly 14, B M 12 AL, Hasting 11 AL, Randall 7 AL Buris 5 AL, Nancy Ann 1 AL
* 1870 - Living in Covington Co., AL - Ballard, B. R. 52 SC, Nancy 54 GA, Jane 28 AL, Sarah A. 24 AL, Butler BB 21 AL, Benj. R. 16, B. L. G. 14 AL, Ann 11 AL, T. 50 AL
* 1880 - Living in Covington Co., AL- Ballard, Randall 69 NC NC NC farmer, Nancy 64 GA VA VA, Benjamin 20 AL, Sarah 30 GA, Burrus 24 AL

Children of BENJAMIN BALLARD and SARAH JONES are:

      i.   ELIZABETH LANIE[7] BALLARD, b. 14 Nov 1833, Oakey Streak, Covington Co., AL; d. 13 Feb 1860, Oakey Streak, Covington Co., AL.

         Notes for ELIZABETH LANIE BALLARD:
         Source: Libb (libb@alaweb.com)

         More About ELIZABETH LANIE BALLARD:
         Burial: Oakey Streak Cem in Covington Co., AL

        ii.   JOSEPH HARDY "BUCK" BALLARD, b. 22 May 1835, Oakey Streak, Covington Co., AL; d. 1860, Civil War.

        iii. POLLY SUSANA BALLARD, b. 23 Jun 1837, Oakey Streak, Covington Co., AL; d. 15 Nov 1840, Oakey Streak, Covington Co., AL.

             More About POLLY SUSANA BALLARD:

             Burial: Oakey Streak Cem in Covington Co., AL

38.   iv.   EVANS COLEMAN BALLARD, b. 09 Mar 1840, Oakey Streak, Covington Co., AL; d. 04 May 1913, Blackrock, Crenshaw Co., AL.

39.   v.   NANCY JANE BALLARD, b. 02 May 1842, Oakey Streak, Covington Co., AL; d. 1919, Oakey Streak, Covington Co., AL.

        vi. PRESLEY PRESTON BALLARD, b. 05 Jun 1844, Oakey Streak, Covington Co., AL; d. 1860, Civil War.

40.   vii. SARAH ANN BALLARD, b. 24 Feb 1846, Oakey Streak, Covington Co., AL; d. 1917, Oakey Streak, Covington Co., AL.

41.   viii. BENJAMIN RANDAL "BUTLER" BALLARD, b. 05 Mar 1849, Oakey Streak, Covington Co., AL; d. Bet. 1918 - 1919.

42.   ix. HASTING URIAH GILCHRIST BALLARD, b. 13 Jul 1851, Oakey Streak, Covington Co., AL; d. 07 Mar 1935, Oakey Streak, Covington Co., AL.

43.   x.   BURSE LASTING GALE BALLARD, b. 19 Jun 1856, Oakey Streak, Covington Co., AL; d. Aft. 1930.

        xi. NANCY ANN BALLARD, b. 06 Apr 1859, Oakey Streak, Covington Co., AL; d. 29 Oct 1910, Oakey Streak, Covington Co., AL.

11. MARY ANN[6] BALLARD (SILAS JOSEPH HARDY[5], BENJAMIN[4], JOHN[3], JOSEPH[2], JOHN[1]) was born Abt. 1812. She married DANIEL GREEN 20 Feb 1833 in Montgomery AL. He was born Abt. 1812.

Notes for MARY ANN BALLARD:
Source: Ron Head (ronhead@knology.net)

Children of MARY BALLARD and DANIEL GREEN are:
        i.   WILLIAM[7] GREEN, b. Abt. 1834.
        ii. JOHNATHAN GREEN, b. Abt. 1835.

12. WILLIAM W.[6] BALLARD (SILAS JOSEPH HARDY[5], BENJAMIN[4], JOHN[3], JOSEPH[2], JOHN[1]) was born Bet. 1812 - 1813 in GA, and died Aft. 1850. He married (1) SARAH LOUISA CAMPBELL 06 Jul 1837 in Montgomery Co., AL. She was born 1818 in SC or NC, and died Aft. 1850. He married (2) REBECCA WILEY 14 Jan 1858 in Montgomery Co., AL. He married (3) EMELINE D. MURPHY 14 Nov 1860 in Montgomery Co., AL.

Notes for WILLIAM W. BALLARD:
Source: 1850-1860 Montgomery County Alabama Federal Census Record, Ron Head (ronhead@knology.net)

* 1850 - Living in Montgomery Co., AL - Ballard, Wm. W. 38 Farmer GA, Sarah 32, Margaret A. 12, Geo W. 10, Lucy A. 8, Frances 6, Benj 4, Jno 2, Margarette Campbell 18, Silas Ballard 24 AL, George Moses AL
* 1860 - Living in Montgomery Co., AL - Ballard, W W 48 teamster, GW 20, Frances J 17, John H 12, James B 21

Children of WILLIAM BALLARD and SARAH CAMPBELL are:

        i.   MARGARET A.[7] BALLARD, b. 1838, AL.
        ii. JAMES B. BALLARD, b. 1839, AL; d. Aft. 1860.
        iii. GEORGE W. BALLARD, b. 28 Oct 1839, AL; d. 07 Jan 1876; m. ELLEN C. BONHAM, 05 Dec 1867; b. 1847; d. 1871.
        iv. LUCY A. BALLARD, b. 1842, AL.

    v.   FRANCES BALLARD, *b. 1844, AL; d. Aft. 1860.*
   vi. BENJAMIN "BENJ" BALLARD, *b. 1846, AL.*
  vii. JOHN BALLARD, *b. 1848, AL; d. Aft. 1860.*

13. JONATHAN O.[6] BALLARD, DR. (SILAS JOSEPH HARDY[5], BENJAMIN[4], JOHN[3], JOSEPH[2], JOHN[1]) *was born 1813 in SC, and died Abt. 1855 in Crenshaw Co., AL. He married (1)* SUZANNA CAROLINE BURNETT *Bet. 1830 - 1832. She was born Abt. 1813. He married (2)* MARTHA JOSEY *1847 in Covington Co., AL. She was born Abt. 1820 in Covington Co., AL, and died Bef. 1860.*

Notes for JONATHAN O. BALLARD, DR.:
Source: Jan M. Ballard (72753.3121@compuserve.com), Libb (libb@alaweb.com), 1860 Covington County Alabama Federal Census
* 1860 - Covington Co., AL - His sons, Jonathan 12, Joseph 10, Arthur 8 living in home of John Josey

Children of JONATHAN BALLARD *and* SUZANNA BURNETT *are:*
        i.   TIMOTHY S.[7] BALLARD, *b. 1831.*
44.   *ii.* MATILDA CAROLINE BALLARD, *b. 02 Jun 1833, 6/21/1838; d. 1901.*
      iii. ANN E. BALLARD, *b. 1834.*
     iv. MARY SUSANNE BALLARD, *b. 1835; m.* THOMAS GREEN REYNOLDS, *1865.*
      v. JOHN A. BALLARD, *b. 1840.*
     vi. AMANDA BALLARD, *b. 18 Feb 1841; d. 10 Dec 1901; m.* MR. PARKER.

Children of JONATHAN BALLARD *and* MARTHA JOSEY *are:*
45.   *vii.* JONATHAN "JOHN LEE"[7] BALLARD, JR., *b. 09 Apr 1847, Oakey Streak, Covington Co., AL; d. 08 Sep 1927, Jackson Clarke Co., AL.*
   viii. JOSEPH BALLARD, *b. 1849; d. Aft. 1860.*
     ix. ARTHUR BALLARD, *b. 1852, AL; d. Aft. 1860.*

14. TEMPERANCE TABITHA[6] BALLARD (SILAS JOSEPH HARDY[5], BENJAMIN[4], JOHN[3], JOSEPH[2], JOHN[1]) *was born 22 Oct 1821 in Conecuh Co., AL, and died 05 Mar 1898 in Jun 13, 1897 AL. She married* KINYARD DAVID WIGGINS, *son of* ELISHEU WIGGINS *and* MARGARET KINNARD. *He was born Abt. 1803 in NC, and died 29 Aug 1893 in AL.*

Notes for TEMPERANCE TABITHA BALLARD:
Source: Joe Webb, (res00jqu@gte.net), 1880 Conecuh County Alabama Federal Census Records
* 1880 - Living in Jamestown, Conecuh Co., AL - Wiggons, Temperance 57 AL AL AL, Tempey 32 AL AL AL, Michal 21 AL, Alford 19 AL, Marshal 19 AL twins, George 15 AL, Kinard 35 AL, Flora 3 AL

More About TEMPERANCE TABITHA BALLARD:
Burial: Mt. Union Cemetery, Conecuh Co., AL

Notes for KINYARD DAVID WIGGINS:
Source: Joe Webb, 1860-1870 Conecuh County Alabama Federal Census Records
* 1860 - Living in Conecuh Co., AL - Wiggins, Kenard 52 farmer NC, Tempa 37 AL, Tabitha 10 FL, Tempa 15 AL, Kenard 7 FL, Susan 13 AL, Catharine 5 FL, Frances 12 AL, Wm. 4 AL, Michael 7/12 AL
* 1870 - Living in Oldtown, Conecuh Co., AL - Wiggins, Kenard 75 NC, Tempa 49 AL, Tempa 25, Susan H 23 AL, Frances 20 AL, Tabitha 18 FL, Kenard 16 FL, Catherine 14 FL, Wm P M 12 AL, James A 8 AL, John M 8 AL, George E 5 AL

Children of TEMPERANCE BALLARD *and* KINYARD WIGGINS *are:*
        i.   KINYARD[7] WIGGINS, *b. Abt. 1845, FL; d. Aft. 1880; m.* MARY E. COLEMAN, *24 Nov 1874.*
       ii. TEMPERANCE "TEMPEY" WIGGINS, *b. Abt. 1846, Conecuh Co., AL; d. Aft. 1880.*

	iii.	SUSAN H. WIGGINS, *b. Abt. 1847, Conecuh Co., AL; d. Aft. 1870.*
	iv.	AMELIA FRANCES WIGGINS, *b. Abt. 1848, Conecuh Co., AL; d. Aft. 1870; m. COLEMAN.*
	v.	TABITHA WIGGINS, *b. Abt. 1850, FL; d. Aft. 1870.*
46.	*vi.*	FLORA KATHERINE WIGGINS, *b. 1856, Conecuh Co., AL; d. 15 Jul 1915, River Falls, Covington Co., AL.*
47.	*vii.*	WILLIAM P. WIGGINS, *b. 04 May 1857, Conecuh Co., AL; d. Aft. 1880.*
48.	*viii.*	MICHAEL O. WIGGINS, *b. Abt. 1860, Conecuh Co., AL; d. Aft. 1889.*
	ix.	JAMES ALFORD WIGGINS, *b. Abt. 1861, Conecuh Co., AL; d. Aft. 1880.*
	x.	JOHN MARSHALL WIGGINS, *b. 04 May 1862, Conecuh Co., AL; d. Aft. 1870.*
	xi.	GEORGE E. WIGGINS, *b. Abt. 1865, Conecuh Co., AL; d. Aft. 1880.*

15. SILAS H.[6] BALLARD (SILAS JOSEPH HARDY[5], BENJAMIN[4], JOHN[3], JOSEPH[2], JOHN[1]) *was born 22 Oct 1823 in AL, and died 01 Jan 1906 in TX. He married* MILDRED "MILLY" ANN WALLER *07 Sep 1850 in Montgomery Co., AL. She was born 23 Dec 1833 in AL, and died 24 Jan 1904 in TX.*

Notes for SILAS H. BALLARD:
Source: 1850-1880 Montgomery County Alabama Federal Census Records, 1900 Taylor County Texas Federal Census Records
* 1850 - Living in Montgomery Co., AL- with brother William W. Ballard - Ballard Silas 24 AL
* 1860 - Living in Montgomery Co., AL - Ballard, Silas 32 AL, Milly A. 28 AL, Jesse 7 AL, Charles W. 5 AL, Martha 4/12 AL, Benjamin Payne
* 1870 - Living in Montgomery Co., AL - Ballard, S 45 farmer AL, Mildrid 35 AL, Martha 10, Georgiana 9 AL, Marietta 4 AL, Francis 8 AL
* 1880 - Living in Lavaca Co., TX - Ballard, H Silas 58 farmer AL GA GA, Millie A 48 AL GA GA, Georgia A 16 AL, Etta 12 AL, Elizabeth 11 AL Betsie 45 servant AL
* 1900 - Living in Abilene, Taylor Co., TX - Ballard, Silas - Oct 1823 AL GA GA, Mildred - Dec 1834 AL GA GA

More About SILAS H. BALLARD:
Burial: Abilene Municipal Cemetery, Abilene, Taylor Co., TX

More About MILDRED "MILLY" ANN WALLER:
Burial: Abilene Municipal Cemetery, Abilene, Taylor Co., TX

Children of SILAS BALLARD *and* MILDRED WALLER *are:*
	i.	JESSE[7] BALLARD, *b. 1853, Montgomery Co., AL; d. Aft. 1860.*
	ii.	CHARLES BALLARD, *b. 1855, Montgomery Co., AL; d. Aft. 1860.*
	iii.	MARTHA ANN BALLARD, *b. 18 Jan 1861, Montgomery Co., AL; d. 23 Dec 1923, Tom Green Co., TX; m.* FRANK STINCHCOMB; *b. 18 May 1856, AL; d. 09 Apr 1928, TX.*

> *Notes for* MARTHA ANN BALLARD:
> *Source: Tom Green County Texas Standard Certificate of Death*
>
> *More About* MARTHA ANN BALLARD:
> *Burial: Abilene Municipal Cemetery, Abilene, Taylor Co., TX*
>
> *More About* FRANK STINCHCOMB:
> *Burial: Abilene Municipal Cemetery, Abilene, Taylor Co., TX*

	iv.	FRANCIS BALLARD, *b. 1862, Montgomery Co., AL; d. Aft. 1870.*
	v.	GEORGIANA BALLARD, *b. 04 Jul 1862, Montgomery Co., AL; d. 14 Sep 1940, Taylor Co., TX; m.* OLLIE EUGENE BROOKS; *b. 1886; d. 03 Jun 1962.*

> *Notes for* GEORGIANA BALLARD:
> *Source: Taylor County Texas Standard Certificate of Death*

More About GEORGIANA BALLARD:
Burial: Abilene Municipal Cemetery, Abilene, Taylor Co., TX

More About OLLIE EUGENE BROOKS:
Burial: Abilene Municipal Cemetery, Abilene, Taylor Co., TX

vi.   MARY ETTA BALLARD, b. 04 Oct 1866, Montgomery Co., AL; d. 19 May 1941, Jones Co., TX; m. SCOTT.

Notes for MARY ETTA BALLARD:
Source: Jones County Texas Standard Certificate of Death

vii.   ELIZABETH BALLARD, b. Abt. 1869, Montgomery Co., AL; d. Aft. 1880.

16.   ELIJAH⁶ BALLARD (JOSHUA⁵, BENJAMIN⁴, JOHN³, JOSEPH², JOHN¹) *was born 1815 in GA, and died 1883. He married MARY THANIE MCEWEN. She was born Abt. 1815 in GA, and died Aft. 1870.*

Notes for ELIJAH BALLARD:
Source: 1850 & 1870 Campbell County Georgia Federal Census Records, 1860 Carroll County Georgia Federal Census Records
* 1850 - Living in Campbell Co., GA - Eli Ballard 25 GA, Thaney G. 36 GA, Benj. F. 14 GA, Robert W. 12 GA, Wesley 10 GA, Cassinda 8 GA, Elizabeth 5 GA, Martha J. 3 GA, Rachel 1 GA
* 1860 - Living in Carroll Co., GA - Eli Ballard 45 GA, Thena 45 GA, Robt. M. 22 GA, Wesley C. 20 GA, Cassinda 28 GA, Elizabeth 16 GA, Martha 14 GA, Rachel 12 GA, Maria GA, Catherine 8 GA, Joshua 5 GA
* 1870 - Living in Campbell Co., GA - Ballard, Eli 60 farmer GA, Thana 56 GA, Elisa 21 GA, Mariah 16 GA, Cathrine 14 GA, Joshua 12 GA, Lucinda 12 GA

Notes for MARY THANIE MCEWEN:
Name could also be McClure or Sethenia McVen 1836

Children of ELIJAH BALLARD and MARY MCEWEN are:
49.   i.   BENJAMIN FRANK⁷ BALLARD, b. 16 Feb 1832, Atlanta, Fulton Co., GA; d. 06 Jul 1905, Hot Springs, Garland Co., AR.
         ii.   ROBERT BALLARD, b. 1838, GA; d. 1861, Civil War, Lynchburg, VA.
50.   iii.   WESLEY C. BALLARD, b. 16 Dec 1839, GA; d. 24 Mar 1909, Cass Co., TX.
51.   iv.   CASSANDRA CASSIDY BALLARD, b. 16 Apr 1845, GA; d. 27 Jun 1917.
         v.   ELIZABETH BALLARD, b. 1844, GA; d. Aft. 1860.
         vi.   MARTHA JANE BALLARD, b. 1846, GA; d. Aft. 1860; m. WILLIAM CROOKE, Spring Gardens, Cherokee Co, AL.
52.   vii.   RACHEL BALLARD, b. Bet. 1844 - 1848, GA; d. Aft. 1891.
         viii.   MARIA BALLARD, b. 1850, GA; d. Aft. 1860.
         ix.   CATHERINE BALLARD, b. 1852, GA; d. Aft. 1860; m. WILLIAM WHITLEY, Salt Springs, GA.
53.   x.   JOSHUA BALLARD, b. 1855.

17.   ARMISTEAD⁶ BALLARD (JOSHUA⁵, BENJAMIN⁴, JOHN³, JOSEPH², JOHN¹) *was born 07 Aug 1819 in GA, and died 13 Sep 1893. He married (1) NANCY GRIFFITH 23 Aug 1856 in Fulton Co., GA. She was born Abt. 1836, and died Bef. 1880. He married (2) MARY R. BARFIELD 15 Sep 1874 in Campbell Co., GA. She was born 1837 in GA, and died 1900.*

Notes for ARMISTEAD BALLARD:
Source- 1880 Campbell Georgia Federal Census Records

* 1860 - Living in Campbell Co., GA - Bullard, Armstead 31, Nancy 42, Levi 5, Elizabeth 3, Joshua 1, Sarah

Blackburn 11, John Brown 3
* 1870 - Living in Campbell Co., GA - Ballard, A (hard to read) 53 Farmer GA, Nancy 54 GA, Levi 14 GA, Elisa 13 domestic servant GA, Joshua 11 GA
* 1880 - Living in Campbell Co., GA - Ballard, Armstead 60 farmer GA, Mary R 42 GA, Annie 11 GA, John 2 GA

More About ARMISTEAD BALLARD:
Burial: Piney Woods Baptist Church Cemetery, Rico, Fulton Co., GA

Notes for MARY R. BARFIELD:
Source: 1900 Campbell County Georgia Federal Census Records

* 1900 - Living in Fairburn, Campbell Co., GA with her daughter Annie Carmichael and her family - Ballard, Mary R 64

Children of ARMISTEAD BALLARD and NANCY GRIFFITH are:

	i.	ELIZABETH[7] BALLARD, b. Abt. 1857, Campbell Co., GA; d. Aft. 1870.
54.	ii.	LEVI BALLARD, b. 06 Nov 1854, Campbell Co., GA; d. Aft. 1870.
55.	iii.	JOSHUA BALLARD, b. 01 Aug 1859, Campbell Co., GA; d. 1936, AR.

Children of ARMISTEAD BALLARD and MARY BARFIELD are:

56.	iv.	ANNA[7] BALLARD, b. Jul 1876, Campbell Co., GA; d. Aft. 1900.
	v.	JOHN BALLARD, b. 17 Mar 1878, Campbell Co., GA; d. 22 Jan 1892.

> *More About JOHN BALLARD:*
> *Burial: Piney Woods Baptist Church Cemetery, Rico, Fulton Co., GA*

	vi.	CHILD BALLARD, b. Campbell Co., GA; d. Bef. 1900.

18. MORTON[6] BALLARD (JOSHUA[5], BENJAMIN[4], JOHN[3], JOSEPH[2], JOHN[1]) was born 1821 in GA, and died 02 Apr 1903 in AR. He married MARTHA SHACKELFORD 02 Dec 1840 in Campbell Co., GA. She was born Abt. 1826 in GA.

Notes for MORTON BALLARD:
Source: 1850, 1860 Campbell County Georgia Federal Census Records

* 1850 - Living in Campbell Co., GA - Ballard, Morton 30 GA, Martha 24 GA, Malissa 2 GA, *Anna Blackmon 10 GA
* 1860 - Living in Campbell Co., GA - Ballard, Morton 40 GA

Child of MORTON BALLARD and MARTHA SHACKELFORD is:
> i. MALISSA[7] BALLARD, b. 1848.

19. OBEDIAH[6] BALLARD (JOSHUA[5], BENJAMIN[4], JOHN[3], JOSEPH[2], JOHN[1]) was born 1823 in GA, and died 1894 in Cleveland Co., AR. He married LOTTIE HUNTER. She was born 1826, and died 1884.

Notes for OBEDIAH BALLARD:
Source: Beverly Killian (beverlykillian@starband.net) 1880 Cleveland County Arkansas Federal Census Records

* 1880 - Living in Cleveland Co., AR (Dorsey township) - Ballard, Obediah 57 GA GA GA, Chollotie 34 GA GA GA., Joshua (nephew) 20 GA GA GA., MA(daughter) 4 AR GA GA, Malinda 3 AR GA GA
* There is also a LD Ballard 26 GA GA GA., living with the Nichols family. There is a Malon Ballard 64 GA GA GA., and Samanthy 38 Al., SC, Al.

Children of OBEDIAH BALLARD and LOTTIE HUNTER are:
>   i.   BETTIE[7] BALLARD, b. Abt. 1843; m. SAM FENISON, Bunn, Dallas Co, AR.
>   ii. MALINDA BALLARD, b. Abt. 1850; m. JOHN FENISON, 22 Sep 1895, Cleveland Co., AR; b. Abt. 1850.

20. ABRAHAM[6] BALLARD (JOSHUA[5], BENJAMIN[4], JOHN[3], JOSEPH[2], JOHN[1]) *was born 1830 in Gwinnett Co., GA, and died Aft. 1860 in Civil War. He married DELANA JANE MADERIA. She was born 1835 in GA, and died Aft. 1860.*

Notes for ABRAHAM BALLARD:
Source: 1860 Campbell County Georgia Federal Census Records

* 1860 - Living in Campbell Co., GA - Ballard, Abraham 30 GA, Jane 25 GA, Joshua 6 GA, Sarah E. 5 GA, Eliza 5 GA, Lucinda 2 GA, Jesse Harper 25 GA, Sabey Harper 18 GA
* Moved to Randolph Co., GA

Children of ABRAHAM BALLARD and DELANA MADERIA are:

57.   i.   JOSHUA[7] BALLARD, b. Bet. 1851 - 1854, Randolph Co., AL; d. Feb 1917, Randolph Co., AL.
>   ii.   MALINDA BALLARD, b. Bet. 1854 - 1855; d. 08 Nov 1930, Baldwin Co., GA; m. JAMES HAMMOND; b. Abt. 1850.
>   iii. SARAH E. BALLARD, b. 1855, GA; d. 13 Jun 1931; m. (1) GEORGE BRYANT; m. (2) WILLIAM RICHARDS; b. Abt. 1850.
>   iv.   ELIZA BALLARD, b. Abt. 1857, GA; d. Aft. 1860.
>   v.   LUCINDA BALLARD, b. 1858, GA; d. Aft. 1860; m. NATHANIEL H. WILKES.
>   vi.   FANNIE BALLARD, b. Aft. 1860; m. (1) JEFFERSON DAVIS BRYANT; m. (2) EVERETT PARR; b. Abt. 1855.

21. LEVI[6] BALLARD (JOSHUA[5], BENJAMIN[4], JOHN[3], JOSEPH[2], JOHN[1]) *was born 22 Nov 1833 in Anniestown, Gwinnett Co., GA, and died 20 Mar 1921 in Palmetto, Campbell Co., GA. He married SARAH SMITH HARRISON 17 Dec 1861 in Fulton Co., GA, daughter of NATHANIAL HARRISON and SARAH SMITH. She was born 20 Nov 1835 in GA, and died 1904.*

Notes for LEVI BALLARD:
Source: Death Certificate, 1860 Calhoun County Arkansas Federal Census Records, 1870-1880 Campbell County Georgia Federal Census Records

* 1858 -United with Ramah Baptist Church, baptized by Rev. John S. Dodd
* Moved to Hampton, Calhoun Co., AR back to Palmetto Co., GA
* 1860 - Living in Calhoun Co., AR - Ballard, Levi 37, Sarah 38, Edgar 7, Violet 5, Nathan 3, Cora 2, Maude 6/12
* Moved to Hampton, Calhoun Co., AR, back to Palmetto County, Georgia.
* 1861 - Civil War: 1861 8th Arkansas Rgmt; major in 56th Arkansas Rgmt, retired as captain. Active in GA politics of Palmetto County
* 1870 - Living in Campbell Co., GA - Ballard, Levi 37 farmer, Sarah 34 GA, Edgar 7 GA, Volet 5 GA, Nathan 3 GA, Ora 2 GA, Maude 6/12
* 1880 - Living in Campbell Co., GA - Ballard, Levi 46, Sarah S 44, Edgar L 17, Valetta A 15, Nathaniel H 13, Cora V 12, Mable C 5, Maud A 10, Jacob H 3
* 1884-1885 - Served as a representative in the Lower House of General Assembly
* 1888-1889 - Served in the senate

More About LEVI BALLARD:
Burial: Ramah Baptist Ch., Palmetto GA

Children of LEVI BALLARD and SARAH HARRISON are:
>   i.   EDGAR LAWRENCE[7] BALLARD, b. 29 Sep 1862, GA; d. 14 Aug 1895, New Orleans, LA.

Notes for EDGAR LAWRENCE BALLARD:
Lawyer in Burnett, TX

    ii.   LEVI BALLARD, b. Abt. 1863, GA.

Notes for LEVI BALLARD:
Levi, Jr, Sarah, and Margaret triplets

    iii.   SARAH BALLARD, b. Abt. 1864, GA.
    iv.   VILLETA ADELAIDE BALLARD, b. May 1864, GA; d. Aft. 1870; m. CHARLES B. MOSEBY, 1885.
    v.   MARGARET BALLARD, b. Abt. 1865, GA.
    vi.   LILLIE BRANCH BALLARD, b. Abt. 1866, GA.
58.   vii.   NATHANIEL HARRISON BALLARD, b. 22 Dec 1866, Pumpkintown Plantation, Randolph Co, GA; d. 09 Feb 1936, Jacksonville, Duval Co., FL.
    viii.   CORA VIRGINIA BALLARD, b. 02 Aug 1868, GA; d. Aft. 1880; m. THOMAS P. ARNOLD, 12 Sep 1880; b. Abt. 1860; d. 07 Mar 1930.
    ix.   ALICE MAUDE BALLARD, b. 1870, GA; d. Aft. 1880; m. CHARLES HUDSON.
    x.   MABEL ELIZABETH BALLARD, b. 18 Aug 1875; d. Aft. 1880; m. RUSH IRVIN.
    xi.   JACOB HOWARD BALLARD, b. 28 Sep 1876, GA; d. 11 Dec 1963, Palmetto GA.

22. AMANDA JANE[6] BALLARD (JOHN[5], BENJAMIN[4], JOHN[3], JOSEPH[2], JOHN[1]) was born Abt. 1822. She married EDMOND A. ADAMS 06 Sep 1846 in Carroll Co., GA. He was born Abt. 1816.

Notes for AMANDA JANE BALLARD:
Source: Peggy Chapman (pbchapman@door.net)

Notes for EDMOND A. ADAMS:
Source: 1850 Pike County Arkansas Federal Census Records, 1860-1880 Fannin County Texas Federal Census Records, Peggy B. Chapman (pbchapman@door.net) , Marriage CD#4
* 1850 - Living in Pike Co., AR, Adams, E. H. 21, farmer, TN, Amanda J. 25, GA, _ana A. 3, GA, Sarah E. 1, GA
* 1860 - Living in Fannin Co., TX - Adams, E.H. 31 TN, A.J. 34, fe GA, S.A. 13, fe, GA, S.E. 11, fe,GA, Wm. R. 9, AR, John C. 8, AR, Mary A.C. 6, AR Edmond M. [sic] 4, AR, Laura E. 2, AR, Arabella 6/12, AR
* 1870 - Living in Fannin Co., TX - Adams, E.H 41 TN, Amanda J. 45, GA. Wm. A. 19, AR, John C. 17, AR, Edmund 15, AR, Laura E. 12, Bell Z? 10, TX, Baswell or Basman 2, TX
* 1880 - Living in Fannin Co., TX Adams, E.W. 29, nursery man, farmer, school teacher. AR TN GA - Sallie B. 20, wife TN NC Adams, E.H. 51, farmer, nurseryman TN SCTN, Ella L. 38, wife, MO KY VA, Bascom L. 12, son, farm laborer, b TX TN GA, S.A. Johnson 30, boarder, laborer NY Switzerland NY, Mary Roberts 14, mulato, servant, TX

Children of AMANDA BALLARD and EDMOND ADAMS are:
    i.   LOU ANA[7] ADAMS, b. 1847, Carroll Co., GA; d. 1879, Fannin Co., TX; m. JOHN W. OLDS, 02 Jun 1869, Fannin Co., TX.
    ii.   SARAH E. ADAMS, b. 1849, Carroll Co., GA; m. FRANCIS C. WHITE, 15 Sep 1870, Fannin Co., TX.
    iii.   WILLIAM A. ADAMS, b. 1850, Pike Co., AR; m. SARAH MCDADE.
    iv.   JOHN C. ADAMS, b. Abt. 1852, Pike Co., AR.
    v.   MARY ADAMS, b. 1853, Pike Co., AR; d. 1861, Fannin Co., TX.
    vi.   EDMOND WISE ADAMS, b. 24 Nov 1855, Pike Co., AR; d. 11 Mar 1914, Fannin Co., TX; m. SARAH BARTHENA STIMPSON; b. Abt. 1853.

       More About EDMOND WISE ADAMS:
       Burial: Willow Wild Cemetery, Bonham Fannin Co., TX

    vii.   LAURA E. ADAMS, b. 1857, Pike Co., AR; d. Abt. 1920, Fannin Co., TX; m. WILLIAM STIMPSON; b. Abt. 1855.

More About LAURA E. ADAMS:
Burial: Willow Wild Cemetery, Bonham, Fannin Co., TX

    viii.   ARABELLA Z. ADAMS, *b. 1860, Fannin Co., TX; m.* JOHN BETTIS.
     ix.   BASCOM LEE ADAMS, *b. 1867, Fannin Co., TX; d. 1945, Bonham, Fannin Co., TX.*

    More About BASCOM LEE ADAMS:
    Burial: Willow Wild Cemetery, Bonham, Fannin Co., TX

23. EUPHRONIAS FRANKLIN[6] BALLARD (JOHN[5], BENJAMIN[4], JOHN[3], JOSEPH[2], JOHN[1]) *was born 1837 in GA, and died Aft. 1860. He married* ADELLINE DAVIS *24 Jan 1860 in Carroll Co., GA. She was born 1836 in GA, and died 14 Aug 1910 in TX.*

Notes for EUPHRONIAS FRANKLIN BALLARD:
Source: Pension records, 1860 Carroll County GA Federal Census Records
* Ballard, Adeline 05495 - Claimant: Ballard, Adeline - Pension Number: 05495 Co.: Henderson - Husband: Euphronius Franklin
* 1860 - Living in Carroll Co., GA - Ed F. Ballard 27 GA Farmer, Adeline 24 TN

Notes for ADELLINE DAVIS:
Source: 1900 Henderson County Texas Federal Census Records
* 1900 - Living in Henderson Co., TX - Ballard, Mrs. A - Jan 1836 wd TN VA TN, Fannie - Feb 1862 GA, Elizabeth - May 1834 sister TN, Lila Niece - Apr 1881 TX

Child of EUPHRONIAS BALLARD and ADELLINE DAVIS is:
    i.   FANNIE[7] BALLARD, *b. Feb 1862, GA; d. 26 Mar 1935, TX.*

24. JAMES A.[6] BALLARD (JESSE[5], BENJAMIN[4], JOHN[3], JOSEPH[2], JOHN[1]) *was born 1825, and died Bef. 1870. He married* SARAH "SALLIE" E. HARRIS *30 Nov 1865 in Morgan Co., GA. She was born Abt. 1825.*

Children of JAMES BALLARD and SARAH HARRIS are:
    i.   OSCAR[7] BALLARD, *b. Abt. 1866.*
    ii.   MATTIE BALLARD, *b. Abt. 1867.*

25. WILLIAM W.[6] BALLARD (JESSE[5], BENJAMIN[4], JOHN[3], JOSEPH[2], JOHN[1]) *was born 1829, and died Bef. 1860. He married* SARAH WEST *21 Dec 1854 in Morgan Co., GA. She was born Abt. 1834, and died Aft. 1870.*

Notes for SARAH WEST:
Source: 1860-1870 Morgan County Georgia Federal Census Records
* 1860 - Living in Mann, Morgan Co., GA - Living with her parents William and Parthena West - Ballard, Sarah P 28, Benjamin S 4, William W 3
* 1870 - Living in Morgan Co., GA - Living with her parents. - Ballard, Sarah 38, Emma L 25, Hugh O 22, Benjamin 14, Willy W 13 (I'm assuming two of these may be children of her brother in law that also died)

Children of WILLIAM BALLARD and SARAH WEST are:
    i.   BENJAMIN "BENNIE"[7] BALLARD, *b. Abt. 1855, Morgan Co., GA; d. Aft. 1870; m.* JAMES AINSLIE.
    ii.   WILLIAM BALLARD, *b. Abt. 1856, Monroe Co., VA; d. Aft. 1870.*

    Notes for WILLIAM BALLARD:
    Moved to Hawthorne, FL never married

26. ELIZABETH[6] BALLARD (JESSE[5], BENJAMIN[4], JOHN[3], JOSEPH[2], JOHN[1]) *was born 1856 in GA, and died 1936. She married JOHN T. NOLES in Walton, GA. He was born 12 Aug 1858, and died 05 Mar 1928.*

More About ELIZABETH BALLARD:
Burial: Madison Historic Cemetery, Madison, Morgan Co., GA

More About JOHN T. NOLES:
Burial: Madison Historic Cemetery, Madison, Morgan Co., GA

Child of ELIZABETH BALLARD and JOHN NOLES is:

  i.   EFFIE MAE[7] NOLES, *b. 31 Aug 1884; d. 04 Jun 1924, Madison, Morgan Co., GA; m. RUFUS H. HIGGINBOTHAM; b. 23 Apr 1879, GA; d. 29 Aug 1952.*

        More About EFFIE MAE NOLES:
        Burial: Madison Historic Cemetery, Madison, Morgan Co., GA

        More About RUFUS H. HIGGINBOTHAM:
        Burial: Madison Historic Cemetery, Madison, Morgan Co., GA

27. ROAN B.[6] BALLARD (JESSE[5], BENJAMIN[4], JOHN[3], JOSEPH[2], JOHN[1]) *was born 28 Feb 1860 in lived in Waycross, Ware Co., GA, and died 16 Mar 1927 in Ware Co., GA. He married HARRIET E. "HATTIE" GOODRICH. She was born Feb 1862 in GA, and died Aft. 1900.*

Notes for ROAN B. BALLARD:

Source: 1900 Ware County Georgia Federal Census Records, Ware County Georgia Standard Certificate of Death
* 1900 - Living in Way Cross, Ware County GA - Ballard, Roan 1860 GA, Hattie - Feb 1862 GA, Ira - Sep 1884 GA, Edward - July 1886 GA, Bessie - Aug 1887 GA

Children of ROAN BALLARD and HARRIET GOODRICH are:

  i.   IRA MASON[7] BALLARD, *b. Sep 1884, GA; d. Aft. 1900.*
  ii.   EDWARD B. BALLARD, *b. 25 Jul 1887, Waycross, Ware Co., GA; d. 21 Jul 1932, Atlanta, Fulton Co., GA.*

        Notes for EDWARD B. BALLARD:
        Source: Fulton County Georgia Certificate of Death

  iii. ELIZABETH "BESSIE" BALLARD, *b. 01 Aug 1888, Waycross, Ware Co., GA; d. Aft. 1900.*

        Notes for ELIZABETH "BESSIE" BALLARD:
        Source: Social Security Application

28. LENORA[6] BALLARD (JESSE[5], BENJAMIN[4], JOHN[3], JOSEPH[2], JOHN[1]) *was born 07 Feb 1864 in GA, and died 24 Apr 1946. She married WILLIAM THOMAS CULPEPPER. He was born 20 Aug 1860, and died 12 Oct 1894.*

Notes for LENORA BALLARD:
Source: 1930 Morgan County Georgia Federal Census Records
* 1930 - Living in Madison, Morgan Co., GA - Culpepper, Lenora B 62 wd GA GA GA

More About LENORA BALLARD:
Burial: Madison Historic Cemetery, Madison, Morgan Co., GA

More About WILLIAM THOMAS CULPEPPER:
Burial: *Williams Creek Baptist Church Cemetery, Norwood, Warren Co., GA*

Child of LENORA BALLARD and WILLIAM CULPEPPER is:
     i. ROSSER⁷ CULPEPPER, *b. 09 Aug 1893; d. 06 Feb 1972.*

             More About ROSSER CULPEPPER:
             Burial: *Madison Historic Cemetery, Madison, Morgan Co., GA*

29. ALBERT C.⁶ BALLARD (WILLIAM⁵, BENJAMIN⁴, JOHN³, JOSEPH², JOHN¹) *was born 1842 in GA, and died Aft. 1900. He married VICTORIA. She was born Jun 1843 in GA, and died Aft. 1900.*

Notes for ALBERT C. BALLARD:
Source- 1880-1900 Morgan County Georgia Federal Census Records
* 1880 - Living in Morgan Co., GA - Ballard, Albert 37, Victoria 36, Cora 17, Zannie 13, Osborn 6
* 1900 - Living in Hello, Morgan Co., GA - Ballard, Albert 1844, Zennia - Sep 1866, Osborn 1874, Maggie Jan 1882

Children of ALBERT BALLARD and VICTORIA are:
     i. CORA⁷ BALLARD, *b. 1863; d. Aft. 1880.*
     ii. ZENNIE BALLARD, *b. Sep 1866; d. Aft. 1900.*
     iii. OSBORN S. BALLARD, *b. 1874; d. Aft. 1900.*
     iv. MAGGIE BALLARD, *b. Jan 1882; d. Aft. 1900.*

30. OSBORN S.⁶ BALLARD (WILLIAM⁵, BENJAMIN⁴, JOHN³, JOSEPH², JOHN¹) *was born 1850 in GA, and died Aft. 1920. He married MATTIE BELDING 03 Sep 1874 in Morgan Co., GA. She was born 1856 in GA, and died Aft. 1920.*

Notes for OSBORN S. BALLARD:
Source: 1880-1920 Morgan County Georgia Federal Census Records

* 1880 - Living in Morgan Co., GA - Ballard, Osborn 30, Mattie 24, Sidney 4, Carrie 2
* 1900 - Living in Morgan Co., GA - (horrible penmanship - hard to read) - Ballard, Obuse, 49 yrs GA GA GA, Mattie - Aug 1855 GA GA GA, Sidney - Oct 1874 GA, Carry - Aug 1872? GA, Josie - Dec 1886 GA, Josier - Dec 1886 GA, Elrene - Dec 1894 GA
* 1910 - Living in Morgan Co., GA - Ballard, O. S 60 GA GA GA, Mattie 54 GA GA GA, Sidney 30 GA, Carrie 27 GA, Josie 25 GA, Irene 19 GA (next door Jack Ballard 36
* 1920 - Living in Morgan Co., GA - Ballard, O. S 69, Mattie 64, Sidney A 44, Josie 34, Irene 23

Children of OSBORN BALLARD and MATTIE BELDING are:

     i. ALBERT SIDNEY⁷ BALLARD, *b. 17 Oct 1875, Morgan Co., GA; d. Aft. 1920.*

             Notes for ALBERT SIDNEY BALLARD:
             Source: WWI Draft Registration Card

     ii. CARRIE BALLARD, *b. Aug 1878, GA; d. Aft. 1910.*
     iii. IRENE BALLARD, *b. Dec 1892, GA; d. Aft. 1920.*
     iv. JOSIE BALLARD, *b. Dec 1886, GA; d. Aft. 1920.*

31. EVAN POWELL⁶ BALLARD (GEORGE WASHINGTON GREENE⁵, BENJAMIN⁴, JOHN³, JOSEPH², JOHN¹) *was born 13 Dec 1850 in GA, and died 01 Jan 1899. He married MARTHA THEODOSIA BROWN in Morgan Co., GA. She was born 28 Mar 1858 in GA, and died 02 May 1881.*

Notes for EVAN POWELL BALLARD:
Source- 1880 Morgan County Georgia Federal Census Records
* 1880 - Living in Morgan Co., GA with mother in law Lucy Brown - Ballard, Evan P 29, M Theodosia 22, Chas H 4

More About EVAN POWELL BALLARD:
Burial: Brown Family Cemetery, Brownwood, Morgan Co., GA

More About MARTHA THEODOSIA BROWN:
Burial: Brown Family Cemetery, Brownwood, Morgan Co., GA

Children of EVAN BALLARD and MARTHA BROWN are:
59.   i.   CHARLES H.[7] BALLARD, b. 14 Oct 1873; d. 10 May 1948.
        ii. SIMEON EDWARD BALLARD, b. 26 Nov 1877; d. 26 Apr 1878.

               More About SIMEON EDWARD BALLARD:
               Burial: Brown Family Cemetery, Brownwood, Morgan Co., GA

32. GEORGE HENRY[6] BALLARD (GEORGE WASHINGTON GREENE[5], BENJAMIN[4], JOHN[3], JOSEPH[2], JOHN[1]) was born 24 Mar 1856 in GA, and died 03 Aug 1932 in Monticello, Jasper Co, GA. He married EMILY JANE HEARD. She was born Abt. 1856 in Newton, GA, and died Bef. 1900.

Children of GEORGE BALLARD and EMILY HEARD are:
        i.   WILLIE J.[7] BALLARD, b. Nov 1882, GA; d. Aft. 1900.
        ii. ELIZABETH "LIZZY" BALLARD, b. May 1888, GA; d. Aft. 1900.
        iii. ALICE MABEL BALLARD, b. 21 Oct 1884; d. 13 Feb 1955, Monticello, GA.
60.   iv. MARION ERNEST BALLARD, b. 05 Nov 1892; d. 23 Oct 1954, Monticello, GA.

33. WILLIAM "WILLIE" EDGAR[6] BALLARD (GEORGE WASHINGTON GREENE[5], BENJAMIN[4], JOHN[3], JOSEPH[2], JOHN[1]) was born 07 Jun 1857 in GA, and died 30 Nov 1929 in Monticello, Jasper Co., GA. He married (1) KATE DOZIER. She was born 02 Dec 1866 in GA, and died 23 Sep 1903 in Monticello, Jasper Co., GA. He married (2) ALICE HEARD. She was born 25 Apr 1873, and died 20 Apr 1946.

Notes for WILLIAM "WILLIE" EDGAR BALLARD:
Source: 1900 Jasper County Georgia Federal Census Records
* 1900 - Living in Monticello, Jasper Co., GA - Ballard, WE - June 1857 married 15 yrs GA, Katie - Dec 1867 GA 3 ch 3 living, Spieghts - Mar 1887 GA, Dol W - Sep 1890 GA, Edgar D - Dec 1899 GA

Children of WILLIAM BALLARD and KATE DOZIER are:
61.   i.   GEORGE SPEIGHTS[7] BALLARD, b. 12 Mar 1887, GA; d. Aft. 1900.
        ii. ADOLPHUS W. BALLARD, b. Sep 1890, GA; d. Aft. 1900; m. NELL BALLARD, 21 Oct 1919; b. Abt. 1888; d. Aft. 1910.
        iii. EDGAR D. BALLARD, b. 04 Dec 1899, GA; d. Aft. 1900.

Child of WILLIAM BALLARD and ALICE HEARD is:
62.   iv. WILLIAM HEARD[7] BALLARD, b. 15 Dec 1910; d. 19 Aug 1956, Monticello, GA.

34. JOHN PORTER[6] BALLARD (GEORGE WASHINGTON GREENE[5], BENJAMIN[4], JOHN[3], JOSEPH[2], JOHN[1]) was born 1860 in GA, and died Aft. 1870. He married HANNAH TAPPEN. She was born Abt. 1855.

Children of JOHN BALLARD *and* HANNAH TAPPEN *are:*
>   i.   PAUL[7] BALLARD, b. Abt. 1875.
>   ii.   ELIZABETH BALLARD, b. Abt. 1876.
> iii.   PORTER BALLARD, b. Abt. 1877.
>   iv.   RANDOLPH BALLARD, b. Abt. 1878.

35. BENJAMIN WALTER[6] BALLARD (GEORGE WASHINGTON GREENE[5], BENJAMIN[4], JOHN[3], JOSEPH[2], JOHN[1]) *was born 28 Jun 1863 in Madison GA, and died 26 Sep 1927 in Atlanta, Fulton Co., GA. He married* MAUDE AUGUSTA KENNER *02 Dec 1885, daughter of* WILLIAM KENNER *and* LUCRETIA TIBBS. *She was born 07 Jul 1866 in AL, and died Aft. 1920.*

Notes for BENJAMIN WALTER BALLARD:
Source: 1900-1920 Fulton County Georgia Federal Census Records
* 1900 - Living in Atlanta, Fulton Co., GA - Ballard, Benjamin W - June 1863, Maud - July 1866, Adline - Sep 1886, Nellie - May 1890
* 1910 - Living in Atlanta, Fulton Co., GA - Ballard, Walter 45, Maude 42 4 ch 2 living, Nell 19
* 1920 - Living in Atlanta, Fulton Co., GA - Ballard, Benjamin 57, Maud 53

Children of BENJAMIN BALLARD *and* MAUDE KENNER *are:*
>   i.   ALLENE CLAY[7] BALLARD, b. 21 Sep 1886, GA; d. Aft. 1920; m. CHARLES M. MARSHALL; b. 1883, GA; d. Aft. 1920.
>
>   *Notes for* CHARLES M. MARSHALL:
>   *Source: 1910-1920 Fulton County Georgia Federal Census Records*
>   ** 1910 - Living in Atlanta, Fulton Co., GA - Marshall, Chas M 27 GA, Alena 23 GA*
>   ** 1920 - Living in Atlanta, Fulton Co., GA - Marshall, Charles 37, Alline 33*
>
>   ii.   NELL BALLARD, b. Abt. 1888; d. Aft. 1910; m. ADOLPHUS W. BALLARD, 21 Oct 1919; b. Sep 1890, GA; d. Aft. 1900.
> iii.   LOUISE ELIZABETH BALLARD, b. Abt. 1895, Atlanta, Fulton Co., GA; d. 07 Jul 1895.
>   iv.   BENJAMIN WALTER BALLARD, b. 22 Jul 1897; d. 28 May 1898.

Generation No. 4

36. ZACHARIAH TAYLOR[7] BALLARD (JOHN S.[6], SILAS JOSEPH HARDY[5], BENJAMIN[4], JOHN[3], JOSEPH[2], JOHN[1]) *was born 02 Mar 1852 in AL, and died 15 Oct 1932 in Montgomery Co., AL. He married (1)* REBECCA N. HOLMAN *17 Jul 1873 in Montgomery Co., AL. She was born Abt. 1848. He married (2)* A. D. HOLMAN *18 May 1884 in Montgomery Co., AL. She was born Abt. 1850. He married (3)* CLEMENTINE COLUMBIA HASSEY *11 Jun 1885 in Montgomery Co., AL. She was born Jun 1862 in AL, and died Aft. 1920.*

Notes for ZACHARIAH TAYLOR BALLARD:
Source:1880 & 1930 Montgomery County Alabama Federal Census, 1900-1920 Crenshaw County Alabama Federal Census Records, Ron Head (ronhead@knology.net)
* 1880 - Living in Montgomery Co., AL - Ballard, Zachariah 29 farmer AL SC SC, R N 21 AL GA GA, Annie 1 AL, JL 5/12 AL, AD Holman 17 sister in law AL, Ellen Johns 50 aunt AL, Charles John cousin 3 AL
* 1900 - Living in Rutledge, Crenshaw Co., AL - Ballard, Zachariah T - Mar 1852 AL, Columbia C - June 1862 AL, Preston - June 1880 AL, Christofer W - July 1886 AL, Kirby T - June 1889 AL, Libera - Oct 1893 AL, William B - June 1896 AL, Cleone F - Oct 1897 AL, Eliza J Hassey mo in law Aug 1834 AL SC SC, Sharlott T Adams - Mar 1832 AL SC SC
* 1910 - Living in Rutledge, Crenshaw Co., AL - Ballard, Zach T 57 married 2 x AL SC SC, Columes C 47 AL, Christopher W 24, Liberia 16, Burbon 14, Cleone 12, Brince L 8, Bibb 3, Hugh D 1 6/12, Eliza Hassey 74 mother in law, Doris Adams aunt 77
* 1920 - Living in Rutledge, Crenshaw Co., AL - Ballard, Zachery T 67, Clementine 57, William B 23, Brints L 17, Bibb H 13, Hugh D 11

* 1930 - Living in Walkers, Montgomery Co., AL - Ballard, Z T 78, C C 68, Hugh Dent Ballard 21

More About ZACHARIAH TAYLOR BALLARD:
Burial: Greenwood Cemetery, Montgomery Co., AL

Children of ZACHARIAH BALLARD and REBECCA HOLMAN are:
  i.   ANNIE[8] BALLARD, b. 24 Feb 1877, AL; d. 21 Jan 1977; m. SOL EXAVIER BRINSFIELD; b. 07 Nov 1872, AL; d. 23 Mar 1951.

       Notes for ANNIE BALLARD:
       Source: Ron Head (ronhead@knology.net)

       More About ANNIE BALLARD:
       Burial: Greenwood Cemetery, Montgomery Co., AL

       More About SOL EXAVIER BRINSFIELD:
       Burial: Greenwood Cemetery, Montgomery Co., AL

  ii. PRESTON HALLMAN BALLARD, b. 07 Jan 1880, AL; d. 30 Jan 1962; m. (1) FLORENCE KING, 1902; b. 1883, AL; d. 1928; m. (2) MARGARET ELDRIDGE, 08 Feb 1929; b. 18 Sep 1901; d. 12 Oct 1992.

       Notes for PRESTON HALLMAN BALLARD:
       Source: 1910 Crenshaw County Alabama Federal Census Records, Ron Head (ronhead@knology.net)

       * 1910 - Living in Luverne, Crenshaw Co., AL - Ballard, Preston 30 AL AL AL, Florence 27 AL FL FL, Rutledge H 5 AL, Mary F 3 AL

       More About PRESTON HALLMAN BALLARD:
       Burial: Emmaus Cemetery, Luverne, Crenshaw Co., AL

       More About MARGARET ELDRIDGE:
       Burial: Emmaus Cemetery, Luverne, Crenshaw Co., AL

Children of ZACHARIAH BALLARD and CLEMENTINE HASSEY are:
  iii. CHRISTOPHER WREN[8] BALLARD, b. 25 Jul 1886, Crenshaw Co., AL; d. 15 Jan 1957, Chilton Co., AL.
  iv. KIRBY TYSON BALLARD, b. Jan 1889, Crenshaw Co., AL; d. 08 May 1934, Montgomery Co., AL; m. FRANCES MORGAN; b. 05 May 1874, TX; d. 04 Nov 1938, Montgomery Co., AL.

       More About KIRBY TYSON BALLARD:
       Burial: Greenwood Cemetery, Montgomery Co., AL

       More About FRANCES MORGAN:
       Burial: Greenwood Cemetery, Montgomery Co., AL

  v.   LIBERIA P. BALLARD, b. 14 Oct 1893, Crenshaw Co., AL; d. 06 Jan 1923, Dallas Co., TX; m. CLAUDE G. WELSH; b. 03 Apr 1886, IL; d. 30 May 1972, San Antonio, Bexar Co., TX.

       More About LIBERIA P. BALLARD:
       Burial: Greenwood Cemetery, Montgomery Co., AL

       More About CLAUDE G. WELSH:
       Burial: Ft. Sam Houston National Cemetery, San Antonio, Bexar Co., TX

     vi.   WILLIAM BOURBON BALLARD, b. 20 Jan 1896, Crenshaw Co., AL; d. 25 Sep 1956, Gregg Co., TX.

    vii.   CLEONE F. BALLARD, b. 02 Oct 1897, Crenshaw Co., AL; d. 09 Oct 1987, Montgomery Co., AL.

        More About CLEONE F. BALLARD:
        Burial: Greenwood Cemetery, Montgomery Co., AL

    viii.   BRENTS LARRIMORE BALLARD, b. 13 Mar 1902, Crenshaw Co., AL; d. 03 Aug 1958, Tarrant Co., TX.

        More About BRENTS LARRIMORE BALLARD:
        Burial: Smithfield Cemetery, North Richland Hills, Tarrant Co., TX

    ix.   BIBB HUNTER BALLARD, b. 16 Oct 1906, Crenshaw Co., AL; d. 06 Oct 2007, Dallas Co., TX.

        More About BIBB HUNTER BALLARD:
        Burial: Restland Memorial Park, Dallas Co., TX

    x.   HUGH DENT BALLARD, b. 22 Nov 1908, Crenshaw Co., AL; d. 06 Sep 2000, TX.

        More About HUGH DENT BALLARD:
        Burial: Restland Memorial Park, Dallas Co., TX

37. THOMAS EDWARD[7] BALLARD (JOHN S.[6], SILAS JOSEPH HARDY[5], BENJAMIN[4], JOHN[3], JOSEPH[2], JOHN[1]) was born 24 Jan 1854 in Montgomery Co., AL, and died 27 Jul 1939 in Caldwell Co., TX. He married ALBERTA ANNETTE HICKS 16 Dec 1877 in Montgomery Co., AL, daughter of JOHN HICKS and MELISSA ADAMS. She was born 17 May 1853 in Montgomery Co., AL, and died 13 Mar 1928 in Lockhart Co., TX.

Notes for THOMAS EDWARD BALLARD:

Source: 1880 Montgomery County Alabama Federal Census Records, Alice Ballard (bottleneck19@yahoo.com)
* 1880 - Living in Tuckers, Montgomery Co., AL - Ballard, Thomas E 25, Alberta A 27, Erin 2, Berta 8/12

Notes for ALBERTA ANNETTE HICKS:
Source: Alice Ballard (bottleneck19@yahoo.com)

Children of THOMAS BALLARD and ALBERTA HICKS are:

     i.   ERIN[8] BALLARD, b. 26 Nov 1878, AL; d. Aft. 1880.
    ii.   BERTA BALLARD, b. 18 Feb 1880, AL; d. Aft. 1880.
    iii.   ESMA BALLARD, b. 03 Oct 1881, AL.
    iv.   RAY BALLARD, b. 28 Nov 1883, AL.
    v.   RALPH BALLARD, b. 09 Oct 1885, AL.
    vi.   LIDIE BALLARD, b. 29 Jan 1888, AL.
    vii.   JOHN BALLARD, b. 18 Apr 1890, AL.
    viii.   HENDRIS BALLARD, b. 22 Mar 1896, AL.
    ix.   GUSTA BALLARD, b. 14 Oct 1899, AL.

38. EVANS COLEMAN[7] BALLARD (BENJAMIN RANDALL[6], SILAS JOSEPH HARDY[5], BENJAMIN[4], JOHN[3], JOSEPH[2], JOHN[1]) was born 09 Mar 1840 in Oakey Streak, Covington Co., AL, and died 04 May 1913 in Blackrock, Crenshaw Co., AL. He married (1) NANCY HENRIETTA LASSITER 25 Oct 1865 in or 12/27 Butler Co., AL. She was born 21 Jul 1844 in AL, and died 20 Mar 1883. He married (2) GERINA CAROLINE MOORE 29 Mar 1884, daughter of ASA MOORE and GERINDA SIZEMORE. She was born 09 Mar 1850 in Talbot Co., GA, and died 26 Oct 1924 in Rutledge, Crenshaw Co., AL.

Notes for EVANS COLEMAN BALLARD:
Source: The Andulusia Star News submitted by Jan Ballard, 1880-1910 Crenshaw County Alabama Federal Census Records, Phil Ballard (pballard@crenshaw-schools.org)
* 1870 - Living in Crenshaw Co., AL - Ballard, EC 30, Nancy 25, Thomas 3, Anna 6/12, Matthew Lasiter 20
* 1880 - Living in Rutledge, Crenshaw County Alabama - Ballard, Evan 40, Lucy 36, Thomas 13, Anna 1, Randal 7, John 8, Viola 7, George 5, Charles 3, not named 6/12 (f)
* 1900 - Living in Roberson, Crenshaw Co., AL - Ballard, Evan - Mar 1840, Urina C - Mar 1851, Viola D - Oct 1872, Nancy H - Jan 1880, Gerena E - Nov 1886, Jacob - May 1891
* 1910 - Living in Rutledge, Crenshaw Co., AL - Ballard, Evan C 70 AL NC GA, Garina C 58 GA GA GA, Luda V 36 AL, George C 34 AL

More About EVANS COLEMAN BALLARD:
Burial: Blackrock Cemetery, Crenshaw Co., AL

More About NANCY HENRIETTA LASSITER:
Burial: Black Rock Cemetery, Black Rock, Crenshaw Co., AL

Notes for GERINA CAROLINE MOORE:
Source: 1920 Crenshaw County Alabama Federal Census Records
* 1920 - Living in Rutledge, Crenshaw Co., AL - Ballard, Mrs. Caroline 58 wd, Jacob 25, Annie May dau in law 33, Bernette 7, Myrtle M 6, Tina S 4

Children of EVANS BALLARD and NANCY LASSITER are:

    i.   THOMAS JEFFERSON[8] BALLARD, b. 1867, Blackrock, Crenshaw Co., AL; d. 1912, Rutledge Cemetery Crenshaw Co., AL; m. SARAH ALICE GANEY; b. 1868; d. 1912.

    Notes for THOMAS JEFFERSON BALLARD:
    Source: 1900 Crenshaw County Alabama Federal Census Records, 1910 Coffee County Alabama Federal Census Records, Jennifer "Joan" Ballard Stewart (jenniferbstewart@bellsouth.net)
    * 1900 - Living in Roberson, Crenshaw Co., AL - Ballard, Thomas J - Dec 1866 md 9 yrs, Sarah A - Mar 1868 - 7 children 6 living, Ema - Nov 1891, Fletcher - Jan 1894, Homer - May 1895, Tessey - Apr 1896, Rhobes - Jan 1898, Guy - Aug 1899
    * 1910 - Living in Old Town, Coffee Co., AL - Ballard, Thomas J 43 AL, Sarah A 42 (12 children 10 living), Fletcher 16, Omer 14 AL, Mary R 11 AL, Guy G 10 AL, Chalmer P 9 AL, Lollie A 8, Trudie E 6 AL, Cubie F 3 AL

    More About SARAH ALICE GANEY:
    Burial: Rutledge Primitive Baptist Church Cemetery, Rutledge, Crenshaw Co., AL

    ii.   EVAN COLEMAN BALLARD, b. 15 Feb 1868, Crenshaw Co., AL; d. 1868.
    iii.   ANNA BALLARD, b. 18 Nov 1869, Crenshaw Co., AL; d. 22 Jan 1939, Black Rock, Crenshaw Co. AL; m. JOSEPH E. DEEN; b. Abt. 1865.

    More About ANNA BALLARD:
    Burial: Black Rock Cemetery, Black Rock, Crenshaw Co. AL

    iv.   BENJAMIN "RANDALL" BALLARD, b. 03 Mar 1871, Crenshaw Co., AL; d. 10 Jul 1936; m. TABITHA OWEN, 28 Sep 1893, Crenshaw Co., AL; b. 01 Mar 1875, TX; d. 10 Jul 1936.

    Notes for BENJAMIN "RANDALL" BALLARD:
    Source: 1900-1910 Coffee County Alabama Federal Census Records, Rosie Wells
    * 1900 - Living in Old Town, Coffee Co., AL - Ballard, Benjamin R - Mar 1871 AL AL AL, Tabbie - Mar 1875 TX, Layman L - July 1894 AL, Babe - Sept 1897 AL, George C. brother - Feb 1875 AL AL AL
    * 1910 - Living in Old Town, Coffee Co., AL - Ballard, Benjamin R 39 AL, Tabitha B 35 TX, Layman

L 15 AL, Emmit W 12 AL, Mary G 4 AL not named female 2/12 AL
* 1920 - Living in Old Town, Coffee Co., AL - Ballard, Randal, Tabbie 45, Emmit 22, Gladis 14,
Grady 9, Connie 8 niece
* 1930 - Living in Old Town, Coffee Co., AL - Ballard, BR 59, Tabbie B 55, Emett 32, Connie 19,
Homer 35 nephew

More About BENJAMIN "RANDALL" BALLARD:
Burial: Alberton Cemetery, Coffee Co., AL

More About TABITHA OWEN:
Burial: Alberton Cemetery, Coffee Co., AL

    v.   VIOLA DELULA BALLARD, b. 03 Oct 1873, Crenshaw Co., AL; d. 14 Jan 1946; m. JOHN D. THOMAS.

More About VIOLA DELULA BALLARD:
Burial: Chapel Hill Baptist Cemetery, Crenshaw Co., AL

    vi.   JOHN BEAUEGARD BALLARD, b. 1876, Crenshaw Co., AL; m. EMILY OWENS.
   vii.   CHARLIE MONROE BALLARD, b. 10 Jul 1877, Crenshaw Co., AL; d. 27 Dec 1918, Crenshaw Co., AL;
       m. LENA CLEMENTINE GREGORY, 25 Jul 1898; b. 16 May 1876; d. 17 Mar 1961.

Notes for CHARLIE MONROE BALLARD:
Source: 1900-1920 Crenshaw County Alabama Federal Census Records
* Was a farmer and owned several hundred acres of land in Chapel Hill community. Donated land
for Chapel Hill Baptist Church.
* 1900 - Living in Roberson, Crenshaw Co., AL - Ballard, Charles M - July 1875, Tiney - May 1880,
Sherman A - May 1899
* 1920 - Living in Rutledge, Crenshaw Co., AL - Ballard, Mrs Tina or Lina 41 wd, Raymond 16,
Leon C 15, Dollie 13, Duffie 13, Crawsey 5, Allen 3 8/12, Demsey 1 2/12

  viii.   GEORGE COLUMBUS BALLARD, b. 13 Feb 1879, Crenshaw Co., AL; d. 1928; m. MARY ANNA RAYBON;
       b. 1885, AL; d. Aft. 1930.

Notes for GEORGE COLUMBUS BALLARD:
Source: 1920-1930 Crenshaw County Alabama Federal Census Records
* 1920 - Living in Rutledge, Crenshaw Co., AL - Ballard, George C 44 AL, Mary A 38 AL, Gracie
13, Gady 10, Bee 9, Grover 6, Ila 3

Notes for MARY ANNA RAYBON:
Source: 1930 Crenshaw County Alabama Federal Census Records
* 1930 - Living in Rutledge, Crenshaw Co., AL - Ballard, Annah 45 AL, Gracie 25 AL, Grodie 20 AL
Bee 19 AL George 16 AL, Ilie 14 AL, Hazel 10 AL

    ix.   NANCY HENRIETTA BALLARD, b. 15 Jan 1880, Crenshaw Co., AL; m. MILLER BYRD.

Notes for MILLER BYRD:
Source: Phil Ballard (pballard@crenshaw-schools.org)

    x.   MINNIE BALLARD, b. 06 Jun 1881, Crenshaw Co., AL.

Children of EVANS BALLARD and GERINA MOORE are:
    xi.   EVANS COLEMAN[8] BALLARD, b. 1885, Crenshaw Co., AL.
   xii.   EMMA GERINA BALLARD, b. 06 Nov 1887, Crenshaw Co., AL; d. 22 Sep 1913; m. JOHN DANIEL
       THOMAS; b. 25 Mar 1878; d. 07 Apr 1958.

More About EMMA GERINA BALLARD:
Burial: Chapel Hill Baptist Cemetery, Crenshaw Co., AL

More About JOHN DANIEL THOMAS:
Burial: Chapel Hill Baptist Cemetery, Crenshaw Co., AL

    xiii.   JACOB "JAKE" BALLARD, b. 31 May 1891, Crenshaw Co., AL; d. 24 Jul 1959; m. ANNIE MAE MORGAN; b. 29 Sep 1889; d. 08 Jul 1976.

Notes for JACOB "JAKE" BALLARD:
Source: 1920 Crenshaw County Alabama Federal Census Records

* 1920 - Living in Crenshaw Co., AL - Living with mother and is family - Ballard, Jacob 25 AL, Annie May 33, Bernette 7, Myrtle 6, Tina 4

More About JACOB "JAKE" BALLARD:
Burial: Rutledge Primitive Baptist Church Cemetery, Rutledge, Crenshaw Co., AL

More About ANNIE MAE MORGAN:
Burial: Rutledge Primitive Baptist Church Cemetery, Rutledge, Crenshaw Co., AL

39. NANCY JANE[7] BALLARD (BENJAMIN RANDALL[6], SILAS JOSEPH HARDY[5], BENJAMIN[4], JOHN[3], JOSEPH[2], JOHN[1]) was born 02 May 1842 in Oakey Streak, Covington Co., AL, and died 1919 in Oakey Streak, Covington Co., AL. She married WILLIAM D. HAMMOND. He was born 14 Jul 1819, and died 29 Aug 1879.

Notes for NANCY JANE BALLARD:
Source: 1880 Geneva County Alabama Federal Census Records, Norma Hammond McLoughlin (mclou@hal-pc.org), Joe Webb

* 1880 - Living in Geneva Co., AL - Hammond, Nancy J 38 farmer AL AL AL, Elizabeth 7 FL, William T 6 FL, Catherine 5 AL, Joseph M 4 AL, Willie J 10/12 AL

More About NANCY JANE BALLARD:
Burial: Geneva Co., AL

More About WILLIAM D. HAMMOND:
Burial: Geneva Co., AL

Children of NANCY BALLARD and WILLIAM HAMMOND are:

    i.   ELIZABETH PERELEE[8] HAMMOND, b. 06 Aug 1872, Geneva Co., AL; d. Aft. 1880; m. DANIEL BISHOP MERCHANT; b. 20 Dec 1870.
    ii.   WILLIAM TAYLOR HAMMOND, b. 19 Nov 1873, Geneva Co., AL; d. Aft. 1880; m. CHARITY FUFORD; b. 20 Aug 1877.
    iii.   CATHERINE HAMMOND, b. 1875, Geneva Co., AL; d. Aft. 1880; m. ANGUS P. VAUGHN; b. Apr 1870.
    iv.   JOSEPH HAMMOND, b. 1876, Geneva Co., AL; d. Aft. 1880; m. HENRIETTA HALL; b. 1880.
    v.   WILLIE J. HAMMOND, b. 1876, Geneva Co., AL; d. Aft. 1880; m. (1) JEPTHA P. DENARD; m. (2) SID HOLMAN.

40. SARAH ANN[7] BALLARD (BENJAMIN RANDALL[6], SILAS JOSEPH HARDY[5], BENJAMIN[4], JOHN[3], JOSEPH[2], JOHN[1]) was born 24 Feb 1846 in Oakey Streak, Covington Co., AL, and died 1917 in Oakey Streak, Covington Co., AL. She married JEREMIAH "JERRY" APLIN. He was born 1851 in AL, and died Aft. 1880.

Children of SARAH BALLARD and JEREMIAH APLIN are:
    i.   JOHN[8] APLIN, b. 1863.
    ii. RANDAL APLIN, b. 1869.

41. BENJAMIN RANDAL "BUTLER"[7] BALLARD (BENJAMIN RANDALL[6], SILAS JOSEPH HARDY[5], BENJAMIN[4], JOHN[3], JOSEPH[2], JOHN[1]) was born 05 Mar 1849 in Oakey Streak, Covington Co., AL, and died Bet. 1918 - 1919. He married MARY ELIZABETH ETHERIDGE 1870. She was born 1850 in GA, and died Aft. 1900.

Notes for BENJAMIN RANDAL "BUTLER" BALLARD:
Source: 1880 -1900 Covington County Alabama Federal Census Records
* 1880 - Living in Covington Co., AL - Ballard, Butler 30 farmer AL NC GA, Mary E. 30 GA, John 7 AL, Elexander ;6 AL, Greenberry 5 AL, Hardy 6 AL
* 1900 - Living in Westover, Covington Co., AL - Ballard, Butler B - Mar 1849, Mary E - Aug 1848, Sellers - Mar 1875, Benjamin - June 1881, fe - Sept 1883, male - Mar 1862 (48 yrs)

Children of BENJAMIN BALLARD and MARY ETHERIDGE are:
    i.   JOHN DANIEL[8] BALLARD, b. 1871, AL; m. CELIA BOLDEN.
    ii. PRESTON GREENBERRY BALLARD, b. Jan 1873, AL; d. Aft. 1900; m. (1) SALLY GARRETT; b. Nov 1874, AL; d. Aft. 1900; m. (2) DORA CRAIG BAILEY.

         Notes for PRESTON GREENBERRY BALLARD:
         Source: 1900 Covington County Alabama Federal Census Records
         * 1900 - Living in Westover, Covington Co., AL - Ballard, Green - Jan 1873 AL AL AL, Sallie - Nov 1874 AL, Berry L - Dec 1896 AL, Mary - Apr 1900 AL

    iii. JAMES ALEXANDER OLIVER BALLARD, b. Dec 1876, AL; d. Feb 1912; m. CAROLINE "CARRIE" VICTORY JACKSON; b. 11 Jul 1876; d. 09 Jun 1943.

         Notes for JAMES ALEXANDER OLIVER BALLARD:
         Source: 1900 Covington County Alabama Federal Census Records, Eddy Ballard (woballard@yahoo.com)
         * 1900 - Living in Red Level, Covington Co., AL - Ballard, Alexander A - Dec 1876 AL AL AL, Carrie V - July 1876, Robert - Apr 1898, Benjamin - Feb 1900

         Notes for CAROLINE "CARRIE" VICTORY JACKSON:
         Source: Eddy D. Ballard (Woballard@yahoo.com)

    iv. HARDY SELLERS BALLARD, b. Mar 1875, AL; d. Aft. 1920; m. ELLA MCCARTER; b. 1873; d. Aft. 1920.

         Notes for HARDY SELLERS BALLARD:
         Source: 1910-1920 Covington County Alabama Federal Census Records
         * 1910 - Living in Hamptonville, Covington Co., AL - Ballard, HS 37 (married 10) 5 children - 4 living, Ella 27, Fenis 8, Ima 7, Feona 5, Marshall 10/12
         * 1920 - Living in River Falls, Covington Co., AL - Ballard, Hardy 43, Ella A 38, Phennie 18, Rooth 16, Phronnie 14, Marshal 10, Euveda 5

    v.   BENJAMIN CUMBLE BALLARD, b. Jun 1881, Covington Co., AL; d. Aft. 1900.
    vi. SARAH ANTIONETTE BALLARD, b. Sep 1883, Covington Co., AL; d. Aft. 1900; m. WILLIAM BARNES.

42. HASTING URIAH GILCHRIST[7] BALLARD (BENJAMIN RANDALL[6], SILAS JOSEPH HARDY[5], BENJAMIN[4], JOHN[3], JOSEPH[2], JOHN[1]) was born 13 Jul 1851 in Oakey Streak, Covington Co., AL, and died 07 Mar 1935 in Oakey Streak, Covington Co., AL. He married (1) MARY E. BOYKIN. He married (2) SARAH STRICKLAND 1870. She was born

1847 in AL, and died Aft. 1880. He married (3) MINNIE BARROW Bef. 1891. She was born Abt. 1860, and died Bef. 1920. He married (4) NANCY Bef. 1900. She was born Dec 1861, and died Aft. 1900.

Notes for HASTING URIAH GILCHRIST BALLARD:
Source: 1880-1920 Covington County Alabama Federal Census Records
* 1880 - Living in Covington Co., AL - Ballard, Haston 24 farmer AL NC GA, Sarah J. 33 AL GA GA, Calvin M. 7 AL
* 1900 - Living in Westover, Covington Co., AL - Ballard, Hastings - June 1851 AL TN AL, Nancy - Dec 1861, Malachi - Jan 1881, William J - Apr 1893
* 1920 - Living in Westover, Covington Co., AL - Ballard, Hastings G 68 wd, Malichi 28 wd

Child of HASTING BALLARD and SARAH STRICKLAND is:
      i.   CALVIN M.[8] BALLARD, b. 1863, AL; d. Aft. 1880.

Children of HASTING BALLARD and MINNIE BARROW are:
      ii.   CALVIN M.[8] BALLARD, b. 1889, AL; d. 1891.
      iii.   MALACHI C. BALLARD, b. Jan 1891, AL; d. 1969; m. LENA; b. 1905; d. Aft. 1930.

          Notes for MALACHI C. BALLARD:
          Source: 1930 Covington County Alabama Federal Census Records
          * 1930 - Living in Westover, Covington Co., AL - Ballard, Mal C 38, Lena 25, Ramond 8, Lois 7, Wilson 3 2/12, Haston G 78 father

      iv.   WILLIAM JENKINS BALLARD, b. Apr 1893, AL; d. 1969; m. SARAH; b. 1895; d. Aft. 1930.

          Notes for WILLIAM JENKINS BALLARD:
          Source: 1930 Covington County Alabama Federal Census Records
          * 1930 - Living in Westover, Covington Co., AL - Ballard, Jenkins W 37, Sarah 35, Clyde 16, Emmett 5

43. BURSE LASTING GALE[7] BALLARD (BENJAMIN RANDALL[6], SILAS JOSEPH HARDY[5], BENJAMIN[4], JOHN[3], JOSEPH[2], JOHN[1]) *was born 19 Jun 1856 in Oakey Streak, Covington Co., AL, and died Aft. 1930. He married LOLA B.. She was born Oct 1871, and died Aft. 1930.*

Notes for BURSE LASTING GALE BALLARD:
Source: 1900-1930 Covington County Alabama Federal Census Records
* 1900 - Living in Westover, Covington Co., AL - Ballard, Burrues L - June 1857, Lola B - Oct 1871, Ella - June 1885 AL, Adella - Feb 1891 AL, David - Aug 1892 AL, Delaney - Mar 1894 AL, Minnie R - Feb 1896 AL, Ella - Apr 1898
* 1920 - Living in Westover, Covington Co., AL - Ballard, Burrus L 63, Lula B 48, Adella 28, Dave P 27, Delaney M 25, Jermome F 18, BV 16, Ada E 12, Elvie 8, Selmer 6
* 1930 - Living in Westover, Covington Co., AL - Ballard, BL 73 AL LB 58 AL, Ella 40, Adella 38, Dove 37, Jerrome 28, Ada 23, Elba E 18, Selmer 17

Children of BURSE BALLARD and LOLA B. are:
      i.   ELLA[8] BALLARD, b. Jun 1885, Covington Co., AL; d. Aft. 1900.
      ii.   ADELLA BALLARD, b. Feb 1891, Covington Co., AL; d. Aft. 1930.
      iii.   DAVID BALLARD, b. Aug 1892, Covington Co., AL; d. Aft. 1900.
      iv.   DAVE P. BALLARD, b. 1893, Covington Co., AL; d. Aft. 1920.
      v.   DELANEY BALLARD, b. Mar 1894, Covington Co., AL; d. Aft. 1920.
      vi.   MINNIE R. BALLARD, b. Feb 1896, Covington Co., AL; d. Aft. 1900.
      vii.   ELLA BALLARD, b. Apr 1898, Covington Co., AL; d. Aft. 1930.
      viii.   JEROME F. BALLARD, b. 1902, Covington Co., AL; d. Aft. 1930.

    ix.   *B. V. BALLARD, b. 1904, Covington Co., AL; d. Aft. 1920.*
    x.   *ADA E. BALLARD, b. 1908, Covington Co., AL; d. Aft. 1930.*
    xi.   *SELMER BALLARD, b. 1914, Covington Co., AL; d. Aft. 1930.*

44. MATILDA CAROLINE[7] BALLARD (JONATHAN O.[6], SILAS JOSEPH HARDY[5], BENJAMIN[4], JOHN[3], JOSEPH[2], JOHN[1]) *was born 02 Jun 1833 in 6/21/1838, and died 1901. She married SOLOMON EALUM 12 Mar 1848. He was born 15 Sep 1825 in AL, and died 04 Mar 1893 in Of Butler Co., AL.*

Notes for MATILDA CAROLINE BALLARD:
Source: Jack D. Mathis (jmathisd@aol.com), Matt Grantham (Mattnapa@aol.com)

More About MATILDA CAROLINE BALLARD:
Burial: Consolation Cemetery Butler Co., AL

Notes for SOLOMON EALUM:
Source: 1860-1880 Covington County Alabama Federal Census Records
* 1860 - Living in Covington Co., AL - Ealum, Solomon 37 AL, Matilda C 24, Ambrose J 10, Susannah 8, Mary E 4
* 1870 - Living in Covington Co., AL - Elam, S 44, Mary C 38, Susan 18, Mary 13, Emma C 11, James 10, Eliza A 7, Edward 17
* 1880 - Living in Covington Co., AL - Elam, Solomon 54, Matilda C 46, James R 18, Eliza 16, Evey C 5

More About SOLOMON EALUM:
Burial: Consolation Cemetery Butler Co., AL

Children of MATILDA BALLARD and SOLOMON EALUM are:
    i.   *AMBROSE J.[8] EALUM, b. 1850, Covington Co., AL; d. Aft. 1860.*
    ii.   *SUSANNAH EALUM, b. 1852, Covington Co., AL; d. Aft. 1870.*
    iii.   *EDWARD EALUM, b. 1853, Covington Co., AL; d. Aft. 1870.*
    iv.   *MARY E. EALUM, b. 1856, Covington Co., AL; d. Aft. 1880.*
    v.   *EMMA C. EALUM, b. 1860, Covington Co., AL; d. Aft. 1870.*
    vi.   *JAMES ROBERT EALUM, b. 1860, Covington Co., AL; d. Aft. 1880.*
    vii.   *EVA C. EALUM, b. 1875, Covington Co., AL; d. Aft. 1870.*
    viii.   *IRVIN EALUM, b. 1879, Covington Co., AL; d. Aft. 1880.*

45. JONATHAN "JOHN LEE"[7] BALLARD, JR. (JONATHAN O.[6], SILAS JOSEPH HARDY[5], BENJAMIN[4], JOHN[3], JOSEPH[2], JOHN[1]) *was born 09 Apr 1847 in Oakey Streak, Covington Co., AL, and died 08 Sep 1927 in Jackson Clarke Co., AL. He married MARY ANNA GOODLOE 13 May 1875 in Suggsville, Clarke Co., AL, daughter of BENJAMIN GOODLOE and MARTHA STARKE. She was born 11 Nov 1858 in Suggsville, Clarke Co., AL, and died 10 Aug 1933 in Jackson, Clarke Co., AL.*

Notes for JONATHAN "JOHN LEE" BALLARD, JR.:
Source: 1880 Monroe County Alabama Federal Census Records, 1900-1920 Clarke County Alabama Federal Census Records, Jan M. Ballard (72753.3121@compuserve.com), Teena Schroeder (RSTS@worldnet.att.net)

* 1880 - Living in Claiborne, Monroe Co., AL - Ballard, John L 31 AL VA AL, Mary 21 AL VA SC, John L Jr 7/12 Nov AL
* 1900 - Living in Jackson, Clarke Co., AL - Ballard, John L - Apr 1847 AL SC AL, Mary J - Nov 1858 AL VA SC, John L Jr. - Oct 1879 AL, Charles L - Jul 1881 AL, Samuel G - Sept 1883 AL, Joe R - Feb 1886 AL, Vivian G - May 1888 AL, Fanny S - Aug 1890 AL, Stan R - Oct 1893 AL, Flora M - Aug 1896 AL, Henry J - May 1899 AL
* 1910 - Living in Jackson, Clarke Co., AL - Ballard, John L 66 AL NC SC, Mary G 52 AL VA Sc, Joe R 28 AL, Vivian G 21 AL, Fannie A 19 AL, Reeves S 16 AL, Flora Mae 13, Henry J 10 AL, Minnie
* 1920 - Living in Jackson, Clarke Co., AL - Ballard, John R 72 AL NC SC, , Mary 62 AL VA SC, Henry 20 AL, Minnie R 19 AL

Children of JONATHAN BALLARD and MARY GOODLOE are:

   i.   MARTHA[8] BALLARD, b. Abt. 1877, Monroe Co., AL.

   ii.   JOHN LEE BALLARD, JR., b. 06 Oct 1879, Purdue Hill, Monroe Co., AL; d. 07 Feb 1951, Vicksburg, MS; m. CLARA MAUDE CURRY, 12 Jun 1906, Mobile AL; b. 01 Dec 1883, McIntosh, Washington Co., AL; d. 22 Oct 1970, ,Vicksburg, Warren Co., MS.

        Notes for JOHN LEE BALLARD, JR.:
        Source: 1920 St. Laundry Parish Louisiana Federal Census Records, Jan M. Ballard (72753.3121@compuserve.com)
        * 1920 - Living in Opelousas, St. Landry Par., LA - Ballard, John L 40, Clara 36, Mary Kate 11, John Lee Jr 10, Edward 9, Frank C 7, Clara Maude 5 Hubert Earl 2 2//12, Paul Eugene 5/12
        * 1930 - Living in Warren Co., MS - Ballard, John L 50 AL AL AL, Clara M 46, Edward C 19 LA, Frank C 18 LA, C Maude 15 LA, Herbert E 12 LA, Paul E 10 LA, William J 8 LA, Ruth 5 LA

   iii.   CHARLES LEVENS BALLARD, b. 06 Jul 1881, Monroe Co., AL; d. Aft. 1900.
   iv.   SAMUEL GAILLARD BALLARD, b. 23 Aug 1884, Monroe Co., AL; d. Aft. 1900.
   v.   JOSEPH ROCKWELL BALLARD, b. 02 Feb 1885, Purdue Hill, Monroe Co., AL; d. 28 Jan 1952; m. MAMIE FLORENCE DUKE; b. 1894, AL; d. Aft. 1930.

        Notes for JOSEPH ROCKWELL BALLARD:
        Source: 1920-1930 Clarke County Alabama Federal Census Records, Teena Schroeder (RSTS@worldnet.att.net)
        * 1920 - Living in Jackson, Clarke Co., AL - Ballard, Joe R 33 AL, Mamie 26 AL, Joseph D 6, Catherine 4 2/12, Morgan 1
        * 1930 - Living in Jackson, Clarke Co., AL - Ballard, Joseph R 42, Mary D 37, Joseph R Jr 16, Catherine 14, Morgan D 11, Fred J 1 10/12

   vi.   FRANCIS "FANNIE" ANGES BALLARD, b. 12 Aug 1887, AL; d. Aft. 1910.
   vii.   VIVIAN GOODLOE BALLARD, b. 20 May 1889, AL; d. Aft. 1910.
   viii.   STARK RIVES BALLARD, b. Oct 1893, AL; d. Aft. 1910; m. LUCRETIA ANN MAYHAM, 20 Feb 1932, Buffalo NY; b. 18 Jun 1895, Buffalo, Erie Co, NY.

        Notes for STARK RIVES BALLARD:
        Source: Teena Schroeder (RSTS@att.net)

   ix.   FLORA MARY BALLARD, b. 09 Aug 1896, AL; d. Aft. 1910.
   x.   HENRY SAVAGE BALLARD, b. May 1899, AL; d. Aft. 1910.
   xi.   MINNIE BALLARD, b. 1901, Clarke Co., AL; d. Aft. 1910.

46. FLORA KATHERINE[7] WIGGINS (TEMPERANCE TABITHA[6] BALLARD, SILAS JOSEPH HARDY[5], BENJAMIN[4], JOHN[3], JOSEPH[2], JOHN[1]) *was born 1856 in Conecuh Co., AL, and died 15 Jul 1915 in River Falls, Covington Co., AL. She married JOHN HENRY C. DONALDSON 25 Nov 1878 in Evergreen, Conecuh Co., AL. He was born 07 Feb 1832 in Coffee Co., AL, and died 29 Apr 1904 in Covington Co., AL.*

More About FLORA KATHERINE WIGGINS:
Burial: Mt. Union Cemetery, Conecuh Co., Al

More About JOHN HENRY C. DONALDSON:
Burial: Family cemetery Evergreen Conecuh Co., AL

Children of FLORA WIGGINS and JOHN DONALDSON are:

   i.   SUSAN SAMANTHA[8] DONALDSON, b. 02 Dec 1879, Cohassett, Conecuh Co., AL; d. 04 Feb 1969, Andalusia, Covington Co., AL; m. COLONEL D. LORD; b. 04 Oct 1873; d. 03 Sep 1953.

More About SUSAN SAMANTHA DONALDSON:
Burial: 06 Feb 1969, Fairmont Cemetery Red Level, Covington Co., AL

More About COLONEL D. LORD:
Burial: Mt. Union Cemetery, Conecuh Co., AL

     ii. KINYARD DAVID DONALDSON, b. 15 Oct 1881, Cohassett, Conecuh Co., AL; d. 01 Jul 1948; m. ELIZABETH MURREY; b. Abt. 1900; d. 01 Jul 1948.
     iii. NANCY JANE DONALDSON, b. 04 Jan 1885, Cohassett, Conecuh Co., AL; d. 01 May 1977; m. WALTER AMMONS; b. Abt. 1883; d. May 1977.
     iv. JAMES WILBER DONALDSON, b. 18 Aug 1889, Hurbert, Conecuh Co., AL; d. 29 May 1976, MS; m. NORA LUCUS.
     v. FRONIE ELIZABETH DONALDSON, b. 12 Dec 1893, Hurbert, Conecuh Co., AL; d. 21 Nov 1977; m. WILLIAM BARTON; b. Abt. 1891; d. 21 Nov 1977.
     vi. WILLIE BENJAMIN DONALDSON, b. 10 Apr 1895, Hurbert, Conecuh Co., AL; d. 02 Jul 1961, Andalusia, Covington Co., AL; m. VIRGIE MAE; b. Abt. 1920; d. 02 Jul 1961.

47. WILLIAM P.[7] WIGGINS (TEMPERANCE TABITHA[6] BALLARD, SILAS JOSEPH HARDY[5], BENJAMIN[4], JOHN[3], JOSEPH[2], JOHN[1]) was born 04 May 1857 in Conecuh Co., AL, and died Aft. 1880. He married DICEY ANN SHEFFIELD 04 May 1877 in AL. She was born 25 Dec 1858, and died Aft. 1880.

Notes for WILLIAM P. WIGGINS:
Source: 1880 Conecuh County Alabama Federal Census Records
* 1880 - Living in Jamestown, Conecuh Co., AL - Wiggons, William P 23 Laborer AL AL AL, Disey 22 AL AL AL, James 2 AL, William 1 AL

Children of WILLIAM WIGGINS and DICEY SHEFFIELD are:
     i. JAMES[8] WIGGINS, b. Abt. 1878, Conecuh Co., AL; d. Aft. 1880.
     ii. WILLIAM WIGGINS, b. Abt. 1879, Conecuh Co., AL; d. Aft. 1880.

48. MICHAEL O.[7] WIGGINS (TEMPERANCE TABITHA[6] BALLARD, SILAS JOSEPH HARDY[5], BENJAMIN[4], JOHN[3], JOSEPH[2], JOHN[1]) was born Abt. 1860 in Conecuh Co., AL, and died Aft. 1889. He married SARA "SALLY" HENDRIX.

Notes for MICHAEL O. WIGGINS:
Source: Joe Webb

Children of MICHAEL WIGGINS and SARA HENDRIX are:
     i. MARY[8] WIGGINS, b. Abt. 1878.
     ii. ADA WIGGINS, b. 1880.
     iii. ARRIE WIGGINS, b. 1882.
     iv. WILLIAM KINNARD WIGGINS, b. 1887.
     v. GEORGE WIGGINS, b. 1889.

49. BENJAMIN FRANK[7] BALLARD (ELIJAH[6], JOSHUA[5], BENJAMIN[4], JOHN[3], JOSEPH[2], JOHN[1]) was born 16 Feb 1832 in Atlanta, Fulton Co., GA, and died 06 Jul 1905 in Hot Springs, Garland Co., AR. He married ELIZA STRICKLAND 21 Nov 1856 in Fulton Co., GA. She was born 12 Jan 1828 in GA, and died 22 Apr 1928.

Notes for BENJAMIN FRANK BALLARD:
Source: LLoyd Russel Ballard, 1860 Campbell County Georgia Federal Census Records, 1870 Bradley County Arkansas Federal Census Records, 1880 Saline County Arkansas Federal Census Records, 1900 Garland County Arkansas Federal Census Records

Civil War 56th AR Rgmt . Living as of 1888 Hot Springs, AR. Frank killed man in heat and passion and self-defense Fulton Co, GA, & fled to AR.
1860 - Living in Campbell Co., GA - Ballard, Benjamin F. 24 GA, Eliza 22 GA, Julia 1 GA
1870 - Living in Bradley Co., AR - Ballard, Benj 33 Farm laborer GA, Eliza 31 GA, Julia 11 GA, Seany 9, GA, Mary 6 GA, Etta 5 GA, Russer 2
1880 - Living in Saline Co., AR - Ballard, Benj. 41 farmer , Eliza 40, Cena 19, Mary 15, Eddie 12, Russie 10, John 9, Alfonsa 3

More About BENJAMIN FRANK BALLARD:
Burial: Greenwood Cemetery, Hot Springs, Garland Co., AR

Notes for ELIZA STRICKLAND:
Source: 1910 Garland County Arkansas Federal Census Records
1910 - Living in Hot Springs, Garland Co., AR - Ballard, Eliza 77 GA GA GA wd 5 children 4 living, Alphonse 30

More About ELIZA STRICKLAND:
Burial: Greenwood Cemetery, Hot Springs, Garland Co., AR

Children of BENJAMIN BALLARD and ELIZA STRICKLAND are:

     i.   JULIAN[8] BALLARD, b. Abt. 1857, GA; d. Bef. 1889.
     ii.   CENA BALLARD, b. Nov 1869, GA; d. Aft. 1900.
    iii.   ELI F. BALLARD, b. 1861, GA; d. Aft. 1870.
    iv.   MARTHA J. BALLARD, b. Abt. 1863, GA; d. Bef. 1889.
     v.   EDDIE BALLARD, b. Feb 1866, GA; d. Aft. 1900.
    vi.   MARY BALLARD, b. Abt. 1865, AL; d. Aft. 1900.
    vii.   GEORGE R. BALLARD, b. 1866, GA; d. Aft. 1870.
   viii.   RUSSIE E. BALLARD, b. Nov 1869, GA; d. Aft. 1900.
    ix.   JOHN W. BALLARD, b. 11 May 1874, AR; d. 07 Jul 1941.

          More About JOHN W. BALLARD:
          Burial: Greenwood Cemetery, Hot Springs, Garland Co., AR

     x.   ALPHONSO BALLARD, b. Apr 1881, AR; d. 11 Oct 1918, AR.

          More About ALPHONSO BALLARD:
          Burial: Greenwood Cemetery, Hot Springs, Garland Co., AR

50. WESLEY C.[7] BALLARD (ELIJAH[6], JOSHUA[5], BENJAMIN[4], JOHN[3], JOSEPH[2], JOHN[1]) *was born 16 Dec 1839 in GA, and died 24 Mar 1909 in Cass Co., TX. He married LOUISE JANE GILLEY. She was born 1845 in GA, and died Aft. 1870.*

Notes for WESLEY C. BALLARD:
Source: Ken & Janiece Keener (kenkeener@pdq.net), 1870 Campbell County Georgia Federal Census Records, 1880-1900 Cass County Texas Federal Census Record
1870 - Living in Campbell Co., GA - Ballard, Wesley 27 farm labor, Jane 25 GA, Mary 3
1880 - Living in Cass Co., TX - Ballard, W. B 39 farmer GA GA GA, Jane 31 GA, Elizabeth 12, California 10 GA, William 7 GA, Eli 1 TX
1900 - Living in Cass Co., TX - Ballard, Wesley - Dec 1839 GA GA GA, Sarah - Jan 1869 TX GA GA, Eli - Aug 1787 TX, Anna D - Jan 1898 TX

Children of WESLEY BALLARD and LOUISE GILLEY are:

     i.   MARY[8] BALLARD, b. 1863.
     ii.   DELILAH CALIFORNIA "CALLIE" BALLARD, b. 23 Oct 1869, Atlanta GA; d. Jan 1949, Texarkana, TX;

m. SAMUEL BOLIVAR HARRELSON; b. Sep 1860, TX; d. 1967.

Notes for SAMUEL BOLIVAR HARRELSON:
Source: 1900 Cass County Texas Federal Census Records
* 1900 - Living in Cass Co., TX - Haralson, Simeon - Sep 1860 TX NC SC, Callie - Oct 1860, Adolphus - Jan 1890, William H - Sep 1891, Lilie P - Oct 1892, Robert A - Mar 1896, John - May 1898

  iii.   *WILLIAM R. BALLARD, b. 29 Apr 1873, GA; d. 1956, Texarkana TX; m. ANNIE LEE; b. 1875; d. 1920.*
  iv.   *ELI BALLARD, b. Aug 1878, Cass Co., TX; d. Aft. 1930; m. MITTIE, 1904, TX; b. 1888; d. Aft. 1930.*

Notes for ELI BALLARD:
Source: 1910-1930 Cass County Texas Federal Census Records
* 1910 - Living in Atlanta, Cass Co., TX - Ballard, Ely 31 married 6 years TX GA GA, Mittie 22 TX GA GA, Lottie M 1 TX
* 1920 - Living in Cass Co., TX - Ballard, Ely 41, Mittie 32, Lottie Mar 12
* 1930 - Living in Cass Co., TX - Ballard, Eli 51 TX, Mittie 42 TX, Lottie M 20 TX

51.   *CASSANDRA CASSIDY[7] BALLARD (ELIJAH[6], JOSHUA[5], BENJAMIN[4], JOHN[3], JOSEPH[2], JOHN[1]) was born 16 Apr 1845 in GA, and died 27 Jun 1917. She married JOHN GRUBBS 05 Dec 1867 in Cedartown, Carroll Co., GA. He was born 1833, and died Aft. 1880.*

Notes for JOHN GRUBBS:
Source: 1870 Carroll County Georgia Federal Census Records, 1880 Douglas County Georgia Federal Census Records

* 1870 - Living in Villa Rica, Carroll Co., GA - Grubbs, John 37miller GA, Cassinda 23 GA, Eli T 1, Frances 9
* 1880 - Living in Douglas Co., GA - Grubbs, John 47 works in mill, Cassinda 35, Eli Talton 11, Mary E 9, John M 7, Winnie E 5, Frances T 3, Hiram W 4/12

Children of CASSANDRA BALLARD and JOHN GRUBBS are:
  i.   *ELI TALTON[8] GRUBBS, b. 1869, GA; d. Aft. 1880.*
  ii.   *MARY E. GRUBBS, b. 1871, GA; d. Aft. 1880.*
  iii.   *JOHN GRUBBS, b. 1873, GA; d. Aft. 1880; m. SARAH GRIFFIN.*
  iv.   *WINNIE E. GRUBBS, b. 1875, GA; d. Aft. 1880.*
  v.   *FRANCES T. GRUBBS, b. 1877, GA; d. Aft. 1880.*
  vi.   *HIRAM W. GRUBBS, b. 1880, GA; d. Aft. 1880.*

52.   *RACHEL[7] BALLARD (ELIJAH[6], JOSHUA[5], BENJAMIN[4], JOHN[3], JOSEPH[2], JOHN[1]) was born Bet. 1844 - 1848 in GA, and died Aft. 1891. She married JOHN WASHINGTON HALLMAN in Bremen, GA. He was born 1842, and died Aft. 1891.*

Notes for JOHN WASHINGTON HALLMAN:
Source: 1880 Douglas County Georgia Federal Census Records

* 1880 - Living in Douglas Co., GA - Hallman W 38, Rachel 26, Henry 11, M. M 7, Eli 5, Latitia 2

Children of RACHEL BALLARD and JOHN HALLMAN are:
  i.   *ROBERT HENRY[8] HALLMAN, b. 14 Nov 1870, Winston, Douglas Co., GA; d. Aft. 1880.*
  ii.   *ELIJAH "ELI" HALLMAN, b. 17 Jun 1875, Winston, Douglas Co., GA; d. Aft. 1880.*
  iii.   *LATITIA "TISHIE" HALLMAN, b. 01 Aug 1877, Winston, Douglas Co., GA; d. Aft. 1880.*
  iv.   *MARGARET HALLMAN, b. 24 Feb 1878, Winston, Douglas Co., GA; d. Aft. 1880.*
  v.   *WILLIAM HALLMAN, b. 1879, Douglas Co., GA; d. Aft. 1880.*

vi.   JOHN WESLEY HALLMAN, b. 19 Oct 1882, Bremen, Haralson Co., GA.
vii. BEULAH HALLMAN, b. 09 Apr 1891, Bremen, Haralson Co., GA.

53. JOSHUA[7] BALLARD (ELIJAH[6], JOSHUA[5], BENJAMIN[4], JOHN[3], JOSEPH[2], JOHN[1]) was born 1855. He married EVELINE CHANDLER. She was born Abt. 1850.

Children of JOSHUA BALLARD and EVELINE CHANDLER are:
i.   HOYT[8] BALLARD, b. Abt. 1875.
ii.   MARSHALL BALLARD, b. Abt. 1876.
iii. LEVI BALLARD, b. Abt. 1877.
iv.   JOHN BALLARD, b. Abt. 1878.

54. LEVI[7] BALLARD (ARMISTEAD[6], JOSHUA[5], BENJAMIN[4], JOHN[3], JOSEPH[2], JOHN[1]) was born 06 Nov 1854 in Campbell Co., GA, and died Aft. 1870. He married MAMIE CATHEY.

Children of LEVI BALLARD and MAMIE CATHEY are:
i.   CARDIE[8] BALLARD.
ii.   BEATRICE BALLARD.
iii. ANDIE BALLARD.
iv.   VALETA BALLARD.
v.   DESSIE BALLARD.

55. JOSHUA[7] BALLARD (ARMISTEAD[6], JOSHUA[5], BENJAMIN[4], JOHN[3], JOSEPH[2], JOHN[1]) was born 01 Aug 1859 in Campbell Co., GA, and died 1936 in AR. He married FANNIE MCCOY. She was born Apr 1870 in AR, and died Aft. 1930.

Notes for JOSHUA BALLARD:
Source: 1900-1930 Cleveland County Arkansas Federal Census Records, Susan Fisher (sfisher102759MI@comcast.net)
* 1900 - Living in Cleveland Co., AR - Ballard, Joshua - Aug 1859 GA GA AL, Fannie B - Apr 1870 AR, Temora C - Mar 1887 AR, Carl A - July 1889 AR, Vollie M - Aug 1897 AR
* 1910 - Living in Redland, Cleveland Co., AR - Ballard, Joshua 55 GA, Fannie R 40 7 children 4 living AR, Collie 20, Lloyd 7, Neil 2
* 1920 - Living in Redland, Cleveland Co., AR - Ballard, Josh 60 GA GA AL, Fannie 50 AR, Loyd 16 AR, Neal 12 AR
* 1930 - Living in Redland, Cleveland Co., AR - Ballard, Josh 70, Fannie R 60, Neal 22

Children of JOSHUA BALLARD and FANNIE MCCOY are:

i.   TEMORE[8] BALLARD, b. Mar 1887, Redland, Cleveland Co., AR; d. Aft. 1900.
ii.   COLLIE ARMSTEAD BALLARD, b. Jul 1889, Redland, Cleveland Co., AR; d. Aft. 1930; m. AVY MAE ROGERS.

Notes for COLLIE ARMSTEAD BALLARD:
Source: Susan Fisher (sfisher102759MI@comcast.net)

iii. VOLLIE M. BALLARD, b. Aug 1897, Redland, Cleveland Co., AR; d. Aft. 1900.
iv.   LLOYD BALLARD, b. 1903, Redland, Cleveland Co., AR; d. Aft. 1930; m. PEARL; b. 1900; d. Aft. 1930.

Notes for LLOYD BALLARD:
Source: 1930 Cleveland County Arkansas Federal Census Records

* 1930 - Living at Redland, Cleveland Co., AR - Ballard, Loyd 26 AR, Pearl 30 AR

    v.   NEAL BALLARD, b. 1908, Redland, Cleveland Co., AR; d. Aft. 1930.

56. ANNA[7] BALLARD (ARMISTEAD[6], JOSHUA[5], BENJAMIN[4], JOHN[3], JOSEPH[2], JOHN[1]) *was born Jul 1876 in Campbell Co., GA, and died Aft. 1900. She married JOSEPH BARTOW CARMICHAEL 02 Oct 1894 in Coweta GA. He was born Jul 1861 in GA, and died Aft. 1900.*

Notes for JOSEPH BARTOW CARMICHAEL:
Source: 1900 Campbell County Georgia Federal Census Records
* 1900 - Living in Fairburn, Campbell Co., GA - Carmichael, Joseph B - July 1861 GA SC GA, Annie - July 1876 - 3 children 3 living GA GA GA John H - Sept 1895 GA, N L - Nov 1897 GA, Essie - Apr 1900 GA, Mary R. Ballard mother in law - Feb 1836 - 3 children 1 living GA GA GA

Children of ANNA BALLARD and JOSEPH CARMICHAEL are:
    i.   JOHN H.[8] CARMICHAEL, b. Sep 1895, Campbell Co., GA; d. Aft. 1900.
    ii.   N. L. CARMICHAEL, b. Nov 1897, Campbell Co., GA; d. Aft. 1900.
    iii.   ESSIE CARMICHAEL, b. Apr 1900, Campbell Co., GA; d. Aft. 1900.

57. JOSHUA[7] BALLARD (ABRAHAM[6], JOSHUA[5], BENJAMIN[4], JOHN[3], JOSEPH[2], JOHN[1]) *was born Bet. 1851 - 1854 in Randolph Co., AL, and died Feb 1917 in Randolph Co., AL. He married HELEN ELIZABETH BURSON. She was born 07 Jan 1842, and died 28 Apr 1909 in Randolph Co., AL.*

More About JOSHUA BALLARD:
Burial: Big Springs Baptist Church, Randolph Co., AL

More About HELEN ELIZABETH BURSON:
Burial: Big Springs Baptist Church, Randolph Co., AL

Children of JOSHUA BALLARD and HELEN BURSON are:
    i.   GEORGE[8] BALLARD, b. 23 Oct 1872, Randolph Co., AL; d. 26 Feb 1960.

        More About GEORGE BALLARD:
        Burial: Big Springs Bapt. Church, Randolph Co., AL

    ii.   LUCINDA "LOU" BALLARD, b. 30 Nov 1874, Randolph Co., AL; d. 21 Aug 1916; m. JOHN BOWMAN.
    iii.   JAMES M. BALLARD, b. 16 Jun 1876, Randolph Co., AL; d. 11 Aug 1938; m. ANNIE EULA; b. 1884; d. 1957.

        Notes for JAMES M. BALLARD:
        Source: 1920 Randolph County Alabama Federal Census Records
        * 1920 - Living in Lamar, Randolph Co., AL - Ballad, James M 43 AL, Eulas 34 GA, James E 4 AL, Mary 1 10/12 AL

        More About JAMES M. BALLARD:
        Burial: Big Springs Baptist Church, Randolph Co., AL

        More About ANNIE EULA:
        Burial: Big Springs Baptist Church, Randolph Co., AL

    iv.   OLIVER LEVI BALLARD, b. 03 Jan 1877, Randolph Co., AL; d. 11 Aug 1951; m. LINNIE; b. Randolph Co., AL.
    v.   WILLIAM JACKSON BALLARD, b. 21 Apr 1878, Randolph Co., AL; d. 02 Apr 1921, Randolph Co., AL;

  m. NANCY GERTRUDE FINCHER; b. 17 Apr 1884; d. 13 Jan 1973.

  Notes for WILLIAM JACKSON BALLARD:
  Source: 1910 Randolph County Alabama Federal Census Records
  * 1910 - Living in Lamar, Randolph Co., AL - Ballard, William J. 30 AL, Nana G 25, Lera L 8 AL, Era 6 AL, Jasper W 3 AL, Wilmer E 10/12 AL
  * 1930 - Living in High Shoals, Randolph Co., AL - Ballard, William 50 AL, Girtrud 46, Jasper 23, Lucile 16, James 14, Ralph 12, Mary

  vi. PEARL BALLARD, b. Abt. 1879, Randolph Co., AL.
  vii. SARAH JANE BALLARD, b. 08 Mar 1881, Randolph Co., AL; m. WARREN BAILY.
 viii. LINNE ANN BALLARD, b. 13 Mar 1883, Randolph Co., AL; m. (1) MILTON P. WALDREP; b. 26 Jul 1880; d. 02 Mar 1961; m. (2) MR. CROKER, Bef. 1902; m. (3) MR. DAVIS, Bef. 1908; b. Abt. 1880; d. Bef. 1910.

  Notes for LINNE ANN BALLARD:
  Source: 1910 Randolph County Alabama Federal Census Records

  * 1910 - Living in Randolph Co., AL - Davis, Linie A 25 wd, Nesbit 2, Clara Croker 8, J. P 4, Fay 11 step son, George W Ballard 39 brother, James M 33 brother, Bud Waldrop 28 wd boarder

  ix. ALMA BALLARD, b. 10 Sep 1885, Randolph Co., AL; d. 1886.
  x. NATHANIEL JOSHUA BALLARD, b. 06 Mar 1887, Randolph Co., AL; d. 10 Oct 1940, Coweta Co., GA; m. MOLLIE LOUISE SIMPSON; b. 23 Mar 1884, Coweta Co., GA; d. 16 Apr 1964, Coweta Co., GA.

58. NATHANIEL HARRISON[7] BALLARD (LEVI[6], JOSHUA[5], BENJAMIN[4], JOHN[3], JOSEPH[2], JOHN[1]) was born 22 Dec 1866 in Pumpkintown Plantation, Randolph Co, GA, and died 09 Feb 1936 in Jacksonville, Duval Co., FL. He married FRIEDA GEISSLER. She was born Abt. 1870, and died 11 May 1936 in Atlanta, Fulton Co., GA.

More About NATHANIEL HARRISON BALLARD:
Burial: Ramah Baptist Church Cemetery, Palmetto, Fulton Co., GA

Children of NATHANIEL BALLARD and FRIEDA GEISSLER are:

  i. FRIEDA[8] BALLARD, b. 15 Feb 1898; d. 16 Sep 1901.
  ii. SARAH HARRISON BALLARD, b. 07 Mar 1899; d. Bef. 1954; m. JOHN F. EVERETT; b. Abt. 1895.
  iii. ANNA BANG BALLARD, b. 11 Jun 1900; d. 29 May 1907.
  iv. LEVI BALLARD, b. 09 Sep 1902, Lexington, GA; m. KATHLEEN NELSON, 30 Jul 1930.
  v. MARGARET HILL BALLARD, b. 16 Mar 1904; m. J. LEROY HOLCOMBE, 26 Dec 1935; b. Abt. 1900.
  vi. HERMAN O. GEISSLER BALLARD, b. 15 Sep 1905.
  vii. DAVIDSON FULCO BALLARD, b. 18 Feb 1909; m. VIRGINIA LOUISE HALL; b. 21 Feb 1912, Atmore, Escambia Co., AL; d. 29 Jun 1984, GA.

59. CHARLES H.[7] BALLARD (EVAN POWELL[6], GEORGE WASHINGTON GREENE[5], BENJAMIN[4], JOHN[3], JOSEPH[2], JOHN[1]) was born 14 Oct 1873, and died 10 May 1948. He married BERTHA CAMPBELL. She was born Abt. 1875.

Children of CHARLES BALLARD and BERTHA CAMPBELL are:
  i. EVAN FRANK[8] BALLARD, b. 30 Jun 1905; m. DIANA ARMITAGE; b. Canada.
  ii. MAUDE BALLARD, b. 15 Feb 1919.

60. MARION ERNEST[7] BALLARD (GEORGE HENRY[6], GEORGE WASHINGTON GREENE[5], BENJAMIN[4], JOHN[3], JOSEPH[2], JOHN[1]) was born 05 Nov 1892, and died 23 Oct 1954 in Monticello, Jasper Co., GA. He married (1) ANNA HARRELL. He *married (2) ELIZABETH P. LANE. She was born 25 May 1912.*

Child of MARION BALLARD and ANNA HARRELL is:
      i.   ANNA[8] BALLARD.

61. GEORGE SPEIGHTS[7] BALLARD (WILLIAM "WILLIE" EDGAR[6], GEORGE WASHINGTON GREENE[5], BENJAMIN[4], JOHN[3], JOSEPH[2], JOHN[1]) was born 12 Mar 1887 in GA, and died Aft. 1900. He married MAUDE BENTON.

Notes for GEORGE SPEIGHTS BALLARD:
Banker, probably buried in Monticello, Jasper Co., GA

Children of GEORGE BALLARD and MAUDE BENTON are:
      i.   GEORGE SPEIGHTS[8] BALLARD, b. 27 Jul 1919.

          Notes for GEORGE SPEIGHTS BALLARD:
          He published the notes of Nathaniel H. & Levi Ballard in 1947. Graduated from Harvard living in Houston, TX as of 1959

     ii.   LUCIAN BENTON BALLARD, b. 02 May 1922; m. ELIZABETH BENTON THOMPSON.

62. WILLIAM HEARD[7] BALLARD (WILLIAM "WILLIE" EDGAR[6], GEORGE WASHINGTON GREENE[5], BENJAMIN[4], JOHN[3], JOSEPH[2], JOHN[1]) was born 15 Dec 1910, and died 19 Aug 1956 in Monticello, Jasper Co., GA. He married ANNIE KINGMAN MALONE. She was born 11 Nov 1915.

Children of WILLIAM BALLARD and ANNIE MALONE are:
      i.   WILLIAM HEARD[8] BALLARD, b. 1936; d. Vietnam.

          Notes for WILLIAM HEARD BALLARD:
          Graduated from Naval Academy in 1959. Per USNA he is deceased. Possible Vietnam.

     ii.   NANCY ANN BALLARD, b. 1937; m. PHILLIP HELLER BUCHEN; b. Abt. 1935.
    iii.   ROBERT WALTER BALLARD, b. 24 Dec 1939, Monticello, Jasper Co., GA; m. MARY ANN BLACKWELL; b. 02 Feb 1941.

          Notes for ROBERT WALTER BALLARD:
          Pharmacist living as of 1972 Edmonton, GA. Possibly Eatonton, Putnam Co., GA.

     iv.   RANDOLPH MALONE BALLARD, b. 22 Nov 1946; d. 29 Sep 1955.
      v.   EVAN ADOLPHUS BALLARD, b. 1950.

Edward Ballard

Generation No. 1

1. EDWARD[1] BALLARD *was born 03 May 1798 in ME, and died 31 Jul 1855 in Columbia Co., GA. He married* ELIZABETH GIBSON *06 Apr 1834 in Columbia Co., GA. She was born 18 May 1802 in Appling, Columbia Co., GA, and died 08 May 1872 in Appling, Columbia Co., GA.*

Notes for EDWARD BALLARD:
Source: 1850 Columbia County Georgia Federal Census Records, Georgia Marriages to 1850
* 1850 - Living in Columbia Co., GA - Ballard, Edward 51 planter ME, Elizabeth 48 GA, Ida 15 GA, Alva 13 GA, Ware 7 GA, Vale 2 GA, Benjiman E. Pearre 26

Children of EDWARD BALLARD *and* ELIZABETH GIBSON *are:*

    i.   IDA[2] BALLARD, *b. 25 Dec 1834, Columbia Co., GA; d. 02 Jun 1857; m.* WILLIAM WOOD, *19 Apr 1856, Columbia Co., GA; b. Abt. 1830.*

    ii. ALVAN BALLARD, *b. 07 Oct 1836, Columbia Co., GA; d. 23 Oct 1857.*

    iii. EDWARD BALLARD, *b. 03 Feb 1838, Columbia Co., GA; d. 16 Jul 1845, Columbia Co., GA.*

2.   iv. WARE BALLARD, *b. 16 May 1843, Columbia Co., GA; d. 19 Dec 1909, Baldwin Co., GA.*

    v. IKE VALE BALLARD, *b. 09 Oct 1847, Columbia Co., GA; d. 07 Jan 1919, Columbia Co., GA; m.* KATE EVELYN TRIPPE, *27 Nov 1878, Columbia Co., GA; b. 13 Aug 1850, GA; d. 31 Oct 1898, Columbia Co., GA.*

    Notes for IKE VALE BALLARD:
    Source: 1880 - 1910 Columbia County Georgia Federal Census Records
    * 1880 - Living in Columbia Co., GA - Ballard, Isaac 31 farmer GA MD GA, Kate 78 GA GA GA, Susan E Trippe mother GA VA VA
    * 1900 - Living in Columbia Co., GA - Ballard, Ike V - boarder - Oct 1847 - 52 GA GA GA farmer
    * 1910 - Living in Columbia Co., GA - Ballard, Ike V 63 - boarder wd GA GA GA retired Merchant dry goods

    More About IKE VALE BALLARD:
    Burial: Harlem Memorial Cemetery, Harlem, Columbia Co., A

Generation No. 2

2. WARE[2] BALLARD (EDWARD[1]) *was born 16 May 1843 in Columbia Co., GA, and died 19 Dec 1909 in Baldwin Co., GA. He married* MATTIE ROANA BENTON *26 Mar 1866 in Columbia Co., GA. She was born 20 Sep 1845 in GA, and died 16 Aug 1925.*

Notes for WARE BALLARD:
Source: 1880 Columbia County Georgia Federal Census Records , 1900 Aiken County South Carolina Federal Census Records

* 1880 - Living in Columbia Co., GA - Ballard, Wave 37 Farmer GA ME GA, Mattie 35 GA GA GA, Floyd 11 GA, Ada 9 GA, Guy 7 GA
* 1900 - Living in Schultz, Aiken Co., SC - Bullard, Ware - May 1843 GA GA GA, Mattie R - Oct 1844 - 5 children 4 living GA GA GA, Ada C - Nov 1871 GA, Guy A - May 1873 GA, Marion - Feb 1885 GA

More About WARE BALLARD:
Burial: Sunset Hill Cemetery, North Augusta, Aiken Co., SC

Notes for MATTIE ROANA BENTON:
Source: 1910 Aiken County South Carolina Federal Census Records
* 1910 - Living in Schultz, Aiken Co., SC - Ballard, Martha R 64 wd GA NC SC, Ada H 39 GA, Maran B 24 GA
* 1920 - Living in Aiken Co., SC - Ballard, Mattie R 75 GA living with her daughter Ada Nixon

More About MATTIE ROANA BENTON:
Burial: Sunset Hill Cemetery, North Augusta, Aiken Co., SC

Children of WARE BALLARD and MATTIE BENTON are:

  i.   *FEMALE³ BALLARD, b. 1867, Columbia Co., GA; d. 1867.*
  ii. *FLOYD BALLARD, b. 1869, Columbia Co., GA.*
  iii. *ADA H. BALLARD, b. 20 Nov 1870, Columbia Co., GA; d. 30 Jul 1951; m. JOSEPH J. NIXON, Bet. 1910 - 1920; b. 14 Jan 1874, SC; d. 29 Dec 1947.*

      More About ADA H. BALLARD:
      Burial: Sunset Hill Cemetery, North Augusta, Aiken Co., SC

      Notes for JOSEPH J. NIXON:
      Source: 1920 - 1930 Aiken County South Carolina Federal Census Records
      * 1920 - Living in North Augusta, Aiken Co., SC - Nixon, J J 46 SC SC SC Merchant, Wholesale Groc, Ada B 47 GA, Hattie L 19, J J Jr. 18, Gladys 15, Mattie R. Ballard mother in law 75 GA, Maron Ballard 34 GA Dressmaker
      * 1930 - Living in North Augusta, Aiken Co., SC - Nixon, Joseph J 57 SC Merchant wholesale Grocery, Ada B 58, Marian sister in law 45 GA

      More About JOSEPH J. NIXON:
      Burial: Sunset Hill Cemetery, North Augusta, Aiken Co., SC

3.   iv. *GUY EDWARD BALLARD, b. 16 May 1872, Columbia Co., GA; d. 15 Dec 1943, Aiken Co., SC.*
      v.   *MARIAN BENTON BALLARD, b. Feb 1885, Columbia Co., GA; d. 24 May 1959, Richmond Co., GA.*

      Notes for MARIAN BENTON BALLARD:
      Sources: Aiken County Georgia Federal Census Records

      * She is listed on census Records in her sister Ada Nixon's home up to 1930
      * 1940 - Living in Aiken Co., SC - Ballard, Marian boarder 55 GA teacher public school

Generation No. 3

3. *GUY EDWARD³ BALLARD (WARE², EDWARD¹) was born 16 May 1872 in Columbia Co., GA, and died 15 Dec 1943 in Aiken Co., SC. He married ANNA LOUISE SANDSTROM Aft. 31 Oct 1900 in Augusta, Richmond Co., GA. She was born 24 Mar 1881, and died 26 Jun 1946 in North Augusta, Aiken Co., SC.*

Notes for GUY EDWARD BALLARD:
Source: 1910-1940 Aiken County South Carolina Federal Census Records

* 1910 - Living in Schultz, Aiken Co., SC - Ballard, Guy E 37, Annie L 28, Marta L 7, Guy E Jr. 3, Robt M 2
* 1920 - Living in North Augusta, Aiken Co., SC - Ballard, Guye 46 GA, Annie L 37 RI, Martha 17 GA, Edward G 13 SC, Robert M 12 SC, Babel 6 SC, Ware Wilder 1 7/12 SC
* 1930 - Living in North Augusta, Aiken Co., SC - Ballard, Guy E 58 GA, Annie 48 RI, Guy E Jr. 23 SC , Robert M 21 SC, Mable G 16 SC, Wave W 11 SC
* 1940 - Living in North Augusta, Aiken Co., SC - Ballard, Guy E Sr 67 GA, Anna L 57 RI, Wave W 21 SC

More About GUY EDWARD BALLARD:

Burial: Sunset Hill Cemetery, North Augusta, Aiken Co., SC

Notes for ANNA LOUISE SANDSTROM:
Source: Aiken County South Carolina Standard Certificate of Death

More About ANNA LOUISE SANDSTROM:
Burial: Sunset Hill Cemetery, North Augusta, Aiken Co., SC

Children of GUY BALLARD and ANNA SANDSTROM are:

      i.   MARTHA[4] BALLARD, b. 21 Sep 1902, North Augusta, Aiken Co., SC; d. 22 Apr 1979, Spartanburg Co., SC.

      ii.   GUY EDWARD BALLARD, JR., b. 08 Jun 1906, North Augusta, Aiken Co., SC; d. 15 Jun 1988, Aiken Co., SC; m. FAY SHEALY, 02 Aug 1935; b. 04 Jul 1910; d. 15 Jun 1988, North Augusta, Aiken Co., SC.

           More About GUY EDWARD BALLARD, JR.:
           Burial: Sunset Hill Cemetery, North Augusta, Aiken Co., SC

4.   iii.   ROBERT MARION BALLARD, b. 02 Dec 1907, North Augusta, Aiken Co., SC; d. 29 Dec 2008, Rome, Floyd Co., GA.

      iv.   MABLE GRACE BALLARD, b. 21 Apr 1913, Aiken Co., SC; d. 04 Feb 1989; m. ROBERT J. HOLLINGSWORTH; b. 18 Dec 1906, Fulton Co., GA; d. 02 May 1959.

           Notes for ROBERT J. HOLLINGSWORTH:
           Source: 1940 New York County, New York Federal Census Records
           * 1940 - Living in New York City, New York Co., NY - Hollingsworth, Robt T 33 Atlanta Fulton Co., GA - Purchasing Agent Auto Parts, Mabel 26 Aiken Co., SC

      v.   WAVE WILDER BALLARD, b. 14 Oct 1918, Aiken Co., SC; d. 08 Sep 1986, Aiken Co., SC.

Generation No. 4

4. ROBERT MARION[4] BALLARD (*GUY EDWARD[3], WARE[2], EDWARD[1]*) was born 02 Dec 1907 in North Augusta, Aiken Co., SC, and died 29 Dec 2008 in Rome, Floyd Co., GA. He married LENA LUCILLE SCOTT 26 May 1934 in Augusta, Richmond Co., GA. She was born 09 Feb 1913 in Richmond Co., GA, and died 09 Apr 1989 in Rome, Floyd Co., GA.

Notes for ROBERT MARION BALLARD:
Source: 1940 Richmond County Georgia Federal Census Records, Obituary

* 1940 - Living in Augusta, Richmond Co., GA - Ballard, Robert 32 born SC, Lena 27 GA , Robert Jr 4 GA. Anna E, 2 GA, Helen L 1 GA
* 2008 - Obituary -- Robert Marion Ballard, Sr., 101, of Riverwood Retirement Center, Rome Georgia, passed away Monday Evening, December 29, 2008 at Rome's' Floyd Medical Center.
Mr. Ballard was born in North Augusta, Aiken County, South Carolina on December 2, 1907 the son of the late Guy Edward Ballard and Anna L Sandstrom Ballard.
He was married to Lena Lucile Scott on May 26, 1934. He was preceded in death by his wife of 54 years, Lena Scott Ballard in 1989, and a daughter, Dixie B. Morton (Mike) in 2005. He is survived by his children, Robert M Ballard, Jr (Mozelle) of Thomson, GA, Elizabeth B. Moore (William) of Hendersonville, TN, Helen B. Portman (William) of Hendersonville, TN, Judith B Dempsey of Rome, GA and Jack E. Ballard, Sr. of Rome, GA. He is also survived by 15 grandchildren and 21 great-grandchildren.
Mr. Ballard retired in 1972 as Division Meter Superintendant after 45 years of service with Georgia Power Company. After retirement he was known by many in the Rome area as "the Clock Doctor" for his work on time

pieces. He worked on clocks until the age of 95 when failing vision hampered his abilities. He was also an avid fisherman all his life.

Upon moving to Rome in 1943, he became a member of Rome's First United Methodist Church. He served his church as Lay Speaker, member of the Official Board, member of The Adult Fellowship Class, and member of the Chancel Choir. He also was Vice President of Travelers Protective Association, Director of United Cerebral Palsy Chapter, and Member of Georgia Chapter of International Association of Electrical Inspectors.

While active in the Civitan Civic Club, he served as Vice-President and President of the Rome Civitan Club. Mr. Ballard was also Civitan's Georgia District Governor for 1958-59.

He will be remembered for his love of music, his church, his family and the spoken and written word.

The family will receive friends at Daniel's Funeral Home on Wednesday, December 31st from 4:00 to 6:00 p.m.

Funeral services will be Thursday, January 1, 2009 at 2:00 p.m. in the sanctuary of Rome First United Methodist Church. Mr. Ballard's son-in-law, the Rev. William M. Portman is officiating.

Honorary pallbearers will be Adult Fellowship Class of FUMC.

Interment will be at Westover Cemetery, Augusta, Georgia on Friday, January 2, 2009 at 2:00pm with visitation following the burial.

In lieu of flowers, memorials may be sent to The Choir Fund at Rome First United Methodist Church, P O Box 628, Rome, GA 30162-0628

Children of ROBERT BALLARD and LENA SCOTT are:

    i.   *ROBERT BALLARD[5] JR., b. Abt. 1936, Augusta, Richmond Co., GA; d. Aft. 1940.*

    ii.   *ANNA E. BALLARD, b. Abt. 1938, Augusta, Richmond Co., GA; d. Aft. 1940.*

    iii.   *HELEN L. BALLARD, b. Abt. 1939, Augusta, Richmond Co., GA; d. Aft. 1940.*

    iv.   *DIXIE BALLARD, b. 29 Jan 1943, Augusta, Richmond Co., GA; d. 05 Nov 2005, Floyd Co., GA.*

Hiram Ballard

Generation No. 1

1. HIRAM[1] BALLARD was born Abt. 1800 in SC. He married HASSEY ARMSTRONG. She was born Abt. 1800 in GA.

Child of HIRAM BALLARD and HASSEY ARMSTRONG is:
2.   i.   THOMAS WINFIELD[2] BALLARD, b. 20 Feb 1828, Walton or Gwinnett Co., GA; d. 04 Jul 1902, Thomas Co., GA.

Generation No. 2

2. THOMAS WINFIELD[2] BALLARD (HIRAM[1]) was born 20 Feb 1828 in Walton or Gwinnett Co., GA, and died 04 Jul 1902 in Thomas Co., GA. He married JANE REBECCA HAWTHORNE 02 Aug 1846 in Muscogee Co., GA. She was born 1830 in Marion Co., GA, and died Aft. 1880.

Notes for THOMAS WINFIELD BALLARD:
Source: 1850 Muscogee County Georgia Federal Census Records, 1870-1900 Thomas County Georgia, Patrick Ballard (pjb7454@aol.com), (pjballard@hotmail.com), (pjballard@mindspring.com)
* 1850 - Living in McNortons, Muscogee Co., GA - Ballard, Thomas 22 Farmer b. Walton Co., GA, Jane 20 b. Marion Co., GA (Next door to Nancy Ballard 44 b Jackson Co., GA, Mary 17 Laurens Co. GA, Celia 14 Laurens Co., GA, Hazentine 12 b. Gwinnett Co., GA, Mahaley 10 b. Gwinnett Co., GA
* 1870 - Living in Ochlocknee, Thomas Co., GA - Ballard, Thomas 42 GA, Jane 40 GA, Clara I 17 GA, Alexander 15 GA, Lafayette 13 GA, Hiram 16
* 1880 - Living in Cairo, Thomas Co., GA - Ballard, Thomas 53 GA SC GA, Jane 50 GA, Hiram 20 GA
* 1900 - Living in Cairo, Thomas Co., GA - Ballard, Thomas W - Feb 1828 GA SC GA, Jane - May 1830 - 6 Children 3 living GA GA GA, Lou Butler servant

More About THOMAS WINFIELD BALLARD:
Burial: Magnolia Plantation Cemetery, Thomasville, Thomas Co., GA

Children of THOMAS BALLARD and JANE HAWTHORNE are:

        i.   CLARA I.[3] BALLARD, b. Abt. 1853, Cairo, Thomas Co., GA; m. B. F. BOON, 17 Feb 1870, Thomas Co., GA.
3.   ii. ALEXANDER BALLARD, b. 1854, Cairo, Thomas Co., GA; d. 1900, Grady Co., GA.
4.   iii. STEPHEN LAFAYETTE BALLARD, b. 18 Feb 1857, Cairo, Thomas Co., GA; d. 30 Nov 1918, Grady Co., GA.
5.   iv. HIRAM BALLARD, b. 24 Sep 1859, Cairo, Thomas Co., GA; d. 11 Feb 1902, Thomas Co., GA.
       v. EDDIE ADOPTED WINN, b. Abt. 1866; d. 1955.

Generation No. 3

3. ALEXANDER[3] BALLARD (THOMAS WINFIELD[2], HIRAM[1]) was born 1854 in Cairo, Thomas Co., GA, and died 1900 in Grady Co., GA. He married SALLIE. She was born Bet. 1855 - 1856 in GA, and died Aft. 1900.

Notes for ALEXANDER BALLARD:
Source- 1880 - 1900 Thomas County Georgia Federal Census Records

* 1880 - Living in Cairo, Thomas Co., GA - Ballard, Alexander 26 GA farmer, Sallie 23, Clara B. 3/12
* 1900 - Living in Cairo, Thomas Co., GA - Ballard, Ellick - Jan 1854 GA GA GA, Sallie - Dec 1856 - 6 children 6 living GA GA GA, Clarra - Feb 1880 GA, Milton fe - July 1884 GA, Thomas - Oct 1887 GA, Lela - Sept 1890 GA,

John - July 1893 GA, Sallie - May 1898 GA

Children of ALEXANDER BALLARD and SALLIE are:

    i. CLARA[4] BALLARD, b. 04 Feb 1880, Thomas Co., GA; d. 24 May 1968, Grady Co., GA; m. J. OLIVER EARWOOD; b. Abt. 1874; d. Aft. 1930.

      Notes for CLARA BALLARD:
      Source: 1940 Thomas County Georgia Federal Census Records, Grady County Georgia Death Index
      * 1940 - Living in Coolidge, Thomas Co., GA - Earwood, Clara 60 wd GA

      Notes for J. OLIVER EARWOOD:
      Source: 1930 Grady County Georgia Federal Census Records
      * 1930 - Living in Pine Park, Grady Co., GA - Earwood, J. Oliver 56 GA GA GA, Clara 50 GA GA GA

    ii. MILTON MAE BALLARD, b. 29 Jul 1884, Thomas Co., GA; d. 21 Mar 1975, Jefferson Co., GL.
    iii. THOMAS WILLIAM BALLARD, b. 24 Oct 1887, Thomas Co., GA; d. 1973, Cairo, Grady Co., GA; m. MARY HOOKS; b. 1890; d. 1976.

      Notes for THOMAS WILLIAM BALLARD:
      Source: WWI Draft Registration Card

      More About THOMAS WILLIAM BALLARD:
      Burial: Bold Springs Cemetery, Cairo, Grady Co., GA

      More About MARY HOOKS:
      Burial: Bold Springs Cemetery, Cairo, Grady Co., GA

6.   *iv. LELA BALLARD, b. Sep 1890, Thomas Co., GA; d. 15 Sep 1920, Grady Co., GA.*
    v. JOHN BALLARD, b. Jul 1893, Thomas Co., GA; d. Aft. 1900.
    vi. SALLIE BALLARD, b. 23 May 1897, Thomas Co., GA; d. 28 Aug 1924, Grady Co., GA.

4. STEPHEN LAFAYETTE[3] BALLARD (THOMAS WINFIELD[2], HIRAM[1]) *was born 18 Feb 1857 in Cairo, Thomas Co., GA, and died 30 Nov 1918 in Grady Co., GA. He married LINNIE SUSAN BARWICK. She was born Bet. 1856 - 1857 in GA, and died 31 Dec 1904 in Grady Co., GA.*

Notes for STEPHEN LAFAYETTE BALLARD:
Source- 1880-1900 Thomas County Georgia Federal Census Records, 1910 Grady County Georgia Federal Census Records

* 1880 - Living in Thomas Co., GA - Ballard, Lafayette 24 farmer GA, Susan 24 GA, Eveline 4 GA, William T. 3 GA, John M. 2 GA, James Dillon 1/12 GA
* 1900 - Living in Thomas Co., GA - Ballard, Lafayette - Feb 1857 GA GA GA farming, Lineoneilis - April 1857 GA GA GA, Evie - Aug 1875 GA, Willie T - Oct 1876 GA, John M - Mar 1878 GA, James W - May 1880 GA, Mamie Susan - Mar 1883 GA, Maggie - April 1875 GA, Bessie - Apr 1885 GA, Tellie - Sept 1887 GA, Louie - Nov 1890 GA
* 1910 - Living in Pine Park, Grady Co., GA - Ballard, Lafayette with his daughter Maggie

Children of STEPHEN BALLARD and LINNIE BARWICK are:

    i. EVALINE " EVIE"[4] BALLARD, b. 25 Aug 1875, Thomas Co., GA; d. 18 Aug 1965; m. GRAHAM W. STUBBS; b. Abt. 1875.
7.   *ii. WILLIAM THOMAS BALLARD, b. 20 Oct 1876, Thomas Co., GA; d. 19 Feb 1963, Ft. White, Columbia Co., FL.*

8. iii.   JOHN MORGAN BALLARD, b. 26 Mar 1878, Thomas Co., GA; d. 14 Apr 1958, Montgomery Co., AL.
    iv.   JAMES DILLAN BALLARD, b. 04 May 1880, Thomas Co., GA; d. 14 Mar 1946, GA; m. (1) PAULA HAGGARD; m. (2) LEOLA CONLEY.
    v.   MAMIE SUSAN BALLARD, b. 01 Mar 1883, Thomas Co., GA; d. 01 Dec 1967, Thomas Co., GA; m. BENJAMIN F. BUTLER; b. 1865.
    vi.   BESSIE BALLARD, b. Apr 1885, Thomas Co., GA; d. Aft. 1900.
    vii.   MAGGIE BALLARD, b. Apr 1885, Thomas Co., GA; d. Aft. 1920; m. BUSH.

    Notes for MAGGIE BALLARD:
    Source: 1910 Grady County Georgia Federal Census Records

    * 1910 - Living in Pine Park, Grady Co., GA - Ballard, Maggie 25 GA GA GA, Lafayette father 53 wd GA US GA, Wyman W Stubbs nephew 16 FL NC GA, Clyde Griffin boarder

    viii.   TELLIE BALLARD, b. Sep 1887, Thomas Co., GA; d. 02 Aug 1900, Thomas Co., GA.
    ix.   LOIS BALLARD, b. Nov 1890, Thomas Co., GA; d. 07 Feb 1919, Columbia Co., FL.

5. HIRAM³ BALLARD (THOMAS WINFIELD², HIRAM¹) was born 24 Sep 1859 in Cairo, Thomas Co., GA, and died 11 Feb 1902 in Thomas Co., GA. He married JULIA FERRIS. She was born 11 May 1859 in GA, and died 02 Aug 1903 in GA.

Notes for HIRAM BALLARD:
Source: 1900 Thomas County Georgia Federal Census Records, Patrick Ballard (PJB7454@aol.com), Find A Grave

* 1900 - Living in Cairo, Thomas Co., GA- Ballard, Hiram B - Sept 1859 40 GA GA GA farming, Jullia F - April 1862 38 7 children 7 living, Roy V - Oct 1881 18 GA, Lota - Jan 1883 17 GA, Feris F - May 1888 12 GA, Herman B - July 1890 GA 9, Fannie 6 - Oct 1893 GA, Bob - July 1897 2 GA, Alexis - Oct 1899 7/12 GA

More About HIRAM BALLARD:
Burial: Magnolia Plantation Cemetery, Thomasville, Thomas Co., GA

More About JULIA FERRIS:
Burial: Magnolia Plantation Cemetery, Thomasville, Thomas Co., GA

Children of HIRAM BALLARD and JULIA FERRIS are:

9. i.   ROY VASCO⁴ BALLARD, b. 27 Oct 1881, Thomas Co., GA; d. 1931.
    ii.   LOTA BALLARD, b. 26 Jan 1884, Thomas Co., GA; d. 03 Jun 1964, Thomas Co., GA; m. CURTIS PALMER, 1908, Thomas Co., GA; b. 30 Apr 1888, Decatur Co., GA; d. 05 Dec 1948, Gulf Co., FL.

    More About LOTA BALLARD:
    Burial: Midway Baptist Church Cemetery, Thomas Co., GA

    More About CURTIS PALMER:
    Burial: Midway Baptist Church Cemetery, Thomas Co., GA

    iii.   JULIE FERRIS BALLARD, b. 11 May 1887, Thomas Co., GA; d. 02 Aug 1903.

    More About JULIE FERRIS BALLARD:
    Burial: Magnolia Plantation Cemetery, Thomasville, Thomas Co., GA

    iv.   MONNA BALLARD, b. 07 May 1889, Thomas Co., GA; d. 18 Jul 1890.

More About MONNA BALLARD:
Burial: Magnolia Plantation Cemetery, Thomasville, Thomas Co., GA

10.	v.	HERMAN BROWN BALLARD, b. 19 Jul 1891, Thomas Co., GA; d. 26 Dec 1962, Lakeland, Polk Co., FL.
	vi.	FANNIE BALLARD, b. Oct 1893, Thomas Co., GA; d. Aft. 1900.
	vii.	BOB BALLARD, b. Jul 1897, Thomas Co., GA; d. Aft. 1900.
	viii.	ALEXIS BALLARD, b. Oct 1899, Thomas Co., GA; d. Aft. 1900.

Generation No. 4

6. LELA[4] BALLARD (ALEXANDER[3], THOMAS WINFIELD[2], HIRAM[1]) was born Sep 1890 in Thomas Co., GA, and died 15 Sep 1920 in Grady Co., GA. She married BISHOP MARVIN STRINGER. He was born Abt. 1886 in GA, and died Aft. 1920.

Notes for BISHOP MARVIN STRINGER:
Source: 1920 Grady County Georgia Federal Census Records
* 1920 - Living in Pine Park, Grady Co., GA - Stringer, Marvin B 34 GA, Leila 30 GA, Cora 8 GA, Clancy 4 GA, Christin 1 GA

Children of LELA BALLARD and BISHOP STRINGER are:

	i.	CORA ELIZABETH[5] STRINGER, b. 1912, Grady Co., GA; d. 07 Apr 1938, Thomas Co., GA.
	ii.	CLANCY ADEL STRINGER, b. 18 Sep 1915, Grady Co., GA; d. 01 May 1990.
	iii.	MAMIE CHRISTINE STRINGER, b. 28 Jun 1918, Grady Co., GA; d. 09 Sep 2004.

7. WILLIAM THOMAS[4] BALLARD (STEPHEN LAFAYETTE[3], THOMAS WINFIELD[2], HIRAM[1]) was born 20 Oct 1876 in Thomas Co., GA, and died 19 Feb 1963 in Ft. White, Columbia Co., FL. He married SALLY ISABELLE DAVIS. She was born 02 Feb 1882, and died 26 Jan 1941.

Notes for WILLIAM THOMAS BALLARD:
Source: 1910 Charlton County Georgia Federal Census Records, 1920 Columbia County Florida Federal Census Records, 1930 - 1940 Ware County Georgia Federal Census Records
* 1910 - Living in Thick Branch, Charlton Co., GA -Ballard, William T 34, Sallie 24, Thelma 5, Carl 2
* 1920 - Living in Ft. White, Columbia Co., FL - Ballard, William 43, Sallie 38, Thelma 15, Carl 12, Josie M 8, Myrtle 7
* 1930 - Living in Waycross, Ware Co., GA - Ballard, William T 53, Sallie 48, Carl T 21, Josie M 19, Myrtle 16, Sarah 9, Mary S 6, Ruby 18 dau in law 18 AL
* 1940 - Living in Waycross, Ware Co., GA - Ballard, William T 63, Sarah 57, Sarah 20, Mary Sere 16

More About WILLIAM THOMAS BALLARD:
Burial: Ft. White City Cemetery, Columbia Co., FL

More About SALLY ISABELLE DAVIS:
Burial: Ft. White City Cemetery, Columbia Co., FL

Children of WILLIAM BALLARD and SALLY DAVIS are:

	i.	THELMA[5] BALLARD, b. Abt. 1905, Ft. White, Columbia Co., FL; d. Aft. 1920; m. THOMAS J. DENNIS, 24 Oct 1921, Columbia Co., FL.
	ii.	CARL THOMAS BALLARD, b. 26 Apr 1908, Ft. White, Columbia Co., FL; d. 13 Feb 2007, Waycross, Ware Co., GA.

More About CARL THOMAS BALLARD:
Burial: Greenlawn Cemetery, Waycross, Ware Co., GA

   iii. JOSIE M. BALLARD, b. 09 Aug 1910, Ft. White, Columbia Co., FL; d. 10 Oct 1990, Waycross, Ware Co., GA; m. ARTHUR V. SWEAT; b. 1906.

   iv. MYRTLE BALLARD, b. 03 Aug 1913, Ft. White, Columbia Co., FL; d. 09 Feb 1938, FL; m. KINARD.

   v. MARY SUE BALLARD, b. 19 May 1923, Ft. White, Columbia Co., FL; d. 29 Nov 2014, Lake City, Columbia Co., FL; m. ODEST LEO DUREN; b. 21 Apr 1916, Columbia Co., FL; d. 28 Jul 1999.

More About ODEST LEO DUREN:
Burial: Oak Grove Cemetery, Providence, Union Co., FL

   vi. SARAH E. BALLARD, b. Abt. 1921, Ft. White, Columbia Co., FL; d. Aft. 1940.

8. JOHN MORGAN[4] BALLARD (STEPHEN LAFAYETTE[3], THOMAS WINFIELD[2], HIRAM[1]) was born 26 Mar 1878 in Thomas Co., GA, and died 14 Apr 1958 in Montgomery Co., AL. He married CAMMIE O. WHITE. She was born 19 Feb 1885, and died 25 Aug 1953 in AL.

Notes for JOHN MORGAN BALLARD:
Source: LDS IGI, 1910 Thomas County Georgia Federal Census Records, 1920-1940 Montgomery County Alabama Federal Census Records

* 1910 - Living in Thomasville, Thomas Co., GA - Ballard, John M 32, Cammie O 25, Willie C. 7, Ethel L 4
* 1920 - Living in Montgomery Co., AL - Ballard, John 42 GA, Cammie 35 AL, Wyley 17 AL, Ethel 14 AL, Mary Son 9 AL, Roberta 7 AL, Jessie Louise 4 6/12 AL
* 1930 - Living in Montgomery Co., AL - Ballard, John M 52 GA GA GA, Cammie 45 Al GA AL, Jessie L 14 AL
* 1940 - Living in Montgomery Co., AL - Ballard, John M 62, Cammie O 55

More About JOHN MORGAN BALLARD:
Burial: Greenwood Cemetery, Montgomery, Montgomery Co., AL

More About CAMMIE O. WHITE:
Burial: Greenwood Cemetery, Montgomery, Montgomery Co., AL

Children of JOHN BALLARD and CAMMIE WHITE are:
   i. JOHNNIE[5] BALLARD, b. Thomas Co., GA.

   ii. WILEY OLAN BALLARD, b. 31 Dec 1902, Pine Park, Grady Co., GA; d. 05 Jan 1978; m. MYRTLE LYNN JOINER, 29 Apr 1922, Montgomery Co., AL; b. 04 Sep 1906, Al; d. 31 May 1982, Montgomery Co., AL.

Notes for WILEY OLAN BALLARD:
Source: 1930 Montgomery County Alabama Federal Census Records

* 1930 - Living in Montgomery, Montgomery Co., AL - Ballard, Wiley O 28 GA GA AL, Myrtle 23 AL GA AL, Betty Jean 3 5/12 AL, Wylene 2 2/12 AL

More About WILEY OLAN BALLARD:
Burial: Greenwood Cemetery, Montgomery, Montgomery Co., AL

More About MYRTLE LYNN JOINER:
Burial: Greenwood Cemetery, Montgomery, Montgomery Co., AL

   iii. ETHEL LEE BALLARD, b. 24 Jun 1905, Thomasville, Thomas Co., GA; d. 07 Nov 1964; m. JOHN F. GRIDER, 02 May 1923, Montgomery Co., AL; b. 04 Sep 1900; d. 25 Mar 1969.

More About ETHEL LEE BALLARD:
Burial: Greenwood Cemetery, Montgomery, Montgomery Co., AL

Notes for JOHN F. GRIDER:
Source: 1930 Montgomery County Alabama Federal Census Records
* 1930 - Living in Montgomery Co., AL - Grider, John T 29 AL AL AL, Ethel 25 AL AL AL, Sara 6 AL, Mary 3 AL

More About JOHN F. GRIDER:
Burial: Greenwood Cemetery, Montgomery, Montgomery Co., AL

    iv.   MARY SUE BALLARD, b. 29 Jul 1910, Thomasville, Thomas Co., GA; d. 03 Jul 1996, Montgomery Co., AL; m. OLIVER J. DAVIS, 02 Feb 1929, Montgomery Co., AL; b. 1911; d. 1990.

More About MARY SUE BALLARD:
Burial: Greenwood Cemetery, Montgomery, Montgomery Co., AL

More About OLIVER J. DAVIS:
Burial: Greenwood Cemetery, Montgomery, Montgomery Co., AL

    v.   ROBERTA BALLARD, b. 12 Apr 1913, AL; d. 10 Apr 1966; m. (1) JAMES C. MATHEWS; m. (2) HERMAN WEEDON.
    vi.   JESSIE LOUISE BALLARD, b. 31 Jul 1915, AL; d. 04 Sep 1988, Montgomery Co., AL.

9. ROY VASCO[4] BALLARD (HIRAM[3], THOMAS WINFIELD[2], HIRAM[1]) was born 27 Oct 1881 in Thomas Co., GA, and died 1931. He married CORA V. LEE HADDOCK 09 May 1906 in Suwannee Co.,, FL. She was born Abt. 1888 in GA, and died Aft. 1930.

Notes for ROY VASCO BALLARD:
Source: 1910-1920 Thomas County Georgia Federal Census Records, 1930 Dade County Florida Federal Census Records
* 1910 - Living in Thomasville, Thomas Co., GA - Ballard, Roy V 28, Cora V 22, Howard 1
* 1920 - Living in Thomasville, Thomas Co., GA - Ballard, Roy V 38, Cora l 30, Howard 11, Eveline 5
* 1930 - Living in Miami, Dade Co., FL - Ballard, Roy V 48, Cora Lee 40, Howard R 21, Evelyn 15

More About ROY VASCO BALLARD:
Burial: Antioch Baptist Church Cemetery, Live Oak, Suwannee Co. FL

Children of ROY BALLARD and CORA HADDOCK are:
    i.   HOWARD ROY[5] BALLARD, b. Abt. 1909, GA; d. Aft. 1930; m. DORIS VALERIE RYAN, 23 Jun 1938, Richmond, VA.
    ii.   EVELINE BALLARD, b. 25 May 1914, Thomasville, Thomas Co., GA; d. 20 Jan 2002; m. EVERETT ALVA CLAY, 05 Oct 1937, Dade Co., FL; b. 23 Feb 1914, Tampa, FL.

10. HERMAN BROWN[4] BALLARD (HIRAM[3], THOMAS WINFIELD[2], HIRAM[1]) was born 19 Jul 1891 in Thomas Co., GA, and died 26 Dec 1962 in Lakeland, Polk Co., FL. He married MARY PEARL BONNER 27 Jul 1920 in Thomas Co., GA. She was born 28 Jul 1900 in GA, and died 30 Dec 1980.

Notes for HERMAN BROWN BALLARD:
Source: 1930- 1940 Polk County Florida Federal Census Records, 1935 Polk County Florida State Census Records, Patrick Ballard (pjballard@mindspring.com)
* 1930 - Living in Lakeland, Polk Co., FL - Ballard, Herman B 38 GA GA FL, Mary P 29 GA AL GA, Charles H 8 GA, Roy L 5 FL, Robert A 1 FL, Myra Wadell 40 roomer, Mary Wadell 14 roomer

1935 - Living in Polk Co., FL - Ballard, Herman B 43, Mary P 34, Chas H 13, Roy L 10, Robert A 6
1940 - Living in Lakeland, Polk Co., FL - Ballard, Herman B 48 GA, Mary P 39 GA, Charles H 19 GA, Roy L 15 FL, Robert A 11 FL, James H 4 GL, George F 10/12 FL, Marjorie E Bryant sister in law 34 GA, Pace Bryant nephew 7 GA

More About HERMAN BROWN BALLARD:

Burial: Oak Hill Burial Park, Lakeland, Polk Co., FL

More About MARY PEARL BONNER:

Burial: Oak Hill Burial Park, Lakeland, Polk Co., FL

Children of HERMAN BALLARD *and* MARY BONNER *are:*

     i.   CHARLES HERMAN[5] BALLARD, *b.* 20 May 1919, Pine Park, Grady Co., GA; *d.* 26 Apr 2004.

          Notes for CHARLES HERMAN BALLARD:
          Source: Social Security Records

    ii. ROY LANE BALLARD, *b.* 1924, Lakeland, Polk Co., FL; *d.* Aft. 1940.
   iii. ROBERT AMES BALLARD, *b.* 08 Dec 1928, Lakeland, Polk Co., FL; *d.* 10 Mar 1999.

          Notes for ROBERT AMES BALLARD:
          Source: Social Security Records

    iv. GERALD THORNTON BALLARD, *b.* 1930, Lakeland, Polk Co., FL.
     v. JAMES H. BALLARD, *b.* 15 Jul 1935, Lakeland, Polk Co., FL; *d.* 14 Oct 2009, Lakeland, Polk Co., FL; *m.* DOROTHY.

          More About JAMES H. BALLARD:
          Burial: Oak Hill Burial Park, Lakeland, Polk Co., FL

    vi. GEORGE F. BALLARD, *b.* 1940, Lakeland, Polk Co., FL; *d.* Aft. 1940.

Humphrey Ballard

Generation No. 1

1. HUMPHREY[1] BALLARD *was born Abt. 1735 in NC, and died Aft. 1801 in Wilkes Co., GA. He married* EDNEY. *She was born 1750, and died Aft. 1801.*

Notes for HUMPHREY BALLARD:
Source: Jane Sisolak, (tsisolak@swbell.net) LDS Films# 908813 "Ballard Family Lineages", Nathan Ballard of Wilkes Co., GA supplied by Kathy Ballard, Some Early Tax Digests of Georgia by Ruth Blair 1971, Some early tax digests of Georgia / collected and edited by Ruth Blair. -- Vidalia, GA : Georgia Genealogical Reprints, c1971 pages 258-260

* DNA for this family is in the Ballard Project group III, which is also the group where we find William Ballard and Philadelphia and the Lincoln County North Carolina
* Note - There appears to be a connection between this Humphrey Ballard with Reuben Ballard that lived in NC, GA and died in Kentucky and also Miles Ballard of NC to Pike Co., GA
* 1770 - Bute Co. NC, DB-3, page 315. 25 March 1770. William Smith, Planter, to Christopher Strother, both of Bute Co. 200 Pds. for 200 A. on SS Tar River & on the River. Wit: William Tabb, Humphrey Ballard, Thos. Bell. Proved by Thomas Bell, Esq., Bute Aug. Court 1771, Ben McCulloch, C.C. Reg: 20 Nov. 1771, James Johnson, P.R.
* 1771 - Bute. Co. NC, 15 May 1771 Humphrey Ballard to William Walker's Church; 10S, English money for 1 ac. with house and spring. Signed Humphrey Ballard. Rec. 31 July 1771, page 260, Bute - Warren County Deed, 1765 to 1783. Film # 0454305
* 1773 - Warren Co. NC, 4 Dec 1773 Humphrey Ballard to Jacob Crocker (?); L100 for 186 acres on south side of Giles Creek; a 1/3 portion of former tract Rec. 21 Oct. 1777. Vol. 6, p. 202. Warren County Deed, 1776-1783, Film # 0020067
* 1778 - Montgomery Co. NC, Buys 200 acres on north side of Gallon Creek/Yadkin River, adjacent to Mark Bennett & John Edwards. Wit. Solomon Bennett and Nathan Ballard
* 1783 - Montgomery Co. NC Records 111 acres on NE side Yadkin; Grant # 118; adj. John Harris & McCullock; wit. Thompson Clemmons & Chappell.
* 1787 - GA - Purchased land from Saunders Walker on Fishing Creek, adj. John Milner and John Edwards.
* 1792 - Wilkes Co., GA - Humphrey Ballard land in Wilkes Co on Fishing Creek waters joining John Milliner & John Smith 200 acres (2st quality) Oak & Hickory lands 1 white male >21, 1 negro, land tax: 30L, person's tax 4s, 1.75d
(Note his neighbors - Reubin Ballard land in Wilkes Co on Fishing Creek waters joining Jessey Herd & Joseph Anthony 343 Acres (1st quality) Oak & Hickory lands 1 white male >21, land tax: 51L,9s, person's tax 4s,3d, Jeremiah Bentley land in Wilkes Co on Fishing Creek joining Reuben Ballard & Joseph Blakely 176 Acres (1st quality) 17(2nd) Oak & Hickory lands 1 white male >21, land tax: 39L,12s, person's tax 3s,6.5d)
* 1801 - Wilkes County Georgia Will Book 1792-1801 - Humphrey Ballard's Will
I, Humphrey Ballard, being weak and poorly in body but of sound mind and memory and knowing the mortality of my body and that it is appointed for man to die do make and ordain this my last will and testament in manner and form following, Viz.
Item: I give and bequeath to my son Nathan Ballard one bed and furniture and large pewter dish to him and his heirs forever. That is the said bed and furniture and dish my son Nathan is not to have til after the decease of me and my wife.
Item: I give and bequeath to my son Philip Ballard fifty dollars being a part of a note I have on my son Nathan of two hundred dollars and sixteen dollars also being the (can't make out word) of the above two hundred dollar note for one year.
Item. I give and bequeath to my son Benjamin Ballard one hundred and fifty dollars this of the note due me of Nathan Ballard and one feather bed and furniture one brown filly colt and (can't make out these two words) of my lawful property after the decease of me and my wife to him and his heirs forever.
Lastly: I constitute and appoint my son Philip Ballard my sole Executor of this my last will and testament and

hereby disannul and revoke all former wills and testaments hereby ratifying this my last will and testament. In witness whereof I hereunto set my hand and seal this 19th of September 1800.
Signed Humphrey (his x mark) Ballard
Sealed, signed and acknowledged in presence of: Josiah Gordin, John DYSON, J. P.
Recorded: July 22, 1801
State of Georgia, Wilkes County: Personally appeared in open court John Dyson and being duly sworn saith that he saw the within named Humphrey Ballard sign seal publish and declare the foregoing instrument of writing to be his last will and testament and that the time of his so doing he was...

* Wilkes County Deed Books A-VV -- 1784 - 1806 - By Michal Martin Farmer, page 821 - Deed Book VV -- 1804-1806 - Page 428 22 March 1799, Humphrey Ballard and Edney, his wife, to Phillip Ballard, all of Wilkes County, for $200, Leggett Branch of Fishing Creek, 50 Acres, part of 200 acres granted to Sanders Walker and sold by Walker to said Humphrey Ballard, adjacent Phillip and Nathan Ballard. (signed) Humphrey Ballard, Edney (her X mark) Ballard. Witnesses: Lewis C. Davis, Nathan Ballard. Proved by Lewis C. DAVIS, 24 February 1806, William Sansom. J. I. C.

* Wilkes County Deed Books A-VV -- 1784 - 1806, By Michael Martin Farmer, page 682-683 - Deed Book SS 1801-1802 - Page 306. 4 December 1788, Reuben Ballard to Jeremiah Bentley, both of Wilkes County, Georgia, for L100, 76 acres in Wilkes County on Heard Mill Creek, part of a survey granted to Solomon Palmer and sold by deed to said Reuben Ballard, on and up branch. Reuben Ballard and Apsilla his wife (signed Reuben (his R mark) Ballard, Apsilla (her A mark) Ballard. Witnesses: Stephen Heard, Humphrey Ballard, Sanders Walker. Oglethorpe County, Georgia: Proved by Sanders Walker, 24 March 1802, John Lumpkin, J. I. C. Recorded 2 July 1802.
* I believe he is the son of Lewis Ballard that was in Bute County but moved to Lincoln Co., NC

Children of HUMPHREY BALLARD *and* EDNEY *are:*

     i.   BENJAMIN² BALLARD, *b. Abt. 1770; d. Aft. 1801.*

        Notes for BENJAMIN BALLARD:
        Source: Wilkes County, Georgia Deed Books A-VV", by Michael Martin Farmer, page 287, Wilkes Co., Georgia Deed Books A-VV", by Michael Martin Farmer, page 219, Early Records of Georgia, Wilkes Co.,, Vol. II", by Grace Gillam Davison, page 106

        * 1791 - Page 431. 19, Dec 1791 Benjamin Ballard and Catherine, his wife, to John Kelly, All Wilkes County, for L45, patented to Ballard on Kemps Creek, part of 146 acres, adjacent Goldwire, Henry Leverett, John Ashmore, and Levin Parkerson, 62 acres. (signed) Benjamin Ballard, Catherine (his X mark) Ballard. Witnesses: Peter Smith, Catherine Smith, B. (Benjamin) Catchings, J.P. Registered 26 Jan 1793.
        * 1791 - Page 240 28, February 1791, Benjamin Ballard to Levin Parkerson, both of Wilkes County for L5, patented to Ballard on Kemps Creek, adj. East by said Parkerson, West by said Ballard, John Ashmore, 55 acres. Benjamin Ballard. Witnesses: Peter Smith, Thomas (his X mark) Green, Benjamin Catchings, J. P. Registered 6 June 1791.
        * 1791 - Page 240 -- Ballard, Benjamin to Levin Parkerson 55 acres on waters of Kemp's Creek adj. lands of both parties. Feb. 28, 1791. Peter Smith, Thomas Green, Benjamin Catchings, J.P. Test.

2.   ii.   PHILLIP BALLARD, *b. Abt. 1770, Wilkes Co., GA; d. Bef. 1837.*
3.   iii. NATHAN BALLARD, *b. Abt. 1772, Wilkes Co., GA; d. 1803, Will probated 3/7/1803 Wilkes Co., GA.*

Generation No. 2

2. PHILLIP² BALLARD (HUMPHREY¹) *was born Abt. 1770 in Wilkes Co., GA, and died Bef. 1837. He married* MARY PETTIT. *She was born Abt. 1780, and died Aft. 01 Aug 1837 in Pike Co., GA.*

Notes for PHILLIP BALLARD:
Source: Jane Sisolak (tsisolak@swbell.net), BJSGen@aol.com

Notes for MARY PETTIT:
Source: Pike County Probate Court Will Book C

* 1837 - Written: August 1 1837 Recorded: November 3 1837 - State of Georgia Pike County
In the name of God Amen, I Mary Ballard of said State and County being of advanced age and knowing that I must shortly depart this life deem it right and proper both as respects myself and my family - that I should make a disposition of the property with which a kind providence has blest me therefore make this my last Will and Testament hereby revoking all others heretofore made by me.
Item 1st: I desire and direct that my body be buried in a decent Christian like manner suitable to my circumstances and condition in life.
Item 2nd: I desire and direct that all my just debts be paid without delay by my executors herein after appointed.
Item 3rd: I will give and bequeath to my beloved son Phillip Ballard a Negro boy about fifteen years of age by the named of George Washington commonly known by the name of George - I also will, give and bequeath to my beloved son Phillip Ballard another Negro by the name of John Henry about twelve years of age commonly called by the name of Henry.
Item 4th: I give, will and bequeath to my beloved son James Ballard, Francis, a Negro girl about fourteen years of age and I also give and bequeath and will to my beloved son James Ballard another Negro boy by the name of Ham (?) about ten years of age.
Item 5th: I will, give and bequeath to my beloved daughter Edna May(?) Osborn the wife of Green B. Osborn a Negro boy by the name of Parris about eight years old.
Item 6th: I will and bequeath and direct that Fanny, a Negro woman about fifty years of age and Cyrus(?) a Negro boy eight years of age be sold at the highest bidder at public out cry by my executor herein after named and the proceeds thereof equally divided by my executors between the following of
my named children and grand son John Thomas Ballard, son of my deceased son John Ballard, Jane Trammel(?) my daughter, wife of __?__ B. Trammel, Sarah Davis, my daughter, wife of Simon Davis, Gideon Ballard, my son, Elizabeth Brumbelow, wife of Ezikiel(?) Brumbelow, Samantha Robertson, wife of Green B. Robertson, Mary Upchurch, wife of Lumsford Upchurch and John Thomas Ballard son of my deceased son John Ballard and my grand son.
Item 7th: I will that the part coming to my daughter Elizabeth Brumbelow be given in trust that the same be free from and exempt from the present or future liabilities of her said husband.
Item 8th: I hereby constitute and appoint my sons Phillip Ballard and James Ballard my executors of this my last Will and Testament. August 1st 1837. Mary Ballard Signed sealed declared and published by Mary Ballard as her last Will and Testament in the presence of us the Subscribers who subscribe our names here to in the presence of said Teastor at her special instance and request and of each other.
August 1st 1837   Thomas D. King   James Hancock   George B. James

State of Georgia - Pike County - We James Hancock and George B. James do solemnly swear that we saw Mary Ballard sign seal and declare and publish and declare this writing to be and contain her will at the time thereof she was of sound disposing mind and memory and that she did it freely without compulsion to the best of our knowledge and belief and that we saw Thomas D. King Esq. sign the same as witness called in open court this 3rd day of November 1837. James Hancock George B. James Wiley E. Mangham

State of Georgia Pike County - We Phillip Ballard and James Ballard do solemnly swear that this writing contains the true last Will and Testament of Mary Ballard late of said County deceased as far as we know or believe and that we will well and truely execute the same by paying first the debts and then the legacies contained in said will as far as her goods and chattels will .... and that we will make a true and perfect inventory of all such goods and chattels so help us God. Sworn to and subscribed Phillip Ballard   James Ballard   Received the 12th November 1837

Children of PHILLIP BALLARD and MARY PETTIT are:

4.   i.   JANE[3] BALLARD, b. Abt. 1798, Wilkes Co., GA; d. Aft. 1850.
5.   ii.   JOHN BALLARD, b. Abt. 1799, Wilkes Co., GA; d. Bef. 1837.
6.   iii. SARAH BALLARD, b. 17 Aug 1800, Wilkes Co., GA; d. 25 Nov 1886.
7.   iv.   GIDEON BALLARD, b. Bet. 1801 - 1810; d. Aft. 1840.
            v.   EDNA MAY BALLARD, b. Abt. 1809; d. Aft. 1837; m. GREEN B. OSBORN.

      vi.   ELIZABETH BALLARD, *b. Abt. 1810; m. EZEKIAL BRUMBELOW.*

     vii. MARY A. BALLARD, *b. Abt. 1815; m. LUNCEFORD UPCHURCH, 30 Jan 1834, Newton Co. GA; b. Abt. 1810.*

8.   *viii.* PHILLIP BALLARD, *b. Abt. 1817, Putnam GA; d. Aft. 1880.*

     ix. SAMANTHA BALLARD, *b. Abt. 1820; m. GREEN ROBERTSON.*

9.   *x.*   JAMES HENRY BALLARD, *b. 30 Nov 1821, GA; d. Aft. 1880.*

3. NATHAN[2] BALLARD (HUMPHREY[1]) *was born Abt. 1772 in Wilkes Co., GA, and died 1803 in Will probated 3/7/1803 Wilkes Co., GA. He married (1) MARY. He married (2) NANCY MILNER 1784, daughter of JOHN MILNER. She was born Abt. 1774.*

Notes for NATHAN BALLARD:
Source: Wilkes County Georgia Will Book 1791-1819 pg 57-58, Kathy Ballard, Allan L. Bentley (abentley@bellsouth.net)
* 1800 - July 7, living in Guilford Co., NC - Deep River Monthly Meeting - Nathan Ballard offered a paper to this meeting condemning his misconduct in thinking one of his fellow men & taking too much strong drink which was e read. This meeting not being free to accept it, appoints Edward Bond, Jehu Wickersham & John Hunt to visit him on the occasion & report their care & sense to next meeting.
* 1803 - Feb 9, Wilkes Co., GA Will Book pg 57 - State of Georgia, Wilkes County - In the name of God Amen, I Nathon Ballard of the county aforesaid being infirm in body but of Sound and disposing mind do make this my last will and testament in the manner and form following. After paying all my Just debts by my Executors Therein after mentioned I do lend unto my beloved wife Mary Ballard the house and Land whereon I do now live during her widowhood and if She should inter marry during her widowhood and if should Intermarry the said Land and Premises shall be sold by my Executors and the money Equally divided between my wife and four children To Wit, John Ballard, James Ballard, Edna and Nancy. Also I do give and bequeath to my wife One boy man saddle and bridle two Feather Bed and Furniture. The first choice with the flock of and Too Choice coults and colors fur head of sheep Two sows and twelve pigs one pine Chest and can two Choice Tables One pine cupboard and Furniture Two choice Pots & skillet and frying pan and all the Peuter I have also and Bar. I have Plow and two shovel Ploughs and the best Pair of Gears, One Grubbing Hoe wheel and cards an one and looking glass also all the residue of my also the residue of my Estate shall be sold and Equally distributed amongst my four children above mentioned also amongst my four children above mentioned also that it shall be understood by my Executors that the child above named Edna is to be maintained and Supported by my Present wife during her widowhood. I (?) then appoints and Constitute my Trusty Friend John Dyson, Boling Anthony and John Cooper Esgn, Executors of my last Will and Testament. In Witness whereof I have here unto set my hand and Seal this 9 day of February 1808 (signed) Nathon Ballard (seal an mark) Witnessed by Philip Ballard, Josiah Gardiao
* 1803 - March 7 - Personally appeared in open Court Phillip Ballard and Josiah Gardian (?) Two of the subscribing Witnesses to the within will and by duly sworn saw that they saw Nathan Ballard Sign Seal Published declare the within (?) Testaments of writing to be his last will and Testament & that at the time of his so doing he was of sound Disposing mind and memory. Sworn before me this 7th of March 1803 Phillip Ballard Josiah Gardian (?), Da Percell C (/) Co? Recorded 25 July 1806

Children of NATHAN BALLARD and NANCY MILNER are:

10.   *i.*   JAMES[3] BALLARD, *b. 25 Sep 1790, Wilkes Co., GA; d. 1870, AL.*

     ii. JOHN BALLARD, *b. Abt. 1791, Wilkes Co., GA; d. 1817, Jones Co., GA.*

    iii. EDNA BALLARD, *b. Abt. 1795, Wilkes Co., GA; d. Aft. 1803; m. (1) JOHN B. ROSE, 22 Oct 1818; m. (2) HENRY CLEMONS, 01 Jul 1819.*

    iv. NANCY BALLARD, *b. Abt. 1796, Wilkes Co., GA; d. Aft. 1803; m. JOHN BAPTIST ROSSEE, 22 Oct 1818, Wilkes Co., GA.*

     v. MARY BALLARD, *b. Abt. 1798, Wilkes Co., GA; d. Bef. 1803; m. CHARLES DUKE.*

Generation No. 3

4. JANE[3] BALLARD (PHILLIP[2], HUMPHREY[1]) *was born Abt. 1798 in Wilkes Co., GA, and died Aft. 1850. She married*

ALFRED BELL TRAMMEL. He was born Abt. 1795, and died Aft. 1850.

Notes for ALFRED BELL TRAMMEL:
Source: 1850 Pike County Georgia Federal Census Records
* 1850 - Living in Pike Co., GA - Tramell, Alfred B 55 farmer GA, Jane 52 GA, Sarah 20 GA, John 17 GA, Elizabeth 15 GA, Alfred 10 GA, Martha J 6 GA, Jessee Davis 35

Children of JANE BALLARD and ALFRED TRAMMEL are:

11.	i.	NANCY[4] TRAMMEL, b. Abt. 1828, GA; d. Aft. 1850.
	ii.	SARAH TRAMMEL, b. Abt. 1829, GA; d. Aft. 1850.
	iii.	JOHN TRAMMEL, b. Abt. 1831, GA; d. Aft. 1850.
	iv.	ELIZABETH TRAMMEL, b. Abt. 1835, GA; d. Aft. 1850.
12.	v.	ALFRED BELL TRAMMEL, b. Abt. 1838, GA; d. Aft. 1870.
	vi.	MARTHA J. TRAMMEL, b. Abt. 1842, GA; d. Aft. 1850.

5. JOHN[3] BALLARD (PHILLIP[2], HUMPHREY[1]) *was born Abt. 1799 in Wilkes Co., GA, and died Bef. 1837.*

Child of JOHN BALLARD is:

      i.   JOHN THOMAS[4] BALLARD, b. Bef. 1837.

6. SARAH[3] BALLARD (PHILLIP[2], HUMPHREY[1]) *was born 17 Aug 1800 in Wilkes Co., GA, and died 25 Nov 1886. She married SIMEON DAVIS. He was born 02 Feb 1800 in Hancock Co., GA, and died 15 Nov 1889 in Columbia Co., AR.*

More About SARAH BALLARD:
Burial: Shiloh Cemetery, Waldo Co., AR

Children of SARAH BALLARD and SIMEON DAVIS are:

      i.   JOSEPH ADKINS[4] DAVIS, b. 26 Apr 1827, Monroe Co., GA.
     ii.   MARY E. DAVIS, b. 16 Oct 1828, GA.
    iii.   PHILLIP DAVIS, b. Abt. 1830, GA.
    iv.   MARTHA DAVIS, b. 30 May 1832, GA.
     v.   ELIZABETH DAVIS, b. 27 Jun 1836, GA.
    vi.   AMANDA DAVIS, b. 13 May 1838, GA.
   vii.   FRANCES JANE DAVIS, b. 14 Jan 1839, Wilkes Co., GA.
  viii.   JOHN MATTHIAS DAVIS, b. 24 May 1840.
    ix.   DUDLEY H. DAVIS, b. 24 Sep 1842.

7. GIDEON[3] BALLARD (PHILLIP[2], HUMPHREY[1]) *was born Bet. 1801 - 1810, and died Aft. 1840. He married ELIZABETH TAYLOR 25 Dec 1833 in Newton Co., GA. She was born Abt. 1811, and died Aft. 1840.*

Notes for GIDEON BALLARD:
Source :1840 Newton County Georgia Federal Census Records
* 1840 - Living in Newton Co., Georgia - Free White Persons - Males - Under 5:   1
Free White Persons - Males - 5 thru 9:   1,   Free White Persons - Males - 30 thru 39:   1
Free White Persons - Females - Under 5:   2,   Free White Persons - Females - 20 thru 29:   1
Persons Employed in Agriculture: 1,   No. White Persons over 20 Who Cannot Read and Write: 1
Free White Persons - Under 20:   4,   Free White Persons - 20 thru 49:   2
Total Free White Persons: 6,   Total All Persons - Free White, Free Colored, Slaves: 6

Children of GIDEON BALLARD and ELIZABETH TAYLOR are:

      i.   MALE[4] BALLARD, b. Abt. 1834, Newton Co., GA.

    ii.   MALE BALLARD, b. Abt. 1836, Newton Co., GA.
    iii. FEMALE BALLARD, b. Abt. 1838, Newton Co., GA.
    iv. FEMALE BALLARD, b. Abt. 1837, Newton Co., GA.

8. PHILLIP[3] BALLARD (PHILLIP[2], HUMPHREY[1]) *was born Abt. 1817 in Putnam GA, and died Aft. 1880. He married* MARTHA GILLESPIE *31 Dec 1851 in Pike Co., GA. She was born 1828 in SC, and died Bet. 1870 - 1880.*

Notes for PHILLIP BALLARD:
Source: 1860 - 1870 Pike County Georgia Federal Census Records, 1880 Cass County Texas Federal Census Records
* 1860 - Living in Pike Co., GA - Ballard, Philip 40 GA, MA 31 SC, MT 8GA, MF 6 GA, JR 1 GA, Sarah 17 GA
* 1870 - Living in Pointer, Pike Co., GA - Ballard, Philip 53 GA painter, Martha 42 SC, Mary 17 GA, Martha 15, GA, John R. 11 GA, Rufus 8 GA, Lois 6 GA, Lelah 3 GA
* 1880 - Living in Cass Co., TX - Ballard, Phil 61 GA NC SC farmer, Rufus 19 GA, Lois 15 GA, Louisiana 13 GA

Children of PHILLIP BALLARD and MARTHA GILLESPIE are:

13.   *i.*   MARY J.[4] BALLARD, b. 09 Oct 1853, Putnam Co., GA; d. 30 Aug 1930, Marshall, Harrison Co., TX.
        ii. MARTHA F. " MATTIE" BALLARD, b. 31 Aug 1854, GA; d. 01 May 1937, Greenville Co., SC; m. HARVEY P. HALL.

            Notes for MARTHA F. " MATTIE" BALLARD:
            Source: Greenville County South Carolina Standard Certificate of Death

       iii. JOHN R. BALLARD, b. 1859, GA; d. Aft. 1870.
       iv. RUFUS BALLARD, b. 1862, GA; d. Aft. 1880.
14.   *v.*   LOIS BALLARD, b. 04 Dec 1864, GA; d. 23 Mar 1931, Karnes Co., TX.
       vi. LELAH LOUISIANA BALLARD, b. 03 Oct 1866, GA; d. 25 Dec 1965; m. GEORGE WASHINGTON BLACK; b. 04 May 1851, Franklin Co., GA; d. 01 Jan 1911, Hardeman Co., TX.

            More About LELAH LOUISIANA BALLARD:
            Burial: Leagueville Cemetery, Henderson Co., TX

            More About GEORGE WASHINGTON BLACK:
            Burial: Bell Cemetery, Cass Co., TX

9. JAMES HENRY[3] BALLARD (PHILLIP[2], HUMPHREY[1]) *was born 30 Nov 1821 in GA, and died Aft. 1880. He married* REBECCA ANN FRANCES JACKSON *24 Sep 1848 in Newton Co., GA. She was born Abt. 1830, and died Aft. 1880.*

Notes for JAMES HENRY BALLARD:
Source: 1870 Oktibbeha County Mississippi Federal Census Records, 1880 Clay County Mississippi Federal Census Records

* 1870 - Living in Oktibbeha Co., MS - Ballard, James 48 GA, Rebecca 38 GA, Josaphine 18 GA, Albert 16 GA, Emma R 13 GA, Etney E 10 MS, James H 7 MS, Mary E 4 MS
* 1880 - Living in Clay Co., MS - Ballard, James 59 farmer GA VA SC, Rebecca A 47 GA GA GA, Josephine 26 GA, Albert W 25 GA, Emma R 22 GA, Edna E 20 MS, James H 16 MS, Mary A. E 13 MS

Children of JAMES BALLARD and REBECCA JACKSON are:

       i.   MARY ANN ELIZABETH[4] BALLARD, b. 11 Feb 1851, Pike Co., GA.
       ii. JOSEPHINE BALLARD, b. 09 Feb 1852, Barnesville. Lamar Co., GA; d. Aft. 1900.
       iii. ALBERT WRIGHT BALLARD, b. 21 Dec 1853, Barnesville. Lamar Co., GA; d. Aft. 1880.

    iv.   GEORGE ANN BALLARD, b. 19 Dec 1855, Barnesville. Lamar Co., GA.

    v.   EMMA REBECCA BALLARD, b. 28 Aug 1857, Barnesville. Lamar Co., GA; d. Aft. 1880.

    vi.   EDNA ELEANOR BALLARD, b. 07 May 1861, Clay Co., MS; d. Aft. 1880; m. JOHN E. BLACKBURN, 04 Mar 1886, West Point, Clay Co., MS; b. Abt. 1855.

Notes for EDNA ELEANOR BALLARD:
Source: Automated Archives CD#5 Marriages

    vii.   JAMES HENRY BALLARD, b. 30 Oct 1863, MS; d. Aft. 1880; m. LUCINDA F. REED, 24 Nov 1886, Clay Co., MS; b. Abt. 1866.

Notes for JAMES HENRY BALLARD:
Source: LDS-IGI Records, Automated Archives CD#5 Marriages

    viii.   MARY A. E. BALLARD, b. Abt. 1867, MS; d. Aft. 1880.

10. JAMES[3] BALLARD (NATHAN[2], HUMPHREY[1]) was born 25 Sep 1790 in Wilkes Co., GA, and died 1870 in AL. He married AMELIA "EMILY" TAYLOR 27 Jun 1816 in Jones Co., GA. She was born 1800 in GA, and died 1880 in AL.

Notes for JAMES BALLARD:
Source: Toni Norris Verbois, 1850 Coosa County Alabama Federal Census Records, 1860 Tallapoosa Alabama Federal Census Records, Jones County Georgia Marriage Records, 1870 Elmore County Alabama Federal Census Records, Alabama Surname Files Expanded - 1702-1981
* 1816 - June 1816 - Jones Co., GA - James Ballard & Amelia Taylor. To any Judge of the Superior or Inferior Court, Justice of the peace, ordained Minister of the Gospel, you or either of you are hereby authorized to Join in Matrimony James Ballard & Amelia Taylor, and this shall be your authority for the same and you will after this Solemnization return this to me, properly certified in order to be recorded. Given under my hand & Seal at Office this 25th June 1816 - A Carter CCO (seal)
* 1816 - June 25 - James Ballard & Amelia Taylor, Georgia, Jones County. To any Judge of the Superior or Inferior Court, Justice of the peace, ordained Ministers of the Gospel. You or either of you are hereby authorized to Join in Matrimony James Ballard & Amelia Taylor and this shall be your authority for the same and you will after this Solemnization return this to me properly certified in order to be recorded. Given under my hand & Seal at Office this 25th June 1816. A Carter CCO (seal)
* 1816 - June 27 - Jones Co., GA - By Authority of license the within named James Ballard & Amelia Taylor were Joined in Matrimony before me this 27th June 1816 J F Zachry, JP
* 1850 - Living in Coosa Co., AL - Ballard, James 59 farmer GA, Emily 50 GA, Emily 20 GA, Miriam 17 GA, Joseph 15 GA, William 14 AL, Gilbert 12 AL, Rebecca 6 AL
* 1860 - Living in Tallapoosa Co., AL - Ballard, James 70 farmer GA, Emily 60 AL, Emily 30 AL, Joseph 26 AL, Gilbert 21 AL, Rebecca 17 AL (John William Ballard son of James and Emily is living next door)
* 1870 - Living in Elmore Co., AL - Ballard, Emily (James is not there)

Notes for AMELIA "EMILY" TAYLOR:
Source: 1870 Elmore County Alabama Federal Census Records
* 1870 - Living in Elmore Co., AL - Ballard, Emily 70 keeping House GA, Emily 38 AL, Rebecca 23 AL, Martha Lee 53 GA, Henry Lee 19

Children of JAMES BALLARD and AMELIA TAYLOR are:

15.   i.   MARTHA[4] BALLARD, b. 07 May 1817, Jones Co., GA; d. 22 Nov 1894.

    ii.   JOHN BALLARD, b. 1819, Jones Co., GA; d. 18 Sep 1861; m. MARGARET; b. 1816, GA; d. Aft. 1850.

Notes for JOHN BALLARD:
Source: 1850 Coosa County Alabama Federal Census Records
* 1850 - Living in Coosa, Coosa Co., AL - Ballard, John 31 teacher GA, Margaret 24 GA (living next door to his parents)

16.	iii.	JAMES T. BALLARD, b. 09 Mar 1823, Lowndes Co., AL; d. 1878, Madison Co., AR.
	iv.	EMILY BALLARD, b. 1830, GA; d. Aft. 1870.
	v.	MIRIAM BALLARD, b. 27 Sep 1832, Jones Co., GA; d. 14 Jul 1897, Pike Co., Al; m. STEPHEN B. RAY, 11 Apr 1855, Coosa Co., AL; b. 28 Apr 1832; d. 10 Mar 1916.

More About MIRIAM BALLARD:
Burial: Pilgrims Rest Cemetery, Dozier, Covington Co., AL

Notes for STEPHEN B. RAY:
Source: 1880 Pike County Alabama Federal Census Records
* 1880 - Living in Dixons, Pike Co., AL - Ray, Seven B, Miriam, William E, James M, Thomas, Martha F Hollis, David R Hollis, Minnie Lee Hollis

More About STEPHEN B. RAY:
Burial: Pilgrims Rest Cemetery, Dozier, Covington Co., AL

	vi.	JOSEPH BALLARD, b. 1834, GA; d. Aft. 1860.
17.	vii.	WILLIAM JOHN BALLARD, b. 1837, AL; d. 18 Sep 1861, Winchester, Frederick Co., VA.
	viii.	GILBERT BALLARD, b. 1839, GA; d. Aft. 1860.
	ix.	REBECCA BALLARD, b. 1843, AL; d. Aft. 1860.

Generation No. 4

11. NANCY[4] TRAMMEL (JANE[3] BALLARD, PHILLIP[2], HUMPHREY[1]) was born Abt. 1828 in GA, and died Aft. 1850. She married KING DAVID HUCKABY. He was born 1825 in GA, and died Aft. 1880.

Notes for KING DAVID HUCKABY:
Source: 1880 Pike County Georgia Federal Census Records
* 1880 - Living in Pike Co., GA - Huckaby, King D 55 GA GA, Mary A 35 GA, Amanda 15 GA, Susan 14 GA, George 12 GA, Mary 10 GA, King D 7 GA, William M 5, John 4mo, Jeff D 18 GA

Children of NANCY TRAMMEL and KING HUCKABY are:
	i.	CHARLES THOMAS[5] HUCKABY, b. Dec 1851, GA; d. 17 Nov 1926, Fulton Co., GA.
	ii.	WILLIAM P. HUCKABY, b. 1853, GA.
	iii.	SARAH E. HUCKABY, b. Abt. 1855, GA.
	iv.	JOSEPH DAVIS HUCKABY, b. 1857.
	v.	JEFFERSON DAVIS HUCKABY.

12. ALFRED BELL[4] TRAMMEL (JANE[3] BALLARD, PHILLIP[2], HUMPHREY[1]) was born Abt. 1838 in GA, and died Aft. 1870. He married JANE. She was born Abt. 1845.

Notes for ALFRED BELL TRAMMEL:
Source: 1870 Sabine Parish Louisiana Federal Census Records
* 1870 - Living in Sabine Par., LA - Trammel A. B 31 GA, Jane 25 GA, Andrew 8 LA, Augustus 4 LA, Leroy L 2 LA

Children of ALFRED TRAMMEL and JANE are:
	i.	ANDREW[5] TRAMMEL, b. Abt. 1862, LA; d. Aft. 1870.
	ii.	AUGUSTUS TRAMMEL, b. Abt. 1866, LA; d. Aft. 1870.
	iii.	LEROY L. TRAMMEL, b. Abt. 1868, LA; d. Aft. 1870.

13. MARY J.[4] BALLARD (*PHILLIP[3], PHILLIP[2], HUMPHREY[1]*) was born 09 Oct 1853 in Putnam Co., GA, and died 30 Aug 1930 in Marshall, Harrison Co., TX. She married *JAMES R. RUSSELL* 05 Dec 1875 in Pike Co., GA. He was born Oct 1850 in Montgomery Co., AL, and died Aft. 1880.

Notes for MARY J. BALLARD:
Source: Pike County Georgia Marriage Records, Harrison County Texas Standard Certificate of Death, lcunnin1@bellsouth.net
Return of a Marriage. To the Ordinary of Pike County, State of Georgia
1. Full name of groom: James R. Russell,   2. Place of residence: Douglassville, Cass Co. Texas
3. Age: Age 25 years,   4. Color: White
5. Occupation: Farmer,   6. Place of birth - State or Country: Montgomery Co. Ala
7. Father's name: W.L. Russell,   8. Mother's maiden name: S.E. Howell
9. Full name of bride: Mary T. Ballard,   10. Maiden name if a widow:
11. Place of residence: Pike Co. Georgia,   12. Age: Age 23 years
13. Color: White,   14. Place of birth - State or Country: Putnam Co. Ga.
15. Father's name: Phillip Ballard, 16. Mother's maiden name: Martha A. Gillespie
I hereby certify that James R. Russell and Mary T. Ballard were joined in marriage by me, in accordance with the laws of the State of Georgia, in the State of Georgia, in the county of Pike this 5 day of Dec, 1875. - J.M. Bolton

Notes for JAMES R. RUSSELL:
Source: 1880 Cass County Texas Federal Census Records

* 1880 - Living in Cass Co., TX - Russell, James 27 AL AL AL, Mary 25 GA VA GA, Lois 5 TX, Walter 3 TX, William 1 TX

Children of MARY BALLARD and JAMES RUSSELL are:
    i.   LOIS[5] RUSSELL, b. 1875, TX; d. Aft. 1880.
    ii. WALTER RUSSELL, b. 1877, TX; d. Aft. 1880.
    iii. WILLIAM RUSSELL, b. 1879, TX; d. Aft. 1880.

14. LOIS[4] BALLARD (*PHILLIP[3], PHILLIP[2], HUMPHREY[1]*) was born 04 Dec 1864 in GA, and died 23 Mar 1931 in Karnes Co., TX. She married *JAMES T. JONES*. He was born Abt. 1864 in TX, and died Aft. 1910.

Notes for LOIS BALLARD:
Source: Karnes County Texas Standard Certificate of Death

Notes for JAMES T. JONES:
Source: 1900 Choctaw Nation Indian Territory, 1910 Karnes County Texas Federal Census Records
* 1900 - Living in Lehigh, Choctaw Nation, Indian Territory - Jones, Jas T 36 TX miner, Loris 36 3 children 1 living GA GA GA, Fuller 15 TX
* 1910 - Living in Karnes Co., TX - Jones, James T 48 TX OH IL, Lois 46 - 3 children 1 living GA GA GA, Fuller 25 TX, David F brother 59 TX, Faustino Lopez lodger 25

Child of LOIS BALLARD and JAMES JONES is:

    i.   VINCENT FULLER[5] JONES, b. 17 Jan 1885, TX; d. 04 May 1950, Tom Green Co., TX; m. EFFIE BELLE MORGAN; b. 16 Aug 1893, TX; d. 05 Oct 1972, TX.

       Notes for VINCENT FULLER JONES:
       Source: 1920 - 1940 Karnes County Texas Federal Census Records
       * 1920 - Living in Karnes Co., TX - Jones, Vincent F.35, TX; Effie B., 25, TX; Vivian, 6, TX; Eugen, 4 6/12, TX; Ema M., 2 11/12, TX; Mabel, 10/12, TX

* *1930 - Karnes Co., TX - Jones, Fuller 44, TX; Belle, 35, TX; Vivian, 16, TX; Eula, 14, TX; Ima, 13, TX; Myrtle, 11, TX; Loureto, 10, TX; Ruth, 7, TX; Martha, 5, TX; Annie B., 2, TX; Opal, 0, TX*
* *1940 Karnes Co., TX - Jones, Fuller 54, TX; Bell, 46, TX; Iona, 22, TX; Martha, 15, TX; Anna Bell, 12, TX; Opal, 11, TX; Eva, 9, TX*

More About VINCENT FULLER JONES:
Burial: Runge City Cemetery, Runge, Karnes Co., TX

More About EFFIE BELLE MORGAN:
Burial: Runge City Cemetery, Runge, Karnes Co., TX

15. MARTHA[4] BALLARD (JAMES[3], NATHAN[2], HUMPHREY[1]) *was born 07 May 1817 in Jones Co., GA, and died 22 Nov 1894. She married JAMES W. LEE 29 Oct 1840 in Chambers Co., AL. He was born 11 May 1815 in NC, and died 24 Jul 1866 in AL.*

Notes for JAMES W. LEE:
Source: 1850-1860 Coosa County Alabama Federal Census Records
* *1850 - Living in Coosa, Coosa Co., AL - Lee, James W 35, Martha Lee 33, Anna E. 9, Benjn F 7, James A 5, Thomas 3, Mary C. 1*
* *1860 - Living in Coosa Co., AL- Lee, James W 45, Martha 43, Anne E 18, B V 16, James A 15, Thomas P 14, Mary C 12, HD 10*

Children of MARTHA BALLARD and JAMES LEE are:

18.   i.   ANNE ELIZABETH[5] LEE, b. 02 Sep 1841, AL; d. 19 Mar 1902.
        ii.   BENJAMIN FRANKLIN LEE, b. 20 Feb 1843, Al; d. 09 Jan 1911, Los Angeles Co., CA.
       iii.   JAMES A. LEE, b. 12 Dec 1844, Al; d. 12 Jul 1862, VA.
       iv.   THOMAS LEE, b. 10 Mar 1847, Al; d. 12 Jul 1920, NM.
        v.   MARY C. LEE, b. 20 Dec 1848, Al; d. 1898, GA.
       vi.   HENRY LEE, b. Abt. 1851; d. Aft. 1870.

16. JAMES T.[4] BALLARD (JAMES[3], NATHAN[2], HUMPHREY[1]) *was born 09 Mar 1823 in Lowndes Co., AL, and died 1878 in Madison Co., AR. He married (1) FRANCES ELIZABETH BETTS 10 Apr 1855 in Coosa Co., AL, daughter of JOHN W. BETTS. She was born 06 Mar 1831 in GA, and died 1864. He married (2) LUCINDA BETTS 11 Jun 1865 in Coosa Co., AL, daughter of JOHN W. BETTS. She was born 1844, and died Aft. 1880 in Living in Madison Co., AR.*

Notes for JAMES T. BALLARD:
Source: Coosa County Alabama Marriage Records, Jerry Frazier (jfrazier@marin.k12.ca.us), Shirley A. Goings Lindsey (wlindsey@msn.com), Jenny Graham (JENNY.D.GRAHAM@cpmx.saic.com), 1860 Tallapoosa Alabama Federal Census Records
* *1860 - Living in Tallapoosa AL- Ballard, James L. 38 farmer GA, Francis E. 29 GA, Ann 3 AR, John 1 AL*
* *1865 - Coosa Co., AL - Ballard, James T to Lucinda Betts - State of Alabama Coosa County. To any ordained or Licensed Minister of the Gospel Judge the Supreme Circuit or Probate Court or any Justice of the Peace for Said County Greeting. You are hereby Authorized to Sodomize the rites of matrimony Between James T Ballard and Lucinda Betts and this Shall be your Sufficient Authority for so doing. Given under hand this 28th day of September 1865. A. A. M. Millan Judge of. (?) The above named parties were married by me on this 11 day of June 1865. Joel B. Sayers M G*

Notes for FRANCES ELIZABETH BETTS:
Source: 1880 Madison County Arkansas Federal Census Records, Alabama Marriage Index

* *1880 - Living in Lamar, Madison Co., AR - Ballard, Lucinda 34 AL, Jno A 20 AR AL AL (step son), Stephen B 18 AR (step son), Lizzie M 14 AR, Mary 12 AR, Susan 10 AR, James A 6 AR, Ellen 4 AR*

Notes for LUCINDA BETTS:
Source: 1880 Madison County Arkansas Federal Census Records
* 1880 - Living in Lamar, Madison Co., AR - Ballard, Lucinda 34 AL, Jno A 20 step son AR AL AL, Stephen B 18 step son AR AL AL, Lissie M 14 AL, Mary 12 AL, Susan 10 AR, James A 6 AR, Ellen 4 AR

Children of JAMES BALLARD and FRANCES BETTS are:
	i.	WILLIAM D.[5] BALLARD, b. 1856, AL or AR; d. 1857, AR.
19.	ii.	ANNE ELIZABETH BALLARD, b. 06 Aug 1857, AR or AL; d. 25 Apr 1936, Dallas Co., TX.
20.	iii.	JOHN ALLEN BALLARD, b. 30 Jul 1859, Sitha, Crawford Co., AR; d. 13 Apr 1924, Van Buren, Crawford Co., AR.
21.	iv.	STEPHEN B. BALLARD, b. Aug 1861, AR; d. Bet. 1887 - 1888, Madison Co., AR.
	v.	EMILY F. BALLARD, b. 1863, AR; d. 1863, AR.

Children of JAMES BALLARD and LUCINDA BETTS are:
22.	vi.	MARTHA ELIZABETH "LISSIE"[5] BALLARD, b. May 1866, AR; d. 12 Sep 1949, Lamar Co., TX.
23.	vii.	MARIAM MARY BALLARD, b. 20 Feb 1868, AL; d. 25 Dec 1895, Madison Co., AR.
	viii.	SARAH SUSIE BALLARD, b. 21 Jul 1870, AR; d. Aft. 1880, Lamar Co., TX; m. MR CLARK.
24.	ix.	JAMES ALLEN BALLARD, b. 30 Dec 1874, AR; d. 06 Aug 1962, Paris, Lamar Co., TX.
25.	x.	ELLEN BALLARD, b. 1877, AR; d. Aft. 1892, AR.

17. WILLIAM JOHN[4] BALLARD (JAMES[3], NATHAN[2], HUMPHREY[1]) was born 1837 in AL, and died 18 Sep 1861 in Winchester, Frederick Co., VA. He married FRANCES EMILY STRINGER, daughter of ANDERSON STRINGER and SARAH STERLING. She was born 04 Sep 1840, and died Aft. 1860.

Notes for WILLIAM JOHN BALLARD:
Source: Toni Norris Verbois (toni_verbois@yahoo.com), Pedigree Chart of John R. Ballard, 1860 Tallapoosa Alabama Federal Census Records

* 1860 - Living in Tallapoosa Co., AL - Ballard, William J 25 farmer, Frances E. 20 , William 8/12

Children of WILLIAM BALLARD and FRANCES STRINGER are:
| 26. | i. | WILLIAM LAFAYETTE[5] BALLARD, b. 15 Jan 1860, Tallapoosa Co., AL; d. 17 Jan 1931, Mira, Caddo Co., LA. |
| | ii. | SAMUEL J. BALLARD, b. 13 Aug 1861, AL. |

Generation No. 5

18. ANNE ELIZABETH[5] LEE (MARTHA[4] BALLARD, JAMES[3], NATHAN[2], HUMPHREY[1]) was born 02 Sep 1841 in AL, and died 19 Mar 1902. She married WILLIAM FREDERIC DIDEN. He was born 23 Jan 1827 in England, and died 12 Sep 1902 in Milton, Santa Rosa Co., FL.

Notes for ANNE ELIZABETH LEE:
Source: 1880 Santa Rosa County Florida Federal Census Records

* 1880 - Living in Santa Rosa Co., FL - Diden, Anna E 37 AL NC GA, Anna 10 FL England AL, William F 8 FL, Mary E 6 FL, Thomas F 4 FL, David 4 FL, David 2 FL, Martha 62 mother GA GA GA

More About ANNE ELIZABETH LEE:
Burial: Milton Cemetery, Milton, Santa Rosa Co., FL

More About WILLIAM FREDERIC DIDEN:
Burial: Milton Cemetery, Milton, Santa Rosa Co., FL

Children of ANNE LEE and WILLIAM DIDEN are:

    i.   ANNIE[6] DIDEN, b. 1869, FL; d. 1926; m. JOHN H. GRIFFITH; b. 1868; d. 1954.

        More About ANNIE DIDEN:
        Burial: Milton Cemetery, Milton, Santa Rosa Co., FL

        More About JOHN H. GRIFFITH:
        Burial: Milton Cemetery, Milton, Santa Rosa Co., FL

    ii.   WILLIAM FREDERICK DIDEN, b. 15 Jun 1871, FL; d. 21 Apr 1944; m. PEARL JONES; b. 30 Dec 1877; d. 22 Nov 1949.

        More About WILLIAM FREDERICK DIDEN:
        Burial: Milton Cemetery, Milton, Santa Rosa Co., FL

        More About PEARL JONES:
        Burial: Milton Cemetery, Milton, Santa Rosa Co., FL

    iii.   MARY ELIZABETH DIDEN, b. 15 May 1874, Milton, Santa Rosa Co., FL; d. 24 Apr 1970, Milton, Santa Rosa Co., FL; m. JESSE EDWARD ALLEN; b. 21 Feb 1872; d. 04 Feb 1928.

        More About MARY ELIZABETH DIDEN:
        Burial: Milton Cemetery, Milton, Santa Rosa Co., FL

        More About JESSE EDWARD ALLEN:
        Burial: Milton Cemetery, Milton, Santa Rosa Co., FL

    iv.   THOMAS FRANK DIDEN, b. 17 Jan 1876, Milton, Santa Rosa Co., FL; d. 26 Apr 1889, Milton, Santa Rosa Co., FL.

        More About THOMAS FRANK DIDEN:
        Burial: Milton Cemetery, Milton, Santa Rosa Co., FL

    v.   DAVID CLEVELAND DIDEN, b. 25 Sep 1878, Milton, Santa Rosa Co., FL; d. 14 Nov 1936, Milton, Santa Rosa Co., FL; m. FANNIE S.; b. 31 Mar 1884; d. 30 Aug 1966.

        More About DAVID CLEVELAND DIDEN:
        Burial: Milton Cemetery, Milton, Santa Rosa Co., FL

        More About FANNIE S.:
        Burial: Milton Cemetery, Milton, Santa Rosa Co., FL

19. ANNE ELIZABETH[5] BALLARD (JAMES T.[4], JAMES[3], NATHAN[2], HUMPHREY[1]) was born 06 Aug 1857 in AR or AL, and died 25 Apr 1936 in Dallas Co., TX. She married WILLIAM ZACHARIAH GOINGS. He was born 13 Dec 1854 in AR, and died 06 Aug 1899 in TX.

Notes for ANNE ELIZABETH BALLARD:
Source: 1900 Hunt County Texas Federal Census Records, 1910-1920 Dallas County Texas Federal Census Records, 1930 El Paso County Texas Federal Census Records, Death Certificate
* 1900 - Living in Hunt Co., TX - Goings, Anna - Aug 1856 wd AR AL AL farmer, John 1881 AR AR AR farm laborer, Stevens 1877 AR farm laborer, Edward 1884 AR, Adolphus 1887 AR, Ida 1889 AR, Maud 1890 AR, Eva 1893 AR, Malvern 1895 AR, Hallie 1897 AR, Jordan, Will son in law TX Mollie 1875 AR,, Authur 4 AR
* 1910 - Living in Dallas Co., TX - Goings, Malvin 15, TX AR (hard to read), Anna mother 52 wd 11 children, 10 living AR AL AL, Hattie 12 TX AR AR

1920 - Living in Dallas Co., TX - Going Annie 62 WD AR, Edward son 34 AR, Maudie granddaughter 13 TX, Cecil 11 granddaughter TX, Myrtle 9 granddaughter TX, Georgia granddaughter 3 11/12 TX, Eva Dinley dau 28 wd AR, and 3 roomers
1930 - Living in El Paso Co., TX - Goings, Edward 45 wd AR AR AR, Annie 72 wd AR AR AR

More About ANNE ELIZABETH BALLARD:
Burial: Laurel Land Memorial Park, Dallas, Dallas Co., TX

Notes for WILLIAM ZACHARIAH GOINGS:
Source: 1880 Logan County Arkansas Federal Census Records, 1900 Hunt County Texas Federal Census Records
1880 - Living in Mountain, Logan Co., AR - Goings, WZ 25 farmer AR, Ann 22 AL AL AL, Mollie 5 AR AR AR, James 3 AR AR AR, Stephen 1 AR AR AR

Children of ANNE BALLARD and WILLIAM GOINGS are:

    i.   MARY ISABELLE[6] GOINGS, b. 04 Sep 1875, AR; d. 1968, LA CA; m. ROY JORDAN.
   ii.   JAMES MONROE GOINGS, b. 28 Apr 1877, AR; d. 31 Jul 1899, AR.
  iii.   WILLIAM STEVEN GOINGS, b. 1879, AR; d. Aft. 1900.
  iv.   JOHN LAFAYETTE GOINGS, REV., b. 24 Apr 1881, AR; d. 04 Jun 1950, Dallas, Collin Co., TX; m. MARY; b. 1893, MO; d. Aft. 1930.

        Notes for JOHN LAFAYETTE GOINGS, REV.:
        Source: Dallas County Texas Certificate of Death

        More About JOHN LAFAYETTE GOINGS, REV.:
        Burial: Crown Hill Memorial Park, Dallas Co., TX

    v.   EDWARD JACKSON GOINGS, b. 17 May 1884, AR; d. 01 Aug 1966, LA CA.
   vi.   EDGAR ADOLPHUS GOINGS, b. 23 Feb 1887, AR; d. 14 Mar 1928, El Paso Co., TX; m. PRECIOUS CORA McCLENDON; b. 11 Feb 1890, AR; d. 03 Jan 1972, Dallas Co., TX.

        Notes for EDGAR ADOLPHUS GOINGS:
        Source: El Paso County Texas Standard Certificate of Death

        More About EDGAR ADOLPHUS GOINGS:
        Burial: Laurel Land Memorial Park, Dallas, Dallas Co., TX

        More About PRECIOUS CORA McCLENDON:
        Burial: Laurel Land Memorial Park, Dallas, Dallas Co., TX

  vii.   IDA LOU GOINGS, b. 30 Jan 1889, Poughkeepsie, AR; d. 17 May 1972, Dallas Co., TX; m. ALBERT CARL BROOKS; b. 30 Oct 1888, TX; d. 23 Oct 1972, Dallas Co., TX.

        Notes for IDA LOU GOINGS:
        Source: Dallas County Texas Certificate of Death

        More About IDA LOU GOINGS:
        Burial: Grove Hill Memorial Park

 viii.   MAUD GOINGS, b. 1890, AR; d. Aft. 1900.
   ix.   EVA MARIE GOINGS, b. 20 Mar 1893, AR; d. Jan 1975, Dallas Co., TX; m. DINLEY.
    x.   MALVERN GOINGS, b. 19 Jan 1895, TX; d. 21 May 1968, Titus Co., TX.
   xi.   HATTIE MAY GOINGS, b. 27 Jun 1897, TX; d. 03 Apr 1992, Dallas Co., TX; m. GUY EVAN DAY; b. 1891; d. 1940.

20. JOHN ALLEN[5] BALLARD (JAMES T.[4], JAMES[3], NATHAN[2], HUMPHREY[1]) *was born 30 Jul 1859 in Sitha, Crawford Co., AR, and died 13 Apr 1924 in Van Buren, Crawford Co., AR. He married* MELVINA C. DOTSON *14 Aug 1882 in Sharp Co., AR. She was born 31 Jan 1864 in Sitka, Sharp Co., AR, and died 09 Jun 1934 in Mulberry, Crawford Co., AR.*

Notes for JOHN ALLEN BALLARD:
Source: 1900 Franklin County Arkansas Federal Census Records, 1910 Crawford County Arkansas Federal Census Records, Arkansas Death Records, Find A Grave.
* 1900 - Living in Mulberry, Franklin Co., AR - Ballard, John A 1859 AL GA AL farmer, Melvina 1864 AR TN TN, Myrtle L 1884 AR, Willis 1896 AR, Lewis 1898 AR, Walker 1890 AR, Gertie 1893 AR, Thomas 1897 AR
* 1910 - Living in Maxey, Crawford Co., AR - Ballard, J A 51, MC 46, Wilt 22, Tome 13, Floyd 7, Sam 6, Edison 2
* 1924 - Died in Crawford Co., AR

More About JOHN ALLEN BALLARD:
Burial: Rankin Cemetery, Lone Elm, Franklin Co., AR

More About MELVINA C. DOTSON:
Burial: Rankin Cemetery, Lone Elm, Franklin Co., AR

Children of JOHN BALLARD *and* MELVINA DOTSON *are:*

  i.   E. B.[6] BALLARD, *b. 07 Jun 1883, Sharp Co., AR; d. 07 Jun 1883, Sharp Co., AR.*
 ii.   MYRTLE LEE BALLARD, *b. 07 Jul 1884, Sitka Sharp Co., AR; d. 10 Dec 1903, Reno Lamar Co TX.*
iii.   WILLIAM STEVEN BALLARD, *b. 25 May 1886, Evening Shade, Sharp Co., AR; d. 07 Mar 1947, Fullerton, Orange Co., CA; m.* LELIA WEYMOUTH UPTON, *Oct 1917; b. 10 Feb 1901, Crawford Co., AR; d. 23 Dec 1987, Orange Co., CA.*

       Notes for WILLIAM STEVEN BALLARD:
       Source: 1920 Crawford County Arkansas Federal Census Records, 1930 Orange County California Federal Census Records, WWII Draft Registration Cards

       * 1920 - Living in Van Buren, Crawford Co., AR - Ballard, W S 33 AR AR AR, Lelia 19 AR AR AR, Beuford 1 8/12 /E
       * 1930 - Living in Fullerton, Orange Co., CA - Ballard, William S 43 AR AR AR, Buford 11 AR AR AR, Bernaldine 10 AR AR AR, Eugene 7 AR AR AR, William Nelson 59 lodger CO

 iv.   LEWIS NELSON BALLARD, *b. 27 Sep 1888, Sharp Co., AR; d. 01 Jul 1975, Van Buren, Crawford Co., AR; m.* JESSIE ANN CARTY, *25 Dec 1912, Lone Elm, Franklin Co AR; b. 18 Jul 1893, Franklin Co., AR; d. 09 Sep 1990, Van Buren, Crawford Co., AR.*

       Notes for LEWIS NELSON BALLARD:
       Source: 1920-1930 Crawford County Arkansas Federal Census Records

       * 1920 - Living in Maxey, Crawford Co., AR - Ballard, Louis N 30 AR AR AR, Jessie A 26 AR AR AR, Hazel 5 AR, Hubert W 3 AR, Olan P 11/12 AR
       * 1930 - Living in Maxey, Crawford Co., AR - Ballard, Louis 41 AR AR AR, Jessie 36 AR AR AR, Hazel 16 AR, Hubert 13 AR, Olan 11 AR, James 9 AR, Junior 6 AR, Jessie M 3 AR, William F 4/12 AR

       More About LEWIS NELSON BALLARD:
       Burial: Rankin Cemetery, Lone Elm, Franklin Co., AR

       More About JESSIE ANN CARTY:
       Burial: Rankin Cemetery, Lone Elm, Franklin Co., AR

  v.   J. WALKER BALLARD, *b. 09 Sep 1890, Sitka, Sharp Co., AR; d. 04 Mar 1901, Franklin Co., AR.*

More About J. WALKER BALLARD:
Burial: Rankin Cemetery, Lone Elm, Franklin Co., AR

vi. GERTRUDE MAY BALLARD, b. 04 Oct 1893, Madison Co., AR; d. 22 Dec 1903, Reno Lamar Co TX.

vii. THOMAS JEFFERSON BALLARD, b. 14 Sep 1897, Elkins AR; d. 03 Apr 1970, Van Buren Crawford Co., AR; m. FLOSSIE DELLA WEST, 22 Jun 1931, Mulberry Crawford Co., AR; b. 05 Jul 1903, Mulberry Crawford Co., AR; d. 12 May 1965, Van Buren Crawford Co., AR.

viii. FLOYD BALLARD, b. 29 Sep 1900, Mulberry Crawford Co., AR; d. 16 Aug 1981, Bixby Tulsa OK; m. LENA COX, 04 Sep 1924, Mulberry Crawford Co., AR; b. 13 Jun 1898; d. 26 Mar 1983.

ix. SAM BALLARD, b. 07 Jul 1903, Reno Lamar Co TX; d. 09 Apr 1909, Mulberry Crawford Co., AR.

More About SAM BALLARD:
Burial: Rankin Cemetery, Lone Elm, Franklin Co., AR

x. CARL EDISON BALLARD, b. 19 Jul 1907, Reno, Lamar Co., TX; d. 04 Apr 1909, Mulberry Crawford Co., AR.

More About CARL EDISON BALLARD:
Burial: Rankin Cemetery, Lone Elm, Franklin Co., AR

21. STEPHEN B.[5] BALLARD (JAMES T.[4], JAMES[3], NATHAN[2], HUMPHREY[1]) was born Aug 1861 in AR, and died Bet. 1887 - 1888 in Madison Co., AR. He married SARAH ELIZABETH "LIZZIE" JEFFERS. She was born May 1864 in Madison Co., AR, and died Aft. 1900.

Notes for SARAH ELIZABETH "LIZZIE" JEFFERS:
Source: 1900 Madison County Arkansas Federal Census Records

* 1900 - Living in Lamar, Madison Co., AR - Bell, Charles J, Sarah E, Lester L, Elbert A, Mary E., Fred B, James E, Ballard, John M step son - Apr 1884 AR, Everett L step son - Oct 1877 AR

Children of STEPHEN BALLARD and SARAH JEFFERS are:

i. WILLIAM[6] BALLARD, b. 1881; d. 1881.

ii. FRANCES ELLA BALLARD, b. 25 Apr 1882, Paris, Logan Co., AR; d. 08 Sep 1983, Riverside Co., CA; m. THOMAS WILBURN GRAHAM, 01 Jan 1898, Washington Co., AR; b. Feb 1873, Washington Co., AR; d. Feb 1941, Riverside CA.

iii. JOHN MELVIN BALLARD, b. Apr 1884, AR; d. Aft. 1900; m. INA HOLMSLEY; b. Abt. 1886.

iv. EVERETT LEROY BALLARD, b. 1888, Madison Co., AR; d. Aft. 1900; m. (1) ELIZABETH JEFFERS; b. Abt. 1890; m. (2) OLIE DINE COUNTS.

22. MARTHA ELIZABETH "LISSIE"[5] BALLARD (JAMES T.[4], JAMES[3], NATHAN[2], HUMPHREY[1]) was born May 1866 in AR, and died 12 Sep 1949 in Lamar Co., TX. She married JEFFERSON DAVID CARLISLE 14 Jan 1886 in Franklin Co. AR. He was born Aug 1861 in MS, and died 1910 in AR.

Notes for JEFFERSON DAVID CARLISLE:
Source: 1900 Lamar County Texas Federal Census Records, 1910 Franklin County Arkansas Federal Census Records

* 1900 - Living in Lamar Co., TX - Carlisle, Jeff 38, Lizzie 34, Ellis 11, Nora 9, Maude 4, Ella 1
* 1910 - Living in Franklin Co., AR - Carlile, Jeff D 48 MS TN AL, Martha E 43 AL US US 9 children - 5 living, Ellis M 21 AR, Nora L 19 AR, Maud 14 TX, Ella 10 TX, Selma 7 TX, Lewis Ballard 21 AR hired man

Children of MARTHA BALLARD and JEFFERSON CARLISLE are:

i. ELLIS M.[6] CARLISLE, b. 02 Dec 1888, AR; d. 21 Sep 1954, CA.

     ii.   NORA LEE CARLISLE, b. 07 Dec 1889, AR; d. 13 Apr 1982, Mansfield, Tarrant Co., AR; m. MILLER.

          Notes for NORA LEE CARLISLE:
          Source: Tarrant County Texas Certificate of Death

    iii.   MAUDE CARLISLE, b. 14 Apr 1896, TX; d. Aft. 1910.
    iv.   ELLA CARLISLE, b. 04 Mar 1899, TX; d. 16 May 1980; m. KITCHENS.

          Notes for ELLA CARLISLE:
          Source: Social Security Death Records, Bexar County Texas Death records

     v.   SELMA CARLISLE, b. 1903, TX; d. 1927.

23.   MARIAM MARY[5] BALLARD (JAMES T.[4], JAMES[3], NATHAN[2], HUMPHREY[1]) was born 20 Feb 1868 in AL, and died 25 Dec 1895 in Madison Co., AR. She married EPHRAIM GAINES 24 Dec 1884. He was born 28 Dec 1854, and died 27 Apr 1929.

Notes for MARIAM MARY BALLARD:
Source: Bill & Dorothy Dareing (deebee@ntin.net), Karen Weeks (Kweeks58@aol.com)

Notes for EPHRAIM GAINES:
Source: Bill & Dorothy Dareing (deebee@ntin.net)

Children of MARIAM BALLARD and EPHRAIM GAINES are:

     i.   LAURA G.[6] GAINES, b. 31 Oct 1885, Webb City Madison Co., AR; d. 04 Aug 1984, Wesley Cemetery.; m. MILLAGE L. MCELHANEY, 11 Oct 1905; b. 20 Feb 1881, Madison Co., AR; d. 06 Aug 1926, Wesley Cemetery..

          Notes for LAURA G. GAINES:
          Source: Bill & Dorothy Dareing (deebee@ntin.net), Karen Weeks (Kweeks58@aol.com)

          Notes for MILLAGE L. MCELHANEY:
          Source: Karen Weeks (Kweeks58@aol.com)

     ii.   WILLIAM FRANK GAINES, b. 11 Jul 1887; m. (1) CORA JEFFRIES; m. (2) DELLA EUBANKS.

          Notes for WILLIAM FRANK GAINES:
          Source: Bill & Dorothy Dareing (deebee@ntin.net)

    iii.   MARY ETTA GAINES, b. 31 May 1889; d. 20 Sep 1975; m. WILLIAM SYLVESTER KIRKSEY, 30 Nov 1906.

          Notes for MARY ETTA GAINES:
          Source: Bill & Dorothy Dareing (deebee@ntin.net)

     iv.   NORA ALICE GAINES, b. 11 Feb 1893.

          Notes for NORA ALICE GAINES:
          Source: Bill & Dorothy Dareing (deebee@ntin.net)

     v.   DELLA GAINES, b. 11 Feb 1893; d. 13 Nov 1893.

24. JAMES ALLEN[5] BALLARD (JAMES T.[4], JAMES[3], NATHAN[2], HUMPHREY[1]) *was born 30 Dec 1874 in AR, and died 06 Aug 1962 in Paris, Lamar Co., TX. He married* DORA ELVIRA HALL *06 Nov 1904 in Franklin Co., AR. She was born 22 May 1881 in Fayetteville AR, and died 03 Nov 1969 in Paris, Lamar Co., TX.*

Notes for JAMES ALLEN BALLARD:
Source: Jerry Frazier

More About JAMES ALLEN BALLARD:
Burial: Hopewell Cemetery. Lamar Co TX

More About DORA ELVIRA HALL:
Burial: Hopewell Cemetery. Lamar Co TX

Children of JAMES BALLARD *and* DORA HALL *are:*
- i. ORVEL OTTO[6] BALLARD, *b. 29 Jul 1905, Reno TX; d. 30 Jan 1978, Paris, Lamar Co., TX; m.* ROSIE HELEN MORTON; *b. 05 Nov 1916, Sallisaw, Sequoyah Co., OK; d. Lamar Co., TX.*

  Notes for ROSIE HELEN MORTON:
  Obituary - Rosie Ballard, 81, Rt. 5, Paris, TX, died Thursday, Nov. 13, 1997, at her home. Services will be at 10 a.m. Saturday, Nov. 15, at Bright-Holland Funeral Home Chapel with Haskell England officiating. Burial will be in Hopewell Cemetery. The family will receive friends from 6-8 p.m. Friday at the funeral home. She was born Nov. 5, 1915, in Sallisaw, Okla., to Hershel and Willie Culvert Morton. She was a homemaker and member of Bonham Street Church of Christ. She married Orvel Ballard April 11, 1934. After his death in 1978, she married A.C. Ballard April 26, 1982. Surviving are her husband of 15 years, A.C. Ballard; six sons and daughters-in-law, Cecil and Josephine Ballard of Alba, Willard and Veronica Ballard of Reno, Hershel and Margaret Ballard of Paris, Dewayne and Kathy Ballard of Atlas, Orvell and Bonnie Ballard of Paris and Larry and Doreen Ballard of Paris; a daughter and son-in-law, Wanda and Jim Montgomery of Paris; five stepsons, Jerry Ballard of Brookston, Clayton Ballard of Paris, Freddy Ballard of Brookston, Kenneth Ballard of Brookston, and Rickey Ballard of Brookston; three step daughters, Linda Ashford of Reno, Peggy Dixon of Slate Shoals and Brenda Johnson of Paris; 37 grandchildren; 44 great-grandchildren; and two great- great- grand children; and two brothers-in-law, Ruben Allen of Paris and Milford Aubrey of Carrollton. She was preceded in death by two sisters and one brother.

- ii. BEN GRADEN BALLARD, *b. 27 Mar 1907.*
- iii. LYDIA IOMA BALLARD, *b. 27 Dec 1908, AR; d. 05 Mar 1984, Lamar Co., TX; m.* ROY LEE BRYAN; *b. 11 Oct 1902; d. 29 Sep 1988.*
- iv. OSCAR LEE BALLARD, *b. 05 Nov 1911; d. 23 Jun 1983, Paris, Lamar Co., TX.*
- v. AXIE ELLEN BALLARD, *b. 04 Mar 1915, Franklin Co., AR; d. 26 Dec 1925, Garrets, Bluff Co., TX.*
- vi. ODIS NELSON BALLARD, *b. 04 Mar 1917, Lamar Co., TX; d. 1967; m.* IDELL F. MAGGARD; *b. 11 Jun 1920; d. 05 Mar 1979.*
- vii. ARCHIE CLAYTON BALLARD, *b. 20 Sep 1918, Lamar Co., TX; d. 06 Aug 1962, Paris, Lamar Co., TX; m.* LARENE DOROTHY UTZ; *b. 21 Feb 1920, Shady Grove Lamar Co TX; d. 11 Nov 1981, Paris Lamar Co TX.*

25. ELLEN[5] BALLARD (JAMES T.[4], JAMES[3], NATHAN[2], HUMPHREY[1]) *was born 1877 in AR, and died Aft. 1892 in AR. She married* COLUMBUS GRAHAM *26 Jun 1892 in Washington Co., AR. He was born 25 Sep 1867 in AR, and died 14 Apr 1957 in Tulare Co., CA.*

Notes for COLUMBUS GRAHAM:

Source: 1900-1910 Washington County Arkansas Federal Census Records, Tulare County California Death Index, 1930 Tulare County California Federal Census Records
* 1900 - Living in Springdale, Washington Co., AR - Graham, Columbus - Sept 1870 AR MO AR farmer,

Ellen - Sep 1877 AR AR AR, Pearl 3 - Nov 196, Almon - July 1899 11/12AR
* 1910 - Living in Elm Springs, Washington Co., AR - Graham, Columbus 40 AR Unknown, IL farmer, Ellen 34 - 4 children 4 living AR , Pearl 13 AR, Alma 10 AR, Clarence 7 AR, Edith 3 AR
* 1930 - Living in Visalia, Tulare Co., Ca - Graham, Columbus S 60 AR IL IL Gardener

Children of ELLEN BALLARD and COLUMBUS GRAHAM are:

    i.   HELEN PEARL[6] GRAHAM, b. 25 Nov 1896, Pulaski Co., CA; d. 05 Mar 1950, Waukena, Tulare Co., CA; m. GEORGE WASHINGTON HALSTEAD; b. 29 Sep 1898, Visalia, Tulare Co., CA; d. 24 Nov 1953, Visalia, Tulare Co., CA.

        More About HELEN PEARL GRAHAM:
        Burial: Visalia Public Cemetery, Visalia, Tulare Co., CA

        More About GEORGE WASHINGTON HALSTEAD:
        Burial: Visalia Public Cemetery, Visalia, Tulare Co., CA

    ii.   ALMA AVIS GRAHAM, b. 12 Jul 1899, AR; d. 24 Aug 1984, Santa Cruz, CA; m. ARCHIBALD C. WALL.

        Notes for ALMA AVIS GRAHAM:
        Source: California Death Records, Social Security Records

    iii.   CLARENCE R. GRAHAM, b. 22 Jan 1902, Springdale, Washington Co., AR; d. 23 Dec 1975.

        Notes for CLARENCE R. GRAHAM:
        Source: WWII Draft Registration Cards

        More About CLARENCE R. GRAHAM:
        Burial: Los Angeles National Cemetery, LA Co., CA

    iv.   EDITH GRAHAM, b. Abt. 1907, AR; d. Aft. 1910.

26. WILLIAM LAFAYETTE[5] BALLARD (WILLIAM JOHN[4], JAMES[3], NATHAN[2], HUMPHREY[1]) was born 15 Jan 1860 in Tallapoosa Co., AL, and died 17 Jan 1931 in Mira, Caddo Co., LA. He married (1) AMERICA ALICE WALDROUP 12 Oct 1883 in Sulphur, Miller Co., AR, daughter of JOHN WALDROUP and LUCINDA SAMS. She was born 03 Mar 1869 in Lafayette Co., AR, and died 03 Jan 1904 in Sulphur, Miller Co., AR. He married (2) SARAH TENCIE BROWN Aft. 1904. She was born 18 Dec 1878, and died 06 Jun 1930.

Notes for WILLIAM LAFAYETTE BALLARD:
Source: Find A Grave, 1900 Miller County Arkansas Federal Census Records, 1910 Caddo Parish Louisiana Federal Census Records, Mt. Zion Cemetery Miller County Arkansas records, Toni Norris Verbois (toni_verbois@yahoo.com)

* 1900 - Living in Sulphur, Miller Co., AR - Ballard, William L Jan 1859 AL farmer, America A Mar 1869 AR, John W Dec 1889, Fannie L Apr 1896, Miron J Oct 1898 AR
* 1910 - Living in Caddo Parish, LA - Ballard, William L md 2x, Lensie Ballard 32 md 3x 8 children 5 living, Fannie 14, Miran 11, Nellie 9, Dnaa 6, Thelma 3, Vera 1, Lillie Tidwell 14, Bessie Tidwell 11, Myrtle Tidwell 8

More About WILLIAM LAFAYETTE BALLARD:
Burial: Mt. Zion Cemetery. Doddridge Miller Co. AR

More About AMERICA ALICE WALDROUP:
Burial: Mt. Zion Cemetery. Doddridge Miller Co. AR

More About SARAH TENCIE BROWN:

Burial: Munnerlyn Chapel Cemetery. Mira LA

Children of WILLIAM BALLARD and AMERICA WALDROUP are:

     i.   ANNA LEE[6] BALLARD, b. 21 Oct 1886, Sulphur, Miller Co., AR; d. 04 Jul 1895, Sulphur, Miller Co., AR.

         More About ANNA LEE BALLARD:
         Burial: Mt. Zion Cemetery. Doddridge Miller Co. AR

    ii.   JOHN WILLIAM BALLARD, b. 19 Dec 1889, Doddridge, Miller Co., AR; d. 14 Sep 1960, Shreveport, Caddo Parish, LA; m. SARAH O'NORA WYNN, 24 Dec 1911, Mira, Caddo Co., LA; b. 01 Dec 1892, Mira, Caddo Parish, LA; d. 20 Jan 1978, Hosston, Caddo Parish, LA.

         Notes for JOHN WILLIAM BALLARD:
         Source: Toni Norris Verbois (toni_verbois@yahoo.com)

         More About JOHN WILLIAM BALLARD:
         Burial: Vivian Cemetery. Caddo Co., LA

         More About SARAH O'NORA WYNN:
         Burial: Vivian Cemetery. Parish, LA

   iii.   HILSON L. BALLARD, b. 03 Jun 1893, Sulphur, Miller Co., AR; d. 12 Jul 1896, Sulphur, Miller Co., AR.

         More About HILSON L. BALLARD:
         Burial: Mt. Zion Cemetery. Doddridge Miller Co. AR

    iv.   FANNIE LEE BALLARD, b. 24 Apr 1896, Sulphur, Miller Co., AR; d. 04 Feb 1994, Bastrop, Bossier Parish LA; m. WILLIAM HARDY GRAVES, 09 Mar 1913; b. 04 Jun 1890; d. 17 Jul 1957.

         More About FANNIE LEE BALLARD:
         Burial: Munnerlyn Chapel Cemetery. Mira LA

     v.   MIRON JOB BALLARD, b. 18 Oct 1898, Sulphur, Miller Co., AR; d. 18 Sep 1972, Prescott, Nevada Co., AR; m. MARY PEARSON; b. 1895, LA; d. 29 Mar 1974, Starr City, AR.

         More About MIRON JOB BALLARD:
         Burial: Bluff City Cemetery., Bluff City, Nevada Co., AR

         More About MARY PEARSON:
         Burial: Bluff City Cemetery. AR

    vi.   NELLIE BLANCHE BALLARD, b. 24 Mar 1901, Black Diamond Miller Co., AR; d. 14 Jan 2000; m. CURTIS C. LEACH, SR.; b. 17 Sep 1890, Florien LA; d. 10 Jul 1975, Shreveport, Caddo Parish, LA.

         More About NELLIE BLANCHE BALLARD:
         Burial: Centuries Memorial. Park, Shreveport, Caddo Parish, LA

         More About CURTIS C. LEACH, SR.:
         Burial: Centuries Memorial. Park Cemetery., Shreveport, Caddo Parish, LA

   vii.   DENA AMERICA BALLARD, b. 21 Dec 1903, Sulphur, Miller Co., AR; d. 15 Mar 1992, Memphis, Shelby Co., TN; m. MURRAY BEASLEY.

More About DENA AMERICA BALLARD:
Burial: Forest Hill Cemetery., South, Memphis, Shelby Co., TN

Children of WILLIAM BALLARD and SARAH BROWN are:

viii. THELMA[6] BALLARD, *b. 27 Jan 1907, Ida, Caddo Parish, LA; d. 28 Nov 1981, Shreveport, Caddo Parish, LA; m. JIM DINKINS; d. 13 Sep 1973, Shreveport, Caddo Parish, LA.*

More About THELMA BALLARD:
Burial: Forest Park Cemetery, Shreveport, Caddo Parish, LA

More About JIM DINKINS:
Burial: Forest Park Cemetery, Shreveport, Caddo Parish, LA

ix. VERA M. BALLARD, *b. 26 Apr 1909, Mira, Caddo Parish LA; d. 01 Feb 1951, Shreveport, Caddo Parish, LA; m. JOHN B. HILL, 17 Aug 1927, Caddo Parish, LA; b. 26 Jun 1907; d. 25 Jan 1944.*

More About VERA M. BALLARD:
Burial: Hosston Cemetery., Caddo Parish., LA

More About JOHN B. HILL:
Burial: Hosston Cemetery., Caddo Parish., LA

x. SARAH LOUISE BALLARD, *b. 30 May 1911, Mira, Caddo Parish LA; d. 02 Jan 2009, Shreveport, Caddo Parish, LA; m. (1) ASBURY BLANTON FULLILOVE; m. (2) CLIFTON C. KEY.*

More About SARAH LOUISE BALLARD:
Burial: Forest Park East Cemetery., Shreveport, Caddo Parish, LA

xi. RAYMOND W. BALLARD, *b. 10 Feb 1913, Ida, Caddo Parish, LA; d. 05 Nov 1938, Lincoln Parish, LA; m. GERTRUDE HOLMAN.*

More About RAYMOND W. BALLARD:
Burial: Munnerlyn Chapel, Cemetery., Ido, Caddo Parish, LA

xii. SAMUEL L. BALLARD, *b. 27 Feb 1915, Mira, Caddo Parish LA; d. 14 Jun 1974, Carlsbad Co., NM; m. KATHLENE KREBS.*

More About SAMUEL L. BALLARD:
Burial: Sunset Gardens Cemetery., Carlsbad, Carlsbad Co., NM

James Ballard

Generation No. 1

1. JAMES[1] BALLARD *was born Abt. 1754, and died 1826 in Taliaferro Co., GA.*

Notes for JAMES BALLARD:
Source: Phyllis Bauer

Children of JAMES BALLARD are:

2.   i.   ELIJAH W.[2] BALLARD, *b. 19 May 1782, NC; d. 25 Dec 1852, Fayette Co., GA.*
      ii.   JAMES BALLARD, *b. Bet. 1784 - 1790.*

Generation No. 2

2. ELIJAH W.[2] BALLARD (JAMES[1]) *was born 19 May 1782 in NC, and died 25 Dec 1852 in Fayette Co., GA. He married* SARAH TABITHA WELDON. *She was born 01 May 1792 in NC, and died 09 Jan 1864 in Fayette Co., GA.*

Notes for ELIJAH W. BALLARD:
Source: 1850 Fayette County Georgia Federal Census Records, Phillis J. Bauer, Melissa Brandt (missmissy104@hotmail.com), Ruby Beaver (rbeaver@duracom.net) Barbara Fincher (bpdf@gnat.net), (sjcaseyjr@email.msn.co), Kenneth Cook (Kcook@peoplescom.net), Lynn B. Cunningham (lcunnin1@bellsouth.net)

* 1850 - Living in Fayette Co., GA - Ballard, Elijah 63 NC farmer, Sarah 58 NY, San Buffington 22 GA

More About ELIJAH W. BALLARD:
Burial: Old Ballard Cemetery, Fayette Co., GA

Notes for SARAH TABITHA WELDON:
Source: Lynn B. Cunningham (lcunnin1@bellsouth.net)

More About SARAH TABITHA WELDON:
Burial: Old Ballard Cemetery, Fayette Co., GA

Children of ELIJAH BALLARD and SARAH WELDON are:

      i.   LUCINDA THOMPSON[3] BALLARD, *b. Abt. 1810.*

            Notes for LUCINDA THOMPSON BALLARD:

            Source: Ballard-Ballord Bits pg 328-329 X2241 & X 2242, Buffington Family by C.D. Rhame, R. H. Palmer & RM Buffinton, 1965, pg. 76

3.   ii.   JOHN JASPER BALLARD, *b. 12 Nov 1812, Greene Co., GA; d. 15 Jul 1864, Richmond, Henrico Co., VA (Civil War).*
4.   iii. ELIJAH W. BALLARD, *b. 1816, Greene Co., GA; d. 1885, Hopkins Co., TX.*
5.   iv.   WILLIAM BARNES BALLARD, *b. 12 Mar 1818, Greene Co., GA; d. 31 Mar 1886, 1888 Green Co., GA or Pike Co., GA.*
6.   v.   THOMAS WELDON BALLARD, *b. 20 Dec 1820, Greene Co., GA; d. 30 Mar 1887, Fayette Co., GA.*
7.   vi.   JAMES H. BALLARD, *b. 24 Feb 1822, Greene Co., GA; d. Aft. 1850.*
8.   vii. DANIEL G. S. BALLARD, *b. 09 Nov 1823, Greene or Fayette Co., GA; d. 21 Apr 1867, Pike Co., GA.*
      viii. ELIZABETH A. BALLARD, *b. Abt. 1826, Greene Co., GA.*
      ix.   MARTHA JANE BALLARD, *b. 1828.*

x.   MARGARET KATHERINE BALLARD, b. 1831.

Generation No. 3

3. JOHN JASPER[3] BALLARD (ELIJAH W.[2], JAMES[1]) was born 12 Nov 1812 in Greene Co., GA, and died 15 Jul 1864 in Richmond, Henrico Co., VA (Civil War). He married NANCY MCKNIGHT 17 Oct 1833 in Taliaferro Co., GA. She was born 1809 in Washington Co., GA, and died 15 Nov 1876 in Ballard Hill, Pike Co., AL.

Notes for JOHN JASPER BALLARD:
Source: 1850 Fayetteville Fayette County Georgia Federal Census Records, Ballard-Ballord Bits page 115 M1, Phyllis Bauer, Beverly Killian (beverlykillian@starband.net)
* Lived in Fayetteville Fayette Co., GA. Moved to Milo and then Springhill Pike Co., AL. Served 18 months in Army of Northern VA CSA and d. in Richmond, Henrico Co., VA.
* 1850 - Living in Fayette Co., GA - (Ballard is looking like Bullard but when compared to other "a"s on the page, it is an "a" and not a "u") Ballard John J. 38 GA, Nancy 41 GA, Martin 12 GA, Jackson 8 GA, John 5 GA, Sarah Ann 3 GA, Lewis 2 GA, and Zachry T. 3\4 GA
* 1864 - Died in the Civil War having served in Company G, 2nd Regiment, GA Volunteer Inf., Army Northern VA CSA Muscogee Co., GA Columbus Guards, Private Feb 1, 1864 Winder Hosp. Richmond VA July 15, 1864

More About JOHN JASPER BALLARD:
Burial: Hollywood Cemetery, Richmond, Richmond City, VA

Notes for NANCY MCKNIGHT:
Source: 1870 Pike County Alabama Federal Census Records
* 1870 - Living with son James P. Ballard in Pike Co., AL

Children of JOHN BALLARD and NANCY MCKNIGHT are:
9.   i.   WILLIAM ELIJAH[4] BALLARD, b. 19 Jul 1834, Fayette Co., GA; d. 24 Nov 1874, AL.
           ii.   ROBERT SAMUEL BALLARD, b. 08 Mar 1835, Fayette Co., GA; d. 31 Aug 1857.
          iii.   MARTIN BALLARD, b. Abt. 1837, Fayette Co., GA; d. Aft. 1872; m. MOLLIE, 05 Sep 1872, Pickensville, Pickens Co., AL; b. 05 Aug 1852, Pickens Co., AL.
          iv.   MARY ELIZABETH BALLARD, b. 03 Apr 1838, Fayette Co., GA.
10.   v.   JAMES PURIFOY BALLARD, b. 10 Apr 1840, Fayette Co., GA; d. Abt. 1893, Copperas Cove, Coryell Co., TX.
          vi.   JACKSON BALLARD, b. 1842, Fayette Co., GA; d. Aft. 1850.
          vii.   SARAH JANE CATHERINE "KATY" BALLARD, b. 27 May 1842, Fayette Co., GA; d. 03 May 1901, Troy, Pike Co., AL.
11.   viii.   THOMAS WELDON BALLARD, b. 02 May 1844, Fayetteville Fayette Co., GA; d. 05 May 1910, lived in Pike Co., AL.
          ix.   MARTHA BELLAH BALLARD, b. 23 May 1847, Fayette Co., GA.
           x.   LEWIS BALLARD, b. Abt. 1848, Fayette Co., GA.
12.   xi.   JULIA ANN BALLARD, b. 14 Jan 1849, Fayetteville Fayette Co., GA; d. 18 Jan 1909.
          xii.   ZACHARY T. BALLARD, b. 1850, Fayette Co., GA.
         xiii.   DANIEL GASTON STANLEY BALLARD, b. 15 Nov 1850, Fayette Co., GA.
13.   xiv.   JOHN JASPER BALLARD, b. 28 Sep 1853, Fayette Co., GA; d. 27 Oct 1918.

4. ELIJAH W.[3] BALLARD (ELIJAH W.[2], JAMES[1]) was born 1816 in Greene Co., GA, and died 1885 in Hopkins Co., TX. He married (1) MARY BLOODWORTH 24 Aug 1837 in Wilkinson Co., GA, daughter of HENRY BLOODWORTH and ELIZABETH TEMPLES. She was born 1816 in Wilkinson Co., GA, and died 1853 in Wilkinson Co., GA. He married (2) SARAH EMILY GOLDEN 27 Apr 1853 in Wilkinson Co., GA. She was born Abt. 1835 in Garrard Co., KY, and died Aft. 1880 in TX.

Notes for ELIJAH W. BALLARD:
Source: 1850 Wilkinson County Georgia Federal Census Records, 1860 Bradley Arkansas Federal Census Records,

1870 Hopkins County Texas Federal Census Records, 1880 Delta County Texas Federal Census Records, Melissa Brandt (e-mell@home.com), Ruby Beaver (rbeaver@duracom.net), Paul Wilhite, (backpages@earthlink.net), Kenneth Cook (Kcook@peoplescom.net), Beverly Killian (beverlykillian@starband.net), (lcunnin1@bellsouth.net), Ancestry.com marriage record

* 1850 - Living in Wilkinson Co., GA - Ballard, Elijah 33 GA, Mary 35 GA, Mariah D.11 GA, William C Q 10 GA, James W 7 GA, Timothy C 5 GA, John M GA, Henry E. S 1 GA

* 1860 - Living in Miller, Bradley AR - Ballard, Elijah 42, Sarah E 25, James W. 19, Timothy 17, John N.15, Henry C.12, Permelia A. 11, Gillis N. 8, Jesse T. 7, Mary E. 4, and Seaborn H. 1.

* 1870 - Living in Hopkins Co., TX - Ballard, Elijah 53 farmer GA, Sarah E 36 GA, Timothy C 27 farmer GA, Laura 19 TX, Permelia A 17 GA, Gillis M 16 GA., Mary E 11 GA, Sebern H 10 AR, Sarah 8 AR, Rueben W 4 AR, Isaac 2 TX

* 1880 - Living in Delta Co., TX - Ballard, Elijah W. 64 GA, Sarah E. 45 GA, Sarah E. 16 AR, Ruben W. 15 AR, Isaac V. 12 TX, Fannie G. 9 TX, Robert E. 5 TX, Renfrow, William W. 14 AR, Renfrow, James H. 11 TX

Children of ELIJAH BALLARD and MARY BLOODWORTH are:

	i.	MARIAH I.[4] BALLARD, b. Abt. 1839, GA; d. Aft. 1850.
	ii.	WILLIAM BALLARD, b. Abt. 1840, GA; d. Aft. 1850.
14.	iii.	TIMOTHY C. BALLARD, b. 11 Nov 1844, GA; d. 05 Dec 1895, Commerce, Hunt Co., TX.
	iv.	JAMES W. BALLARD, b. Abt. 1845, GA; d. Aft. 1860.
	v.	JOHN N. BALLARD, b. 1846, GA; d. Aft. 1860.

> *Notes for JOHN N. BALLARD:*
> *Source: Civil War Pension Index supplied by JONESY6IRON@aol.com*
> *Name of Holder: Ballard, John N.*
> *Name of Dependent: Father, Ballard Elijah*
> *Service: (two lines; writing is so broken, can't read them)*
> *Date of Filing: (looks like 1890 Sept 16*
> *Class: ?,   Application No. : ?   Certificate No. : 301634 (hard to read)*

	vi.	HENRY C. BALLARD, b. 1848, GA; d. Aft. 1860.
	vii.	PERMILIA "PAM" M. BALLARD, b. 1849, GA; d. 25 Apr 1886, Hopkins Co., TX.
	viii.	GILLIS MARION BALLARD, b. 1852, GA; d. 18 Dec 1931, Hamilton Co., TX.
	ix.	JESSE T. BALLARD, b. 1853, GA; d. Aft. 1860.

Children of ELIJAH BALLARD and SARAH GOLDEN are:

15.	x.	MARY E.[4] BALLARD, b. 1854, TX; d. Aft. 1880.
16.	xi.	SEABORN H. BALLARD, b. 02 Nov 1859, GA; d. 11 Apr 1914, OK.
17.	xii.	REUBEN WESLEY BALLARD, b. 21 Jan 1864, Pine Bluff, Jefferson Co., AR; d. 21 Nov 1937, Dustin, Hughes Co., OK.
	xiii.	SARAH E. BALLARD, b. 1862, AR; d. Aft. 1880.
18.	xiv.	ISAAC VINSON BALLARD, b. 18 Jul 1867, Hunt Co., TX; d. 04 Aug 1941, Caddo Parish, LA.
	xv.	FANNIE G. BALLARD, b. 1871, TX; d. Aft. 1880.
19.	xvi.	ROBERT LEE BALLARD, b. 27 Jan 1874, TX; d. 26 May 1931, Grayson Co., TX.
	xvii.	ANDREW JACKSON BALLARD, b. 1881, TX; d. 12 Sep 1917; m. EMMIE LOU EVANS.

5. WILLIAM BARNES[3] BALLARD (ELIJAH W.[2], JAMES[1]) *was born 12 Mar 1818 in Greene Co., GA, and died 31 Mar 1886 in 1888 Green Co., GA or Pike Co., GA. He married (1) MARTHA JANE UNITY PATTON 02 Dec 1841 in Fayette Co., GA, daughter of JAMES PATTON and ELIZABETH HUNT. She was born 19 Sep 1825 in Jasper Co., GA, and died 17 Oct 1857 in Fayette Co., GA. He married (2) SUSAN J. S. ALLEN 30 Oct 1858 in Pike Co., GA, daughter of ABRAHAM ALLEN and MARTHA MARSHALL. She was born 13 May 1840 in GA, and died 17 May 1911 in Pike Co., GA.*

Notes for WILLIAM BARNES BALLARD:
Source: Lynn B. Cunningham (lcunnin1@bellsouth.net), 1850 Fayette County Georgia Federal Census Records,

1860, 1870, 1880 Pike County Georgia Federal Census Records
* *1850 - Living in Fayette Co., GA - Ballard, William., 30 M, Farmer, $1800, GA, Ballard, Martha, 24, F, GA, Ballard, James P or D. 7, M, GA, Ballard, Elijah, 6, M, GA, Ballard, Elizabeth A, 4, F, GA, Thomas W., 2, M, GA, Daniel G., 2/12, M, GA*
* *1860 - Living in Pike Co., GA - Ballard, William B., 42 M, Farmer Ballard, Susan J.S. 20, F, Ballard, James P. 16, M Ballard, Elijah, 15, M, Farm Laborer, Ballard, Elizabeth A. 13, F, Ballard Thomas W. 11, M Ballard, Abraham S.A., 9/12, M*
* *1870 - Living in Pike Co., GA - Ballard, William B. 52 M, W, Farmer, Ballard, Susan J.S. 30, F, W, Keeping House, Ballard Thomas W. 21, M, W, Farm Laborer, Ballard, Isabella, 19, F, W, At Home (wife of Thomas) Ballard, William B. 13, M, W, Farm Laborer, Ballard, Abraham S. 10, M, W, Farm Laborer John H. 4, M, W, Martha S. 7, F, W (daughter of Daniel G.S. Ballard)*
* *1880 - Living in Pike Co., GA - Ballard, William 62 GA, Farming GA MO GA Susan 40, GA NC NC, Abram S. 20 GA GA GA, John Ballard 14, GA GA GA Martha 8, GA GA GA Young D. 6, GA GA GA Charles W. 1, GA GA GA*
* *From Will of William B. Ballard (written in 1885): Codicil to the Last Will and Testament of William B. Ballard. Owing to my son James P. Ballard having lost his eye sight, I will and devise the clause of the seventh item of this my will changed where it says my son James P. keep the estate together in the event of the death of my wife and pay out as directed in the 5th item. I devise and will that in the event of the death of my wife, all my estate both real and personal except under previous direction of my will sold by trustees hereinafter appointed and divided equally among my children. I hereby appoint my son Thomas W. Ballard, Jr. and Drewy S. Allen trustees.... Will is signed by R.V. - Reid, William O. Gwyn, Harry Wells. Other signatures by: A.S. Allen, M.A.E. Stegar, Robert H. Allen*

More About WILLIAM BARNES BALLARD:
Burial: Allen Cemetery Williamson Pike Co., GA

Notes for MARTHA JANE UNITY PATTON:
Source: Doris (DorisKF@adelphia.net)

More About MARTHA JANE UNITY PATTON:
Burial: Old Ballard Cemetery. Fayette Co., GA

More About SUSAN J. S. ALLEN:
Burial: Allen Family Cemetery Pike Co., GA

Children of WILLIAM BALLARD and MARTHA PATTON are:
20.   i.   JAMES PATTON[4] BALLARD, b. 05 Sep 1840, 1843 Fayette Co., GA; d. 22 Aug 1912, Pike Co., GA.
21.   ii.   ELIJAH BALLARD, b. 11 Nov 1844, Fayette Co., GA; d. 31 Dec 1919.
22.   iii.   ELIZABETH A. BALLARD, b. 18 Nov 1846, Fayette Co., GA; d. Aft. 1880, Joaquin, Shelby Co., TX.
23.   iv.   THOMAS W. BALLARD, b. 20 Nov 1848, Fayette Co., GA; d. 09 Dec 1904.
          v.   DANIEL G. BALLARD, b. 1850, Fayette Co., GA; d. Aft. 1850.
24.   vi.   WILLIAM BARNES BALLARD, b. 19 Aug 1857, Pike Co., GA; d. 19 Jul 1933, Pike Co., GA.

Children of WILLIAM BALLARD and SUSAN ALLEN are:
25.   vii.   ABRAHAM "ABE" S.[4] BALLARD, b. 09 Aug 1859, Pike Co., GA; d. 21 Jun 1915, Pike Co., GA.
26.   viii.   JOHN HARVEY BALLARD, b. 17 Aug 1864, Pike Co., GA; d. 17 Dec 1948, Pike Co., GA.
         ix.   YOUNG DREWRY BALLARD, b. 16 Mar 1874, Pike Co., GA; d. 17 Nov 1931, Pike Co., GA; m. ROXIE ADDIE BALLARD, 02 Mar 1899, Pike Co., GA; b. 13 Oct 1880, Fayette Co., GA; d. 13 Apr 1971, Pike Co., GA.

          More About YOUNG DREWRY BALLARD:
          Burial: Williamson Methodist Church Cemetery, Pike Co., GA

          More About ROXIE ADDIE BALLARD:
          Burial: Williamson Methodist Church Cemetery, Pike Co., GA

    x.   CHARLES WESLEY BALLARD, *b. Abt. 1879, Pike Co., GA; d. 29 Jun 1937, Pike Co., GA; m. IDA V. BANKS, 30 May 1900, Pike Co., GA; b. 16 Aug 1878, GA; d. 20 Oct 1921, Pike Co., GA.*

    Notes for CHARLES WESLEY BALLARD:
    Source: Lynn B. Cunningham (lcunnin1@bellsouth.net)

    More About CHARLES WESLEY BALLARD:
    Burial: Williamson Methodist Church Cemetery, Pike Co., GA

    More About IDA V. BANKS:
    Burial: Williamson Methodist Church Cemetery, Pike Co., GA

6. THOMAS WELDON[3] *BALLARD (ELIJAH W.[2], JAMES[1]) was born 20 Dec 1820 in Greene Co., GA, and died 30 Mar 1887 in Fayette Co., GA. He married* ELIZABETH JANE ALLEN *04 Sep 1845 in Pike Co., GA, daughter of* YOUNG ALLEN *and* JANE MOORE. *She was born 26 Apr 1827 in GA, and died 21 Apr 1892 in Fayette Co., GA.*

Notes for THOMAS WELDON BALLARD:
Source: Valkere4@aol.com, Lynn B. Cunningham (lcunnin1@bellsouth.net), 1850 Pike County Georgia Federal Census Records, 1860-1880 Fayette County Georgia Federal Census Record
* 1850 - Living in Pike Co., GA - Ballard, Thomas W. 29 GA, Elizabeth 23 GA, Sarah J. 3 GA, Washington 1 GA, Jane Allen 54 NC
* 1860 - Living in Fayette Co., GA - Ballard, T. W. 39 GA, E. J. 33 GA, Sarah Jane 12 GA, Washington A. 11 GA, Mary W. 7 GA, Martha N 6 GA, Elijah M. 3 GA, Elizabeth R. 1 GA
* 1870 - Living in Fayette Co., GA - Ballard, Thos W. 49 GA, Elizabeth 43 GA, Wm. A. 21 GA, Jas W. 14 GA, Elizabeth M. 13 GA, M.N 15 (Martha Nancy) GA, E. Rebeca 11 GA, Addie T. 6 GA, Annie 2 GA
* 1880 - Living in Fayette Co., GA - Ballard, Thomas 59 Farmer GA NC NC, Elizabeth 53 GA NC NC, Addie 16 GA, Annie 12 GA

More About THOMAS WELDON BALLARD:
Burial: Old Ballard Cemetery., Fayette Co., GA

Notes for ELIZABETH JANE ALLEN:
Source: Obituary in the Pike County Journal
* 1892 - The Pike County Journal - Zebulon, Pike County, GA April 29 -
Mrs. Elizabeth Ballard - On the 21st, Mrs. Elizabeth Ballard of Fayette Co., a sister of Capt. As. S. Allen of this county, passed from life unto death after a short illness. At the time of her death she was on a visit to her daughter Mrs. John F. Dickinson, at Griffin. She was seized with a violent coughing spell and her daughter ran to her and while supporting her mother's head in her arms, the candle of life went out. Mrs. Ballard was in her 65th year and had been a consistent member of the Methodist Church for many years. She was loved and respected by all that knew her. The remains were buried at the Old homestead in Fayette County on the 23rd. The Journal tenders sympathy to the bereaved relatives.

More About ELIZABETH JANE ALLEN:
Burial: Old Ballard Cemetery., Fayette Co., GA

Children of THOMAS BALLARD *and* ELIZABETH ALLEN *are:*
      i.   LUM[4] *BALLARD, b. Bet. 1845 - 1865.*
27.   *ii.* SARAH JANE BALLARD, *b. 30 Aug 1847, Pike Co., GA; d. 28 May 1909, Fayette Co., GA.*
28.   *iii.* WASHINGTON AUGUSTUS BALLARD, *b. 31 Mar 1849, Fayette Co., GA; d. 28 Jul 1919, Fayette Co., GA.*
29.   *iv.* MARY WELDON BALLARD, *b. 15 Dec 1852, Fayette Co., GA; d. 19 Aug 1929, Griffin, Spalding Co., GA.*
      v. MARTHA NANCY BALLARD, *b. 12 Oct 1854, GA; d. 08 May 1906; m.* MANLEY.

More About MARTHA NANCY BALLARD:
Burial: Old Ballard Family Cemetery, Woolsey, Fayette Co., GA

      vi.   JAMES W. BALLARD, b. Abt. 1856, GA; d. Aft. 1870.
30.   vii.   ELIJAH MADDOX BALLARD, b. 17 Dec 1856, GA; d. 10 Dec 1933, Fayette Co., GA.
     viii. ELIZABETH REBECCA BALLARD, b. Abt. 1858, GA; d. Aft. 1870.
     ix.   ADDIE THOMAS BALLARD, b. 19 Jun 1863, Fayette Co., GA; d. 30 Jun 1919, Fayette Co., GA; m. (1) CHARLES MCFARLAND; m. (2) WILLIAM WALTER CHAMPION, 25 Oct 1887, Fayette Co., GA; b. 05 Feb 1869, GA; d. 02 Aug 1923, AL.

          More About ADDIE THOMAS BALLARD:
          Burial: Old Ballard Cemetery., Fayette Co., GA

          More About CHARLES MCFARLAND:
          Burial: Old Ballard Cemetery., Fayette Co., GA

     x.   ANNIE A. BALLARD, b. 20 Jul 1867, Fayetteville, Fayette Co., GA; d. 30 Jun 1919; m. WILLIAM WALTER CHAMPION; b. 05 Feb 1869.

          More About ANNIE A. BALLARD:
          Burial: Opp City Cemetery, Covington Co., AL

7. JAMES H.[3] BALLARD (ELIJAH W.[2], JAMES[1]) *was born 24 Feb 1822 in Greene Co., GA, and died Aft. 1850. He married* SARAH A. *25 Oct 1838 in Taliaferro Co., GA. She was born 1819, and died Aft. 1850.*

Notes for JAMES H. BALLARD:
Source: 1850 Pike County GA Federal Census Records

* 1850 - Living in Pike Co., GA - Ballard, James H. 31 mechanic GA, Sarah A. 31 GA, Elizabeth 12 GA, John 7 11 GA, Jas. T. 9 GA, Sarah H. 7 GA, Mary A. 5 GA, Martha 2 GA, Jariett M. 8/12 GA

Children of JAMES BALLARD *and* SARAH A. *are:*
     i.   ELIZABETH[4] BALLARD, b. 1838, GA; d. Aft. 1850.
     ii.   JOHN JASPER BALLARD, b. 1839, GA; d. Aft. 1850.
     iii. JAMES S. BALLARD, b. 1841, GA; d. Aft. 1850.
     iv. SARAH BALLARD, b. 1843, GA; d. Aft. 1850.
     v.   MARY A. BALLARD, b. 1845, GA; d. Aft. 1850.
     vi. MARTHA A. BALLARD, b. 1848, GA; d. Aft. 1850.
     vii. HARRIET M. BALLARD, b. 1850, GA; d. Aft. 1850.

8. DANIEL G. S.[3] BALLARD (ELIJAH W.[2], JAMES[1]) *was born 09 Nov 1823 in Greene or Fayette Co., GA, and died 21 Apr 1867 in Pike Co., GA. He married (1)* REBECCA JANE ALLEN *Bef. 1847. She was born 1831 in GA, and died Aft. 1860. He married (2)* CORNELIA ALLEN *13 Apr 1865 in Pike Co., GA, daughter of* JOHN ALLEN *and* MARY JACKSON. *She was born 22 Sep 1839 in Pike Co., GA, and died 31 Oct 1913 in Coweta Co., GA.*

Notes for DANIEL G. S. BALLARD:

Source: Lynn Cunningham (lcunnin1@mail.atl.bellsouth.net), 1860 Pike County Georgia Federal Census Records
* 1860 - Living in Pike Co.,. GA - Daniel G S 36 GA, Rebecca 34 GA, Sarah E. 12 GA, Nancy J. 10 GA, Elijah 8 GA, Joseph W. 4 GA, Ophelia GA

More About DANIEL G. S. BALLARD:
Burial: Drewry Allen Cemetery Williamson Pike Co., GA

More About REBECCA JANE ALLEN:
Burial: Drewry Allen Cemetery Williamson Pike Co., GA

Notes for CORNELIA ALLEN:
Source: 1870 Pike County Georgia Federal Census Records, (lcunnin1@bellsouth.net), 1880 Coweta County Georgia Federal Census Records
* 1870 - Living in Pike Co., GA - Green, Hartford 57 lawyer GA, Cornelia 31 GA, Rebecca A 30, Pinie 27 GA, Maudie 19 GA, Charles W 16 GA, Mattie L 11 GA, Mary B 1 GA, Carrie Ballard 4 GA, Melia Willis 20 b domestic servant, Willie 7/2 mul
* 1880 - Living in Coweta Co., GA - Green, Cornelia A 40 GA GA GA, Carrie D Ballard 14 GA GA GA

Children of DANIEL BALLARD and REBECCA ALLEN are:
31.   i.   SARAH E.[4] BALLARD, b. 17 Oct 1847, Pike Co., GA; d. 14 Feb 1938, Pike Co., GA.
        ii.   NANCY "NANNIE" JANE BALLARD, b. 1849, Pike Co., GA; d. Aft. 1860.

          More About NANCY "NANNIE" JANE BALLARD:
          Burial: Dreioa Allen Cemetery Williamson, Pike Co., GA

       iii.   ELIJAH BALLARD, b. 1852, Pike Co., GA; d. Aft. 1860.

          Notes for ELIJAH BALLARD:
          Source: Cemetery Stone says the is the son of Dan and Rebecca but supplies no dates.

          More About ELIJAH BALLARD:
          Burial: Pines Golf and Country Club Cemetery, Reidsboro, Pike Co., GA

32.   iv.   JOSEPH W. BALLARD, b. 23 Jul 1855, Pike Co., GA; d. 25 Apr 1923, Fayette Co., GA.
       v.   ELIZA OPHELIA BALLARD, b. Abt. 1859, Pike Co., GA; d. Aft. 1860.
      vi.   MARTHA S. BALLARD, b. 1863, Pike Co., GA; m. W. SCOTT STARR, 26 Feb 1881, Pike Co., GA; b. Abt. 1860.

          Notes for MARTHA S. BALLARD:
          Source: Lynn B. Cunningham (lcunnin1@bellsouth.net)

Child of DANIEL BALLARD and CORNELIA ALLEN is:
33.   vii.   CARRIE S.[4] BALLARD, b. 06 Jan 1866, Pike Co., GA; d. 04 Feb 1927, Fulton Co., GA.

Generation No. 4

9.   WILLIAM ELIJAH[4] BALLARD (JOHN JASPER[3], ELIJAH W.[2], JAMES[1]) was born 19 Jul 1834 in Fayette Co., GA, and died 24 Nov 1874 in AL. He married SUSAN JANE BANKS 03 Oct 1858 in Pike Co., AL. She was born Abt. 1845 in AL, and died 28 Oct 1874 in AL.

Notes for WILLIAM ELIJAH BALLARD:
Source: 1860 Pike County Alabama Federal Census Records, 1870 Crenshaw County Alabama Federal Census Records, Phyliss Bauer
* 1860 - Living in Pike Co., AL - Ballard, Wm E. 25, Susan J 15, John Jasper 5/12
* 1870 - Living in Crenshaw Co., AL - Ballard, William E 35 Teaching School AL, Susan 30 AL, John 7 AL, Robert 5 AL, Jamy 3 AL, Dora 1 AL

More About WILLIAM ELIJAH BALLARD:
Burial: Ballard, Hill Cemetery, Pike Co., AL

Children of WILLIAM BALLARD and SUSAN BANKS are:

      i.   JOHN JASPER[5] BALLARD, b. Feb 1860, Pike Co., AL; d. Aft. 1860.
      ii.   ROBERT BALLARD, b. Abt. 1863, Pike Co., AL; d. Bef. 1880, Pike Co., AL.

           Notes for ROBERT BALLARD:
           Source: 1880 Pike County Alabama Federal Census Records
           * 1880 - Living in Pike Co., AL - Ballard, Robert 16 painter AL GA AL (Living with his uncle and aunt Coleman and Martha Carpenter

34.   iii.   DORA BALLARD, b. 03 Apr 1869, Pike Co., AL; d. 21 Feb 1922, Karnes City, Karnes Co., TX.
      iv.   JAMES BALLARD, b. Abt. 1870, Pike Co., AL; m. NETTIE BANKS.
35.   v.   MAUDE VICTORIA BALLARD, b. 28 Oct 1874, Pike Co., AL; d. 19 Dec 1909, Marianna, Jackson Co., FL.

10. JAMES PURIFOY[4] BALLARD (JOHN JASPER[3], ELIJAH W.[2], JAMES[1]) was born 10 Apr 1840 in Fayette Co., GA, and died Abt. 1893 in Copperas Cove, Coryell Co., TX. He married CLARA ANN E. WATKINS. She was born 20 Feb 1843 in Macon Co., GA, and died 23 Jun 1908 in Pike Co., AL.

Notes for JAMES PURIFOY BALLARD:
Source: Phyllis Bauer, (cunningham53@bellsouth.net) 1870 Pike County Alabama Federal Census Records
* 1870 - Living in Pike Co., AL - Ballard, James P. 30 farmer GA, Clara 27 GA, Mollie 1 AL, Nancy 60 GA

Notes for CLARA ANN E. WATKINS:
Source: Pike County Alabama Federal Census Records, Obituary (cunningham53@bellsouth.net)
* 1880 - Living in Danbury's Pike Co., AL - Ballard, Clara A. 31, Mary Etta 8, John 6, James 4
* Montgomery Advertiser - June 28, 1908 - Obituary - Mrs. Ballard Dead - A Good Woman of Bilo Has Passed Away -
* Troy, June 24 - Mrs Clara Ballard of Milo died Monday night at the home of her son, John Ballard. Mrs. Ballard was a native of Georgia but moved to this State when a young girl and was the daughter of Alfred Watkins. She was 65 years old and had been quite ill for quite a while. She was a devoted member of the Baptist Church of Milo, where the funeral occurred yesterday afternoon; the service being conducted by Rev. B H Lynch. She is survived by three children. Mrs. John Macon, John Ballard and Earnest Ballard.

Children of JAMES BALLARD and CLARA WATKINS are:
36.   i.   MARY ETTA "MOLLIE"[5] BALLARD, b. 27 Apr 1869, Pike Co., AL; d. 14 Sep 1948, Pike Co., AL.
37.   ii.   JOHN ALFRED BALLARD, b. 04 Jun 1871, Spring Hill, Pike Co., AL; d. 07 Dec 1946, Pike Co., AL.
      iii.   THOMAS BALLARD, b. 25 Aug 1874, Pike Co., AL.
38.   iv.   JAMES ERNEST BALLARD, b. 05 Dec 1876, Pike Co., AL; d. 16 Jul 1952.

11. THOMAS WELDON[4] BALLARD (JOHN JASPER[3], ELIJAH W.[2], JAMES[1]) was born 02 May 1844 in Fayetteville Fayette Co., GA, and died 05 May 1910 in lived in Pike Co., AL. He married JANE CATHERINE SIMMONS 10 Jul 1864 in Pike Co., AL, daughter of ISAAC SIMMONS and ELIZABETH FOWLER. She was born 22 Dec 1833 in Dallas Co., AL, and died 20 Jun 1911.

Notes for THOMAS WELDON BALLARD:
Source: Ballard-Ballord Bits page 115 M2, Phyllis Bauer, 1870-1900 Pike County Alabama Federal Census Records

* 1870 - Living in Pike Co., AL - Ballard, Thomas 26 GA, Jane C. 36 AL, Lula 3 AL, Lilla A. 1 AL
* 1880 - Living in Pike Co., AL - Ballard, T W. 36, Jane 47, Lula 13, Lilla 11, Victor 9, Hubert 7, Eugene 3, step children: Theodore Gibson 26, Elizabeth 21, Adalaide 20 AL
* 1900 - Living in Pike Co., AL - Ballard, Thomas W - May 1844 GA GA GA , Jane C - Dec 1833 - 10 children 10 living AL NC NC, Herbert W, - May 1873 ALW. Eugene - July 1876 AL, Lula C Wilson - July 1866 AL 3 children 3 living, James T Wilson - Mar 1884 AL, Mary Jane Wilson - Feb 1886 AL, Lucien C. Wilson - Dec 1887 AL

Children of THOMAS BALLARD and JANE SIMMONS are:

39.	i.	LULA CATHERINE[5] BALLARD, b. 21 Jul 1866, Milo, Pike Co., AL; d. 1915.
40.	ii.	LILLIAN CORNELIA "LILLIE" BALLARD, b. 27 Jul 1868, Milo, Pike Co., AL; d. Aft. 1911.
41.	iii.	THOMAS VICTOR "VIC" BALLARD, b. 03 Jan 1871, Milo, Pike Co., AL; d. 30 Nov 1928, Pike Co., AL.
42.	iv.	HERBERT WELDON BALLARD, b. 08 May 1873, Milo, Pike Co., AL; d. 1946, Pike Co., AL.
43.	v.	WALTER EUGENE BALLARD, b. 25 Jul 1876, Springhill, Pike Co., AL; d. 08 Mar 1954.

12. JULIA ANN[4] BALLARD (JOHN JASPER[3], ELIJAH W.[2], JAMES[1]) was born 14 Jan 1849 in Fayetteville Fayette Co., GA, and died 18 Jan 1909. She married WILLIAM J. BLAN 13 Dec 1869 in Pike Co., AL. He was born 18 Apr 1845 in Macon Co., AL, and died 24 Jun 1904 in Troy, Pike Co., AL.

Notes for JULIA ANN BALLARD:
Source: Phylis Bauer

More About JULIA ANN BALLARD:
Burial: Oakwood Cemetery, Troy, Pike Co., AL

Notes for WILLIAM J. BLAN:
Source: 1880 Pike County Alabama Federal Census Records
* 1880 - Living in Troy, Pike Co., AL - Blan, William J 35 AL SC SC, Julia 30 GA GA GA, Katie 9 AL, Willie 5 AL, Sidney H 3 AL (Living as boarders with the Coward family)

More About WILLIAM J. BLAN:
Burial: Oakwood Cemetery, Troy, Pike Co., AL

Children of JULIA BALLARD and WILLIAM BLAN are:

> i. SIDNEY HERBERT[5] BLAN, b. Abt. 1870, Pike Co., AL.
> ii. KATIE BLAN, b. 06 Apr 1871, Pike Co., AL; d. 10 Feb 1953.
> iii. WILLIE MARY BLAN, b. 22 Jun 1874, Troy, Pike Co., AL; d. 17 Mar 1956, Fulton Co., GA; m. LEWIS ALVEY HANCHEY; b. 19 Apr 1868, Pike Co., AL; d. 21 Apr 1908, Pike Co., AL.
>
> > *More About WILLIE MARY BLAN:*
> > *Burial: College Park Cemetery, College Park, Fulton Co., GA*
> >
> > *More About LEWIS ALVEY HANCHEY:*
> > *Burial: Oakwood Cemetery, Troy, Pike Co., AL*
>
> iv. LUCILLE BLAN, b. 21 Sep 1881, Pike Co., AL; d. 25 Apr 1970; m. JAMES COSBY SAWTELL; b. 05 May 1875, Cuthbert, Randolph Co., GA; d. 13 Nov 1909, Troy, Pike Co., AL.
>
> > *More About LUCILLE BLAN:*
> > *Burial: Oakwood Cemetery, Troy, Pike Co., AL*

13. JOHN JASPER[4] BALLARD (JOHN JASPER[3], ELIJAH W.[2], JAMES[1]) was born 28 Sep 1853 in Fayette Co., GA, and died 27 Oct 1918. He married (1) LAUREN TINA "TINNIE" E. NIXON 18 May 1873 in Pike Co., AL. She was born 15 Jun 1854, and died 27 Jun 1886. He married (2) ALICE G BILLUPS 10 Mar 1887 in Troy, Pike Co., AL. She was born 12 May 1864 in Sumter Co., AL, and died 14 Apr 1916.

Notes for JOHN JASPER BALLARD:
Source: 1880-1900 Pike County Alabama Federal Census Record, 1910 Covington County Alabama Federal Census Records
* 1880 - Living in Troy, Pike Co., AL - Ballard, John J 25 Clerk in store GA GA GA, Laurentina 24 AL LA LA, Mattie 4 AL

* 1900 - Living in Troy, Pike Co., AL - Ballard, John J - Sept 1853 - AL, Alice 4 children 3 living AL GA GA Salesman, Ana - Aug 1880 AL, Emmet D - Feb 1883 AL, Addie E - Jan 1889 AL, Emmet D - Feb 1883 AL, Addie E - Jan 1889 AL, Gertrude - July 1890 AL, Irma L - Aug 1892 AL
* 1910 - Living in Andalusia, Covington Co., AL - Ballard, J. J 56 AL GA GA, Alice 45 - 6 children 3 living AL AL AL, Trudie 20 AL, Irma 17 AL, Ruth 9 AL

More About JOHN JASPER BALLARD:
Burial: Oakwood Cemetery, Pike Co., AL

More About LAUREN TINA "TINNIE" E. NIXON:
Burial: Oakwood Cemetery, Troy, Pike Co., AL

More About ALICE G BILLUPS:
Burial: Oakwood Cemetery, Troy, Pike Co., AL

Children of JOHN BALLARD and LAUREN NIXON are:
    i.   MATTIE[5] BALLARD, b. Abt. 1876, Pike Co., AL; d. Aft. 1880.
    ii. ANNA BALLARD, b. Abt. 1881, Pike Co., AL; d. Aft. 1900.
    iii. ERNEST D. BALLARD, b. Abt. 1883, Pike Co., AL; d. Aft. 1900.

Children of JOHN BALLARD and ALICE BILLUPS are:
    iv. ADDIE ETHEL[5] BALLARD, b. 31 Jan 1889, Pike Co., AL; d. 01 Aug 1905.

         More About ADDIE ETHEL BALLARD:
         Burial: Oakwood Cemetery, Troy, Pike Co., AL

    v.   GERTRUDE VIVIAN "TRUDIE" BALLARD, b. 28 Jul 1890, Pike Co., AL; d. 10 Mar 1937; m. WALTER CLIFTON PAYNE, DR., 14 Jul 1915, Andalusia, Covington Co., AL; b. Abt. 1891, AL; d. Aft. 1920.

         More About GERTRUDE VIVIAN "TRUDIE" BALLARD:
         Burial: St. John's Cemetery, Pensacola, Escambia Co., FL

         Notes for WALTER CLIFTON PAYNE, DR.:
         Source: 1920 Escambia County Florida Federal Census Records

         * 1920 - Living in Pensacola, Escambia Co., FL - Payne, Walter Clifton 29 AL AL AL, Gertrude V 28 AL AL AL, Ruth Ballard 18 sister in law AL

         More About WALTER CLIFTON PAYNE, DR.:
         Burial: St. John's Cemetery, Pensacola, Escambia Co., FL

    vi. JOHN BALLARD, b. 20 Dec 1894, Pike Co., AL; d. 01 Jan 1897.

         More About JOHN BALLARD:
         Burial: Oakwood Cemetery, Troy, Pike Co., AL

    vii. IRMA L. BALLARD, b. Abt. 1897, Pike Co., AL; d. Aft. 1910.
    viii. REX BALLARD, b. 20 Sep 1898, Pike Co., AL; d. 20 Oct 1899.

         More About REX BALLARD:
         Burial: Oakwood Cemetery, Troy, Pike Co., AL

    ix. RUTH BALLARD, b. Abt. 1901, Pike Co., AL; d. Aft. 1910.

14. TIMOTHY C.[4] BALLARD (ELIJAH W.[3], ELIJAH W.[2], JAMES[1]) was born 11 Nov 1844 in GA, and died 05 Dec 1895 in

Commerce, Hunt Co., TX. He married LAURA BRYMER *19 Jun 1870 in Hopkins Co., TX, daughter of* JACKSON BRYMER *and* JENNETY WARD. *She was born 25 Dec 1850 in IN, and died 02 Jan 1939 in Pecan St. Commerce, Hunt Co., TX.*

Notes for TIMOTHY C. BALLARD:
Source: Ruby Beaver (rbeaver@duracom.net), 1870 Hopkins County Texas Federal Census Records, 1880 Texas Federal Census Soundex Records, 1900 Hunts County Texas Federal Census Records
* 1870 - Living in Hopkins Co., TX with parents - Ballard, Timothy C 27, Laura 19
* 1880 - Living in Hunts Co., TX - Ballard, Timothy 35 GA GA GA, Laura 28 IN LA IN, Olive J 8 TX, Alice B 5 TX, Mary A 1 TX

More About TIMOTHY C. BALLARD:
Burial: Sonora Cemetery, Fairlie, Hunt Co., TX

Notes for LAURA BRYMER:
Source: 1900 Hunts County Texas Federal Census Records, 1910-1920 Delta County Texas Federal Census Records, Hunt County Texas Standard Certificate of Death
* 1900 - Living in Hunts Co., TX - Ballard, Laura Dec 1850 TX, TN IN, Delie P - Dec 1879 TX GA TX, Ada - Oct 1881 TX, Willie - Nov 1885 TX, Laurie L.- July 1887 TX, Wills Ward - 1871 (son in law) TX, Amy Laurie grand daughter Jan 1893 TX, Jimmie J. grandson Mar 1895 TX
* 1910 - Living in Delta Co., TX - Ballard, Ballard, John 25, Laura mother 55 wd, Annie L sister 22, Joseph Bryner grandfather 86 wd
* 1920 - Living in Delta Co., TX - Ballard, John W 33, Laura 69 mother

More About LAURA BRYMER:
Burial: Sonora Cemetery, Hunt Co., TX

Children of TIMOTHY BALLARD *and* LAURA BRYMER *are:*
      i.   ADA MAE⁵ BALLARD, *b. 07 Oct 1871, TX; d. Aft. 1900.*
      ii. OLIVE JENETTA BALLARD, *b. 06 May 1872, TX; d. 1896, Hunt Co., TX.*
44.   iii. ALICE BELL BALLARD, *b. 02 Dec 1874, TX; d. 1914.*
      iv. MARY ADELIA BALLARD, *b. 20 Dec 1878, TX; d. 07 Dec 1955, Dallas Co., TX; m.* JAMES GILBERT, *23 Dec 1900, Hunt Co., TX; b. 12 Jun 1880, Hardin Co., TN; d. 22 Dec 1931, Hunt Co., TX.*
      v. JOHN WILLIAM BALLARD, *b. 10 Nov 1884, Hunt Co., TX; d. 09 Mar 1963, Commerce, Hunt Co., TX; m.* LOTTIE SMITH, *19 Oct 1921, Hunt Co., TX.*

         Notes for JOHN WILLIAM BALLARD:
         Source: 1910 Delta County Texas Federal Census Records, Hunt County Texas Certificate of Death, WWII Draft Registration Card, WWI Draft Registration Card
         * 1910 - Living in Delta Co., TX - Ballard, John 25, Laura mother 55 wd, Annie L sister 22, Joseph Bryner grandfather 86 wd
         * 1920 - Living in Delta Co., TX - Ballard, John W 33, Laura 69 mother

         More About JOHN WILLIAM BALLARD:
         Burial: Rosemound Cemetery, Commerce, TX

45.   vi. ANNA LAURIE BALLARD, *b. 30 Jul 1887, TX; d. Aft. 1910.*

15. MARY E.⁴ BALLARD (ELIJAH W.³, ELIJAH W.², JAMES¹) *was born 1854 in TX, and died Aft. 1880. She married* ELIAS R. WARD *03 Sep 1874. He was born 1855 in IN, and died Aft. 1880.*

Notes for ELIAS R. WARD:
Source: 1880 Delta County Texas Federal Census Records
* 1880 - Living in Delta Co., TX - E. R. Ward 25 IN IN IN, Mary E 22 TX IN GA, JM 5 (m), ME 5/12 January TX

Children of MARY BALLARD and ELIAS WARD are:
    i.   *J. M.[5] WARD, b. 1875, TX; d. Aft. 1880.*
    ii.   *M. E. WARD, b. 1870, TX; d. Aft. 1880.*

16. *SEABORN H.[4] BALLARD (ELIJAH W.[3], ELIJAH W.[2], JAMES[1]) was born 02 Nov 1859 in GA, and died 11 Apr 1914 in OK. He married JOSEPHINE BRAKE Abt. 1880, daughter of JASPER BRACKS. She was born 08 Dec 1863 in TX, and died 09 Aug 1948 in Sumerton, Yuma Co., AZ.*

Notes for SEABORN H. BALLARD:
Source: Beverly Killian (beverlykillian@starband.net), 1900 Hopkins County Texas Federal Census Record, 1910 McClain County Oklahoma Federal Census Records
* 1900 - Living in Hopkins Co., TX - Ballard, Sebern Nov 1859 AR, Josaphine Dec 1863 TX, John G - Oct 1884, Polly - June 1886 TX, Evlenor - July 1889 TX, Elic H - June 1890, Earsley O - Feb 1897 TX, Myrtle - Dec 1898
* 1910 - Living in Colbert, McClain Co., OK - Ballard, S. H 50 married 31 yrs AR, Josephine 46 - 14 children - 11 living TX, Harvey 18 AR, Ursley 13 TX, Mertle 11 TX, Jewell 9 TX, Burton 6 TX, Lottie 4 TX

More About SEABORN H. BALLARD:
Burial: Antlers City Cemetery, Pushmataha Co., OK

Notes for JOSEPHINE BRAKE:
Source: 1920-1930 Pushmataha County Oklahoma Federal Census Records
* 1920 - Living in Antlers, Pushmataha Co., OK - Ballard, Josie 56 TX, Burton 15 LA, Lottie 14 AR
* 1930 - Living in Antlers, Pushmataha Co., OK - Ballard, Josephine 66 wd TX TX AR, Lottie Laney 24 WD AR AR TX, Clariette 5 AR

More About JOSEPHINE BRAKE:
Burial: Antlers City Cemetery, Pushmataha Co., OK

Children of SEABORN BALLARD and JOSEPHINE BRAKE are:
46.   i.   *WILLIAM ELIJAH[5] BALLARD, b. 20 Nov 1882, Collin Co TX; d. 22 Dec 1951, Little Rock Pulaski Co., AR.*
       ii.   *JOHN G. BALLARD, b. Oct 1884, TX; d. Aft. 1900.*

           Notes for JOHN G. BALLARD:
           Source: Beverly Killian (beverlykillian@starband.net)

       iii.   *POLLY BALLARD, b. 29 Jun 1887, Peerless, Hopkins Co., TX; d. 18 Dec 1973; m. MILTON B. SMITH; b. 1866.*

           Notes for POLLY BALLARD:
           Source: Social Security Application

           More About POLLY BALLARD:
           Burial: Mt. Zion Cemetery, Doddridge, Miller Co. AR

47.   iv.   *EVLENOR O. BALLARD, b. Jul 1889, TX; d. Aft. 1920.*
       v.   *ELIC H. BALLARD, b. Jun 1890, TX; d. Aft. 1900.*
48.   vi.   *HARVEY E. BALLARD, b. 1892, AR; d. Aft. 1920.*
       vii.   *URSLEY O. BALLARD, b. Feb 1897, TX; d. Aft. 1910.*
       viii.   *MYRTLE BALLARD, b. Dec 1898, TX; d. Oct 1918.*

           Notes for MYRTLE BALLARD:
           Source: Beverly Killian (beverlykillian@starband.net)
           Antlers American, Oct.10,1918: Miss Myrtle Ballard about age 20, died at the home of her sister, Mrs. M. Crownover, Last Friday afternoon. Buried Antlers City cemetery.

More About MYRTLE BALLARD:
Burial: Antlers City cemetery

  ix.   JEWEL BALLARD, *b. 1900, TX; d. Aft. 1910.*
   x.   BURTON BALLARD, *b. 1904, LA; d. Aft. 1920.*
  xi.   LOTTIE BALLARD, *b. 1906, AR; d. Aft. 1920, 8.*

17. REUBEN WESLEY[4] BALLARD (ELIJAH W.[3], ELIJAH W.[2], JAMES[1]) *was born 21 Jan 1864 in Pine Bluff, Jefferson Co., AR, and died 21 Nov 1937 in Dustin, Hughes Co., OK. He married* LENORAH CLEMENTINE CROCKETT *28 Jul 1889 in Delta, TX, daughter of* JASPER CROCKETT *and* EASTER SNEED. *She was born 07 Sep 1872 in 9/7/1872 on stone - Mt. Pleasant Titus Co TX, and died 15 Dec 1964 in Wetumka, Hughes Co., OK.*

Notes for REUBEN WESLEY BALLARD:
Source:1910 Red River County Texas Federal Census Records, 1920 Pittsburg County Oklahoma Federal Census Records, 1930 Hughes County Oklahoma Federal Census Records, Paul Wilhite, (backpages@earthlink.net)
* 1910 - Living in Red River Co., TX - Ballard, Reuben W 46 (m1), AR GA GA, Renora 36 8 children 4 living TX MO TN, Charlie (f) 12 LA, Alsie 10 LA, Beattrice 4 TX, Benetta 2 TX
* 1920 - Living in Cabaniss, Pittsburg Co., OK - Ballard, Ruben W 55 AR GA GA, Lenorah C 45 TX IL IL, Beatrice D 14 AR, Mernetta 12, Thirsten J 10, Lenorah 5, Geneva 2, Jasper M Crockett 72 wd father in law IL TN KY
* 1930 - Living in Dustin, Hughes Co., OK - Ballard, Ruben W 66 AR GA GA, Lenora 55 TX IL TN, Thirston 18 TX, Genevia 12 OK

More About REUBEN WESLEY BALLARD:
Burial: Weturnka Cemetery, Hughes Co., OK

Children of REUBEN BALLARD *and* LENORAH CROCKETT *are:*

    i.   CHARLOTTE DENA[5] BALLARD, *b. 07 Feb 1898, LA; d. 08 Oct 1975; m.* WILLIAM JEREMIAH BUCHANAN; *b. 31 Mar 1865, Madison Co., IA; d. 27 Aug 1951, Haskell Co., OK.*

        More About CHARLOTTE DENA BALLARD:
        Burial: Old Cache Cemetery, Keota, Haskell Co., OK

        More About WILLIAM JEREMIAH BUCHANAN:
        Burial: Old Cache Cemetery, Keota, Haskell Co., OK

   ii.   ALICE ARVELLA BALLARD, *b. 15 Jul 1899, LA; d. 20 Aug 1975; m.* GEORGE WASHINGTON KINDRED, *06 Sep 1914, Sequoyah, OK; b. 09 Apr 1878, Denton Co., TX; d. 04 Nov 1960, Hughes Co., OK.*

        More About ALICE ARVELLA BALLARD:
        Burial: Fairview Cemetery, Hughes Co., OK

        Notes for GEORGE WASHINGTON KINDRED:
        Source: 1920 Tarrant County Texas Federal Census Records

        * 1920 - Living in Tarrant Co., TX - Kinred, George 42, Alcie A 19, Amy R 1, Beatrice

        More About GEORGE WASHINGTON KINDRED:
        Burial: Fairview Cemetery, Hughes Co. OK

  iii.   BEATRICE D. BALLARD, *b. 02 Jan 1902, AR; d. 01 Nov 1984, Hughes Co., OK; m.* LURTA NESTER; *b. 18 Aug 1888; d. 03 Sep 1983.*

        More About BEATRICE D. BALLARD:
        Burial: Wetumka, Hughes Co., OK

     iv.   *BENNETTA BALLARD, b. 1908, TX; d. Aft. 1920.*

     v.   *THIRSTON BALLARD, b. 1910, TX; d. Aft. 1930.*

     vi.   *LENORAH CLEMENTINE BALLARD, b. 26 Jan 1915, Wetumka, Hughes Co., OK; d. 01 Nov 1996, Wetumka, Hughes Co., OK; m. (1) FINCH; m. (2) JESS ALEXANDER WILHITE, 14 Feb 1929, Wetumka, Hughes Co., OK; b. 19 Nov 1906, Gerty Hughes Co OK; d. 14 Feb 1929, Wetumka, Hughes Co., OK.*

        More About LENORAH CLEMENTINE BALLARD:
        Burial: Wetumka, Hughes Co., OK

     vii.   *GENEVA BALLARD, b. 26 Jul 1918, OK; d. 06 Nov 1985; m. DELBERT KERN, 16 Oct 1933, Hughes Co., OK; b. 07 Sep 1914; d. 23 Aug 1979.*

        More About GENEVA BALLARD:
        Burial: Wetumka, Hughes Co., OK

        More About DELBERT KERN:
        Burial: Wetumka, Hughes Co., OK

18. *ISAAC VINSON[4] BALLARD (ELIJAH W.[3], ELIJAH W.[2], JAMES[1]) was born 18 Jul 1867 in Hunt Co., TX, and died 04 Aug 1941 in Caddo, LA. He married PIETY FRANCES TRANT 06 Aug 1891 in Caddo Parish, LA. She was born Aug 1874 in AL, and died 28 Oct 1963 in Pettis, MO.*

Notes for ISAAC VINSON BALLARD:
Source: 1900 Upshur County Texas Federal Census Records, 1910 Cass County Texas Federal Census Records, 1920 Morris County Texas Federal Census Records

* 1900 - Living in Upshur Co., TX - Ballard, Isaac 1870 TX, Piety - Aug 1874 AL, Orbie 1894 TX, Bessie - Dec 1897 TX
* 1910 - Living in Cass Co., TX - Ballard, Isac B 31 TX, Pida 30 AL 30, Orbie 14 12 TX, Bessie 12 TX, Lossie 8 TX, Mattie 6 TX, Gilbert 5 TX
* 1920 - Living in Morris Co., TX - Ballard, Isac B 53 TX, Piely 44 AL, Mattie 16 TX, Gilbert 14 TX

Children of ISAAC BALLARD and PIETY TRANT are:
     i.   *ORBIE JAMES[5] BALLARD, b. 08 Nov 1895, TX; d. 1980, Jefferson Co., CO; m. BLANCHE.*
     ii.   *BESSIE BALLARD, b. Dec 1897, TX; d. Aft. 1910.*
     iii.   *ISAAC LONNIE BALLARD, b. 12 Jan 1902, Upsur Co., TX; d. 01 Mar 1980, LA Co., CA; m. MARCELLA IDA STEFFEN; b. 13 Jun 1915; d. 18 Dec 1995, Forest Lawn Memorial Park, Cypress, Orange Co., CA.*

        More About ISAAC LONNIE BALLARD:
        Burial: Forest Lawn Memorial Park, Cypress, Orange Co., CA

     iv.   *MATTIE BALLARD, b. 31 Dec 1904, Cass Co., TX; d. 22 Feb 1996, Pettis, MO.*
     v.   *GILBERT BALLARD, b. 1905, TX; d. Aft. 1920.*

19. *ROBERT LEE[4] BALLARD (ELIJAH W.[3], ELIJAH W.[2], JAMES[1]) was born 27 Jan 1874 in TX, and died 26 May 1931 in Grayson Co., TX. He married EMMA GLOVER 02 Jan 1894 in Lincoln Co., AR. She was born 28 Feb 1876 in AR, and died 12 Nov 1959 in Pittsburg Co., OK.*

Notes for ROBERT LEE BALLARD:

Source: beverlykillian@starband.net (Beverly Killian), 1900 Jefferson County Arkansas Federal Census Records,

1910 McClain County Oklahoma Federal Census Records, 1920 Red River County Texas Federal Census Records
* 1900 - Living in Plum Bayou, Jefferson Co., AR - Ballard, Robert L - Jan 1874 TX GA GA, William E - Feb 1876 AR GA AR, Beney O - Sept 1877 AR TX AR, Johney L J - July 1899 AR, John H Pain boarder, William Dendy boarder
* 1910 - Living in Colbert Census McClain Co. OK - Ballard, RL 36 TX GA GA, Emma 34 AR AR AR, Bennie 11 LA TX AR, Lee 8 LA TX AR, Wm 3/4 TX TX AR
* 1920 - Living in Red River Co., TX - Ballard, R. L 45 TX, Willie E 45 AR, Francis L 17, Clarence W 10, Isac D 6 TX, Allaner B 3 TX

More About ROBERT LEE BALLARD:
Burial: Ulan Cemetery, Ulan, Pittsburg Co., OK

More About EMMA GLOVER:
Burial: Ulan Cemetery, Ulan, Pittsburg Co., OK

Children of ROBERT BALLARD and EMMA GLOVER are:
  i. BENNIOLA "BENNIE"[5] BALLARD, b. Sep 1897, AR; d. 27 Feb 1949, NM.
  ii. JOHNEY L. J. BALLARD, b. Jul 1899, AR; d. Aft. 1910.
  iii. FRANCES LEE BALLARD, b. 02 May 1902, LeFlore Co., OK; d. Jul 1982, Tulsa, OK.
  iv. ISAAC BALLARD, b. 05 Jan 1913, TX; d. 10 Oct 1986; m. GOLDIE DUCKWORTH; b. 05 May 1914; d. 05 Feb 2003.

    More About ISAAC BALLARD:
    Burial: Ulan Cemetery, Ulan, Pittsburg Co., OK

    More About GOLDIE DUCKWORTH:
    Burial: Ulan Cemetery, Ulan, Pittsburg Co., OK

  v. WILLIAM CLARENCE BALLARD, b. 16 Jul 1909, Blossom, Lamar Co., TX; d. 27 Jul 1976, Pittsburg Co., OK; m. CLARA BEATRICE AUTREY, 16 Feb 1929, Pittsburg, OK; b. 19 Apr 1909, OK; d. 20 Apr 1984.

    Notes for WILLIAM CLARENCE BALLARD:
    Source: 1930 Pittsburg County Oklahoma Federal Census Records
    * 1930 - Living in Bucklucksy, Pittsburg Co., OK - Ballard, Clarence 20, Beatrice 20

    More About CLARA BEATRICE AUTREY:
    Burial: Ulan Cemetery, Ulan, Pittsburg Co., OK

  vi. ALLANDER B. BALLARD, b. 1917, TX; d. Aft. 1920.

20. JAMES PATTON[4] BALLARD (WILLIAM BARNES[3], ELIJAH W.[2], JAMES[1]) *was born 05 Sep 1840 in 1843 Fayette Co., GA, and died 22 Aug 1912 in Pike Co., GA. He married SARAH W. RIVERS 02 Dec 1866 in Pike Co., GA. She was born 27 Oct 1839 in GA, and died 09 Jun 1918 in Pike Co., GA.*

Notes for JAMES PATTON BALLARD:
Source: Lynn B. Cunningham (lcunnin1@bellsouth.net), 1880 Pike County Georgia Federal Census Records

* Lynn says that he was blind. Her source - Article in Pike County Journal in Zebulon GA Friday October 23, 1891
* 1880 - Living in Pike County GA - J. P. Ballard 36 GA, Sarah 37 GA, Lucy 6 GA, J. D. McDonell 11, W. B. Ballard 22 GA

More About JAMES PATTON BALLARD:
Burial: Williamson Methodist Church Cemetery, Pike Co. GA

More About SARAH W. RIVERS:
Burial: Williamson Methodist Church Cemetery, Pike Co. GA

Child of JAMES BALLARD and SARAH RIVERS is:
      i.   LUCY[5] BALLARD, b. Abt. 1874.

21. ELIJAH[4] BALLARD (*WILLIAM BARNES[3], ELIJAH W.[2], JAMES[1]*) *was born 11 Nov 1844 in Fayette Co., GA, and died 31 Dec 1919. He married ELIZA JANE LONGACRE, daughter of URIAH LONGACRE and HARRIETT HOOPER. She was born 26 Jul 1849 in Shelby Co., TX, and died 26 Apr 1934 in Panola Co., TX.*

Notes for ELIJAH BALLARD:
Source: Lynn Cunningham (lcunnin1@bellsouth.net), Dr. John Ballard
* 1862 - Military service began with the 44th Georgia in the Civil War 6/28/1862- 4/9/1865

More About ELIJAH BALLARD:
Burial: Waldrop Cemetery, Fair Play, Panola Co., TX

Notes for ELIZA JANE LONGACRE:
Source: William David Farnham (ww2x57@aol.com)

More About ELIZA JANE LONGACRE:
Burial: Waldrop Cemetery, Panola Co., TX

Children of ELIJAH BALLARD and ELIZA LONGACRE are:
      i.   JOHN THOMAS[5] BALLARD, b. 1872; d. 27 Mar 1937; m. JULIA ESTHER BROOKS; b. 28 Mar 1874, Panola Co., TX; d. 16 Feb 1960, Pasadena, Harris Co., TX.

            More About JOHN THOMAS BALLARD:
            Burial: Waldrop Cemetery, Fair Play, Panola Co., TX

     ii.   EUNICE COOPER BALLARD, b. 08 Dec 1879, Beckville, Panola Co., TX; d. 26 Sep 1961, Houston, Harris Co., TX; m. J. W. COOPER; b. 1876; d. 1926.

            More About EUNICE COOPER BALLARD:
            Burial: Waldrop Cemetery, Fair Play, Panola Co., TX

            More About J. W. COOPER:
            Burial: Waldrop Cemetery, Fair Play, Panola Co., TX

22. ELIZABETH A.[4] BALLARD (*WILLIAM BARNES[3], ELIJAH W.[2], JAMES[1]*) *was born 18 Nov 1846 in Fayette Co., GA, and died Aft. 1880 in Joaquin, Shelby Co., TX. She married JOSEPH OLIVER BECKHAM 14 Dec 1865 in Pike Co., GA. He was born 31 Oct 1844 in Pike Co., GA, and died 12 Mar 1895 in Ringgold, Bienville Parish, LA.*

Notes for JOSEPH OLIVER BECKHAM:
Source: 1870 Claiborne Parish Louisiana, 1880 Lincoln Parish Louisiana
* 1870 - Living in Claiborne Parish LA - Beckham, J O 26 farmer GA, Elizabeth A 24 GA, Stephen 4 GA, William R 2 GA, Joseph 11/12 LA
* 1880 - Living in Lincoln Parish, LA - Bickham, Joseph 35 Farmer GA, Elizabeth 37 GA, Steven E 14 GA, W. B 11 GA, Joseph O 9 GA, Anna M 7 LA, Fletcher H 4 LA

More About JOSEPH OLIVER BECKHAM:
Burial: Springhill Cemetery, Ringgold Bienville Parish, LA

Children of ELIZABETH BALLARD and JOSEPH BECKHAM are:
  i. STEPHEN E.[5] BECKHAM, *b. 1867, Pike Co., GA; d. Aft. 1880.*
  ii. WILLIAM B. BECKHAM, *b. 14 Sep 1869, Pike Co., GA; d. Aft. 1880.*
  iii. JOSEPH OLIIVER BECKHAM, *b. 1870, Pike Co., GA; d. 14 Feb 1946, Bienville Parish, LA.*

    More About JOSEPH OLIIVER BECKHAM:
    Burial: Springhill Cemetery, Ringgold Bienville Parish, LA

  iv. ANNIE MAE BECKHAM, *b. 25 Mar 1873, Claiborne Parish, LA; d. 25 Jan 1947, Carroll Parish, LA; m. JOHN W. HINTON; b. 28 Mar 1869, Bienville Parish, LA; d. 28 Oct 1951, West Carroll Parish, LA.*

    More About ANNIE MAE BECKHAM:
    Burial: Springhill Cemetery, Ringgold Bienville Parish, LA

    More About JOHN W. HINTON:
    Burial: Springhill Cemetery, Ringgold Bienville Parish, LA

  v. FLETCHER HENRY BECKHAM, *b. 11 Oct 1875, LA; d. 06 May 1928; m. MINNIE SANDERS; b. 09 Jul 1884; d. 18 Jan 1969.*

    More About FLETCHER HENRY BECKHAM:
    Burial: Springhill Cemetery, Ringgold Bienville Parish, LA

    More About MINNIE SANDERS:
    Burial: Springhill Cemetery, Ringgold Bienville Parish, LA

  vi. ADDIE FLORENCE BECKHAM, *b. Nov 1882, LA; d. 12 Mar 1938; m. DANIEL E. BLAKE; b. 25 Nov 1875; d. 19 Oct 1954.*

    More About ADDIE FLORENCE BECKHAM:
    Burial: Bethlehem Cemetery, Calvin, Winn Parish, LA

    More About DANIEL E. BLAKE:
    Burial: Bethlehem Cemetery, Calvin, Winn Parish, LA

23. THOMAS W.[4] BALLARD (WILLIAM BARNES[3], ELIJAH W.[2], JAMES[1]) *was born 20 Nov 1848 in Fayette Co., GA, and died 09 Dec 1904. He married ISABELLA "BELL" D. WILDER 30 Nov 1869 in Pike Co. GA, daughter of JAMES WILDER and MARY. She was born 30 May 1853 in GA, and died 01 Apr 1886.*

Notes for THOMAS W. BALLARD:
Source: Lynn B. Cunningham (lcunnin1@bellsouth.net), 1880 Fayette County Georgia Federal Census Records, Ruhi19@cox.net

* 1869 - Pike Co. GA Book page 357 - To any Judge, Justice of the Peace or Minister of the Gospel you are hereby authorized to join Thomas W. Ballard and Isabella D. Wilder in the Holy Estate of Matrimony according to the constitution and Laws of this state and for doing this shall be your sufficient license. Given under my hand this 30th day of Nov 1869. J. J. Harpy, Ordy. I certify that Thomas W. Ballard and Isabella D. Wilder were duly joined in Matrimony by me the 30th day of Nov. 1869. E. Britian, MG, Recorded Jany 11th 1871 J. J. Harper, Ordy.
* 1880 - Living in Fayette Co. GA - Ballard, Thomas 30 farmer GA GA GA, Belle 27 GA GA GA, James 9 GA GA GA, Mary 3 GA GA GA

Children of THOMAS BALLARD and ISABELLA WILDER are:

49. i. JAMES W.[5] BALLARD, *b. 31 Jan 1871, GA; d. 04 Jun 1923, Pike Co., GA.*
    ii. MARY BALLARD, *b. 1873, GA.*

50. iii. MABEL WILDER BALLARD, b. 15 Aug 1877, GA; d. 30 Mar 1926, DeKalb Co., GA.
     iv. THOMAS B. BALLARD, b. Oct 1880, GA.
     v. ELIJAH BALLARD, b. Oct 1882, GA.

24. WILLIAM BARNES[4] BALLARD (WILLIAM BARNES[3], ELIJAH W.[2], JAMES[1]) was born 19 Aug 1857 in Pike Co., GA, and died 19 Jul 1933 in Pike Co., GA. He married EMILY KATIE HUCKABY 1881 in Pike Co., GA, daughter of EDWARD HUCKABY and LUCY W.. She was born 22 Oct 1855 in GA, and died 11 Nov 1886 in Pike Co., GA.

Notes for WILLIAM BARNES BALLARD:
Source: Lynn B. Cunningham (lcunnin1@bellsouth.net), 1880 Pike County Federal Census Records

* 1880 - Living with his brother James Patton Ballard's family in Pike County GA.

More About WILLIAM BARNES BALLARD:
Burial: Hollonville Cemetery, Pike Co., GA

More About EMILY KATIE HUCKABY:
Burial: Hollonville Cemetery, Pike Co., GA

Children of WILLIAM BALLARD and EMILY HUCKABY are:
     i. ANNIE ELIZABETH "BESSIE"[5] BALLARD, b. 04 Nov 1882, Pike Co., GA; d. 08 Feb 1965, Pike Co., GA; m. CHARLES EVAN OXFORD; b. 16 May 1888; d. 11 Apr 1962, Monroe Co., GA.

         More About ANNIE ELIZABETH "BESSIE" BALLARD:
         Burial: Magnolia Cemetery, Concord, Pike Co., GA

         More About CHARLES EVAN OXFORD:
         Burial: Magnolia Cemetery, Concord, Pike Co., GA

     ii. MARY ELLA BALLARD, b. 15 Nov 1884, Pike Co., GA; d. 27 Nov 1974.

         Notes for MARY ELLA BALLARD:
         Source: Lynn B. Cunningham (lcunnin1@bellsouth.net)

         More About MARY ELLA BALLARD:
         Burial: Hollonville Cemetery, Pike Co., GA

     iii. LUCY K. BALLARD, b. 28 Oct 1886, Pike Co., GA; d. 01 Jun 1887, Pike Co., GA.

         More About LUCY K. BALLARD:
         Burial: Hollonville Cemetery, Pike Co., GA

25. ABRAHAM "ABE" S.[4] BALLARD (WILLIAM BARNES[3], ELIJAH W.[2], JAMES[1]) was born 09 Aug 1859 in Pike Co., GA, and died 21 Jun 1915 in Pike Co., GA. He married ANNIE ELIZA HARRISON. She was born Oct 1863 in GA, and died 12 Apr 1949 in Pike Co., GA.

Notes for ABRAHAM "ABE" S. BALLARD:
Source: 1900 - 1910 Pike County Georgia Federal Census Records, Lynn B. Cunningham (lcunnin1@bellsouth.net)

* 1900 - Living in Williamson, Pike Co., GA - Ballard, Abraham S 40 - Aug 1859 GA GA GA, Annie Elza 37 - Oct 1863 - 8 children 7 living GA GA GA, Lola 12 - July 1887 GA, May 11 - Feb 1889 GA, Estelle 9 - Jun 1891 GA, Miller C 7 - Apr 1893 GA, Susan 5 - Jan 1895 GA, Rubie C 3 - Jan 1897 GA, Abraham A 2/12 - Apr 1900 GA
* 1910 - Living in Zebulon, Pike Co., GA - Ballard, Abe S 51 GA GA GA, Liza 47 - 8 children 8 living GA GA GA,

May 21 GA, Estella 7 GA, Miller 17 GA, Susie 15 GA, Rubie 13 GA, Abie 10 GA, Marvin 2 GA

More About ABRAHAM "ABE" S. BALLARD:
Burial: Zebulon Methodist Church Cemetery, Pike Co., GA

More About ANNIE ELIZA HARRISON:
Burial: Zebulon Methodist Church Cemetery, Pike Co., GA

Children of ABRAHAM BALLARD and ANNIE HARRISON are:
  i.   LOLA⁵ BALLARD, b. 20 Jul 1887, Pike Co., GA; d. 13 Apr 1929, GA; m. RAYMOND HILL DICKINSON; b. 12 Jan 1885, GA; d. 10 Nov 1945, GA.

       More About RAYMOND HILL DICKINSON:
       Burial: Williamson UMC Cemetery, Pike Co., GA

  ii. MAY BALLARD, b. Feb 1889, Pike Co., GA; d. Aft. 1920.
  iii. ESTELLE BALLARD, b. Jan 1891, Pike Co., GA; d. 1939; m. WILLIAM EDGAR HAMMOND; b. 1888; d. 1970.

       More About ESTELLE BALLARD:
       Burial: Zebulon Methodist Church Cemetery, Pike Co., GA

       More About WILLIAM EDGAR HAMMOND:
       Burial: Zebulon Methodist Church Cemetery, Pike Co., GA

  iv. MILLER CALTON BALLARD, b. Apr 1893, Pike Co., GA; d. 05 Mar 1952, Floyd Co., GA; m. HARRIET BOWEN; b. 1900; d. 1992.

       Notes for MILLER CALTON BALLARD:
       Source: 1920 Pike County Georgia Federal Census Records
       * 1920 - Living in Zebulon, Pike Co., GA - Ballard Miller 26 Carlton 19, Eliza mother 56 wd, May 5, Abie 19, Marvin 12

       More About HARRIET BOWEN:
       Burial: Zebulon Methodist Church Cemetery, Pike Co., GA

  v.   SUSAN BALLARD, b. 28 Jan 1895, Pike Co., GA; d. 20 Nov 1963; m. WILLIAM JEFF BUSH; b. 26 Sep 1891; d. 08 Jun 1964.

       More About SUSAN BALLARD:
       Burial: Zebulon Methodist Church Cemetery, Pike Co., GA

       More About WILLIAM JEFF BUSH:
       Burial: Zebulon Methodist Church Cemetery, Pike Co., GA

  vi. RUBY BALLARD, b. Jan 1897, Pike Co., GA; d. Aft. 1910.
  vii. ABRAHAM ALLEN BALLARD, b. 19 Apr 1900, Pike Co., GA; d. Aft. 1920; m. TOMMIE LEE MORRIS; b. 09 Jul 1902; d. 03 Jan 1993.

       More About TOMMIE LEE MORRIS:
       Burial: McDonough Cemetery, Henry Co., GA

  viii. MARVIN BALLARD, b. 1908, GA; d. Aft. 1920.

26. JOHN HARVEY⁴ BALLARD (WILLIAM BARNES³, ELIJAH W.², JAMES¹) *was born 17 Aug 1864 in Pike Co., GA, and* *died 17 Dec 1948 in Pike Co., GA. He married MARTHA RENDA BANKS. She was born 15 Jul 1867 in GA, and died 17 Aug 1951 in Pike Co., GA.*

Notes for JOHN HARVEY BALLARD:
Source: 1910 -1930 Pike County Georgia Federal Census Records, Lynn B. Cunningham (lcunnin1@bellsouth.net)

* 1910 - Living in Concord, Pike Co., GA - Ballard, John H 45, Mattie R 41, Ramon W 12, George H 10, Mary S 7, Annie K 5, Charles Y 3, Bob B 2
* 1920 - Living in Zebulon, Pike Co., GA - Ballard, John H 53, Martha 50, George 19, Mary 16, Kate 14, Charles 13, Bob 11, Sarah 9
* 1930 - Living in Williamson, Pike Co., GA - Ballard, John H 64, Martha R 60, George H 28, Young C 23, Robt B 20, Chas W 51, Raymond 31

More About JOHN HARVEY BALLARD:
Burial: Magnolia Cemetery, Pike Co., GA

More About MARTHA RENDA BANKS:
Burial: Magnolia Cemetery, Pike Co., GA

Children of JOHN BALLARD and MARTHA BANKS are:

     i.   WILLIAM RAMOND[5] BALLARD, b. 03 Oct 1898, Pike Co., GA; d. 27 Apr 1968, Lamar Co., GA.

        More About WILLIAM RAMOND BALLARD:
        Burial: Magnolia Cemetery, Concord, Pike Co., GA

     ii.   GEORGE HARVEY BALLARD, b. 01 Aug 1900, Pike Co., GA; d. Aft. 1930; m. MARY K.; b. 24 Jul 1909; d. 23 Apr 1990.

        Notes for GEORGE HARVEY BALLARD:
        Source: WWI Draft Registration Cards

        More About GEORGE HARVEY BALLARD:
        Burial: Upson Memorial Garden, Thomston, Upson Co., GA

        More About MARY K.:
        Burial: Upson Memorial Garden, Thomston, Upson Co., GA

    iii.   MARY S. BALLARD, b. Abt. 1903, Pike Co., GA; d. Aft. 1920.

    iv.   ANNIE KATE BALLARD, b. 1906, Pike Co., GA; d. 18 Feb 1985, Lamar Co., GA; m. JESSE DOUGLAS WILLIAMS; b. 30 Nov 1899, Pike Co., GA; d. 05 Mar 1985, Lamar Co., GA.

        More About ANNIE KATE BALLARD:
        Burial: Magnolia Cemetery, Concord. Pike Co., GA

        More About JESSE DOUGLAS WILLIAMS:
        Burial: Magnolia Cemetery, Concord, Pike Co., GA

     v.   CHARLES YOUNG BALLARD, b. 1906, Pike Co., GA; d. 1961; m. KATHRYN BROCK; b. 1909; d. 2002.

        More About CHARLES YOUNG BALLARD:
        Burial: Griffin Memorial Gardens, Griffin, Spalding Co., GA

        More About KATHRYN BROCK:
        Burial: Griffin Memorial Gardens, Griffin, Spalding Co., GA

vi.   ROBERT BANKS BALLARD, b. 11 Apr 1908, Pike Co., GA; d. 13 Jun 1942, Pike Co., GA.

Notes for ROBERT BANKS BALLARD:
Source: WWII Draft Cards

More About ROBERT BANKS BALLARD:
Burial: Magnolia Cemetery, Concord, Pike Co., GA

vii.   SARA BALLARD, b. 05 Apr 1910, Pike Co., GA; d. 18 Oct 1993; m. CLEVELAND G. ARMISTEAD; b. 19 Sep 1906; d. 07 Mar 1978.

More About SARA BALLARD:
Burial: Williamson UMC Cemetery, Pike Co., GA

More About CLEVELAND G. ARMISTEAD:
Burial: Williamson, UMC Cemetery, Pike Co., GA

27.   SARAH JANE[4] BALLARD (THOMAS WELDON[3], ELIJAH W.[2], JAMES[1]) was born 30 Aug 1847 in Pike Co., GA, and died 28 May 1909 in Fayette Co., GA. She married ALONZO O. GAY 13 Dec 1865 in Fayette Co., GA. He was born 20 Jun 1844 in GA, and died 19 Dec 1911 in Fayette Co., GA.

More About SARAH JANE BALLARD:
Burial: Woolsey Cemetery, Fayette Co., GA

Notes for ALONZO O. GAY:
Source: 1880 Spalding County Georgia Federal Census Records
* 1880 - Living in Spalding Co., GA - Gay, Alonzo O. 35 farmer GA GA GA, Sarah J 33 GA GA GA, Martha E 13 GA, George T 10 GA, Fannie 8 GA, Nancy W 6 GA, Young A 3 GA, infant 3//12 March GA

More About ALONZO O. GAY:
Burial: Woolsey Cemetery, Fayette Co., GA

Children of SARAH BALLARD and ALONZO GAY are:
i.   MARTHA E.[5] GAY, b. Abt. 1867, GA; d. Aft. 1880.
ii.   GEORGE T. GAY, b. Abt. 1870, GA; d. Aft. 1880.
iii. FANNIE GAY, b. Abt. 1872, Spalding Co., GA; d. Aft. 1880.
iv.   NANCY W. GAY, b. 1874, GA; d. 19 Jan 1940, GA; m. ARTICE N. DAY; b. 06 Feb 1895; d. 14 May 1966.

More About NANCY W. GAY:
Burial: Woolsey Cemetery, Fayette Co., GA

More About ARTICE N. DAY:
Burial: Oak Ridge Cemetery, Tift Co. GA

v.   YOUNG ALONZO GAY, b. 24 Aug 1877, GA; d. 05 Aug 1902, Fayette Co., GA.

More About YOUNG ALONZO GAY:
Burial: Woolsey Cemetery, Fayette Co., GA

vi.   LINNIE GAY, b. 25 Sep 1882, Spalding Co., GA; d. 16 Jan 1963, Fayette Co., GA; m. MORTIMER G.SAMS; b. 09 Dec 1883; d. 04 Sep 1953.

More About LINNIE GAY:
Burial: Woolsey Cemetery, Fayette Co., GA

More About MORTIMER G.SAMS:
Burial: Woolsey Cemetery, Fayette Co., GA

28. WASHINGTON AUGUSTUS[4] BALLARD (THOMAS WELDON[3], ELIJAH W.[2], JAMES[1]) was born 31 Mar 1849 in Fayette Co., GA, and died 28 Jul 1919 in Fayette Co., GA. He married ADA "ADDIE" ELVIRA LUCKIE. She was born 30 Oct 1855 in GA, and died 11 Apr 1913.

Notes for WASHINGTON AUGUSTUS BALLARD:
Source: 1880 Federal Census Soundex Records - Georgia
* 1880 - Living in Fayette County Georgia - Washington 31 GA, Addie E. 24 GA, Lennsden 1 GA

More About ADA "ADDIE" ELVIRA LUCKIE:
Burial: Antioch Baptist Church Cemetery, Woolsey, Fayette Co., GA

Children of WASHINGTON BALLARD and ADA LUCKIE are:
　　　i.　LUMSDEN[5] BALLARD, b. 03 Feb 1879, GA; d. 06 Dec 1902.

　　　　　More About LUMSDEN BALLARD:
　　　　　Burial: Antioch Baptist Church Cemetery, Woolsey, Fayette Co., GA

　　　ii.　CLIFFORD A. BALLARD, b. 18 Nov 1883; d. 14 Apr 1975; m. (1) MYRTLE; b. 29 May 1886; d. 05 Aug 1914; m. (2) MAMIE BELLE MAYS; b. 11 May 1891; d. 19 Aug 1967.

　　　　　More About CLIFFORD A. BALLARD:
　　　　　Burial: Woolsey Cemetery, Fayette Co., GA

　　　　　More About MYRTLE:
　　　　　Burial: Woolsey Cemetery, Fayette Co., GA

　　　　　More About MAMIE BELLE MAYS:
　　　　　Burial: Woolsey Cemetery, Fayette Co., GA

29. MARY WELDON[4] BALLARD (THOMAS WELDON[3], ELIJAH W.[2], JAMES[1]) was born 15 Dec 1852 in Fayette Co., GA, and died 19 Aug 1929 in Griffin, Spalding Co., GA. She married (1) JOHN FRANKLIN DICKINSON. He died 14 Feb 1914 in Griffin, Spalding Co., GA. She married (2) OSWELL T. MALONE. He was born 26 Sep 1849, and died 28 Aug 1884.

Notes for MARY WELDON BALLARD:
Source: Spalding County Georgia Certificate of Death

More About JOHN FRANKLIN DICKINSON:
Burial: Old Ballard Family Cemetery, Woolsey, Fayette Co., GA

More About OSWELL T. MALONE:
Burial: Old Ballard Family Cemetery, Woolsey, Fayette Co., GA

Children of MARY BALLARD and JOHN DICKINSON are:
　　　i.　OLLIE[5] DICKINSON.
　　　ii.　EFFIE PAULINE DICKINSON, b. 26 Sep 1870, Pike Co., GA; d. 16 Jan 1958, Griffin, Spalding Co., GA.

　　　　　More About EFFIE PAULINE DICKINSON:
　　　　　Burial: Oak Hill Cemetery, Griffin, Spalding Co., GA

Child of MARY BALLARD and OSWELL MALONE is:
    iii. ANNIE[5] MALONE, b. 03 Nov 1883; d. 1970.

        More About ANNIE MALONE:
        Burial: Old Ballard Family Cemetery, Woolsey, Fayette Co., GA

30. ELIJAH MADDOX[4] BALLARD (*THOMAS WELDON[3], ELIJAH W.[2], JAMES[1]*) *was born 17 Dec 1856 in GA, and died 10 Dec 1933 in Fayette Co., GA. He married (1) SARAH ELDER 22 Jan 1888 in Spalding Co., GA. She was born 26 Apr 1860 in GA, and died 30 May 1893 in Fayette Co., GA. He married (2) MINNIE DAVIS 31 Jan 1894 in Fayette Co., GA. She was born Abt. 1870.*

Notes for ELIJAH MADDOX BALLARD:
Source: 1880 Fayette County Georgia Federal Census Records
* 1880 - Living in Fayette Co., GA - Ballard, Elijah 23 Farmer GA GA GA, Sarah 21 GA GA GA

More About ELIJAH MADDOX BALLARD:
Burial: Old Ballard Family Cemetery, Woolsey, Fayette Co., GA

More About SARAH ELDER:
Burial: Old Ballard Family Cemetery, Woolsey, Fayette Co., GA

Children of ELIJAH BALLARD and SARAH ELDER are:
    i. ROXIE ADDIE[5] BALLARD, b. 13 Oct 1880, Fayette Co., GA; d. 13 Apr 1971, Pike Co., GA; m. YOUNG DREWRY BALLARD, 02 Mar 1899, Pike Co., GA; b. 16 Mar 1874, Pike Co., GA; d. 17 Nov 1931, Pike Co., GA.

        More About ROXIE ADDIE BALLARD:
        Burial: Williamson Methodist Church Cemetery, Pike Co. GA

        More About YOUNG DREWRY BALLARD:
        Burial: Williamson Methodist Church Cemetery, Pike Co. GA

    ii. ELIZABETH REBECCA BALLARD, b. 11 Sep 1883; d. 29 Oct 1952; m. JAMES LANGFORD BOYNTON; b. 07 Jun 1880; d. 02 Apr 1956.

        More About ELIZABETH REBECCA BALLARD:
        Burial: Forsyth City Cemetery, Monroe Co., GA

        More About JAMES LANGFORD BOYNTON:
        Burial: Forsyth City Cemetery, Monroe Co., GA

    iii. JAMES ELDER BALLARD, b. 06 Sep 1888; d. 21 Nov 1962; m. RUTHA DAVIS; b. 15 Nov 1892; d. 22 Apr 1945.

        More About JAMES ELDER BALLARD:
        Burial: Culloden City Cemetery, Monroe Co., GA

        More About RUTHA DAVIS:
        Burial: Culloden City Cemetery, Monroe Co., GA

31. SARAH E.[4] BALLARD (*DANIEL G. S.[3], ELIJAH W.[2], JAMES[1]*) *was born 17 Oct 1847 in Pike Co., GA, and died 14 Feb 1938 in Pike Co., GA. She married JAMES H. HOWELL 22 Dec 1868 in Pike Co. GA. He was born 21 Jan 1843 in GA, and died 24 Oct 1911 in Pike Co., GA.*

Notes for SARAH E. BALLARD:
Source: Lynn B. Cunningham (lcunnin1@bellsouth.net), 1880 Zebulon Pike County GA Federal Census Records
* 1880 - James H. Howell 37 GA, Sarah E. 31 GA, Mary 10 GA, William D. 7 GA, Annie O. 5 GA, James 1 GA, O.E. 21 GA

More About SARAH E. BALLARD:
Burial: Zebulon Methodist Church Cemetery., Pike Co., GA

Child of SARAH BALLARD and JAMES HOWELL is:
      i.   MARY R.⁵ HOWELL, b. Abt. 1870, Pike Co., GA.

32. JOSEPH W.⁴ BALLARD (DANIEL G. S.³, ELIJAH W.², JAMES¹) was born 23 Jul 1855 in Pike Co., GA, and died 25 Apr 1923 in Fayette Co., GA. He married ALMETA W. STEGAR. She was born 01 May 1859 in Pike Co., GA, and died 18 Apr 1892 in Fayette Co., GA.

Notes for JOSEPH W. BALLARD:
Source: 1880 Federal Census Soundex Georgia, Lynn B. Cunningham (lcunnin1@bellsouth.net)
* 1880 - Living in Fayette County Georgia - Joseph W. Ballard 24 GA, Almeta W. 21, GA, Mary L. 2 GA, Ernest B. 2/12, Martha S. 17 GA, Matthew Adams 19 GA,

More About JOSEPH W. BALLARD:
Burial: Zebulon Methodist Church Cemetery., Pike Co., GA

More About ALMETA W. STEGAR:
Burial: Zebulon Methodist Church Cemetery., Pike Co., GA

Children of JOSEPH BALLARD and ALMETA STEGAR are:

      i.   MARY⁵ BALLARD, b. 1878.
     ii.   EARNEST B. BALLARD, b. 15 Apr 1880; d. 22 Feb 1940; m. MARY OPHELIA; b. 05 Jul 1880; d. 12 Apr 1926.

         Notes for EARNEST B. BALLARD:
         Source: BJSGen@aol.com (cemetery submission)

         More About EARNEST B. BALLARD:
         Burial: Inman Cemetery Fayette Co., GA

         More About MARY OPHELIA:
         Burial: Inman Cemetery Fayette Co., GA

    iii.   REBECCA BALLARD, b. 19 Oct 1887, GA; d. 08 Jun 1888, Fayette Co., GA.

33. CARRIE S.⁴ BALLARD (DANIEL G. S.³, ELIJAH W.², JAMES¹) was born 06 Jan 1866 in Pike Co., GA, and died 04 Feb 1927 in Fulton Co., GA. She married JOSEPH ARTHUR SASSER 24 Feb 1891 in Coweta Co., GA. He was born 21 Jul 1861 in GA, and died 20 May 1928.

Notes for CARRIE S. BALLARD:
Source: Obituary

The Atlanta Constitution - 5 Feb 1927 - Mrs. J.A. Sasser Dies After Long Illness
Mrs. Joseph Arthur Sasser, of 401 Ponce de Leon avenue, died Friday morning at 11 o'clock at a private hospital here after a prolonged illness. Mrs Sasser, before her marriage was Miss Carrie Ballard, daughter of the late Mrs. Cornelia A. Green, of Senoia, and step-daughter of Judge Hartford Green. She attended high school in Senoia, Ga.,

going later from there to the LaGrange Female college where she proved exceedingly talented in literature and also won several medals in music. She was graduated from the college, sharing highest honors with a classmate. Her education was completed with a post-graduate course at Peabody in Nashville. Mrs. Sasser was a leading factor in religious, charitable and educational work in Senoia, and upon moving to Atlanta many years ago devoted much of her time to like activities, until her health failed. She was a member of St. Marks Methodist church, a member of the D.A.R. and a member of the U.D.C. She is survived by her husband, J.A. Sasser, a well known Atlantan, one son, J.A. Sasser, Jr., and a first cousin now residing in Atlanta, Mrs. Effie Bloodworth Butner, the wife of F.M. Butner. Services will be held this afternoon at 3 o'clock from the residence, 401 Ponce de Leon avenue. Rev. W.L. Buren of St. Marks Methodist church, conducting.

More About CARRIE S. BALLARD:
Burial: Senoia City Cemetery, Coweta Co., GA

Notes for JOSEPH ARTHUR SASSER:
Source: 1900 Coweta County Georgia Federal Census Records
* 1900 - Living in Senoia, Coweta Co., GA - Sassor J. A - July 1862 GA, C B - Jan 1866 - 3 children, 1 living, GA, no name female - May 1899 GA, CA Green sister - Sep 1839 GA
* 1910 - Living in Atlanta, Fulton Co., GA - Sasser, Joseph A 44 GA, Carrie B 38 - 5 children 1 living GA, Joseph A Jr. 4, Mrs. Comelia Green mother in law 70 wd, Dora Holbrook servant, Mary Campbell Nurse

More About JOSEPH ARTHUR SASSER:
Burial: Senoia City Cemetery, Coweta Co., GA

Children of CARRIE BALLARD and JOSEPH SASSER are:
    i.   CORNELIA⁵ SASSER, b. 18 Oct 1885; d. 22 Aug 1888.
    ii.   MARY E. SASSER, b. 31 Aug 1897; d. 26 May 1898.

        More About MARY E. SASSER:
        Burial: Senoia City Cemetery, Coweta Co., GA

    iii. CARRIE BALLARD SASSER, b. 08 May 1900; d. 15 Mar 1901.

        More About CARRIE BALLARD SASSER:
        Burial: Senoia City Cemetery, Coweta Co., GA

    iv. JOSEPHINE SASSER, b. 20 Aug 1902; d. 19 Jan 1904.

        More About JOSEPHINE SASSER:
        Burial: Senoia City Cemetery, Coweta Co., GA

    v.   JOSEPH ARTHUR SASSER, b. 1906; d. 1935.

        More About JOSEPH ARTHUR SASSER:
        Burial: Senoia City Cemetery, Coweta Co., GA

Generation No. 5

34. DORA⁵ BALLARD (WILLIAM ELIJAH⁴, JOHN JASPER³, ELIJAH W.², JAMES¹) *was born 03 Apr 1869 in Pike Co., AL, and died 21 Feb 1922 in Karnes City, Karnes Co., TX. She married AUGUSTINE "GUSTAVE" PENIX 20 Jan 1891 in Pike Co., AL. He was born 14 Oct 1863, and died 11 Aug 1920.*

Notes for DORA BALLARD:
Source: 1880 Pike County Alabama Federal Census Records
* 1880 - Living in Pike Co., AL - (parents are deceased - she is living with family - Rice, William R 51, Kate 38, Dora Ballard 10 niece

More About DORA BALLARD:
Burial: Karnes City Cemetery, Karnes City, Karnes Co., TX

Notes for AUGUSTINE "GUSTAVE" PENIX:
Source: 1900-1910 Montgomery County Alabama Federal Census Records, Pike County Alabama Marriage Records
* 1900 - Living in Montgomery Co., AL - Penix, Augustan 37 - Set 1862 - TN, Dora 31 - Apr 1869 AL 3 children 3 living, Hilda 7 Apr 1893 AL, Richard 4 July 1895 AL, Dollie 11/12 - June 1899 AL
* 1910 - Living in Montgomery Co., AL - Penix, A 47 AL AL AL, Dora 41 - 4 children 4 living AL AL AL, Hilda 17 Al, Rich 15 AL, Nellie 11 AL, Maud B 4/12

More About AUGUSTINE "GUSTAVE" PENIX:
Burial: Karnes City, Karnes Co., TX

Children of DORA BALLARD and AUGUSTINE PENIX are:

    i.   HILDA AGATHA[6] PENIX, b. 17 Apr 1893, Montgomery Co., AL; d. May 1979, Etowah Co., AL; m. JOSEPH LUCIEN BROWN; b. 07 May 1892, Etowah Co., AL; d. 02 Jul 1963, Etowah Co., AL.

        More About HILDA AGATHA PENIX:
        Burial: Forrest Cemetery, Gadsden, Etowah Co., AL

        More About JOSEPH LUCIEN BROWN:
        Burial: Forrest Cemetery, Gadsden, Etowah Co., AL

    ii.   RICHARD RICE PENIX, b. 12 Jul 1894, Montgomery Co., AL; d. 25 Jul 1958, Bexar Co., TX.

        Notes for RICHARD RICE PENIX:
        Source: Bexar County Certificate of Death

    iii.   NELL PENIX, b. 09 Jun 1899, Montgomery Co., AL; d. 19 Dec 1941, Bexar Co., TX; m. FLORIAN FRANK KOLODZIE; b. 04 Oct 1896, Karnes City, Karnes Co., TX; d. 30 Dec 1963, Karnes City, Karnes Co., TX.

        More About NELL PENIX:
        Burial: Karnes City Cemetery, Karnes City, Karnes Co., TX

    iv.   MAUD B. PENIX, b. 1910, Montgomery Co., AL; d. Aft. 1910.

35. MAUDE VICTORIA[5] BALLARD (WILLIAM ELIJAH[4], JOHN JASPER[3], ELIJAH W.[2], JAMES[1]) was born 28 Oct 1874 in Pike Co., AL, and died 19 Dec 1909 in Marianna, Jackson Co., FL. She married FREDRICK STEPHEN BISHOP 01 Jun 1892 in Barbour Co., AL. He was born 27 Apr 1871 in Clayton, Barbour Co., AL, and died 07 Apr 1942 in Marianna, Jackson Co., FL.

Notes for MAUDE VICTORIA BALLARD:
Source: Phillis Bauer

More About MAUDE VICTORIA BALLARD:
Burial: Riverside Cemetery, Marianna, Jackson Co., FL

Notes for FREDRICK STEPHEN BISHOP:
Source: 1910-1920 Jackson County Florida Federal Census Records
* 1910 - Living in Jackson Co., FL - boarder in the Pooser house - Biship, Fred S 39 wd AL AL AL, Bernard 16 AL, Winnie 15 AL, Louise 5 FL, Mildred 3 FL
* 1920 - Living in Jackson Co., FL - Bishop, Fred 48 wd AL, Bernard 26 AL, Louise 14 FL, Mildred 12 FL

More About FREDRICK STEPHEN BISHOP:
Burial: Riverside Cemetery, Marianna, Jackson Co., FL

Children of MAUDE BALLARD and FREDRICK BISHOP are:

    i. THOMAS BERNARD[6] BISHOP, *b. 11 Jun 1893, Clayton, Barbour Co., AL; d. 19 Aug 1973, Chattahoochee, Gadsden Co., FL; m. WILMA AMELIA SILLS, 23 Sep 1923, Bainbridge Seminole Co., GA; b. 26 Oct 1903, Sills Jackson Co., FL; d. 08 Jun 1984, Marianna, Jackson Co., FL.*

        Notes for THOMAS BERNARD BISHOP:
        Source: Phyllis Bauer

    ii. WINNIE KATHLEEN BISHOP, *b. 05 Aug 1894, Clayton, Barbour Co., AL; d. 07 Aug 1991, Bluntstown, Calhoun Co., FL; m. GORDAN MCCAULEY, 1918; b. 03 May 1891; d. 22 Nov 1951.*

        More About WINNIE KATHLEEN BISHOP:
        Burial: Oaklawn Cemetery, Jacksonville, Duval Co., FL

        More About GORDAN MCCAULEY:
        Burial: Oaklawn Cemetery, Jacksonville, Duval Co., FL

    iii. LOUISE WEAVER BISHOP, *b. 07 Apr 1905, Marianna, Jackson Co., FL; d. 24 Nov 1938; m. BURRELL THOMAS ALFORD, 22 Jul 1930, Jackson Co FL; b. 02 Dec 1904, FL; d. Oct 1991.*

    iv. MILDRED BALLARD BISHOP, *b. 28 Feb 1907, Marianna, Jackson Co., FL; d. 13 Jun 2006; m. PEBBLE CURTIS STONE, Calhoun Co FL; b. 08 Jan 1907, Jackson Co FL.*

        More About MILDRED BALLARD BISHOP:
        Burial: Riverside Cemetery, Marianna, Jackson Co., FL

    v. MAUDE VICTORIA BISHOP, *b. 19 Dec 1909, Marianna, Jackson Co., FL; d. 14 Aug 1977, Marianna, Jackson Co., FL.*

        More About MAUDE VICTORIA BISHOP:
        Burial: Riverside Cemetery, Marianna, Jackson Co., FL

36. MARY ETTA "MOLLIE"[5] BALLARD (*JAMES PURIFOY*[4], *JOHN JASPER*[3], *ELIJAH W.*[2], *JAMES*[1]) *was born 27 Apr 1869 in Pike Co., AL, and died 14 Sep 1948 in Pike Co., AL. She married JOHN P. MACON 18 Oct 1883 in Pike Co., AL. He was born 07 Feb 1855 in Pike Co., AL, and died Bet. 1920 - 1930 in Pike Co., AL.*

More About MARY ETTA "MOLLIE" BALLARD:
Burial: Spring Hill Cemetery, Troy, Pike Co., AL

Notes for JOHN P. MACON:
Source: 1900-1920 Pike County Alabama Federal Census Records

* 1900 - Living in Spring Hill, Pike Co., AL - Macon, John P - Feb 1855 GA GA GA, Mary E - Apr 1869 - 8 children 6 living - AL GA GA, Leola - Oct 1884 AL, Clara E - Sept 1886 AL, Clara E - Sep 1886 AL, John J - Nov 1890 AL, Leila - Mar 1895 AL, Ernest Apr 1897 AL, not named daughter - Apr 1900 AL
* 1910 - Living in Spring Hill, Pike Co., AL - Macon, John 55 GA GA GA, Mollie 41 - 14 children 9 living AL GA GA, Ola 25 AL, Jake 19 AL, Ila 15 AL, Ernest 13, Ida 10 AL, May 7 AL, Era 4 AL, Arthur 1 5/12 AL
* 1920 - Living in Spring Hill, Pike Co., AL - Macon, John 64 AL AL AL, Mary E 50 AL AL AL, AAda 19 AL, May 16 AL, Eva 13 AL, Arthur 10 AL, Norah 6 AL

More About JOHN P. MACON:
Burial: Spring Hill Cemetery, Troy, Pike Co., AL

Children of MARY BALLARD and JOHN MACON are:

      i.   LEOLA "OLA"[6] MACON, b. 10 Oct 1884, Pike Co., AL; d. 02 Jan 1968, Pike Co., AL; m. DANIEL BRADLEY COSKREY, Mar 1937, Pike Co., AL; b. 30 Jul 1889, Pike Co., AL; d. 09 Jul 1966, Pike Co., AL.

          More About LEOLA "OLA" MACON:
          Burial: Spring Hill Cemetery, Troy, Pike Co., AL

          More About DANIEL BRADLEY COSKREY:
          Burial: Spring Hill Cemetery, Troy, Pike Co., AL

     ii.   CLARA ELIZABETH MACON, b. Abt. 1887, Pike Co., AL; d. 02 Mar 1964, Troy, Pike Co., AL.

          Notes for CLARA ELIZABETH MACON:
          Source: Pike County Alabama Death Records

    iii.   JOHN JAKE MACON, b. Abt. 1891, Pike Co., AL; d. Aft. 1910.
     iv.   LEILA MACON, b. Abt. 1895, Pike Co., AL; d. Aft. 1910.
      v.   ERNEST MACON, b. 14 Apr 1897, Pike Co., AL; d. 20 Mar 1957, Pike Co., AL; m. MARGARET ETHEL ABERCROMBIE, 23 Dec 1919, Pike Co., AL; b. 30 Dec 1896, Pike Co., AL; d. 24 Mar 1986, Pike Co., AL.

          More About ERNEST MACON:
          Burial: Spring Hill Cemetery, Troy, Pike Co., AL

          More About MARGARET ETHEL ABERCROMBIE:
          Burial: Spring Hill Cemetery, Troy, Pike Co., AL

     vi.   IDA MACON, b. Abt. 1900, Pike Co., AL; d. Aft. 1920.
    vii.   MAY MACON, b. Abt. 1903, Pike Co., AL; d. Aft. 1920.
   viii.   ERA MACON, b. Abt. 1906, Pike Co., AL; d. Aft. 1920.
     ix.   ARTHUR MACON, b. 21 Dec 1910, Pike Co., AL; d. 23 Sep 1991; m. LUCILLE W. BRYON, 07 Sep 1946, Union Springs, Bullock Co., AL; b. 11 Nov 1910; d. 23 Jun 1989.

          Notes for ARTHUR MACON:
          Source: 1930 Pike County Alabama Federal Census Records
          * 1930 - Living in Spring Hill, Pike Co., AL - Macon, Arthur 20 AL, Mollie - mother 60 wd AL, Lois sister 15 AL

          More About ARTHUR MACON:
          Burial: Riverdale Cemetery, Columbus Muscogee Co., GA

          More About LUCILLE W. BRYON:
          Burial: Riverdale Cemetery, Columbus, Muscogee Co., GA

      x.   NORAH MACON, b. Abt. 1912, Pike Co., AL; d. Aft. 1920.
     xi.   LOIS MACON, b. Abt. 1915, Pike Co., AL; d. Aft. 1930.

37. JOHN ALFRED[5] BALLARD (*JAMES PURIFOY[4], JOHN JASPER[3], ELIJAH W.[2], JAMES[1]*) *was born 04 Jun 1871 in Spring Hill Pike Co., AL, and died 07 Dec 1946 in Pike Co., AL. He married NANCY ELLA AGNES BENNETT 06 Feb 1896 in Spring Hill Pike Co., AL. She was born 06 Dec 1874 in Pike Co., AL, and died 10 Feb 1955.*
Notes for JOHN ALFRED BALLARD:
Source: 1900 - 1930 Pike County Alabama Federal Census Records, Phyliss Bauer
* 1900 - Living in Pike Co., AL - Ballard, John A 28 - June 1871 AL GA GA, Nancy E 25 - Dec 1874 2 children 1

living - AL SC AL, Ewell 1 - Aug 1898 AL, Clara 57 - Feb 1843 5 children 3 living Mother GA NC GA, J. Earnest - brother 23 - Dec 1876 AL GA GA
* 1910 - Living in Spring Hill, Pike Co., AL - Ballard, John A 37 AL GA GA, Nancy 34 - 7 children 5 living AL NC AL, Euell 11 AL, Lorene 8 AL, James 6 AL, Nell 4 AL Myrus 2 AL
* 1920 - Living in Spring Hill, Pike Co., AL - Ballard, John 48 AL, Nannie 44 AL, Ewel 21 AL, Lorene 18 AL, James 16 AL, Nell 14 AL, Mirus 11 AL, Julia 9 AL, John 6 AL
* 1930 - Living in Spring Hill, Pike Co., AL - Ballard, John A 58 AL AL AL, Nannie 54 AL SC AL, Euell F 30 AL, Jim A 26 AL, Myrus 22 AL, John Jr. 16 AL, Ada Davis sister in law 63 AL SC AL

More About JOHN ALFRED BALLARD:
Burial: Spring Hill Cemetery, Troy, Pike Co., AL

More About NANCY ELLA AGNES BENNETT:
Burial: Spring Hill Cemetery, Troy, Pike Co., AL

Children of JOHN BALLARD and NANCY BENNETT are:

  i.   HOWARD BENNETT[6] BALLARD, b. 20 Oct 1896, Pike Co., AL; d. 10 Mar 1900.
  ii.   EWELL FRANCIS BALLARD, b. 20 Aug 1898, Pike Co., AL; d. 29 Nov 1953.
  iii. LULA KATHERINE BALLARD, b. 17 Jun 1900, Pike Co., AL; d. 06 Feb 1901.
  iv.   WILLIE LORENE "MAMMY" BALLARD, b. 06 Dec 1901, Spring Hill Pike Co., AL; d. 27 Dec 1973, Pike Co., AL; m. LEONARD GOLDEN ABERCROMBIE; b. 19 Sep 1895, Barbour Co., AL; d. 06 Dec 1963, Troy, Pike Co., AL.

        More About WILLIE LORENE "MAMMY" BALLARD:
        Burial: Spring Hill Cemetery, Troy, Pike Co., AL

        More About LEONARD GOLDEN ABERCROMBIE:
        Burial: Spring Hill Cemetery, Troy, Pike Co., AL

  v.   JAMES ALFRED "JIM" BALLARD, b. 10 Mar 1904, Pike Co., AL; d. 04 Jan 1956.
  vi.   CLARA ELINOR "NELL" BALLARD, b. Abt. 1906, Pike Co., AL; d. Aft. 1920.
  vii. MYRUS CECIL "TOBY" BALLARD, b. 22 Mar 1908, Pike Co., AL; d. 11 Dec 1963.
  viii. JULIA BALLARD, b. Abt. 1911, Pike Co., AL; d. Aft. 1920.
  ix.   JOHN BALLARD, b. Abt. 1914, Pike Co., AL; d. Aft. 1930.

38. JAMES ERNEST[5] BALLARD (JAMES PURIFOY[4], JOHN JASPER[3], ELIJAH W.[2], JAMES[1]) was born 05 Dec 1876 in Pike Co., AL, and died 16 Jul 1952. He married ALMA WHEELER 08 Oct 1893. She was born 27 Feb 1882 in AL, and died 21 Jul 1958.

Notes for JAMES ERNEST BALLARD:
Source: 1910-1930 Pike County Alabama Federal Census Records
* 1910 - Living in Spring Hill, Pike Co., AL - Ballard, James E 33 AL GA GA, Alma 27 - 3 children 3 living AL AL AL, Eric 5 AL, Rex 2 AL, Emma 2 AL
* 1920 - Living in Troy, Pike Co., AL - Ballard, Ernest 43 AL AL AL, Alma 37 AL AL AL, Eric 15 AL, Rex 11 AL, Emma 11 AL, Emma Wheeler 58 mother in law, Mamie Jenkins 18 boarder
* 1930 - Living in Troy, Pike Co., AL - Ballard, Ernest 54 AL, Alma 48 AL, Eric 26 AL, Rex 22 AL, Wesley Dorrell 23 son in law AL, Emma Dorrell 22 dau AL

More About JAMES ERNEST BALLARD:
Burial: Oakwood Cemetery, Troy, Pike Co., AL

More About ALMA WHEELER:
Burial: Oakwood Cemetery, Troy, Pike Co., AL

Children of JAMES BALLARD and ALMA WHEELER are:

   i.   JAMES ERIC[6] BALLARD, b. 30 Dec 1904, Pike Co., AL; d. 11 May 1965; m. EVELYN DOWLING.

         Notes for JAMES ERIC BALLARD:
         Source: Melissa Dantzler (MELISABOP@aol.com)

   ii.   LITTLETON REX BALLARD, b. 13 Mar 1908, Pike Co., AL; d. Jan 1959; m. FERRELL ZRINGAN.
   iii. EMMA CLARA BALLARD, b. Abt. 1908, Pike Co., AL; d. Aft. 1930; m. WESLEY W. DORRELL; b. Abt.
         1910, AL; d. 08 Aug 1959.

39. LULA CATHERINE[5] BALLARD (THOMAS WELDON[4], JOHN JASPER[3], ELIJAH W.[2], JAMES[1]) was born 21 Jul 1866 in Milo, Pike Co., AL, and died 1915. She married ASA WILSON. He was born Abt. 1865, and died Bef. 1910.

Children of LULA BALLARD and ASA WILSON are:
   i.   JAMES "JIM" TOM[6] WILSON, b. 1884, Pike Co., AL; d. Aft. 1900.
   ii.   MARY JANE WILSON, b. 03 Feb 1886, Pike Co., AL; d. 29 May 1969, Pike Co., AL; m. JAMES SMART.
   iii. LUCIAN CLOVIS WILSON, b. 13 Dec 1887, Pike Co., AL; d. 21 Jul 1961, Pike Co., AL; m. ADELINE
         BURNEY.

40. LILLIAN CORNELIA "LILLIE"[5] BALLARD (THOMAS WELDON[4], JOHN JASPER[3], ELIJAH W.[2], JAMES[1]) was born 27 Jul 1868 in Milo, Pike Co., AL, and died Aft. 1911. She married JESSE ASBURY SIMMONS.

Children of LILLIAN BALLARD and JESSE SIMMONS are:
   i.   BALLARD[6] SIMMONS.
   ii.   WILFRED SIMMONS.
   iii. WILMA SIMMONS.

41. THOMAS VICTOR "VIC"[5] BALLARD (THOMAS WELDON[4], JOHN JASPER[3], ELIJAH W.[2], JAMES[1]) was born 03 Jan 1871 in Milo, Pike Co., AL, and died 30 Nov 1928 in Pike Co., AL. He married ADA JANNEY. She was born 07 Aug 1873, and died 09 Aug 1956 in Pike Co., AL.

Notes for THOMAS VICTOR "VIC" BALLARD:
Source: 1910 Norfolk County Virginia Federal Census Records
* 1910 - Living in Norfolk Co., VA - Ballard, Thomas V 36 AL AL AL, Ada E 35 - 2 children 2 living TN TN TN, Thomas J 7 District of Columbia, Martha J 12 DC and 2 boarders

More About THOMAS VICTOR "VIC" BALLARD:
Burial: Oakwood Cemetery, Troy, Pike Co., AL

More About ADA JANNEY:
Burial: Oakwood Cemetery, Troy, Pike Co., AL

Children of THOMAS BALLARD and ADA JANNEY are:

   i.   MARTHA JANE[6] BALLARD, b. 25 Jun 1897, DC; d. 24 Feb 1983, FL; m. W. JOE CODY.
   ii.   THOMAS BALLARD, b. 28 Oct 1902, DC; d. 24 Sep 1982, FL; m. HATTIE SUE WEST.

42. HERBERT WELDON[5] BALLARD (THOMAS WELDON[4], JOHN JASPER[3], ELIJAH W.[2], JAMES[1]) was born 08 May 1873 in Milo, Pike Co., AL, and died 1946 in Pike Co., AL. He married JOHNNIE MAE CULVER 25 Nov 1912 in Maplesville AL. She was born 01 May 1883 in Perote Bullock Co., AL, and died 01 Mar 1976 in Dothan Houston Co., AL.

Notes for HERBERT WELDON BALLARD:

Source: Jim and Terri Tait (jtait@hiwaay.net)

Alabama Official and Statistical Register, 1907 State of AL Dept of Archives and History, compiled by Thomas M. Owen, L.L, D. Director, Brown Publishing Co, Montgomery, AL, 1907 p. 113:
Legislative Department, Pike Co.
Herbert Weldon Ballard of Troy, Pike county was born at Milo in that county, April 8, 1873 and is the son of Thomas Weldon and Jane C. (Simmons) Ballard and the grandson of John J. and Nancy (McNight) Ballard, and of Issac and Elizabeth (Fowler) Simmons, who emigrated about 1817 from North Carolina to Dallas county, and thence to Milo, Pike Co.. John J. Ballard lived at Fayettville, Georgia until 1854, when he removed to Milo, Pike county; and served eighteen months in the Army of Northern Virginia and died of a fever in Richmond. Thomas Weldon Ballard, his son, was born in Fayetteville, Georgia and moved in 1854 with his father to Milo. He also served eighteen months in the Confederate army; lost a leg from a wound received in the battle of Murfreesboro, Tenn; and was tax collector of Pike county for two terms. The Ballards are of Scotch descent, the first ancestor settling in N.C. Herbert W. Ballard received his elementary education in the common schools of Pike county; and attended the State Normal School at Troy two years, finishing his junior year in 1894; in 1895 he took a course in the Atlanta Business College, but was compelled to leave on account of eye trouble, from which, however, he ultimately recovered. In the spring of 1901 he entered upon the life insurance business in which work he canvassed all the adjacent counties. Mr. Ballard has for year taken an active interest in agricultural pursuits. He is a Democrat; and is unmarried.

More About HERBERT WELDON BALLARD:
Burial: Oakwood Cemetery, Troy, Pike Co., AL

More About JOHNNIE MAE CULVER:
Burial: Oakwood Cemetery, Troy, Pike Co., AL

Child of HERBERT BALLARD and JOHNNIE CULVER is:
>   i.   CATHERINE[6] BALLARD, b. 28 Jan 1914, Pike Co., AL; m. SAMUEL JULIUS CASEY, 31 May 1934, Troy AL; b. 01 Mar 1911; d. 21 Aug 1993, Dead Lakes FL.

43. WALTER EUGENE[5] BALLARD (THOMAS WELDON[4], JOHN JASPER[3], ELIJAH W.[2], JAMES[1]) *was born 25 Jul 1876 in Springhill, Pike Co., AL, and died 08 Mar 1954. He married* LAURA ADELE MCGAUGH *18 Jan 1901 in Lowndes Co. AL, daughter of* WILLIAM MCGAUGH *and* MARGARET MCLEMORE. *She was born 1876 in Lowndes Co., AL, and died 23 Sep 1959.*

Notes for WALTER EUGENE BALLARD:
Source: 1920, 1930 Montgomery County Alabama Federal Census Records, Ballard-Ballord Bits page 115 M5, Phyllis Bauer, Lowndes Co. Alabama Marriage Records
* 1901 - Married to Laura Adel McGaugh January 18, 1901 Lowndes Co. AL. Married by E. R. Eldridge, book C
* 1920 - Living in Cloverdale Montgomery Co., AL - Ballard, Eugene 42 AL, Laura 42 AL, Eliza 17 AL, Eugene 12 AL, Margret 8 AL, Victor AL
* 1930 - Living in Montgomery Co., AL - Ballard, Eugene 52 AL, Adele 51 AL , Elisabeth M. 27 AL, Eugene Jr. 21 AL, Margaret A. 19 AL, Victor H. 19 AL

Children of WALTER BALLARD and LAURA MCGAUGH are:
>   i.   MARY ELIZABETH "LIBBA"[6] BALLARD, b. 25 Oct 1902, Montgomery AL.
>   ii. WALTER EUGENE "GENE" BALLARD, b. 18 Jun 1908, Prattville Autauga Co., AL; d. Aft. 1973, lived in Montgomery Co., AL; m. ELEANOR FARREL BOWEN, Nov 1935, NC.
>
>   *Notes for WALTER EUGENE "GENE" BALLARD:*
>   *Source: Ballard-Ballord Bits page 115 M9*
>
>   iii. MARGARET ADELE BALLARD, b. 27 Jan 1911, Prattville Autauga Co., AL; m. LAWRENCE HALL MARKS, 17 Aug 1935, Montgomery AL; b. Mar 1911, Montgomery AL; d. 19 Dec 1995.

iv.   VICTOR HERBERT BALLARD, b. 27 Jan 1911, Prattville Autauga Co., AL.

44. ALICE BELL[5] BALLARD (TIMOTHY C.[4], ELIJAH W.[3], ELIJAH W.[2], JAMES[1]) was born 02 Dec 1874 in TX, and died 1914. She married JAMES AUGUSTA LILLY 12 Aug 1891 in Hunt Co., TX, son of ROBERT LILLY and ANN DOUGLAS. He was born 09 May 1859 in AL, and died 20 Apr 1947 in Commerce, Hunt Co., TX.

More About ALICE BELL BALLARD:
Burial: Rosemound Cemetery, Commerce, Hunt Co., TX

Notes for JAMES AUGUSTA LILLY:
Source: Hunt County Texas Death Certificate, 1910-1920 Hunt County Texas Federal Census Records

* 1910 - Living in Hunt Co., TX - Little, James A 51, Alice B 35, George H 17, Annie L 15, Robert E 13, James A 10, Wayla L 7, Curtis A 4
* 1920 - Living in Hunt Co., TX - Little, James A 60 AL, Fannie 44 AL, George H 28 TX, James A 19 TX, Wava Lee 17 TX, Curtis A 14 TX, Elton C 6 TX

More About JAMES AUGUSTA LILLY:
Burial: Rosemound Cemetery, Commerce, Hunt Co., TX

Children of ALICE BALLARD and JAMES LILLY are:

   i.   GEORGE HOMER[6] LILLY, b. 09 Sep 1892, Commerce, Hunt Co., TX; d. 25 Jun 1971, Commerce, Hunt Co., TX.

       Notes for GEORGE HOMER LILLY:
       Source: Hunt County Texas Certificate of Death

  ii.   ROBERT EMERSON LILLY, b. 28 Jan 1897, Commerce, Hunt Co., TX; d. 17 Oct 1972, Dallas Co., TX.

       Notes for ROBERT EMERSON LILLY:
       Source: Dallas County Texas Certificate of Death

 iii.   JAMES AUGUSTA LILLY, b. 09 Apr 1900, Commerce, Hunt Co., TX; d. 14 Oct 1970, Sulphur Springs, Hopkins Co., TX.

       Notes for JAMES AUGUSTA LILLY:
       Source: Hopkins County Texas Certificate of Death

  iv.   CURTIS ANDERS LILLY, b. 27 Aug 1905, Commerce, Hunt Co., TX; d. 24 Mar 1973, Commerce, Hunt Co., TX.

       Notes for CURTIS ANDERS LILLY:
       Source: Commerce Hunt County Texas Certificate of Death

   v.   WAYA L. LILLY, b. Abt. 1913, Commerce, Hunt Co., TX; d. Aft. 1920.
  vi.   ELTON CARR LILLY, b. 16 May 1912, Commerce, Hunt Co., TX; d. Aft. 1940.

       Notes for ELTON CARR LILLY:
       Source: WWII Draft Cards

45. ANNA LAURIE[5] BALLARD (TIMOTHY C.[4], ELIJAH W.[3], ELIJAH W.[2], JAMES[1]) was born 30 Jul 1887 in TX, and died Aft. 1910. She married WILLS WARD. He was born 1871 in TX, and died Aft. 1900.

Notes for ANNA LAURIE BALLARD:
Source: 1900 Hunts County Texas Federal Census Records
* *1900 - Living in Hunts County TX - Ballard, Laura - Dec 1851, Delia - Dec 1879, Ada - Oct 1881, Willie - Nov 1885, Laurie L - July 1881, Wills Ward son in law 1871, Amy Laurie - Jan 1893, Jimmie J - Mar 1895*

More About ANNA LAURIE BALLARD:
Burial: (can't be the mother of his two children)

Children of ANNA BALLARD and WILLS WARD are:
> i. AMY LAURIE[6] WARD, b. Jan 1893; d. Aft. 1900.
> ii. JIMMIE J. WARD, b. Mar 1895; d. Aft. 1900.

46. WILLIAM ELIJAH[5] BALLARD (SEABORN H.[4], ELIJAH W.[3], ELIJAH W.[2], JAMES[1]) *was born 20 Nov 1882 in Collin Co TX, and died 22 Dec 1951 in Little Rock Pulaski Co., AR. He married (1)* NANCY CATHERINE GIBSON *Bef. 1907. She died Aft. 1907 in OK. He married (2)* DORA TURNER COLBERT *Bef. 1916. She was born 1884, and died Aft. 1930.*

Notes for WILLIAM ELIJAH BALLARD:
Source: Beverly Killian (beverlykillian@starband.net), 1920, 1930 Lee County Arkansas Federal Census Records
* *1920 - Living in Lee County Arkansas - Ballard, William E 37 TX US TX, Dora L 35 AR US TX, Dora M Colbert 12 step child AR, Fannie 10 step child AR, Rosa L 6 step child AR, Winnie M Ballard 12 OK, Bluford H 4 8/12 zok*
* *1930 - Living in Lee Co., AR. ,Hampton - Township Ballard, W. E. 47, TX TX TX, Dora 46, Leon(fe) 17, Blufford 14, Fay (fe) (she is a grandchild) 5, LA TX AR*

Child of WILLIAM BALLARD and NANCY GIBSON is:
> i. WINNIE MAE[6] BALLARD, b. 03 Dec 1907, Antlers OK; d. 28 Mar 1968; m. JOSEPH ELIHU GUIN; b. 16 Jun 1900; d. 06 Jul 1964.

Children of WILLIAM BALLARD and DORA COLBERT are:
> ii. DORA COLBERT[6] (STEP), b. 1913.
> iii. ROSA LEON COLBERT (STEP), b. 1914.
> iv. FANNIS COLBERT (STEP), b. 1915.
> v. BLUEFORD HAROLD BALLARD, b. 16 Mar 1916, OK; d. 17 Jan 1978, Los Angeles, CA; m. MARTHA WHITE.

>> *Notes for BLUEFORD HAROLD BALLARD:*
>> *Source: Beverly Killian (beverlykillian@starband.net)*

47. EVLENOR O.[5] BALLARD (SEABORN H.[4], ELIJAH W.[3], ELIJAH W.[2], JAMES[1]) *was born Jul 1889 in TX, and died Aft. 1920. He married* MOLLIE. *She was born 1898 in KY, and died Aft. 1920.*

Notes for EVLENOR O. BALLARD:
Source: 1920-1930 Yuma County Arizona Federal Census Records, Beverly Killian (beverlykillian@starband.net)

* *1920 - Living in Crane, Yuma County AZ - Ballard, E O Ballard 23, Mollie 22, Nellie 2 1/12, Seaborn 8/12, Elizabetrh Ballew 52 mother*
* *1930 - Living in Somerton, Yuma County AZ - Ballard, Ersley O 33 TX TX TX, Mollie 32 OK KY MO, Bernice 12 OK, Seaborn 10 OK, Claudie 8 AZ, Larry 3 AZ*

Children of EVLENOR BALLARD and MOLLIE are:
> i. BERNICE[6] BALLARD, b. 1918, OK; d. Aft. 1930.

      ii.   SEABORN BALLARD, *b. 1920, OK; d. Aft. 1930.*
      iii. CLAUDIE BALLARD, *b. 1922, AZ; d. Aft. 1930.*
      iv. LARRY BALLARD, *b. 1927, AZ; d. Aft. 1930.*

48. HARVEY E.[5] BALLARD (SEABORN H.[4], ELIJAH W.[3], ELIJAH W.[2], JAMES[1]) *was born 1892 in AR, and died Aft. 1920. He married* HALEY. *She was born 1900 in TX, and died Aft. 1920.*

Notes for HARVEY E. BALLARD:
Source: Beverly Killian, 1920 Pushmataha Oklahoma Federal Census Records

* 1920 - Living in Antlers twp, Pushmataha County OK - Ballard, Harvey E 28 AR TX TX, Haley 20 TX TX TX, Josephine 2 OK AR TX, Irene 1 OK AR TX

Children of HARVEY BALLARD *and* HALEY *are:*
      i.   JOSEPHINE[6] BALLARD, *b. 1918, OK; d. Aft. 1920.*
      ii. IRENE BALLARD, *b. 1919, OK; d. Aft. 1920.*

49. JAMES W.[5] BALLARD (THOMAS W.[4], WILLIAM BARNES[3], ELIJAH W.[2], JAMES[1]) *was born 31 Jan 1871 in GA, and died 04 Jun 1923 in Pike Co., GA. He married* LUCY CRAWFORD *15 Dec 1897 in Pike Co., GA. She was born 03 Feb 1880 in GA, and died 21 Feb 1978 in DeKalb Co., GA.*

Children of JAMES BALLARD *and* LUCY CRAWFORD *are:*

      i.   THAD C.[6] BALLARD, *b. Abt. 1903, Pike Co., GA; d. 29 Jan 1962, Bibb Co., GA.*
      ii. MARY LENA BALLARD, *b. Abt. 1908, Pike Co., GA.*

50. MABEL WILDER[5] BALLARD (THOMAS W.[4], WILLIAM BARNES[3], ELIJAH W.[2], JAMES[1]) *was born 15 Aug 1877 in GA, and died 30 Mar 1926 in DeKalb Co., GA. She married* THOMAS JESSE ROBERTSON *11 Oct 1900 in Pike Co., GA. He was born 10 Oct 1875 in GA.*

Children of MABEL BALLARD *and* THOMAS ROBERTSON *are:*

      i.   CHARLOTTE ISABEL[6] ROBERTSON, *b. 02 Jul 1905, Pike Co., GA; d. 15 Jul 1981, Upson Co., GA.*
      ii. MATTIE RUTH ROBERTSON, *b. Abt. 1910, Pike Co., GA.*

James Ballard

Generation No. 1

1. JAMES[1] BALLARD *was born Abt. 1775 in NC, and died Mar 1847 in Wilkinson Co., GA. He married (1) WIFE NUMBER ONE. She was born 1785 in SC, and died Aft. 1860. He married (2) MARGIANA BRADY 01 Jan 1827 in Wilkinson Co., GA. She was born 1773 in GA, and died Aft. 1850.*

Notes for JAMES BALLARD:
Source: Angela Eppley (chrokeez2@hotmail.com), Deb VandenBos (DebbieD30@aol.com), 1840 Itawamba County Mississippi, Randal Wiginton (Wiginton@bellsouth.net), 1850 Marion County Alabama Federal Census Records, Wilkinson County Georgia Marriage Records
* 1850 - Living in Marion Co., AL - Ballard, James 72 farmer SC, Martha 63, Jeremiah 79 AL

Notes for WIFE NUMBER ONE:
Source: 1860 Itawamba County Mississippi Federal Census Records
* 1860 - Living in Itawamba Co., MS with daughter Ursual and family.

Children of JAMES BALLARD and WIFE ONE are:

2.	i.	URSULA M.[2] BALLARD, b. 13 Dec 1806, SC; d. 05 May 1861, Itawamba Co., MS.
3.	ii.	LEVI GARRISON BALLARD, b. 23 Mar 1807, SC; d. Aft. 1860.
4.	iii.	WESLEY BALLARD, b. 1812, SC; d. Aft. 1860, Hardeman Co., TN.
	iv.	LUCRETIA BALLARD, b. Abt. 1815; m. WILLIAM WIGGINSTON, 03 May 1836, Blount Co., AL; b. 1801, SC; d. Itasca Co., TX.

More About LUCRETIA BALLARD:
Burial: Pleasant Ridge Cemetery. Hamilton, Marion Co., AL

More About WILLIAM WIGGINSTON:
Burial: Itasco Cemetery

5.	v.	ELIZABETH BALLARD, b. Aug 1820, GA; d. Aft. 1870.
	vi.	ANDREW BALLARD, b. 1822, SC.
6.	vii.	ISAAC ASBURY BALLARD, b. 06 Apr 1822, GA; d. 15 Dec 1902, Hamilton, Marion Co, AL; Stepchild.
7.	viii.	DANIEL MILTON BALLARD, b. 15 Mar 1827, GA; d. 16 Dec 1901.
8.	ix.	JESSE BALLARD, b. 1828, GA; d. Aft. 1860.

Children of JAMES BALLARD and MARGIANA BRADY are:

| 9. | x. | ARTIMISSA[2] BALLARD, b. 1821, of Wilkinson Co., GA; d. Aft. 1870. |
| 10. | xi. | JAMES BALLARD, b. Abt. 1804, GA; d. Aft. 1860. |

Generation No. 2

2. URSULA M.[2] BALLARD (JAMES[1]) *was born 13 Dec 1806 in SC, and died 05 May 1861 in Itawamba Co., MS. She married JAMES WIGGINSTON 11 Aug 1831 in Blount Co., AL. He was born 1804 in TN, and died 17 Mar 1872 in Itawamba Co., MS.*

Notes for URSULA M. BALLARD:
Source: 1860 Itawamba County, Mississippi Federal Census Records

More About URSULA M. BALLARD:
Burial: Mt. Pleasant Methodist Church, Itawamba Co., MS

Notes for JAMES WIGGINSTON:
Source: 1850-1860 Itawamba County Mississippi Federal Census Records
* 1850 - Living in Itawamba Co., MS - Wigginton, James 42 TN, Ursula 31 SC, James 17 AL, Levi 11 AL, Canzada 9 AL, Isaac 7 MS, Samuel 5 AL
* 1860 - Living in Itawamba Co., MS - Wiggenton, Jas 32 TN, Urshulu 47 SC, Canzada 18 MS, Eli M 20 AL, Isaac R 16 AL, Saml J 14 AL, Thos R 9 MS, Martha Ballard 73 SC

More About JAMES WIGGINSTON:
Burial: Mt. Pleasant Meth. Itawamba Co., MS

Children of URSULA BALLARD and JAMES WIGGINSTON are:

       i.   JAMES PLEASANT³ WIGGINSTON, b. 1833, Itawamba Co., MS; d. Aft. 1850; m. JANE.
      ii. MISS WIGGINSTON, b. 1834, Itawamba Co., MS.
11.   iii. LEVI M. WIGGINSTON, b. 1839, Itawamba Co., MS; d. Bet. 1850 - 1870.
      iv. CANZANDA F. WIGGINSTON, b. 08 Dec 1842, Itawamba Co., MS; d. 23 Jan 1910, Tremont Itawamba Co., MS; m. DAVID G. WHEELER, 13 Oct 1864, Itawamba Co., MS; b. 04 Apr 1839.

           More About CANZANDA F. WIGGINSTON:
           Burial: Mt. Pleasant Meth. Itawamba Co., MS

      v. ISAAC RILEY WIGGINSTON, b. 1845, Itawamba Co., MS; d. 25 Dec 1949, Texola, Beckham Co., OK; m. EASTER ANN ROBISON; b. 26 Apr 1846, Itawamba Co., MS; d. 05 Apr 1915.

           More About ISAAC RILEY WIGGINSTON:
           Burial: Mt. Pleasant Meth. Itawamba Co., MS

           More About EASTER ANN ROBISON:
           Burial: Mt. Pleasant Meth. Itawamba Co., MS

      vi. SOLOMAN JONES WIGGINSTON, b. 23 Dec 1846, Itawamba Co., MS; d. 20 Feb 1921, Itasca Hill Co TX; m. ELIZABETH JANE ROBINSON; b. 19 Apr 1844, AL; d. 25 Jan 1889, Marion Co., AL.
     vii. THOMAS RAY WIGGINSTON, b. 08 Oct 1850, Itawamba Co., MS; d. 06 Aug 1937, Itawamba Co., MS; m. PAMELA ELMIRA STONE; b. 19 Jan 1846; d. 11 Dec 1898, Itawamba Co., MS.

           Notes for THOMAS RAY WIGGINSTON:
           Source: 1870 Itawamba County Mississippi Federal Census Records
           * 1870 - Living in Itawamba Co., MS with brother Levi

           More About THOMAS RAY WIGGINSTON:
           Burial: Mt. Pleasant Meth. Itawamba Co., MS

           More About PAMELA ELMIRA STONE:
           Burial: Mt. Pleasant Meth. Itawamba Co., MS

   viii. MARCUS DEE WIGGINSTON, b. 1865, Itawamba Co., MS; d. 03 Sep 1928, Itawamba Co., MS; m. NANCY JANE FRIDAY; b. 1869, Itawamba Co., MS.
     ix. EMILY VALDORA WIGGINSTON, b. 06 Dec 1868, Itawamba Co., MS; d. 25 Dec 1925; m. JOHN FRANKLIN FRIDAY; b. 10 Apr 1860, Itawamba Co., MS; d. 1935, Itawamba Co., MS.
      x. MELISSA JANIE WIGGINSTON, b. 1872, Itawamba Co., MS; d. 1939; m. THOMAS F. FRIDAY, 02 Jan 1890, Itawamba Co., MS; b. 1866, Itawamba Co., MS; d. 1935.

           More About MELISSA JANIE WIGGINSTON:
           Burial: Mt. Pleasant Methodist Church Cemetery, Itawamba Co., MS

           More About THOMAS F. FRIDAY:
           Burial: Mt. Pleasant Methodist Church Cemetery, Itawamba Co., MS

3. LEVI GARRISON[2] BALLARD (JAMES[1]) was born 23 Mar 1807 in SC, and died Aft. 1860. He married MARY ANN BURNS 11 Apr 1827 in Blount Co., AL. She was born 07 Feb 1810 in NC, and died Aft. 1860.

Notes for LEVI GARRISON BALLARD:
Source: 1850-1860 Marion County Alabama Federal Census Records, Vicki Whaley (Whaley6@aol.com), Marcelle Lewis (airnet@prodigy.net), Blount County Tennessee Marriage Bond between Joseph Burns and Levy G Ballard
* 1827 - Blount Co., AL Marriage Bond - State of Alabama, Blount County AL - To any of the Judges of Said State any Justice of the Peace of Said County or any Ordained or Licensed Minister of the Gospel Legally authorized. These are to authorize you or either of you to Solemnize the rites of matrimony between Levy G Ballard and Mary Burns of Said County agreeable to the Statute in Such case made and provided. Given at the office of the Clerk of the County Consent of Said County this 2nd day of April 1827. (Clerks name is hart to read).
I certify that I Solemnized the rites of matrimony Between the above named Levy G Ballard and Mary Burns in the 11 th day of April 1827. Given under my hand the 11th day of April 1827. Henry McPherson. Justice Peace Blount. The following consent now Given to by Joseph Burnes. ??? please to let Levi G Ballard have Lison to marry any Burns this from under Nancy Burnes hand
Know all men by there presents that we Levi G Ballard and Joseph Burns of Blount County State of Alabama are held held firmly bound unto the Govenor of Said State for the time being and his successors in office in the Sum of two hundred Dollars for the use of Said State for the payment of which well and truly to be made we bind ourselves and our heirs jointly and Severally, witness our hands and Seals this 2nd day of April 1827. The condition of the above obligation is Such that the Said Levy G. Ballard hath this day prayed and License from the Clerk of the County Court of Said County to be married to Mary Burns. Now if there be no Lawful cause to obstruct Said marriage, the above obligation to be void, otherwise to remain in full force. Levi G Ballard (seal), Joseph (x) Burns (seal). Test. (hard to read)
* 1850 - Living in Marion Co., AL - Ballard, L. G. 45 farmer SC, James W 20 AL, Mary A 40 NC, Joseph 28 AL, Elizabeth 14 AL, Alfred 12 MS, Asberry 10 MS, Levi G 6 AL, Jesse 2 AL
* 1860 - Living In Marion Co., AL - Ballard, Garrison 54 Farmer NC, Mary 50 NC, Asberry 18 AL, Albert 14 AL, Levi 11 AL, Jesse 10 AL.

Children of LEVI BALLARD and MARY BURNS are:
12. i. JAMES W.[3] BALLARD, b. 1830, AL; d. Aft. 1880.
13. ii. JOSEPH BALLARD, b. 1832, AL; d. Bet. 1860 - 1870, Franklin Co., AL.
14. iii. ELIZABETH BALLARD, b. 1836, AL; d. 1922.
     iv. ALFRED BALLARD, b. 1838, AL; d. Aft. 1860.
15. v. ISAAC ASBERRY BALLARD, b. 23 Mar 1841, AL; d. 03 Jun 1912, Marion Co., AL.
     vi. ALBERT BALLARD, b. 1846, AL.
16. vii. LEVI GARRISON BALLARD, b. Bet. 1846 - 1848, AL; d. Aft. 1900.
     viii. TIPSON BALLARD, b. 1850, AL.

4. WESLEY[2] BALLARD (JAMES[1]) was born 1812 in SC, and died Aft. 1860 in Hardeman Co., TN. He married MANERVA BYRNES 01 Oct 1840 in Itawamba Co., MS. She was born 1828 in SC, and died Aft. 1860 in Hardeman Co., TN.

Notes for WESLEY BALLARD:
Source: 1850 Itawamba County Mississippi Federal Census Records, 1860 Hardeman County TN Census Records, Angela Eppley (chrokeez2@hotmail.com)
* 1850 - Living in Itawamba Co., MS - Ballard, Wesley 32 SC, Minerva 32 SC, Tabitha, 8 MS, Adeline 7 MS, Francis 5 AL, George 4 MS, Livi 2 MS, Drucilla 6/12 MS
* 1860 - Living in Salisbury, Hardeman Co., TN - Ballard, Wesley 42, Minerva 41, Tabitha A. 18, Adaline 17, Francis M. 14, George M. 13, Levi 12, Mary E 8, James 5, John 3, Martha 1

Children of WESLEY BALLARD and MANERVA BYRNES are:
17. i. TABITHA A.[3] BALLARD, b. 1842, MS; d. Aft. 1880.
18. ii. ADALINE BALLARD, b. 1843, Itawamba Co., MS; d. 1890, TN.

19. iii. *LEVI D. BALLARD, b. 1848, MS; d. Aft. 1880.*
    iv. *FRANCIS M. BALLARD, b. 1845, AL; d. Aft. 1860.*
    v. *GEORGE M. BALLARD, b. 1846, MS; d. Aft. 1860.*
    vi. *DRUCILLA BALLARD, b. 1850, MS; d. Aft. 1850.*
    vii. *MARY E. BALLARD, b. 1852, MS; d. Aft. 1880.*
    viii. *JAMES "JIM" BALLARD, b. 1855, MS; d. Aft. 1860.*
    ix. *JOHN BALLARD, b. 1857; d. Aft. 1880.*
    x. *MARTHA BALLARD, b. 1859; d. Aft. 1860.*

5. ELIZABETH[2] BALLARD (JAMES[1]) *was born Aug 1820 in GA, and died Aft. 1870. She married WILLIAM PANNELL 26 May 1840 in Blount Co., AL. He was born Abt. 1820 in TN or KY, and died Aft. 1870.*

Notes for WILLIAM PANNELL:
Source: 1850-1860 Marion County Alabama Federal Census Records
* 1850 - Living in Marion Co., AL- Pannel, William 29 TN, Elizabeth 30 GA, James R 8 MS, Daniel M M 7 MS, Martha Ann 5 MS, Jeremiah J 4 MS, Usley M AL
* 1860 - Living in Marion Co., AL - Pannel, William 40 farmer KY, Elizabeth 39 GA, James 17 MS,. Daniel 16 MS, Martha 15 MS, Jeremiah 15 GA, Usley 10 AL, George 8 AL, Lucretia 6 AL, Nancy 4 AL, Levi 2 AL, Mary 1 AL

Children of ELIZABETH BALLARD and WILLIAM PANNELL are:
    i. *JAMES RILEY[3] PANNELL, b. 1841, MS; d. Aft. 1860.*
    ii. *DANIEL M. PANNELL, b. Abt. 1844, MS; d. Aft. 1860.*
    iii. *MARTHA ANN PANNELL, b. 1845, MS; d. Aft. 1860.*
    iv. *JEREMIAH J. PANNELL, b. 1845, MS; d. Aft. 1860.*
    v. *URSLEY MATILDA PANNELL, b. 27 Jan 1850, AL; d. Aft. 1860.*
    vi. *GEORGE POTTER PANNELL, b. 1852, AL; d. Aft. 1860.*
    vii. *LUCRETIA PANNELL, b. 1854, AL; d. Aft. 1860.*
    viii. *NANCY PANNELL, b. 1856, AL; d. Aft. 1860.*
    ix. *LEVI GARRISON PANNELL, b. 1858, AL; d. Aft. 1860.*
    x. *MARY PANNELL, b. 1859, AL; d. Aft. 1860.*

6. ISAAC ASBURY[2] BALLARD (JAMES[1]) *was born 06 Apr 1822 in GA, and died 15 Dec 1902 in Hamilton, Marion Co, AL. He married (1) MARY "POLLY" MARKHAM 25 Jan 1848 in Itawamba Co., MS. She was born 1826 in TN. He married (2) HARRIET STEPHENS 1853. She was born 03 Sep 1836 in AL or MS, and died 22 Feb 1910.*

Notes for ISAAC ASBURY BALLARD:
Source: Helen J. Hopewell, Joyce Sanders fgs, 1850 Itawamba County MS, 1860 Marion County Alabama Federal Census Records, Angela Eppley (chrokeez2@hotmail.com), 1880 Marion County Alabama Federal Census Records, LDS-IGI Records, Angela Eppley (chrokeez2@hotmail.com), Automated Archives CD#5 Marriages
* 1850 - Living in Itawamba Co., MS - Ballard, Isaac 29 farmer GA, Mary 24 TN, Nancy 1 MS
* 1860 - Living in Pikeville, Marion Co., AL- Ballard, Isaac 38 GA, Harriet 23 MS, Nancy 11 AL, Susan 6 AL, William 4 AL, Francis 2 AL, Sarah 10/12 AL
* 1880 - Living in Marion Co., AL - Ballard, Isaac 58 GA NC NC, Harriet 44 AL SC SC, Martha J. 18 AL, George W. 14 AL, Darrell (or Daniel) 12 AL, Melvena 7 AL, Marion M. 5 Rosetta V. 9/12 AL daughter 10

More About ISAAC ASBURY BALLARD:
Burial: Smyrna Methodist Church Cemetery, Marion Co., AL

More About HARRIET STEPHENS:
Burial: Smyrna Cemetery, Marion Co., AL

Child of ISAAC BALLARD and MARY MARKHAM is:
    i. *NANCY[3] BALLARD, b. 1849, AL.*

Children of ISAAC BALLARD and HARRIET STEPHENS are:

　　　ii.　SUSAN[3] BALLARD, b. 1854, AL; m. JOHN T. POLLARD.
20.　iii.　WILLIAM ADNEY BALLARD, b. 10 Jan 1856, AL; d. 10 Jun 1929.
21.　iv.　FRANCES BALLARD, b. 22 Oct 1857, Marion Co., AL; d. 14 Feb 1936, Marion Co., AL.
　　　v.　SARAH BALLARD, b. 1860, Marion Co., AL; m. MR. POLLARD.
　　　vi.　MARTHA JANE BALLARD, b. 28 May 1862, Marion Co., AL; d. 18 Dec 1947, Jefferson Co., AL; m. KENNETH RILEY MILLICAN; b. 14 Sep 1861, Carroll Co., GA; d. 15 Nov 1945, Marion Co., AL.

　　　More About MARTHA JANE BALLARD:
　　　Burial: Hamilton City Cemetery, Hamilton, Marion Co., AL

　　　More About KENNETH RILEY MILLICAN:
　　　Burial: Hamilton City Cemetery, Marion Co., AL

　　　vii.　J. S. BALLARD, b. 19 Apr 1864, Marion Co., AL; d. 03 Aug 1876.

　　　More About J. S. BALLARD:
　　　Burial: Smyrna Cemetery, Marion Co., AL

22.　viii.　GEORGE WASHINGTON BALLARD, b. 23 Apr 1866, Marion Co., AL; d. 01 Jul 1936, Marion Co., AL.
23.　ix.　DANIEL "DAN" MONROE BALLARD, b. 24 Jun 1867, Marion Co., AL; d. 07 Feb 1943, AL.
　　　x.　FEMALE BALLARD, b. 1870, AL.
　　　xi.　MELVENA BALLARD, b. 1873, AL.
　　　xii.　MARION M. BALLARD, b. 01 Jun 1875, AL; d. 19 Mar 1965; m. HOLLIE; b. 22 Feb 1880; d. 19 Jan 1965.

　　　More About MARION M. BALLARD:
　　　Burial: Smyrna Cemetery, Marion Co., AL

　　　More About HOLLIE:
　　　Burial: Smyrna Cemetery, Marion Co., AL

　　　xiii.　H. W. BALLARD, b. 29 Jul 1877, Marion Co., AL; d. Dec 1877.

　　　More About H. W. BALLARD:
　　　Burial: Smyrna Methodist Church Cemetery.

　　　xiv.　ROSETTA V. BALLARD, b. 13 Sep 1880, Marion Co., AL; d. 09 Aug 1898.

　　　More About ROSETTA V. BALLARD:
　　　Burial: Smyrna Methodist Church Cemetery.

7. DANIEL MILTON[2] BALLARD (JAMES[1]) *was born 15 Mar 1827 in GA, and died 16 Dec 1901. He married* ELLEN MIREN, *daughter of* SARAH MIREN. *She was born 1832 in GA, and died 14 Mar 1908.*

Notes for DANIEL MILTON BALLARD:
Source: 1860 Winston County Alabama Federal Census Records, 1870-1900 Marion County Alabama Federal Census Records, 1880 Marion County Alabama Federal Census Records, Find A Grave
* 1850 - Living in Marion Co., AL - Ballard, Milliton 24 GA, Elizabeth 21 AL
* 1860 - Living in Winston Co., AL - Ballard, Milleton 35 GA, Ellen 27 AL, William F 7 AL, Phebe 5 AL, Isaac T 1 AL, Sarah A 1 AL
* 1870 - Living in Marion Co., AL - Ballard, M 46 AL, Emma 30 AL, Wiliam F 19 AL, Ballard T 15 AL, Isaac T 12 AL, Sallie A 9 AL, Albert 6 AL, Erasmus 4 AL, Garrison 2 AL
* 1880 - Living in Marion Co., AL with wife, children, mother in law and grand children - Ballard, Daniel 55 GA, Ellen 48 GA, Tinsley 21 AL(twins) Sarah An 21 AL, Allis 19 AL, Ellen, Clary Ann 15 AL , John R 12 AL, Isabell 11

AL, Alvin 8 AL, Mother in Law Sarah Miren, son in law Wather Mays, daughter Fabey and her children by Walter: Isabell and William
* 1900 - Living in Rye, Marion Co., AL - Ballard, Milton M - June 1833 GA GA GA farming, Ellen - Apr 1832 - 8 children 8 living GA GA GA

More About DANIEL MILTON BALLARD:
Burial: Ballard Cemetery, Hamilton, Marion Co., AL

More About ELLEN MIREN:
Burial: Ballard Cemetery, Hamilton, Marion Co., AL

Children of DANIEL BALLARD and ELLEN MIREN are:

       i.   WILLIAM F.³ BALLARD, b. 30 Nov 1848, AL; d. 29 Sep 1928, Marion Co., AL; m. TEMPERANCE "TEMPA"; b. 1856, AL; d. Aft. 1910.

          Notes for WILLIAM F. BALLARD:
          Source: 1880-1910 Marion County Alabama Federal Census Records
          * 1880 - Living in Marion Co., AL - Ballard, William F 28 farmer AL AL AL, Tempy 28 AL NC NC
          * 1900 - Living in Marion Co., AL - Ballard, William 48 - Jul 1851 AL GA GA, Tampa 48 - Apr 1852 AL GA GA 1 child, 1 child living
          * 1910 - Living in Marion Co., AL - Ballard, William F 57 AL GA GA, Temperance 54 AL NC GA 1 child 0 living

          More About WILLIAM F. BALLARD:
          Burial: Smyrna Cemetery, Marion Co., AL

24.   ii.   FEBBIE BALLARD, b. 17 May 1856, Pontotoc Co., MS; d. 03 Jul 1941, Crystal, Atoka Co., OK.
25.   iii.   SARAH ANN BALLARD, b. 15 Jan 1859, Marion Co., AL; d. 08 Jun 1934, Marion Co., AL.
26.   iv.   MARY ALICE BALLARD, b. 1861, AL; d. 1954.
       v.   ELLEN OREY BALLARD, b. 1863, AL; d. Aft. 1880.
27.   vi.   ISAAC TINSLEY BALLARD, b. 1863, AL; d. 1941.
       vii.   ALBERT BALLARD, b. 1864, AL; d. Aft. 1880.
       viii.   CLARA ANN BALLARD, b. 1865, AL; d. Aft. 1880; m. ALEX BERRYHILL.
       ix.   ERASMUS BALLARD, b. 1866, AL; d. Aft. 1870.
28.   x.   JOHN ROE BALLARD, b. 11 Jul 1867, AL; d. 24 Nov 1915, Lamar Co., AL.
       xi.   GARRISON BALLARD, b. 1868, AL; d. Aft. 1880.
       xii.   IDA BELLL BALLARD, b. 21 Mar 1870, AL; d. 05 Aug 1916; m. JAMES ELLIS RYE, 05 Jan 1888; b. 04 Apr 1869; d. 04 Sep 1945.

          More About IDA BELLL BALLARD:
          Burial: Kingsville Cemetery, Detroit, Lamar Co., AL
          More About JAMES ELLIS RYE:
          Burial: Kingsville Cemetery, Detroit, Lamar Co., AL

       xiii.   ALVIN BALLARD, b. 10 May 1874, AL; d. 21 Jan 1955, Hamilton, Marion Co., AL; m. MAUDE MURRAY; b. 09 Dec 1874; d. 01 Aug 1947, Hamilton, Marion Co., AL.

8. JESSE² BALLARD (JAMES¹) was born 1828 in GA, and died Aft. 1860. He married ELIZABETH HOGLIN 28 Mar 1848 in Itawamba Co., MS. She was born 1827 in AL, and died Aft. 1860.

Notes for JESSE BALLARD:
Source: LDS-IGI Records, Joyce Sanders, 1850 Itawamba County Mississippi Federal Census Records, 1860 Hemstead County Arkansas Federal Census Records, Angela Eppley (chrokeez2@hotmail.com), Automated Archives CD#5 Marriages
* 1850 - Living in Itawamba Co., MS - Ballard, Jessie 22 farmer GA, Elizabeth 23 AL, Martha 2 MS, Anthony 5/12 MS

1860 - Living in Hempstead Co., AR - Ballard, Jesse A. 35 GA, Elizabeth 34 AL, Martha 12 MS, Anthony 10 MS, Elean 8 MS, ?Uitman 6 MS, James 4 MS

Children of JESSE BALLARD and ELIZABETH HOGLIN are:
  i. MARTHA[3] BALLARD, b. 1848, MS. d. aft 1860
  ii. ANTHONY BALLARD, b. 1850, MS. d. after 1860
  iii. JAMES BALLARD, b. 1856, MS. d. after 1860

9. ARTIMISSA[2] BALLARD (JAMES[1]) was born 1821 in of Wilkinson GA, and died Aft. 1870. She married DANIEL MCCOOK. He was born Abt. 1811 in GA, and died 1881 in Wilkinson Co., GA.

Notes for ARTIMISSA BALLARD:
Source: Dana Sullivan (Sullivan@gibralter.net), Debra Veazey (debivz@charter.net), Family Data Collection - Births - Ancestry.com

Notes for DANIEL MCCOOK:
Source: 1850-1870 Wilkinson County Georgia Federal Census Records
1850 - Living in Wilkinson Co., GA - McCook, Danile 39 GA, Artimisay 29 GA, James W 9 GA, Mary 8 GA, Loucinda 5 GA, Daniel 3 GA, Hershal V 6 GA, Margery Ballard 77 GA, Jane Brady 39 GA
1860 - Living in Bloodworth, Wilkinson Co., GA - McCook, Daniel 50 farmer GA, Artimissa 40 GA, James B 18 GA, Mary 17 GA, Lucinda 15 GA, Daniel 12 GA, Hershal V I 10 GA, Francis M 8 GA, Narcissa 6 GA, George W 4 GA, Manerva 2 GA
1870 - Living in Wilkinson Co., GA - Mccook, Danl 58 farmer GA, Artemissa 51 GA, Daniel 22 works on farm GA, H J 20 (male) GA, Frances 19 GA, Narcissa 17 GA, George W 14 GA, Minerva 13 GA, Carrie 7 GA

Children of ARTIMISSA BALLARD and DANIEL MCCOOK are:
  i. JAMES[3] MCCOOK, b. 1841, GA; d. 02 May 1864, Richmond VA.

   More About JAMES MCCOOK:
   Burial: Hollywood Cemetery, Richmond, Richmond City, VA

29. ii. MARY MCCOOK, b. 20 Jan 1843, Wilkinson Co., GA; d. 01 May 1911, Wilkinson Co., GA.
  iii. LUCINDA MCCOOK, b. 23 Oct 1845, GA; d. Aft. 1860.
  iv. DANIEL MCCOOK, b. 28 Dec 1847, GA; d. Aft. 1870.
30. v. HERSHALL JOHNSON MCCOOK, b. 1849, GA; d. 1923.
  vi. FRANCIS MCCOOK, b. 1852, GA; d. Aft. 1870.
  vii. FRANK MCCOOK, b. 1854, GA.
  viii. GEORGE MCCOOK, b. 1856, GA; d. Aft. 1870.
  ix. JOHN W. MCCOOK, b. 1856, GA.
  x. NARCISSUS MCCOOK, b. 1856, GA; d. Aft. 1870.
  xi. ARTIMISSA MCCOOK, b. 1858, GA.
  xii. MINERVA MCCOOK, b. 1858, GA; d. Aft. 1870.
  xiii. CARRIE MCCOOK, b. 20 Oct 1863, GA; d. Aft. 1870.

10. JAMES[2] BALLARD (JAMES[1]) was born Abt. 1804 in GA, and died Aft. 1860. He married (1) MARTHA BRADY 01 Jan 1827 in Wilkinson Co., GA. She died Abt. 1843. He married (2) ALLEY BRADY 18 Jan 1844 in Upson Co., GA. She was born Abt. 1806, and died Aft. 1880.

Notes for JAMES BALLARD:
Source: James Ballard (mballard_1@email.msn.com), 1860 Upson County Georgia Federal Census Records
* DNA puts this branch matching William Ballard and Philadelphia
1850 - Living in (?) Co., GA - Ballard, James Ballard 46 Farmer GA, Ally 46 GA, Mahaly J. 18 GA, Martha M. 16 GA, Josephus 12 GA, Cicero 12 GA, Edmund 10 GA, Elizabeth 9 GA, Mary J. 12 GA, Wright, Jno 21 GA, Hester A. 19 GA, Whitfield, George 1 GA

* 1860 - Living in Upson Co., GA - James Ballard 63 GA, A 50 GA, Ed 20 GA, M J 28 GA, E 17 GA

Children of JAMES BALLARD and MARTHA BRADY are:

31.	i.	JAMES THOMAS[3] BALLARD, b. Abt. 1828, Gaston Co., NC; d. 24 Jul 1863, Chattanooga, Hamilton Co., TN.
	ii.	MAHALA JANE BALLARD, b. 18 Oct 1831, Upson Co., GA; d. 19 Dec 1908, Lineville, Clay Co., AL; m. THOMAS H. FOSTER, 09 Dec 1866, Upson Co., GA; b. 24 Dec 1835, Jasper Co., GA; d. 02 May 1926, Clay Co., GA.

More About MAHALA JANE BALLARD:
Burial: Providence Cemetery, Clay Co., AL

32.	iii.	MARY JANE BALLARD, b. 11 Dec 1839, Upson Co., GA; d. 15 May 1920, Troup Co., GA.
	iv.	MARTHA M. BALLARD, b. 05 Oct 1834, Upson Co., GA; d. 29 Dec 1908, Clay Co., GA; m. WILLIAM SMITH, 10 Dec 1857, Upson Co., GA; b. 05 Feb 1835, Upson Co., GA; d. 19 Apr 1923.
33.	v.	JOSEPH BALLARD, b. Abt. 1837, GA; d. Bef. 1880.
34.	vi.	CICERO BALLARD, b. Abt. 1838, GA; d. 08 May 1917.
	vii.	EDMUND BALLARD, b. Abt. 1840; d. Aft. 1861; m. FRANCES E. BRADY, 06 Oct 1861, Upson Co., GA; b. Abt. 1840.
	viii.	ELIZABETH BALLARD, b. Abt. 1843, GA; d. Aft. 1860; m. HARVEY M. TEAL, 12 Aug 1860, Upson Co., GA; b. Abt. 1835.

Generation No. 3

11. LEVI M.[3] WIGGINSTON (URSULA M.[2] BALLARD, JAMES[1]) was born 1839 in Itawamba Co., MS, and died Bet. 1850 - 1870. He married (1) MELISSA ROBINSON. She was born 1845, and died Aft. 1870. He married (2) FANNIE E..

Notes for LEVI M. WIGGINSTON:
Source: 1870 - Living in Itawamba County Mississippi Federal Census Records
* 1870 - Living in Itawamba Co., MS - Wigginton, Levy 31, Melissa 22, Mary 4, Thomas 20

Child of LEVI WIGGINSTON and MELISSA ROBINSON is:

	i.	MARY[4] WIGGINSTON, b. 1866; d. Aft. 1870.

12. JAMES W.[3] BALLARD (LEVI GARRISON[2], JAMES[1]) was born 1830 in AL, and died Aft. 1880. He married SARAH B. Abt. 1855. She was born 1825 in AL, and died Aft. 1880.

Notes for JAMES W. BALLARD:
Source: 1860-1880 Marion County Alabama Federal Census Records
* 1860 - Living in Marion Co. AL - Ballard, James 29 Farmer AL, Sarah 35 GA, Clary 14 AL, Mary 13 AL,, Sarah 6 AL, Samuel 4 AL
* 1870 - Living in Marion Co. AL - Ballard, J. W. 38 AL, Sallie 46 AL, Sallie J. 17 AL, Wm. 14 AL, Edward 7 AL, John 3 AL
* 1880 - Living in Marion Co. AL - Ballard, James 49, Sarah 55, Issac 16, John 13

Children of JAMES BALLARD and SARAH B. are:

	i.	SARAH J.[4] BALLARD, b. 1854; d. Aft. 1870.
	ii.	SAMUEL BALLARD, b. 1856, AL; d. Aft. 1860.
	iii.	WILLIAM BALLARD, b. 1856.
	iv.	JOHN BALLARD, b. Bet. 1863 - 1865, AL; d. Aft. 1880.
35.	v.	ISAAC EDWARD. BALLARD, b. 1864, AL; d. Aft. 1900.

13. JOSEPH[3] BALLARD (LEVI GARRISON[2], JAMES[1]) was born 1832 in AL, and died Bet. 1860 - 1870 in Franklin Co.,

AL. He married LUCRETIA. She was born 1830 in AL, and died Aft. 1910.

Notes for JOSEPH BALLARD:
Source: 1860 Marion County Alabama Federal Census Records
* 1860 - Living in Marion Co., AL - Ballard, Joseph 27 farmer AL, Lucretia 30 AL, Martha 8 AL, Eady 5 AL, America 4 AL, William 2 AL, Mary E. 13 AL

Notes for LUCRETIA:
Source: 1870-1900 Marion County Alabama Federal Census Records
* 1870 - Living in Marion Co., AL - Ballard, L 39 AL, Jane 16 AL, MA 14 AL, ME 10 AL, JW 8 AL
* 1880 - Living in Marion Co., AL - Ballard, Lucricia 47 AL, NC, NC, Joseph 16 son AL, AL, AL
* 1900 - Living in Marion Co., AL - Ballard, Lucrecie - Mar 1830 AL KY AL, James T. Kennedy nephew - June 1875 AR, Lucie A C Cantrell niece - Nov 1879 AL

Children of JOSEPH BALLARD and LUCRETIA are:
      i.   MARY E.[4] BALLARD, b. Abt. 1847, Marion Co., AL.
      ii.   MARTHA JANE BALLARD, b. 18 Jan 1853, Marion Co., AL; d. 16 May 1890, Marion Co., AL; m. JAMES CANTRELL; b. Abt. 1854, AL; d. Aft. 1880.

          Notes for JAMES CANTRELL:
          Source: 1880 Marion County Alabama Federal Census Records
          * 1880 - Living in Marion Co., AL - Cantrell, James T 26 farmer AL SC GA, Susan M J 27 AL AL AL, Mary E V 6 MS, John D 5 AL, Leander F 3 AL, Lucy A C 7/12 AL

      iii.   EADY BALLARD, b. 21 Feb 1855, Marion Co., AL; d. 25 Sep 1890, Marion Co., AL; m. BENNETT CANTRELL; b. 02 Sep 1851, Marion Co., AL; d. 28 Nov 1939, Hackleburg, Marion Co., AL.

          Notes for BENNETT CANTRELL:
          Source: 1880 Marion County Alabama Federal Census Records
          * 1880 - Living in Marion Co., AL - Cantrell, Bennett P 28 farmer AL SC GA, Edy M 25 AL SC SC, Lucreta J 6, Sarah A 1 AL

36.   iv.   AMERICA M. BALLARD, b. 15 Feb 1857, Marion Co., AL; d. 20 Feb 1936, Marion Co., AL.
      v.   SARAH E. BALLARD, b. 20 Jun 1861, Marion Co., AL; d. 08 Jul 1963; m. WILLIAM LUNSFORD; b. 1860; d. Bef. 1910.
37.   vi.   JOSEPH BALLARD, b. 09 Oct 1863, Marion Co., AL; d. 12 Aug 1908, Marion Co., AL.

14. ELIZABETH[3] BALLARD (LEVI GARRISON[2], JAMES[1]) was born 1836 in AL, and died 1922. She married ERASMUS ASA MIXON. He was born 1831, and died 1903.

Notes for ELIZABETH BALLARD:
Source: Marcelle Lewis (airnet@prodigy.net)

Child of ELIZABETH BALLARD and ERASMUS MIXON is:
      i.   CLARA ANNIE[4] MIXON, b. 1856.

15. ISAAC ASBERRY[3] BALLARD (LEVI GARRISON[2], JAMES[1]) was born 23 Mar 1841 in AL, and died 03 Jun 1912 in Marion Co., AL. He married MAHALA CAROLINE STIDHAM. She was born 11 Jun 1843 in AL, and died 24 Jan 1939 in Marion Co., AL.

Notes for ISAAC ASBERRY BALLARD:
Source: 1880-1900 Marion County AL Federal Census Records, Automated Archives CD, Vicki Whaley (Whaley6@aol.com)
* 1880 - Living in Marion Co., AL - Ballard, Isaac Asberry 40 AL AL AL, Mahala 37 AL AL AL, Albert J. 18 AL, Mary L. 14 AL, Anny I. 10 AL, Thomas W. 7 AL, Magnola E. 5 AL, Thomas W. AL

* 1900 - Living in Marion Co., AL - Ballard, Isaac M. March 1841 AL AL AL married 39 years, Mahala C June 1843 56 8 children AL AL AL, Magnolia E March 1876 24 AL, Darthula O March 1882 AL, Nettie M Mar 1888 AL

Children of ISAAC BALLARD and MAHALA STIDHAM are:

38.	i.	ALBERT JAMES[4] BALLARD, b. 19 Oct 1862, AL; d. 26 Dec 1912, Marion AL.
	ii.	MARY LOUELLA BALLARD, b. 1866, AL; d. 1936; m. WESLEY A. LINDSEY, 22 Dec 1887, Marion Co., AL; b. 1866; d. 1944.
	iii.	ANNIE ISABELLA BALLARD, b. 03 May 1870, AL; d. Apr 1959; m. JAMES M. LINDSAY, 23 Oct 1887, Marion Co., AL; b. 1864; d. 1936.
39.	iv.	THOMAS WINSTON BALLARD, b. 1873, AL; d. 1909.
	v.	MAGNOLIA E. BALLARD, b. 10 Mar 1876, AL.
	vi.	LULA EVELINA BALLARD, b. 30 Aug 1879, AL; d. 06 Feb 1962; m. HENRY DALTON LINDSEY, 01 Feb 1900, Marion Co., AL; b. 1870; d. 1942.
	vii.	DARTHULA BALLARD, b. 1882; m. MARTIN HARDEN; b. 1885; d. 1956.
	viii.	NETTIE MARCELLE BALLARD, b. 1887; d. 1972; m. THOMAS ROY MCCLAIN; b. 1888; d. 1977.

16. LEVI GARRISON[3] BALLARD (LEVI GARRISON[2], JAMES[1]) was born Bet. 1846 - 1848 in AL, and died Aft. 1900. He married ATHERILLA "ATHA" GAMILL 16 Jul 1868 in Hardin Co., TN. She was born 1850 in TN, and died Aft. 1900.

Notes for LEVI GARRISON BALLARD:
Source:1870-1880, Hardin County Tennessee Federal Census Records, 1900-1910 Chester County Tennessee Federal Census Records
* 1870 - Living in Hardin Co., TN - Ballard, Levi 23 AL, Atharilla 19 TN
* 1880 - Living in Hardin Co., TN - Ballard, 34 MS labor, Atha 30 TN, James 9 TN, Annie 7 TN, Sarah 4 TN, Colum 4/12 TN
* 1900 - Living in Chester Co., TN - Ballard Levi 1846 AL GA GA, Athalila 1850 TN, Robert E 1883 TN, Annie 1887 TN, Allien H? 1889 TN
* 1910 - Living in Chester Co., TN - Ballard, Levi G 64 married 2 times, married 42 years, AL GA GA, Al 60 married 1 time 42 years old TN, TN, TN

Children of LEVI BALLARD and ATHERILLA GAMILL are:

	i.	JAMES[4] BALLARD, b. 1873, TN. d. aft. 1880
	ii.	ANNIE BALLARD, b. 1873, TN. d. Aft. 1880
	iii.	SARAH BALLARD, b. 1876, TN. d. Aft. 1880
	iv.	COLUMBUS BALLARD, b. 1878, AR. d. Aft. 1880
40.	v.	ROBERT E. BALLARD, b. 1883, TN; d. Aft. 1910.
	vi.	ANNIE Z. BALLARD, b. 1887. d. Aft. 1900
	vii.	ALICE H. BALLARD, b. 1889, TN; d. 1946, Chester Co., TN; m. JOHN HARRISON SMITH; b. 29 Nov 1889, Chester Co., TN; d. 1962, Chester Co., TN.

17. TABITHA A.[3] BALLARD (WESLEY[2], JAMES[1]) was born 1842 in MS, and died Aft. 1880. She married DAVID W. "DAVE" NICHOLS 11 Feb 1864 in Union Co., IL. He was born 1832 in NY, and died Aft. 1880.

Notes for DAVID W. "DAVE" NICHOLS:
Source: 1870 Washington County Illinois Federal Census Records, 1880 Jefferson County Illinois Federal Census Records
* 1870 - Living in Washington Co., IL - Nichols 38 NY, Tabitha 28 MS, Laura B 5 IL, Luretta 4 IL, Andrew 3/12, Levi Ballard 22 MS
* 1880 - Living in DeSota, Jefferson Co., IL - Nichols, David 48 machinist NY NY NY, Ballard 38 MS AL AL, Laura B 14 IL, Lauretta 12 IL, Adam B 10, Leo B 8 IL (next door to Levi D. Ballard

Children of TABITHA BALLARD and DAVID NICHOLS are:

	i.	LAURA B.[4] NICHOLS, b. Bet. 1865 - 1866, IL; d. Aft. 1880.
	ii.	LAURETTA NICHOLS, b. 1868, IL; d. Aft. 1880.

iii. ANDREW NICHOLS, b. 1870, IL; d. Aft. 1880.
iv. LEO NICHOLS, b. 1872, IL; d. Aft. 1880.

18. ADALINE[3] BALLARD (WESLEY[2], JAMES[1]) was born 1843 in Itawamba Co., MS, and died 1890 in TN. She married JOHN A. LINEBERRY 13 Aug 1861 in Wayne Co., TN. He was born 1846 in Wayne Co., TN, and died 1902 in TN.

More About ADALINE BALLARD:
Burial: Culp's Chapel, Cemetery, Perry Co., TN

Notes for JOHN A. LINEBERRY:
Source: 1870-1880 Wayne County Tennessee Federal Census Records
* 1870 - Living in Wayne Co., TN - Lineberry, John 24 farmer TN, Adaline 22 TN, Lilly L B 5 TN, Mary E 4 MS, Fannie P 3 TN, Rebecca O 5/12 TN
* 1880 - Living in Wayne Co., TN - Linebury, John 35 farmer TN TN TN, Adline 32 TN TN TN, Lillie 16 TN, Bettie 14 TN, Fannie P 12 TN, Becka A 10 TN, Florence 8 TN, Orlean 8/12 TN. Allice 5 TN

More About JOHN A. LINEBERRY:
Burial: Culp's Chapel, Cemetery, Perry Co., TN

Children of ADALINE BALLARD and JOHN LINEBERRY are:
      i. LILLY LEE B.[4] LINEBERRY, b. 24 Apr 1862, Hardin Co., TN; d. 16 Sep 1946, Gibson Co., TN; m. (1) GEORGE SMITH ORR; b. 1866; m. (2) WILLIAM A. FRAZIER, 05 Sep 1897, Perry Co., TN; b. 20 Dec 1867.
      ii. MARY ELIZABETH "BETTIE" LINEBERRY, b. 14 Dec 1866, MS; d. 23 Aug 1934, Pemiscot Co., MO; m. JEFFREY CLIFTON; b. 1863.
      iii. FRANNIE PERMELIA LINEBERRY, b. 1869, Wayne Co., TN; d. 01 May 1955, TN.
      iv. REBECCA A. " BECKA LINEBERRY, b. 1870, Wayne Co., TN; d. Aft. 1880.
41.   v. FLORENCE LINEBERRY, b. 03 Oct 1872, Wayne Co., TN; d. 07 Aug 1947.
      vi. ALICE LINEBERRY, b. 1875, Wayne Co., TN; d. Aft. 1880.
      vii. ORLEAN LINEBERRY, b. 06 Feb 1880, Clifton, Wayne Co., TN; d. 15 Aug 1967, Mississippi Co., AR; m. JAMES THOMAS HALFORD; b. 03 Feb 1880, Wayne Co., TN; d. Jun 1970, Mississippi Co., AR.

        More About ORLEAN LINEBERRY:
        Burial: Bassett Cemetery, Bassett, Mississippi Co., AR

        More About JAMES THOMAS HALFORD:
        Burial: Bassett Cemetery, Bassett, Mississippi Co., AR

19. LEVI D.[3] BALLARD (WESLEY[2], JAMES[1]) was born 1848 in MS, and died Aft. 1880. He married ALIDA FOWLER 05 Jul 1873 in Collinsville, Madison Co., IL. She was born 1856 in IL, and died Aft. 1900.

Notes for LEVI D. BALLARD:
Source: 1870 Washington County Illinois Federal Census Records, 1880 Missouri Federal Census Records Soundex, Samatha (SamBailey5@aol.com)
* 1870 - Living in Washington Co., IL - Ballard, Levi 22 MS works on farm of sister Tabitha Nichols
* 1880 - Living in Jefferson Co., MO - Ballard, Levi D 30 MS, AL, AL, Alida 24 IL IL IL, Alonzo 6 IL, Albert 1 IL

Notes for ALIDA FOWLER:
Source: 1900 Madison County Illinois Federal Census Records
* 1900 - Living in Madison Co., IL with parents: Ballard, Lida Nov 1855 IL, Daisy Dec 1881 IL TN IL, William Mar 1885 IL TN IL, William Ma 1885, Harry Oct 1891 IL TN IL, Benjamin 1878 IL TN IL

Children of LEVI BALLARD and ALIDA FOWLER are:
42.   i. ALONZO[4] BALLARD, b. 1874, Madison Co., IL.

43.   *ii.*   ALBERT "BERT" BALLARD, b. 25 Jul 1878, Madison, IL; d. 15 Jan 1948, Lima, Allen Co., OH.
         iii.   DAISY BALLARD, b. 1881.
         iv.   WILLIAM BALLARD, b. 1884.
         v.   HARRY BALLARD, b. 1891.

20.   WILLIAM ADNEY[3] BALLARD (ISAAC ASBURY[2], JAMES[1]) was born 10 Jan 1856 in AL, and died 10 Jun 1929. He married (1) SADIE BYRD Abt. 1876. She was born 07 Jul 1854 in AL, and died 05 Jul 1894 in Marion Co., AL. He married (2) SYBLE P. Bef. 1900. She was born Aug 1852 in MS, and died Aft. 1920.

Notes for WILLIAM ADNEY BALLARD:
Source: 1880-1910 Marion County Alabama Federal Census Records
* 1880 - Living in Marion Co., AL - Ballard, Adney W. 24 (hard to read) 24, Bell, Pearl 2, Sindy Lee 45 aunt AL MS MS
* 1900 - Living in Bexar, Marion Co., AL - Ballard, William A - Jan 1856 AL AL AL, Cylva P - Aug 1852 MS N SC, Elmira I -Aug 1877 AL AL AL, Joseph L. Middleton - Apr 1877 AL GA GA
* 1910 - Living in Hamilton, Marion Co., AL - Ballard, William A 53 AL AL AL, Sibbie 54 no children MS TN SC, Jesse D Arnold 53 wd boarder
* 1920 - Living in Hamilton, Marion Co., AL - Ballard, Adney 62 AL AL AL, Sid... (hard to read) 65

More About WILLIAM ADNEY BALLARD:
Burial: Smyrna Cemetery, Marion Co., AL

More About SADIE BYRD:
Burial: Smyrna Cemetery, Marion Co., AL

Children of WILLIAM BALLARD and SADIE BYRD are:
         i.   BELLE[4] BALLARD, b. 1877, AL; m. JOSEPH L. MIDDLETON, 07 Sep 1900, Marion Co., AL; b. Apr 1877, AL.
         ii.   ELMIRA I. BALLARD, b. 11 Aug 1876; d. 04 Jan 1968; m. JOSEPH LAFAYETTE MIDDLETON; b. 21 Apr 1877; d. 07 Apr 1939.

                 More About ELMIRA I. BALLARD:
                 Burial: Smyrna Cemetery, Marion Co., AL

                 More About JOSEPH LAFAYETTE MIDDLETON:
                 Burial: Smyrna Cemetery, Marion Co., AL

44.   *iii.*   ELIZABETH PEARL BALLARD, b. Mar 1878, AL.

21.   FRANCES[3] BALLARD (ISAAC ASBURY[2], JAMES[1]) was born 22 Oct 1857 in Marion Co., AL, and died 14 Feb 1936 in Marion Co., AL. She married WILLIAM WASHINGTON SANDERSON. He was born 11 Nov 1848, and died 1900 in Marion Co., AL.

More About FRANCES BALLARD:
Burial: Smyrna Cemetery, Marion Co., AL

Child of FRANCES BALLARD and WILLIAM SANDERSON is:
         i.   LULA BELL[4] SANDERSON, m. HENRY AMY PERSER.

22.   GEORGE WASHINGTON[3] BALLARD (ISAAC ASBURY[2], JAMES[1]) was born 23 Apr 1866 in Marion Co., AL, and died 01 Jul 1936 in Marion Co., AL. He married JULLIETT JETTA CATHERINE OWENS. She was born 13 Jul 1867 in AL, and died 18 Jun 1959 in Jefferson Co., AL.

Notes for GEORGE WASHINGTON BALLARD:

Source: 1900-1930 Marion County Alabama Federal Census Records
* 1900 - Living in Hamilton, Marion Co., AL - Ballard, George W - Apr 1866 34 AL AL AL Farmer, Getta C 32 - July 1867 AL GA SC - 8 children 4 living, Bessie - Jan 1888 12 AL, Isac F - July 1893 AL 6, Vinnie M - Apr 1897 3 AL, George D - Apr 1900 2/12 AL
* 1910 - Living in Barnesville, Marion Co., AL - Ballard, George W 43 AL AL AL Farmer, Jetta C 42 AL GA SC, Isaac F 16 AL, Ninnie M 13 AL, Mintie C 8, Eva 2 AL, Claude O. 8/12 AL
* 1920 - Living in Hamilton, Marion Co., AL - Ballard, George W 53 AL AL AL farmer, Jetta 52 AL GA SC, Evie 12 AL
* 1930 - Living in Hamilton, Marion Co., AL - Ballard, George W 63 AL AL AL, Jetta 61 AL GA SC, Eva 22 AL

More About GEORGE WASHINGTON BALLARD:
Burial: Smyrna Cemetery, Marion Co., AL

More About JULLIETT JETTA CATHERINE OWENS:
Burial: Smyrna Cemetery, Marion Co., AL

Children of GEORGE BALLARD and JULLIETT OWENS are:
  i.   KATIE[4] BALLARD, b. 07 Nov 1885, Marion Co., AL; d. 08 Jun 1887.

        More About KATIE BALLARD:
        Burial: Smyrna Cemetery, Marion Co., AL

  ii.   MAUD BALLARD, b. 1887, Marion Co., AL; d. 08 Sep 1887.

        More About MAUD BALLARD:
        Burial: Smyrna Cemetery, Marion Co., AL

  iii. NINNIE MAE BALLARD, b. 13 Apr 1887, Marion Co., AL; d. 09 Feb 1998, Jefferson Co., AL; m. ALBERT MARTIN.

        More About NINNIE MAE BALLARD:
        Burial: Midway UMC, Adamsville, Jefferson Co., AL

  iv.   BESSIE BALLARD, b. 31 Jan 1889, Marion Co., AL; d. 04 Jan 1979; m. LEONARD BURLESON, 03 Feb 1907, Marion Co., AL.

        More About BESSIE BALLARD:
        Burial: 100F Cemetery, Greenwood, Leflore Co., MS

  v.   VERNIE BALLARD, b. 23 Nov 1890, Marion Co., AL; d. Aft. 1910.

        More About VERNIE BALLARD:
        Burial: Smyrna Cemetery, Marion Co., AL

  vi.   ISAAC FAUST BALLARD, b. 12 Jul 1893, Marion Co., AL; d. 21 Aug 1977; m. ERAH.

        Notes for ISAAC FAUST BALLARD:
        Source: 1930 Marion County Alabama Federal Census Records
        * 1930 - Living in Hamilton, Marion Co., AL - Ballard, Faust 36 AL AL AL, Erah 28 AL AL AL (living next door to George W.

        More About ISAAC FAUST BALLARD:
        Burial: Pleasant Hill Cemetery, Bethel, Turner Co., GA

  vii. PAUL BALLARD, b. 11 Aug 1895, Marion Co., AL.

More About PAUL BALLARD:
Burial: Smyrna Cemetery, Marion Co., AL

    viii.   GEORGE DEWEY BALLARD, *b. 01 Apr 1899, Marion Co., AL.*

More About GEORGE DEWEY BALLARD:
Burial: Smyrna Cemetery, Marion Co., AL

    ix.   EVAH E. BALLARD, *b. 08 Nov 1907, Marion Co., AL; d. 24 Jul 1962; m. JAMES DYER.*

More About EVAH E. BALLARD:
Burial: Smyrna Cemetery, Marion Co., AL

    x.   CLAUDE O. BALLARD, *b. 1910, Marion Co., AL; d. 24 Sep 1910, Marion Co., AL.*

23. DANIEL "DAN" MONROE[3] BALLARD *(ISAAC ASBURY[2], JAMES[1])* was born 24 Jun 1867 in Marion Co., AL, and died 07 Feb 1943 in AL. He married MARGRET M. WRIGHT 1885, daughter of MILES WRIGHT and MELINDA GREY. She was born 12 Sep 1863 in AL, and died 25 Oct 1952 in Hamilton Marion Co., AL.

Notes for DANIEL "DAN" MONROE BALLARD:
Source: 1900-1910 Marion County Alabama Federal Census Records, Angela Eppley (chrokeez2@hotmail.com)
* 1900 - Living in Rye, Marion Co., AL - Ballard, Daniel M - June 1848, Margeret M - Sep 1863, Dovie - July 1886, Dee A - Jan 1888, Effie - Aug 1889, Lolas J - June 1894, Frank - Nov 1898
* 1910 - Living in Monroe Co., AL - Ballard, Daniel M 41, Margaret 46, Lola 14, Luna 9, ruby 8, Gertrude 4

More About DANIEL "DAN" MONROE BALLARD:
Burial: Smyrna Cemetery, Marion Co., AL

Notes for MARGRET M. WRIGHT:
Source: Angela Eppley (chrokeez2@hotmail.com)

Children of DANIEL BALLARD and MARGRET WRIGHT are:
45.   *i.*   DOVIE[4] BALLARD, *b. Jul 1886, AL; d. Aft. 1900.*
46.   *ii.*   DEE CURTIS BALLARD, *b. 06 Jan 1888, AL; d. 09 Mar 1986.*
47.   *iii.*   EFFIE BALLARD, *b. Aug 1889, AL; d. Aft. 1900.*
48.   *iv.*   LOLA BALLARD, *b. 05 Jun 1894, AL; d. Aft. 1910.*
    v.   FRANK BALLARD, *b. Nov 1898, AL; d. Aft. 1900.*
    vi.   LUNA BALLARD, *b. 12 Jul 1900, AL; d. Aft. 1910.*
49.   *vii.*   RUBY BALLARD, *b. 10 Mar 1902, AL; d. Aft. 1910.*
    viii.   GERTRUDE BALLARD, *b. 10 Mar 1902, AL; d. Aft. 1910; m. SHORTY MILLIGAN; b. 1903; d. 1957.*

24. FEBBIE[3] BALLARD *(DANIEL MILTON[2], JAMES[1])* was born 17 May 1856 in Pontotoc Co., MS, and died 03 Jul 1941 in Crystal, Atoka Co., OK. She married WALTER MAYS. He was born 1856 in AL, and died 1902 in Choctaw Co., OK.

More About FEBBIE BALLARD:
Burial: Crystal Cemetery, Atoka Co., OK

More About WALTER MAYS:
Burial: Springs Chapel Cemetery, Hugo, Choctaw Co., OK

Children of FEBBIE BALLARD and WALTER MAYS are:
    i.   ISABELL[4] MAYS, *b. 1875, AL.*
    ii.   WILLIAM MAYS, *b. 1877, AL.*

25. SARAH ANN[3] BALLARD (DANIEL MILTON[2], JAMES[1]) was born 15 Jan 1859 in Marion Co., AL, and died 08 Jun 1934 in Marion Co., AL. She married GEORGE WASHINGTON RYE. He was born 18 Jun 1859 in Marion Co., AL, and died 25 May 1934 in Marion Co., AL.

More About SARAH ANN BALLARD:
Burial: Cooper Cemetery, Marion Co., AL

More About GEORGE WASHINGTON RYE:
Burial: Cooper Cemetery, Marion Co., AL

Children of SARAH BALLARD and GEORGE RYE are:
    i.   INFANT[4] RYE, b. 09 Jan 1887, Marion Co., AL; d. 09 Jan 1887.

        More About INFANT RYE:
        Burial: Cooper Cemetery, Marion Co., AL

    ii.   ROSA BELLE RYE, b. 19 Aug 1888, Marion Co., AL; d. 30 Mar 1962; m. ROSCO B. BROWN, 1904; b. 1883.
    iii.   AUSTIN RYE, b. 26 Jul 1890, Marion Co., AL; d. 02 Jan 1972, Escambia Co., FL.
    iv.   WILLIAM M. RYE, b. 30 May 1893, Marion Co., AL; d. 31 Aug 1992, Marion Co., AL.

        More About WILLIAM M. RYE:
        Burial: Cooper Cemetery, Marion Co., AL

    v.   CORNELIA RYE, b. 24 Mar 1898, Marion Co., AL; d. 02 Jul 1898, Marion Co., AL.

        More About CORNELIA RYE:
        Burial: Cooper Cemetery, Marion Co., AL

    vi.   WESLEY ASBURY RYE, b. 29 Mar 1898, Marion Co., AL; d. 22 Apr 1990.

        More About WESLEY ASBURY RYE:
        Burial: Ballard Cemetery, Hamilton, Marion Co., Al

    vii.   MARIETTA RYE, b. 19 Mar 1901, Marion Co., AL; d. 04 Mar 1997, Fulton Co., GA; m. ANDREW WASHINGTON KARR; b. 18 Oct 1898, AL; d. 30 Jun 1978.

        More About ANDREW WASHINGTON KARR:
        Burial: Cooper Cemetery, Marion Co., AL

    viii.   KEFFER RYE, b. 20 Sep 1903, Marion Co., AL; d. 22 Oct 1985, Lamar Co., AL; m. JESSIE DUKE; b. 07 Jun 1905; d. 15 Jan 1981, Lamar Co., AL.

        More About KEFFER RYE:
        Burial: Ballard Cemetery, Hamilton, Marion Co., AL

        More About JESSIE DUKE:
        Burial: Ballard Cemetery, Hamilton, Marion Co., Al

26. MARY ALICE[3] BALLARD (DANIEL MILTON[2], JAMES[1]) was born 1861 in AL, and died 1954. She married GIDEON LEWIS. He was born 03 Jul 1864 in Lamar Co., AL, and died 13 May 1929 in Marion Co., AL.

More About MARY ALICE BALLARD:
Burial: Ballard Cemetery, Hamilton, Marion Co., AL

More About GIDEON LEWIS:

Burial: Ballard Cemetery, Hamilton, Marion Co., AL

Children of MARY BALLARD and GIDEON LEWIS are:

    i.   ETTA[4] LEWIS, b. 23 Sep 1883, Marion Co., AL; d. 01 Jan 1974; m. WILLIAM NORTHINGTON.

         More About ETTA LEWIS:
         Burial: Rudicell Cemetery, Marion Co., AL

    ii. ELLIE LEWIS, b. 22 Feb 1886, Marion Co., AL; d. 18 Jan 1976; m. MARY NORTHINGTON; b. 1884.

         More About ELLIE LEWIS:
         Burial: Rudicell Cemetery, Marion Co., AL

    iii. ROY LEWIS, b. 04 Mar 1897, Marion Co., AL; d. 29 Jun 1952, Hamilton, Marion Co., AL.

         More About ROY LEWIS:
         Burial: Ballard Cemetery, Hamilton, Marion Co., AL

    iv. VETO LEWIS, b. 06 May 1901, Marion Co., AL; d. 14 Jan 1905.

         More About VETO LEWIS:
         Burial: Ballard Cemetery, Hamilton, Marion Co., AL

27. ISAAC TINSLEY[3] BALLARD (DANIEL MILTON[2], JAMES[1]) *was born 1863 in AL, and died 1941. He married ALICE. She was born 1871, and died 1926.*

Notes for ISAAC TINSLEY BALLARD:
Source: 1910 Bowie County Texas Federal Census Records
* 1910 - Living in Bowie Co., TX - Ballard, Isaac 55 AL AL AL, Alice 47 AL, James 25 AL, Lee R 21 TX, Florence 17 TX, Devoe 14 TX, Margaret 12 TX, Sam 8, Veto 6 TX, Frank nephew 23 AL

Children of ISAAC BALLARD and ALICE are:

    i.   JAMES[4] BALLARD, b. 1885, AL; d. Aft. 1910.
    ii. LEE R. BALLARD, b. 1889, TX; d. Aft. 1910.
    iii. FLORENCE BALLARD, b. 1893, TX; d. Aft. 1910.
    iv. DEVOE BALLARD, b. 1896, TX; d. Aft. 1910.
    v.   MARGARET BALLARD, b. 1898, TX; d. Aft. 1910.
    vi. SAM BALLARD, b. 1902, TX; d. Aft. 1910.
    vii. VETO BALLARD, b. 1904, TX; d. Aft. 1910.

28. JOHN ROE[3] BALLARD (DANIEL MILTON[2], JAMES[1]) *was born 11 Jul 1867 in AL, and died 24 Nov 1915 in Lamar Co., AL. He married MARTHA JANE PALMER 03 Jan 1889. She was born 20 Oct 1870 in Marion Co., AL, and died 04 Sep 1967 in Marion Co., AL.*

Notes for JOHN ROE BALLARD:
Source: 1900-1910 Marion County Alabama Federal Census Records, Find A Grave
* 1900 - Living in Rye, Marion Co., AL - Ballard, John R - July 1867, Martha J - Oct 1870, Maloritie - Nov 1888, Fleeter - Nov 1892, Artie V - July 1896, Alexander M - Sept 1898
* 1910 - Living in Rye, Marion Co., AL - Ballard, John R 43 AL, Martha J 39, Fleda j 16, Ida V 13, Henry W 12, Martha J 8, Victor 1 6/12

More About JOHN ROE BALLARD:
Burial: Ballard Cemetery, Hamilton, Marion Co., AL

More About MARTHA JANE PALMER:

Burial: Ballard Cemetery, Hamilton, Marion Co., AL

Children of JOHN BALLARD *and* MARTHA PALMER *are:*

50.   i.   MELVERDIA[4] BALLARD, *b. 09 Nov 1889, Marion Co., AL; d. 15 Oct 1985, Hamilton, Marion Co., AL.*

       ii.   FLEETA BALLARD, *b. 02 Nov 1893, Marion Co., AL; d. 02 Nov 1987, Detroit, Lamar Co., AL; m.* JAMES B. DALTON; *b. 15 Dec 1891; d. 21 Feb 1948.*

More About FLEETA BALLARD:
Burial: Ballard Cemetery, Hamilton, Marion Co., AL

More About JAMES B. DALTON:
Burial: Ballard Cemetery, Hamilton, Marion Co., AL

51.   iii.   ARTIE IDA V. BALLARD, *b. 29 Jul 1896, Marion Co., AL; d. 27 Jun 1954.*
52.   iv.   ALEXANDER HENRY BALLARD, *b. 25 Sep 1898, Marion Co., AL; d. 31 Oct 1967.*

       v.   MARTHA JANE BALLARD, *b. 01 Jun 1902, Marion Co., AL; d. 15 Aug 1962, AL; m.* V. BRYAN GREGORY; *b. 21 Jul 1900, AL; d. 02 Feb 1969, Marion Co., AL.*

More About MARTHA JANE BALLARD:
Burial: Carter Cemetery, Detroit, Lamar Co., AL

More About V. BRYAN GREGORY:
Burial: Carter Cemetery, Detroit, Lamar Co., AL

       vi.   VICTOR HOLLIS BALLARD, *b. 12 Sep 1908, Marion Co., AL; d. 16 May 1987, Marion Co., AL.*

More About VICTOR HOLLIS BALLARD:
Burial: Ballard Cemetery, Hamilton, Marion Co., AL

       vii.   GOLIE BALLARD, *b. 28 Dec 1910, Detroit, Lamar Co., AL; d. 13 Aug 1996, Lamar Co., AL; m.* NELL ROSE JACKSON; *b. 23 Jul 1915, Lamar Co., AL; d. 27 Apr 1989, Monroe Co., MS.*

More About NELL ROSE JACKSON:
Burial: Sulligent City Cemetery, Lamar Co., AL

      viii.   GERTRUDE IDA BALLARD, *b. 28 Dec 1913, Marion Co., AL; d. 18 Jan 1998, Hamilton, Marion Co., AL; m.* LYMAN RAY; *b. 01 Oct 1912, Lamar Co., AL; d. 05 Apr 1957, Marion Co., AL.*

More About LYMAN RAY:
Burial: Hamilton City Cemetery, Hamilton, Marion Co., AL

29. MARY[3] MCCOOK (ARTIMISSA[2] BALLARD, JAMES[1]) *was born 20 Jan 1843 in Wilkinson Co., GA, and died 01 May 1911 in Wilkinson Co., GA. She married* JAMES H. BLOODWORTH *24 Dec 1868 in Wilkinson Co., GA. He was born 26 Dec 1841 in Wilkinson Co., GA, and died 29 Oct 1924 in Wilkinson Co., GA.*

More About MARY MCCOOK:
Burial: Nunn-Wheeler Cemetery, Toomsboro, Wilkinson Co., GA

Notes for JAMES H. BLOODWORTH:
Source: Standard Certificate of Death, Wilkinson County Georgia Marriage Records, 1880 Wilkinson County Georgia Federal Census Records
* 1880 - Living in Wilkinson Co., GA - Bloodsworth, James 35 Farming GA GA GA, Mary 30 GA GA GA, Carrie A 8 GA, Permelia 6 GA, Daniel A 4 GA, James O 2 GA
* 1900 - Living in Wilkinson Co., GA - Bloodworth, James H 57 - Dec 1843 GA, Mary 56 - Jan 1845 - 8 children 7 living GA, Mollie 20 - Feb 1880 GA, George 17 - May 1883 GA, Berdie 16 - Apr 1884 GA, Lonzo 17 servant

More About JAMES H. BLOODWORTH:
Burial: Nunn-Wheeler Cemetery, Toomsboro, Wilkinson Co., GA

Children of MARY McCOOK and JAMES BLOODWORTH are:
      i.   CARRIE[4] BLOODWORTH, b. Abt. 1872, Wilkinson Co., GA; d. Aft. 1880.
     ii.   PERMELIA BLOODWORTH, b. Abt. 1874, Wilkinson Co., GA; d. Aft. 1880.
   iii.   DANIEL A. BLOODWORTH, b. Abt. 1876, Wilkinson Co., GA; d. Aft. 1880.
   iv.   JAMES O. BLOODWORTH, b. Abt. 1878, Wilkinson Co., GA; d. Aft. 1880.
    v.   MARY J. BLOODWORTH, b. Abt. 1880, Wilkinson Co., GA; d. Aft. 1900.
   vi.   GEORGE BLOODWORTH, b. May 1883, Wilkinson Co., GA; d. Aft. 1900.
  vii.   BERDIE BLOODWORTH, b. Apr 1884, Wilkinson Co., GA; d. Aft. 1900.

30. HERSHALL JOHNSON[3] McCOOK (ARTIMISSA[2] BALLARD, JAMES[1]) was born 1849 in GA, and died 1923. He married (1) SARAH BRASWELL. She was born 29 Apr 1859 in GA, and died 25 Mar 1888. He married (2) VICTORIA BRASWELL. She was born Oct 1862, and died Aft. 1900.

Notes for HERSHALL JOHNSON McCOOK:
Source: 1880-1900 Wilkinson County Georgia Federal Census Records
* 1880 - Living in Wilkinson Co., GA - McCook, Hersel 30 GA GA GA, Sarrah 21 GA GA GA, Iveson L 1 GA GA GA, Victoria L Brunswell 19 sister GA GA GA
* 1900 - Living in Wilkinson Co., GA - McCook, Daniel (????) Dec 1850, Vicktoria - Oct 1862, Iverson L - Dec 1879, Daisy V - Sep 1881, Robert H - Oct 1883, James B - Aug 1891, Temperence - Dec 1894, Daniel W - Aug 1896, Viney M - Feb 1899 GA

Children of HERSHALL McCOOK and SARAH BRASWELL are:
53.   i.   IVERSON L.[4] McCOOK, b. 09 Dec 1878, GA; d. 29 Dec 1955.
        ii.   DAISY VICTORIA McCOOK, b. 22 Sep 1880, GA; d. Aft. 1900.
       iii.   FRANK BALLARD McCOOK, b. 10 Oct 1882.
       iv.   SALLIE D. McCOOK, b. 16 Mar 1888.

Children of HERSHALL McCOOK and VICTORIA BRASWELL are:
     v.   ROBERT HERSHEL[4] McCOOK, b. 09 Aug 1890, Wilkinson Co., GA; d. Aft. 1900.
   vi.   JAMES B. McCOOK, b. Aug 1891, Wilkinson Co., GA; d. Aft. 1900.
  vii.   LITTLE ROY McCOOK, b. 03 Aug 1892, Wilkinson Co., GA.
 viii.   TEMPERANCE ARTIMISSA McCOOK, b. 14 Dec 1893, Wilkinson Co., GA; d. Aft. 1900.
   ix.   DANIEL WATSON McCOOK, b. 05 Aug 1896, Wilkinson Co., GA; d. Aft. 1900.
    x.   VENNIE MARVIN McCOOK, b. 28 Feb 1899, Wilkinson Co., GA; d. Aft. 1900.

31. JAMES THOMAS[3] BALLARD (JAMES[2], JAMES[1]) was born Abt. 1828 in Gaston Co., NC, and died 24 Jul 1863 in Chattanooga, Hamilton Co., TN. He married SUSAN BRADY 08 Jan 1856 in Upson Co., GA. She was born 27 Jul 1836 in Upson Co., GA, and died 11 May 1893 in GA.

Notes for JAMES THOMAS BALLARD:
Source: James Ballard (mballard_1@email.msn.com), 1860 Upson County Georgia Federal Census Records
* 1860 - Living in Upson Co., GA - Ballard, J. T. 22 GA, S. 23 GA, J A 3 GA, E 3 GA, G M. 7 GA (next door to his parents)

More About JAMES THOMAS BALLARD:
Burial: Hendricks Baptist Church Cemetery, Thomaston, Upson Co., GA

More About SUSAN BRADY:
Burial: Hendricks Baptist Church Cemetery, Thomaston, Upson Co., GA

Children of JAMES BALLARD and SUSAN BRADY are:

54.   i.   JAMES ALFRED[4] BALLARD, b. 10 Oct 1856, Upson Co., GA; d. 30 Jul 1929, AL.

      ii.   G. M. BALLARD, b. 1857, Upson Co., GA; d. Aft. 1860.

      iii.   LOU ELLA BALLARD, b. 25 Jul 1859, Upson Co., GA; d. 01 Oct 1930, GA; m. JOSHUA R. GORDY, 18 Aug 1875, Upson Co., GA; b. 18 Nov 1857, Upson Co., GA; d. 21 May 1932, Troup Co., GA.

          More About LOU ELLA BALLARD:
          Burial: Hillview Cemetery, LaGrange, Troup Co., GA

          More About JOSHUA R. GORDY:
          Burial: Hillview Cemetery, LaGrange, Troup Co., GA

      iv.   ANN OPHELIA BALLARD, b. 13 Nov 1860, Upson Co., GA; d. 28 Jan 1934, Upson Co., GA; m. DAVID C. ELLERBEE, 17 Apr 1878, Upson Co., GA; b. 19 Jan 1858, Upson Co., GA; d. 06 Dec 1936, GA.

          More About ANN OPHELIA BALLARD:
          Burial: Hendricks Baptist Church Cemetery, Thomaston, Upson Co., GA

          More About DAVID C. ELLERBEE:
          Burial: Hendricks Baptist Church Cemetery, Thomaston, Upson Co., GA

32.   MARY JANE[3] BALLARD (JAMES[2], JAMES[1]) *was born 11 Dec 1839 in Upson Co., GA, and died 15 May 1920 in Troup Co., GA. She married* WILLIAM MADDEN CHIPMAN. *He was born 04 Jul 1840 in AL, and died 15 Mar 1920 in Troup Co., GA.*

More About MARY JANE BALLARD:
Burial: Hillview Cemetery, LaGange, Troup Co., GA

Notes for WILLIAM MADDEN CHIPMAN:
Source: 1880 Upson County Georgia Federal Census Records, 1900 Troup County Georgia Federal Census Records
* 1880 - Living in Flint, Upson Co., GA - Chipman, Wm M 40 farmer MS SC SC, Mary J 42 GA GA GA, Lullulah S 15, Francis M 13, William 11, Martha F 10, Julius L 7, Alonzo 5, Georgia G 1, Ally Ballard 74 blind
* 1900 - Living in LaGrange, Troup Co., GA - Chipman, Will - July 1840 GA GA GA, Mollie wife - Dec 1839 GA GA GA, Mollie dau in law - July 1872 GA, Farris - June 1893, Frank - Dec 1895, Eva - May 1897, Berta - Jay 1875 GA, :Joseph - Sep 1893 GA , George - May 1899 GA

More About WILLIAM MADDEN CHIPMAN:
Burial: Hillview Cemetery, LaGange, Troup Co., GA

Children of MARY BALLARD and WILLIAM CHIPMAN are:

      i.   LULLULAH[4] CHIPMAN, b. Abt. 1865, GA.

      ii.   FRANCIS CHIPMAN, b. 21 Sep 1866, AL; d. 09 Jul 1896.

          More About FRANCIS CHIPMAN:
          Burial: Hillview Cemetery, LaGange, Troup Co., GA

      iii.   WILLIAM CHIPMAN, b. 09 Feb 1869, GA; d. 09 Apr 1929, Atlanta, Fulton Co., GA; m. LISIE A. WOODSON; b. 07 Mar 1871; d. 20 Apr 1941.

          More About LISIE A. WOODSON:
          Burial: Magnolia Cemetery, Atlanta, Fulton Co., GA

      iv.   MARTHA F. CHIPMAN, b. 09 Jan 1871, Meriwether Co., GA; d. 14 Jan 1934, Troup Co., GA.

More About MARTHA F. CHIPMAN:
Burial: Hillview Cemetery, LaGange, Troup Co., GA

    v.   JULIUS L. CHIPMAN, b. 01 Mar 1873, Meriwether Co., GA; d. 09 Nov 1899.

More About JULIUS L. CHIPMAN:
Burial: Hillview Cemetery, LaGange, Troup Co., GA

    vi.   ALONZO W. CHIPMAN, b. 28 Mar 1874, Meriwether Co., GA; d. 09 Nov 1943.

More About ALONZO W. CHIPMAN:
Burial: Hillview Cemetery, LaGange, Troup Co., GA

    vii.   JIMMIE CHIPMAN, b. Abt. 1877, Meriwether Co., GA.
    viii.   GEORGIA G. CHIPMAN, b. 31 Mar 1879, Meriwether Co., GA; d. 09 Mar 1949, GA.

More About GEORGIA G. CHIPMAN:
Burial: Hillview Cemetery, LaGange, Troup Co., GA

33. JOSEPH[3] BALLARD (JAMES[2], JAMES[1]) was born Abt. 1837 in GA, and died Bef. 1880. He married MARY FULTON 22 Aug 1858 in Upson Co., GA. She was born Abt. 1839 in GA, and died Aft. 1880.

Notes for JOSEPH BALLARD:
Source: 1860 Upton County Georgia Federal Census Records
* 1860 - Living in Upton Co., GA - Ballard, Joseph 23 GA, Mary 21 GA (next door to his parents)

Notes for MARY FULTON:
Source: 1880 Upson County Georgia Federal Census Records
* 1880 - Living in Flint, Upson Co., GA - Ballard, Mary 44 pauper GA, Jennie 19 GA, Mary F 17 GA, :Josie 15 GA, Cicero B 12 GA, Susan 9 GA, Zola 7 GA

Children of JOSEPH BALLARD and MARY FULTON are:
    i.   VIRGINIA "JENNIE"[4] BALLARD, b. Abt. 1861, GA; d. Aft. 1880; m. WILLIAM MILLER, 13 Jul 1884, Upson Co., GA.
    ii.   MARY F. BALLARD, b. Abt. 1863, GA; d. Aft. 1880.
    iii.   JOSIE BALLARD, b. Abt. 1865, GA; d. Aft. 1880.
    iv.   CICERO B. BALLARD, b. Abt. 1868, GA; d. Aft. 1880.
    v.   SUSAN BALLARD, b. Abt. 1871, GA; d. Aft. 1880.
    vi.   ZOLA BALLARD, b. Abt. 1873, GA; d. Aft. 1880.

34. CICERO[3] BALLARD (JAMES[2], JAMES[1]) was born Abt. 1838 in GA, and died 08 May 1917. He married MARY ADALINE ALLEN 29 Nov 1868 in Burnet Co., TX. She was born 15 Jul 1831 in MS, and died 18 Apr 1917 in Bell Co., TX.

Children of CICERO BALLARD and MARY ALLEN are:
    i.   EDDY[4] BALLARD, b. 22 Oct 1869, Lampasas Co., TX; d. 19 Apr 1917, Temple, Bell Co., TX.
    ii.   DEBORAH ANNIE BALLARD, b. 12 May 1872, Lampasas Co., TX; m. ASA N. GALLAWAY, 23 Dec 1890.
    iii.   FANNY MAY BALLARD, b. 20 May 1874, Lampasas Co., TX; m. JOSH T. BRISTOW, 07 Sep 1893.

Generation No. 4

35. ISAAC EDWARD.[4] BALLARD (JAMES W.[3], LEVI GARRISON[2], JAMES[1]) was born 1864 in AL, and died Aft. 1900. He married TERESA C.. She was born 1851, and died Aft. 1900.

Children of ISAAC BALLARD *and* TERESA C. *are:*
     i.   HENRY T.[5] BALLARD, b. Jun 1883, AL; d. Aft. 1900.
    ii. AUSTIN BALLARD, b. Feb 1886, AL; d. Aft. 1900.
   iii. HATTIE O. BALLARD, b. May 1882, AL; d. Aft. 1900.
   iv. JAMES O. BALLARD, b. Feb 1890, AL; d. Aft. 1900.
    v. TOBY BALLARD, b. Mar 1891, AL; d. Aft. 1900.
   vi. BOOKER E. BALLARD, b. Oct 1894, AL.

36. AMERICA M.[4] BALLARD (JOSEPH[3], LEVI GARRISON[2], JAMES[1]) *was born 15 Feb 1857 in Marion Co., AL, and died 20 Feb 1936 in Marion Co., AL. She married* JOSHUA GANN. *He was born Jun 1855, and died Aft. 1900.*

Notes for JOSHUA GANN:
Source: 1900 Marion County Alabama Federal Census Records
* 1900 - Living in Hackleburg, Marion Co., AL - Gram, Joshua - June 1855 AL TN AL farmer, America M - Feb 1857 AL AL AL, William L - Feb 1880 AL, Sarah A - Mar 1886 AL, Orlena A - Mar 1887 AL, Ellie M - Jun 1890 AL, James A G - Sep 1892 AL, Joshua A - 1894 AL

Children of AMERICA BALLARD *and* JOSHUA GANN *are:*
     i.   WILLIAM L.[5] GANN, b. 15 Feb 1880, Marion Co., AL; d. 23 Aug 1951, Hamilton, Marion Co., AL.
    ii. SARAH A GANN, b. 06 Nov 1886, Marion Co., AL; d. 16 Dec 1963; m. JAMES ROBERT HICKS; b. 10 Mar 1880, GA; d. 07 Aug 1958, AL.
   iii. ORLENA A. GANN, b. 21 Mar 1887, Marion Co., AL; d. 29 Nov 1954; m. THOMAS BROOKS.
   iv. ELLIE M. GANN, b. 23 Jan 1891, Marion Co., AL; d. 1975, Marion Co., AL; m. JORDON SULLINS.
    v. JAMES A. G. GANN, b. 11 Sep 1892, Marion Co., AL; d. 13 Jun 1978, AL.
   vi. JOSHUA A. GANN, b. 15 Dec 1895, Marion Co., AL; d. 18 Dec 1972.

37. JOSEPH[4] BALLARD (JOSEPH[3], LEVI GARRISON[2], JAMES[1]) *was born 09 Oct 1863 in Marion Co., AL, and died 12 Aug 1908 in Marion Co., AL. He married* JUDY LOU ELLA COLE *24 Aug 1887 in Marion Co., AL. She was born 15 Jan 1871 in AL, and died 17 Jan 1960 in Birmingham, Jefferson Co., AL.*

Notes for JOSEPH BALLARD:
Source: 1900 Marion County Alabama Federal Census Records
* 1900 - Living in Hackleburg Marion Co., AL - Ballard Joseph - Oct 1863 AL, Julie L - Jan 1874 AL 4 children 4 living, Minnie L - Mar 1888 AL, John Walter - Apr 1891 AL, Mary E - Nov 1893 AL, Jeneva - Aug 1896 AL, Oscar B Wilson laborer

Children of JOSEPH BALLARD *and* JUDY COLE *are:*
     i.   MINNIE L.[5] BALLARD, b. Mar 1888, AL; d. Aft. 1900.
    ii. JOHN WALTER BALLARD, b. 11 Apr 1891, AL; d. 16 Feb 1963, Smith Co., TX.

              Notes for JOHN WALTER BALLARD:
              Source: Smith County Texas Certificate of Death

   iii. MARY E. BALLARD, b. Nov 1893, AL; d. Aft. 1900.
   iv. JENEVA BALLARD, b. Aug 1896, AL; d. Aft. 1900.

38. ALBERT JAMES[4] BALLARD (ISAAC ASBERRY[3], LEVI GARRISON[2], JAMES[1]) *was born 19 Oct 1862 in AL, and died 26 Dec 1912 in Marion AL. He married* MARY AMY MOORE. *She was born 06 Feb 1860, and died 07 Feb 1945 in Marion AL.*

Notes for ALBERT JAMES BALLARD:
Source: 1900 Marion County Alabama Federal Census Records
* 1900 - Living in Marion Co., AL - Ballard, Albert J Oct 1862 married 19 years AL AL AL, Mary A Feb 1861

9 children AL AL GA, James B - June 1881 AL, Larence L - May 1884 AL, Reah A - July 1886, Van B - Nov 1888 AL, Ollie W - June 1890 AL, Henry C - Apr 1893 AL, Daniel M - Dec 1898 AL

Children of ALBERT BALLARD and MARY MOORE are:

55.   i.   JAMES BERRY[5] BALLARD, b. 08 Jun 1881, Marion Co., AL; d. 06 Nov 1958, Crockett Co., TN.
          ii. LAWRENCE LEE BALLARD, b. 10 May 1884; d. 07 Mar 1978; m. ETHEL GERTRUDE HOLLAND; b. Abt. 1884.
          iii. ANNIE REAH BALLARD, b. 12 Jul 1885, Marion Co., AL; d. 21 Dec 1978, Marion AL; m. WILLIAM M. LINDSEY.
          iv. VAN BUREN BALLARD, b. 30 Nov 1888; d. 21 Dec 1978, Marion AL; m. OLLIE HALL.
          v.   OLLIE W. BALLARD, b. 10 Jan 1890, Marion Co., AL; d. 04 Feb 1985, Marion Co., AL; m. TOMMIE B. MCCARLEY.
          vi. HENRY CLEBURN BALLARD, b. 29 Apr 1893, Marion Co., AL; d. 27 Jul 1963, Marion AL; m. (1) GLOW ETTA WEBB; b. Abt. 1895; m. (2) LINNIE STONE.
          vii. DANIEL M. BALLARD, b. 23 Feb 1894, Marion Co., AL; d. 16 Jan 1987, Crockett TN; m. IVIE HOLLIDAY.
          viii. CARTIE BALLARD, b. 29 Jun 1897, Marion Co., AL; d. 20 Mar 1917, Marion Co., AL.
          ix. TINNIE BALLARD, b. 12 Jul 1901, Marion Co., AL; d. 08 Jan 1965, Marion Co., AL; m. IRA J. CRAPO.

39.   THOMAS WINSTON[4] BALLARD (ISAAC ASBERRY[3], LEVI GARRISON[2], JAMES[1]) was born 1873 in AL, and died 1909. He married FLORENCE ELMINA EMERSON 04 Jun 1899 in Marion Co., AL. She was born 1876, and died 1947.

Notes for THOMAS WINSTON BALLARD:
Source: Vicki Whaley (Whaley6@aol.com), 1900 Marion County Alabama Federal Census Records
* 1900 - Living in Marion Co., AL - Ballard, Thomas W Aug 1873 AL AL AL, Florence E Oct 1876 AL, AL, AL

Children of THOMAS BALLARD and FLORENCE EMERSON are:

56.   i.   MAUDIE JANE[5] BALLARD, b. 31 Jan 1904, Marion Co., AL; d. 20 Apr 1971.
          ii. CARL BALLARD, m. ELLIS SPRUELL.
          iii. WARD BALLARD, m. LONA RUDICELL.
          iv. COY BALLARD, m. ALMA.
          v.   FRED BALLARD, m. AILEEN.

40.   ROBERT E.[4] BALLARD (LEVI GARRISON[3], LEVI GARRISON[2], JAMES[1]) was born 1883 in TN, and died Aft. 1910. He married ELLEN Abt. 1905 in TN. She was born 1884 in TN, and died Aft. 1900.

Child of ROBERT BALLARD and ELLEN is:
          i.   JAMES[5] BALLARD, b. 1901.

41.   FLORENCE[4] LINEBERRY (ADALINE[3] BALLARD, WESLEY[2], JAMES[1]) was born 03 Oct 1872 in Wayne Co., TN, and died 07 Aug 1947. She married ELISHA ANDREW WILEY. He was born 13 Aug 1869 in Perry Co., TN, and died 28 Jan 1960 in Memphis, Shelby Co., TN.

More About FLORENCE LINEBERRY:
Burial: Memorial Park Cemetery., Memphis, Shelby Co., TN

Children of FLORENCE LINEBERRY and ELISHA WILEY are:
          i.   NOAH SIDNEY[5] WILEY, b. 20 Oct 1894; d. 24 Mar 1956; m. MARY LOUIS ROBBERTS; b. 30 Jan 1896, Greene Co., IA; d. 12 Oct 1990, Memphis, Shelby Co., TN.

          More About NOAH SIDNEY WILEY:
          Burial: Memorial Park Cemetery., Memphis, Shelby Co., TN

          More About MARY LOUIS ROBBERTS:
          Burial: Memorial Park Cemetery, Memphis, Shelby Co., TN

ii. PERNIE A. WILEY, b. 25 Jul 1902, AR; d. 01 Feb 1988, Memphis, Shelby Co., TN.

More About PERNIE A. WILEY:
Burial: Memorial Park Cemetery., Memphis, Shelby Co., TN

42. ALONZO[4] BALLARD (LEVI D.[3], WESLEY[2], JAMES[1]) was born 1874 in Madison Co., IL. He married CORA. She was born Oct 1877 in MO, and died Aft. 1900.

Notes for ALONZO BALLARD:
Source: 1900 Marion County Missouri Federal Census Records, WWI Draft Registration Card
* 1900 - Living in Jasper, Marion Co., MO - Ballard, Alonzo P. Jan 1872 IL IL IL, Cora Oct 1877 MO NY GA, Deen H (f) Jan 1900 MO

More About ALONZO BALLARD:
Burial: New St. Marcus Cemetery and Mausoleum, Afton, St. Louis Co., MO

Child of ALONZO BALLARD and CORA is:
i. DEEN H.[5] BALLARD, b. Jan 1900, MO; d. Aft. 1900.

43. ALBERT "BERT"[4] BALLARD (LEVI D.[3], WESLEY[2], JAMES[1]) was born 25 Jul 1878 in Madison, IL, and died 15 Jan 1948 in Lima, Allen Co., OH. He married JEWELL SEWERT 21 Jan 1899 in Green Cp., MO. She was born 27 Feb 1879 in St. Louis Co., MO, and died 21 Apr 1952 in Wyandotte, Wayne Co., MI.

Notes for ALBERT "BERT" BALLARD:
Source: 1900-1930 Madison County Illinois Federal Census Records, 1940 Allen County Ohio Federal Census Records, WWI Draft Registration Card
* 1900 - Living in Madison Co., IL - Ballard, Bert A July 1878 IL TN IL, Jewell Feb 1879 IL, Fern Jan 1900
* 1910 - Living in Madison Co., IL - Ballard, Bert 37 married 11 years IL IL IL, Jewell 30 - 4 children MO OH Germany, Fern 10 IL IL MO, Fredie 7 IL, Charlotte 4 IL, Drew 1 IL
* 1918 - WWI Draft Registration Card - Albert Bonhlo Ballard - born July 25, 1878 coal miner living in Powell, Collinsville, IL - Nearest relative Jewell Ballard wife
* 1920 - Living in Madison Co., IL - Ballard, A. B 41 IL IL IL machinist railroad, Jewell 41 MO MI MO, Fred 17 IL, Charlotte 15 IL, Andrew 10 IL, Helen 8 IL
* 1930 - Living in Alton, Madison Co., IL - Ballard, Albert 52 IL IL IL, Jewel 51 MO MO CT, Helen Skipper (dau) 18 IL, Charley Skipper 22 (son in law) OH, Nancy Lu 21, Skipps Ballard 21 IL, Virginia 20 (dau in law), Jeanetta Ballard 4 gd, Ondge Trowbudge 20 boarder
* 1940 - Living in Lima, Allen Co., OH with daughter Charlotte and her husband Harry Lewis

More About ALBERT "BERT" BALLARD:
Burial: Woodlawn Cemetery, Lima, Allen Co., OH

More About JEWELL SEWERT:
Burial: Woodlawn Cemetery, Lima, Allen Co., OH

Children of ALBERT BALLARD and JEWELL SEWERT are:
      i. FERN[5] BALLARD, b. Jan 1900, IL or IN; d. Aft. 1910.
57.   ii. FRED W. BALLARD, b. 22 Feb 1903, IL; d. 1974, Greene Co., IL.
58.   iii. CHARLOTTE ALBERTA BALLARD, b. 1906, IL; d. Aft. 1940.
      iv. ANDREW "DREW" BALLARD, b. 1909, IL; d. Aft. 1910.
59.   v. HELEN G. BALLARD, b. 09 Nov 1911, IL; d. 20 Aug 2003, Madison Co., IL.

44. ELIZABETH PEARL[4] BALLARD (WILLIAM ADNEY[3], ISAAC ASBURY[2], JAMES[1]) was born Mar 1878 in AL. She married HENRY W. WRIGHT 18 Jan 1894 in Marion Co., AL. He was born Jan 1876.

Child of ELIZABETH BALLARD and HENRY WRIGHT is:
    i.   SEBORN V.[5] WRIGHT, b. Mar 1896, Marion Co., AL.

45.   DOVIE[4] BALLARD (DANIEL "DAN" MONROE[3], ISAAC ASBURY[2], JAMES[1]) was born Jul 1886 in AL, and died Aft. 1900. She married GEORGE RIDINGS. He was born 1888.

Notes for DOVIE BALLARD:
Source: Angela Eppley (chrokeez2@hotmail.com)

Children of DOVIE BALLARD and GEORGE RIDINGS are:
    i.   MARVIN[5] RIDINGS.
    ii.   LOY RIDINGS.
    iii. JACK RIDINGS.
    iv.   GOLDEN RIDINGS.
    v.   BONNIE RIDINGS.
    vi.   HATTIE RIDINGS.
    vii. RUBY LEE RIDINGS.
    viii. LILLIE RIDINGS.

46.   DEE CURTIS[4] BALLARD (DANIEL "DAN" MONROE[3], ISAAC ASBURY[2], JAMES[1]) was born 06 Jan 1888 in AL, and died 09 Mar 1986. He married ALDIE LEE FORESTER, daughter of GENE FORESTER and MARY MCLEROY. She was born 21 Sep 1891, and died 03 Oct 1977.

More About DEE CURTIS BALLARD:
Burial: Barnesville Cemetery, Marion Co., AL

More About ALDIE LEE FORESTER:
Burial: Barnesville Cemetery, Marion Co., AL

Children of DEE BALLARD and ALDIE FORESTER are:
    i.   TROY[5] BALLARD, b. 11 Sep 1906, Marion Co., AL; d. 22 Jun 1978, Lee Co., MS.
    ii.   CHLOE BALLARD, b. 26 Feb 1908; d. 1978; m. J. RAMON SANDERSON; b. 1905; d. 1990.

          More About J. RAMON SANDERSON:
          Burial: Hamilton Memory Gardens, Weston, Marion Co., AL

    iii. ROY BALLARD, b. 17 Dec 1909.
    iv.   IRENE BALLARD, b. 18 Nov 1911; d. 05 Sep 1969; m. HORSEA PARMEER.
    v.   GLEN BALLARD, b. 24 Sep 1913; d. 01 Jun 1994.

          More About GLEN BALLARD:
          Burial: Barnesville Cemetery, Marion Co., AL

    vi.   GIRTHIE BALLARD, b. 02 Dec 1915; d. 04 Sep 2007, Hamilton, Marion Co., AL; m. MILLARD H. WOODS; b. 12 May 1907; d. 28 Sep 1967.

          More About GIRTHIE BALLARD:
          Burial: Barnesville Cemetery, Marion Co., AL

          More About MILLARD H. WOODS:
          Burial: Barnesville Cemetery, Marion Co., AL

vii.   CLEETA BALLARD, b. 08 Mar 1918; d. 20 Jul 2011, Marion Co., AL; m. CECIL DUPREE WOODS; b. 18 Nov 1916; d. 05 Jul 1960.

More About CLEETA BALLARD:
Burial: Barnesville Cemetery, Marion Co., AL

More About CECIL DUPREE WOODS:
Burial: Barnesville Cemetery, Marion Co., AL

viii.   HECTOR BALLARD, b. 12 Jan 1920.
ix.   EDWARD LEE BALLARD, b. 04 Jan 1922; d. 12 Apr 1976.

More About EDWARD LEE BALLARD:
Burial: Barnesville Cemetery, Marion Co., AL

x.   LYMAN BALLARD, b. 03 Apr 1924, Marion Co., AL; d. 08 Feb 2001, Hamilton, Marion Co., AL; m. OPAL RAE WHITEHEAD.
xi.   BERLON BALLARD, b. 20 Apr 1926; d. 12 Jun 1997; m. WILMA LEE HIGHTOWER; b. 10 Oct 1930, Marion Co., AL; d. 03 Aug 2009, Marion Co., AL.

More About BERLON BALLARD:
Burial: Barnesville Cemetery, Marion Co., AL

More About WILMA LEE HIGHTOWER:
Burial: Barnesville Cemetery, Marion Co., AL

xii.   WORLIE BALLARD, b. 01 Mar 1928; m. DOROTHY LOUISE CHUNN.
xiii.   MARY DENE BALLARD, b. 1930.
xiv.   SARAH JEAN BALLARD, b. 1931.
xv.   EMMA LENE BALLARD, b. 12 Nov 1932; d. 26 Feb 2016; m. JACK THORNE; b. 03 Jan 1935, Franklin Co., AL; d. 25 Jun 2005, Franklin Co., AL.

More About JACK THORNE:
Burial: Franklin Memory Gardens, Russellville, Franklin Co., AL

xvi.   CURTIS FAY BALLARD, b. 19 Apr 1937.

47. EFFIE[4] BALLARD (DANIEL "DAN" MONROE[3], ISAAC ASBURY[2], JAMES[1]) was born Aug 1889 in AL, and died Aft. 1900. She married DALE BYRD. He was born 1890, and died 1928.

Children of EFFIE BALLARD and DALE BYRD are:
i.   EVA[5] BYRD.
ii.   REBURN BYRD.

48. LOLA[4] BALLARD (DANIEL "DAN" MONROE[3], ISAAC ASBURY[2], JAMES[1]) was born 05 Jun 1894 in AL, and died Aft. 1910. She married RICHARD CALVIN GREEN.

Children of LOLA BALLARD and RICHARD GREEN are:
i.   JESMA CLATIS[5] GREEN, b. 28 Jun 1915, Hamilton AL; d. 1961, Campbell MO; m. JAMES CHARLES TUCK.
ii.   SULA MAE GREEN, b. 28 Dec 1919; d. 1959.
iii.   HELEN MARIE GREEN, b. 16 Jul 1924.
iv.   HERMENIA LOUISE GREEN, b. 13 Dec 1927; d. 1949.
v.   LOLA PEARL GREEN, b. 21 Feb 1929.

49. RUBY[4] BALLARD (DANIEL "DAN" MONROE[3], ISAAC ASBURY[2], JAMES[1]) was born 10 Mar 1902 in AL, and died Aft.

1910. She married CLYDE HARNE. He was born 1894, and died 1965.

Children of RUBY BALLARD and CLYDE HARNE are:
    i.   DOROTHY[5] HARNE.
    ii. DOUGLAS HARNE.

50. MELVERDIA[4] BALLARD (JOHN ROE[3], DANIEL MILTON[2], JAMES[1]) *was born 09 Nov 1889 in Marion Co., AL, and died 15 Oct 1985 in Hamilton, Marion Co., AL. She married MURAW H. REAL. He was born 1889, and died 1946.*

More About MELVERDIA BALLARD:
Burial: Kingsville Cemetery, Detroit, Lamar Co., AL

Notes for MURAW H. REAL:
Source: 1930-1940 Marion County Alabama Federal Census Records
* 1930 - Living in Rye, Marion Co., AL - Real, Muraw 41 AL AL AL, Melverdia 70 AL AL AL, Middleton 19 AL, Lehern 18 AL, Annie L 16 AL, Nellie M 12 AL, John H 9 MS, Dexter 7 AL
* 1940 - Living in Rye, Marion Co., AL - Real, Muraw H 51 AL, Melverdia 50 AL, Nellie M 22 AL, John H 19 MS, Dexter D 17 AL

Children of MELVERDIA BALLARD and MURAW REAL are:
    i.   JAMES M.[5] REAL, b. 14 Jul 1910, Marion Co., AL.
    ii. LEEBURN REAL, b. 28 Sep 1911, Marion Co., AL.
    iii. ANNIE LEE REAL, b. 03 Jan 1914, Marion Co., AL; d. 15 Feb 1980, Marion Co., AL.
    iv. NELLIE REAL, b. 08 Aug 1917, Marion Co., AL; d. 13 Oct 2010.
    v. JOHN REAL, b. Abt. 1921, Marion Co., AL; d. Aft. 1940.
    vi. DEXTER D. REAL, b. Abt. 1923, Marion Co., AL; d. Aft. 1940.

51. ARTIE IDA V.[4] BALLARD (JOHN ROE[3], DANIEL MILTON[2], JAMES[1]) *was born 29 Jul 1896 in Marion Co., AL, and died 27 Jun 1954. She married MARVIN BROWN. He was born 02 Jul 1891 in AL, and died 08 Dec 1976.*

Notes for ARTIE IDA V. BALLARD:
Source: 1940 Monroe County Mississippi Federal Census Records
* 1940 - Living in Monroe Co., MS - Brown, Marvin 48 AL farmer, Artie V 43 AL, Milton 20 AL, Dorothy 14 AL, Gera 10AL

More About ARTIE IDA V. BALLARD:
Burial: Peace Chapel Cemetery, Smithville, Monroe Co., MS

Notes for MARVIN BROWN:
Source: 1920 Marion County Alabama Federal Census Records
* 1920 - Living in Rye, Marion Co., AL - Brown, Marvin 28 AL, Artier 23 AL, Jessimer 4 4/12 AL, Ruby Maxine 1 4/12 AL

More About MARVIN BROWN:
Burial: Peace Chapel Cemetery, Smithville, Monroe Co., MS

Children of ARTIE BALLARD and MARVIN BROWN are:
    i.   JESSIMER[5] BROWN, b. Abt. 1915, Marion Co., AL; d. Aft. 1920.
    ii. RUBY MAXINE BROWN, b. Abt. 1918, Marion Co., AL; d. Aft. 1920.
    iii. MILTON BROWN, b. Abt. 1920, Marion Co., AL; d. Aft. 1940.
    iv. DOROTHY BROWN, b. Abt. 1926, Marion Co., AL; d. Aft. 1940.
    v. GERA BROWN, b. Abt. 1930, Marion Co., AL; d. Aft. 1940.

52. ALEXANDER HENRY[4] BALLARD (JOHN ROE[3], DANIEL MILTON[2], JAMES[1]) *was born 25 Sep 1898 in Marion Co., AL,* *and died 31 Oct 1967. He married FLORA HALL. She was born 26 Oct 1898 in Hamilton, Marion Co., AL, and died 21 Oct 1996 in Marion Co., AL.*

Notes for ALEXANDER HENRY BALLARD:
Source: 1920 Marion County Alabama Federal Census Records, 1930-1940 Lamar County Alabama Federal Census Records
* 1920 - Living in Rye, Marion Co., AL - Ballard, Alex H 21 farmer AL, Flora 21 AL
* 1930 - Living in Millville, Lamar Co., AL - Ballard, Alexander H 31 AL, Flora 31 AL, Joyce B 8 AL., Janina J 4/12 AL
* 1940 - Living in Millville, Lamar Co., AL - Ballard, Alexander 41 AL, Flora 41 AL, Joyce 18 AL, Jania 10 AL

More About ALEXANDER HENRY BALLARD:
Burial: Ballard Cemetery, Hamilton, Marion Co., AL

More About FLORA HALL:
Burial: Ballard Cemetery, Hamilton, Marion Co., AL

Children of ALEXANDER BALLARD and FLORA HALL are:
>   i.   JOYCE[5] BALLARD, b. Abt. 1922, AL; d. Aft. 1940.
>   ii. JANIA BALLARD, b. Abt. 1930, AL; d. Aft. 1940.

53. IVERSON L.[4] McCOOK (HERSHALL JOHNSON[3], ARTIMISSA[2] BALLARD, JAMES[1]) *was born 09 Dec 1878 in GA, and died 29 Dec 1955. He married NELLIE GRANTHAM. She was born 10 Jun 1887, and died 30 Mar 1952.*

Child of IVERSON McCOOK and NELLIE GRANTHAM is:
>   i.   IRA[5] McCOOK, b. 16 Jan 1920; m. ANNETTE BUCHANS; b. 20 Nov 1922.

54. JAMES ALFRED[4] BALLARD (JAMES THOMAS[3], JAMES[2], JAMES[1]) *was born 10 Oct 1856 in Upson Co., GA, and died 30 Jul 1929 in AL. He married LUGENIA FRANCES WILLIAMS 09 Jan 1878 in Upson Co., GA, daughter of WILLIAM WILLIAMS and ELIZABETH WYATT. She was born 12 Jan 1862 in Upson Co., GA, and died 12 Apr 1936 in Calhoun Co., AL.*

Notes for JAMES ALFRED BALLARD:
Source: 1880 Upson County Georgia Federal Census Records, 1900-1910 Clay County Alabama Federal Census Records, James Ballard (mballard_1@email.msn.com)
* 1880 - Living in Flint, Upson Co., GA - Ballard, James 23 farm laborer GA GA GA, Lou 18 GA GA GA
* 1900 - Living in Fox Creek, Clay Co., AL - Ballard, James A - Oct 1856 GA GA GA, Francis - Jan 1862 GA GA GA, William - Sept 1881 GA, Bennet F - Feb 1886 GA, Nathan - Dec 1887 GA, Emett - May 1890 GA, John A. Williams - Jan 1872 brother in law GA, Harris W. Williams - Apr 1837 wd father in law GA
* 1910 - Living in Clay Co., AL - Ballard, James A 53 GA GA GA, Lou F 48 - 8 children 4 living, Emmett 19 GA, Benjamin F 26, Mary I 24 AL

More About LUGENIA FRANCES WILLIAMS:
Burial: Blue Eye Cemetery, Talladega Co., AL

Children of JAMES BALLARD and LUGENIA WILLIAMS are:
60.	i.	WILLIAM THOMAS[5] BALLARD, b. 17 Sep 1880, Upson Co., GA; d. 05 Mar 1953, Lineville, Clay Co., AL.
61.	ii.	BENJAMIN FRANKLIN BALLARD, b. 15 Feb 1884, Meriweather Co., GA; d. 19 Nov 1956, Anniston, Calhoun Co., AL.
	iii.	NATHAN BALLARD, b. 23 Dec 1888, GA; d. 02 Nov 1936; m. CORA BROOKS; b. 09 Apr 1891, Weston GA; d. 20 Dec.
62.	iv.	JAMES EMMETT BALLARD, b. 13 May 1890, GA; d. 18 Apr 1954, Lineville, Clay Co., AL.

Generation No. 5

55. JAMES BERRY[5] BALLARD (ALBERT JAMES[4], ISAAC ASBERRY[3], LEVI GARRISON[2], JAMES[1]) *was born 08 Jun 1881 in Marion AL, and died 06 Nov 1958 in Crockett TN. He married* ALICE ELMIRA COCHRAN *01 Jan 1907. She was born 07 Dec 1886 in MS, and died 14 Jan 1971 in Stigler Haskell OK.*

Children of JAMES BALLARD *and* ALICE COCHRAN *are:*
     i.   LETHA[6] BALLARD, *b. Bet. 1908 - 1928.*
    ii.   LURAL JETTRA BALLARD, *b. Bet. 1908 - 1928.*
   iii. JAMES ELIOT BALLARD, *b. Bet. 1908 - 1928.*
    iv. TALTON BALLARD, *b. Bet. 1908 - 1928.*
    v.   LONA GERTRUDE, *b. 13 Oct 1909.*

56. MAUDIE JANE[5] BALLARD (THOMAS WINSTON[4], ISAAC ASBERRY[3], LEVI GARRISON[2], JAMES[1]) *was born 31 Jan 1904 in Marion Co., AL, and died 20 Apr 1971. She married* WILLIE RENON NORTON.

Child of MAUDIE BALLARD *and* WILLIE NORTON *is:*
63.   i.   BETTY JANE[6] NORTON.

57. FRED W.[5] BALLARD (ALBERT "BERT"[4], LEVI D.[3], WESLEY[2], JAMES[1]) *was born 22 Feb 1903 in IL, and died 1974 in Greene Co., IL. He married (1)* MINA M. SIEBENMANN. *She was born 1905. He married (2)* VIVIAN CLARK *Aft. 1930. She was born 1906, and died 1988.*

Notes for FRED W. BALLARD:
Source: 1930 Madison County Illinois Federal Census Records
* 1930 - Living in Alton, Madison Co., IL - Ballard, Fred 27 IL IL MO, Vivian 22 IL IL IL, Doris G 4 9/12 IL, Shirley F 1 11/12 IL

Children of FRED BALLARD *and* VIVIAN CLARK *are:*
     i.   DORIS JEAN[6] BALLARD, *b. 18 Jul 1925, Madison Co., IL; d. 2003.*
    ii.   SHIRLEY F. BALLARD, *b. 06 Apr 1928, Madison Co., IL; d. 2018, Madison Co., IL; m.* WILLIAM ENNIS.
   iii. DALE BALLARD, *b. 22 Aug 1930, Madison Co., IL; d. 16 Sep 1950, Korean war.*

58. CHARLOTTE ALBERTA[5] BALLARD (ALBERT "BERT"[4], LEVI D.[3], WESLEY[2], JAMES[1]) *was born 1906 in IL, and died Aft. 1940. She married (1)* HARRY CARTER LEWIS *Abt. 1930. He was born 1898 in NY, and died Aft. 1940. She married (2)* ELBERT R. WALL *22 Oct 1949 in Lucas Co., OH.*

Notes for HARRY CARTER LEWIS:
Source: 1940 Allen County Ohio Federal Census Records
* 1940 - Living in Lima, Allen Co., OH - Lewis, Harry 42 NY, Charlotte 34 IL, Tommy 9 IL, Dick 1 OH, Bert Ballard father in law 62 IL, Jewell mother in law 60 MO

Children of CHARLOTTE BALLARD *and* HARRY LEWIS *are:*
     i.   TOMMY[6] LEWIS, *b. 1931, IL; d. Aft. 1940.*
    ii.   DICK LEWIS, *b. 1939, OH; d. Aft. 1940.*

59. HELEN G.[5] BALLARD (ALBERT "BERT"[4], LEVI D.[3], WESLEY[2], JAMES[1]) *was born 09 Nov 1911 in IL, and died 20 Aug 2003 in Madison Co., IL. She married* CHARLES SKIPPER. *He was born 26 Mar 1908 in OH, and died 1979 in Madison Co., IL.*

More About HELEN G. BALLARD:
Burial: Valhalla Memorial Park and Mausoleum, Godfrey, Madison Co., IL

Notes for CHARLES SKIPPER:
Source: 1940 Madison County Illinois Federal Census Records
* 1940 - Living in Alton, Madison Co., IL - Skipper, Charles 31 OH, Helen 28 IL, Nancy L 10 IL, Norma J 9 IL

Children of HELEN BALLARD and CHARLES SKIPPER are:
     i.   NANCY L.[6] SKIPPER, b. Abt. 1930, IL; d. Aft. 1940.
    ii.   NORMA J. SKIPPER, b. Abt. 1931, IL; d. Aft. 1940.

60. WILLIAM THOMAS[5] BALLARD (*JAMES ALFRED[4], JAMES THOMAS[3], JAMES[2], JAMES[1]*) was born 17 Sep 1880 in Upson Co., GA, and died 05 Mar 1953 in Lineville, Clay Co., AL. He married MARTHA EMMA SMITH 09 Dec 1903. She was born 14 Oct 1885 in AL, and died 31 Mar 1969 in AL.

Notes for WILLIAM THOMAS BALLARD:
Source: 1910 Clay County Alabama Federal Census Records
* 1910 - Living in Clay Co., AL - Ballard, William T 29 GA, Martha E 23 3 child/living AL, Lavelle 5 AL, Smith 3 AL, Byron 7/12 AL

Children of WILLIAM BALLARD and MARTHA SMITH are:
     i.   LAVELLE[6] BALLARD, b. 1905, Clay Co., AL.
    ii.   SMITH BALLARD, b. 1907, Clay Co., AL.
   iii.   BYRON BALLARD, b. 1909, Clay Co., AL.

61. BENJAMIN FRANKLIN[5] BALLARD (*JAMES ALFRED[4], JAMES THOMAS[3], JAMES[2], JAMES[1]*) was born 15 Feb 1884 in Meriweather Co., GA, and died 19 Nov 1956 in Anniston, Calhoun Co., AL. He married MARY ISABELL PATTERSON 26 Dec 1909 in Talladega Co., AL. She was born 29 Mar 1885 in Talladega Co., AL, and died 17 Apr 1971 in Anniston Calhoun Co., AL.

More About BENJAMIN FRANKLIN BALLARD:
Burial: Forestlawn Gardens and Mausoleum, Anniston, Calhoun Co., AL

More About MARY ISABELL PATTERSON:
Burial: Forestlawn Gardens and Mausoleum, Anniston, Calhoun Co., AL

Children of BENJAMIN BALLARD and MARY PATTERSON are:
     i.   JAMES DUDLEY[6] BALLARD, b. 05 May 1913, Clay Co., AL; d. 15 Apr 1983, Anniston, Calhoun Co., AL; m. MARY LOU NORTON; b. 25 Dec 1913, Anniston, Calhoun Co., AL; d. 19 Mar 2014, Anniston, Calhoun Co., AL.

        More About JAMES DUDLEY BALLARD:
        Burial: Forestlawn Gardens and Mausoleum, Anniston, Calhoun Co. AL

    ii.   ELMER GERALD BALLARD, b. 1918, Clay Co., AL; d. 1997; m. CATHERINE KNIGHT; b. 23 Feb 1923; d. 28 Sep 2008.

        More About ELMER GERALD BALLARD:
        Burial: Forestlawn Gardens and Mausoleum, Anniston, Calhoun Co., AL

        More About CATHERINE KNIGHT:
        Burial: Forestlawn Gardens and Mausoleum, Anniston, Calhoun Co., AL

   iii.   DAVID ALEXANDER BALLARD, b. 13 Sep 1921, Clay Co., AL; d. 23 Jul 2014, St. Clair Co., AL; m. MARTHA BLACK; b. 14 Mar 1924; d. 30 Aug 2011.

        More About DAVID ALEXANDER BALLARD:

Burial: Forestlawn Gardens and Mausoleum, Anniston, Calhoun Co., AL

More About MARTHA BLACK:
Burial: Forestlawn Gardens and Mausoleum, Anniston, Calhoun Co., AL

62. JAMES EMMETT[5] BALLARD (JAMES ALFRED[4], JAMES THOMAS[3], JAMES[2], JAMES[1]) *was born 13 May 1890 in GA, and died 18 Apr 1954 in Lineville, Clay Co., AL. He married ROSE L. SIMS. She was born 24 Oct 1892 in AL, and died 17 Sep 1977 in Lineville Clay Co., AL.*

Notes for JAMES EMMETT BALLARD:
Source: 1920-1930 Clay County Alabama Federal Census Records

* 1920 - Living in Copper Mine, Clay Co., AL - Ballard, Emett 29 AL, Rosie L 27 AL, Alma E 5 AL, Mary S 3 6/12 AL, Francis L 1/12
* 1930 - Living in Copper Mine, Clay Co., AL - Ballard, Emmett 39 GA, Rosa 35 AL, Alma E 14 AL, Mary S 13 AL, Lucile 9 AL hard to read female 7 AL

Children of JAMES BALLARD and ROSE SIMS are:

     i.   ALMA E.[6] BALLARD, b. 1915, Clay Co., AL; d. Aft. 1930.
    ii.   MARY S. BALLARD, b. 1916, Clay Co., AL; d. Aft. 1930.
   iii. FRANCIS LUCILE BALLARD, b. 1920, Clay Co., AL; d. Aft. 1930.
   iv. FEMALE BALLARD, b. 1923, Clay Co., AL; d. Aft. 1930.

Generation No. 6

63. BETTY JANE[6] NORTON (MAUDIE JANE[5] BALLARD, THOMAS WINSTON[4], ISAAC ASBERRY[3], LEVI GARRISON[2], JAMES[1]) *She married WILLIAM JAMES TURMAN, SR..*

Child of BETTY NORTON and WILLIAM TURMAN is:
     i.   VICKI DELEIGH[7] TURMAN, m. LLOYD ALLEN PENNY.

James H. Ballard

Generation No. 1

1. JAMES H.[1] BALLARD *was born 24 Feb 1815 in Wilkinson Co., GA, and died 25 Feb 1855 in Tuscaloosa Co., AL. He married* NANCY A. FARMER *25 Oct 1838 in Taliaferro Co., GA. She was born 15 Oct 1822 in GA, and died 01 Apr 1873 in Tuscaloosa Co., AL.*

Notes for JAMES H. BALLARD:
Source: Eunice Brown (Eunice M@webtv.net), Beverly Killian (beverlykillian@starband.net), William David Farnham (WW2X57@aol.com)

* 1850 - Living in Tuscaloosa Co., AL - Ballard, James H. 35 GA farmer, Nancy A 27 AL, Herman O 10 AL, Elijah 7 AL, Sarah 5 AL, William H 2 AL, Henry 8/12 AL

More About JAMES H. BALLARD:
Burial: Mount Pleasant Shakerag Cemetery Tuscaloosa, Tuscaloosa Co., AL

Notes for NANCY A. FARMER:
Source: Tuscaloosa County Alabama Federal census Records

* 1860 - Living in Tuscaloosa Co., AL - Ballard, Nancy 37 F GA Planter, Thomas 19 M GA, Elijah 16 M AL, Sarah 14 F AL, William 12 M AL, Henry 10 M AL, Josiah 07 M AL, James 05 M AL

More About NANCY A. FARMER:
Burial: Mount Pleasant Shakerag Cemetery Tuscaloosa, Tuscaloosa Co., AL

Children of JAMES BALLARD *and* NANCY FARMER *are:*

2.	i.	THOMAS DANIEL[2] BALLARD, *b. Mar 1841, AL; d. 11 Apr 1901.*
3.	ii.	ELIJAH JASPER BALLARD, *b. 23 Sep 1843, AL; d. 26 Sep 1894, Howard Co., TX.*
	iii.	SARAH ELIZABETH BALLARD, *b. 1846, AL; d. 1922; m.* JOSEPH HEWETT.

More About SARAH ELIZABETH BALLARD:
Burial: Hillcrest Cemetery, Temple, Bell Co., TX

4.	iv.	WILLIAM HARVEY BALLARD, *b. 15 Apr 1848, Tuscaloosa Co., AL; d. 23 Jan 1930, Electra, Wichita Co., TX.*
5.	v.	HENRY DAVID BALLARD, *b. 11 Mar 1850, Tuscaloosa Co., AL; d. 04 May 1931, El Paso Co., TX.*
	vi.	JOSIAH BALLARD, *b. 1853, Tuscaloosa Co., AL; d. Aft. 1870.*
	vii.	JAMES C. BALLARD, *b. 16 Dec 1853, Tuscaloosa Co., AL; d. 24 Nov 1942, El Paso, El Paso Co., TX.*

Notes for JAMES C. BALLARD:
Source: El Paso County Texas Standard Certificate of Death

More About JAMES C. BALLARD:
Burial: Evergreen Cemetery

Generation No. 2

2. THOMAS DANIEL[2] BALLARD (JAMES H.[1]) *was born Mar 1841 in AL, and died 11 Apr 1901. He married* CHLOE BELL POWELL. *She was born 11 Aug 1846 in MS, and died 08 Feb 1930.*

Notes for THOMAS DANIEL BALLARD:
Source: 1870-1880 Lee County Mississippi Federal Census Records, 1900 Dallas County Texas Federal Census Records

* 1870 - Living in Lee Co., MS - Ballard, Thos D 29 farmer GA, Isabella C 24 MS, Willie 6 MS, Buna M 9/12 MS
* 1880 - Living in Lee Co., MS - Ballard, Thomas 39 farmer GA GA GA, Belle 34 MS NC NC, Buner 11 MS, Lon 7 MS, Dona 4 MS, Fletcher 2 MS, Ollie 7/12 MS, Willie Coggins MS
* 1900 - Living in Dallas Co., TX - Ballard, Thomas D - Mar 1841 GA GA GA farmer, Chloe B - Aug 1845 MS NC NC 11 children 9 living, Buna M. McCarty (dau) Dec 1864 wd MS 4 children 4 living, Thomas S Ballard - Oct 1873 MS, Mary O - Oct 1879 MS, Ella M - May 1883 MS, Myrlte E - Dec 1887 MS, David G - July 1889 MS, Marty, Dennis S gs - Dec 1889 MS, Fay B gd - Feb 1892 MS, Thomas H gs - Oct 1894 TX, Jimmie E - Aug 1896 TX

More About THOMAS DANIEL BALLARD:
Burial: Britton Cemetery Ellis Co., TX

Notes for CHLOE BELL POWELL:
Source: 1910 Ellis County Texas Federal Census Records
* 1910 - Living in Ellis Co., TX - Ballard, Chloe B 63, Ella M 26, Annie M 22, David G 20, Dennis L. McCarty 20, Foy B. McCarty 18, Thomas N 14

More About CHLOE BELL POWELL:
Burial: Britton Cemetery Ellis Co., TX

Children of THOMAS BALLARD *and* CHLOE POWELL *are:*

     i.   BUNA M.[3] BALLARD, b. Dec 1869, Lee Co., MS; d. Aft. 1900; m. MCCARTY; d. Bef. 1900.
    ii.   THOMAS LON BALLARD, b. 30 Oct 1873, Lee Co., MS; d. 16 Aug 1930.

        Notes for THOMAS LON BALLARD:
        Source: Ellis County Texas Standard Certificate of Death

    iii.   DONA BALLARD, b. Abt. 1876, Lee Co., MS.
    iv.   JOHN FLETCHER BALLARD, b. 24 Jan 1877, Lee Co., MS; d. 20 Mar 1958, Ellis Co., TX; m. ADDIE ODESSA MCGEE; b. 01 Sep 1889; d. 19 Nov 1966, Ft. Worth, Tarrant Co., TX.

        More About JOHN FLETCHER BALLARD:
        Burial: Britton Cemetery, Ellis Co., TX

        More About ADDIE ODESSA MCGEE:
        Burial: Britton Cemetery, Ellis Co., TX

    v.   MARY OLLIE BALLARD, b. Oct 1879, Lee Co., MS; d. Aft. 1900.
    vi.   ELLA MAY BALLARD, b. 23 May 1883, Lee Co., MS; d. 01 Oct 1935, Dallas Co., TX; m. LONZO BURLESON RICKETTS; b. 19 Mar 1883; d. 29 Dec 1963, Dallas Co., TX.

        Notes for ELLA MAY BALLARD:
        Source Dallas County Standard Certificate of Death

        More About ELLA MAY BALLARD:
        Burial: Laurel Land Memorial Park Dallas, Dallas Co., TX

        More About LONZO BURLESON RICKETTS:
        Burial: Laurel Land Memorial Park Dallas, Dallas Co., TX

    vii.   MYRTLE ANNIE BALLARD, b. 31 Dec 1887, Lee Co., MS; d. 16 May 1971, Mansfield, Tarrant Co., TX;

m. *JESSIE LEA CHRISMAN; b. 1889; d. 1958.*

Notes for MYRTLE ANNIE BALLARD:
Source: Tarrant County Texas Certificate of Death

More About MYRTLE ANNIE BALLARD:
Burial: Britton Cemetery., Ellis Co., TX

   viii.   DAVID GRADY BALLARD, *b. 03 Jul 1889, Mooreville, Lee Co., MS; d. 17 Dec 1960, Mansfield, Tarrant Co., TX.*

      More About DAVID GRADY BALLARD:
      Burial: Britton Cemetery, Ellis Co., TX

3. ELIJAH JASPER[2] BALLARD (JAMES H.[1]) *was born 23 Sep 1843 in AL, and died 26 Sep 1894 in Howard Co., TX. He married MARY AMANDA DARDEN. She was born 21 Jan 1846 in Tuscaloosa Co., AL, and died 11 Nov 1911 in Big Spring, Howard Co., TX.*

Notes for ELIJAH JASPER BALLARD:
Source: 1870 Lee County Mississippi Federal Census Records, 1880 Bell County Texas Federal Census Records, William David Farnham (WW2X57@aol.com)

* 1870 - Living in Lee Co., MS - Ballard, Elijah J 26 farmer GA, Amanda 23 AL, Nancy 48 GA, David 21 AL, Josiah 18 AL, James 16 MS
* 1880 - Living in Bell Co., TX - Ballard, E J 34 farmer GA GA GA, Mary A 34 AL GA SC, Claud 10 MS, Stellea 7 MS, Norah 4 TX

More About ELIJAH JASPER BALLARD:
Burial: Mt. Olive Cemetery, Big Spring, Howard Co., TX

More About MARY AMANDA DARDEN:
Burial: Mt. Olive Cemetery, Big Spring, Howard Co., TX

Children of ELIJAH BALLARD and MARY DARDEN are:

    i.   CLAUDE ASA[3] BALLARD, *b. 10 Nov 1870, Tupelo, Lee Co., MS; d. 21 Sep 1951, Howard Co., TX; m. NOVA S. HICKMAN; b. 05 Jun 1886, Greensburg, Kiowa Co., KS; d. 16 Jan 1963, Sweetwater, Nolan Co., TX.*

      More About CLAUDE ASA BALLARD:
      Burial: Trinity Memorial Park, Big Spring, Howard Co., TX

      More About NOVA S. HICKMAN:
      Burial: Trinity Memorial Park, Big Spring, Howard Co., TX

   ii.   NANCY STELLA BALLARD, *b. 27 May 1873, Lee Co., MS; d. 07 Oct 1957, Big Spring, Howard Co., TX; m. JOSEPH CALLAWAY.*

      More About NANCY STELLA BALLARD:
      Burial: Mt. Olive Cemetery, Big Spring, Howard Co., TX

   iii.   LORA ETHEL BALLARD, *b. 13 Jan 1876, Falls Co., TX; d. 18 Apr 1954, Big Spring, Howard Co., TX.*

      More About LORA ETHEL BALLARD:

Burial: Mt. Olive Cemetery, Big Spring, Howard Co., TX

4. WILLIAM HARVEY[2] BALLARD (*JAMES H.[1]*) *was born 15 Apr 1848 in Tuscaloosa Co., AL, and died 23 Jan 1930 in Electra, Wichita Co., TX. He married* MARY ELLEN SAVAGE *28 Nov 1867 in Lee Co., MS. She was born 19 Jun 1850 in AL, and died 10 Dec 1916 in TX.*

Notes for WILLIAM HARVEY BALLARD:
Source: LDS-IGI records, Eunice Brown (Eunice M@webtv.net), Find A Grave, Automated Archives Marriage CD#5, 1880 Barren Creek Baxter County Arkansas Federal Census Records, 1900 Dallas County Texas Federal Census Records, 1910 Jones County Texas Federal Census Records
* 1870 - Living in Barren Creek, Baxter Co., AR - Ballard, William 20 AL, Mary E 20 AL, Sarah 1 MS
* 1880 - Living in Barren Creek, Baxter Co., AR - Ballard, Wm. H 31 AL, Mary E 28 AL, Sarah A 11 MS, Harvey M 8 AR, James 5 AR, Cora 2 AR, Luther A 1 AR
* 1900 - Living in Dallas Co., TX - Ballard, William H - Apr 1849 AL GA GA, Mary E - June 1850 AL SC SC, Luther A - Mar 1879 AR, Donnie M (f) - June 1881 AR, Sammie D - Sep 1886 TX, Henry T - Nov 1887 TX, Lee R - May 1889 TX, Jessie V (m) Aug 1892 TX
* 1910 - Living in Jones Co., TX - Ballard, William H 62, Mary E 69, Jesse V 17

More About WILLIAM HARVEY BALLARD:
Burial: Highland Cemetery, Iowa Park, Wichita Co., TX

More About MARY ELLEN SAVAGE:
Burial: Highland Cemetery, Iowa Park, Wichita Co., TX

Children of WILLIAM BALLARD *and* MARY SAVAGE *are:*

	i.	SERA ARMETA MAGODLEN[3] BALLARD, b. 05 Apr 1869, MS; d. Aft. 1880.
6.	ii.	HARVEY MORRIS BALLARD, b. 01 Feb 1871, Mt. Home, Barren Creek twp. Marion Co., AR; d. 19 Nov 1938, Rialto San Bernardino Co., CA.
	iii.	THEDAR JACKSON BALLARD, b. 26 Mar 1872.
7.	iv.	JAMES "JIM" BALLARD, b. 23 Jan 1875, Mt. Pleasant, Izard Co., AR; d. Aft. 1910.
	v.	CORRIE MARGARET BALLARD, b. 10 Nov 1877, AR; d. Aft. 1880.
8.	vi.	LUTHER ANDREW BALLARD, b. 01 Mar 1879, Baxter Co., AR; d. 13 Mar 1960, El Paso Co., TX.
	vii.	MARY CALDONIA "DONNIE" BALLARD, b. Bet. 15 - 16 Jun 1881, AR; d. 15 Apr 1962, Ft. Worth, Tarrant Co., TX; m. PETTY.

Notes for MARY CALDONIA "DONNIE" BALLARD:
Source: Death Certificate

More About MARY CALDONIA "DONNIE" BALLARD:
Burial: Highland Cemetery, Iowa Park, Wichita Co., TX

	viii.	PEARL EMMA JANE BALLARD, b. 14 Sep 1883, AR.
9.	ix.	DAVID SAMUEL BALLARD, b. 29 Sep 1886, TX; d. Aft. 1910.
	x.	HENRY TOMAS BALLARD, b. 16 Nov 1888, TX; d. Aft. 1900.
	xi.	ROBERT LEE BALLARD, b. 26 May 1890, TX; d. 30 Oct 1958.

More About ROBERT LEE BALLARD:
Burial: Highland Cemetery, Iowa Park, Wichita Co., TX

	xii.	JESSIE VANBUREN BALLARD, b. 09 Aug 1892, TX; d. Aft. 1910.

5. HENRY DAVID[2] BALLARD (JAMES H.[1]) *was born 11 Mar 1850 in Tuscaloosa Co., AL, and died 04 May 1931 in El Paso Co., TX. He married MARY SAFRONIA CONGER. She was born 25 Jun 1859 in Weatherford, Parker Co., TX, and died 28 Apr 1951 in El Paso Co., TX.*

Notes for HENRY DAVID BALLARD:
Source: El Paso County Texas Standard Certificate of Death, 1880 Ellis County Texas Federal Census Records, 1900 Hill County Texas Federal Census Records, 1910-1930 El Paso County Texas Federal Census Records

* 1880 - Living in Ellis Co., TX - Ballard, Henry 30 farmer TN, Mollie 21 TX, Olvian 1 TX, Eula 5 days TX
* 1900 - Living in Hill Co., TX - Ballard Henry 1850 -AL GA GA farmer, Mollie 1859 TX MO AR, Olin 1878 TX, Eulah L 1880 TX, Irma 1881 TX, Clinton 1883 TX, Ila 1884 TX, Cearcy 1886 TX, Vera 1895
* 1910 - Living in El Paso Co., TX - Ballard, Henry D 60 AL, Mollie 50 TX, Olin 31 TX, Clinton 21 TX, Cearcy 23 TX, Vera 15 TX
* 1920 - Living in El Paso Co., TX - Ballard, Henry D 69, Mary 60, Vera 33
* 1930 - Living in El Paso Co., TX - Ballard, Henry D 80, Mary S 70

More About HENRY DAVID BALLARD:
Burial: Restlawn Memorial Park El Paso, El Paso Co., TX

More About MARY SAFRONIA CONGER:
Burial: Restlawn Memorial Park El Paso, El Paso Co., TX

Children of HENRY BALLARD and MARY CONGER are:
  i.   OLIN WELLBORNE[3] BALLARD, *b. 10 Sep 1878, Red Oak, Ellis Co., TX; d. 27 Jan 1950, Howard Co., TX.*

      More About OLIN WELLBORNE BALLARD:
      Burial: Restlawn Memorial Park El Paso, El Paso Co., TX

  ii. EULAH L. BALLARD, *b. 1880, Ellis Co., TX; d. Aft. 1900.*
  iii. ARMA BALLARD, *b. 1881, TX; d. Aft. 1900.*
  iv. CLINTON BALLARD, *b. 1883, TX; d. Aft. 1910.*
  v.   ILA BALLARD, *b. 1884, TX; d. Aft. 1900.*
  vi. SEARCY EUGENE BALLARD, *b. 08 Dec 1886, Red Oak, Ellis Co., TX; d. 06 Jul 1981, Abilene, Taylor Co., TX.*

      More About SEARCY EUGENE BALLARD:
      Burial: Round Mound Cemetery., Hamby, Jones Co., TX

  vii. VERA BALLARD, *b. 1895, TX; d. Aft. 1920.*

Generation No. 3

6. HARVEY MORRIS[3] BALLARD (WILLIAM HARVEY[2], JAMES H.[1]) *was born 01 Feb 1871 in Mt. Home, Barren Creek twp. Marion Co., AR, and died 19 Nov 1938 in Rialto San Bernardino Co., CA. He married RETTA EUGENIA HOLLAND 03 Oct 1894. She was born 01 Feb 1871 in Hood TX, and died 01 Oct 1964 in Seaside, Monterey Co., CA.*

Notes for HARVEY MORRIS BALLARD:
Source: 1900 Ellis County Texas Federal Census Records, 1910 Taylor County Texas Federal Census Records, 1920 Wichita County Texas Federal Census Records, 1930 San Bernardino County California Federal Census Records, Eunice Brown (Eunice M@webtv.net)
* 1900 - Living in Ellis Co., TX - Ballard, Harvey M - Feb 1871 AR AL AL, Retta E - Sep 1873 TX IL IA, Morris E - July 1895 TX AR TX, Lucy E - Dec 1897 TX AR TX, Ora - Aug 1899 TX AR TX

* 1910 - Living in Taylor Co., TX - Ballard, H M 39 AR AL AL, R E 37 TX IL IA, Morris 14 TX, Louie 12 TX, Ora 10 TX, Lorena 8 TX, Wallie G 7 TX
* 1930 - Living in Bloomington, San Bernardino Co., CA - Ballard, Harvey M 59 AR, Retta E 35 TX, Oliver L E 33 TX, Willie I 26 TX, Emma E 6 granddaughter OK, Wilbur Grandson 3 OK
* 1940 - Living in Wichita Co., TX - Ballard, Harvey M 49 AR, Retta 46 TX, Morris 25 TX, Louie 23 TX, Ora 20 TX, Florina 18 TX, Idell 16 TX, and boarders: Madison E Brown 20, Albert Smith 43, Earl Greathouse 19, Sherman Richards 31

More About HARVEY MORRIS BALLARD:
Burial: Rialto Park Cemetery, Rialto, San Bernardino Co., CA

Notes for RETTA EUGENIA HOLLAND:
Source: 1940 San Bernardino California Federal Census Records
* 1940 - Living in Rialto, San Bernardino Co., CA - Ballard, Retta 66, Idell Rich 38, Pat Rich 35, Emma Tomblinson 17, Wilber Tomblinson 13

More About RETTA EUGENIA HOLLAND:
Burial: Rialto Park Cemetery, Rialto, San Bernardino Co., CA

Children of HARVEY BALLARD and RETTA HOLLAND are:
      i.   MORRIS EUGENE[4] BALLARD, b. 04 Jul 1895, TX; d. 14 Apr 1958; m. EMMA.

           More About MORRIS EUGENE BALLARD:
           Burial: LA National Cemetery, LA Co., CA

      ii.   OLIVER LOUIE BALLARD, b. 25 Dec 1896, Tarrant Co., TX; d. 19 Feb 1968, San Bernardino Co., CA; m. LILLIAN RHODES; b. 1892; d. 1977.

           More About OLIVER LOUIE BALLARD:
           Burial: Green Acres Memorial. Park and Mortuary, Bloomington, San Bernardino Co., CA

           More About LILLIAN RHODES:
           Burial: Green Acres Memorial. Park and Mortuary, Bloomington, San Bernardino Co., CA

    iii.   MARY ORZILLA BALLARD, b. 17 Aug 1899, TX; m. WALTER MARION TOMBLINSON.
    iv.   KITTY LORENA BALLARD, b. 23 Jun 1901, TX; d. 10 Dec 1992, San Bernardino Co., CA; m. MATISON ELI BROWN.
     v.   WILLIE IDELL BALLARD, b. 15 Nov 1903, TX; d. Aft. 1930; m. ERVIN FRANCIS TOMBLINSON.

7. JAMES "JIM"[3] BALLARD (WILLIAM HARVEY[2], JAMES H.[1]) was born 23 Jan 1875 in Mt. Pleasant, Izard Co., AR, and died Aft. 1910. He married ANNIE. She was born 1877 in TX, and died Aft. 1910.

Notes for JAMES "JIM" BALLARD:
source: 1910 Jones County Texas Federal Census Records

* 1910 - Living in Jones County TX - Ballard, James 34 AR, Annie 33 TX, Lottie 12 TX, Minnie 6 TX

Children of JAMES BALLARD and ANNIE are:
      i.   LOTTIE[4] BALLARD, b. 1898, TX; d. Aft. 1910.
      ii.   MINNIE BALLARD, b. 1904, TX; d. Aft. 1910.

8. LUTHER ANDREW[3] BALLARD (WILLIAM HARVEY[2], JAMES H.[1]) was born 01 Mar 1879 in Baxter Co., AR, and died 13 Mar 1960 in El Paso Co., TX. He married OLA ELLER MURDOCK. She was born 15 Feb 1885 in Johnson Co., TX, *and died 31 Oct 1962 in Wichita Falls, Wichita Co., TX.*

Notes for LUTHER ANDREW BALLARD:
Source: 1910-1920 Jones County Texas Federal Census Records

* 1910 - Living in Hamlin, Jones Co., TX - Ballard, Uther A 29 AR, Ola 24 TX, Lucile 2 TX
* 1920 - Living in Hamlin, Jones Co., TX - Ballard, Luther 39, Ala 32, Lucile 11, Curtis 8, Eliz. Murdock 58 Wd
mother in law

More About LUTHER ANDREW BALLARD:
Burial: Anthony Community Cemetery., Anthony, Dona Ana Co. NM

More About OLA ELLER MURDOCK:
Burial: Crestview Memorial. Park, Wichita Falls, Wichita Co., TX

Children of LUTHER BALLARD and OLA MURDOCK are:

      i. LUCILLE[4] BALLARD, b. 25 Aug 1907, Mitchell Co., TX; d. 15 Dec 1990, Wichita Falls, Wichita Co., TX; m. DAVIS J. SMITH; b. 1907; d. 1997.

          More About LUCILLE BALLARD:
          Burial: Crestview Memorial Park, Wichita Co., TX

      ii. CURTIS BALLARD KOURI, b. 24 Nov 1912, TX; d. 03 Mar 1990, Wichita Falls, Wichita Co., TX.

          More About CURTIS BALLARD KOURI:
          Burial: Crestview Memorial Park, Wichita Falls, Wichita Co., TX

9. DAVID SAMUEL[3] BALLARD (WILLIAM HARVEY[2], JAMES H.[1]) was born 29 Sep 1886 in TX, and died Aft. 1910. He married IDA. She was born 1887 in TX, and died Aft. 1910.

Child of DAVID BALLARD and IDA is:
      i. PASCAL[4] BALLARD, b. 1908, TX; d. Aft. 1910.

John Ballard

Generation No. 1

1. JOHN[1] BALLARD *was born Bet. 1820 - 1826 in NC, and died Aft. 1880. He married* ELIZABETH "BETSEY". *She was born Nov 1822 in NC, and died Aft. 1910.*

Notes for JOHN BALLARD:
Source: 1850-1880 Union County Georgia Federal Census Records
* 1850 - Living in Union Co., GA - Ballard, John 31 farmer NC, Elizabeth 25 NC, Lavada 4 GA, Sarah 2, GA, Joseph 10/12 GA
* 1860 - Living in Union Co., GA - Ballard, John 34 NC, Betsy 32 NC, Lavada 18 NC, Sarah 11 GA, Joseph 10 GA, Wm. 9 GA, Julia Ann 7 GA, Caledonia 5 GA, Navada 1 GA
* 1870 - Living in Union Co., GA - Ballard, John 50 farmer NC, Elizabeth 45 NC, Julia 15 GA, Calegonia 13 GA, Emeline 11 GA, Dulcena 9 GA, Vianna 7 GA, Sherman 4 GA
* 1880 - Living in Gum Log, Union Co., GA - Ballard, John 60, Elizabeth 55, Sarah 30, Caldonia E 28, Emeline 26, Dulcina 24, Vienna 22, Andrew S 13

Notes for ELIZABETH "BETSEY":
Source: 1900-1910 Union County Georgia Federal Census Records
* 1900 - Living in Gum Log, Union Co., GA - Ballard, Elizabeth - Nov 1822, Susannah E - July 1868, Vianna - Apr 1865
* 1910 - Living in Gumlog, Union Co., GA - Ballard, Lizzie 13 ch 9 living NC NC NC, Emmeline 40 GA NC NC

Children of JOHN BALLARD and ELIZABETH "BETSEY" are:

	i.	LAVADA[2] BALLARD, b. Bet. 1847 - 1848, NC; d. Aft. 1860.
	ii.	SARAH BALLARD, b. 1849, GA.
2.	iii.	JOSEPH T. "JOE" BALLARD, b. Jun 1849, GA; d. 09 Jul 1936, Cleveland, Bradley Co., TN.
	iv.	WILLIAM BALLARD, b. 1851, GA.
	v.	JULIA ANN BALLARD, b. 1853, GA; d. Aft. 1870.
	vi.	CALEDONIA BALLARD, b. 1855, GA; d. Aft. 1880.
	vii.	KANSADA BALLARD, b. 1859, GA.
3.	viii.	DULCENA BALLARD, b. 1861, GA; d. Aft. 1900.
	ix.	VIENNA LUCINDA BALLARD, b. 15 Feb 1863, Union Co. GA; d. 26 Jun 1923; m. DOLPH MARION RHINEHART; b. 1850; d. Aft. 1920.

> Notes for VIENNA LUCINDA BALLARD:
> Source: Union County Georgia Standard Certificate of Death
>
> Notes for DOLPH MARION RHINEHART:
> Source: 1920 Union County Georgia Federal Census Records
> * 1920 - Living in Ivylog, Union Co., GA - Rinehart, Marion 70 NC NC NC, Viana 54 GA NC NC

4.	x.	ANDREW SHERMAN BALLARD, b. 01 Jan 1863, Union Co., GA; d. 21 Sep 1932.
	xi.	SUSANNAH E. BALLARD, b. Jul 1868, GA; d. Aft. 1900.

Generation No. 2

2. JOSEPH T. "JOE"[2] BALLARD (JOHN[1]) *was born Jun 1849 in GA, and died 09 Jul 1936 in Cleveland, Bradley Co., TN. He married (1)* EMELINE LEDFORD. *She was born 1855 in AL, and died 1934. He married (2)* LIDIA M. *Abt. 1869. She was born 1849 in GA, and died Aft. 1870.*

Notes for JOSEPH T. "JOE" BALLARD:
Source- 1870-1900 Union County Georgia Federal Census Records

1870 - Living in Union Co., GA - Ballard, Joseph 21 farmer, GA, Lidia 21 GA
1880 - Living in Union Co., GA - Ballard, Joseph 29 Farmer GA NC NC, Emeline 25 AL, NC NC, William 10 GA,
Thomas C. 8 GA, James M. 6 GA, Daniel A. 4 GA, Georgia A. 3 GA, Laura 1 GA, Mary 3/12 GA
1900 - Living in Union Co., GA - Ballard, Jos W - June 1849 GA, Emiline ? NC GA NC, Robert 0 Sept 1889 NC,
Lassie A 1884, Cora or Cassa - July 1886 NC, Mallie M - Aug 1881 NC
1930 - Living in Bradley Co., TN with his son Thomas C. Ballard

More About JOSEPH T. "JOE" BALLARD:
Burial: Bethel Cemetery, Bradley Co., TN

More About EMELINE LEDFORD:
Burial: Bethel Cemetery, Bradley Co., TN

Children of JOSEPH BALLARD and EMELINE LEDFORD are:

    i.   WILLIAM³ BALLARD, b. 1870, GA.
   ii. THOMAS CLEAMON BALLARD, b. 1872, GA; d. 28 Apr 1953, Bradley Co., TN; m. NANCY EMALINE
       LEDFORD; b. 1873, NC; d. 1965.

       Notes for THOMAS CLEAMON BALLARD:
       Source: 1900 Clay County North Carolina Federal Census Records, 1910 -1920 Cherokee County
       North Carolina Federal Census Records, 1930 Bradley County Tennessee Federal Census Records,
       Bradley County Certificate of Death
       1900 - Living in Clay Co. NC - Ballard, Thomas - Mar 1871 NC NC NC, Nancy - Nov 1871 NC
       NC NC, Vester - Oct 1893 NC, Walter - Apr 1896 NC, Robbie - Sept 1898 NC
       1910 - Living in Valley Town, Cherokee Co., NC - Ballard, Thomas C 39 NC NC GA, Nancy E 37
       NC NC NC, Lester 17 NC, Walter E 14 NC, Jessie R 11 NC, Marvin D 7 NC, Lillie A 3 NC, Everett
       H 9/12 NC, Sheradan Petterson 18 NC boarder
       1920 - Living in Valley Town, Cherokee Co., NC - Ballard, Thomas 50 NC GA GA, Nancy 48 NC
       NC NC, Walter 23 NC, Dewey 16 NC, Lillie 14 NC , Everett 11 NC, Fred 6 NC
       1930 - Living in Bradley Co., TN - Ballard, Thomas C 59 NC GA GA, Nancy 57 NC NC GA, Evert
       H 20 NC, Fred P 16 NC, Joseph T father 91 GA England England, Emaline mother 85 NC NC NC

       More About THOMAS CLEAMON BALLARD:
       Burial: Lebanon Baptist Cemetery, Cleveland, Bradley Co., TN

       More About NANCY EMALINE LEDFORD:
       Burial: Lebanon Baptist Cemetery, Cleveland, Bradley Co., TN

   iii. GEORGIA A. BALLARD, b. 1873, GA.
   iv. JAMES M. BALLARD, b. 1874, GA.
    v. DANIEL A. BALLARD, b. 1876, GA.
   vi. LAURA BALLARD, b. 1879, GA; d. Aft. 1880.
  vii. MARY B. BALLARD, b. 07 Feb 1881, Union Co., GA; d. 03 Apr 1926, Valleytown, Cherokee Co., NC;
       m. JAMES M. HENDERSON; b. Abt. 1873, GA; d. Aft. 1920.

       Notes for MARY B. BALLARD:
       Source: Cherokee County North Carolina Standard Certificate of Death

       More About MARY B. BALLARD:
       Burial: Valleytown Cemetery, Cherokee Co., NC

       Notes for JAMES M. HENDERSON:
       Source: 1910 Clay County North Carolina Federal Census Records, 1920 Cherokee County North
       Carolina Federal Census Records
       1910 - Living in Shooting Creek, Clay Co., NC - Henderson, J M GA NC GA , Mary E 30 - 2
       children 2 living A GA GA, Dollie 9 GA, Lillie 5 NC

* 1920 - Living in Valley Town, Cherokee Co., NC - Henderson, Mary 37 GA, Dollie 18 GA, Mattie 7 NC, Joseph 6 NC

   viii.   CORA BELLE BALLARD, *b. 31 Jul 1886, Murphy Clay, NC; d. 11 May 1950.*

      Notes for CORA BELLE BALLARD:
      Source: Social Security Records

      More About CORA BELLE BALLARD:
      Burial: Bethel Cemetery, Bradley Co., TN

   ix.   ROBERT BALLARD, *b. Sep 1889, NC.*

3. DULCENA[2] BALLARD (JOHN[1]) *was born 1861 in GA, and died Aft. 1900. She married* ROBERT A. COFFEY. *He was born Apr 1841, and died Aft. 1900.*

Notes for ROBERT A. COFFEY:
Source: 1900-1910 Union County Georgia Federal Census Records
* 1900 - Living in Gum Log, Union Co., GA - Coffey, Robert A - Apr 1841 GA NC NC, Dulcena - Mar 1861 - 4 children 2 living GA NC NC, Martha - Oct 1888 GA GA GA, John H. S - Apr 1890 GA GA GA, John father - Aug 1809 wd NC NC England
* 1910 - Living in Gumlog, Union Co., GA - Coffey, Robert 40 70 md 2x GA NC GA, Dulcina 49 - 4 children 2 living GA NC US, John 20 GA

Children of DULCENA BALLARD *and* ROBERT COFFEY *are:*
   i.   MARTHA[3] COFFEY, *b. Oct 1888, Union Co., GA; d. Aft. 1900.*
   ii.   JOHN HENRY COFFEY, *b. 02 Apr 1890, Union Co., GA; d. 18 Jun 1957, Fannin Co., GA; m.* HENRIETTA COCHRAN; *b. 09 Mar 1898; d. 03 Feb 1924, Fannin Co., GA.*

      More About JOHN HENRY COFFEY:
      Burial: Hemptown Baptist Church Cemetery, Hemp, Fannin Co., GA

      More About HENRIETTA COCHRAN:
      Burial: Hemptown Baptist Church Cemetery, hemp, Fannin Co., GA

4. ANDREW SHERMAN[2] BALLARD (JOHN[1]) *was born 01 Jan 1863 in Union Co., GA, and died 21 Sep 1932. He married (1)* SARAH *Bef. 1910. She was born 1865 in GA, and died Aft. 1910. He married (2)* DELILA GRIGGS *Bef. 1920. She was born 18 Oct 1861, and died 03 May 1945. He married (3)* MARY ANN *Bef. 1930. She was born 1866, and died Aft. 1930.*

Notes for ANDREW SHERMAN BALLARD:
Source: 1910, 1920 Union County Georgia Federal Census Records
* 1910 - Living in Gunlog, Union Co., GA - Ballard, Sherman 40 GA, Sarah 45, Vinie 16, Donie 13, Maggie 11, Maude 9, Gracie 7, Fred 5, Henry 2
* 1920 - Living in Union Co., GA - Ballard, Sherman 53, Lila 52, Vina 26, David 22, Maggie 19, Maude 17, Grace 15, Fred 13, Henry 11
* 1930 - Living in Gum Log, Union Co., GA - Ballard, Sherman A 52, Mary Ann 64, Dovie Jane 27, Maggie V 27, Maudie 23, Gracie 22, Henry 20

More About ANDREW SHERMAN BALLARD:
Burial: Pine Log Baptist Church Cemetery, Brasstown, Clay Co., NC

More About DELILA GRIGGS:
Burial: Pine Log Baptist Church Cemetery, Brasstown, Clay Co., NC

Children of ANDREW BALLARD and SARAH are:

    i.   LIZZIE[3] BALLARD, b. Abt. 1892, GA; d. Aft. 1910.

   ii.   VINNIE BALLARD, b. 1894, GA; d. 13 Feb 1973.

       More About VINNIE BALLARD:
       Burial: Pine Log Baptist Church Cemetery, Brasstown, Clay Co., NC

  iii.   DOVIE JANE BALLARD, b. 1896, GA; d. 19 Feb 1939.

       More About DOVIE JANE BALLARD:
       Burial: Pine Log Baptist Church Cemetery, Brasstown, Clay Co., NC

  iv.   MAGGIE BALLARD, b. 22 Feb 1898, GA; d. 25 Dec 1989; m. JULIUS C. FOSTER; b. 26 Sep 1878; d. 24 Jun 1949.

       More About MAGGIE BALLARD:
       Burial: Pine Log Baptist Church Cemetery, Brasstown, Clay Co., NC

       More About JULIUS C. FOSTER:
       Burial: Woods Grove Memorial Cemetery, Towns Co., GA

   v.   MAUDE BALLARD, b. 25 Jun 1900, GA; d. 11 Dec 1988.

       More About MAUDE BALLARD:
       Burial: Pine Log Baptist Church Cemetery, Brasstown, Clay Co., NC

  vi.   GRACE BALLARD, b. 1905, GA; d. Aft. 1910.

 vii.   FRED BALLARD, b. 06 Apr 1905, GA; d. 23 Dec 1940, Murphy, Cherokee Co., NC.

       Notes for FRED BALLARD:
       Source: Cherokee County North Carolina Death Certificates

       More About FRED BALLARD:
       Burial: Pine Log Baptist Church Cemetery, Brasstown, Clay Co., NC

 viii.   HENRY R. BALLARD, b. 16 Apr 1908, GA; d. 15 Aug 1955; m. BLONNIE S.; b. 28 May 1911.

       More About HENRY R. BALLARD:
       Burial: Pine Log Baptist Church Cemetery, Brasstown, Clay Co., NC

       More About BLONNIE S.:
       Burial: Pine Log Baptist Church Cemetery, Brasstown, Clay Co., NC

Joseph Ballard

Generation No. 1

1. JOSEPH[1] BALLARD was born 05 Dec 1820 in Campbell Co., TN, and died 25 Apr 1907 in Bartow Co., GA. He married MARGARET COUNTRYMAN 02 Feb 1841 in Bartow Co., GA. She was born Abt. 1820 in GA, and died 18 Sep 1897.

Notes for JOSEPH BALLARD:
Source: 1850 Cherokee County Georgia Federal Census Records, 1860 Gordon County Georgia Federal Census Records, 1880-1900 Bartow County Georgia Federal Census Records, Georgia Marriages 1699-1944, Find A Grave

* 1850 - Living in Cherokee District GA - listed 2 x with differences -
#1 Ballard, Joseph 29 TN, Margaret 21 GA, Mary A. 7 GA, Melinda 3 GA, James M. 2 GA, Jane 1 GA, Listing
#2 Ballard, Joseph 29 TN, Margaret 20 GA, Mary H. 7 GA, Malinda 5 GA, James M 4 GA, Eliza J. 1 GA
* 1860 - Living in Gordon Co., GA - Ballard, Joseph 41 TN, Margaret 29 GA, Mary A. 29? GA, Mary A. 17 GA, Malinda 15 GA, James M. 13 GA, Eliza J. 10 GA, John H. 8 GA, George W. 6 GA, Joseph K 2 GA
* 1870 - Living in Bartow Co., GA - Ballard, Joseph 54 , Margeret 41 GA, Louisa 20 (Eliza??) GA, John H. 19, George W. 16, Kelly 12 GA, William 10 GA, Rhody 6 GA, Thomas 2 GA
* 1880 - Living in Bartow Co., GA - Ballard, Joseph 60 farmer TN VA VA, Margaret 50 GA GA GA, William 19 GA, Rhoda 14 GA, Thomas 11 GA, Emma 9 GA
* 1900 - Living in Euharlee, Bartow Co., GA - Ballard, Joe - Dec 1820, Emma - Apr 1872 (dau), Fred Swanson grandson - Aug 1879, Nannie - Dec 1877

More About JOSEPH BALLARD:
Burial: Euharlee Presbyterian Cemetery Euharlee, Bartow Co., GA

More About MARGARET COUNTRYMAN:
Burial: Euharlee Presbyterian Cemetery Euharlee, Bartow Co., GA

Children of JOSEPH BALLARD and MARGARET COUNTRYMAN are:

2.	i.	MALINDA[2] BALLARD, b. 01 Jul 1841, Gordon Co., GA; d. 01 Jan 1929, Altoona, Blount Co., AL.
	ii.	MARY A. BALLARD, b. 11 Oct 1843, Gordon Co., GA; d. 15 Nov 1896, Gordon Co., GA.
	iii.	ELIZA JANE BALLARD, b. 1849, Gordon Co., GA; d. Aft. 1860.
3.	iv.	JAMES M. BALLARD, b. 1851, Gordon Co., GA; d. 08 Apr 1922, Gordon Co., GA.
4.	v.	JOHN H. BALLARD, b. 05 Feb 1852, Gordon Co., GA; d. 17 Nov 1909, Blount Co., AL.
	vi.	GEORGE WASHINGTON BALLARD, b. Dec 1854, Gordon Co., GA.
5.	vii.	JOSEPH KELLY BALLARD, b. 23 Apr 1859, Gordon Co., GA; d. 18 Nov 1942, Memphis, Shelby Co., TN.
6.	viii.	WILLIAM BALLARD, b. Jun 1861, Gordon Co., GA; d. 20 Apr 1929, Allen Co., KY.
7.	ix.	RHODA BALLARD, b. 1866, Gordon Co., GA; d. 27 Feb 1942.
8.	x.	THOMAS BALLARD, b. 25 Sep 1869, Gordon Co., GA; d. 03 Mar 1917, Floyd Co., GA.
	xi.	EMMA BALLARD, b. 1871, GA; d. Aft. 1900.

Generation No. 2

2. MALINDA[2] BALLARD (JOSEPH[1]) was born 01 Jul 1841 in Gordon Co., GA, and died 01 Jan 1929 in Altoona, Blount Co., AL. She married SINGLETON ALLEN DECKER 09 Jan 1866 in Gordon Co., GA. He was born 1840 in Bartow Co., GA, and died 1900 in Marshall Co. AL.

Notes for MALINDA BALLARD:

Source: Blount County Alabama Death Certificate

More About MALINDA BALLARD:
Burial: Ebenezer Methodist Cemetery, Snead, Blount Co. AL

Notes for SINGLETON ALLEN DECKER:
Source: 1860 Marshall County Alabama Federal Census Records, 1870-1880 Bartow County Georgia Federal Census Records
* 1860 - Living in Marshall Co., AL - Living with his parents Allen W Dicker and Elizabeth and siblings
* 1870 - Living in Bartow Co., GA - Decker, Singleton A 30 farmer GA, Malinda 23 GA, Margaret E 3 GA, Georgian 1 GA
* 1880 - Living in Adairsville, Bartow Co., GA - Decar, Singleton 34, Malinda 32, Mary 2, Allice 4, William 1

More About SINGLETON ALLEN DECKER:
Burial: Ebenezer Methodist Cemetery, Snead, Blount Co. AL

Children of MALINDA BALLARD and SINGLETON DECKER are:
    i.   MARGARET E.³ DECKER, b. Abt. 1867, GA; d. Aft. 1870.
   ii.   GEORGIAN DECKER, b. Abt. 1869, GA; d. Aft. 1870.
  iii.   MARY DECKER, b. Abt. 1873, GA; d. Aft. 1880.
  iv.   ALICE DECKER, b. Abt. 1876, GA; d. Aft. 1880.
   v.   WILLIAM F. DECKER, b. 03 Nov 1879, GA; d. 12 Apr 1962; m. ORA MAE CAMPBELL; b. 07 May 1890; d. 27 Dec 1963.

        More About WILLIAM F. DECKER:
        Burial: Ebenezer Methodist Cemetery, Snead, Blount Co. AL

        More About ORA MAE CAMPBELL:
        Burial: Ebenezer Methodist Cemetery, Snead, Blount Co. AL

  vi.   ALVIN C. DECKER, b. 07 Apr 1882, GA; d. 07 May 1939; m. MOLLY; b. 1881; d. 1956.

        More About MOLLY:
        Burial: Ebenezer Methodist Cemetery, Snead, Blount Co. AL

 vii.   ULYESS W. DECKER, b. 1887, GA; d. 31 Mar 1973.

        More About ULYESS W. DECKER:
        Burial: Bethel Church Cemetery, Snead, Blount Co., AL

3. JAMES M.² BALLARD (JOSEPH¹) was born 1851 in Gordon Co., GA, and died 08 Apr 1922 in Gordon Co., GA. He married NANCY ANGELINE HORTON. She was born 1850 in GA, and died Aft. 1910.

Notes for JAMES M. BALLARD:
Source: 1870 Gordon County Georgia Federal Census Records, 1880-1910 Bartow County Georgia Federal census Records

* 1870 - Living in Gordon Co., GA - Ballard, James 22 GA farming, Angeline 20 GA, Salon 8/12 GA
* 1880 - Living in Stilsboro, Bartow Co., GA - Ballard, James M 29, Angeline 21, Lolie 12, Wesley 10, Lizzie 8, Walter 6, Lila 4
* 1900 - Living in Bartow Co., GA - Ballard, James M 52, Angie A 43, Joseph W 25, Lizabeth 24, Lela 20, Catherine 17, Malinda 15, Monroe 12, Waterman 4
* 1910 - Living in Bartow Co., GA - Living with daughter Kate Pavoloski

Children of JAMES BALLARD and NANCY HORTON are:

    i.   LOLIE[3] BALLARD, b. 1868, Bartow Co., GA; d. Aft. 1880.

   ii. WESLEY BALLARD, b. 1870, Bartow Co., GA; d. Aft. 1880.

  iii. ELIZABETH "LIZZIE" BALLARD, b. 1872, Bartow Co., GA; d. Aft. 1900.

  iv. JOSEPH WALTER BALLARD, b. 1874, Bartow Co., GA; d. Aft. 1900.

   v. LILA BALLARD, b. 1876, Bartow Co., GA; d. Aft. 1900.

  vi. CATHERINE "KATE" BALLARD, b. Abt. 1883, Bartow Co., GA; d. Aft. 1910; m. JOHN PAVOLOSKI; b. Abt. 1882, GA; d. Aft. 1910.

Notes for JOHN PAVOLOSKI:
Source: 1910 Bartow County Georgia Federal Census Records
* 1910 - Living in Bartow Co., GA - Pavoloski, John 28 GA, Germany Germany, Kate 24 - 3 children 2 living GA GA GA, Maxie 4 GA, Ruby 2 GA, James M Ballard father in law 62 GA TN GA , Angeline mother in law 53 - 9 children 9 living GA NC NC

  vii. MALINDA BALLARD, b. Abt. 1885, Bartow Co., GA; d. Aft. 1900.

 viii. WATERMAN BALLARD, b. Abt. 1896, Bartow Co., GA; d. Aft. 1900.

  ix. MONROE BALLARD, b. Abt. 1898, Bartow Co., GA; d. Aft. 1900.

4. JOHN H.[2] BALLARD (*JOSEPH[1]*) was born 05 Feb 1852 in Gordon Co., GA, and died 17 Nov 1909 in Blount Co., AL. He married MALINDA CAROLINE SWANSON 07 Oct 1873 in Bartow Co., GA. She was born 12 Feb 1854 in Cherokee Co., GA, and died 08 Aug 1923 in Blount Co., AL.

Notes for JOHN H. BALLARD:
Source: 1880-1900 Bartow County Georgia Federal Census Records, Annie B. Maner
* 1880 - Living in Adairsville, Bartow Co., GA, Ballard, John H. 26 laborer GA GA GA, Malinda A. GA NC NC, Joseph E. 5 GA, Jas A. 4 GA, John H. 2 GA, Wm. A 6/12 GA
* 1900 - Living in Euharlee, Bartow Co., GA - Ballard, John H - Feb 1854 GA TN GA, Malinda C - Feb 1854 - 11 children 11 living GA NC GA, James - Oct 1875, Andrew - Nov 1879, Julie - Oct 1881, Oscar - Jan 1884, Earle - Feb 1886, Emma - Dec 1888, Mannie - Feb 1893, Fannie - June 1896

More About JOHN H. BALLARD:
Burial: Ebenezer Methodist Cemetery, Snead, Blount Co., AL

Notes for MALINDA CAROLINE SWANSON:
Source: 1910 Blount County Alabama Federal Census Records

* 1910 - Living in Campbells, Blount Co., AL - Ballard, Malinda 56, Emma 23, Marlin 19, Mamie 17, Fannie 14, Julia Lamb 28

More About MALINDA CAROLINE SWANSON:
Burial: Ebenezer Methodist Cemetery, Snead, Blount Co., AL

Children of JOHN BALLARD and MALINDA SWANSON are:

    i.   FRANK[3] BALLARD, b. Abt. 1871, Bartow Co., GA.

   ii. JACK BALLARD, b. Abt. 1873, Bartow Co., GA.

  iii. JOSEPH E. BALLARD, b. Abt. 1874, Bartow Co., GA; d. Aft. 1900.

  iv. JAMES ASBURY BALLARD, b. 25 Oct 1875, Bartow Co., GA; d. 27 Dec 1954; m. PEARL ELIZABETH; b. 04 Aug 1895; d. 22 Jun 1947.

More About JAMES ASBURY BALLARD:
Burial: Ebeneer Methodist Cemetery, Snead, Blount Co., AL

More About PEARL ELIZABETH:

Burial: Bethel Church Cemetery, Snead Blount Co., AL

v.   JOHN H. BALLARD, b. 1878, Bartow Co., GA; d. Aft. 1880.
vi. WILLIAM ANDREW BALLARD, b. 28 Nov 1879, Bartow Co., GA; d. 12 Aug 1954, Dutton, Jackson Co., AL; m. MAMIE FERGUSON; b. 17 Aug 1886, St. Clair Co., AL; d. 14 Dec 1975, Dutton, Jackson Co., AL.

More About WILLIAM ANDREW BALLARD:
Burial: Dutton Methodist Church Cemetery, Jackson Co., AL

More About MAMIE FERGUSON:
Burial: Dutton Methodist Church Cemetery, Jackson Co., AL

vii. JULIE SWANSON BALLARD, b. Oct 1881, Bartow Co., GA; d. Aft. 1910; m. LAMB.
viii. EARL BALLARD, b. Feb 1886, Bartow Co., GA; d. Aft. 1900; m. DILULA; b. Abt. 1892, GA.

Notes for EARL BALLARD:
Source: 1910 Blount County Alabama Federal Census Records
* 1910 - Living in Blount Co., AL - Ballard, Earl 24 GA GA GA, Dilula 18 AL AL AL

ix. EMMA SWANSON BALLARD, b. Dec 1888, Bartow Co., GA; d. Aft. 1910.
x.   MARTIN BALLARD, b. 1891, Bartow Co., GA; d. Aft. 1910.
xi. MINNIE SWANSON BALLARD, b. Feb 1893, Bartow Co., GA; d. Aft. 1910.
xii. FANNIE BALLARD, b. Jun 1896, Bartow Co., GA; d. Aft. 1910.

5.   JOSEPH KELLY[2] BALLARD (JOSEPH[1]) was born 23 Apr 1859 in Gordon Co., GA, and died 18 Nov 1942 in Memphis, Shelby Co., TN. He married EMMA E. CARNES. She was born 1862 in GA, and died Aft. 1930.

Notes for JOSEPH KELLY BALLARD:
Source: 1880 Bartow County Georgia Federal Census Records, 1910 -1920 Clay County Mississippi Federal Census Records,1930 Madison County Tennessee Federal Census Records, 1940 Jackson County Alabama Federal Census Records, Shelby County Tennessee Certificate of Death, agordontx@earthlink.net

* 1880 - Living in Bartow Co., GA - Ballard, J. K. 21 farming GA TN GA, Emma 18 GA GA GA
* 1900 - Living in Marman Springs, Monroe Co., MS - Ballard, Joseph K - June 1861 39 GA SC SC machinist, Emma L - Dec 1862 - 37 - 7 children 6 living GA GA NC, Charles H - Dec 1880 19 GA, Richard B - Nov 1886 GA, Thomas K - Aug 1889 GA, Rolf L - July 1893 AL, Claudie - Jan 1900 4/12 MS
* 1910 - Living in West Point, Clay Co., MS - Ballard, Joseph K 51 GA GA GA, Emma L 47 - 6 children 6 living GA GA GA, Thomas K 20 GA, Ralph L 16 AL, Claud 10 MS
* 1920 - Living in West Point, Clay Co., MS - Ballard, Joseph K 59 GA, Emma L 57 GA, Richard B 33 GA Claud 20 MS, Mary L 21 dau in law.
* 1930 - Living in Jackson, Madison Co., TN - Ballard, Joseph K 70 GA TN GA, Emma 68 GA GA GA
* 1940 - Living in Stevenson, Jackson Co., AL - Ballard, RB 52 GA, Myrtle J 35 AL, J K father 81 wd GA

More About JOSEPH KELLY BALLARD:
Burial: West Point Cemetery, West Point, MS

Children of JOSEPH BALLARD and EMMA CARNES are:
9.   i.   CHARLES HENRY[3] BALLARD, b. 1880, GA; d. 1956, MS.
     ii. LUCIOUS MEMORY BALLARD, b. 18 Aug 1884, Kingston, GA; d. Bef. 1900.

     Notes for LUCIOUS MEMORY BALLARD:
     Source: Social Security Application

iii.   RICHARD BERRY BALLARD, b. 29 Nov 1886, GA; d. 22 Jun 1963, Jefferson Co., AL; m. MYRTLE J.; b. Abt. 1905, AL; d. Aft. 1940.

Notes for RICHARD BERRY BALLARD:
Source: 1940 Jackson County Alabama Federal Census Records, Alabama Death Records
* 1940 - Living in Stevenson, Jackson Co., AL - Ballard, RB 52 GA, Myrtle J 35 AL, J K father 81 wd GA

10.   iv.   RALPH LEE BALLARD, b. 11 Jul 1893, AL; d. Aug 1971, West Point, Clay Co., MS.
      v.   CLAUDE BALLARD, b. 1900, MS; d. Aft. 1920; m. MARY LENA ASKEW; d. Aft. 1920.
      vi.   THOMAS KELLY BALLARD, b. 20 Aug 1889, GA; d. 1998, TN; m. (1) MARY FRANCES BOND; m. (2) CARRIE SUE STAYTON, 03 Jun 1917, St. Francis Co., AR.

Notes for THOMAS KELLY BALLARD:
Source: 1930 Etowah County Alabama Federal Census Records, 1940 Madison County Tennessee Federal Census Records
* 1930 - Living in Gadsden, Etowah Co., AL - Ballard, Thomas 40, Carrie S 40, Thoms K 10, Lelia C. Nunn 56, Rufus Cottingham 58
* 1940 - Living in Jackson, Madison Co., TN Ballard, Thomas Kelly 51 Mill Foreman, Carrie 51 AR, Tommy 20

6.   WILLIAM[2] BALLARD (JOSEPH[1]) was born Jun 1861 in Gordon Co., GA, and died 20 Apr 1929 in Allen Co., KY. He married NANCY "NANNIE". She was born Aug 1870, and died Aft. 1900.

Notes for WILLIAM BALLARD:
Source: 1900 Bartow County Georgia Federal Census Records
* 1900 - Living in Euharlee, Bartow Co., GA - Ballard, William - June 1861, Nannie - Aug 1870, Eunice - Dec 1888, Lee - Aug 1890, Alfred - Apr 1892, Joe - June 1894, Bryant - Oct 1896, Bessie - Nov 1898

Children of WILLIAM BALLARD and NANCY "NANNIE" are:
      i.   EUNICE[3] BALLARD, b. Dec 1888, Bartow Co., GA; d. Aft. 1900.
      ii.   LEE BALLARD, b. Aug 1890, Bartow Co., GA; d. Aft. 1900.
      iii.   ALFRED BALLARD, b. Apr 1892, Bartow Co., GA; d. Aft. 1900.
      iv.   JOE BALLARD, b. Jun 1894, Bartow Co., GA; d. Aft. 1900.
      v.   BRYANT BALLARD, b. Oct 1896, Bartow Co., GA; d. Aft. 1900.
11.   vi.   BESSIE BALLARD, b. 22 Nov 1898, Bartow Co., GA; d. 21 Jan 1996, Cobb Co., GA.

7.   RHODA[2] BALLARD (JOSEPH[1]) was born 1866 in Gordon Co., GA, and died 27 Feb 1942. She married ELIAS C. CARNES. He was born 08 Aug 1859 in GA, and died 11 Sep 1947 in Floyd Co., GA.

More About RHODA BALLARD:
Burial: East View Cemetery, Rome, Floyd Co., GA

Notes for ELIAS C. CARNES:
Source: 1920 Floyd County Georgia Federal Census Records

* 1920 - Living in Etowah, Floyd Co., GA - Carnes, Elias 60 GA, Rhody 52 GA, Thomas 20 GA, Frank 21 GA, Walter 16 GA
* 1930 - Living in Armuchee, Floyd Co., GA - Carnes, Elias C 70 GA, Rhoda 61 GA, James F 31 GA, Manny 29 dau in law GA, James 2 GA grandson

More About ELIAS C. CARNES:
Burial: East View Cemetery, Rome, Floyd Co., GA

Children of RHODA BALLARD and ELIAS CARNES are:

     i.   THOMAS T.³ CARNES, b. 13 Feb 1894, Bartow Co., GA; d. 17 Jun 1950, Floyd Co., GA; m. BESSIE EDWARDS; b. 1905.

     ii. ANNIE MAE CARNES, b. 26 Aug 1895; d. 27 Sep 1980; m. LEMUEL A. PADGETTE.

         More About ANNIE MAE CARNES:
         Burial: Evergreen Cemetery, Fitzgerald, Ben Hill Co., GA

12.   iii. JAMES FRANKLIN CARNES, b. 22 Jul 1900, GA; d. 22 May 1982.

     iv. WALTER CARNES, b. 11 Sep 1901, GA; d. 12 Jun 1987, Floyd Co., GA; m. HENRIETTA; b. 1908.

         More About WALTER CARNES:
         Burial: Sunset Hills Memorial Gardens Cemetery

8. THOMAS² BALLARD (JOSEPH¹) *was born 25 Sep 1869 in Gordon Co., GA, and died 03 Mar 1917 in Floyd Co., GA. He married MATTIE. She was born Apr 1874 in GA, and died Aft. 1900.*

Notes for THOMAS BALLARD:
Source: 1900 Bartow County Georgia Federal Census Records
* 1900 - Living in Euharlee, Bartow Co., GA - Ballard, Thomas - Sept 1868 GA TN GA, Mattie - Apr 1874 GA GA GA, Smyley D - Apr 1898, Stanley - Jan 1900

More About THOMAS BALLARD:
Burial: Myrtle Hill Cemetery Rome, Floyd Co GA

Children of THOMAS BALLARD and MATTIE are:

     i.   SMYLEY D.³ BALLARD, b. 04 Apr 1889, Bartow Co., GA; d. 22 Oct 1960, Floyd Co., GA.

         More About SMYLEY D. BALLARD:
         Burial: East View Cemetery Rome, Floyd Co GA

     ii. STANLEY BALLARD, b. Jan 1900, Bartow Co., GA; d. Aft. 1900.

Generation No. 3

9. CHARLES HENRY³ BALLARD (JOSEPH KELLY², JOSEPH¹) *was born 1880 in GA, and died 1956 in MS. He married EMILY JANE EASTER. She was born 1880, and died 1935 in MS.*

Children of CHARLES BALLARD and EMILY EASTER are:

     i.   EVELYN AILEEN⁴ BALLARD, b. 1911.

     ii. JOHN KELLY BALLARD, b. 1904.

     iii. ELIZAETH JANE BALLARD, b. 1916.

10. RALPH LEE³ BALLARD (JOSEPH KELLY², JOSEPH¹) *was born 11 Jul 1893 in AL, and died Aug 1971 in West Point, Clay Co., MS. He married LULA CALVERT. She was born Abt. 1895 in MS, and died 07 Feb 1990 in West Point, Clay Co., MS.*

Notes for RALPH LEE BALLARD:

Source: 1930-1940 Clay County Mississippi Federal Census Records, Social Security Death Index
* 1930 - Living in West Point, Clay Co., MS - Ballard, Ralph 36 AL GA GA, Lula 35 MS MS AL, Cecile E. 10 MS AL MS

* 1940 - Living in West Point, Clay Co., MS - Ballard, Ralph L 46 AL, Lula C 46 MS, Cecile E 20 MS

Child of RALPH BALLARD and LULA CALVERT is:

     i.   CECILE[4] BALLARD, b. 14 Feb 1920, MS; d. 10 Sep 2000.

          Notes for CECILE BALLARD:
          Source: Social Security Death Index

11. BESSIE[3] BALLARD (WILLIAM[2], JOSEPH[1]) *was born 22 Nov 1898 in Bartow Co., GA, and died 21 Jan 1996 in Cobb Co., GA. She married DANIEL WEBSTER POPHAM. He was born 1891.*

Notes for DANIEL WEBSTER POPHAM:

Source: 1920-1940 Bartow County Georgia Federal Census Records

* 1920 - Living in Taylorsville, Bartow Co., GA - Popham, W. Dorn 27, Bessie 21, WD 4, Watson 2
* 1930 - Living in Taylorsville, Bartow Co., GA - Popham, Dan W 37, Bessie 30, W D 14, Walton 12, Paul 10, Margie 7, Jeri Dean 5, Cecil 3, Jewel 1
* 1940 - Living in Taylorsville, Bartow Co., GA - Pophan, Dan 46, Bessie 30, Walton 22, Margie 18, Jeraldine 15, Cecil 12, Jewel 10, Lura 8, Rachel 4

Children of BESSIE BALLARD and DANIEL POPHAM are:

     i.   W. D.[4] POPHAM.
     ii. WALTON POPHAM.
     iii. PAUL POPHAM.
     iv. MARGIE POPHAM.
     v. JERALDINE POPHAM.
     vi. CECIL POPHAM.
     vii. JEWEL POPHAM.
    viii. LURA POPHAM.
     ix. RACHEL POPHAM.

12. JAMES FRANKLIN[3] CARNES (RHODA[2] BALLARD, JOSEPH[1]) *was born 22 Jul 1900 in GA, and died 22 May 1982. He married MARY LEE ALFORD. She was born 05 Feb 1901 in GA, and died 01 Jul 1996 in Bartow Co., GA.*

More About JAMES FRANKLIN CARNES:
Burial: East View Cemetery, Rome, Floyd Co., GA

Child of JAMES CARNES and MARY ALFORD is:
     i.   JAMES A.[4] CARNES, b. 1927, GA; d. Aft. 1930.

Miles Ballard

Generation No. 1

1. MILES[1] BALLARD *was born 1800 in NC, and died 1865 in Pike Co., or Butler Co., GA. He married (1) EVELINA BILLINGSLEY Abt. 1827, daughter of ELIAS BILLINGSLEY and LUCY POWELL. She was born 13 Apr 1809 in NC, and died 19 Jul 1854 in Pike Co., GA. He married (2) ELIZABETH KNIGHT 08 Nov 1855 in Fayette Co., GA. She was born Abt. 1830 in Fayette Co., GA, and died Abt. 1863 in Fayette Co., GA.*

Notes for MILES BALLARD:
Source: Lynn B. Cunningham (lcunnin1@mail.atl.bellsouth.net) D. Richard Ballard, Edward Wayne Ballard, Annie B. Maner (AManer@msn.com), History of Anson Co. Chapter 17 Letters from Mexico page 90-97 and page 108. 1830, 1840, 1850 Pike County Georgia Federal Census Records, 1860 Butler Co. Alabama Federal Census Records
* I am not sure if this is one man, Miles Ballard, or two different men with the same name.
* 1830 - Living in Pike Co., GA - Ballard, Miles Ballard (age) 40-50 = m-1, (age) 30-40 = f-1, (age) under 5= m-1 and f-1
* 1840 - Living in Pike Co., GA - Ballard, Miles, plus 3 males, 4 females
* 1850 - Living in Pike Co., GA - Ballard, Miles 50,farmer Estate Value = $1250 NC, Eveline 40 NC, Lucy A 16 GA, Powell 14 GA, Henry 8 GA , Lafayette 6 GA, James 4 GA, Amanda, 2 GA, Susan 1 GA
* 1855 - Pike Co., GA Marriage Book - Georgia Vital Statistics, #0325801, page 479: Georgia, Pike Co. - To any Minister of the Gospel, Judge, Justice of the Inferior Court, or Justice of the Peace. You are hereby authorized to join Miles Ballard and Elizabeth C. Knight in the Holy State of Matrimony according to the Constitution and laws of this State and for so doing this shall be your Sufficient License. Given under my hand and Seal, this sixth day of November 1855 - Joseph C. Bickham, C.C.O. (Seal) Georgia, Fayette Co. I do certify that Miles Ballard and Elizabeth C. Knight were duly joined in Matrimony by me this eighth day of November 1855. G. Leach, M.G.- Recorded 21st Nov. 1855 J. C. Bickham
* 1860 - Living in Butler Co., AL - Ballard, Miles 1801 NC, E. Ballard 1811 GA, ML (m) 1844, JP (m) 1846, AF (f) 1847, SE (f) 1849 GA, LA (f) 1857 GA, FJ (m) 1859 AL
* 1860 - Two of his children are listed as still living in Pike County GA with Marcus L. Billingsly 34 - Sarah A. 8GA, John 6 GA. Their paternal grandfather is also in the same home, Elias Billingsley 81 NC

Children of MILES BALLARD and EVELINA BILLINGSLEY are:

2.	i.	ROBERT W.[2] BALLARD, b. 25 Aug 1829, Pike Co., GA; d. 04 Mar 1897, Carroll Co., GA.
3.	ii.	ELIZA JANE BALLARD, b. 1832, Pike Co., GA; d. Aft. 1880.
4.	iii.	LUCY A. BALLARD, b. 1834, Pike Co., GA or NC.
5.	iv.	POWELL F. BALLARD, b. 15 Jan 1837, 1835 Pike Co., GA; d. 03 Nov 1877, Pike Co., GA.
	v.	HENRY BALLARD, b. 1842, Pike Co., GA; d. 26 Jun 1862, Cold Harbor, Hanover Co., VA civil war; m. NANCY BETHENA KENDRICK, 02 Mar 1862, Pike Co., GA; b. Abt. 1844, GA.
	vi.	MILES LAFAYETTE BALLARD, b. 1844, Pike Co., GA; d. 26 Jun 1862, Ellison's Mill, Richmond, VA.
6.	vii.	JAMES POLK BALLARD, b. 26 Jun 1846, Pike Co., GA; d. 28 Jan 1906, Zebulon, Pike Co., GA.
	viii.	AMANDA SARAH BALLARD, b. 1848, Pike Co., GA; m. JOHN HALE.
7.	ix.	SUSAN EVELINA BALLARD, b. 1849, Pike Co., GA; d. 24 Apr 1924, Zebulon, Pike Co., GA.
	x.	SARAH A. BALLARD, b. 1852, Pike Co., GA.
8.	xi.	JOHN H. BALLARD, b. 01 May 1854, Pike Co., GA; d. 22 Jan 1886, Pike Co., GA.

Children of MILES BALLARD and ELIZABETH KNIGHT are:

9.	xii.	LUCY ANN[2] BALLARD, b. 24 Feb 1856, Pike Co., GA; d. 26 Nov 1923, Escambia Co., Pensacola or Leesbury, Lake Co FL.
10.	xiii.	FRANKLIN JEFFERSON BALLARD, b. 22 Feb 1859, Mobile Co., AL; d. 17 Sep 1938, OK City, OK.
11.	xiv.	WILLIAM SOLOMON BALLARD, b. 03 Jun 1861, AL; d. 16 Dec 1936, Hunt Co., TX.

Generation No. 2

2. ROBERT W.[2] BALLARD (MILES[1]) *was born 25 Aug 1829 in Pike Co., GA, and died 04 Mar 1897 in Carroll Co., GA. He married (1)* NANCY H. TURNER *16 Dec 1849 in Pike Co., GA, daughter of* SHADRACH TURNER *and* SARAH SNELGROVE. *She was born 1833 in Pike Co., GA, and died Aft. 1860. He married (2)* SUSAN A. CHILDS OR LYNCH *20 Dec 1864 in Pike Co., GA. She was born 12 Mar 1830 in GA, and died 29 Jun 1911.*

Notes for ROBERT W. BALLARD:
Source: 1860 Pike County Georgia Federal Census Records, Nancy Turner Grogan (bilgro@netdoor.com), Lynn B. Cunningham (lcunnin1@mail.atl.bellsouth.net) Nancy Turner Grogan (bilgro@netdoor.com)

* 1850 - Living in Pike Co., GA - Ballard, Robert, 20, Overseer, NC Nancy B., 17, F, W, GA
* 1860 - Living in Pike Co., GA - Ballard, Robert W., 30, Farmer, Value Real Estate = $750, Value Personal Estate = $528, NC, Nancy H., 27, F, W, GA John G., 9, M, W, GA, Job T., 5, GA, Mary J., 2, GA Walter S., 3/12, GA
* 1870 - Living in Pike Co., GA - Ballard, Robert, 39, Farmer, Val. Real Estate = $800, Val. Pers. Estate = $400, GA, Susan, 39, Keeping House, GA, Job, 15, Attending School, GA, Mary G., Attending School, GA, Walter, 9, Attending School, GA, Ledia, 2, GA
* 1875 - He Moved to Carroll County, Georgia in the Fall of 1875
* 1880 - Living in Carroll Co., GA - Ballard, R.W., 51, Farmer, GA, SC, SC, Ballard, Susan A., W, F, 51, Wife, GA, GA, GA, Ballard, Lela, 12, Dau. GA, Ballard, Robert Lee, 8, Son, GA

More About ROBERT W. BALLARD:

Burial: New Hope United Methodist Church Cemetery Carroll Co., GA

More About SUSAN A. CHILDS OR LYNCH:

Burial: New Hope United Methodist Church Cemetery. Carroll Co., GA

Children of ROBERT BALLARD *and* NANCY TURNER *are:*

       i.   JOHN G.[3] BALLARD, *b. 1851, Pike Co., GA.*

12.   ii. JOB TURNER BALLARD, *b. 05 Nov 1854, Pike Co., GA; d. 19 Jan 1929, Pike Co., GA.*

      iii. MARY JANE BALLARD, *b. 1858, Pike Co., GA; d. 02 Oct 1923, Jefferson Co., AL; m. (1)* FREDERICK WILLIAMSON, *24 Dec 1882, Carroll Co., GA; m. (2)* DAVID B. KUGLAR, *12 Jan 1898, Carroll Co., GA.*

            More About MARY JANE BALLARD:
            Burial: Carrolton City Cemetery, Carroll Co., GA

13.   iv. WALTER SCOTT BALLARD, *b. 22 Feb 1860, Pike Co., GA; d. 20 Dec 1944, Pike Co., GA.*

Children of ROBERT BALLARD *and* SUSAN LYNCH *are:*

14.   v. LELA[3] BALLARD, *b. 08 Mar 1866, Pike Co., GA; d. 17 Feb 1955, Carroll Co., GA.*

      vi. ROBERT LEE BALLARD, *b. 03 May 1869, Pike Co., GA; d. 02 Feb 1933, Franklin Heard Co., GA; m.* IDA L. WALKER, *03 Jan 1899, Carroll Co., GA; b. Sep 1888, GA; d. 10 Nov 1954, Carroll Co., GA.*

3. ELIZA JANE[2] BALLARD (MILES[1]) *was born 1832 in Pike Co., GA, and died Aft. 1880. She married* WILLIAM R. LYNCH *17 Oct 1848 in Pike Co., GA. He was born 1828 in GA, and died Aft. 1880.*

Notes for WILLIAM R. LYNCH:
Source: Lynn Cunningham, 1850-1880 Pike County Georgia Federal Census Records

* 1848 - Georgia, Pike County- To any Minister of the Gospel, Judge, Justice of the Inferior Court, or Justice of the Peace. You are hereby authorized to join William A. Lynch and Eliza Jane Ballard in the Holy State of Matrimony according to the Constitution and laws of this State and for so doing this shall be your sufficient License. Given under my hand and seal this 16th day of October 1848.
Wiley E. Mangham C.C.O.

* 1848 - Georgia, Pike County - I do certify that William R. Lynch and Eliza Jane Ballard were duly joined in matrimony by me this 17th day of October 1848. B.H. White, J.P. Recorded 13th June 1849
W.E. Mangham, C.C.O.
* 1850 - Living in Pike Co., GA - Linch, William, 22, M, Laborer, GA, Elizabeth, 18, GA
* 1860 - Living in Pike Co., GA - Lynch, William 32 farmer GA, Eliza J 27 GA, Wiley 9 GA, Charles R 4 GA, William 2 GA, Lucy A 1/12 GA
* 1870 - Living in Pike Co., GA - Linch, William 42 farmer GA, Eliza J 39 GA, Wiley 19 GA, Charles 13 GA, William 11 GA, Lucy 9 GA, Lula 3 GA, Barto 1 GA
* 1880 - Living in Pike Co., GA - Lnch, William R 53 Laborer GA GA GA, Eliza 50 GA NC NC Lula C 12 GA, Calvin B 10 GA, Emma L 7 GA, Sarah 4 GA

Children of ELIZA BALLARD and WILLIAM LYNCH are:

    i.   JAMES WILEY[3] LYNCH, b. 20 Feb 1851, Pike Co., GA; d. 23 Dec 1939, Pike Co., AL; m. SUSAN.

        Notes for JAMES WILEY LYNCH:
        Source: Pike County Georgia Certificate of Death

   ii. CHARLES B. LYNCH, b. Abt. 1856, Pike Co., GA; d. Aft. 1870.
  iii. WILLIAM L. LYNCH, b. 27 Mar 1857, Pike Co., GA; d. 22 Mar 1924, Griffin, Spalding Co., GA.
  iv. LUCY A. LYNCH, b. 18 Jan 1861, Pike Co., GA; d. 04 Jul 1940, Pike Co., GA; m. THOMAS FRANK KENDRICK; b. 01 May 1853; d. 17 Nov 1930.

        Notes for LUCY A. LYNCH:
        Source: Pike County Georgia Certificate of Death

        More About LUCY A. LYNCH:
        Burial: Beulah Baptist Church Cemetery, Lifsey, Pike Co., GA

    v. LULU LYNCH, b. Abt. 1867, Pike Co., GA; d. Aft. 1880.
   vi. CALVIN BARTO LYNCH, b. Abt. 1869, Pike Co., GA; d. Aft. 1880.
  vii. EMMA L. LYNCH, b. Abt. 1873, Pike Co., GA; d. Aft. 1880.
 viii. SARAY LYNCH, b. Abt. 1876, Pike Co., GA; d. Aft. 1880.

4. LUCY A.[2] BALLARD (MILES[1]) was born 1834 in Pike Co., GA or NC. She married STEPHEN KIRK 06 Jan 1853 in Carroll Co., GA. He was born Abt. 1830 in GA, and died 27 Jul 1862.

Child of LUCY BALLARD and STEPHEN KIRK is:

15.   i. SAVANNAH ALICE[3] KIRK, b. 20 Dec 1859, GA; d. 22 Dec 1952, Pike Co., GA.

5. POWELL F.[2] BALLARD (MILES[1]) was born 15 Jan 1837 in 1835 Pike Co., GA, and died 03 Nov 1877 in Pike Co., GA. He married MARY FRANCES GREEN 07 Nov 1856 in Pike Co., GA, daughter of MOUNTAIN GREEN and POLLY. She was born 22 Sep 1837 in Pike Co., GA, and died 24 Mar 1924 in Pike Co., GA.

Notes for POWELL F. BALLARD:

Source: M. G. Wayne Ballard, Annie B. Maner, D Richard Ballard, 1860, 1870 Pike County Georgia Federal Census Records, Lynn B. Cunningham (lcunnin1@bellsouth.net), History of Anson Co NC pg 1665
* 1860 - Living in Pike Co., GA - Page 69, - Ballard, Powell F. 25 GA Farmer, Mary F. 21 GA, Mary E. 2 GA, Richard S., 9/12 GA
* 1862 - Enlisted 4 March 1862 as a Private served Georgia H Co. 44th Inf Reg. GA
* 1866 - Sold homeplace in Pike Co., GA adjoining Mr. Mountain Kendrick and Mrs. Mitt (Langford) Kendrick to Tom Roan
* 1870 - Living in Pike Co., GA - Ballard, Powell F. 35 GA, Farmer, Mary F. 32 GA, Mary E., 12 Attending School GA, Richard S., 10 Attending School, GA, Frances B., 8, Attending School GA, William P., 3, GA, Emma, 2, GA, Warner, John, 22, GA, Lifsey, Benjamin, 12, GA
* 1877 - Powell Ballard was murdered.

More About POWELL F. BALLARD:
Burial: Ballard Green Cemetery, Zebulon, Pike Co., GA

Notes for MARY FRANCES GREEN:
Source: 1880-1910 Pike County Georgia Federal Census Records, Pike County Georgia Standard Certificate of Death

* 1880 - Living in Pike Co., GA - Ballard, Mary 92 GA farmer, Richard S 21 GA, Fannie B 19 GA, William 15 GA, Emma 12 GA, Rebecca 9 GA, James 7 GA, Teressa 5 GA, Elizabeth 2 GA
* 1910 - Living in Pike Co., GA - Living with her son William P. Ballard

More About MARY FRANCES GREEN:
Burial: Ballard Green Cemetery, Zebulon, Pike Co., GA

Children of POWELL BALLARD and MARY GREEN are:

      i.   HENRY J.[3] BALLARD, b. Bet. 1854 - 1864, Pike Co., GA.
      ii. MARY EVELYN BALLARD, b. 18 Oct 1857, Pike Co., GA; d. 18 Sep 1949, Pike Co., GA; m. (1) JAMES FRANKLIN MCKINLEY, 23 Dec 1875, Pike Co., GA; b. 12 Mar 1855, Pike Co., GA; d. 30 Nov 1892, Pike Co., GA; m. (2) ELIJAH MCKINLEY, 02 Jan 1902, Pike Co., GA; b. 26 Jun 1854, Pike Co., GA; d. 03 Oct 1933, Pike Co., GA.

          More About MARY EVELYN BALLARD:
          Burial: McKinley Family Cemetery, Zebulon, Pike Co., GA

          More About JAMES FRANKLIN MCKINLEY:
          Burial: McKinley Family Cemetery, Zebulon, Pike Co., GA

          More About ELIJAH MCKINLEY:
          Burial: McKinley Family Cemetery, Zebulon, Pike Co, GA

16.   iii. RICHARD STEPHEN BALLARD, b. 05 Aug 1859, Pike Co., GA; d. 10 May 1940, Pike Co., GA.
       iv. FRANCES B. BALLARD, b. 28 May 1861, Pike Co., GA; d. 12 Jul 1919, Nacogdoches Co TX; m. ALONZO A. MCKINLEY, 17 Nov 1880, Pike Co., GA; b. 16 Nov 1860, Pike Co., GA; d. 28 Dec 1917, Nacogdoches Co TX.
17.   v.   WILLIAM POWELL BALLARD, b. 28 Feb 1866, Pike Co., GA; d. 27 Sep 1917, Pike Co., GA.
18.   vi. SARAH EMMA BALLARD, b. 16 May 1868, Pike Co., GA; d. 13 May 1940, Pike Co., GA.
       vii. REBECCA BALLARD, b. 1870, Pike Co., GA; d. 31 May 1940, Pike Co., GA; m. THOMAS MCCORD; b. 07 Nov 1869, GA; d. 23 Nov 1942.

          More About THOMAS MCCORD:
          Burial: Bethel Baptist Church Cemetery, Milner, Lamar Co., GA
      viii. GERTRUDE "TRUDA" TERESA BALLARD, b. 16 Apr 1875, Pike Co., GA; d. 30 Aug 1961, Griffin GA; m.

EDWARD LEROY MCKINLEY, 01 Dec 1901, Pike Co., GA; b. 03 May 1878, GA; d. 23 Mar 1952, Pike Co., GA.
ix. JAMES P. BALLARD, b. 02 Nov 1877, 1873 Pike Co., GA; d. 18 Nov 1892, Pike Co., GA.
x. ELIZABETH BUSSEY BALLARD, b. 20 Apr 1878, Pike Co., GA; d. 04 Jul 1955, Pike Co., GA; m. RICHARD ALDINE MCKINLEY, 07 Apr 1907, Pike Co., GA; b. Dec 1882, Pike Co., GA; d. 29 Mar 1951, Pike Co., GA.

6. JAMES POLK[2] BALLARD (MILES[1]) was born 26 Jun 1846 in Pike Co., GA, and died 28 Jan 1906 in Zebulon, Pike Co., GA. He married KATHERINE "KITTIE" MATILDA AVERY 18 Oct 1870 in Pike Co., GA. She was born 1851 in GA, and died 11 Nov 1889 in Pike Co., GA.

Notes for JAMES POLK BALLARD:
Source- 1880 -1900 Pike County Georgia Federal Census Soundex Georgia, Lynn B. Cunningham (lcunnin1@bellsouth.net)

* 1880 - Living in Pike Co., GA - Ballard, Ballard, James P 34, Kittie 29, Evey 8, Mary W 5, Luie C 3
* 1900 - Living in Pike Co., GA - Ballard, James P - Jun 1842 GA NC GA, Eva 24 - Jul 1875 GA, Mary W 22 - Sep 1877 GA, Laurie C 19 - Jun 1880 GA, Essie 16 - Apr 1884 GA
* 1906 - Pike County Times-Journal, Zebulon, Ga., Friday, February 2, 1906 - Death of J.P. Ballard - James Polk Ballard died at his home in Zebulon Sunday morning. He had been in bad health for several months and his death has been expected at any time during the last month. He was born in 1842 [?] and had lived in Zebulon since 1867. He was married to Miss Kittie Avery in 1870, she dying in 1888. Four children were born to them, Misses Eva, Mary Will, Mrs. Louie Foster, and Miss Essie. Funeral services were held at the Methodist church Monday afternoon, conducted by Rev. F.W. McCleskey, after which he was buried in the Methodist cemetery. The town and community feel for the daughters and extend them sympathy. (Transcribed by Lynn Ballard Cunningham)

More About JAMES POLK BALLARD:
Burial: Zebulon Methodist Church Cemetery, Zebulon, Pike Co., GA

More About KATHERINE "KITTIE" MATILDA AVERY:
Burial: Zebulon Methodist Church Cemetery, Zebulon, Pike Co., GA

Children of JAMES BALLARD and KATHERINE AVERY are:
i. EVA[3] BALLARD, b. 19 Jul 1871, Pike Co., GA; d. 26 Feb 1950, Pike Co., GA.

Notes for EVA BALLARD:
Source: 1910-1930 Pike County Georgia Federal Census Records

* 1910 - Living in Zebulon, Pike Co., GA - Ballard, Eva 35 GA GA GA, Mary sister 32 GA, Essie sister 23 GA, plus two boarders
* 1920 - Living in Zebulon, Pike Co., GA - Ballard, Eva 45 GA GA GA, Mary Willie 42 sister GA GA GA and 1 boarder
* 1930 - Living in Zebulon, Pike Co., GA - Ballard, Eva 56 GA plus 1 boarder

More About EVA BALLARD:
Burial: Zebulon Methodist Church Cemetery, Zebulon, Pike Co., GA

ii. AVERY BALLARD, b. 1872, Pike Co., GA; d. Aft. 1880.
iii. MARY WILLIE BALLARD, b. 01 Sep 1874, Pike Co., GA; d. 21 Aug 1925, Pike Co., GA.

More About MARY WILLIE BALLARD:
Burial: Zebulon Methodist Church Cemetery, Zebulon, Pike Co., GA

19. iv. LOUIE CLYDE BALLARD, b. 02 Jun 1880, Pike Co., GA; d. 14 Apr 1946, Pike Co., GA.

     v.   ESSIE BALLARD, *b. 14 Apr 1883, Pike Co., GA; d. 15 Aug 1911, Pike Co., GA.*

          More About ESSIE BALLARD:
          Burial: Zebulon Methodist Church Cemetery, Zebulon, Pike Co., GA

7. SUSAN EVELINA[2] BALLARD (MILES[1]) *was born 1849 in Pike Co., GA, and died 24 Apr 1924 in Zebulon, Pike Co., GA. She married* HENRY HARPER *22 Dec 1867 in Pike Co., GA. He was born 15 Sep 1845 in Pike Co., GA, and died 16 Feb 1904 in Dodge Co., GA.*

Notes for SUSAN EVELINA BALLARD:
Source: The Pike County Journal (Lynn Cunningham)

* Obit - Friday, Apr. 18, 1924 - Mrs. S.E. Harper Dies On Friday - Mrs. S.E. Harper died at the home of her nephew, W.S. Ballard of near Zebulon, after a brief illness of four days. Passing away just as the day dawned last Friday morning. Mrs. Harper was reared in old Pike county and had many relatives and friends who will regret to hear of her death. She was the widow of the late Henry Harper and a sister of the late Powell, Robert, James P. And John Ballard, also a sister of Mrs. William Lynch and Mrs. William Hales, all deceased. She was the mother of J.H. Harper. Fourteen grandchildren and several nieces and nephews survive her. [Transcribed 7/4/2007 Lynn Cunningham]

Notes for HENRY HARPER:
Source: 1880 Pike County Georgia Federal Census Records, 1900 Dodge County Georgia Federal Census Records

* 1880 - Living in Pike Co., GA - Harper, Henry 35, Susan 30, Selina J 12, James 8, John 2, Walter Ballard 20
* 1900 - Living in Eddins, Dodge Co., GA - Harper, Henry S 54, Susan E 49

More About HENRY HARPER:
Burial: Bowers Cemetery, Empire, Dodge Co., GA

Children of SUSAN BALLARD *and* HENRY HARPER *are:*

        i.   SELINA J.[3] HARPER, *b. Abt. 1868, Pike Co., GA; d. Aft. 1880.*
      ii.   JOHN HARPER, *b. Abt. 1871, Pike Co., GA; d. Aft. 1880.*
    iii. JAMES HARPER, *b. Abt. 1872, Pike Co., GA; d. Aft. 1880.*

8. JOHN H.[2] BALLARD (MILES[1]) *was born 01 May 1854 in Pike Co., GA, and died 22 Jan 1886 in Pike Co., GA. He married* SARAH ALICE CAPEL. *She was born 04 Jun 1858 in Pike Co., GA, and died 21 Jul 1899 in Pike Co., GA.*

Notes for JOHN H. BALLARD:
Source: 1880 Pike County Georgia Federal Census Records, Lynn B. Cunningham (lcunnin1@bellsouth.net)
* 1880 - Living in Pike Co., GA - Ballard, John H 26, Allice 22, Emma 3, Maud C 1

More About JOHN H. BALLARD:
Burial: Mt. Olive Baptist Church Cemetery, Molena, Pike Co., GA

More About SARAH ALICE CAPEL:
Burial: Mt. Olive Baptist Church Cemetery, Molena, Pike Co., GA

Children of JOHN BALLARD *and* SARAH CAPEL *are:*
        i.   EMMA[3] BALLARD, *b. 1877, Pike Co., GA; d. Aft. 1880, FL; m. F. H.* CONNALLY, *25 Dec 1898, Pike Co., GA; b. Abt. 1878.*

ii.   MAUDE C. BALLARD, b. Abt. 1879, Pike Co., GA; d. Aft. 1880; m. CHARLES DAYTON HOWELL, 23 Dec 1897, Pike Co., GA.

9. LUCY ANN[2] BALLARD (MILES[1]) was born 24 Feb 1856 in Pike Co., GA, and died 26 Nov 1923 in Escambia Co., Pensacola or Leesbury, Lake Co FL. She married W. J. BLANCHARD 22 Nov 1877 in Butler Co., AL. He was born 1843 in Al, and died Bef. 1900 in FL.

Notes for LUCY ANN BALLARD:
Source: Annie B. Maner (AManer@msn.com)
* 1877 - Marriage License of Lucy Ann Ballard and W. R. Blanchard - The State of Alabama, Butler Co.. To any Ordained or Licensed Minister of the Gospel, Judge of the Circuit or Probate Courts, or Justice of the Peace for said Co. - Greeting: You are hereby Authorized to celebrate the Rites of Matrimony between W. R. Blanchard and Lucy Ann Ballard and this shall be your sufficient authority for so doing. Given under my hand and seal this 22nd day of November AD 1877 and of American Independence the 101 Year. J. L. Powell, Judge of Probate. The above parties were married by me at my office ? (hard to read Misslls??) on the 22nd day of November AD 1877. J. L. Poll Probate Judge.

Child of LUCY BALLARD and W. BLANCHARD is:
20.   i.   GORDON[3] BLANCHARD, b. Jul 1877, Al; d. 24 Jul 1915, Pensacola FL.

10. FRANKLIN JEFFERSON[2] BALLARD (MILES[1]) was born 22 Feb 1859 in Mobile Co. AL, and died 17 Sep 1938 in OK City, OK. He married (1) MARY ELIZABETH BRIDGES 1884 in MS or LA, daughter of GEORGE BRIDGES. She was born 22 Apr 1867 in MS, and died 29 Mar 1915 in Clinton, Hunt Co., TX. He married (2) ANNA LUETISH "LULA" GREEN Abt. 1916, daughter of MATT GREEN and LIZZIE. She was born 16 Jun 1880 in Salem Parish, LA, and died 12 Aug 1936 in OK City, OK Co., OK.

Notes for FRANKLIN JEFFERSON BALLARD:
Source: 1900 Hunt County Texas Federal Census Records, 1910 Collin County Texas Federal Census Records, 1930 Carter County Oklahoma Federal Census Records, Annie B. Maner (AManer@msn.com), Rose Smith Bush, Lynn B. Cunningham (lcunnin1@bellsouth.net)
* 1900 - Living in Hunt Co., TX - Ballard, Franklin J 40 - Feb 1860 AL AL AL, Mary E 34 - Apr 1866 MS GA VA, William P 15 - Mar 1885 LA, Ardelia 13 - Mar 1887 TX, James H 11 - Feb 1889 TX, Lucy G 8 - June 1891 TX, Joseph J 5 - Jan 1895 TX , Lawrence L 1 - June 1898 TX, Florence S 1 - June 1898 TX
* 1910 - Living in Farmersville, Collin Co., TX - Ballard, Franklin J 51 farmer AL GA AL, Lizzie 43 MS GA LA, Lucy 18 LA, Joseph 14 TX, Lawrence 11 TX, Florence 11 TX, Eula M 8 TX, Stella 6 TX, Ruthie 4 TX, Jesse 6/12 TX
* 1930 - Living in Lone Grove, Carter Co., OK - Ballard, Frank J 71 AL AL AL, Lula 48 LA LA AL, Ruby 12 OK, Alton 10 OK, Horice 6 OK, Harold 3 //12 OK

More About FRANKLIN JEFFERSON BALLARD:
Burial: Sunny Lane Cemetery, Oklahoma Co., OK

More About MARY ELIZABETH BRIDGES:
Burial: Old Liberty Cemetery, Farmersville, Caddo Co., TX

Children of FRANKLIN BALLARD and MARY BRIDGES are:

21.   i.   WILLIAM PINKTON[3] BALLARD, b. 13 Mar 1885, LA; d. 13 Sep 1964, Ventura Co., CA.
22.   ii. ARDELIA "DELIA" BALLARD, b. 23 Mar 1887, TX; d. 05 Jun 1950, Caddo Mills, Hunt Co., TX.
23.   iii. JAMES "JIM" HARRISON BALLARD, b. 27 Feb 1889, TX; d. 29 Mar 1976, Lindsey, Tulare Co., CA.
24.   iv. LUCY "MAE" GRAY BALLARD, b. 01 Jun 1892, TX; d. 1948, OK.
25.   v.   JOSEPH "JOE" JEFFERSON BALLARD, b. 29 Jan 1896, TX; d. 02 Jan 1962, OK City, OK.
26.   vi. FLORENCE SUSAN BALLARD, b. 26 Jun 1898, Greenville, Hunt Co., TX; d. 21 Sep 1979, Centerville, Leon Co., TX.

27.   vii.   LAWRENCE LAFAYETTE BALLARD, b. 26 Jun 1898, Greenville, Hunt Co., TX; d. 12 Feb 1966, Norwalk, Los Angeles Co., CA.

28.   viii.   EULA MAE BALLARD, b. 28 Jun 1901, Clinton, Hunt Co., TX; d. 31 Dec 1950, Eddie, NM.

        ix.   STELLA ELIZABETH BALLARD, b. 30 Aug 1903, OK; d. 17 Mar 1987, Astoria, Clatsop Co., OR; m. (1) MR. NOETH; m. (2) MR. CARROLL.

        x.   IMA RUTH BALLARD, b. 29 Mar 1906, OK; d. 06 May 1993, Multnomah Co., OR; m. MARVIN BRODERICK.

More About IMA RUTH BALLARD:

Burial: Lee Mission Cemetery, Salem, Marion Co., OR

29.   xi.   JESSIE MILES BALLARD, b. 08 Aug 1909, Caddo Mills, Hunt Co., TX; d. 25 Jun 1989, Salem, Marion Co., OR.

        xii.   EUGENE "DOLLIE" BALLARD, b. Abt. 1910, OK or TX.

Children of FRANKLIN BALLARD and ANNA GREEN are:

        xiii.   RUBY LOIS[3] BALLARD, b. 22 Nov 1917, OK; d. 15 Oct 1991; m. CLEO SMITH, 13 Apr 1934.

30.   xiv.   WILBERT ALTON BALLARD, b. 17 Aug 1919, Caddo Mills, Hunt Co., TX; d. 26 Oct 1984, Tehama Co., CA.

        xv.   ERNEST BALLARD, b. Abt. 1920, OK.

        xvi.   HORACE WELDON BALLARD, b. 12 Mar 1923, OK; d. Aft. 1930.

        xvii.   HAROLD B. BALLARD, b. 07 Sep 1926, Durant OK; d. Aft. 1930.

11. WILLIAM SOLOMON[2] BALLARD (MILES[1]) was born 03 Jun 1861 in AL, and died 16 Dec 1936 in Hunt Co., TX. He married (1) EMMA C. PRICE 12 Sep 1886 in Hunt Co., TX. She was born 02 May 1867 in LA, and died 17 Dec 1890 in Hunt Co., TX. He married (2) ELIZABETH "ELIZA" ANN BURGHES 26 Jan 1896 in Hunt Co., TX. She was born 17 Mar 1870 in MO, and died 30 Aug 1958 in Dallas, Dallas Co., TX.

Notes for WILLIAM SOLOMON BALLARD:
Source: Hunt County Texas Certificate of Death, 1900-1930 Hunt County Texas Federal Census Records

* 1900 - Living in Hunt Co., TX - Ballard, Wm S 38 June 1861 AL GA AL Family, Eliza A. 24 May 1876 - 2 children 1 living MO MO MO, Annie 12 - Aug 1887 TX, Josie 9 - Dec 1890 TX, Elton 2 - May 1898 TX, Geo Lewis 26 boarder
* 1910 - Living in Hunt Co., TX - Ballard, Will 42 md 2x AL, Lina 34 - 6 children 4 living MO, Elton 11, Mirtle 10 TX, Naoma 5 TX, Frank 2 TX, Ceve Lindsey 24 laborer TX
* 1920 - Living in Hunt Co., TX - Ballard, William S 58 AL GA AL, Lizzie A 42 MO MO TN, Frank B 12 TN, Irene O 9 TX, Ima Lee 2 4/12 TX, Katie M 1/12 TX
* 1930 - Living in Hunt Co., TX - Ballard, William S 69 AL TN AL, Eliza A 53 MO MO MO, Irene 19 TX, Ima L 12 TX, Katie 10 TX, William Ford 27 lodger

More About WILLIAM SOLOMON BALLARD:
Burial: Royce City Cemetery, Royce City, Rockwall Co., TX

More About ELIZABETH "ELIZA" ANN BURGHES:
Burial: Royce City Cemetery, Royce City, Rockwall Co., TX

Children of WILLIAM BALLARD and EMMA PRICE are:
        i.   ANNIE[3] BALLARD, b. 1888, TX.
        ii.   JOSIE BALLARD, b. Dec 1890.

Children of WILLIAM BALLARD and ELIZABETH BURGHES are:

31. iii. WILLIAM ELTON[3] BALLARD, b. 24 May 1898, Hunt Co., TX; d. 17 Jul 1980, Pampa, Gray Co., TX.

  iv. MYRLTE BALLARD, b. Abt. 1900, Hunt Co., TX; d. Aft. 1910.

  v. NAOMA BALLARD, b. Abt. 1905, Hunt Co., TX; d. 25 Oct 1918, Hunt Co., TX.

Notes for NAOMA BALLARD:
Source: Hunt County Texas Standard Certificate of Death

  vi. BENJAMIN FRANKLIN "FRANK" BALLARD, b. 27 Jun 1907, Hunt Co., TX; d. 08 Mar 1983; m. AGNES M. ALLEN; b. 28 Aug 1913; d. 11 Apr 2001.

More About BENJAMIN FRANKLIN "FRANK" BALLARD:
Burial: Royce City Cemetery, Royce City, Rockwall Co., TX

More About AGNES M. ALLEN:
Burial: Royce City Cemetery, Royce City, Rockwall Co., TX

  vii. IRENE O. BALLARD, b. 23 Sep 1910, Hunt Co., TX; d. 16 Dec 1991; m. BILL AKIN, 19 Sep 1931, Rockwall Co., TX; b. 24 Dec 1909; d. 03 Nov 1990.

More About IRENE O. BALLARD:
Burial: Royce City Cemetery, Rockwall Co., TX

More About BILL AKIN:
Burial: Royce City Cemetery, Rockwall Co., TX

32. viii. IMA LEE BALLARD, b. 10 Jun 1917, Hunt Co., TX; d. 20 Nov 2008.

  ix. KATIE M. BALLARD, b. Abt. 1920, Hunt Co., TX; d. Aft. 1930.

Generation No. 3

12. JOB TURNER[3] BALLARD (ROBERT W.[2], MILES[1]) was born 05 Nov 1854 in Pike Co., GA, and died 19 Jan 1929 in Pike Co., GA. He married ELIZABETH JANE BEVIL 02 Nov 1882 in Pike Co., GA. She was born 05 Nov 1864 in Pike Co., GA, and died 25 Jun 1944 in Pike Co., GA.

Notes for JOB TURNER BALLARD:
Source: Lynn Cunningham (lcunnin1@bellsouth.net)

More About JOB TURNER BALLARD:
Burial: Bevil Hawkins Cemetery near Zebulon

Children of JOB BALLARD and ELIZABETH BEVIL are:

  i. NANCY "NANNIE" ELIZABETH[4] BALLARD, b. 28 Apr 1884, Pike Co., GA; d. 08 Jun 1959, Pike Co., GA; m. CLAUDE TURNER BRANCH; b. 28 Nov 1878, SC; d. 28 Sep 1958, Pike Co., GA.

More About NANCY "NANNIE" ELIZABETH BALLARD:
Burial: Eastview Cemetery, Zebulon, Pike Co., GA

More About CLAUDE TURNER BRANCH:
Burial: Eastview Cemetery, Zebulon, Pike Co., GA

  ii. VINIE CAROLINE BALLARD, b. 27 Jul 1885, Pike Co., GA; m. WILL HENRY DUNN, Dec 1906; b. 1884; d. 1950.

More About VINIE CAROLINE BALLARD:
Burial: Eastview Cemetery, Zebulon, Pike Co., GA

More About WILL HENRY DUNN:
Burial: Eastview Cemetery, Zebulon, Pike Co., GA

   iii.   MATTIE BALLARD, *b. 29 Jun 1887, Pike Co., GA; d. 08 Dec 1969; m. ODIS LAMAR SMITH; b. 10 Jul 1878; d. 01 Jan 1930.*

More About MATTIE BALLARD:
Burial: New Hope Baptist Church Cemetery, Zebulon, Pike Co., GA

More About ODIS LAMAR SMITH:
Burial: New Hope Baptist Church Cemetery, Zebulon, Pike Co., GA

   iv.   JOSIE ANN BALLARD, *b. 06 May 1890, Pike Co., GA; d. 10 Nov 1975; m. THOMAS LAFAYETTE JOHNSON, 29 Dec 1907; b. 28 Jan 1889; d. 19 Oct 1964.*
   v.   EVELYN BALLARD, *b. 16 Jun 1893, Pike Co., GA; d. 07 Jun 1963; m. EMMETT BECKHAM, 27 Dec 1914, Zebulon, Pike Co., GA; b. 12 Mar 1887; d. 26 Apr 1973.*

More About EVELYN BALLARD:
Burial: Beckham Cemetery, Concord Pike Co., GA

More About EMMETT BECKHAM:
Burial: Beckham Cemetery, Concord Pike Co., GA

   vi.   IVA BALLARD, *b. 02 Sep 1895, Pike Co., GA; d. 17 Dec 1978, Pike Co., GA.*

More About IVA BALLARD:
Burial: Bevil-Hawkins Family Cemetery, Zebulon, Pike Co., GA

   vii.   ALVEY SCOTT BALLARD, *b. 30 Apr 1899, Pike Co., GA; d. 03 Jun 1972, Cobb Co., GA; m. (1) MILDRED REEVES; b. 12 Oct 1902; d. 23 Jul 1993; m. (2) MARJORIE ALICE HEDDEN, 30 Jan 1945; b. 10 Dec 1917, Love Co., OK; d. 21 Mar 1990, Cobb Co., GA.*

More About MILDRED REEVES:
Burial: Oak Hill Cemetery, Griffin, Spalding Co., GA

   viii.   HARDY BALLARD, *b. 15 Feb 1902, Pike Co., GA; d. 20 Jun 1971; m. EFFIE BASSIETT; b. 06 Sep 1902; d. 12 May 1984.*

More About HARDY BALLARD:
Burial: Griffin Memorial Gardens, Spalding Co., GA

More About EFFIE BASSIETT:
Burial: Griffin Memorial Gardens, Griffin, Spalding Co., GA

13. WALTER SCOTT[3] BALLARD (ROBERT W.[2], MILES[1]) *was born 22 Feb 1860 in Pike Co., GA, and died 20 Dec 1944 in Pike Co., GA. He married SARAH CAROLINE BEVIL 16 Oct 1883 in Pike Co., GA. She was born 05 Mar 1866 in Pike Co., GA, and died 05 Feb 1952 in Pike Co., GA.*

More About WALTER SCOTT BALLARD:

Burial: New Hope Baptist Cemetery, Zebulon, Pike Co., GA

More About SARAH CAROLINE BEVIL:

Burial: New Hope Baptist Cemetery, Zebulon, Pike Co., GA

Children of WALTER BALLARD and SARAH BEVIL are:

> i. ETTA[4] BALLARD, b. 20 Mar 1886, GA; d. 15 Dec 1974, Spalding Co., GA; m. GEORGE MARTIN BARROW; b. 28 Feb 1885, Pike Co., GA; d. 18 Jan 1947, Spalding Co., GA.
>
> 33. ii. JOBE TURNER BALLARD, b. 06 Apr 1892, GA; d. 05 May 1928, Pike Co., GA.

14. LELA[3] BALLARD (ROBERT W.[2], MILES[1]) was born 08 Mar 1866 in Pike Co., GA, and died 17 Feb 1955 in Carroll Co., GA. She married JESSE KUGLAR 26 Aug 1889 in Carroll Co., Ga. He was born 02 Nov 1867 in GA, and died 10 Feb 1937 in Carroll Co., GA.

Notes for LELA BALLARD:
Source: Lynn Ballard Cunningham (lcunnin1@bellsouth.net)

Notes for JESSE KUGLAR:
Source: LDS-IGI

Children of LELA BALLARD and JESSE KUGLAR are:

> i. KATE[4] KUGLAR, b. Abt. 1885, Henry GA.
> ii. PAUL KUGLAR, b. Abt. 1886.
> iii. BONNIE KUGLAR, b. Abt. 1890.

15. SAVANNAH ALICE[3] KIRK (LUCY A.[2] BALLARD, MILES[1]) was born 20 Dec 1859 in GA, and died 22 Dec 1952 in Pike Co., GA. She married RICHARD STEPHEN BALLARD 21 Oct 1880 in Pike Co., GA, son of POWELL BALLARD and MARY GREEN. He was born 05 Aug 1859 in Pike Co., GA, and died 10 May 1940 in Pike Co., GA.

Notes for RICHARD STEPHEN BALLARD:
Source:1880-1930 Pike County Georgia Federal Census Records, Lynn B. Cunningham (lcunnin1@bellsouth.net)

* 1910 - Living in Pike Co., GA - Ballard, Richard 51, Savannah 51, Richard G 23, Nancy Billingly mother in law
* 1920 - Living in Pike Co., GA - Ballard, Richard 63, Savannah 60, Richard G 33, Nancy F Billingsly 83 mo in law
* 1930 - Living in Pike Co., GA - Ballard, Richard 70, Bavanah 70 (with son Richard)

Children of SAVANNAH KIRK and RICHARD BALLARD are:
> i. RICHARD G.[4] BALLARD, b. 12 Mar 1886, Pike Co., GA; d. 26 Aug 1931, Spalding Co., GA.
>
> *More About RICHARD G. BALLARD:*
> *Burial: Ballard Green Cemetery, Zebulon, Pike Co., GA*
>
> 34. ii. WILLIAM P. BALLARD, b. 09 Sep 1881, Pike Co., GA; d. 10 Feb 1971.

16. RICHARD STEPHEN[3] BALLARD (POWELL F.[2], MILES[1]) was born 05 Aug 1859 in Pike Co., GA, and died 10 May 1940 in Pike Co., GA. He married SAVANNAH ALICE KIRK 21 Oct 1880 in Pike Co., GA, daughter of STEPHEN KIRK and LUCY BALLARD. She was born 20 Dec 1859 in GA, and died 22 Dec 1952 in Pike Co., GA.

Notes for RICHARD STEPHEN BALLARD:

Source:1880-1930 Pike County Georgia Federal Census Records, Lynn B. Cunningham (lcunnin1@bellsouth.net)
* 1910 - Living in Pike Co., GA - Ballard, Richard 51, Savannah 51, Richard G 23, Nancy Billingly mother in law
* 1920 - Living in Pike Co., GA - Ballard, Richard 63, Savannah 60, Richard G 33, Nancy F Billingsly 83 mo in law
* 1930 - Living in Pike Co., GA - Ballard, Richard 70, Savanah 70 (with son Richard)

Children are listed above under (15) Savannah Alice Kirk.

17. WILLIAM POWELL[3] BALLARD (POWELL F.[2], MILES[1]) was born 28 Feb 1866 in Pike Co., GA, and died 27 Sep 1917 in Pike Co., GA. He married MARY VIRGINIA "JENNIE" HARRIS 05 Mar 1893 in Pike Co., GA, daughter of HENRY HARRIS and SUSAN HARDEN. She was born 03 Sep 1873 in Pike Co., GA, and died 30 May 1950 in Pike Co., GA.

Notes for WILLIAM POWELL BALLARD:
Source:1910 Pike County Georgia Federal Census Records, Annie Maner, D Richard Ballard

* 1910 - Living in Pike Co., GA - Ballard, William P 44 GA GA GA, Jennie 36 - 7 children 7 living GA GA GA, Zen 15 GA, Arthur 13 GA, Jewell 11 GA, Ollie 8 GA, Ruby 5 GA, Kelly 3 GA, Howard 6/12 GA, Polly 73 mother GA GA GA 9 children 8 living

More About WILLIAM POWELL BALLARD:

Burial: New Hope Cemetery Pike Co., GA

Notes for MARY VIRGINIA "JENNIE" HARRIS:

Source: 1920 - 1930 Pike County Georgia Federal Census Records

* 1920 - Living in Pike Co., GA - Ballard, Jessie V 46, Iva Jewell 20, O. J 18, Ruby M 15, Elton K 14, Howard C 11, Ennis W 8, M Conrad 4
* 1930 - Living in Pike Co., GA - Ballard, M Virginia 46, O J 28, Kelly 24, Mary Jane 22, Ennis 19, Conrad 14

More About MARY VIRGINIA "JENNIE" HARRIS:
Burial: New Hope Baptist Cemetery, Zebulon, Pike Co., GA

Children of WILLIAM BALLARD and MARY HARRIS are:

35.　　　　i.　WILLIAM ZENEFORD[4] BALLARD, b. 10 Aug 1894, Pike Co., GA; d. 24 Apr 1966, Pike Co., GA.
　　　　　ii.　ARTHUR ROLAND BALLARD, b. 20 Feb 1897, Pike Co., GA; d. 24 Apr 1966, Pike Co., GA.

　　　　　　　More About ARTHUR ROLAND BALLARD:
　　　　　　　Burial: New Hope Baptist Cemetery, Zebulon, Pike Co., GA

36.　　　　iii.　IVA JEWELL BALLARD, b. 23 Mar 1899, Pike Co., GA; d. 21 Aug 1997.
　　　　　iv.　OLLIE JAMES BALLARD, b. 26 Dec 1901, Pike Co., GA; d. 05 Sep 1989; m. BENA CLARK; b. 21 Oct 1907; d. 23 Jan 1999.

　　　　　　　More About OLLIE JAMES BALLARD:
　　　　　　　Burial: Oak Hill Cemetery, Griffin, Spalding Co., GA

　　　　　　　More About BENA CLARK:
　　　　　　　Burial: Oak Hill Cemetery, Griffin, Spalding Co., GA

　　　　　v.　RUBY MYRTLE BALLARD, b. 10 Jun 1904, Pike Co., GA; d. 16 Oct 2000; m. W. T. JONES.

　　　　　　　More About RUBY MYRTLE BALLARD:
　　　　　　　Burial: New Hope Baptist Cemetery, Zebulon, Pike Co., GA

     vi.   ELTON KELLY BALLARD, b. 16 Mar 1906, Pike Co., GA; d. 03 Dec 1960, Jacksonville, Duval Co., FL; m. MARY JANE PERKINS.

         More About ELTON KELLY BALLARD:
         Burial: New Hope Baptist Cemetery, Zebulon, Pike Co., GA

     vii.   HOWARD CLAY BALLARD, b. 12 Oct 1908, Pike Co., GA; d. 10 Aug 1985, Pike Co., GA; m. LOUISE HUNTER, 05 Aug 1939; b. 05 Feb 1915, Pike Co., GA; d. 11 Sep 1999, GA.

         More About HOWARD CLAY BALLARD:
         Burial: New Hope Baptist Cemetery, Zebulon, Pike Co., GA

         More About LOUISE HUNTER:
         Burial: New Hope Baptist Cemetery, Zebulon, Pike Co., GA

     viii.   ENNES WENDELL BALLARD, b. 25 Mar 1911, Pike Co., GA; d. 28 Nov 1995, Spaulding Co., GA.

         More About ENNES WENDELL BALLARD:
         Burial: New Hope Baptist Cemetery, Zebulon, Pike Co., GA

     ix.   MARVIN CONRAD BALLARD, b. 25 Apr 1915, Pike Co., GA; d. 02 Sep 2007; m. MARY DAVIS, 04 Jul 1954; b. 02 Jan 1919; d. 27 Oct 2001.

         More About MARVIN CONRAD BALLARD:
         Burial: New Hope Baptist Cemetery, Zebulon, Pike Co., GA

         More About MARY DAVIS:
         Burial: Oak Hill Cemetery, Griffin, Spalding Co., GA

18. SARAH EMMA[3] BALLARD (POWELL F.[2], MILES[1]) was born 16 May 1868 in Pike Co., GA, and died 13 May 1940 in Pike Co., GA. She married JOSEPH BARTOW REEVES 19 Apr 1891 in Pike Co., GA. He was born 08 Dec 1860 in Pike Co., GA, and died 07 Sep 1937 in Pike Co., GA.

Notes for JOSEPH BARTOW REEVES:

Source: 1900 Merewether County Georgia Federal Census Records, 1910 Pike County Georgia Federal Census Records
* 1900 - Living in Merewether Co., GA - Ballard, Joe - Dec 1854, Emma - May 1868, Lena B - May 1892, Trunis - Dec 1893, Horace - Mar 1895, Eugene - June 1896, Billy - Oct 1898
* 1910 - Living in Pike Co., GA - Ballard, Reeves, Joseph B 50, Emma 45, Trumme 16, Horace 15, Eugene 13, W. P 11

Children of SARAH BALLARD and JOSEPH REEVES are:

     i.   LENA BELL[4] REEVES, b. May 1892; d. Aft. 1900; m. COLLIE RUFUS BUCHANAN; b. 1892.
     ii.   TRUMMIE MYRTICE REEVES, b. Dec 1893; d. Aft. 1910; m. JOHN PROCTOR AKIN; b. 1893.
     iii.   JOSEPH HORACE REEVES, b. 04 Mar 1895; d. Aft. 1910; m. JEWELL PERKINS; b. 1895.
     iv.   JAMES EUGENE REEVES, b. Jun 1896; d. Aft. 1910; m. LILLIAN PEARL TOLEN; b. 1897.
     v.   WILLIAM POWELL "BILLY" REEVES, b. Oct 1898; d. Aft. 1910.

19. LOUIE CLYDE[3] BALLARD (JAMES POLK[2], MILES[1]) was born 02 Jun 1880 in Pike Co., GA, and died 14 Apr 1946 in Pike Co., GA. She married ORREN ALLEN FOSTER. He was born 21 Aug 1880 in GA, and died 13 Apr 1968 in Pike Co., GA.

More About LOUIE CLYDE BALLARD:
Burial: Zebulon Methodist Church Cemetery, Zebulon, Pike Co., GA

Notes for ORREN ALLEN FOSTER:
Source: 1910 Pike County Georgia Federal Census Records, 1920 Coweta County Georgia Federal Census Records, 1930 -1940 Monroe County Georgia Federal Census Records

* 1910 - Living in Driver, Pike Co., GA - Foster, Allen 29 GA GA GA, Louie C 29 - 2 children 2 living GA, Dougless 2 GA, Clinton A 1 9/12 GA
* 1920 - Living in Haralson, Coweta Co., GA - Foster, Orren A 39, Louis 39, Douglas 13, Clinton 11, Henry 9, Walter 7, Lizzie 63
* 1930 - Living in Dillard, Monroe Co., GA - Foster, Orren A 49, Louie 49, Douglas J 23, Clenton A 21, Henry K 19, Walter B 17, Martha E 74
* 1940 - Living in Dillard, Monroe Co., GA - Foster O A 59, Louie Clyde 6, Clinton 32, Enes 66

More About ORREN ALLEN FOSTER:
Burial: Zebulon Methodist Church Cemetery, Zebulon, Pike Co., GA

Children of LOUIE BALLARD and ORREN FOSTER are:
      i. DOUGLAS[4] FOSTER, b. Abt. 1908, Pike Co., GA; d. Aft. 1920.
      ii. CLINTON A. FOSTER, b. Abt. 1909, Pike Co., GA; d. Aft. 1940.
      iii. HENRY FOSTER, b. Abt. 1911, GA; d. Aft. 1930.
      iv. WALTER FOSTER, b. Abt. 1913, GA; d. Aft. 1930.

20. GORDON[3] BLANCHARD (LUCY ANN[2] BALLARD, MILES[1]) was born Jul 1877 in Al, and died 24 Jul 1915 in Pensacola FL. He married ANNIE REGINA BOND 06 Aug 1902 in Santa Rosa Co FL. She was born 04 Sep 1887 in Pensacola FL, and died 30 Jul 1962 in Pensacola FL.

Children of GORDON BLANCHARD and ANNIE BOND are:

      i. ESSEX[4] BLANCHARD, b. 1904, FL.
      ii. VIOLETTE BLANCHARD, b. 1910, FL.

21. WILLIAM PINKTON[3] BALLARD (FRANKLIN JEFFERSON[2], MILES[1]) was born 13 Mar 1885 in LA, and died 13 Sep 1964 in Ventura Co., CA. He married KATIE NELLIE TOWNSEND Abt. 1909 in OK. She was born 04 Jul 1885 in Hopkins Co., TX, and died 02 Jun 1960 in Fillmore, Ventura Co., CA.

Notes for WILLIAM PINKTON BALLARD:
Source: 1910 Collin County Texas Federal Census Records, 1920 Hopkins County Texas Federal Census Records, Annie B. Maner (AManer@msn.com)

* 1910 - Living in Collin Co., TX - Ballard, W P 25 TX farmer, Caty N 23 - 2 children 2 living TX, William H 3 TX, Nely M 4/12 TX, Macy A Towsand 62 mother in law 8 children 7 living.
* 1920 - Living in Hopkins Co., TX - Willie 36 LA AL MS grocery, Katie 34 TX LA TX, Willie 12 TX, Nellie 9 TX, Lizzie 8 TX, Valton 5 TX, Murtle 4 TX, Edward 1/12 TX, Nancy Townsen 69 mother in law TX

More About WILLIAM PINKTON BALLARD:
Burial: Bardsdale Cemetery, Fillmore, Ventura Co., CA

More About KATIE NELLIE TOWNSEND:
Burial: Bardsdale Cemetery, Fillmore, Ventura Co., CA

Children of WILLIAM BALLARD and KATIE TOWNSEND are:

           i.   WILLIAM "WILLIE"[4] BALLARD, b. 1910, TX; d. Aft. 1920.
           ii.   NELLIE BALLARD, b. Abt. 1911, TX; d. Aft. 1920.
           iii. MARY ELIZABETH "LIZZIE" BALLARD, b. 01 Nov 1911, Hunt Co., TX; d. 19 Feb 2007, Quarts Hill, Los Angeles Co., CA; m. HUNTER.

                  More About MARY ELIZABETH "LIZZIE" BALLARD:
                  Burial: Joshua Memorial Park, Lancaster, Los Angeles Co., CA

37.   *iv.*   VALTON D. BALLARD, b. 08 Apr 1914, Hopkins Co., TX; d. 13 Sep 2001, CA.
           v.   MYRTLE BALLARD, b. Abt. 1916, TX; d. Abt. 1920; m. LEONARD JOHNSON.
           vi.   JAMES "JIMMIE" EDWARD BALLARD, b. Abt. 1920, TX; d. Aft. 1920; m. VELMA JUANITA; b. 1921; d. 1962.

                  Notes for JAMES "JIMMIE" EDWARD BALLARD:
                  Source: WWII Draft Registration Card
                  * 1940 - Draft Card, residence Fillmore, Ventura CA, wife Velma Juanita

                  More About VELMA JUANITA:
                  Burial: Bardsdale Cemetery, Fillmore, Ventura Co., CA

22. ARDELIA "DELIA"[3] BALLARD (FRANKLIN JEFFERSON[2], MILES[1]) was born 23 Mar 1887 in TX, and died 05 Jun 1950 in Caddo Mills, Hunt Co., TX. She married FRANK MILLER. He was born 1882, and died 1951.

More About ARDELIA "DELIA" BALLARD:
Burial: Odd Fellows Cemetery, Caddo Mills, Hunt Co., TX

More About FRANK MILLER:
Burial: Odd Fellows Cemetery, Caddo Mills, Hunt Co., TX

Children of ARDELIA BALLARD and FRANK MILLER are:
           i.   ETHEL[4] MILLER.
           ii.   ORVILLE MILLER.
           iii. ALICE MILLER.
           iv.   D. H. MILLER.
           v.   ELTON MILLER.

23. JAMES "JIM" HARRISON[3] BALLARD (FRANKLIN JEFFERSON[2], MILES[1]) was born 27 Feb 1889 in TX, and died 29 Mar 1976 in Lindsey, Tulare Co., CA. He married DELLAR LORENA MILLER 29 Feb 1908 in Caddo Mills TX. She was born 27 Feb 1892 in Monroe Co., TN, and died 19 Jun 1979 in Lindsey, Tulare Co., CA.

More About JAMES "JIM" HARRISON BALLARD:
Burial: Lindsay-Strathmore Cemetery, Lindsay, Tulare Co., CA

More About DELLAR LORENA MILLER:
Burial: Lindsay-Strathmore Cemetery, Lindsay, Tulare Co., CA

Children of JAMES BALLARD and DELLAR MILLER are:

           i.   CARL BETHEL[4] BALLARD, b. 24 Jun 1910, Hunts Co., TX; d. 08 Jun 1959, Sebastopol, Sonoma Co., CA; m. MARY LILLY DRAYER; b. 10 Oct 1915, Tulare Co., CA; d. 18 Dec 1979, Sebastopol, Sonoma Co., CA.

                  More About CARL BETHEL BALLARD:

Burial: Druids Occidental Cemetery, Sebastopol, Sonoma Co., CA

More About MARY LILLY DRAYER:
Burial: Druids Occidental Cemetery, Sebastopol, Sonoma Co., CA

- ii. MINERVA LORENA BALLARD, b. Jan 1915, Atoka Co., OK.
- iii. JAMES HARRISON "JAY" BALLARD, b. 1917, Caddo Mills, Hunt Co., TX.
- iv. WILLIAM EUGENE "RED" BALLARD, b. 08 Apr 1921, Goddlett, Hardeman Co., TX; d. 07 Jan 2005, Santa Maria, Santa Barbara Co., CA; m. (1) MARY JEAN DAVIS; b. 14 May 1921, Bartholomew Co., IN; d. 26 Feb 2010, Bartholomew Co., IN; m. (2) MARIAN MAXINE BAILEY; b. 20 Sep 1925, Ringgold Co., IA; d. 08 Aug 1989, Santa Maria, Santa Barbara Co., CA.
- v. MARY ALICE BALLARD, b. 1923, Goddlett, Hardeman Co., TX; d. 1925.
- vi. MARJORIE BALLARD, b. 29 Dec 1926, Ozark, Franklin Co., AR; d. 04 Mar 2013, Santa Rosa, Sonoma Co., CA; m. GOLDEN.

24. LUCY "MAE" GRAY[3] BALLARD (FRANKLIN JEFFERSON[2], MILES[1]) was born 01 Jun 1892 in TX, and died 1948 in OK. She married GILBERT NORRIS 10 Oct 1911 in Hunt Co TX. He was born Abt. 1891.

Children of LUCY BALLARD and GILBERT NORRIS are:
- i. JANELL[4] NORRIS, b. Bet. 1901 - 1910; m. ROBERT BURKHART.
- ii. MARIE NORRIS, b. Bet. 1901 - 1910; m. DEWEY REESE.

25. JOSEPH "JOE" JEFFERSON[3] BALLARD (FRANKLIN JEFFERSON[2], MILES[1]) was born 29 Jan 1896 in TX, and died 02 Jan 1962 in OK City, OK. He married NORA ANNALIZAR STREET 06 Oct 1916 in Durant, Bryan Co., OK. She was born 18 Mar 1895 in TX, and died 26 Mar 1980.

Notes for JOSEPH "JOE" JEFFERSON BALLARD:
Source: 1920 Hunt County Texas Federal Census Records, 1930 - 1940 Oklahoma County Oklahoma Federal Census Records, Annie B. Maner (AManer@msn.com)

* 1920 - Living in Greenville, Hunt Co., TX - Ballard, Joe 24 TX, Nora 25 TX, Alleen 2 OK, Naoma 2/12 TX, Lawrence 21 brother TX
* 1930 - Living in Greely, Oklahoma Co., OK - Ballard, Joe J 35 LA, Nora A 36 TX, Aleen H 12 TX, Ineze E 8 TX, Rachel L 7 OK, Imagene 6 TX, Mildred E 4 3/12 OK, Nadene M 3 OK
* 1940 - Living in Oklahoma, Oklahoma Co., OK - Ballard Joe 44 TX, Nora 45 TX, Namoma 20 TX, Inez 18 TX, Rachel 17 OK, Imagene 16 TX, Mildred 14 OK, Nadene 13 OK, Betty Jo 9 OK, Ruth 5 OK

More About JOSEPH "JOE" JEFFERSON BALLARD:
Burial: Sunny Lane Cemetery, Del City, Oklahoma Co., OK

More About NORA ANNALIZAR STREET:
Burial: Sunny Lane Cemetery, Del City, Oklahoma Co., OK

Children of JOSEPH BALLARD and NORA STREET are:

- i. ALENE[4] BALLARD, b. 30 Aug 1917, Hunt Co., TX; d. 09 Oct 2002; m. JAMES N. WILLIS.

  Notes for ALENE BALLARD:
  Source: Social Security Records

- ii. NAOMI ELIZABETH BALLARD, b. 21 Nov 1919, Hunt Co., TX; d. 06 Sep 2010, Oklahoma Co., OK; m. ANDREW LESTER WILLIAMS; b. 17 Apr 1917, Cleveland Co., OK; d. 20 May 1987, Oklahoma City, OK Co., OK.

More About NAOMI ELIZABETH BALLARD:
Burial: Sunny Lane Cemetery, Oklahoma Co., OK

More About ANDREW LESTER WILLIAMS:
Burial: Sunny Lane Cemetery, Oklahoma Co., OK

iii.   INEZ ELLA BALLARD, b. 08 Jun 1921, Hunt Co., TX; d. 22 Oct 2000; m. JOE ALVARADO; b. 06 Apr 1914, Bexar Co., TX; d. 25 Sep 1984, Oklahoma City, OK Co., OK.

More About INEZ ELLA BALLARD:
Burial: Sunny Lane Cemetery, Oklahoma Co., OK

More About JOE ALVARADO:
Burial: Sunny Lane Cemetery, Oklahoma Co., OK

iv.   RACHEL MAE BALLARD, b. 14 Nov 1922, Ardmore, OK; d. 04 Feb 2001; m. RICHARD HOUSTON WADE, 26 Sep 1941, Oklahoma Co., OK; b. 09 Oct 1921, OK; d. 11 May 2010, Cleveland Co., OK.

Notes for RACHEL MAE BALLARD:
Source: Social Security Records

More About RACHEL MAE BALLARD:
Burial: Sunny Lane Cemetery, Oklahoma Co., OK

More About RICHARD HOUSTON WADE:

Burial: Sunny Lane Cemetery, Oklahoma Co., OK

v.   MILDRED E. BALLARD, b. 03 Dec 1925, OK; d. 26 Apr 1961; m. SHERRILL EDWARD LONGEST, 12 Dec 1945, Oklahoma Co., OK; b. 27 Sep 1924; d. 20 May 1992.

More About MILDRED E. BALLARD:
Burial: Sunny Lane Cemetery, Oklahoma Co., OK

More About SHERRILL EDWARD LONGEST:

Burial: Sunny Lane Cemetery, Oklahoma Co., OK

vi.   NADENE MARGARETTE BALLARD, b. 09 Mar 1927, OK; d. 16 Jul 2004; m. CONNER.

More About NADENE MARGARETTE BALLARD:

Burial: Laurel Land Memorial Park, Dallas Co., TX

vii.   IMOGENE BALLARD, b. 29 Jul 1929, TX; d. 16 Nov 2012, Bacome Muscogee OK; m. RAYMOND O TRACY, 23 May 1945, Oklahoma Co., OK; b. Abt. 1925; d. Bef. 2012.

Notes for IMOGENE BALLARD:
Source: Oklahoma County Oklahoma Marriage Records

More About IMOGENE BALLARD:
Burial: Alta Mesa Memorial Park, Palo Alto, Santa Clara Co., CA

viii.   BETTY JO BALLARD, b. Abt. 1931, OK; d. 14 Jan 1985; m. (1) CARROLL; m. (2) BOB MCCAUGHAN, 12 Jul 1947, Cleveland, OK.

More About BETTY JO BALLARD:
Burial: rose Hills Memorial Park, Los Angeles Co., CA

    ix. RUTH BALLARD, *b. Abt. 1935, OK; d. Aft. 1940.*

26. FLORENCE SUSAN[3] BALLARD (FRANKLIN JEFFERSON[2], MILES[1]) *was born 26 Jun 1898 in Greenville, Hunt Co., TX, and died 21 Sep 1979 in Centerville, Leon Co., TX. She married* WALTON BURPO MASSEY *19 Oct 1913 in Hunt Co., TX. He was born 03 Dec 1893 in Navarro Co., TX, and died 26 Aug 1937 in Gladewater, Gregg Co., TX.*

More About FLORENCE SUSAN BALLARD:

Burial: Bur. Restland Cemetery. Dallas, Dallas Co TX

Notes for WALTON BURPO MASSEY:
Source: 1920-1930 Carter County Oklahoma Federal Census Records, Gregg County Texas Certificate of Death

* 1920 - Living in Ardmore, Carter Co., OK - Massey, Walton B 26 TX, Florence S 21 TX, Leo H 2 3 5/12 OK, Lillie May 1 OK
* 1930 - Living in Morgan, Carter Co., OK - Massey N N 36 TX TX AR, Florence 31 TX AL LA, Leo H 12 OK, May 11 OK, Earl 9 OK, Alton 8 OK, Dorothy 6 OK, June 3 3/12 OK

More About WALTON BURPO MASSEY:
Burial: Bur. Rosedale Cemetery

Children of FLORENCE BALLARD and WALTON MASSEY are:
    i. JOSEPH JEFFERSON[4] MASSEY, *b. 08 Apr 1915.*
    ii. LEO HOWARD MASSEY, *b. 01 Jul 1917, OK; d. Aft. 1930.*
    iii. LILLIE MAE MASSEY, *b. 18 Dec 1918, OK; d. Aft. 1930.*
    iv. WALTER EARL MASSEY, *b. 27 May 1920, OK; d. Aft. 1930.*
    v. ALTON CLIFTON MASSEY, *b. 22 Feb 1922, OK; d. Aft. 1930.*
    vi. DOROTHY EDITH MASSEY, *b. 08 Feb 1924, OK; d. Aft. 1930.*
    vii. CAROL JUNE MASSEY, *b. 03 Dec 1926, OK; d. Aft. 1930.*

27. LAWRENCE LAFAYETTE[3] BALLARD (FRANKLIN JEFFERSON[2], MILES[1]) *was born 26 Jun 1898 in Greenville, Hunt Co., TX, and died 12 Feb 1966 in Norwalk, Los Angeles Co., CA. He married (1)* EULA MAY GRAY *22 Jan 1918 in Bryan Co., TX. She was born 02 Apr 1902 in Hunt Co., TX, and died 1952. He married (2)* OCTIE OREATOR JENNINGS *05 May 1921 in Greenville TX, daughter of* JOHN JENNINGS *and* MINNIE SHIPLEY. *She was born 23 Oct 1905 in Prairie Indian Territory, OK, and died 27 May 1993 in Norwalk, Los Angeles Co., CA.*

Notes for LAWRENCE LAFAYETTE BALLARD:

Source: 1920 Hunt County Texas Federal Census Records, 1940 Oklahoma County Oklahoma Federal Census Records, Bryan County Oklahoma Marriage Records

* 1920 - Living in Greenville, Hunt Co., TX - Ballard, Lawrence 21 TX living with brother Joe
* 1940 - Living in Oklahoma City, Oklahoma Co., OK - Ballard, Laurence L 41 TX, Ortie 36 OK, Geneva 17 OK, Floyd Lee 15 OK, June 8 OK, Gene 8 OK, Laurance Jr 1/12 OK

More About LAWRENCE LAFAYETTE BALLARD:
Burial: Little Lake Cemetery, Santa Fe Springs, Los Angeles Co., CA

More About OCTIE OREATOR JENNINGS:
Burial: Little Lake Cemetery, Santa Fe Springs, Los Angeles Co., CA

Child of LAWRENCE BALLARD and EULA GRAY is:

    i.   LAWRENCE FRANKLIN[4] BALLARD, b. 25 Dec 1918, Greenville TX; d. 12 Feb 1966, Norwalk Los Angeles Co CA; m. MONA NANCE; b. 24 Dec 1923.

Children of LAWRENCE BALLARD and OCTIE JENNINGS are:

    ii.   ANNIE GHNEVA[4] BALLARD, b. 27 May 1922, Carter Co., OK; d. 10 Feb 2012, CA; m. JEFFERSON G. MANER; b. 11 Jan 1919, OK; d. 02 Sep 2011.

        More About ANNIE GHNEVA BALLARD:
        Burial: Riverside National Cemetery, Riverside, Riverside Co., CA

        More About JEFFERSON G. MANER:
        Burial: Riverside National Cemetery, Riverside, Riverside Co., CA

    iii.   FLOYD LEE BALLARD, b. 12 Feb 1925, Carter Co., OK; d. 10 Dec 1998, CA.
    iv.   JOHNNY LEE BALLARD, b. 01 Apr 1929, Carter Co., OK; d. 02 Apr 1930, Ardmore, Carter Co., OK.

        More About JOHNNY LEE BALLARD:
        Burial: Lone Grove Cemetery, Carter Co., OK

    v.   GENE ALLEN BALLARD, b. 14 Dec 1931, Carter Co., OK; d. 1936, Ardmore, Carter Co., OK.
    vi.   JUNE HELEN BALLARD, b. 14 Dec 1931, Carter Co., OK; d. Aft. 1940.
    vii.   EULA YWACHETTE BALLARD, b. 01 Sep 1936, OK; d. 1936.

        More About EULA YWACHETTE BALLARD:
        Burial: Lone Grove Cemetery, Carter Co., OK

    viii.   LAWRENCE LAFAYETTE BALLARD, b. 21 Feb 1940, Oklahoma City, OK Co., OK; d. 29 Nov 1970, Orange Co., CA.

        More About LAWRENCE LAFAYETTE BALLARD:
        Burial: Little Lake Cemetery, Santa Fe Springs, Los Angeles Co., CA

28. EULA MAE[3] BALLARD (FRANKLIN JEFFERSON[2], MILES[1]) *was born 28 Jun 1901 in Clinton, Hunt Co., TX, and died 31 Dec 1950 in Eddie, NM. She married CARL MILLER. He died 05 Dec 1968.*

Children of EULA BALLARD and CARL MILLER are:
    i.   HOLLIS[4] MILLER.
    ii.   WALLACE MILLER.
    iii.   DARWIN MILLER.

29. JESSIE MILES[3] BALLARD (FRANKLIN JEFFERSON[2], MILES[1]) *was born 08 Aug 1909 in Caddo Mills, Hunt Co., TX, and died 25 Jun 1989 in Salem, Marion Co., OR. He married GLADYS 05 Mar 1939. She was born 16 Apr 1918.*

Notes for JESSIE MILES BALLARD:
Source: Annie B. Maner (AManer@msn.com)

More About JESSIE MILES BALLARD:

Burial: Lee Mission Cemetery, Salem, Marion Co., OR

More About GLADYS:
Burial: Lee Mission Cemetery, Salem, Marion Co., OR

Children of JESSIE BALLARD and GLADYS are:
      i.   SANDRA GAE[4] BALLARD.
     ii.   EDWINA RAE BALLARD.
    iii.   JUANITA "NITA" BALLARD.
     iv.   JOYCE MARILYN BALLARD.

30. WILBERT ALTON[3] BALLARD (FRANKLIN JEFFERSON[2], MILES[1]) *was born 17 Aug 1919 in Caddo Mills, Hunt Co., TX, and died 26 Oct 1984 in Tehama Co., CA. He married* OPAL ROSE SHOWALTER *19 Nov 1938 in Oklahoma Co., OK. She was born 15 Oct 1915 in OK, and died 22 Apr 1979 in Fairfield, Solano Co., CA.*

Notes for WILBERT ALTON BALLARD:
Source: 1940 Oklahoma County Oklahoma Federal Census Records, Tehama County California Certificate of Death, WWII Draft Registration Card, WWII Army Enlistment Records Kris839138@aol.com

* 1940 - Living in Oklahoma City, Oklahoma Co., OK - Ballard, Alton 21 OK gardener nursery, Opal 21 OK, William Frank 9/12 OK
* 1940 - Oct 16 - Residence: Bell, CA
* 1944 - July 28, 1944 Enlisted. Resident: Contra Costa CA

More About WILBERT ALTON BALLARD:
Burial: Vacaville - Elmira Cemetery, Solano Co., CA

More About OPAL ROSE SHOWALTER:
Burial: Vacaville - Elmira Cemetery, Solano Co., CA

Children of WILBERT BALLARD and OPAL SHOWALTER are:

      i.   THOMAS[4] BALLARD.
     ii.   WILLIAM FRANK BALLARD, b. Abt. 1939, Oklahoma City, OK Co., OK; d. Aft. 1940.
    iii.   ALTON EUGENE "GENE" BALLARD, b. 30 Dec 1940, Oklahoma City, OK Co., OK; d. 30 Apr 2006.
     iv.   DOROTHY BALLARD, b. 08 Jan 1943, Woodland, Yolo Co., CA; d. 02 Mar 2007; m. (1) JOSEPH SINGLETON III; m. (2) WALTER JOHN UTZ, 30 Aug 1975, Reno, NV; b. 07 May 1924, Germany; d. 26 May 1996.

          More About DOROTHY BALLARD:
          Burial: Vacaville Elmira Cemetery, Solano Co., CA

          More About WALTER JOHN UTZ:
          Burial: Vacaville - Elmira Cemetery, Solano Co., CA

      v.   DAVID BALLARD, b. Abt. 1945.
     vi.   ALMA JUDY BALLARD, b. 05 Apr 1954, Contra Costa, CA.

31. WILLIAM ELTON[3] BALLARD (WILLIAM SOLOMON[2], MILES[1]) *was born 24 May 1898 in Hunt Co., TX, and died 17 Jul 1980 in Pampa, Gray Co., TX. He married* PANSY HAMILTON. *She was born 16 Aug 1902, and died 08 Sep 1988 in Pampa, Gray Co., TX.*

Notes for WILLIAM ELTON BALLARD:
Source: 1940 Motley County Texas Federal Census Records
* 1940 - Living in Motley Co., TX - W. E 42 TX, Pansy 37 TX, W. E. Jr. 17 TX, Mamie 14 TX, Tatsy 12 TX

More About WILLIAM ELTON BALLARD:
Burial: Memory Gardens of Pampa, Gray Co., TX

More About PANSY HAMILTON:
Burial: Memory Gardens of Pampa, Pampa, Gray Co., TX

Children of WILLIAM BALLARD and PANSY HAMILTON are:
>   i.   WILLIAM ELTON[4] BALLARD, JR., b. Abt. 1923, TX; d. Aft. 1940.
>   ii. MAMIE BALLARD, b. Abt. 1924, TX; d. Aft. 1940.
>   iii. PATSY BALLARD, b. Abt. 1918, TX; d. Aft. 1940.

32. IMA LEE[3] BALLARD (WILLIAM SOLOMON[2], MILES[1]) was born 10 Jun 1917 in Hunt Co., TX, and died 20 Nov 2008. She married NOAH DUNNING, REV. 03 Sep 1933 in Rockwall Co., TX. He was born 10 Apr 1913, and died 30 Apr 1962.

More About IMA LEE BALLARD:
Burial: Royce City Cemetery, Royce City, Rockwall Co., TX

More About NOAH DUNNING, REV.:
Burial: Royce City Cemetery, Royce City, Rockwall Co., TX

Children of IMA BALLARD and NOAH DUNNING are:
>   i.   POLLY ANN[4] DUNNING, b. Abt. 1935, Hunt Co., TX.
>   ii. LINDA JOE DUNNING, b. Abt. 1936, Hunt Co., TX.

Generation No. 4

33. JOBE TURNER[4] BALLARD (WALTER SCOTT[3], ROBERT W.[2], MILES[1]) was born 06 Apr 1892 in GA, and died 05 May 1928 in Pike Co., GA. He married ANNIE IONE WILSON. She was born 27 Nov 1893, and died 01 Jun 1977.

More About ANNIE IONE WILSON:
Burial: Davis Family Cemetery, Pike Co., GA

Children of JOBE BALLARD and ANNIE WILSON are:
>   i.   J. W.[5] BALLARD, b. 21 Feb 1910, Pike Co., GA; d. 05 Sep 2001, Pike Co., GA; m. OSSIE REBECCA McCORD; b. 20 Aug 1911.
>   ii. MARY ELIZABETH BALLARD, b. 29 Sep 1914, Pike Co., GA; d. 14 Oct 2013, Griffin, Spalding Co., GA; m. TROY BALLARD; b. 30 Jul 1912, Pike Co., GA; d. 17 Mar 2007.
>
>   *More About TROY BALLARD:*
>   Burial: Mt Gilead Baptist Church Cemetery, Pike Co., GA

34. WILLIAM P.[4] BALLARD (RICHARD STEPHEN[3], POWELL F.[2], MILES[1]) was born 09 Sep 1881 in Pike Co., GA, and died 10 Feb 1971. He married (1) ANNIE Bef. 1910. She was born 1887, and died Aft. 1910. He married (2) SUSIE M. DAVIS Bef. 1920. She was born 01 Oct 1888, and died 11 Nov 1981.

Notes for WILLIAM P. BALLARD:
Source: 1910-1920 Pike County Georgia Federal Census Records

* 1910 - Living in Pike Co., GA - Ballard, William P 28, Annie 23, John H 6, Alva R 4, Allen C 2, Cecil F 5/12
* 1920 - Living in Pike Co., GA - Ballard, William P 38, Susie M 31, John H 16, Roswell 14, Alton 12, Cecil F 10, Troy 7, Bena A 5, Hattie 3 10/12 Oresa 6/12

* 1930 - Living in Pike Co., GA - Ballard, Willie P 44, Susie 48, CF 20, Troy 17, Bena 15, Hattie 13, Oressa 10, Frances 7, Melvil 3 6/12

More About SUSIE M. DAVIS:
Burial: Mt. Gilead Baptist Church Cemetery, Pike Co., GA

Children of WILLIAM BALLARD and ANNIE are:

     i.   JOHN H.[5] BALLARD, b. 29 Oct 1903, Pike Co., GA; d. 12 May 1990, Fulton Co., GA.

    ii. ALVA R. BALLARD, b. 24 May 1906, Pike Co., GA; d. 10 May 1978; m. JEFFIE WARD; b. 30 Jan 1913; d. 16 Mar 2008, Henry Co., GA.

        More About ALVA R. BALLARD:
        Burial: Mt Gilead Baptist Church Cemetery, Pike Co., GA

        More About JEFFIE WARD:
        Burial: Mt Gilead Baptist Church Cemetery, Pike Co., GA

    iii. ALTON POWERLL BALLARD, b. 06 Apr 1908, Pike Co., GA; d. 01 Aug 1938, Appling, Columbia Co., GA; m. EVELYN GRIMES; b. 02 Jun 1912; d. 30 Dec 2000.

    iv. CECIL FRANKLIN BALLARD, b. 03 Oct 1909, Pike Co., GA; d. 24 Jun 2004, Pike Co., GA; m. HELENE REBECCA SIMMONS; b. 23 Aug 1919, Lamar Co., GA; d. 19 Apr 1988, Jones Co., GA.

        More About CECIL FRANKLIN BALLARD:
        Burial: Glen Haven Memorial Garden, Bibb Co., GA

     v. TROY BALLARD, b. 30 Jul 1912, Pike Co., GA; d. 17 Mar 2007; m. MARY ELIZABETH BALLARD; b. 29 Sep 1914, Pike Co., GA; d. 14 Oct 2013, Griffin, Spalding Co., GA.

        More About TROY BALLARD:
        Burial: Mt Gilead Baptist Church Cemetery, Pike Co., GA

    vi. BENA A. BALLARD, b. 02 Aug 1914, Pike Co., GA; d. 09 May 2015, GA; m. JOHN HENRY WILLIAMSON; b. 27 Aug 1917; d. 29 Apr 1987.

        More About BENA A. BALLARD:
        Burial: Glen Haven Memorial Garden, Bibb Co., GA

        More About JOHN HENRY WILLIAMSON:
        Burial: Glen Haven Memorial Garden, Bibb Co., GA

Children of WILLIAM BALLARD and SUSIE DAVIS are:

    vii. HATTIE[5] BALLARD, b. 21 Feb 1916, Pike Co., GA; d. 03 Dec 2002, Pike Co., GA; m. CLARK MITCHELL TURNER; b. 07 Jul 1915, Pike Co., GA; d. 06 Dec 2009, Spalding Co., GA.

        More About CLARK MITCHELL TURNER:
        Burial: Providence First Baptist Church Cemetery, Pike Co., GA

    viii. ORESSA BALLARD, b. 19 Dec 1919, Pike Co., GA; d. 06 Feb 2004, Spalding Co., GA; m. DOUGLAS L. PITTS; b. 30 Oct 1919, Pike Co., GA; d. 29 May 2002, Pike Co., GA.

    ix. FRANCES BALLARD, b. 29 May 1922, Pike Co., GA; d. 05 Feb 2010, Lamar Co., GA; m. HENRY JAMES MILAM; b. 24 Jul 1922; d. 06 Nov 2007.

More About FRANCES BALLARD:
Burial: Greenwood Cemetery, Barnesville, Lamar Co., GA

More About HENRY JAMES MILAM:
Burial: Greenwood Cemetery, Barnesville, Lamar Co., GA

   x.   MELVIL BALLARD, b. 19 May 1926, Pike Co., GA; d. 17 Aug 1995, Pike Co., GA.
   xi.   WILLIAM TURNER BALLARD, b. 25 Jan 1931, Pike Co., GA; d. 25 Nov 1972.

      More About WILLIAM TURNER BALLARD:
      Burial: Oak Hill Cemetery, Griffin, Spalding Co. GA

35. WILLIAM ZENEFORD[4] BALLARD (WILLIAM POWELL[3], POWELL F.[2], MILES[1]) *was born 10 Aug 1894 in Pike Co., GA, and died 24 Apr 1966 in Pike Co., GA. He married SALLIE FANNIE DAVIS 24 Dec 1915 in Pike Co., GA. She was born 07 Oct 1896, and died 10 Sep 1982.*

Notes for WILLIAM ZENEFORD BALLARD:
Source: 1920 - 1930 Pike County Georgia Federal Census Records

* 1920 - Living in Pike County GA - Ballard, William Z 25, Sallie M 23, Mildred 1 3/12
* 1930 - Living in Pike County GA - Ballard, W. Zin 35, Sally F 33, Mildred 11, Gerald 9, Roland 6, Mary Ethel 4 3/12, Davis 2 6/12

More About WILLIAM ZENEFORD BALLARD:
Burial: Oak Hill Cemetery, Griffin, Spalding Co., GA

More About SALLIE FANNIE DAVIS:
Burial: Oak Hill Cemetery, Griffin, Spalding Co., GA

Children of WILLIAM BALLARD and SALLIE DAVIS are:

     i.   MILDRED FRANCES[5] BALLARD, b. 02 Apr 1918, Pike Co., GA; d. 28 Aug 1992, Pike Co., GA; m. JOSEPH CARSON BUFFINGTON; b. 17 Nov 1916; d. 03 Apr 2009.

         More About MILDRED FRANCES BALLARD:
         Burial: New Hope Baptist Cemetery, Zebulon, Pike Co., GA

         More About JOSEPH CARSON BUFFINGTON:
         Burial: New Hope Baptist Cemetery, Zebulon, Pike Co., GA

     ii.   GERALD BALLARD, b. 16 Apr 1920, Pike Co., GA; d. 06 Oct 2002; m. LOUISE STAPLETON; b. 30 Sep 1922, GA; d. 03 May 2013, CA.

         More About GERALD BALLARD:
         Burial: Oak Hill Cemetery, Griffin, Spalding Co,, GA

         More About LOUISE STAPLETON:
         Burial: Oak Hill Cemetery, Griffin, Spalding Co,, GA

     iii.   DOUGLAS ROLAND BALLARD, b. 23 Jun 1923, Pike Co., GA; d. 27 Dec 1987; m. DOROTHY PAULINE WHITTINGTON, 26 May 1945; b. 28 Oct 1919; d. 10 Apr 1995.

         More About DOROTHY PAULINE WHITTINGTON:
         Burial: Oak Hill Cemetery, Griffin, Spalding Co,, GA

     iv.   MARY ETHEL BALLARD, b. 11 Sep 1925, Pike Co., GA; d. 02 Oct 2009, GA.
     v.   JOHN DAVIS BALLARD, b. 08 Mar 1928, Pike Co., GA; d. 04 Sep 2003; m. EULA RUSH; b. 18 Oct 1921; d. 06 Apr 1999.

     More About EULA RUSH:
     Burial: Oak Hill Cemetery, Griffin, Spalding Co,, GA

36. IVA JEWELL[4] BALLARD (WILLIAM POWELL[3], POWELL F.[2], MILES[1]) was born 23 Mar 1899 in Pike Co., GA, and died 21 Aug 1997. She married JEWELL EUGENE SIKES. He was born 23 Sep 1901, and died 16 Aug 1965.

More About IVA JEWELL BALLARD:
Burial: Oak Hill Cemetery, Griffin, Spalding Co., GA

Notes for JEWELL EUGENE SIKES:
Source: 1930 Lamar County Georgia Federal Census Records

* 1930 - Living in Redbone, Lamar Co., GA - Sikes, Eugene J 28 GA GA GA, Jewell 28 GA GA GA, Arthur 5 GA, Kathleen 2 7/12 GA

More About JEWELL EUGENE SIKES:
Burial: Oak Hill Cemetery, Griffin, Spalding Co., GA

Children of IVA BALLARD and JEWELL SIKES are:
     i.   ARTHUR[5] SIKES, b. Abt. 1925, GA; d. Aft. 1930.
     ii.   KATHLEEN SIKES, b. Abt. 1927, GA; d. Aft. 1930.

37. VALTON D.[4] BALLARD (WILLIAM PINKTON[3], FRANKLIN JEFFERSON[2], MILES[1]) was born 08 Apr 1914 in Hopkins Co., TX, and died 13 Sep 2001 in CA. He married LORENA A. CANTRELL 22 Dec 1937 in Carter, OK. She was born 04 Jan 1918 in Newport, OK, and died 05 Feb 2007 in CA.

Notes for VALTON D. BALLARD:
Source: 1940 Ventura County California Federal Census Records

* 1940 - Living in Fillmore, Ventura Co., CA - Ballard, Valton D 26 TX, Lorena A 22 OK, Kenneth B 1 CA

More About VALTON D. BALLARD:
Burial: Pierce Brothers Santa Paula Cemetery, Santa Paula, Ventura Co., CA

More About LORENA A. CANTRELL:
Burial: Pierce Brothers Santa Paula Cemetery, Santa Paula, Ventura Co., CA

Children of VALTON BALLARD and LORENA CANTRELL are:

     i.   KENNETH VALTON[5] BALLARD, b. 1938.
     ii.   RICHARD EUGENE BALLARD, b. 1947.

Ballard

Generation No. 1

1. BALLARD[1] *was born Abt. 1815, and died Bet. 1844 - 1850. He married* ELIZABETH DYLOR. *She was born 1815 in GA, and died Aft. 1880.*

Notes for BALLARD:
He is reported to be Gordon Ballard but I have not been able to document that,

Notes for ELIZABETH DYLOR:
Source: 1850-1880 Upson County Georgia Federal Census Records

* 1850 - Living in Upson Co., GA - Ballard, Elizabeth 35 GA, John 15 GA, William 13, Emily 11, Catharine 7, Simon 5
* 1860 - Living in Upson Co., GA - Ballard, Elizabeth 45 domestic GA, John 24 overseer GA, Wm. R. overseer 22 GA, E. 20 GA, ESC 18 GA, Simeon 16 GA
* 1870 - Living in Upson Co., GA - Ballard, Elizabeth 50 GA, Emaline 31 GA, Catherine 27 GA, Emma 10 GA
* 1880 - Living in Waymanville, Upson Co., GA - Ballard, Elizabeth 64 wd GA GA GA, Catherine 35 GA GA GA, Forest Parker 8 Grandson GA

Children of BALLARD and ELIZABETH DYLOR are:

2.	i.	WILLIAM RILEY[2] BALLARD, *b. 04 Nov 1836, GA; d. 31 Aug 1903.*
3.	ii.	EMALINE "EMILY" BALLARD, *b. 1839, GA; d. Jan 1880.*
	iii.	CATHERINE "KATIE" BALLARD, *b. 15 Dec 1840, GA; d. 27 Nov 1920, Spalding Co., GA.*
4.	iv.	SIMEON L. BALLARD, *b. 1844, GA; d. Bet. 1880 - 1900.*
5.	v.	JOHN BALLARD, *b. 18 Sep 1834, GA; d. 03 Jul 1890.*

Generation No. 2

2. WILLIAM RILEY[2] BALLARD (BALLARD[1]) *was born 04 Nov 1836 in GA, and died 31 Aug 1903. He married* ADELYN MATILDA WOMACK *10 Feb 1861 in Upson Co., GA, daughter of* DEGICHENS WOMACK *and* ELIZABETH. *She was born 1836 in GA, and died Aft. 1888.*

Notes for WILLIAM RILEY BALLARD:
Source: Alan Frederick Ballard (AFBallard@aol.com),1870 - 1880 Upson County Georgia Federal Census Records, 1900 Spalding County Georgia Federal Census Records, Georgia, Find a Grave

* 1870 - Living in Upson Co., GA - Ballard, William 34 GA, Adeline 34 GA, Willie 6 GA, Charlie 5 GA, Edna 2 GA, Martha 3/12 GA GA, John 29, Sarah 25, Laura 6, William 4
* 1880 - Living in Upson Co., GA - Ballard, William R 43 farming GA GA GA, Matilda 44 GA GA GA, Willie 17 GA, Charles 15 GA, Edna 13 GA, Martha A 11 GA, Leonard 8 GA, Wilkes 2 GA
* 1900 - Living in Griffin, Spalding Co., GA - Ballard, W. R Nov 1836 GA GA GA, Adaline - Jan 1865, W. D - Oct 1863, Jessie dau in law - Aug 1863 3 children 3 living GA, Edwin grandson - July 1885, Annie grand du - Nov 1887 GA, Fred grandson July 1895 GA

More About WILLIAM RILEY BALLARD:
Burial: Oak Hill Cemetery, Griffin, Spalding Co., GA

Children of WILLIAM BALLARD and ADELYN WOMACK are:

	i.	JOHN[3] BALLARD, *b. Bet. 1862 - 1882.*
	ii.	LAURA BALLARD, *b. Bet. 1862 - 1882.*
	iii.	MARGARET "MATTIE" BALLARD, *b. Bet. 1862 - 1882; m.* MR. MONROE.

iv. SARAH BALLARD, b. Bet. 1862 - 1882.

6. v. WILLIAM DAVID "WILLIE" BALLARD, b. 15 Oct 1863, Griffin, Spalding Co., GA; d. 24 Dec 1946, Geneva, Seminole Co., FL.

vi. CHARLES BALLARD, b. 1865, Griffin, Spalding Co., GA; d. Aft. 1880.

vii. MAUDE BALLARD, b. 17 Aug 1867, Griffin, Spalding Co., GA; d. 10 Dec 1938, Macon, Bibb Co., GA; m. MR. SANDERS.

More About MAUDE BALLARD:
Burial: Oak Hill Cemetery Griffin, Spalding Co., GA

viii. MARTHA A. BALLARD, b. Bet. 1869 - 1870, Griffin, Spalding Co., GA; d. Aft. 1880.

ix. LEONARD BALLARD, b. 1872, Griffin, Spalding Co., GA; d. Aft. 1880.

x. WILKES BALLARD, b. 1878, Griffin, Spalding Co., GA; d. Aft. 1880.

xi. EDNA BALLARD, b. 26 Mar 1887, Griffin, Spalding Co., GA; d. 10 Dec 1938, Macon, Bibb Co., GA.

3. EMALINE "EMILY"[2] BALLARD (BALLARD[1]) was born 1839 in GA, and died Jan 1880. She married PARKER.

Notes for EMALINE "EMILY" BALLARD:
Source: Mortality Schedule

Child of EMALINE BALLARD and PARKER is:

7. i. FORREST[3] PARKER, b. Nov 1871, GA; d. 1912.

4. SIMEON L.[2] BALLARD (BALLARD[1]) was born 1844 in GA, and died Bet. 1880 - 1900. He married LAURA ANN ELLIOTT 29 Dec 1867 in Upson Co., GA. She was born 01 Mar 1841 in GA, and died 01 Mar 1936 in Griffin, Spalding Co., GA.

Notes for SIMEON L. BALLARD:
Source: 1880 Georgia Federal Census Soundex Records

* 1870 - Living in Upson Co., GA - Ballard, Simeon 21 GA, Laura 25 GA
* 1880 - Living in Upson Co., GA - Ballard, Simeon 36 farming GA GA GA Laura 33 GA GA GA, Morgan 10 GA, Ambrose 7 GA, Milledge 5 GA, Harriett 3 GA, Emma 1 GA

Notes for LAURA ANN ELLIOTT:
Source: 1900 Spalding County Georgia Federal Census Records

* 1900 - Living in Griffin, Spalding Co., GA - Ballard, Laura A - Mar 1840 GA, Hattie - Sept 1880 GA, Edna - July 1882 GA, Mary - July 1883 GA, , Ambrose - Oct 1872 GA, Clemmie dau in law - Nov 1875 GA, Annie L - Aug 1899 GA

More About LAURA ANN ELLIOTT:
Burial: Oak Hill Cemetery, Griffin, Spalding Co., GA

Children of SIMEON BALLARD and LAURA ELLIOTT are:

i. DOUGLAS[3] BALLARD, d. Aft. 1933, of Bemis, TN.

ii. MORGAN L. BALLARD, b. 28 Dec 1870, Upson Co., GA; d. 20 Dec 1934.

More About MORGAN L. BALLARD:

Burial: Oak Hill Cemetery, Griffin, Spalding Co., GA

8. iii. AMBROSE B. BALLARD, b. 27 Jul 1873, Upson Co., GA; d. 03 Jul 1933, East Thomaston, Upson Co., GA.

        iv.   MILLEDGE BALLARD, b. 1875, Upson Co., GA; d. Aft. 1880.

9.   v.   HARRIET "HATTIE" BALLARD, b. 11 Aug 1876, Upson Co., GA; d. 10 Nov 1940.

        vi.   EMMA BALLARD, b. 1879, Upson Co., GA; d. Aft. 1880.

       vii.   EDNA BALLARD, b. Abt. 1882, Upson Co., GA; d. Aft. 1900; m. MR. MCNEIL.

       viii.   MARY BALLARD, b. Jul 1883, Upson Co., GA; d. Aft. 1900; m. MR. O'DELL.

5. JOHN[2] BALLARD (BALLARD[1]) was born 18 Sep 1834 in GA, and died 03 Jul 1890. He married SARAH CATHARINE JERNIGAN 06 Sep 1860 in Upson Co., GA. She was born 05 Nov 1845 in GA, and died 15 Jun 1896.

Notes for JOHN BALLARD:
Source: 1870, 1880 Upson County Federal Census Records
* 1870 - Living in Upson Co., GA - Ballard, John 29 farm hand GA, Sarah 25 GA, Laura 6 GA, William 4 GA
* 1880 - Living in Upson Co., GA - Ballard, John 46 working in Cotton Mill GA, Sarah 38 GA, Laura 16 Cotton Mill GA, William 14 Cotton Mill GA, John Henry 10 GA, Rosealla 7 GA, Minnie 5 GA

More About JOHN BALLARD:
Burial: Oak Hill Cemetery, Griffin, Spalding Co., GA

More About SARAH CATHARINE JERNIGAN:
Burial: Oak Hill Cemetery, Griffin, Spalding Co., GA

Children of JOHN BALLARD and SARAH JERNIGAN are:

       i.   LAURA[3] BALLARD, b. 1864, GA; d. Aft. 1880.

10.   ii.   WILLIAM A. BALLARD, b. 26 Mar 1866, GA; d. 20 Sep 1934.

       iii.   JOHN HENRY BALLARD, b. 1870, GA; d. Aft. 1880.

       iv.   ROZEALIA BALLARD, b. 1873, GA; d. Aft. 1880.

       v.   MINNIE BALLARD, b. 27 Nov 1875, GA; d. 26 Nov 1906; m. JERNIGAN.

           More About MINNIE BALLARD:
           Burial: Oak Hill Cemetery, Griffin, Spalding Co., GA

Generation No. 3

6. WILLIAM DAVID "WILLIE"[3] BALLARD (WILLIAM RILEY[2], BALLARD[1]) was born 15 Oct 1863 in Griffin, Spalding Co., GA, and died 24 Dec 1946 in Geneva, Seminole Co., FL. He married (1) JESSICA JONES 23 Aug 1883 in Upson Co., GA. She was born Aug 1863 in GA, and died 1900 in GA. He married (2) LUGENIA "LULU" LAING Bef. 1904. She was born 17 Jul 1865 in Floyd Co., GA, and died 04 May 1946 in Geneva, Seminole Co., FL.

Notes for WILLIAM DAVID "WILLIE" BALLARD:
Source: 1900 Spalding County Georgia Federal Census Records, 1910 Orange County Florida Federal Census Records, 1920 Seminole County Florida Federal Census Records, Alan Ballard, Winter Park FL (AFBallard@aol.com)

* 1900 - Willie and family are living with parents
* 1910 - Living in Sanford, Orange Co., FL - Ballard, William D 47 GA GA GA, Lulu 42 FL FL FL 2 children 2 living, Homer 6 GA GA FL, Elizabeth 3 GA GA FL, Frederick 15 GA GA GA
* 1920 - Living in Geneva, Seminole Co., FL - Ballard, William D 52 GA, Lula 50 FL, Frederick 25 GA, Homer 16 GA, Elizabeth 13 GA
* 1930 - Living in Geneva, Seminole Co., FL - Ballard, William D 66 GA GA GA, Lula 64 FL Scotland Scotland, Homer 25 GA GA FL

More About WILLIAM DAVID "WILLIE" BALLARD:
Burial: Geneva Cemetery, Geneva, Seminole Co., FL

More About LUGENIA "LULU" LAING:
Burial: Geneva Cemetery, Geneva, Seminole Co., FL

Children of WILLIAM BALLARD and JESSICA JONES are:

	i.	PAUL⁴ BALLARD.
	ii.	EDWIN LESLIE BALLARD, b. 1886, Griffin, Spalding Co., GA; d. 1949; m. ADA.
11.	iii.	FREDERICK "FRED" BALLARD, b. 10 Jul 1894, Griffin, Spalding Co., GA; d. 02 Aug 1954, Geneva, Seminole Co., FL.
12.	iv.	ANNIE BALLARD, b. 27 Nov 1898, Griffin, Spalding Co., GA; d. 27 Apr 1979, Griffin, Spalding Co., GA.

Children of WILLIAM BALLARD and LUGENIA LAING are:

    v.   HOMER⁴ BALLARD, b. 29 May 1904, Griffin, Spalding Co., GA; d. 03 Jul 1973, Seminole Co., FL; m. ALEXIA MEES; b. 21 Aug 1897, KS; d. 28 May 1959, Geneva, Seminole Co., FL.

        More About HOMER BALLARD:
        Burial: Geneva Cemetery, Geneva, Seminole Co., FL

    vi. ELIZABETH BALLARD, b. 1906, Geneva, Seminole Co., FL; d. Aft. 1910; m. JOSHUA BEASLEY.

7. FORREST³ PARKER (EMALINE "EMILY"² BALLARD, BALLARD¹) was born Nov 1871 in GA, and died 1912. He married GLADYS "JIM" HOLLIS. She was born 1863, and died 04 Jan 1937 in Atlanta, Fulton Co., GA.

Notes for FORREST PARKER:
Source: 1900 - 1910 Spalding County Georgia Federal Census Records

* 1900 - Living in Griffin, Spalding Co., GA - Parker Forrest - Nov 1871 GA GA GA cloth room cotton mill, Jim - Feb 1870 AL NC SC, Forrest - June 1898 GA, Margaret - Apr 1900 GA, Katie Ballard - aunt - Oct 1840 GA GA GA
* 1910 - Living in Griffin, Spalding Co., GA - Parker, Forest 33 GA GA GA foreman cloth room, Jim 34 GA GA SC 3 children 3 Living, Forest Jr. 11 GA, Margarete 10 GA, Grace 6 GA, Kate 62 GA aunt

More About FORREST PARKER:
Burial: Oak Hill Cemetery, Griffin, Spalding Co., GA

More About GLADYS "JIM" HOLLIS:
Burial: Oak Hill Cemetery, Griffin, Spalding Co., GA

Children of FORREST PARKER and GLADYS HOLLIS are:
    i.   FORREST⁴ PARKER, b. Jun 1898, GA; d. Aft. 1910.
    ii. MARGARET PARKER, b. Apr 1900, GA; d. Aft. 1910.
    iii. GRACE PARKER, b. 01 Aug 1903, Spalding Co., GA; d. Aug 1988.

8. AMBROSE B.³ BALLARD (SIMEON L.², BALLARD¹) was born 27 Jul 1873 in Upson Co., GA, and died 03 Jul 1933 in East Thomaston, Upson Co., GA. He married A. CLEMIE BRANAN. She was born 08 Nov 1875 in GA, and died 22 Apr 1951.

Notes for AMBROSE B. BALLARD:
Source: 1910 Pulaski County Georgia Federal Census Records, 1920 Spalding County Georgia Federal Census Records, 1930 Upson County Georgia Federal Census Records, File contributed for use in USGenWeb Archives by LisaGraham32@aol.com Lisa Graham

* 1910 - Living in Cary, Pulaski Co., GA - Ballard, Ambros B 37 GA, Carrie 34 - 4 children 4 living, Annie L. 10 GA, Willis H 8 GA, Francis O 4 GA, Gussie V 2 GA, William F Branan father in law 62 wd GA
* 1920 - Living in Africa, Spalding Co., GA - Ballard, Ambro 46 GA Clem 44 wife, Annie L 20 GA, Francis 14 GA, Vera 11 GA, Edna 9 GA, Jewel 5 GA
* 1930 - Living in Thomaston, Upson Co., GA - Ballard, Ambrose57 GA, Clemmie 54 GA, Annie L 30 GA, Edna R 19 GA, Frances 24 GA, Jewel 15 GA, Frank Branan (?) father in law 81 wd GA

Ballard - *Mr. Ambrose B. Ballard age 59 passed away at his residence in East Thomaston Monday evening, July 3, 1933 following several months illness. He leaves his widow, five daughters, Mrs. Sherry Ellerbee, Misses Annie Lou, Frances, Edna Ruth and Jewell Ballard of Thomaston, one son, Mr. Willis H. Ballard of Thomaston; three sisters, Mrs. Hattie Autrey, Mrs. Edna McNeil and Mrs. Mary Odell of Griffin; two brothers, Morgan L. Ballard of Griffin and Douglas Ballard of Bemis, Tenn., his mother, Mrs. Laura Ballard of Griffin and six grandchildren. The funeral was held Tuesday morning at the East Thomaston Baptist for which he had been a faithful member for many years, Reverends C. O. English his pastor, C. B. Ballard of Griffin his Former Pastor and George W. Mitchell who has been one of his closest friends for many years officiated at the funeral. The interment was held in Shiloh Cemetery.*
Other- A.B. Ballard Shiloh Cemetery
7/27/1873- 7/3/1933 Mrs. A. B. Ballard (wife) 11/8/1875- 4/22/1951

More About AMBROSE B. BALLARD:
Burial: Shiloh Cemetery

More About A. CLEMIE BRANAN:

Burial: Shiloh Baptist Church Cemetery, Thomaston, Upson Co., GA

Children of AMBROSE BALLARD and A. BRANAN are:

> i.   SHERRY[4] BALLARD, b. Bet. 1895 - 1920; d. Aft. 1933; m. ELLERBEE.
> ii. ANNIE LOU FRANCES BALLARD, b. 14 Aug 1899, GA; d. 20 Apr 1990; m. SHEPHERD.
>
>   *More About ANNIE LOU FRANCES BALLARD:*
>   *Burial: Yatesville Methodist Church Cemetery, Yatesville, Upson Co., GA*
>
> iii. WILLIS HULLETT BALLARD, b. 24 Feb 1902, GA; d. 13 Oct 1969.
>
>   *More About WILLIS HULLETT BALLARD:*
>   *Burial: Shiloh Baptist Church Cemetery, Thomaston, Upson Co., GA*
>
> iv. FRANCIS OLIVER BALLARD, b. 17 Dec 1905, GA; d. 05 Aug 1976, VA; m. (1) OAKS; m. (2) WALTER CARTER ANSELL, 07 Jun 1955, Portsmouth, VA.
>
>   *Notes for FRANCIS OLIVER BALLARD:*
>   *Source: Marriage Records Application shows she had two previous marriages*
>
>   *More About FRANCIS OLIVER BALLARD:*
>   *Burial: Shiloh Baptist Church Cemetery, Thomaston, Upson Co. GA*
>
> v.   GUSSIE VERA BALLARD, b. Abt. 1908, GA; d. Aft. 1920.
> vi. EDNA RUTH BALLARD, b. Abt. 1911, Spalding Co., GA; d. Aft. 1933.
> vii. JEWELL BALLARD, b. Abt. 1915, Spalding Co., GA; d. Aft. 1933.

9. HARRIET "HATTIE"[3] BALLARD (SIMEON L.[2], BALLARD[1]) *was born 11 Aug 1876 in Upson Co., GA, and died 10 Nov 1940. She married* GEORGE ALEANDER AUTREY. *He was born 16 Apr 1873, and died 03 May 1933.*

More About HARRIET "HATTIE" BALLARD:
Burial: Oak Hill Cemetery, Griffin, Spalding Co., GA

Notes for GEORGE ALEANDER AUTREY:
Source: 1910 Spalding County Georgia Federal Census Records

* 1910 - *Living in Africa, Spalding Co., GA - Awtry, Geo A 38 GA, Hattie 26 GA, Geo R 6 GA, Elmer L 3 GA, Sam D 1 GA, Laura Ballard mother in law 68 wd GA 7 children 6 living*

More About GEORGE ALEANDER AUTREY:
Burial: Oak Hill Cemetery, Griffin, Spalding Co., GA

Children of HARRIET BALLARD and GEORGE AUTREY are:

> i. GEORGE R.[4] AUTREY, b. Abt. 1906, GA; d. Aft. 1910.
> ii. ELMER L. AUTREY, b. Abt. 1907, GA; d. Aft. 1910.
> iii. SAM D. AUTREY, b. Abt. 1908, GA; d. Abt. 1910.

10. WILLIAM A.[3] BALLARD (JOHN[2], BALLARD[1]) *was born 26 Mar 1866 in GA, and died 20 Sep 1934. He married* CORNELIA E KEEN. *She was born 04 Apr 1866, and died 07 Oct 1941.*

Notes for WILLIAM A. BALLARD:
Source: 1900-1920 Spalding County Georgia Federal Census Records

* 1900 - *Living in Africa, Spalding Co., GA - Ballard, Will - Mar 1866, Cornilia - Apr 1866, John W - Oct 1887 GA, Cora L - Dec 1889, Sadie L - May 1893 GA, Effie L - Nov 1896 GA*
* 1910 - *Living in Africa, Spalding Co., GA - Ballard, Wm L 44 GA GA GA, Cornelia E 44 GA GA GA - 5 children 4 living, Cora L 20 GA, Sallie L 17 GA, Effie L 13 GA, Harriet O Reenes 67 wd 8 children 6 living GA GA GA*
* 1920 - *Living in Africa, Spalding Co., GA - Ballard, William A 53 carpenter GA GA GA, Cornelias E 53 GA GA GA*
* 1930 - *Living in Africa, Spalding Co., GA - Ballard, William A 64, Cornelia E 64*

More About WILLIAM A. BALLARD:
Burial: Oak Hill Cemetery, Griffin, Spalding Co., GA

More About CORNELIA E KEEN:
Burial: Oak Hill Cemetery, Griffin, Spalding Co., GA

Children of WILLIAM BALLARD and CORNELIA KEEN are:
> i. JOHN W.[4] BALLARD, b. Oct 1887, Spalding Co., GA; d. Aft. 1900.
> ii. CORA L. BALLARD, b. Dec 1889, Spalding Co., GA; d. Aft. 1910.
> iii. SADIE L. BALLARD, b. May 1893, Spalding Co., GA; d. Aft. 1910.
> iv. EFFIE LOIS BALLARD, b. Nov 1896, Spalding Co., GA; d. Aft. 1910; m. PAUL H. MADDOX.

Generation No. 4

11. FREDERICK "FRED"[4] BALLARD (WILLIAM DAVID "WILLIE"[3], WILLIAM RILEY[2], BALLARD[1]) *was born 10 Jul 1894 in Griffin, Spalding Co., GA, and died 02 Aug 1954 in Geneva, Seminole Co., FL. He married* EDNA GEIGER. *She was born 31 Mar 1900 in Geneva, Seminole Co., FL, and died 28 May 1987 in Orlando, Orange Co., FL.*

Notes for FREDERICK "FRED" BALLARD:
Source: 1930 Seminole County Florida Federal Census Records, Alan Frederick Ballard (AFBallard@aol.com)
* 1930 - *Living in Geneva, Seminole Co., FL - Ballard, Fred 35, Edna 30, George W 7, Edwin R 5, Carl C 1*

More About FREDERICK "FRED" BALLARD:
Burial: Geneva Cemetery, Geneva, Seminole Co., FL

More About EDNA GEIGER:
Burial: Geneva Cemetery, Geneva, Seminole Co., FL

Children of FREDERICK BALLARD and EDNA GEIGER are:

  i. GEORGE WILLIAM[5] BALLARD, b. 30 Jun 1922; d. 13 Jun 1944, Normandy France.

    More About GEORGE WILLIAM BALLARD:

    Burial: Geneva Cemetery, Geneva, Seminole Co., FL

  ii. EDWIN RILEY BALLARD, b. 15 Nov 1923, Geneva, Seminole Co., FL; d. 18 Oct 1989, Maitland, Orange Co., FL; m. GERALDINE MILLER; b. 08 Oct 1928, Grady Co., GA; d. 22 Sep 2009, Maitland, Orange Co., FL.

    More About EDWIN RILEY BALLARD:
    Burial: Palm Cemetery, Winter Park, Orange Co., FL

    More About GERALDINE MILLER:
    Burial: Palm Cemetery, Winter Park, Orange Co., FL

  iii. CARL CECIL BALLARD, b. 07 Apr 1928.

    Notes for CARL CECIL BALLARD:
    Source: Alan Frederick Ballard (AFBallard@aol.com)

12. ANNIE[4] BALLARD (WILLIAM DAVID "WILLIE"[3], WILLIAM RILEY[2], BALLARD[1]) was born 27 Nov 1898 in Griffin, Spalding Co., GA, and died 27 Apr 1979 in Griffin, Spalding Co., GA. She married JAMES CLIFFORD WILLIAMS. He was born 13 Jan 1881 in GA, and died 12 Aug 1937 in Upson Co., GA.

More About ANNIE BALLARD:
Burial: Oak Hill Cemetery., Griffin, Spalding Co., GA

Children of ANNIE BALLARD and JAMES WILLIAMS are:

  i. MARTHA[5] WILLIAMS.
  ii. PAIGE WILLIAMS.
  iii. JAMES C. WILLIAMS.
  iv. MALCOM H. WILLIAMS.
  v. RICHARD COLEMAN WILLIAMS.

Mr. Ballard

Generation No. 1

1. MR.[1] BALLARD *was born Abt. 1800. He married* MARY ANN SUSAN. *She was born Abt. 1809 in GA, and died Bef. Sep 1885 in Bibb Co., GA.*

Notes for MARY ANN SUSAN:

Source: 1850-1870 Vineville Bibb County Georgia Federal Census Records

* *1850 - Living in Bibb Co., GA - Susan Jewell 41, Augustus Ballard 21 Book keeper GA, Walter S. 19 Clerk GA, S. B. 16 male student GA, C. M. 13 male student GA*
* *1860 - Living in Vineville Bibb Co., GA - Jewett, Susan, Julia, Malone, Ballard, Augustus 31 Book keeper GA, Walter 28 Book keeper GA, Cecil 24 Clerk*
* *1870 - Living in Bibb Co., GA - Jewet, Susan 60, Malone 22 clerk in store, Walter S 38 Mule Trader GA, Adrian Jones 56*

* *1883 - Bibb Co., GA - Mrs. Mary A S Jewetts Will - State of Georgia Bibb County } In the name of God Amen. I Mary A. S Jewett of the County and State aforesaid hereby make and publish this my last Will and testament.*
First - I direct my Executors hereinafter Mentioned to pay all My just debts and funeral expenses
Second - I desire My house & lot in Vineville kept together as long as my Son Walter S Ballard lives or disposed of as may be agreed upon by my Executors and the interest or rent of to be equally divided between my Son Walter S Ballard my daughter Leona V Farran and my Son Malone Jewett and at the death of my Son Walter S Ballard pay my Son Malone Jewett what is due him and the remainder if any to be equally divided between my Daughters Leona V Farran & my Son Malone Jewett, if my son Malone Jewett Should die without family or Will 1 bequeath his portion to my Grand Son John Farran and the part i bequeath to my daughter Leona V Farrar to be hers to dispose of as she may choose and the proceeds if old invested as she may desire in no event to be liable for any debt of her husband or any future husband but to be hers to do with as she herself may desire.
Third - I give My Son Walter S Ballard my Silver Table Spoons desert Spoons Tea Spoons to have during his life and at his death to my daughter Leona V Farran. I give my daughter Leona V. Farran my Silver Waiters and Butten dish. I give to my Son Malone Jewett my Silver Ladle, Butten knives, Pie knife Forks Berry Spoon & Sugar Spoon, and if Malone Jewett dies without family or Will to go to my Daughter Leona V Farrar to take Charge of and Keep the Silverware which i have given to my Son Walter S. Ballard and I desire that my daughter Leona V Farran take charge of and keep the Silver Ware i have given to my Son Malone Jewett & give the Same up to him where he may wish her to do so.
Fourth - Should my grand Son John Farran die before he becomes of age, I desire that portion of My Estate that would go be inherited by him to go to my Daughter Leona V. Farran.
Lastly - I appoint Malone Jewett & Leona V Farran as My Exutors and Executrix
In Witness Whereof I have hereto let my hand and Seal and published and declared this instrument to be my last Will and Testament This Third day of January in the year of our Lord Eighteen Hundred and Eighty three in the presence of the persons whose names are Subscribed as attesting Witnesses. Mary A S Jewett.
John S Williams, C. M Farrar, W. A Clarke

* *1885 - Aug 20 - Probate - Georgia Jones County Ordinarys Office At Chambers*
Personally Came John T. Williams and C. M Farran two of the Subscribing Witnesses to this instrument and who after being duly Sworn deposeth and Saith that They Saw Mrs. A. S. Jewett the Testatrix Sign Seal Publish and declare this instrument to be her last Will & Testament that She Signed the Same in our presence & was at the time of Signing the Same of Sound Mind and Memory and in our Judgment Capable of Making her Will & did So freely & Voluntarily that we Signed the Same as Witnesses in his presence & in presence of each other, and W. A. Clark Signed also at Same time, all in her presence, at her request and in the presence of each other on the day Therein Set forth & that Said W. A Clark now resider out of the County & his Signature to this Will is genuine. Sworn to & Subscribed before me Aug 20th 1885, Roland J. Ross Ordinary Jones Co. GA } Jno F. Williams, C. M, Farran

For Order admitting Will to Record See Minutes Court Ordinary at Sept Term 1885 on page 341 & 342. R. T Ross ordinary. Recorded Sept 8 1885 R T Ross Ordinary

Children of MR. BALLARD and MARY SUSAN are:

     i.   AUGUSTUS[2] BALLARD, b. 1829, GA; d. Aft. 1864.

          Notes for AUGUSTUS BALLARD:

          Source: 1864 Georgia Militia Census
          * Aug M Ballard - Bookkeeper b. GA

     ii.   WALTER S. BALLARD, b. 1832, GA; d. Aft. 1880.
     iii.   S. B. BALLARD, b. 1834, GA; d. Aft. 1860.

2.   iv.   LEONA V. BALLARD, b. 27 Jun 1834, GA; d. 12 May 1899.
     v.   CECIL M. BALLARD, b. Bet. 1836 - 1837, GA; d. 1863.

          Notes for CECIL M. BALLARD:
          Source: Georgia Wills and Probate Records 1742-1992
          Name   Cecil M Ballard, Probate Date 4 Jan 1862, Probate Place   Bibb, Georgia, USA
          Inferred Death Year   Abt 1862, Inferred Death Place Georgia, USA
          * Last Will and Testament of C M Ballard - State of Virginia County of Fairfax}. Be it remembered that I Cecil M Ballard First Lieutenant of Company C Eighth Regiment Georgia Volunteers of the county of Bibb and State of Georgia, being of Sound mind and Disposing Memory do make and Declare this as my last Will & Testament hereby revoking any other which may have been before made by me
          Item 1st I desire that all my just debts be paid as soon as possible after my decease.
          Item 2dn I Will and request all my property both real and personal to my Mother Mrs. Susan Jewett and my half brother Owen Malone Jewett to be equally Divided between them both share and Shard alike.
          I hereby appoint my Mother Mrs. Susan Jewett Executrix to my will.
          In Witness whereof I have hereunto set my hands and Seal this the 4th Day of January Eighteen Hundred Sixty Two. C. W. Ballard (mark)
          The foregoing instrument purporting to be the Last Will and Testament of Cecil M Ballard was signed X Sealed by him in our presence and by his request we hereunto affix our Names as Witness thereto in his presence and also in presence of Each other. Henry J. Menards, Thos G Hodgkins, Jno R Hill, Wallace C. Poe, John Wm Blount
          * Georgia, Bibb County} Ordinary office At Chambers August the 6th 1863 Personally came John W Blount & John R Hill Two of the Subscribing Witnesses to the within Will of C. M Ballard late of said County Deceased who being duly sworn Deposes & Says that they Saw C. M. Ballard Sign Seal publish & declare the within instrument as for his last will & Testament and that this was of sound disposing mind & memory and that he signed it freely voluntarily & of his own accord and that the Said Henry J Menards Thomas G Hodgkins and Wallace C Poes Sign the Same as witnesses Menards & Hodgkins has Since died & that we all Signed the Same in the presence of each other & at the request of Said Testator. Sworn to & Subscribed before me this August 6, 1863, Wm Riley Ordinary. Record August 8, 1863. Signed: J W Blount, Jno R. Hill, Wm. Riley

Generation No. 2

2.   LEONA V.[2] BALLARD (MR.[1]) was born 27 Jun 1834 in GA, and died 12 May 1899. She married SAMUEL MINTER FARRAN. He was born 29 Nov 1821, and died 06 May 1877.

Notes for LEONA V. BALLARD:

Source: 1880 Jones County Georgia Federal Census Records
* 1880 - Living in Ethridge, Jones Co., GA - Farrer, Leona 45 GA GA GA, Charles M 20 GA, Walter S Ballard brother 49 GA, Susan Jewett 70 Mother

More About LEONA V. BALLARD:
Burial: Rose Hill Cemetery, Macon, Bibb Co., GA

More About SAMUEL MINTER FARRAN:
Burial: Rose Hill Cemetery, Macon, Bibb Co., GA

Children of LEONA BALLARD and SAMUEL FARRAN are:

     i.   CHARLES MINTER[3] FARRAN, *b. 23 Aug 1859, Bibb Co., GA; d. 26 Nov 1954, Bibb Co., GA; m. TALLULAH SMITH; b. 03 Mar 1871, GA; d. 10 Jan 1942, Jones Co., GA.*

          More About TALLULAH SMITH:
          Burial: Riverside Cemetery, Macon Bibb Co., GA

    ii. JOHN FARRAN.

Whorton Ballard

Generation No. 1

1. WHORTON[5] BALLARD (JESSE[4], JOHN[3], JOSEPH[2], JOHN[1]) *was born 1763 in NC, and died Aft. 1835 in Coweta Co., GA. He married* SALOMA REDWINE *Abt. 1790 in Montgomery Co., NC. She was born Bet. 1766 - 1768 in NC or PA, and died Aft. 1850 in Cobb Co. GA.*

Notes for WHORTON BALLARD:

Source: Irene Kennedy (deceased), Lloyd Russ Ballard, Tex Dick, Oliver Ballard, Hollis Ballard, Evelyn Ballard, Chris Gardner (grasp1@bellsouth.net), Mildred Sparks, Billy and Janie Price, Evelyn Ballard Group sheets, Sara Wilson records, Kathy Ballard (grits111@hotmail.com), E. Dee Varnadore, Mike Montgomery, Valerie Austin (va5303@nersp.nerdc.ufl.edu), Martha Irwin (marirw@yahoo.com), Kelly Hartley (willow1@yahoo.com)

* Tax records show Whorton paying taxes in Franklin County Georgia
* 1786 - 1792 Franklin County deed Book C 42-43 Reuben & wife Absilla Ballard to John and Susannah Palmer.
* 1800 - Living in Montgomery Co., NC
* 1801 - Wilkes Co., NC Book 1792-1801 page 247 Nathan Ballard
* 1803 - Wilkes Co., NC Will Book
* 1804 - Living in Elbert Co., GA
* 1806 - Greene Book WA B page 100 John
* 1806 - 1808 page 57 William Ballard
* 1807 to 1825 - Capt. Browns Dist. and Coker's dist. He paid taxes in Appling County for land he drew in the 1820-21 land lottery sec 13 land lot #356.
* 1811 - Living in Franklin Co., GA
* 1817 - Living in Franklin Co., GA - witness ib Hanes / Ballard land records Aug 19, 1817
* 1819 - 1826 Franklin Co., GA Deed Bk B-96 from Squire and Nancy Markham to James Ballard
* 1823 - Monroe Co., GA paid taxes for Wesly Ballard, for 202 1/2 acres in Monroe County Georgia.
* 1825 - 1829 Franklin Co., GA Deed Bk BB-76 to Samuel Crow from James Ballard & wife Georgia Wills
* 1825 - 1829 Franklin Co., GA Deed Bk BB-14 & 15 from Issac Briggs to Whorton Ballard
* 1826 - Taliaferro Book A page 12
* 1828 - Living in Coweta Co., GA - Assisted in organizing a Methodist Church
* 1830 - Living in Coweta Co., GA
* 1832 - 1835 Franklin Co., GA Deed Bk D-57 from Whorton Ballard to John Carroll
* 1835 - 1837 Franklin Co., GA Deed Bk DD-4 from Whorton Ballard to Thomas Haynes
Other records pertaining to his sons:
* 1844 - Putnam Bk B pg 188
* 1851 - Pike Bk C page 89
* 1853 - Decatur Bk A page 87
* 1855 - Coweta Bk B page 117
* 1855 - Columbia Co., Bk J page 55
* 1860 - Morgan Bk C page 261
* Christened or Baptized Methodist on Cedar Creek.

More About WHORTON BALLARD:

Burial: New Hope Methodist Cemetery. Campbell Co., GA

More About SALOMA REDWINE:
Burial: New Hope Methodist Cemetery. Campbell Co., GA

Children of WHORTON BALLARD *and* SALOMA REDWINE *are:*

2.   i.   LEWIS[6] BALLARD, *b. 1791, Montgomery Co., NC; d. Aft. 1867.*
3.   ii.   JESSE BALLARD, *b. 1792, Montgomery Co., NC; d. 21 Oct 1878, Cedar Creek, Coweta Co., GA.*

4.   iii.   JAMES BALLARD, b. Bet. 1794 - 1797, NC; d. Aft. 1850, Coweta Co., GA.
5.   iv.   WILLIAM ROBERT BALLARD, b. 1796, NC; d. Oct 1855, Coweta Co., GA.
6.   v.   JANE BALLARD, b. 1800, NC; d. 1870, Hopkins TX or Jackson Parish, LA.
7.   vi.   WESLEY BALLARD, b. 10 May 1803, NC; d. 30 Jul 1872, Carroll Co., GA.
8.   vii.   MARY BALLARD, b. 1804, Beaver Dam Creek, Elbert Co., GA; d. 1861.
9.   viii. ELIZABETH BALLARD, b. 16 Jan 1807, Beaver Dam Creek, Elbert Co., GA; d. 26 Nov 1843, Cherokee
              Co., GA.
       ix.   JOHN BALLARD, b. 1809, Beaver Dam Creek, Elbert Co., GA; m. HARRIETT BAILEY, 10 Dec 1829,
              11/26/1829 Coweta Co., GA; b. 16 Jan 1807; d. 26 Nov 1843, Cherokee Co., GA.
       x.   SALOMA BALLARD, b. 1810; m. ALFRED CRAWFORD, 02 Mar 1837, Coweta Co., GA; b. Abt. 1810.
10.   xi.   COLEMAN H. BALLARD, b. 23 May 1810, GA or NC; d. 07 May 1877, Redland, Angelina Co., TX.
11.   xii.   PRISCILLA BALLARD, b. 1812, Beaver Dam Creek, Elbert Co., GA; d. 28 Feb 1888, Jackson Parish,
              LA.

Generation No. 2

2. LEWIS[6] BALLARD (WHORTON[5], JESSE[4], JOHN[3], JOSEPH[2], JOHN[1]) was born 1791 in Montgomery Co., NC, and died Aft. 1867. He married MEEKY DOBBS 25 Sep 1817 in Franklin Co., GA. She was born Abt. 1800, and died Bef. 1850.

Notes for LEWIS BALLARD:
Source: Tara Barrett, Linda Bradberry (LDBrad@aol.com) & (deah_12@hotmail.com)), LDS-IGI, 1830 Franklin County Georgia Federal Census Records, 1840 Gilmer County Georgia Federal census Records, 1850 Marion County Florida Federal Census Records, 1860 Orange County Florida Federal Census Records, 1867 Orange County Florida State Census Records
* 1822 - Living in Franklin Co., GA - Pastor of Poplar Springs Baptist Church
* 1830 - Living in Franklin Co., GA - Ballard, Lewis. 1 male 30-40, 1 female 30-40, 1 male 10-15, 3 males 5-10, 2 males 0-5 and 1 female 0-5.
* 1840 - Living in Gilmer Co., GA - Ballard, Lewis, 0-0-0-0-1 1-0-0-1 - 1 male 20 and under 30 , 1 female under 5, 1 female 20 and under 30
* 1840 - Living in Cass Co., GA - Ballard, Lewis, 1 male 5-10, 2 males 15-20, 3 male 15-20, 1 male 40-50, 1 fe 5-10 & 1 fe 30-40.
* 1850 - Living in Marion Co., FL - Ballard, Lewis 52 NC, Solomon R 30 GA, William L 25 GA, Munroe 19 GA, Mary C. 17 GA, Martha 9 GA
* 1860 - Living in Orange Co., FL - Ballard, Lewis 61 N, Emiline 26 TN, Lewis H 4 TN, Franklin M. 2 FL
* 1867 - Living in Orange Co., FL - Ballard, Lewis 1 over 21, 1 over 18, 0 under 18, 0 males between 13-45

Children of LEWIS BALLARD and MEEKY DOBBS are:
12.   i.   JAMES CLARK[7] BALLARD, b. 1818, Franklin Co., GA; d. Aft. 1860.
       ii.   SOLOMON R. BALLARD, b. 1819, Franklin Co., GA; d. Aft. 1850.
13.   iii.   MORRIS R. BALLARD, b. 04 Mar 1820, Franklin Co., GA; d. 19 Aug 1899, Attala Co., GA.
14.   iv.   WILLIAM L. BALLARD, b. 1828, Franklin Co., GA; d. Aft. 1860.
15.   v.   ALVIN MONROE BALLARD, b. 1831, Franklin Co., GA; d. 08 Aug 1916, Old Myakka, Sarasota Co.,
              FL.
16.   vi.   MARY CATHERINE BALLARD, b. 1832, Franklin Co., GA; d. Aft. 1850.
       vii.   MARTHA C. BALLARD, b. 1841, Franklin Co., GA; d. Aft. 1850.
       viii. LEWIS H. BALLARD, b. 1856, TN; d. Aft. 1860.
       ix.   FRANKLIN M. BALLARD, b. 1858, FL; d. Aft. 1860.

3. JESSE[6] BALLARD (WHORTON[5], JESSE[4], JOHN[3], JOSEPH[2], JOHN[1]) was born 1792 in Montgomery Co., NC, and died 21 Oct 1878 in Cedar Creek, Coweta Co., GA. He married MARY FRANCES BALLENGER 11 Apr 1811 in Elbert Co., GA, daughter of JOHN BALLENGER and LINNIE ?. She was born 1789 in Greenville Co, SC, and died 07 Apr 1877 in GA.

Notes for JESSE BALLARD:
Source: Mike Montgomery, Kathy Ballard, Lloyd Russ Ballard, Tex Dick, Source: Chris Gardner (grasp1@bellsouth.net), Evelyn Ballard Family Group Sheets. Oliver and Hollis Ballard Notes. 1850 Coweta County Georgia Federal Census Records, 1860 Campbell County Georgia Federal Census Records. Will in Coweta County Georgia Book 13 1849-1885 pages 348-349, Kelly Hartley (willow1@yahoo.com)
* 1812 - War of 1812 Pension Application S.O. #25317 S.C. #155 72, B.L.W. #35631-80-50 & #46707-80-55.
* Jesse was a farmer, Methodist Minister and a Miller
* 1804 - Living in Elbert Co., GA
* 1814 - Served under Capt. John Waters Co., Georgia Militia Nov 21 1814 to May 6, 1814.
* 1828 - Moved from Elbert Co., GA to Coweta Co., GA
* 1850 - Living in Coweta Co., GA next door to William Ballard, Jr.- Ballard, Jesse 57 Farmer NC, Mary 59 SC, Martha 21 GA, Thomas S 19 farmer GA, Linney C 17 GA
* 1851 - Living in Coweta Co., GA
* 1856 - Granted 18 March 1856 - Appeared Jesse Ballard 64 years Campbell Co., GA volunteered at the Cross Roads about July 1812 for 6 months. Honerable discharged at Mobile, 1 April 1813. 80 Acres issued under Act of 1852. Warrent disposed of being legally transferred. signed Jesse Ballard witness by John A. Wright, W. F. Ballard
* 1857 - Land Grant - Campbell Co., GA - 80 acres 23 April 1857 Rec. Warrent No 35.62 - 80 c 12 Aug 1851 - Jesse Ballard 59 years old, Coweta Co., GA was Pvt. in Capt John Wate Waters Regt of Troopers commanded by Col. David Booth in for the Brittian. He volunteered at Red Hollow, Franklin Co 11 Nov 1814 for 6 months. Honerable discharged at Ft. Hawkins 14 May 1851. signed Jesse Ballard.
* 1858 - Jesse, Mary, Whorton Fletcher, Sarah Ann, Thomas S., Elizabeth P. & Linny were members of New Hope Methodist Church south of Palmetto, GA in 1858
* 1860 - Living in Campbell Co., GA - Ballard, Jesse 68 GA, Mary 69 GA
* 1870 - Living in Campbell Co., GA - Ballard, Jess 78 Farmer NC, Mary 81 NC
* 1871 - Act of Feb 14, 1871 - #25317 - Jesse Ballard, Campbell Co., GA, Capt John Waters Co., Ala Militia. Discharged April 1811 or 15. Application Pension, 10 Oct 1871 - appeared before Judge R. C. Beavers, Jesse Ballard age 80, Campbell Co., GA declares he is married, that his wife's name was Mary Ballenger to whom he was married at Elbert Co., GA on 11 April 1811 & served full period of 60 days Military service in War of 1812. He went from Elbert Co. in Capt Waters Co. but was residing in Red Hollow in Franklin Co., GA Post Office new is Palmetto, GA. Jesse (his X mark) Ballard, Witness: Wiley Steed, Wiley Hopkins.

More About JESSE BALLARD:
Burial: New Hope United Methodist Church Cemetery, Palmetto, Fulton Co., GA

Notes for MARY FRANCES BALLENGER:
Source: Becky Walker (beckins@sound.net) submitted some obituaries to the Ballard List and below is one pertaining to Mary
* Death and Obituary Notices from The Southern Christian Advocate 1867-1878 Issue of May 22, 1877: Mrs. Mary Ballard, daughter of John Ballenger and wife of Jesse Ballard, was born in South Carolina; died in Campbell county, Ga., April 7, 1877, aged eighty eight years. She was the mother of nine children, for of whom are living and five dead. Stephen Shell.

More About MARY FRANCES BALLENGER:
Burial: New Hope Methodist Cemetery, Palmetto, Fulton Co., GA

Children of JESSE BALLARD and MARY BALLENGER are:
17.   i.   SARAH[7] BALLARD, b. 07 Jun 1814, 6/17 Franklin Co., GA; d. 25 Feb 1853, Campbell Co., GA.
             ii.   MARY BALLARD, b. Abt. 1816.
18.   iii. WILLIAM MOSES BALLARD, b. 1816, Beaver Dam Creek, Elbert Co., GA; d. 21 Oct 1864, Andersonville, Sumter Co., GA.
             iv.   NANCY ADELINE BALLARD, b. Bet. 1820 - 1824, Elbert Co., GA; d. 25 Dec 1864, Coweta Co, GA; m. WILLIAM B. ROBERTSON, 26 Dec 1837, Coweta Co., GA; b. Abt. 1816.

             Notes for WILLIAM B. ROBERTSON:
             Source: CD#4

19.   v.   WHORTON FLETCHER BALLARD, b. 05 Mar 1822, Beaver Dam Creed, Elbert Co., GA; d. 25 Dec 1864, Coweta Co, GA.
        vi. ELIZABETH ANN BALLARD, b. 04 Dec 1825, Beaver Dam Creek, Elbert Co., GA; d. 1850, Campbell Co., GA; m. JOHN F. SMITH, 11 Jul 1844, Coweta Co., GA; b. Abt. 1820.

        Notes for ELIZABETH ANN BALLARD:
        Source: Lloyd Russ Ballard, Evelyn Ballard

        Notes for JOHN F. SMITH:
        Source: 1850 Campbell County Georgia Federal Census Records
        * 1850 - Living in Campbell Co., GA - Smith, Jno F 26 Farmer GA, Elizabeth 21 GA, Martha Ann 4 GA, Wm J 2 GA, Jas W 4/12 GA

        vii. MARTHA FRANCES BALLARD, b. 1828, Beaver Dam Creek, Elbert Co., GA; d. Aft. 1860, TX; m. MATTHEW PFEIFFER, 12 Dec 1851, Coweta Co., GA.
20.   viii. THOMAS SANFORD BALLARD, b. Bet. 1829 - 1831, Beaver Dam Creek, Elbert Co., GA; d. 1883, Lockhart, Caldwell Co., TX.
21.   ix.   LINDA CAROLINE "LINNY" BALLARD, b. 1832, Beaver Dam Creek, Elbert Co., GA; d. 1875.

4. JAMES[6] BALLARD (WHORTON[5], JESSE[4], JOHN[3], JOSEPH[2], JOHN[1]) was born Bet. 1794 - 1797 in NC, and died Aft. 1850 in Coweta Co., GA. He married ELIZABETH 1815. She was born Abt. 1800 in GA, and died Aft. 1850.

Notes for JAMES BALLARD:
Source: 1850-1860 Cobb County Georgia Federal Census Records, Lloyd Russ Ballard, Tex Dick, Oliver Ballard, Hollis Ballard and Mildred Sparks, History of Wilkinson County GA Church Histories, Kathy Ballard (grits111@hotmail.com)
* 1817 - Living in Franklin Co., GA - On Aug 19, 1817 - James Ballard for $150 purchased 105 acres on North Fork Broad River at the mouth of Little River Creek from Squire Marcham and wife Nancy of Franklin Co., GA. Witness: Whorton Ballard, William Hall
* 1818 - Living in Franklin Co., GA - Tax Rolls
* 1821 - Living in Franklin Co., GA - land draw in the 1821 GA land lottery - lots for 202 acres in Monroe Co., GA
* 1830 - Living in Coweta Co., GA
* 1840 - Living in Cobb Co., GA
* 1850 - Living in Cobb Co., GA - Ballard, James 56 NC, Elizabeth 50 GA, Frances 22 GA, James 18 GA, Coleman 15 GA, Westly 18 GA, Elbert 11 GA

Children of JAMES BALLARD and ELIZABETH are:
22.   i.   LEWIS J.[7] BALLARD, b. 1815, GA; d. 20 Nov 1877, Fayette Co., AL.
23.   ii.   WILLIS ASBERRY BALLARD, b. 13 Feb 1822, GA; d. 08 May 1883, Blount Co., AL.
24.   iii. PIETY "PHIDA" WRIGHT BALLARD, b. 11 May 1823, Franklin Co., GA; d. 20 May 1905, Jackson Parish LA.
25.   iv.   WILLIAM REDWINE BALLARD, b. 06 Jan 1827, GA; d. 21 Nov 1906.
        v.   ANN FRANCIS BALLARD, b. Abt. 1828, GA; d. Aft. 1860; m. MR. HURN.
        vi.   JAMES BALLARD, b. Abt. 1832, GA; d. Aft. 1850.
26.   vii. WESTLEY H. BALLARD, b. 1832, GA; d. 1898.
27.   viii. ROBERT COLEMAN BALLARD, b. 13 Jan 1836, Lincoln Co., NC; d. 05 Oct 1917, Leesburg, Cherokee Co., GA.
28.   ix.   ELBERT TAMPLIN BALLARD, b. Abt. 1839, GA; d. 31 Jul 1903.

5. WILLIAM ROBERT[6] BALLARD (WHORTON[5], JESSE[4], JOHN[3], JOSEPH[2], JOHN[1]) was born 1796 in NC, and died Oct 1855 in Coweta Co., GA. He married JULIA ANN MAYFIELD Bet. 1816 - 1819. She was born 02 Apr 1794 in Franklin Co., GA, and died 24 Jun 1874 in Coweta Co., GA.

Notes for WILLIAM ROBERT BALLARD:
Source: 1850 Coweta County Georgia Federal Census Records, Tex Dick, Hollis and Oliver Ballard Notes (Becky Walker submitted Obituary)
* Death and Obituary Notices from the Southern Christian Advocate 1867-1878 issue August 5, 1874
* 1823 - Franklin Co., GA - William Ballard paid taxes
* 1850 - Living in Coweta Co., GA - Bullard, Wm Sr farmer 54 NC, Julia An 54 NC

Notes for JULIA ANN MAYFIELD:
Source: Obituary, waldy@worldnet.att.net (Waldy & Jean Cuevas)
* 1860 - Living with son Wesley Ballard in Talladega Co., AL
* 1874 - Death and Obituary Notices from the Southern Christian Advocate 1867-1878 Issue of August 5, 1874
* Obit Mrs. July Ann Ballard, whose maiden name was Mayfield, was born in Franklin county, Ga., April 2d 1794; was married to William Ballard in 1816; died at the residence of her son William Ballard, in Coweta County, Georgia, June 24th 1874. She had four children; two preceded her to the grave. W. F. S. Powell

Children of WILLIAM BALLARD and JULIA MAYFIELD are:
	i.	SOLOMA[7] BALLARD.
29.	ii.	WESLEY M. BALLARD, b. 1814, GA; d. Aft. 1880.
30.	iii.	WILLIAM R. BALLARD, b. 1826, GA; d. Aft. 1880.
	iv.	MARY ANN BALLARD, b. 1832.

6. JANE[6] BALLARD (WHORTON[5], JESSE[4], JOHN[3], JOSEPH[2], JOHN[1]) was born 1800 in NC, and died 1870 in Hopkins TX or Jackson Parish LA. She married STEPHEN HEARNE 26 Apr 1819 in Franklin Co., GA. He was born 17 Jan 1800 in Elbert Co., GA, and died 01 Nov 1851 in Coweta Co., GA.

Notes for JANE BALLARD:
Source: 1860 Jackson Parish Louisiana, E. Dee Varnadore, Valerie Austin (va5303@nersp.nerdc.ufl.edu)
* 1860 - Living in Jackson Parish, LA - Hearn, Jane 59 domestic NC, Allen, E Ellis 23 Farmer GA, Nan 17 domestic, Augusta A 3/12 (all of this was faded and difficult to read)

Notes for STEPHEN HEARNE:
Source: 1850 Coweta County Georgia Federal Census Records
* 1850 - Living in Coweta Co., GA - Hearn, Stephen 50 Farmer GA, Jane 50 NC, Thomas 18 GA, Eliz F 11 GA, Salena C 9 GA, Nancy C 7 GA

Children of JANE BALLARD and STEPHEN HEARNE are:
31.	i.	HULDA SMITH[7] HEARN, b. 1821, Franklin Co., GA; d. 1856, Chatham, Jackson Parish, LA, bur. Brooklyn Cemetery..
	ii.	OLIVER R. HEARN, REV., b. 17 Feb 1823, Franklin Co., GA; d. 1900, LA; m. NANCY R. CARROLL, 16 Nov 1843, Coweta Co., GA; b. 09 Sep 1826, Franklin Co., GA; d. 06 Sep 1871, LA.
	iii.	ASBURY FLETCHER HEARN, REV., b. 28 Feb 1825, Franklin Co., GA; d. 21 Nov 1883, moved to Jackson Parish, LA in 1857; m. (1) ELIZABETH MARSHAL, 04 Nov 1847; b. Abt. 1825; m. (2) DELLA COMPTON, 29 Jul 1858.
	iv.	ELBERT CRANTON HEARN, REV., b. 01 Jun 1827, Coweta Co, GA; d. 1887, moved to Jackson Parish, LA in 1857; m. HARRIETT BAKER, 1845.
	v.	MADISON HARWELL HEARN, b. 14 Mar 1830, Coweta Co., GA; d. 1862, LA; m. MARY HOOD, LA.
	vi.	THOMAS HEARN, b. Abt. 1832, Coweta Co., GA.
	vii.	ELIZABETH FRANCES HEARN, b. 01 Nov 1837, Coweta Co., GA; d. 11 Nov 1904, Wood Co., TX; m. THOMAS NELSON STEED, 17 May 1855, Coweta Co., GA.
	viii.	SALOMA C. HEARN, b. Abt. 1841, Coweta Co., GA.
32.	ix.	NANCY C. HEARN, b. 09 Feb 1843, Coweta Co., GA; d. 03 Jul 1881.

7. WESLEY[6] BALLARD (WHORTON[5], JESSE[4], JOHN[3], JOSEPH[2], JOHN[1]) was born 10 May 1803 in NC, and died 30 Jul 1872 in Carroll Co., GA. He married WENDY "WINNIE" FLOYD 03 Jun 1830 in Coweta Co., GA, daughter of ELI FLOYD. She was born 27 Feb 1811 in GA, and died 28 Mar 1890 in The first two children by another woman.

Notes for WESLEY BALLARD:
Source: CD#4, Lloyd Russ Ballard, Tex Dick, Hollis and Oliver Ballard, Kathy Ballard, John Robertson (jr@shelby.net) Ballard-Ballord Bits. 1850 Campbell County Georgia Federal Census Records, 1860 Tallapoosa Alabama Federal Census Records
* 1850 - Living in Campbell Co., GA - Ballard, Wesley 47 NC, Winey 38 GA, Owen R. 18 GA, Wm. L. 15 GA, John W. 5 GA, Benjamin 2 GA
* 1860 - Living in Dudleyville, Tallapoosa Co., AL - Ballard, Wesley 57 NC, Wenney 49 GA, John W 15 GA, Benjamin 13 GA

More About WESLEY BALLARD:
Burial: New Hope United Methodist Church Cemetery. Carroll Co., GA

Notes for WENDY "WINNIE" FLOYD:
Source: 1870 Georgia Federal Census Records
* 1870 - Living in Carroll Co., GA - Ballard, Winnie 59 GA, John W 24 GA, Benjamin O 22 GA

More About WENDY "WINNIE" FLOYD:
Burial: New Hope United Methodist Church Cemetery, Carroll Co., GA

Children of WESLEY BALLARD and WENDY FLOYD are:
33.   i.   EDMOND S.[7] BALLARD, b. 1822, NC; d. Aft. 1870.
34.   ii.   THOMAS W. BALLARD, b. Sep 1825, NC; d. 07 Sep 1907, Comanche Co., TX.
       iii.   OWEN R. BALLARD, b. 10 Jul 1832, GA; d. 14 Dec 1857.
       iv.   WILLIAM L. BALLARD, b. 20 Aug 1834, GA; d. 26 May 1860.
35.   v.   JOHN WESLEY BALLARD, b. 07 Dec 1845, Carroll Co., GA; d. 25 Aug 1932, Carroll Co., GA.
       vi.   BENJAMIN O. BALLARD, b. 09 Sep 1847, GA; d. Aft. 1870.

8. MARY[6] BALLARD (WHORTON[5], JESSE[4], JOHN[3], JOSEPH[2], JOHN[1]) was born 1804 in Beaver Dam Creek, Elbert Co., GA, and died 1861. She married ELISHA TATUM 04 Jan 1832 in Coweta Co., GA. He was born 1799, and died 1860 in Coweta Co, GA.

More About MARY BALLARD:
Burial: New Hope Meth. Church Cemetery, Coweta Co., GA

Notes for ELISHA TATUM:
Source Lloyd Russ Ballard, Tex Dick, Hollis and Oliver Ballard , Martha Irwin (marirw@yahoo.com)

Children of MARY BALLARD and ELISHA TATUM are:
36.   i.   MARTHA[7] TATUM, b. 1826, Coweta Co., GA; d. 24 Nov 1878.
       ii.   MARY ELIZABETH TATUM, b. Coweta Co., GA.
       iii.   THOMAS TATUM, b. Coweta Co., GA.
       iv.   NANCY C. TATUM, b. Coweta Co., GA.
       v.   JAMES M. TATUM, b. 1839, Coweta Co., GA; d. 18 Jul 1862, VA.
       vi.   WILLIAM DAVID TATUM, b. Coweta Co., GA.
       vii.   ROBERT PARKS TATUM, b. Coweta Co., GA.
       viii.   JOSEPH F. TATUM, b. 27 Aug 1846, Coweta Co., GA; d. 05 Jan 1928, Fulton Co., GA.

          Notes for JOSEPH F. TATUM:
          Source: Fulton County Georgia Certificate of Death, 1880 Campbell County Georgia Federal Census Record
          * 1880 - Living in Palmetto, Campbell Co., GA - Tatum, Joseph F 33 GA SC GA, Jane 29 sister GA

SC GA, Bruce 23 F niece GA GA GA

More About JOSEPH F. TATUM:
Burial: Hollywood Cemetery, Atlanta, Fulton Co., GA

    ix.   SARAH JANE TATUM, b. Abt. 1849, Coweta Co, GA; d. Aft. 1880.

9. ELIZABETH[6] BALLARD (WHORTON[5], JESSE[4], JOHN[3], JOSEPH[2], JOHN[1]) was born 16 Jan 1807 in Beaver Dam Creek, Elbert Co., GA, and died 26 Nov 1843 in Cherokee Co., GA. She married WILLIAM SAMPLER, REV. 24 Aug 1826 in Gates Co., NC, son of THOMAS SAMPLER and MARY JOHNSTON. He was born 19 Oct 1804 in Wrightsboro, Columbia Co., GA, and died 26 Aug 1855 in Cobb Co., GA.

More About ELIZABETH BALLARD:
Burial: Old Roswell Cemetery, Roswell, Fulton Co, GA

Notes for WILLIAM SAMPLER, REV.:
Source: Lloyd Russell Ballard, Tex Dick, Chris Gardner, Holis and Oliver Ballard Notes, 1850 Cobb County Georgia Federal Census Records, 1855 Cobb County Georgia State Records, Shelea McLaughlin (shelea3@juno.com)

* 1839 - Cherokee Co., GA - Deed Book D. page 469 & 470, Jan 12....from Burl Dobbs to William Sampler of Cobb Co., GA page 301 for sum $350.
* 1850 Cobb Co., GA - Sampler, William 46 GA, Elizabeth 22 GA, Hester Ann 15 GA, Mary C 12 GA, William W 9 GA, Emily V 2 GA, Sarah F 2 GA

Children of ELIZABETH BALLARD and WILLIAM SAMPLER are:
37.   i.   ROBERT JOHNSON[7] SAMPLER, REV., b. 06 Jul 1827, GA; d. 29 Sep 1901.
         ii.   THOMAS GAZAWAY SAMPLER, b. 05 May 1829, GA; d. 17 May 1872.

               More About THOMAS GAZAWAY SAMPLER:
               Burial: Old Roswell Cemetery, Roswell, Fulton Co., GA

         iii.   ELIZABETH SAMPLER, b. Abt. 1830, GA; d. Aft. 1850.
38.   iv.   RANDOLPH COLEMAN SAMPLER, b. 22 Dec 1830, GA.
         v.   AMSEY PARKS SAMPLER, b. 10 Sep 1832, GA; d. Abt. 1847.
39.   vi.   HESTER ANN SAMPLER, b. 24 Sep 1834, Woodstock, Cherokee Co., GA; d. Aft. 1850.
       vii.   TACY JANE SAMPLER, b. 16 Mar 1836, GA; d. 1847.
     viii.   MARY CATHERINE SAMPLER, b. 01 Jul 1838, GA; d. Aft. 1850.
40.   ix.   WILLIAM WESLEY SAMPLER, b. 14 Feb 1841, Cobb Co., GA; d. 10 Jul 1889, Murray Co., GA.
         x.   MARTHA EMALINE SAMPLER, b. 24 Aug 1843, GA; d. 28 Aug 1844.

10. COLEMAN H.[6] BALLARD (WHORTON[5], JESSE[4], JOHN[3], JOSEPH[2], JOHN[1]) was born 23 May 1810 in GA or NC, and died 07 May 1877 in Redland, Angelina Co., TX. He married MARY BOWEN 14 Dec 1833 in Coweta Co., GA. She was born 04 Aug 1802 in SC, and died 02 Nov 1887 in TX.

Notes for COLEMAN H. BALLARD:
Source: 1850 Monroe County Mississippi Federal Census Records, 1860-1870 Angelina County Texas Federal Census Records, Lloyd Russ Ballard, Tex Dick, Oliver and Hollis Ballard, Jim (GuteTag@aol.com)

* 1850 - Living in Monroe Co. MS - Ballard, Coleman H 38 GA, Mary 47 SC, Sarah A 16 GA, Lydia L 13 MS, Lucinda J 7 MS, Wm R Bowen 22 GA
* 1860 - Living in Angelina Co., TX - Ballard, Coleman H. 50 MS, Mary 58 MS, Lydia 21 GA, Mary Stegall 31 MS, Sally 24 GA
* 1870 - Living in Homer, Angelina Co., TX - Ballard, Coleman 58 Farmer GA, Mrs. Marie 66 SC

More About COLEMAN H. BALLARD:
Burial: Walker Cemetery

Children of COLEMAN BALLARD and MARY BOWEN are:

        i.   SARAH A.[7] BALLARD, b. 25 Sep 1834, Coweta Co., GA; d. 15 Jan 1897, Angelina Co., TX; m. HENRY L. STEGALL; b. 09 Nov 1825, Monroe Co., MS; d. 12 Jul 1897, Angelina Co., TX.

            More About SARAH A. BALLARD:
            Burial: Walker Cemetery, Redland, Angelina Co., TX

            More About HENRY L. STEGALL:
            Burial: Walker Cemetery, Redland, Angelina Co., TX

41.   ii.   ELLA LYDIA BALLARD, b. 28 Mar 1837, MS; d. 02 Apr 1913, TX.
        iii.   LUCINDA J. BALLARD, b. Abt. 1843, MS.

11. PRISCILLA[6] BALLARD (WHORTON[5], JESSE[4], JOHN[3], JOSEPH[2], JOHN[1]) *was born 1812 in Beaver Dam Creek, Elbert Co., GA, and died 28 Feb 1888 in Jackson Parish, LA. She married THOMAS HEARN, REV. 1833 in Coweta Co., GA. He was born Abt. 1807, and died Aft. 1870 in Jackson Parish LA.*

Notes for PRISCILLA BALLARD:
Source: 1880 Fulton County Georgia Federal Census Records
* 1880 - Living in Atlanta, Fulton Co., GA - Hearn, Priscilla P 66, Sarah A 39, Jennie C 32, Emma H 24, Narcissa E 27, Gabriella L 25

More About PRISCILLA BALLARD:
Burial: Oakland Cemetery, Atlanta, Fulton Co., GA

Notes for THOMAS HEARN, REV.:
Source: 1850-1860 Campbell County Georgia Federal Census Records, 1870 Fulton County Georgia Federal Census Records

* 1850 - Living in Campbell Co., GA - Hearn, Thos 40 GA, Priscilla 37 GA, Sarah Ann 16 GA, Wm Mc 13 MS, Emily C 11 GA, Mary E 9 GA, Margaret A 4 GA, Narcsa E 1 GA, Jane C 1 GA
* 1860 - Living in Campbell Co., GA - Hearn, Thomas 50, Prissilla 37, Sarah 25, William 24, Emmert 21, Mary 19, Jane 17, Norsira 12, Malissa 10, Prisiller 6
* 1870 - Living in Atlanta, Fulton Co., GA - Hern, Prucila 58, SAF 34, EC 30, JC 24, NE 20, ED 18, Gabrella 16

Children of PRISCILLA BALLARD and THOMAS HEARN are:

        i.   SARAH ANN[7] HEARN, b. Abt. 1834, GA; d. Aft. 1880.
        ii.   WILLIAM HEARN, b. Abt. 1837, GA; d. Aft. 1850.
        iii. EMILY C. HEARN, b. 1839, GA; d. 12 Jan 1897.

            More About EMILY C. HEARN:
            Burial: Oakland Cemetery, Atlanta, Fulton Co., GA

        iv. MARY ELIZABETH HEARN, b. Abt. 1841, GA; d. Aft. 1850.
         v.   JANE C. HEARN, b. Abt. 1843, GA; d. Aft. 1870.
        vi. NARCISSA E. HEARN, b. 1849, GA; d. 14 Jul 1891.

            More About NARCISSA E. HEARN:
            Burial: Oakland Cemetery, Atlanta, Fulton Co., GA

       vii. MALISSA DINK HEARN, b. 1850, GA; d. Aft. 1860.
      viii. GABRIELLA HEARN, b. 1854, GA; d. 20 Sep 1887.

ix.   PRISCILLA HEARN, b. Abt. 1854, GA; d. Aft. 1860.

Generation No. 3

12. JAMES CLARK[7] BALLARD (LEWIS[6], WHORTON[5], JESSE[4], JOHN[3], JOSEPH[2], JOHN[1]) was born 1818 in Franklin Co., GA, and died Aft. 1860. He married ADALINE BEAL 05 Dec 1844 in Marion Co., FL, daughter of HENRY BEAL and NANCY. She was born Abt. 1828 in GA, and died Aft. 1860.

Notes for JAMES CLARK BALLARD:
Source: RAINEYM968@aol.com, 1850 Marion County Florida Federal Census Records, 1860 Orange County Florida Federal Census Records, Kelly Hartley (willow1@yahoo.com)
* 1850 - Living in Marion Co., FL - Ballard, James C 32 GA, Adaline 22 GA, Lewis 5 FL, Henry 3 FL, Nancy Ann 1 F (next door to Lewis Ballard)
* 1860 - Living in Orange Co., FL - Ballard, James C. 41 GA, Adaline 31 GA, Lewis M. 14 FL, Henry 13 FL, Nancy Ann 11 FL, Hiram 6 FL, Mary 5 FL, Eccy 2 FL, James E. 7/12 FL

Children of JAMES BALLARD and ADALINE BEAL are:
42.   i.   LEWIS M.[8] BALLARD, b. Sep 1845, Marion Co., FL.
43.   ii. HENRY LEWIS BALLARD, b. 11 Jan 1847, Marion Co., FL.
44.   iii. NANCY ANN BALLARD, b. 1849, Marion Co., FL.
          iv. HIRAM D. BALLARD, b. 1854, Hawkinsville, Orange Co., FL; m. MOLLIE E. WINDHAM, 15 Jul 1873, Orange Co., FL.

              Notes for HIRAM D. BALLARD:
              Source: RAINEYM968@aol.com

45.   v.   MARY CATHERINE BALLARD, b. 26 Feb 1855, Lake Co., FL; d. 12 Jun 1941, Tavares, Lake Co., FL.
          vi. EXCY R. BALLARD, b. 1858, Hawkinsville, Orange Co., FL; m. JAMES H. HAMILTON, 09 Mar 1876, Orange Co., FL.
46.   vii. JAMES CLARK BALLARD, b. Dec 1859, Hawkinsville, Orange Co., FL.
          viii. ELIZA BALLARD, b. 1861, Hawkinsville, Orange Co., FL.
47.   ix. MEEKY BALLARD, b. 1862, Hawkinsville, Orange Co., FL; d. 20 Jan 1894, Plant City, Hillsborough Co., FL.
          x.   CAROLINE BALLARD, b. 1865, Orange Co., NC; m. WILEY HICKS, 01 Jun 1879, Polk Co., FL.
          xi. IONA BALLARD, b. 27 Feb 1866, Orange Co., NC; d. 28 Feb 1922, Polk Co., FL; m. ANDREW H. SLOAN, 07 Dec 1884, Polk Co., FL.

13. MORRIS R.[7] BALLARD (LEWIS[6], WHORTON[5], JESSE[4], JOHN[3], JOSEPH[2], JOHN[1]) was born 04 Mar 1820 in Franklin Co., GA, and died 19 Aug 1899 in Attala Co., GA. He married (1) REBECCA STONE Bef. 1844. She was born 1819 in SC, and died Aft. 1850. He married (2) LAVINA "VINA" BOND 15 Sep 1856 in Fulton Co., GA, daughter of LINDSEY BOND and SUSANNA SARTIN. She was born 1830 in Franklin Co., GA, and died 1887 in Attala Co., MS.

Notes for MORRIS R. BALLARD:
Source: Tex Dick, Tara Barrett, Joyce Sanders, Amanda Dees, Brenda Rogers (randees@netword-one.com), 1830 Franklin County Georgia Federal Census Records, 1850 DeKalb County Georgia Federal Census Records, 1860 Gilmer County Georgia Federal Census Records, 1870 Winston County Mississippi Federal Census Records, 1880 Attala County Mississippi Federal Census Records, Franklin County Georgia Federal Census Records, Marriages by Martha Walters Acker, Kelly Hartley (willow1@yahoo.com)
* 1850 - Living in DeKalb Co., GA - Ballard, Morris R. 30 GA, Rebecca 30 SC, Martha A 6 GA, Wm. M. 5 GA, John 2 GA
* 1870 - Living in Winston Co., MS - Ballard, Morris 50, Vina 40, Mary 15, Thomas 12, Willis 10, Taylor 8
* 1880 - Living in Attala, Centre Co., MS - Ballard, Morris 60 farmer GA NC GA, Vina 57 (hard to read) GA GA GA, Mary 25 GA, Willis 20 MS, Taylor 18 MS, Harriet 9 MS, Thos Band 12 nephew MS

More About MORRIS R. BALLARD:
Burial: Tabernacle Methodist Church Cemetery

Notes for REBECCA STONE:
Source: Kelly Hartley (willow1@yahoo.com)

Children of MORRIS BALLARD and REBECCA STONE are:
>   i.   MARTHA A.[8] BALLARD, b. 1844, GA; d. Aft. 1850.
>   ii. WILLIAM M. BALLARD, b. 1845, GA; d. Aft. 1850.
> 48.   iii. JOHN YANCY BALLARD, b. May 1848, Franklin Co., GA; d. 12 Mar 1932.
> 49.   iv. JOEL S. BALLARD, b. Aug 1851, Franklin Co., GA; d. 1909, Choctaw Co., MS.
>   v.   MARY BALLARD, b. Abt. 1855, Franklin Co., GA.

Children of MORRIS BALLARD and LAVINA BOND are:
> 50.   vi.   THOMAS M.[8] BALLARD, b. 30 Aug 1857, MS; d. 01 Jul 1926.
> 51.   vii. WILLIS N. BALLARD, b. Jun 1859, MS; d. Aft. 1880.
>   viii. HARRISON TAYLOR BALLARD, b. 15 Oct 1861, MS; d. 15 Nov 1916, Choctaw Co., MS; m. SARAH ALICE WILLIAMS; b. 20 Dec 1868; d. 11 Apr 1950.

> *More About SARAH ALICE WILLIAMS:*
> *Burial: Tabernacle Cemetery, Attala Co., MS*

>   ix.   HARRIET MARGARET BALLARD, b. Abt. 1873, MS; d. Aft. 1880.

14. WILLIAM L.[7] BALLARD (*LEWIS*[6], *WHORTON*[5], *JESSE*[4], *JOHN*[3], *JOSEPH*[2], *JOHN*[1]) was born 1828 in Franklin Co., GA, and died Aft. 1860. He married (1) SOPHIA MORGAN Jul 1853 in Marion Co., FL. She died Bef. 1860. He married (2) ELIZABETH Bef. 1860. She was born 1840 in GA, and died Aft. 1860.

Notes for WILLIAM L. BALLARD:
Source: Kelly Hartley (willow1@yahoo.com) Source: 1860 Orange County Florida Federal Census Records
* 1860 - Living in Orange Co., FL - Ballard, William L. 32 GA, Elizabeth 20 GA, John W. 5 FL, Martha J. 4 FL

Children of WILLIAM BALLARD and SOPHIA MORGAN are:
>   i.   JOHN W.[8] BALLARD, b. 1855, FL; d. Aft. 1860.
>   ii. MARTHA J. BALLARD, b. 1856, FL; d. Aft. 1860.

15. ALVIN MONROE[7] BALLARD (*LEWIS*[6], *WHORTON*[5], *JESSE*[4], *JOHN*[3], *JOSEPH*[2], *JOHN*[1]) was born 1831 in Franklin Co., GA, and died 08 Aug 1916 in Old Myakka, Sarasota Co., FL. He married (1) IDA MAE BICKFORD. She was born 1872. He married (2) JOSEPHINE FORT. He married (3) CELIA ANN WEBB Bef. 1856. She was born Abt. 1835, and died 21 Mar 1927 in Old Myakka, Sarasota Co., FL.

Notes for ALVIN MONROE BALLARD:
Source: 1860 Orange County Florida Federal Census Records 1867 Orange County Florida State Census Records, 1910 Manatee County Florida Federal Census Records, John Ballard (Kindmind1@aol.com)
* Lake County Florida
* 1860 - Living in Orange Co., FL - Ballard, Alvin M. 27 GA Mail Carrier
* 1867 - Living in Orange Co., FL - Ballard, A M 1 over 21, 2 under 21, 1 under 18, 0 under 18, 4 total, 1 male 13-45 years old
* 1910 - Living in Sandy, Manatee Co., FL - Ballard, Alvin M 78 GA NC NC., (hard to read) Celia 63 FL 3 children 2 living

Children of ALVIN BALLARD and CELIA WEBB are:

52. i. PERRY MARVIN[8] BALLARD, b. 1856, FL; d. 14 May 1929, Desoto Co., FL.
53. ii. WILEY WASHINGTON (MASH) BALLARD, b. May 1859, GA; d. Aft. 1945.
54. iii. J. ALVIN "AL" BALLARD, b. Sep 1861, GA; d. Aft. 1900.
     iv. MARY BALLARD, b. 1865.

16. MARY CATHERINE[7] BALLARD (LEWIS[6], WHORTON[5], JESSE[4], JOHN[3], JOSEPH[2], JOHN[1]) was born 1832 in Franklin Co., GA, and died Aft. 1850. She married SEBASTIAN C. WRIGHT. He was born 1829, and died 05 Dec 1862.

Notes for MARY CATHERINE BALLARD:
Source: Kelly Hartley (willow1@yahoo.com)

Notes for SEBASTIAN C. WRIGHT:
Source: 1860 Orange County Florida Federal Census Records
* 1860 - Living in Orange Co., FL - Wright, Sebastian C 31 farmer NC, Mary C 27 GA, William L. 3 TN, Elizabeth J 1 FL

Children of MARY BALLARD and SEBASTIAN WRIGHT are:
     i. WILLIAM L.[8] WRIGHT, b. 1857, TN; d. Aft. 1860.
     ii. ELIZABETH JANE WRIGHT, b. 1859, FL; d. Aft. 1860.
     iii. JOHN H. WRIGHT, b. Abt. 1861; m. DAISY BLOCKER.

17. SARAH[7] BALLARD (JESSE[6], WHORTON[5], JESSE[4], JOHN[3], JOSEPH[2], JOHN[1]) was born 07 Jun 1814 in 6/17 Franklin Co., GA, and died 25 Feb 1853 in Campbell Co., GA. She married JAMES HUMPHREY CARROLL 14 Dec 1834 in Coweta Co., GA. He was born 13 Jan 1812 in Franklin Co., GA, and died 09 Jan 1886 in Fulton Co., GA.

Notes for SARAH BALLARD:
Source: Sarah Wilson, CD#4
* Church Historian of the New Hope Church organized in March 1843 in GA. The Ballard Family joined May 27, 1854 and many were buried in their cemetery. There was a Methodist Episcopal Concord Church, formerly known as the Ballard Church that closed in the Spring of 1854.

More About SARAH BALLARD:
Burial: New Hope United Methodist Church Cemetery, Palmetto, Fulton Co. GA

Notes for JAMES HUMPHREY CARROLL:
Source: 1850 Coweta County Georgia Federal Census Records
* 1850 - Living in Coweta Co., GA - Carrol, James H 38 farmer GA, Sarah 35 GA, William P 14 GA, Mary F 12 GA, Elizabeth R 10, Jesse G 8 GA, Martha A 6, Martha A 6, Susan J 4, Webby B 3 GA, Madison E 3/12 GA

More About JAMES HUMPHREY CARROLL:
Burial: New Hope United Methodist Church Cemetery, Palmetto, Fulton Co., GA

Children of SARAH BALLARD and JAMES CARROLL are:
     i. WILLIAM P.[8] CARROLL, REV., b. 22 May 1836, GA; d. 06 Jul 1915; m. NANCY MCDONALD; b. 15 Aug 1841; d. 08 Nov 1905.

         More About WILLIAM P. CARROLL, REV.:
         Burial: Hebron Cemetery, Terryville, DeWitt Co., TX

         More About NANCY MCDONALD:
         Burial: Hebron Cemetery, Terryville, DeWitt Co., TX

     ii. MARY FRANCES CARROLL, b. 03 Sep 1837, Coweta Co., GA; d. 02 Jul 1910, Palmetto, Fulton Co.,

GA; m. THOMAS JEFFERSON BARFIELD; b. 09 Mar 1834, Jones Co., GA; d. 29 Sep 1924, Palmetto, Fulton Co., GA.

More About THOMAS JEFFERSON BARFIELD:
Burial: Floral Hill Cemetery, Fulton Co., GA

   iii.   ELIZABETH R. CARROLL, b. Abt. 1840, GA; d. Aft. 1850.
   iv.   JESSE G. CARROLL, b. 17 Aug 1841, Coweta Co., GA; d. 18 Jun 1913, McLennan Co., TX; m. FRANCES ELIZABETH ROBINSON; b. 06 May 1836, Coweta Co., GA; d. 12 Dec 1911, McLennan Co., TX.

More About JESSE G. CARROLL:
Burial: Lone Oak Cemetery, Axtell, McLennan Co., TX

   v.   MARTHA ANN CARROLL, b. 29 May 1843, Coweta Co., GA; d. 01 Aug 1917; m. W. M. ATTAWAY; b. 21 Aug 1841; d. 17 Mar 1926.

More About MARTHA ANN CARROLL:
Burial: Mt. Zion Baptist Church Cemetery, Corner, Jefferson Co., AL

More About W. M. ATTAWAY:
Burial: Mt. Zion Baptist Church Cemetery, Corner, Jefferson Co., AL

   vi.   SUSAN JANE CARROLL, b. Oct 1846, Coweta Co., GA; d. 23 Mar 1924, Paulding Co., GA; m. THOMPSON.

More About SUSAN JANE CARROLL:
Burial: Bethany Christian Church Cemetery, Paulding Co., GA

   vii.   WEBBIE P. CARROLL, b. 03 Feb 1848, Coweta Co., GA; d. 14 Jun 1919; m. HENRY H. BARFIELD; b. 26 Aug 1842; d. 11 Jan 1915.

More About WEBBIE P. CARROLL:
Burial: Oakland Cemetery, Atlanta, Fulton Co., GA

More About HENRY H. BARFIELD:
Burial: Oakland Cemetery, Atlanta, Fulton Co., GA

   viii.   MADISON S. CARROLL, b. 16 Jan 1850, GA; d. 22 Apr 1917; m. LOU E. ADERHOLT; b. 04 Mar 1850; d. 13 Jul 1919.

More About MADISON S. CARROLL:
Burial: New Hope United Methodist Church Cemetery, Palmetto, Fulton Co., GA'

More About LOU E. ADERHOLT:
Burial: New Hope United Methodist Church Cemetery, Palmetto, Fulton Co., GA

18. WILLIAM MOSES[7] BALLARD (*JESSE*[6], *WHORTON*[5], *JESSE*[4], *JOHN*[3], *JOSEPH*[2], *JOHN*[1]) *was born 1816 in Beaver Dam Creek, Elbert Co., GA, and died 21 Oct 1864 in Andersonville, Sumter Co., GA. He married JANE "ANNIE" CAROLINE TRIMBLE 21 Nov 1847 in Fayette Co., GA, daughter of MOSES TRIMBLE. She was born 21 Nov 1823 in Red Oak Campbell Co., GA, and died 21 Jan 1870 in Red Oak, Coweta Co., GA.*

Notes for WILLIAM MOSES BALLARD:
Source: Chris Gardner, Billy Price, Frances Puckett, Evelyn Puckett, Evelyn Ballard Family Group records, 1850 Coweta County Georgia Federal census records.

* He was a prison guard.
* Civil War Pvt Co. 1-2nd Regt. Georgia Reserves. 5' 10" tall
* 1850 - Coweta Co., GA - Lived next door to his parents.
* Died in the prison hospital in Americas Georgia

More About WILLIAM MOSES BALLARD:
Burial: Oak Grove Cemetery, Americus, Sumter Co., GA

Notes for JANE "ANNIE" CAROLINE TRIMBLE:
Source: Evelyn Ballard, Frances Puckett

More About JANE "ANNIE" CAROLINE TRIMBLE:
Burial: Mt. Olive Baptist Church Cemetery, East Point, Fulton Co., GA

Children of WILLIAM BALLARD and JANE TRIMBLE are:

55.   i.   WILLIAM MOSES[8] BALLARD, b. 05 Mar 1849, Red Oak Coweta Co., GA; d. 02 Jan 1940, Ohio, Hamilton Co., TX.
          ii.   THOMAS BALLARD, b. Aft. 1850, Coweta Co., GA.

                 Notes for THOMAS BALLARD:
                 Source: Tex Dick

         iii.   SARAH "SALLIE" CATHERINE BALLARD, b. 02 Jan 1854, Coweta Co., GA; d. 26 Apr 1926, Fulton Co., GA; m. WILLIAM CARL LEE; b. Abt. 1850.

                 Notes for SARAH "SALLIE" CATHERINE BALLARD:
                 Source: Fulton County Georgia Standard Certificate of Death

                 More About SARAH "SALLIE" CATHERINE BALLARD:
                 Burial: College Park Cemetery, Fulton Co., GA

56.   iv.   CLAIBORNE "DUTCH" LORENZO BALLARD, b. 05 May 1856, Red Oak, Campbell Co., GA; d. 26 Apr 1937, Clayton Co., GA.
           v.   MARGARET ADELINE BALLARD, b. 15 Aug 1858, Red Oak, Campbell Co., GA; d. 02 Aug 1954, College Park, Clayton Co., GA.

                 Notes for MARGARET ADELINE BALLARD:
                 Source: Evelyn Ballard

                 More About MARGARET ADELINE BALLARD:
                 Burial: Holly Hill Memorial Park, Fairburn, Fulton Co., GA

          vi.   INDIANA ELIZABETH BALLARD, b. 01 Mar 1860, Red Oak Coweta Co., GA; d. 10 Mar 1948, GA; m. (1) ANDREW JACKSON, 1902; m. (2) DAVIS ALEXANDER, 1902; m. (3) J. S. ECHOLS, 1930.

                 Notes for INDIANA ELIZABETH BALLARD:
                 Source: Evelyn Ballard

57.   vii.   MATILDA "MATTIE" LOU EMMA BALLARD, b. 20 Aug 1863, Red Oak Coweta Co., GA; d. 1930, Americus Sumter Co., GA.

19. WHORTON FLETCHER[7] BALLARD (JESSE[6], WHORTON[5], JESSE[4], JOHN[3], JOSEPH[2], JOHN[1]) was born 05 Mar 1822 in Beaver Dam Creed, Elbert Co., GA, and died 25 Dec 1864 in Coweta Co, GA. He married SARAH ANN STAMPS 1849 in Coweta Co., GA. She was born 15 Jan 1823 in Jackson Co., GA, and died 27 Nov 1878 in Carroll Co., GA.

Notes for WHORTON FLETCHER BALLARD:
Source: Lloyd Russ Ballard, Evelyn Ballard Group Sheets, Kathren Karnes (KKarnes867@aol.com), 1850 Coweta
County Georgia Federal Census Records, 1860 Campbell County Georgia Federal Census Records
* 1850 - Living in Coweta Co., GA - Ballard, Whorton F. 28 GA, Sarah A. 26 GA, Mary 2/12 GA
* 1860 - Living in Campbell Co., GA - Ballard, Horton F. GA, Sarah A 27 GA, Mary F 10 GA, James 8 GA, Thomas
P 6 GA, Adeline 5 GA
* Whorton Fletcher Family Bible - owned by Grace Nations, Centralhatchie, GA
Whorton Fletcher Ballard b. 3/5/1822 d. 12/25/1860 m. Sarah Ann Stamps Ballard b. 1/15/1823 d. 11/27/1879.
Their children: Mary Frances b. 3/22/1850, James Madison b. 8/3/1852, Thomas Parks 11/2/1853, Martha Adaline
2/2/1855
Marriages: Isom m. Lula 5/17/1905, Thomas Ballard m. Mary E McCaw 11/9/1876. Their Children: William
Fletcher b. 2/6/1878, Robert L b 1/26/1880, Thomas Isom b. 12/5/1881, Howard Volly b. 4/14/1884, Magie b.
9/10/1886, Jessie Owen b. 1/24/1889. Josie A b. 1/20/1893, M. Hubert b. 8/29/1901, Emma Lou b. 12/28/1906

More About WHORTON FLETCHER BALLARD:
Burial: New Hope United Methodist Church Cemetery, Palmetto, Fulton Co., GA

Notes for SARAH ANN STAMPS:
Source: 1870 Coweta County Georgia Federal Census Records
* 1870 - Living in Coweta Co., GA - Ballard, Sarah A. 46 GA, James 17 GA, Thomas P 16 GA, Martha A. 14 GA

Children of WHORTON BALLARD and SARAH STAMPS are:
58.   i.   MARY FRANCES[8] BALLARD, b. 22 Mar 1850, GA; d. 22 Oct 1930, GA.
59.   ii.   JAMES MADISON BALLARD, b. 03 Aug 1852, Coweta Co, GA; d. 09 Dec 1916, Wood Co. TX.
60.   iii. THOMAS PARKS BALLARD, b. 02 Nov 1853, Coweta Co., GA; d. 07 Sep 1929, Tyus GA.
61.   iv.   MARTHA ADELINE BALLARD, b. 06 Feb 1856, Coweta Co., GA; d. 02 Mar 1939, Carroll Co., GA.

20. THOMAS SANFORD[7] BALLARD (JESSE[6], WHORTON[5], JESSE[4], JOHN[3], JOSEPH[2], JOHN[1]) was born Bet. 1829 - 1831 in
Beaver Dam Creek, Elbert Co., GA, and died 1883 in Lockhart, Caldwell Co., TX. He married ELIZABETH
PERMELIA CONDER 13 Aug 1854 in Campbell Co., GA, daughter of JOHN HOUSTON CONDER. She was born 05 Dec
1836 in Mecklenburg Co., NC, and died 28 Dec 1888 in Caldwell Co., TX.

Notes for THOMAS SANFORD BALLARD:
Source: Mike Montgomery, Oliver and Hollis Ballard Notes, Lloyd Russ Ballard, Tex Dick, Evelyn Ballard, 1860
Upshur County TX Federal Census Records, 1870 Hopkins County Texas Federal Census Records, 1880 Texas
Federal Census Soundex Records, Dean Moore (dean@telemail.com.py)

* Methodist Minister and Civil War Soldier
* Civil War Records of Thomas S. Ballard in Texas - Ballard, Thomas, Pvt. - Griffth, John S., Captain - Rockwall
Calvary, Kaufman Cty, 19th Brigade, TGT. R&F 95; Cc. commissioned June 24, 1861. Co organized under act of
Feb. 15, 1858. Ballard, T. S., Pvt. Cassaway, E. B., Capt. Co. in Col. Clark's Regt., TVI, CSA 1862 in Upshur
County (Enlisted) Age 31 R & F 95 A. H. Reg rs, En of; 1 May 27, 62
* 1860 - Living in Upshur Co., TX - Bullard, T. S 29 GA, Elizabeth 23 NC, Edward 4 GA, Alace 3 GA, John 1 GA
* 1870 - Living in Hopkins Co., TX - Ballard, Thomas 37 GA, Elizabeth 33 NC, Edward 15 GA, Lorena 14 GA, John
12 GA, Thomas 8 TX, William 11 TX, Emily 1 TX
* 1880 - Living in Wilson Co., TX - Ballard, Thomas 49 GA NC NC, Elizabeth 43 NC NC NC, Thomas 17 TX,
William 13 TX, Emily D 11 TX, James 9 TX, Wesley 7 TX, Charles 5 TX, Arthur 2 TX

Notes for ELIZABETH PERMELIA CONDER:
Source: 1850 Coweta County Georgia Federal Census Records
* 1850 - Living in Coweta Co., GA - Conder, John 44 NC, Lecta A 27 NC, Cyrus E 15 NC, Elizabeth P 12 NC, Ida P
10 NC, Susan E 8 GA, Margaret 7 GA, Nancy C 4 GA
Will of Elizabeth Ballard submitted by Mike Montgomery
State of Texas, Caldwell Co.

Know all men by these presents that Elizabeth P. Ballard, surviving wife of Thomas S. Ballard, Sr., Dec'd of Caldwell co, Texas being of sound and dispensing mind. Knowing the uncertainty of life, and the certainty of death, do hereby make disclose and publish this my last will and testament. 1st. I consign my soul to the God who gave it and my body to the grave and I will that my body shall receive a decent burial. 2n.d I will that all my just debts be paid. 3rd. I will and bequeath that my intire estate personal and real and mixed, after the payment of my just debts go and pass to my beloved children share & share alike, my grandchild Wm. M. to take the share that would go to his father Wm. M. Ballard, dec'd were he now living. 4th. It is my will that my sons J. C. and Thos. S. Ballard be and they are hereby named as the executers of this my last will and testament the guardians of the person and estates of my minor children, E. D., J. M., W. C., C. B., A. E., W. H., & R. J. Ballard. 5th. I further will that my entire estate at my death shall be taken by my executors and dispose of the same when and in whatever manner may to them seem best for the best interest of my heirs. And I further will that if they should not conclude to sell the same or such of it as they may not sell that they keep and manage it for the support of my said children & grandchild paying out the net proceeds to said heirs as the same is ready for distributing for year to year. until they may see proper to sell or partition the same. 6th. I further will and direct that my said executors be not required to give any bond as such executors and that no proceedings be had in court relative to my estate except the probating of this will and the filling of an inventory & appraisement of my said estate and the making of a final report of their acts in the premises. 7th. I further will that if from any cause either of my executors should fail to qualify or cease to act as such executor that the other one shall proceed to carry out this will as my sole executer. 8th. I sign this will in the presence of who at my request sign the same with me as subscribing witnesses - thereto-
WITNESS - C. O. Blackwell, H. J. Halo   signed by Elizabeth P. Ballard
* THE STATE OF TEXAS CALDWELL COUNTY
In Co. Court Pertaining to Estates
To the Honorable W. Keyser Judge of the county court of Caldwell county Texas. The petition of Thos. S. & J. C. Ballard citizens of said county respectifully represent that their mother Elizabeth P. Ballard departed this life on the 28th day of Dec. A. D. 1888 at her home in Caldwell county Texas. Leaving a will disposing of her effects, she had some property, personal & real in said county of small value and left several now petitions pray that notice be given that said will be admitted to probate and that petitions be confirmed as excuters of said will which will be herewith filed and guardians of said miners named in said will which will is herewith filed that Elizabeth P. Ballard was the surviving wife of Thos. S. Ballard Sr., deceased, who departed this life of five years ago.
Thomas S. & J. C. Ballard
By Story & Story attys.
ESTATE OF MRS. ELIZABETH P. BALLARD
Pet. to probate will
Recorded filed Jany 5th 1889

Children of THOMAS BALLARD *and* ELIZABETH CONDER *are:*

	i.	EDWARD[8] BALLARD, b. 1855, Campbell Co., GA; d. Bef. 1880.
62.	ii.	LORANAH ALICE BALLARD, b. 20 Dec 1856, Campbell Co., GA; d. 02 May 1930, Temple, Bell Co., TX.
63.	iii.	JOHN COLEMAN BALLARD, b. 28 Sep 1858, Campbell Co., GA; d. 25 Aug 1894.
64.	iv.	THOMAS SANFORD BALLARD, JR., b. 25 Sep 1862, Hopkins TX; d. Abt. 1891, Dripping Springs, Hays Co., TX.
65.	v.	WILLIAM MARVIN BALLARD, b. 1866, Hopkins Co., TX; d. Nov 1886, Caldwell Co., TX.
66.	vi.	EMILY DONA BALLARD, b. 24 Nov 1869, Hopkins Co., TX; d. 20 Mar 1921, San Antonio, Bexar Co., TX.
67.	vii.	JAMES MONROE BALLARD, b. 24 Jan 1870, 3/24/1871 Hopkins Co., TX; d. 21 Nov 1932, Graham, Carter Co., OK.
68.	viii.	WESLEY CHAPIEL BALLARD, b. 19 Jan 1873, Hopkins Co., TX; d. 03 May 1930, Gonzales Co., TX.
69.	ix.	CHARLES BEAMON BALLARD, b. 11 Jun 1875, Hopkins Co., TX; d. 24 Oct 1920, Ardmore, Carter Co., OK.
70.	x.	ARTHUR ELMER BALLARD, b. 20 Aug 1877, Caldwell Co., TX; d. 30 Dec 1944, Belton, Bee Co., TX.
71.	xi.	WALTER HOUSTON BALLARD, b. 29 Jan 1881, Caldwell Co., TX; d. 12 Aug 1944, Caldwell Co., TX.
72.	xii.	ROXANNA J. BALLARD, b. 01 Sep 1882, Lockhart, Caldwell Co., TX; d. 17 Mar 1952, San Angelo, Tom Green TX.

21.   LINDA CAROLINE "LINNY"[7] BALLARD (JESSE[6], WHORTON[5], JESSE[4], JOHN[3], JOSEPH[2], JOHN[1]) was born 1832 in Beaver Dam Creek, Elbert Co., GA, and died 1875.   She married WILLIAM (OR ROBERT) C. PARKER 03 Jun 1855 in Campbell Co., GA.

Notes for LINDA CAROLINE "LINNY" BALLARD:
Source: Evelyn Ballard

Child of LINDA BALLARD and WILLIAM PARKER is:
      i.   SARAH M.[8] PARKER.

22.   LEWIS J.[7] BALLARD (JAMES[6], WHORTON[5], JESSE[4], JOHN[3], JOSEPH[2], JOHN[1]) was born 1815 in GA, and died 20 Nov 1877 in Fayette Co., AL.   He married (1) SARAH GOBER Abt. 1843 in Cobb Co., GA.   She was born Abt. 1824 in GA, and died 1865.   He married (2) MARTHA ANN BARNETT 27 Dec 1866 in Blount Co., AL.   She was born 1830 in GA, and died Aft. 1880.

Notes for LEWIS J. BALLARD:
Source: 1850 Cobb County Georgia Federal Census Records, 1860, 1870 Blount County Alabama Federal Census Records, Lanelle (itzgaby@aol.com)
* More than likely the brother of Wm. R. Ballard married to Julia Boring
* 1850 - Living in Cobb Co., GA - Ballard, Lewis 37 farmer GA, Sarah 30 GA, Jane 10 GA, James 8 GA, Elizabeth 6 GA, Willis 4 GA, John 2 GA
* 1860 - Living in Blount Co., AL - Levi 42 GA, Sarah 36 GA, Jane 15 GA, James 14 GA, Elizabeth 13 GA, Willis 12 GA, Thomas 10 GA, Piety 8 GA, Adaline 7 GA, George 5 GA, Fletcher 1 AL
* 1866 - Levi Married: 27 Dec 1866 Martha Ann Barnett in Blount County, AL Event: Married by in John Thompson, JP (Justice of the Peace)
* 1870 - Living in Blount Co., AL - Ballard, L. J. 52 wagon maker GA, M A 40 GA, Thos 20 GA, PH 10 fe GA, Adeline 17 GA, GW 16 AL, Fletcher 11 AL, Marg 8 AL, Francis 2 fe AL, Catharine Mardis 12, HD Mardis 10 (f)

Notes for MARTHA ANN BARNETT:
Source: 1880 Fayette County Alabama Federal Census Records
* 1880 - Living in Fayette County Alabama - Ballard, Martha A. 50 GA SC SC, Frances M. (f) 12 AL GA GA, Andrew J. 9 AL AL GA

Children of LEWIS BALLARD and SARAH GOBER are:
      i.   JANE[8] BALLARD, b. 1845, GA; d. Aft. 1860.
73.   ii.   JAMES WILLIAM BALLARD, b. 20 Feb 1845, GA; d. 07 Aug 1906, Henderson Co., TX.
74.   iii.   ELIZABETH BALLARD, b. 1847, GA; d. Aft. 1870.
    iv.   JOHN BALLARD, b. Abt. 1848, GA; d. Aft. 1860.
75.   v.   WILLIS ASBURY BALLARD, b. 29 Jun 1848, GA; d. 10 Sep 1923, Collin Co., TX.
    vi.   THOMAS F. BALLARD, b. 1850, GA; d. Aft. 1880.

        Notes for THOMAS F. BALLARD:
        Source: 1880 Fayette County Alabama Federal Census Records
        * 1880 - Living in Fayette Co., AL - Ballard, Thomas F. 30 farmer GA GA GA, Stewart, John M 25, Mary F. 21 AL, AL, AL, Luiza 50 AL, America E 20 AL, Mary A. 11 AL, John W. 9 AL

    vii.   PIETY BALLARD, b. 1852, GA; d. Aft. 1880; m. JOSEPH N. CHAFIN, 17 Nov 1871, Blount Co., AL.
   viii.   ADALINE BALLARD, b. 1853, GA; d. Aft. 1880; m. JAMES M. LAWRENCE, 17 Nov 1871, Blount Co., AL.
76.   ix.   GEORGE W. BALLARD, b. 25 Nov 1854, GA; d. 07 Jun 1918, Coryell Co., TX.
77.   x.   FLETCHER ELSBURY BALLARD, b. 04 Mar 1859, Blount Co., AL; d. 16 Sep 1914, Haskell Co., TX.
    xi.   MARGARET BALLARD, b. 17 Jun 1862, Blount Co., AL; d. 29 Apr 1933; m. WILEY BYNUM, 23 Jan 1878, Fayette Co., AL; b. 1855; d. 1924.

        Notes for WILEY BYNUM:

Source: 1880 Fayette County Alabama Federal Census Records
* 1880 - Living in Fayette Co., AL - Bynum, Wiley 25 Farmer AL AL AL, Margaret U 18 AL GA GA

Children of LEWIS BALLARD and MARTHA BARNETT are:
78.   xii.   FRANCES MINERVA[8] BALLARD, b. 09 Jun 1868, AL; d. 02 Feb 1945, Austin, Travis Co., TX.
79.   xiii.   ANDREW JACKSON BALLARD, b. 01 Aug 1870, AL; d. 01 Oct 1900.

23. WILLIS ASBERRY[7] BALLARD (JAMES[6], WHORTON[5], JESSE[4], JOHN[3], JOSEPH[2], JOHN[1]) was born 13 Feb 1822 in GA, and died 08 May 1883 in Blount Co., AL. He married ELIZABETH BORING 10 Jan 1850 in Cherokee Co., GA. She was born 25 Jan 1827 in GA, and died 29 Jul 1887 in Blount Co., AL.

Notes for WILLIS ASBERRY BALLARD:
Source: Cemetery records found on the Internet by Dr. John Ballard 1850-1860 Cobb County Georgia Federal Census Records, 1870-1880 Blount County Alabama Federal Census Records
* 1850 - Living in Cobb Co. GA - Willis Ballard 29 GA, Elizabeth 22 GA
* 1860 - Living in Cobb Co. GA - Willis Ballard 29, GA Elizabeth 22 GA living next door to Lewis 34 yrs and James 56 years old
* 1870 - Living in Blount Co., AL - Ballard, WA 47 farmer GA, EB 43 GA, AA 14 GA, AH 12 MS, AN 10 MS
* 1880 - Living in Blount Co., AL - Ballard, Willis A 57, Elizabeth 54, Harrison 21, Asbery A. 18

More About WILLIS ASBERRY BALLARD:
Burial: Ebenezer Methodist Cemetery, Snead, Blount Co., AL

More About ELIZABETH BORING:
Burial: Ebenezer Methodist Church Cemetery, Snead, Blount Co., AL

Children of WILLIS BALLARD and ELIZABETH BORING are:
80.   i.   AMAZONIA ANNETTE[8] BALLARD, b. 26 Feb 1856, Cobb Co., GA; d. 04 Apr 1938, Collin Co., TX.
81.   ii.   A. HARRISON "HARRIS" BALLARD, b. 10 Aug 1858, MS; d. 02 Nov 1898, Blount Co., AL.
        iii.   ASBERRY NEWTON BALLARD, b. 21 Mar 1861; d. 05 Jun 1940; m. MARY JANE "MAMIE" FREEMAN; b. 16 Mar 1884; d. 09 Sep 1971.

        Notes for ASBERRY NEWTON BALLARD:
        Source: 1900 -1910 Blount County Alabama Federal Census Records

        * 1900 - Living in Campbells, Blount Co., AL - Ballard, Asburry M 39 - Mar 1861 MS, Mary J 35 - Aug 1864 no children GA, Abby J. Hick 20 hireling
        * 1910 - Living in Campbells, Blount Co., AL - Ballard, AN 49 MS farmer, Emma 45 - 2 children 0 living GA, Viola E 5 bound child AL

        More About ASBERRY NEWTON BALLARD:
        Burial: Ebenezer Methodist Cemetery, Snead, Blount Co., AL

        More About MARY JANE "MAMIE" FREEMAN:
        Burial: Douglas Cemetery, Marshall Co., AL

24. PIETY "PHIDA" WRIGHT[7] BALLARD (JAMES[6], WHORTON[5], JESSE[4], JOHN[3], JOSEPH[2], JOHN[1]) was born 11 May 1823 in Franklin Co., GA, and died 20 May 1905 in Jackson Parish LA. She married LEWIS REDWINE CARROLL 1844. He was born 27 Jul 1821 in Coweta, GA, and died 08 Mar 1892 in Jackson Parish LA.

Notes for PIETY "PHIDA" WRIGHT BALLARD:
May be the dau of James

Notes for LEWIS REDWINE CARROLL:
Source: LDS-IGI 1850 Coweta County Georgia Federal Census Records, 1860 Campbell County Georgia Federal Census Records, 1870 Paulding Co., GA Federal Census Records, 1880 Jackson County Louisiana Federal Census Records
* 1850 - Living in Coweta Co., GA - Carroll, Lewis R 29 GA, Piety 26 GA, Mary N 5 GA, Elizabeth R 2 GA
* 1860 - Living in Campbell Co., GA - Carroll, Lewis 38, Pietty 25, Mary 15, Elizabeth 13, Nancy 10, Emmor 6, Georgia 3
* 1870 - Living in California, Paulding Co., GA - Carroll, Lewis 40, Mariann 24, Elizabeth 22, Nancy 19, Emma 16, Georgia A 13, Jane 10, John 6, James
* 1880 - Living in Jackson Co., LA

Children of PIETY BALLARD and LEWIS CARROLL are:

    i.   MARY ANN[8] CARROLL, b. 20 Apr 1845, Marietta, Cobb Co., GA; d. 14 Jun 1872.
    ii.   ELIZABETH CARROLL, b. 14 Feb 1847, Marietta, Cobb Co., GA; d. 19 Oct 1887.
    iii.   NANCY CARROLL, b. 29 Aug 1850, Marietta, Cobb Co., GA; d. 03 Dec 1916.
    iv.   EMMA H. CARROLL, b. 02 May 1853, Marietta, Cobb Co., GA; d. 29 May 1889.
    v.   GEORGIA CARROLL, b. 23 Jan 1857, Marietta, Cobb Co., GA; d. 22 Sep 1934.
    vi.   LOUISE JANIE CARROLL, b. 14 Dec 1859, Marietta, Cobb Co., GA; d. 16 Sep 1926.
    vii.   JOHN CARROLL, b. 1864, Marietta, Cobb Co., GA; d. 24 Apr 1925.
    viii.   JAMES THOMAS CARROLL, b. 08 Jan 1865, Marietta, Cobb Co., GA; d. 12 Apr 1931.

25. WILLIAM REDWINE[7] BALLARD (JAMES[6], WHORTON[5], JESSE[4], JOHN[3], JOSEPH[2], JOHN[1]) was born 06 Jan 1827 in GA, and died 21 Nov 1906. He married JULIA A. BORING 31 Mar 1853 in AL. She was born Mar 1836 in GA, and died 25 Apr 1927.

Notes for WILLIAM REDWINE BALLARD:
Source: 1870 Blount County Alabama Federal Census Records, 1880-1900 Fayette County Alabama Federal Census Records, Don Ballard (MMDBG@aol.com), Walt (WaltFW@comcast.net)
* More than likely related to Levi Ballard which was also a wagon maker and W. A. Ballard that lived next door to Levi. WA 47 GA, EB 43 GA, AA 14 GA fe, AH 12 ma MS, AN 12 ma MS and also next door living with Kizzy Algood 57 is Amanda 18 MS, E fe AL, Annie 1 AL, IH 1 AL
* 1870 - Living in Blount Co., AL - Ballard, W. R. 44 GA Wagon maker, July 25 GA, Harriet 11 MS, Fletcher 9 MS, Olivia 6 MS, J. W. 4 MS, Lauer 2 AL AC 6/12 AL
* 1880 - Living in Fayette Co., AL - Ballard, William R. 53 farmer GA NC GA, Julia A 43 GA GA GA, Harriette E. 22 MS, John W. 14 MS, Learer A. 12 AL, Kerey C. 10 AL, Henry E. 8 AL, James I - 5 AL, Tallulia 1 AL
* 1882 - Living in Haywood Co., TN
* 1900 - Living in Russell, Fayette Co., AL - Ballard, William H GA SC SC, Julia, - Jan 1875 (12 children 7 living)

More About WILLIAM REDWINE BALLARD:
Burial: Salem Cemetery. Neshoba Co., MS

Notes for JULIA A. BORING:
Source: 1850 Cherokee County Georgia Federal Census Records
* Probable parents: Isaac and Charlotte Boring
* 1850 - Living in Cherokee Co., GA - Boring, Isaac 51 GA, Charlotte 48 SC, Francis A. 20 GA, Sarah F. 17 GA, Julia A. 15 GA, Alex'r N. 10 GA, Samuel H. 8 GA, Savannah 5 GA, Elizabeth Winn 65 SC

More About JULIA A. BORING:
Burial: Bethany Cemetery., Coffee Co., AL

Children of WILLIAM BALLARD and JULIA BORING are:

    i.   CARA B.[8] BALLARD, b. 09 Jun 1855; d. 05 Nov 1858.
    ii.   HARIETTE E. BALLARD, b. 02 May 1858, MS; d. Jun 1927; m. JOSEPH GRIFFITTS, 27 Jun 1899, Denton Co., TX; b. Aug 1842.

Notes for JOSEPH GRIFFITTS:
Source: 1900 Denton County Texas Federal Census Records
* 1900 - Living in Denton Co., TX - Griffitts, Joseph - Aug 1842, Hariett E - May 1858 MS, Martha J Mar 1870 (his daughter)

82.	iii.	WILLIAM FLETCHER BALLARD, b. 13 Nov 1860, MS; d. 24 Jul 1950, Fayette Co., AL.
	iv.	OLIVIA BALLARD, b. 1864, MS; d. Aft. 1870.
83.	v.	JOHN WESLEY BALLARD, b. 17 Nov 1865, MS; d. 23 Jul 1944, Okaloosa Co., FL.
	vi.	LEONER "LORA" BALLARD, b. 16 Mar 1868, MS; d. 08 Feb 1888.
84.	vii.	ARYARIA C. L. BALLARD, b. 24 Apr 1870, AL; d. 03 Dec 1913.
85.	viii.	HENRY ALEXANDER BALLARD, b. 13 Nov 1872, AL; d. 17 Jan 1953, Coryell Co., TX.
	ix.	JAMES "JIM" P. BALLARD, b. 15 Jan 1875, AL; d. 28 Sep 1902; m. LUCY E. MURRY.
	x.	THOMAS BALLARD, b. 08 Mar 1877, AL; d. 15 Jun 1878.
	xi.	TALLULIA "TALLEY" BALLARD, b. 15 Mar 1879, AL; d. 02 Dec 1960; m. MR. DURHAM.
	xii.	GEORGE WASHINGTON BALLARD, b. 10 Aug 1882, TN; d. 30 May 1962.

26. WESTLEY H.[7] BALLARD (JAMES[6], WHORTON[5], JESSE[4], JOHN[3], JOSEPH[2], JOHN[1]) was born 1832 in GA, and died 1898. He married ELIZABETH COWEN 10 Mar 1865 in Blount Co., AL. She was born Abt. 1845, and died Aft. 1880.

Notes for WESTLEY H. BALLARD:
Source: 1870 Henderson County Texas Federal Census Records, 1880 Hunts County Texas Federal Census Records
* 1870 - Living in Henderson Co., TX - Ballard, Wesley 29 black smith GA, Elizabeth 25 AL, Mary E 4 AL, Sarah 3 AR, Fannie E 1 TX
* 1880 - Living in Hunt Co., TX - Ballard, W H 37 GA NC GA, Elizabeth 33 GA KY KY, Mary 14 AL, Ellen 11 TX, Fanny 10 TX, John 7 TX, Willie 7 TX, Jas 4 TX, Ann 2 TX

Children of WESTLEY BALLARD and ELIZABETH COWEN are:

	i.	MARY E.[8] BALLARD, b. 1866, AL; d. Aft. 1880.
	ii.	SARAH BALLARD, b. 1867, AR; d. Aft. 1880.
86.	iii.	FANNIE E. BALLARD, b. 28 Jun 1869, TX; d. 19 Nov 1948, Hunt Co., TX.
	iv.	JOHN BALLARD, b. 1873, TX; d. Aft. 1880.
	v.	WILLIAM "WILLIE" BALLARD, b. 1873, TX; d. Aft. 1880.
	vi.	JAMES BALLARD, b. 1876, TX; d. Aft. 1880.
	vii.	ANN BALLARD, b. 1878, TX; d. Aft. 1880.

27. ROBERT COLEMAN[7] BALLARD (JAMES[6], WHORTON[5], JESSE[4], JOHN[3], JOSEPH[2], JOHN[1]) was born 13 Jan 1836 in Lincoln Co., NC, and died 05 Oct 1917 in Leesburg, Cherokee Co., GA. He married MARTHA ARMINDA BAKER 14 Nov 1854 in Chattooga Co., GA, daughter of LEVI BAKER and PHOEBE TURNER. She was born 20 May 1838 in 1837 Chattooga Co., GA, and died 28 Jun 1921 in Boaz Marshall Co., AL.

Notes for ROBERT COLEMAN BALLARD:
Source: 1850 Cobb County Georgia Federal Census Records, 1860-1870 Chattooga County Georgia Federal Census Records, 1880-1910 Cherokee County Alabama Federal Soundex Census Records, military records, Mildred Sparks, Kathy Ballard (grits111@hotmail.com), pension records

* 1860 - Living in Chattooga Co., GA - Ballard, Robert 24 NC, Martha 23 GA, Narcissa C 4 GA, John S 2 GA, Willard F 1/12 GA
* 1870 - Living in Chattooga Co., GA - Ballard, Robert 34 NC, Martha 33 GA, Narcissus 14 GA, John 12 GA, William 10 GA, Robert 8 GA, Martha 3 GA, Chilecus 1 GA
* 1880 - Living in Cherokee Co., AL - Ballard, Robbert 44, Martha 43 A, Narsns 23, Martha 13, Chelus 11, Tennie 8, Beulah 5, Paul 3, Baxter 1

1900 - Living in Paden, Cherokee Co., AL - Ballard, Robert C - Jan 1836 NC NC NC farmer, Martha A - May 1837 11 children GA GA GA
1910 - Living in Leesburg, Cherokee Co., AL - Ballard, Robt C 74 NC NC VA minister Evangelist, Martha A 72 GA GA GA
Robert Coleman Ballard Pension: Data listed on Original Pension Document dated 4/3/1915 Robert C. Ballard, Leesburg, Alabama Date of birth: Jan 19, 1836 Lincoln Co. NC. Served Second U.S. Volunteer Infantry Co. "D". Enlisted Chattanooga Tenn. Wife's maiden name: Martha Arminda Baker. m. 11/14/1854 Chattoga Co. GA by John Baker, J.P. (states that records destroyed in burning of Court house). No other marriage. Names and dates of birth of children: Narcissus C. Ballard 3/17/1856, John L. Ballard 6/14/1858, Robert C. Ballard 4/25/1862, Millard F. or T. Ballard 5/25/1860, Martha M. Ballard 4/17/1867, Ira C. Ballard 12/3/1868, Tennie Ballard 1/6/1871, Cora Hill Ballard 1/17/1873, Eula Lee Ballard 12/28/1874, Paul C. Ballard 5/20/1876, Baxter J. Ballard 10/3/1878

More About ROBERT COLEMAN BALLARD:
Burial: Cedar Hill Cemetery, Leesburg, Cherokee Co., AL

Notes for MARTHA ARMINDA BAKER:
Source: Mildred Sparks

More About MARTHA ARMINDA BAKER:
Burial: Cedar Hill Cemetery, Leesburg, Cherokee Co., AL

Children of ROBERT BALLARD and MARTHA BAKER are:

	i.	NARCISSUS C. "NARRA"[8] BALLARD, b. 17 Mar 1856, GA; d. Aft. 1880; m. HARVEY E. THOMAS, 18 Apr 1886.
87.	ii.	JOHN LEVI BALLARD, b. 14 Jun 1858, Dalton Whitfield Co., GA; d. 24 Feb 1918, Sacul, Nacogdoches Co., TX.
88.	iii.	MILLARD FILLMORE "MID" BALLARD, b. 20 May 1860, Chattooga Co., GA; d. 14 Oct 1927, Menlo, Chattooga Co., GA.
89.	iv.	ROBERT CHAPMAN BALLARD, JR., b. 25 Apr 1862, GA; d. Aft. 1910.
90.	v.	MARTHA M. "MATTIE" BALLARD, b. 17 Apr 1867, Walker Co., GA; d. 1949, Armuchee, Walker Co., GA.
91.	vi.	IRA CHELEOUS BALLARD, b. 03 Dec 1868, Trion Chattooga, GA; d. 04 Oct 1937, Gadsden, Etowah AL (bur. Forrest Cemetery. Gadsden..
92.	vii.	TENNIE BALLARD, b. 06 Jan 1871, GA; d. 1961, AL.
	viii.	CORA HILL BALLARD, b. 17 Jan 1873; d. Bef. 1880.
93.	ix.	EULA LEE BALLARD, b. 28 Dec 1874, Chattooga Co., GA; d. Aft. 1910, OK.
94.	x.	PAUL CEPHUS BALLARD, b. 20 May 1876, GA or AL; d. 26 Jul 1964, Stockdale, Wilson Co., TX.
	xi.	BAXTER JONES BALLARD, b. 03 Oct 1878, AL; d. 1899; m. SALLY JANE SMITH, 09 Feb 1898, Chattooga Co., GA.

28. ELBERT TAMPLIN[7] BALLARD (JAMES[6], WHORTON[5], JESSE[4], JOHN[3], JOSEPH[2], JOHN[1]) was born Abt. 1839 in GA, and died 31 Jul 1903. He married AMANDA "MANDY" BOOTH 15 Feb 1866 in Blount Co., AL. She was born 1846 in MS, and died 05 Apr 1905.

Notes for ELBERT TAMPLIN BALLARD:
Source: 1870 Blount County Alabama Federal Census Records, 1880 Sumter County Alabama federal census Records, 1900 Tuscaloosa County Alabama Federal Census Records
1870 - Living in Blount Co., AL - Ballard, Elbert 27 blacksmith GA, Amanda 18, Annie 2 JH 1
1880 - Living in Sumter Co., AL - Ballard, ET 37 blacksmith GA, Manda 36 MS, Rolena 12, George W 10 AL, Nancy 6 AL, Minnie 5 AL, Alleck 3 AL

More About ELBERT TAMPLIN BALLARD:
Burial: Cottondale Cemetery, Tuscaloosa Co., AL

More About AMANDA "MANDY" BOOTH:
Burial: Cottondale Cemetery, Tuscaloosa Co., AL

Children of ELBERT BALLARD and AMANDA BOOTH are:

     i.   ANNIE[8] BALLARD, b. 1872, AL; d. 19 Feb 1932, Tuscaloosa Co., AL.

          More About ANNIE BALLARD:
          Burial: Bethel Baptist Church Cemetery, Tuscaloosa Co., AL

     ii. CLARA BALLARD, b. 1868, AL; d. Bef. 1880.
     iii. J. H. BALLARD, b. 1869, AL; d. Aft. 1870.
     iv. GEORGE W. BALLARD, b. 08 Nov 1871, AL; d. 22 Sep 1931, Tuscaloosa Co., AL.

          More About GEORGE W. BALLARD:
          Burial: Tuscaloosa Memorial Park, Tuscaloosa Co., AL

     v.   NANCY BALLARD, b. 02 Nov 1877, AL; d. 27 Aug 1947.

          More About NANCY BALLARD:
          Burial: Cottondale Cemetery, Tuscaloosa Co., AL

     vi. MINNIE BALLARD, b. 1875, AL; d. Aft. 1880.
     vii. ALLECK BALLARD, b. 1877, AL; d. Aft. 1880.
     viii. ROBERT L. BALLARD, b. 1882, AL; d. 22 Oct 1957, Tuscaloosa Co., AL.

29. WESLEY M.[7] BALLARD (WILLIAM ROBERT[6], WHORTON[5], JESSE[4], JOHN[3], JOSEPH[2], JOHN[1]) was born 1814 in GA, and died Aft. 1880. He married NANCY RUSSELL 28 Jun 1848 in Coweta Co., GA. She was born 1817 in NC, and died Aft. 1880.

Notes for WESLEY M. BALLARD:
Source: Marriage CD#4, 1850 Coweta County Georgia Federal Census Records, 1860 Talladega Co., AL Federal Census Records, 1880 Texas Federal Census Soundex Records
* 1850 - Living in Coweta Co., GA - Ballard, Wesley 26 GA, Nancy 23 NC, Wm. H. 1 GA
* 1860 - Living in Talladega Co., AL - Ballard, Wesley M. 36 GA, Nancy 33 GA, William 11 GA, Ellen 6 GA, Frances 3 GA, Emily 10/12 AL, Julia 64 NC
* 1880 - Living in Franklin Co., TX - Ballard, Wesley M 56 NC, Nancey A 53 GA, Julia F Giles 22 AL, Emily J 20, Ollie 6 TX

Children of WESLEY BALLARD and NANCY RUSSELL are:
     i.   WILLIAM[8] BALLARD, b. 1849, GA; d. Aft. 1860.
     ii. JULIA FRANCES BALLARD, b. 1858, GA; d. Aft. 1880; m. GILES.
     iii. EMILY J. BALLARD, b. 1860, AL; d. Aft. 1880.
     iv. OLLIE BALLARD, b. 1873, TX; d. Aft. 1880.
     v.   ELLEN BALLARD, b. 1854, GA; d. Aft. 1860.

30. WILLIAM R.[7] BALLARD (WILLIAM ROBERT[6], WHORTON[5], JESSE[4], JOHN[3], JOSEPH[2], JOHN[1]) was born 1826 in GA, and died Aft. 1880. He married MARY FRANCES ANN STAMPS 07 Jun 1849 in Coweta Co., GA. She was born 1832 in GA, and died Aft. 1880.

Notes for WILLIAM R. BALLARD:
Source: CD#4, 1850, 1870, 1880 Coweta County GA Federal Census Records, 1880 Federal Census Soundex Records - Georgia
* 1850 - Living in Coweta County Georgia - Ballard, Wm. R. 24 GA, Mary 18 GA
* 1870 - Living in Coweta County Georgia - Ballard, Wm R. 43 Shoemaker, Mary A F 39, Alonzo R 12, Willie F 4, Asa T 5/12, Julia A 74

* 1880 - Living in Coweta County Georgia - Ballard, William R. 53 GA NC GA, Mary A 48 GA GA GA, William C 13 GA, Frances 6 GA

Children of WILLIAM BALLARD and MARY STAMPS are:
95.   i.   ROBERT ALONZO[8] BALLARD, DR., b. 01 Jun 1857, GA; d. 01 Sep 1897.
       ii. WILLIAM BALLARD, b. 1864, GA; d. Aft. 1880.
     iii. ASA T. BALLARD, b. 1869, GA; d. Aft. 1870.
     iv. FRANCES E. BALLARD, b. 1874, GA; d. Aft. 1880.

31. HULDA SMITH[7] HEARN (JANE[6] BALLARD, WHORTON[5], JESSE[4], JOHN[3], JOSEPH[2], JOHN[1]) was born 1821 in Franklin Co., GA, and died 1856 in Chatham Jackson Parish LA, bur. Brooklyn Cemetery.. She married JOHN WESLEY CARROLL. He was born 1815, and died 1872.

Notes for HULDA SMITH HEARN:
Source: Valerie Austin (va5303@nersp.nerdc.ufl.edu)

Child of HULDA HEARN and JOHN CARROLL is:
96.   i.   JOHN FRANKLIN[8] CARROLL, b. 27 Nov 1839, Coweta Co., GA; d. 26 Aug 1910, Jackson Parish, LA.

32. NANCY C.[7] HEARN (JANE[6] BALLARD, WHORTON[5], JESSE[4], JOHN[3], JOSEPH[2], JOHN[1]) was born 09 Feb 1843 in Coweta Co., GA, and died 03 Jul 1881. She married (1) ALLEN C. ELLIS Bef. 1865. He was born Abt. 1840 in GA, and died Aft. 1860. She married (2) MALICIAH LANTRIP 1866 in Jackson Parish LA.

Child of NANCY HEARN and ALLEN ELLIS is:
      i.   AUGUSTUA A.[8] ELLIS, b. 1860, Jackson Parish, LA.

33. EDMOND S.[7] BALLARD (WESLEY[6], WHORTON[5], JESSE[4], JOHN[3], JOSEPH[2], JOHN[1]) was born 1822 in NC, and died Aft. 1870. He married LUCRETIA. She was born 1822 in NC, and died Aft. 1860.

Notes for EDMOND S. BALLARD:
Source: Rick Green (rickgreen@ibm.net), 1860 - 1870 Tallapoosa County Alabama Federal Census Records
* 1860 - Living in Tallapoosa Co., AL - Ballard, E. S. 38 NC, Lucretia 38 NC, Mary D. 17 GA, Elizabeth E. 13 GA, Sarah L. 11 GA, Arra A. 10 GA, Carmella 9 GA, Nancy 8 GA, Frances C. 6 GA, Hiram T. 4 GA, Alford O. 1 GA
* 1870 - Living in Tallapoosa Co., AL - Ballard, Edmond 55, Lukie 50, Mary 32, Elizabeth 30, Louisa 27 GA, Aurelia 23 GA, Carmella 21 AL, Nancy 16 AL, Frances 15 AL, Thomas 13 AL, Alfred 11 AL, Sallie 7 AL, Biddie 1 AL

Children of EDMOND BALLARD and LUCRETIA are:
      i.   MARY D.[8] BALLARD, b. 1843, GA; d. Aft. 1870.
     ii. ELIZABETH G. BALLARD, b. 1847, AL; d. Aft. 1870.
   iii. SARAH LOUISA BALLARD, b. Bet. 1843 - 1849, AL; d. Aft. 1870.
   iv. AURELIA A. BALLARD, b. Bet. 1847 - 1850, AL; d. Aft. 1870.
    v. CARMELLA BALLARD, b. Bet. 1849 - 1851, AL; d. Aft. 1870.
   vi. NANCY BALLARD, b. Bet. 1852 - 1854, AL; d. Aft. 1870.
  vii. FRANCES G. BALLARD, b. Bet. 1854 - 1855, AL; d. Aft. 1870.
 viii. HIRAM THOMAS BALLARD, b. Bet. 1856 - 1857, AL; d. Aft. 1870.
97.   ix. ALFRED O. BALLARD, b. 1859, AL; d. Aft. 1887.
     x. SALLIE BALLARD, b. 1863, AL; d. Aft. 1870.
   xi. BIDDIE BALLARD, b. 1869, AL; d. Aft. 1870.

34. THOMAS W.[7] BALLARD (WESLEY[6], WHORTON[5], JESSE[4], JOHN[3], JOSEPH[2], JOHN[1]) was born Sep 1825 in NC, and died 07 Sep 1907 in Comanche Co., TX. He married SUSAN REAMS 18 May 1845 in Meriwether Co., GA. She was born Abt. 1821 in SC, and died Bef. 1900.

Notes for THOMAS W. BALLARD:
Source: John Robertson, 1850 Meriwether County Georgia Federal Census Records, 1860 Tallapoosa County Alabama Federal Census Records
* 1850 - Living in Meriwether Co., GA - Ballard, Thomas 23 NC, Susan 29 SC, John AL, James GA
* 1860 - Living in Tallapoosa Co., AL - Ballard, Thomas W 36 NC, Susan 42 SC, John A. 15 AL, James L 11 GA, Joshua E. 9 AL, Enoch B. 5, William W. 3 AL

Children of THOMAS BALLARD and SUSAN REAMS are:
98.	i.	JOHN EDMOND "DOC"[8] BALLARD, b. 1848, AL; d. 04 Jan 1909, Dadeville, Tallapoosa Co., AL.
	ii.	JOSHUA E. BALLARD, b. 1851, GA; d. Aft. 1860.
99.	iii.	ENOCH BURTON BALLARD, b. 19 Jun 1855, Tallapoosa Co., AL; d. 04 Mar 1914.
	iv.	WILLIAM W. BALLARD, b. 1857, AL; d. Aft. 1860.
100.	v.	JAMES T. BALLARD, b. 1849, Meriwether GA; d. Aft. 1880.

35. JOHN WESLEY[7] BALLARD (WESLEY[6], WHORTON[5], JESSE[4], JOHN[3], JOSEPH[2], JOHN[1]) was born 07 Dec 1845 in Carroll Co., GA, and died 25 Aug 1932 in Carroll Co., GA. He married (1) MILDRED " MILLIE" ANN INGRAM 12 Apr 1871. She was born 24 Aug 1855 in NC, and died 01 Jun 1900. He married (2) CARRIE LANCASTER 15 Jan 1905. She was born 1884, and died 23 Nov 1954.

Notes for JOHN WESLEY BALLARD:
Source: Lloyd Russell Ballard, Tex Dick, Kathy Ballard, 1880 Federal Census Soundex Georgia, 1880 & 1920-1930 Carroll County Georgia Federal Census Records, John Wesley Ballard Bible owned by I N Ballard of Carrollton GA, Kelly Hartley (willow1@yahoo.com)
* 1880 Carroll Co., GA - Ballard, John Wesley 34 school teacher GA SC SC, Millie A 24 NC GA GA, John Wesley 4 GA GA, James Robinson boarder
* 1920 - Living in Carrollton, Carroll Co., GA - Ballard, John W 64 md 2x GA NC GA, Laura C 35 GA GA SC, J Wesley Jr. 34 wd
* 1930 - Living in Carroll Co., GA - Ballard, John W 84 GA NC GA, Cara 55 GA GA GA
* John Wesley Ballard Bible - (submitted to the Ballard List by Jerry Stephens (JerryS4605@aol.com), Possession of 1. N. Ballard, Carrollton, Ga., Copied and contributed by Mrs. Evelyn Ballard of Wink, Texas
John Wesley Ballards father, Wesley Ballard, son of Whorton and Saloma Ballard. Saloma Ballard nee Saloma Redwine, a German Winnie Ballard, nee Winnie Floyd, daughter of Ell Floyd, 3rd son of William Floyd, of N.Y., signed Declaration of Independence July 4, 1776. Eli Floyd's wife was Sarah King, daughter of Richard Bradford and Martha Bradford, nee Threadpeth.
J.W. Ballard's father Wesley Ballard, son of Whorton and Saloma Ballard, nee Saloma Redwine. His mother Winney Ballard nee Winnie Floyd.
Wesley Ballard born May 10, 1803, Winny Ballard born Feb. 27, 1811
Children:
Owen R. born July 10, 1832, William L., born Aug. 20, 1834
John W., born Dec. 7, 1845, Bei-ij. 0. born Sept. 9, 1847
Millie A. [wife of John W. Ballard above], born Aug.24,1855
John Wesley born Dec. 23,1875, Isaac Newton born Sept. 26, 1889
Cora [wife of John Wesley above] born July 10, 1874
Marriages:
John W. Ballard and Mildred A. Ingram April 12, 1871 by David Moore, M.G.
J. W. Ballard and Laura Cora Price July II, 1901 by H. Ashmore, Esq.
Isaac Newton and F. Virginia Young June 30, 1912
son William N. and Minnie Robinson July 1, 1933
Woodrow Ballard and Margaret Bradley July 15, 1947
J. Wesley Ballard and Carrie Lancaster Jan. 15, 1905 by Rev. E. E. Robinson

Deaths:
0. R. Ballard Dec. 14, 1857 - William L. Ballard May 26, 1860
Wesley Ballard July 30, 1872 - Winnie Ballard Mar. 28, 1890
Carrie Ballard Nov. 23, 1954 - Carrie Mae Ballard April 4, 1920
Mildred Ann Ballard June 1, 1900 - John W. Ballard Aug. 25, 1932

More About JOHN WESLEY BALLARD:
Burial: New Hope United Methodist Church Cemetery. Carroll Co., GA

Children of JOHN BALLARD and MILDRED INGRAM are:
101.   i.   JOHN WESLEY[8] BALLARD, b. 23 Dec 1875, GA; d. 25 Aug 1932.
102.   ii.   ISAAC NEWTON BALLARD, b. 26 Sep 1889.

Child of JOHN BALLARD and CARRIE LANCASTER is:
           iii. CARRIE MAE[8] BALLARD, b. 18 Apr 1920, Carrollton, Carroll Co., GA; d. 19 Apr 1920, Carrollton, Carroll Co., GA.

36. MARTHA[7] TATUM (MARY[6] BALLARD, WHORTON[5], JESSE[4], JOHN[3], JOSEPH[2], JOHN[1]) *was born 1826 in Coweta Co, GA, and died 24 Nov 1878. She married JAMES LORENZO IRWIN. He was born 1815 in Wilkes Co., GA, and died 1882 in Fulton Co., GA.*

Notes for JAMES LORENZO IRWIN:
Source: 1850 Coweta County Georgia Federal Census Records, 1860 -1880 Campbell County Georgia Federal Census Records, Martha Irwin (marirw@yahoo.com)

* 1850 - Living in Coweta Co., GA - Irwin, Jas L 33 boot maker GA, Martha 22 GA, Harriet 5 GA, Aabella 3 GA
* 1860 - Living in Campbell Co., GA - Irwin, James L 47, Martha 52, Harriett 14, Arabilla 13, Albert A 5, Mary 3
* 1870 - Living in Campbell Co., GA - Irwin, Jas 53 farm labor, Martha 46, Hariet 25, Arabelle 22, Alonzo 20, Mary 18, Willie 19, Charles 14, Joseph 12
* 1880 - Living in Palmetto, Campbell Co., GA - Irwin, James L 68 farmer, William 18, Charles 14, Lorenza 12

Children of MARTHA TATUM and JAMES IRWIN are:

           i.   WILLIAM DAVID[8] IRWIN, b. 04 Oct 1861, GA; d. 18 Aug 1943; m. MOLLIE ELIZABETH HUNT.
           ii.   HARRIETT PRUDENCE IRWIN, b. 09 May 1844, GA; d. 22 Nov 1943; m. ALFRED TURNER MCDONALD.
           iii. ARABELLA C. IRWIN, b. 1847, GA; d. Aft. 1870; m. SEABORN LONGINO.
           iv.   ALBERT ALONZO IRWIN, b. 1850, GA; d. Aft. 1870.
           v.   MARY JEAN IRWIN, b. 1856, GA; d. 15 Jul 1931.
           vi.   CHARLES EDWIN IRWIN, b. 1866, GA; d. 1903.
           vii. JAMES LORENZO IRWIN, b. 22 Sep 1868, GA; d. 24 Mar 1953.

37. ROBERT JOHNSON[7] SAMPLER, REV. (ELIZABETH[6] BALLARD, WHORTON[5], JESSE[4], JOHN[3], JOSEPH[2], JOHN[1]) *was born 06 Jul 1827 in GA, and died 29 Sep 1901. He married CAROLINE 1844 in Cobb Co., GA. She was born 1826 in SC.*

Notes for ROBERT JOHNSON SAMPLER, REV.:

Source: 1850 Cobb County Georgia Federal Census Records, 1870 Saint Clair County, Alabama Federal Census Records
* 1850 - Living in Roswell, Cobb Co., GA - Sampler, Robert 23 GA, Caroline 24 SC, William P 4 GA, Anderson Hunt 18 GA
* 1870 - Living in St. Clair Co. AL - Sampler, Robert 42 phycician GA, Caroline 24 SC, West, Albert preacher SC, Jane 26 SC

More About ROBERT JOHNSON SAMPLER, REV.:
Burial: Springville Cemetery, St. Clair Co., AL

Child of ROBERT SAMPLER and CAROLINE is:
     i.   WILLIAM P.⁸ SAMPLER, b. Abt. 1846.

38. RANDOLPH COLEMAN⁷ SAMPLER (ELIZABETH⁶ BALLARD, WHORTON⁵, JESSE⁴, JOHN³, JOSEPH², JOHN¹) was born 22 Dec 1830 in GA. He married MARGARETTE FLORIDA. She was born Abt. 1830.

Children of RANDOLPH SAMPLER and MARGARETTE FLORIDA are:
     i.   MARY JANE⁸ SAMPLER, b. Abt. 1850; m. FELIX MOTE, 22 Mar 1874.
     ii. GUS SAMPLER, b. Abt. 1851; m. DORA SAMPSON; b. Abt. 1852.
     iii. SARAH SAMPLER, b. Abt. 1852; m. CHARLIE AUSTIN, 15 Dec 1878.
     iv. DICK SAMPLER, b. Abt. 1853; m. METTIE AUSTIN.
     v. LORENZA DOW SAMPLER, b. Abt. 1854; m. ELIZABETH WARREN.

39. HESTER ANN⁷ SAMPLER (ELIZABETH⁶ BALLARD, WHORTON⁵, JESSE⁴, JOHN³, JOSEPH², JOHN¹) was born 24 Sep 1834 in Woodstock, Cherokee Co., GA, and died Aft. 1850. She married LITTLENTON M. OTWELL Abt. 1855 in Cobb Co., GA. He was born 07 Feb 1829 in Gwinnett Co., GA, and died 1899 in Roswell, Cobb Co., GA.

Notes for LITTLENTON M. OTWELL:
Source: Tex Dick

More About LITTLENTON M. OTWELL:
Burial: Old Roswell Cemetery, Fulton Co., GA

Children of HESTER SAMPLER and LITTLENTON OTWELL are:
103.   i.   MARY JANE⁸ OTWELL, b. Mar 1857, Cobb Co., GA; d. Aft. 1900, GA.
         ii. WILLIAM S. OTTWELL, b. 1859.
         iii. ROBERT JOSEPH OTWELL, b. 1862; m. STACY ELIZABETH HANEY.
104.   iv. CHARLES "CHARLIE" OTWELL, b. Apr 1866, Cobb Co., GA; d. 1936, Cobb Co., GA.
         v. JOHN M. OTWELL, b. 1868.
         vi. BENJAMIN F. OTWELL, b. 1870.

40. WILLIAM WESLEY⁷ SAMPLER (ELIZABETH⁶ BALLARD, WHORTON⁵, JESSE⁴, JOHN³, JOSEPH², JOHN¹) was born 14 Feb 1841 in Cobb Co., GA, and died 10 Jul 1889 in Murray Co., GA. He married MARTHA JANE PATTERSON LEWIS 16 Feb 1861 in Murray Co., GA. She was born 03 Apr 1836, and died 22 Feb 1897 in Murray Co., GA.

More About WILLIAM WESLEY SAMPLER:
Burial: Mt Zion Cemetery, Chatsworth, Murray Co., GA

Children of WILLIAM SAMPLER and MARTHA LEWIS are:
         i.   EDNA⁸ SAMPLER.
         ii. JOHN SAMPLER, b. 1860.
         iii. MARTHA A. SAMPLER, b. 1862.
105.   iv. EMMA LEE SAMPLER, b. 11 May 1873, Murray Co., GA; d. 11 Apr 1946, Glendale, Los Angeles Co., CA.
106.   v. WILLIAM WALDEN SAMPLER, b. 19 Feb 1872, Tunnel Hill, Whitfield Co., GA; d. 10 May 1951, Murray Co., GA.

41. ELLA LYDIA⁷ BALLARD (COLEMAN H.⁶, WHORTON⁵, JESSE⁴, JOHN³, JOSEPH², JOHN¹) was born 28 Mar 1837 in MS, and died 02 Apr 1913 in TX. She married EDWARD L. ROBB Abt. 1863. He was born 15 Jun 1836, and died 03 Mar 1902.

Children of ELLA BALLARD and EDWARD ROBB are:

    i.   ANNIE MARY[8] ROBB, b. 12 Nov 1862; m. STEPHEN JACKSON TREADWELL; b. 06 Oct 1861; d. 13 Jan 1917.

    ii. EDWARD BALLARD ROBB, b. 18 Sep 1865; d. 29 Jan 1924; m. (1) SALLIE C. FOWLER; b. 07 Aug 1866; d. 04 May 1950; m. (2) MARY ANDREW WARREN, 31 Dec 1919; b. 08 May 1878; d. 04 May 1950.

    iii. JOSEPHINE L. ROBB, b. Abt. 1869; m. T B MOORE.

Generation No. 4

42. LEWIS M.[8] BALLARD (*JAMES CLARK[7], LEWIS[6], WHORTON[5], JESSE[4], JOHN[3], JOSEPH[2], JOHN[1]*) was born Sep 1845 in Marion Co., FL. He married SARAH ENGLISH.

Notes for LEWIS M. BALLARD:
Source: Kelly Hartley (willow1@yahoo.com)

Children of LEWIS BALLARD and SARAH ENGLISH are:

    i.   JAMES[9] BALLARD, b. 1870.

    ii. ABBIE BALLARD, b. 1872.

    iii. ADDIE BALLARD, b. 1875.

43. HENRY LEWIS[8] BALLARD (*JAMES CLARK[7], LEWIS[6], WHORTON[5], JESSE[4], JOHN[3], JOSEPH[2], JOHN[1]*) was born 11 Jan 1847 in Marion Co., FL. He married MARY DYESS 31 Jul 1866 in FL.

Notes for HENRY LEWIS BALLARD:
Source: RAINEYM968@aol.com

Children of HENRY BALLARD and MARY DYESS are:

    i.   NANCY CAROLINE[9] BALLARD, b. 28 Jun 1867, Polk Co., FL.

    ii. MARY ELLEN BALLARD, b. 16 Sep 1872, Polk Co., FL.

    iii. JAMES LEWIS BALLARD, b. 13 Jan 1875.

    iv. HERBERT GILSON BALLARD, b. 12 Jul 1877, Polk Co., FL; d. 18 Jul 1959, St. Augustine, St. Johns Co., FL; m. (1) ALLIE BUIE HOWE; b. 1881, FL; m. (2) JANIE THOMAS, 24 Dec 1901, St. Augustine, St. Johns Co., FL; b. 29 Jan 1876, Peniel, Putnam Co., FL; d. 11 Oct 1937, Jacksonville Beach, Duval Co., FL.

        Notes for HERBERT GILSON BALLARD:
        Source: C. Reyes (ranger29@prodigy.net), (RAINEYM968@aol.com)

        More About HERBERT GILSON BALLARD:
        Burial: Peoria Cemetery Doctors Inlet, Clay Co., FL

    v. HIRAM EASSY BALLARD, b. 05 Oct 1882; d. Apr 1968.

    vi. AARON DENNIS BALLARD, b. 31 Jan 1885, FL.

44. NANCY ANN[8] BALLARD (*JAMES CLARK[7], LEWIS[6], WHORTON[5], JESSE[4], JOHN[3], JOSEPH[2], JOHN[1]*) was born 1849 in Marion Co., FL. She married EZEKIEL HULL.

Notes for NANCY ANN BALLARD:
Source: Sandra (rstaylor@ij.net)

Child of NANCY BALLARD and EZEKIEL HULL is:

    i.   JAMES D.⁹ HULL, *b. 14 Feb 1875, Orange Co., FL; d. 10 Nov 1954.*

45. MARY CATHERINE⁸ BALLARD *(JAMES CLARK⁷, LEWIS⁶, WHORTON⁵, JESSE⁴, JOHN³, JOSEPH², JOHN¹) was born 26 Feb 1855 in Lake Co., FL, and died 12 Jun 1941 in Tavares, Lake Co., FL. She married THOMAS ASBURY HUX 07 Sep 1870 in Ft. Mason Lake Co., FL, son of LEVIE HUX and DICEY WARSHAM.*

Notes for MARY CATHERINE BALLARD:
Source: RAINEYM968@aol.com

More About MARY CATHERINE BALLARD:
Burial: Astatula, Lake Co., FL

Children of MARY BALLARD *and* THOMAS HUX *are:*
    i.   JAMES LEVIE⁹ HUX, *b. 03 Oct 1871.*
    ii. ADA BERTHA HUX, *b. 07 Sep 1873.*
    iii. ESTELLA HUX, *b. 06 Mar 1876.*
    iv. THOMAS DRU HUX, *b. 04 Feb 1878.*
    v. MAGGIE MARY HUX, *b. Nov 1880.*
    vi. HIRAM FLEMING HUX, *b. 11 Apr 1889.*
    vii. NELLIE LORORA HUX, *b. 29 Sep 1895.*

46. JAMES CLARK⁸ BALLARD *(JAMES CLARK⁷, LEWIS⁶, WHORTON⁵, JESSE⁴, JOHN³, JOSEPH², JOHN¹) was born Dec 1859 in Hawkinsville, Orange Co., FL. He married (1) JOSEPHINE WILLIAMS 07 May 1885 in Polk Co FL. He married (2) LOLA ELIZABETH PROCTOR 29 Jan 1891 in Bartow, Polk Co., FL.*

Notes for JAMES CLARK BALLARD:
Source: RAINEYM968@aol.com

Children of JAMES BALLARD *and* LOLA PROCTOR *are:*
    i.   EVA⁹ BALLARD, *b. Oct 1891.*
    ii. HIRAM HILLARY BALLARD, *b. 22 Feb 1893.*
    iii. DOC KEELY BALLARD, *b. 05 Jun 1894.*
    iv. ELMO MARION BALLARD, *b. 28 Jan 1897.*
    v. GRADY LEE BALLARD, *b. 05 Apr 1900.*
    vi. AGNES BALLARD, *b. 1902.*
    vii. ALMETA BALLARD, *b. 1904.*
    viii. HORTENSE BALLARD, *b. 1909.*

47. MEEKY⁸ BALLARD *(JAMES CLARK⁷, LEWIS⁶, WHORTON⁵, JESSE⁴, JOHN³, JOSEPH², JOHN¹) was born 1862 in Hawkinsville, Orange Co., FL, and died 20 Jan 1894 in Plant City, Hillsborough Co., FL. She married GEORGE A. DEVANE 29 Nov 1877 in Polk Co FL.*

More About MEEKY BALLARD:
Burial: Mt. Enon Cemetery. Plant City, Hillsborough Co,, FL

Child of MEEKY BALLARD *and* GEORGE DEVANE *is:*
    i.   AUGUSTUS HIRAM⁹ DEVANE.

48. JOHN YANCY⁸ BALLARD *(MORRIS R.⁷, LEWIS⁶, WHORTON⁵, JESSE⁴, JOHN³, JOSEPH², JOHN¹) was born May 1848 in Franklin Co., GA, and died 12 Mar 1932. He married SUSAN BOND 21 Aug 1870 in Winston Co., MS. She was born 1839 in MS.*

Notes for JOHN YANCY BALLARD:
Source: 1870 Winston County Mississippi, 1880 Choctaw County Mississippi Federal Census Records

Children of JOHN BALLARD and SUSAN BOND are:
>   i.   *W. FRANK⁹ BALLARD, b. 1874, MS.*
>   ii. *HARRISON MONROE BALLARD, b. 16 Sep 1875, MS; d. 25 May 1950, Attala MS; m. MINNIE L. BAINE, 1898; b. 15 Jan 1876, MS; d. 27 Jul 1920, Attala MS.*
>
>   *Notes for HARRISON MONROE BALLARD:*
>   *Source: Joyce Sanders Group Sheets,1900, 1910 Attala County Mississippi Federal Census Records, Tabernacle Attala County, Mississippi, Attala County Mississippi Cemeteries page 338 Tabernacle Methodist Church Cemetery, dforcier@harris.com*
>
>   *More About HARRISON MONROE BALLARD:*
>   *Burial: Tabernacle Methodist Church Cemetery Attala MS*
>
>   *More About MINNIE L. BAINE:*
>   *Burial: Tabernacle Methodist Church Cemetery Attala MS*

49.   JOEL S.⁸ BALLARD (MORRIS R.⁷, LEWIS⁶, WHORTON⁵, JESSE⁴, JOHN³, JOSEPH², JOHN¹) *was born Aug 1851 in Franklin Co., GA, and died 1909 in Choctaw Co., MS. He married SARAH FRANCES MILLS 09 Aug 1869 in Winston Co., MS, daughter of HENRY MILLS and ELENDA. She was born 16 Jan 1841 in Kemper Co., MS, and died 12 Apr 1922 in Choctaw Co., MS.*

Notes for JOEL S. BALLARD:
Source: Tara Barrett, Joyce Sanders, 1870 Winston County Mississippi, 1880 Attala County Mississippi, 1900-1910 Choctaw County Mississippi, Amanda Dees (randees@netword-one.com)
* Buried Salem Methodist Church Cemetery in Choctaw Co., MS
* 1880 - Living in Centre, Attala County MS - Ballard, Joel S 28, Sarah F 38, Mary J 9, Jesse C 7, Chas W 5, Newton 2, Newborn 2, Josiah 1, Joanna 1
* 1900 - Living in Choctaw County MS - Ballard, Joe S - Aug 1851 GA GA GA,. Frances - Jan 1840 MS SC GA, Sallie L - Apr 1881 MS, Ella - Feb 1884 MS, Jim C - July 1885

More About JOEL S. BALLARD:
Burial: Salem United Methodist Cemetery Choctaw Co., MS

Children of JOEL BALLARD and SARAH MILLS are:
>   i.   *MARY J.⁹ BALLARD, b. 1871, MS.*
>   ii. *JESSIE CLAYTON BALLARD, b. 1872, Choctaw Co., MS; d. Jun 1938, Attala Co., MS; m. FRANCES "FANNIE" J. SMITH, 19 Jul 1895, Winston Co., MS; b. 1877, Winston Co., MS; d. 26 Feb 1956, St. Louis MO bur. Attala Co., MS.*
>
>   *Notes for JESSIE CLAYTON BALLARD:*
>   *Source: CD# 5 , Tara Barrett, Joyce Sanders, 1900 and 1910 Choctaw Co. Mississippi Census Records, Attala Co. Mississippi Cemetery Records showing Edgefield Cemetery page 82,*
>
>   *More About JESSIE CLAYTON BALLARD:*
>   *Burial: Edgefield Cemetery Attala Co., MS*
>
>   *More About FRANCES "FANNIE" J. SMITH:*
>   *Burial: Edgefield Cemetery Attala Co., MS*

>   iii. *CHARLES WESLEY BALLARD, b. 22 Feb 1875, MS; d. 15 Jul 1953, Choctaw Co., MS; m. ANNIE BERTHA PARKER, 1896, MS; b. 14 Jun 1876, AL; d. 04 Jun 1943.*

Notes for CHARLES WESLEY BALLARD:
Source: 1900-1910 Choctaw County Mississippi Federal Census Records

* 1900 - Living in Choctaw County MS - Ballard, Charles - Feb 1875 MS GA MS, Bertha 1876 AL AL AL, Russell 1897 MS, Ethel - Jan 1899 MS, Bertha

iv.   WILLIAM NEWTON BALLARD, *b. 18 Jul 1877, MS; d. 23 Mar 1953, Montgomery Co., MS; m. (1)* ELLENDER BAY WATERS; *b. 16 Jul 1894; m. (2)* ROSA LEE MALONE, *18 Aug 1899, Winston Co., MS; m. (3)* LULU MAE WATERS, *Bef. 1912; b. 13 Jan 1893, MS; d. 1965.*

Notes for WILLIAM NEWTON BALLARD:
Source: 1820 Choctaw Co. Mississippi Federal Census Records, Amanda Dees (randees@network-one.com)

More About WILLIAM NEWTON BALLARD:
Burial: Bur. Bethel Methodist Church Cemetery in Montgomery Co., Mississippi

More About LULU MAE WATERS:
Burial: Bur. Bethlehem Cemetery. Dover, Hillsborough Co, FL

v.   WILLIS NEWTON BALLARD, *b. 18 Jul 1877, MS; d. 23 Mar 1953, Attala Co., MS; m.* EMMA MASSEY, *19 Jul 1899, Atta. Co., MS; b. 12 Jan 1881; d. 18 Dec 1951, Attala MS.*

More About WILLIS NEWTON BALLARD:
Burial: Bur. McCool Cemetery. Attala Co., MS

More About EMMA MASSEY:
Burial: Bur. McCool Cemetery. Attala Co., MS

vi.   JOANNA BALLARD, *b. 19 Mar 1879, MS; d. 07 Jun 1882, Choctaw Co., MS.*

Notes for JOANNA BALLARD:
Source: Attala County Mississippi Cemeteries

* Choctaw Co., Ballard Cemetery, just over the line from Attala Co, MS
Janna Ballard, Mar 19, 1879 - June 7, 1882, dau of J.S. & S. F. Ballard

vii.   JOSIAH H. BALLARD, *b. 19 Mar 1879, MS; d. 07 May 1956, Choctaw Co., MS; m.* NANCY JANE COLEMAN, *21 Dec 1899, Choctaw Co., MS; b. 16 May 1885, Chester, MS; d. 23 Mar 1935.*

Notes for JOSIAH H. BALLARD:
Source: 1910 Choctaw County Mississippi Federal Census Records, Automated Archives CD#5 Marriages
Burial: Bur. Salem Methodist Church Cemetery in Choctaw Co. Mississippi

viii.   SALLIE BALLARD, *b. Apr 1881, Choctaw Co., MS.*
ix.   ELLA BALLARD, *b. Feb 1884, Choctaw Co., MS.*
x.   JAMES "JIM" C. BALLARD, *b. Jul 1885.*

50.   THOMAS M.[8] BALLARD *(*MORRIS R.[7]*,* LEWIS[6]*,* WHORTON[5]*,* JESSE[4]*,* JOHN[3]*,* JOSEPH[2]*,* JOHN[1]*) was born 30 Aug 1857 in MS, and died 01 Jul 1926. He married* SARAH ELIZABETH AKINS *1877 in MS. She was born Apr 1852 in GA.*

Notes for THOMAS M. BALLARD:

Source: Joyce Sanders, 1880 - 1900 Attala County Mississippi Federal Census Records, 1910-1920 Choctaw County, Mississippi, Tabernacle in Attala County MS Burials, Attala County Mississippi County Cemeteries page 335, Kelly Hartley (willow1@yahoo.com)
* 1880 - Living in Centre, Attala Co., MS - Ballard, Thos M 22 farmer, Sarah E 28, Vila J 3, Florence 1
* 1900 - Living in Attala Co., MS - Ballard, Thomas M - Aug 1857 - 42 MS GA GA, Sarah E - Apr 1852 - 48 10 children 7 living GA GA GA , Lee J - Sept 1880 -19 MS, Thomas W - Feb 1882 - 18 MS, Mandle M 15 - May 1885 MS, Hiram R 11 - Aug 1888 MS, Zackariah T 9 - Oct 1890 MS
* 1910 - Living in Choctaw Co., MS - Ballard, Tom M 53 MS GA GA, Sara E 58 - 10 children 6 living, Hiram 21 MS, Zach 20 MS
* 1920 - Living in Chester, Choctaw Co., MS - Ballard, Thomas M 62, Sarah E 67, Zachariah 23

More About THOMAS M. BALLARD:
Burial: Woodlawn Cemetery, Sumner, Tallahatchie Co., MS

Children of THOMAS BALLARD and SARAH AKINS are:

i.   *VILA J.⁹ BALLARD, b. 28 Feb 1877, MS; d. 27 Dec 1965; m. WILLIAM M. BLAINE; b. 15 Nov 1877; d. 06 May 1949.*

     Notes for VILA J. BALLARD:
     Source: Kelly Hartley (willow1@yahoo.com)

     More About VILA J. BALLARD:
     Burial: Marked Tree Cemetery, Poinsett Co., AR

     More About WILLIAM M. BLAINE:
     Burial: Marked Tree Cemetery, Poinsett Co., AR

ii.   *FLORENCE BALLARD, b. 1879, MS; m. HENRY THREET, 04 Oct 1895, Attala Co., MS; b. Feb 1876.*

     Notes for FLORENCE BALLARD:
     Source: Kelly Hartley (willow1@yahoo.com)

iii.   *LEVI JASPER BALLARD, b. 26 Sep 1880, MS; d. 1892, Attala Co., MS; m. ALNA SHUMAKER, 09 Dec 1900, Attala Co., MS; b. Abt. 1880.*

     More About LEVI JASPER BALLARD:
     Burial: Tabernacle Methodist Church Cemetery

iv.   *THOMAS WEIR BALLARD, b. 25 Feb 1882, MS; d. 12 Mar 1932, Attala Co., MS; m. ANNIE L. RONE; b. 06 Sep 1882; d. 25 Feb 1912.*

     Notes for THOMAS WEIR BALLARD:
     Source: Kelly Hartley (willow1@yahoo.com)

     More About THOMAS WEIR BALLARD:
     Burial: Tabernacle Methodist Church Cemetery

     Notes for ANNIE L. RONE:
     Source: Kelly Hartley (willow1@yahoo.com)

     More About ANNIE L. RONE:
     Burial: Tabernacle Methodist Church Cemetery

v.   *SARAH ALICE BALLARD, b. 30 Nov 1883, MS; d. 06 Aug 1884, Attala Co., MS.*
     Notes for SARAH ALICE BALLARD:
     Source: Kelly Hartley (willow1@yahoo.com)

More About SARAH ALICE BALLARD:
Burial: Tabernacle Methodist Church Cemetery

   vi.   LITTLE BABE BALLARD, b. 28 Jul 1887, MS; d. 28 Jul 1887.

More About LITTLE BABE BALLARD:
Burial: Tabernacle Methodist Church Cemetery

   vii.   HIRAM RHODES BALLARD, b. 05 Aug 1888, MS; d. Feb 1959; m. (1) DOCIA OLIVER; b. 1895; d. 1980; m. (2) MARY; b. 1889.

Notes for HIRAM RHODES BALLARD:
Source: Kelly Hartley (willow1@yahoo.com)

   viii.   ZACHARIAH T. BALLARD, b. 04 Oct 1890, MS; d. Jun 1973; m. MERYL; b. 1904.
   ix.   INFANT BALLARD, b. 28 Feb 1894, MS; d. 28 Feb 1894, Attala Co., MS.

More About INFANT BALLARD:
Burial: Tabernacle Methodist Church Cemetery

51. WILLIS N.[8] BALLARD (MORRIS R.[7], LEWIS[6], WHORTON[5], JESSE[4], JOHN[3], JOSEPH[2], JOHN[1]) *was born Jun 1859 in MS, and died Aft. 1880. He married* IDELLA A. *1894. She was born Mar 1878.*

Notes for WILLIS N. BALLARD:
Source: Joyce Sanders, 1900 Attala Co., MS Census

Child of WILLIS BALLARD and IDELLA A. is:
   i.   THOMAS P.[9] BALLARD, b. Nov 1894, Attala MS.

52. PERRY MARVIN[8] BALLARD (ALVIN MONROE[7], LEWIS[6], WHORTON[5], JESSE[4], JOHN[3], JOSEPH[2], JOHN[1]) *was born 1856 in FL, and died 14 May 1929 in Desoto Co., FL. He married* LUCRETIA A. "CRESSIE" TILLET *04 Feb 1882. She was born Abt. 1856 in FL, and died Aft. 1930.*

Notes for PERRY MARVIN BALLARD:
Source: 1885 Manatee County Florida State Census Records, William (todeb@strato.net), Sue (schappel@indy.rr.com), 1900 Manatee County Florida Federal Census Records, 1920 DeSoto County Florida Federal Census Records
* 1885 - Living in Manatee Co., FL - Ballard, PM 29 FL FL FL, LC 28 AL AL NC, R 14 (f) FL, R 8 (m) FL, W 4 (m) FL
* 1900 - Living in Sandy, Manatee Co., FL - (no dates or locations listed) - Ballard, Perry, Cresie, Milley, Lee, Bill, Mose, Vallie, Carrie
* 1920 - Living in Palmdale, DeSoto Co., FL - Ballard, Perry M 64 FL FL FL, Lucretia A FL FL FL
* 1929 - Florida Death Index, 1877-1998 Record: Perry M Ballard, Death Date: 1929, County of Death: DeSoto, State of Death: Florida, Race: White, Gender: Male

Children of PERRY BALLARD and LUCRETIA TILLET are:
   i.   MILLIE[9] BALLARD.
   ii.   JOHN WESLEY BALLARD, b. 03 Jun 1883, Manatee Co., FL; d. 31 May 1935, Hendry Co., FL; m. MARY JANE TAYLOR; b. 02 Dec 1893, DeSoto Co., FL; d. 25 Jan 1944, Hendry Co., FL.

Notes for JOHN WESLEY BALLARD:
Source: 1920 DeSoto County Florida Federal Census Records, 1930 Glades County Florida Federal Census Records, WWI Draft Registration Card

*1918 - WWI Draft Registration Card - Living in Labelle, Desoto Co., FL - Ballard, John Wesley b. June 10, 36 years old (part of page missing with year of birth), nearest relative Mary Jane, wife
*1920 - Living in Palmdale, DeSoto Co., FL - Ballard, John W 39 FL FL FL, Mary J 26, Letha 10, Luther 8, Dorene 7, Irene 4 6/12, Dempsey 2 2/12, Mary L 1/12
*1930 - Living in Glades Co., FL - Ballard, John W 45 FL FL FL, Mary 35 FL, Edith 19, Edgar 18 FL, Irene 14 FL, Dempsey 13 FL, Mary L 11, Ida M 8 FL, Josephine 6 FL, Bethel A 3 FL, RC 2/12

iii.   MOSES BALLARD, b. 1888, FL; d. Aft. 1900.
iv.   WILLIAM LANGSTON "BILL" BALLARD, b. 17 Jun 1889, Pine Level, Santa Rosa Co., FL; d. 06 Mar 1942, Ft. Denaud, Hendry Co., FL; m. (1) NANCY TAYLOR; m. (2) NANCY DEES, 30 Apr 1915, Lee Co., FL; m. (3) NETTIE FRANCES DOUGLAS, 20 Dec 1919, Lee Co., FL; b. 19 Aug 1905, Alifia River, Hillsborough Co., FL; d. 15 Jan 1978, Ft. Myers, Lee Co., FL.

Notes for WILLIAM LANGSTON "BILL" BALLARD:
Source: 1930 Glades County Florida Federal Census Records
*1930 - Living in Glades Co., FL - Ballard, William 38 FL FL FL, Nellie 24 FL FL FL, Willie 8 FL, Melvin 7 FL, Elizabeth 5 FL, Earnest 2 FL

v.   LEE BALLARD, b. Bef. 1890, FL; d. Aft. 1900.
vi.   FAIT B. BALLARD, b. 08 Jul 1894, LaBelle, Hendry Co., FL; d. Aft. 1935; m. ZORAH BROWNING; b. 1903; d. Aft. 1935.

Notes for FAIT B. BALLARD:
Source: 1930 Hendry County Florida Federal Census Records, 1935 Hendry County Florida State Census Records, WW! Registration Card

*1917-1918 - WWI Registration - Draft Card - Fait Ballard b. July - Murtees FL. Farmer, Single, Living in Labell Co., FL Medium Height, gray eyes, dark brown hair.
*WWI Civilian Draft Registration Card - Ballard, Fait b. July 8, 1894 LaBelle FL
*1930 - Living in Hendry Co., FL - Ballard, Fate B 31 FL FL FL, Zola M 28 FL FL FL, John H 10 FL, Hiram 8 FL, Louis S 6 FL, Fate B 4 3/12 FL, Dorothy B 2 2/12 FL
*1935 - Living in Hendry Co., FL - Ballard, Fate B 40 farmer, Zorah 32, John Harold 15, Hiram 13, Lewis Samuel 11, AL 9, Dorothy Betty 7, Douglass 4, Perry Marvin 2, Verna Lee 0

vii.   CLARA E. BALLARD, b. 17 Mar 1899, FL; d. 16 Aug 1938; m. HEENAN THOMAS WHIDDEN, 18 Oct 1914, Lee Co., FL; b. 22 Oct 1884, FL; d. 22 Jul 1930, Glades Co., FL.

Notes for HEENAN THOMAS WHIDDEN:
Source: 1930 Glades County Florida Federal Census Records

*1930 - Living in Glades Co., FL - Whidden, Heenan 45, Clara 30, Peter 13, Paul 12, Odessa 8, Virginia 5, Solomon 2, Cresie Ballard 80 mother in law FL

viii.   LOUISE BALLARD, b. 1893.
ix.   MARTHA VOLLIE BALLARD, b. Abt. 1894, FL; d. 1937, Lee Co., FL; m. WILLIAM HARLEY AULTMAN, 08 Oct 1908, Lee Co., FL.
x.   ANDAR BALLARD, b. 1894.

53. WILEY WASHINGTON (MASH)[8] BALLARD (ALVIN MONROE[7], LEWIS[6], WHORTON[5], JESSE[4], JOHN[3], JOSEPH[2], JOHN[1]) was born May 1859 in GA, and died Aft. 1945. He married MARTHA CAROLINE "CALLIE". She was born Dec 1859 in GA, and died Aft. 1945.

Notes for WILEY WASHINGTON (MASH) BALLARD:
Source: 1900 - 1930 Manatee County Florida Federal Census Records, 1935 & 1945 Manatee County Florida

State Census Records, John Ballard (Kindmind1@aol.com)
* *1900 - Living in Sandy, Manatee Co., FL - Ballard, Mash - May 1859 GA GA GA, Callie - Dec 1859 GA GA GA, Aford - Aug 1877 FL, Bob - June 1884 FL, Lona - Jan 1890 FL, Fred - Jan 1892 FL, Baby - May 1896 (female)*
* *1910 - Living in Sandy, Manatee Co., FL - Ballard, Wiley W 43 FL GA FL, Callie 41, Lorrie 18 FL, Fred 16 FL, Florence 13 FL, Ira 11 FL, Mickey 8 FL, Ralph 5 FL, Vensent 3 FL*
* *1920 - Living in Myakka, Manatee Co., FL - Ballard, Wash W. 56 FL FL FL, Callie 50 FL FL FL, Vinnie 14 FL, Ralph 16*
* *1930 - Living in Manatee Co., FL - Ballard, Washington W 63 FL GA FL, Martha 68 FL GA GA*
* *1935 - Living in Manatee Co., FL - Ballard, Wiley W 68, Martha C 67*
* *1945 - Living in Manatee Co., FL - Ballard, Washington 78, Martha Caroline 76*

Children of WILEY BALLARD *and* MARTHA *"CALLIE" are:*

i. AFORD[9] BALLARD, *b. Aug 1877, FL.*
ii. BOB BALLARD, *b. Jun 1884, FL.*
iii. ALFRED A. BALLARD, *b. 07 Mar 1888, Manatee Co., FL; d. Aft. 1920; m.* PEARL WEBB; *b. 1891, FL; d. Aft. 1930.*

Notes for ALFRED A. BALLARD:
Source: 1920 DeSoto County Florida Federal Census Records, WWI Civilian Draft Registration
* *WWI - Civilian Draft Registration - Ballard, Alfred A b. Mar 7, 1888 Manatee Co., FL living in De Soto FL*
* *1920 - Living in Pine Level, DeSoto Co., FL - Ballard, Alfred 32 FL, Pearl 29 FL, Ruby 12 FL, Murry 10 FL, Roffie 5 FL, Amie 4 FL*

iv. A. MONROE BALLARD, *b. 1888, FL; m.* MAGGIE RAWLS.
v. LORI BALLARD, *b. 1889, FL; m.* JOHN GOMEZ.
vi. IRA BALLARD, *b. 13 May 1900, FL; d. Aft. 1917.*

Notes for IRA BALLARD:
Source: WWI Draft Registration Card
* *1917 - WWI Draft Registration - Ira Ballard, b. May 13, 1900. Father Wash W. Ballard, medium height, medium build, brown eyes, dark hair*

vii. FLORENCE BALLARD, *b. May 1899, FL.*
viii. MICKEY BALLARD, *b. 1902, FL.*
ix. RALPH BALLARD, *b. 1905, FL.*
x. VINSON BALLARD, *b. 24 Apr 1907, FL; d. Aft. 1935, lived in Manatee Co., FL; m.* ELLA LENORA HENDRY; *b. 1907, FL; d. Aft. 1935.*

Notes for VINSON BALLARD:
Source: 1930 Manatee County Florida Federal Census Records, 1935 & 1945 Manatee County Florida State Census Records, John Ballard (Kindmind1@aol.com)

* *1930 - Living in Myakka, Manatee Co., FL - Ballard, Vinnie 23 FL, Nora 23 FL, Allen 2 5/12 FL, Harry 1 2/12 FL*
* *1935 - Living in Manatee Co., FL - Ballard, Vinnie 28, Lenora 28, Allen 7, Harry 6, Clyde 4, Dave 2, Loure 1*
* *1945 - Living in Manatee Co., FL - Ballard, Vinson 38, Lenora 38, Allen 17, Harry 16, Clyde 14, Dave 13, Lois 11, Alfred 9, Joyce 2*

54. J. ALVIN "AL"[8] BALLARD (ALVIN MONROE[7], LEWIS[6], WHORTON[5], JESSE[4], JOHN[3], JOSEPH[2], JOHN[1]) *was born Sep 1861 in GA, and died Aft. 1900. He married* ELLA. *She was born Jun 1866 in GA, and died Aft. 1900.*

Notes for J. ALVIN *"AL" BALLARD:*

Source: 1900 Manatee County Florida Federal Census Records
* 1900 - Living in Sandy, Manatee Co., FL - Ballard, AL - Sept 1861 GA , Ella - June 1866 GA, Lee - June 1889, Al - June 1891, living next door to Perry Ballard on one side and Mash on the other.
FL

Children of J. BALLARD and ELLA are:
     i.   LEE[9] BALLARD, b. Jun 1889, FL; d. Aft. 1900.
    ii.   AL BALLARD, b. Jun 1891, FL; d. Aft. 1900.

55. WILLIAM MOSES[8] BALLARD (WILLIAM MOSES[7], JESSE[6], WHORTON[5], JESSE[4], JOHN[3], JOSEPH[2], JOHN[1]) was born 05 Mar 1849 in Red Oak Coweta Co., GA, and died 02 Jan 1940 in Ohio, Hamilton Co., TX. He married ANNA ELECTRA CARTER 17 Jul 1873 in Hamilton Co., TX, daughter of JAMES CARTER and ELIZABETH BEAUCHAMP. She was born 25 Apr 1855 in Hamilton Co., TX, and died 25 Mar 1891 in Hamilton Co., TX.

Notes for WILLIAM MOSES BALLARD:
Source: Evelyn Ballard, 1903-1940 Texas Death Index.
* Buried Live Oak Cemetery. Hamilton TX

More About WILLIAM MOSES BALLARD:
Burial: Live Oak Cemetery, Ohio, Hamilton Co., TX

More About ANNA ELECTRA CARTER:
Burial: Live Oak Cemetery, Ohio, Hamilton Co., TX

Children of WILLIAM BALLARD and ANNA CARTER are:
     i.   MARTHA EMMA LOU[9] BALLARD, b. 22 May 1874, Ohio, Hamilton Co., TX; d. 30 May 1964, Live Oak Hamilton Co., TX; m. JOE PLEZ ARNETT, 20 Dec 1891; b. 02 Nov 1868, Louisville, KY; d. 31 Oct 1941, Hamilton Co., TX.

        Notes for MARTHA EMMA LOU BALLARD:
        Source: Evelyn Ballard

        More About MARTHA EMMA LOU BALLARD:
        Burial: Live Oak Cemetery, Ohio, Hamilton Co., TX

        Notes for JOE PLEZ ARNETT:
        Source: Hamilton County Texas Standard Certificate of Death

        More About JOE PLEZ ARNETT:
        Burial: Live Oak Cemetery, Ohio, Hamilton Co., TX

    ii.   JAMES OSCAR BALLARD, b. 08 May 1876, Ohio, Hamilton Co., TX; d. 09 May 1937, Live Oak, Hamilton Co., TX; m. (1) MARGUITE "MAGGIE" LIBBY SCOTT; b. 11 Jul 1878; d. 21 Apr 1931; m. (2) MATTIE HULLUM; b. 15 Nov 1887; d. 20 Jul 1973.

        Notes for JAMES OSCAR BALLARD:
        Source: Evelyn Ballard, (Codeman432@aol.com)

        More About JAMES OSCAR BALLARD:
        Burial: Live Oak Cemetery, Ohio, Hamilton Co., TX

        More About MARGUITE "MAGGIE" LIBBY SCOTT:
        Burial: Live Oak Cemetery, Ohio, Hamilton Co., TX

        More About MATTIE HULLUM:

Burial: Greenwood Cemetery, Teague, Freestone Co., TX

iii. NOAH G. BALLARD, b. 03 Jun 1879, Ohio, Hamilton Co., TX; d. 15 Mar 1882, Live Oak, Hamilton Co., TX.

More About NOAH G. BALLARD:
Burial: Live Oak Cemetery, Ohio, Hamilton Co., TX

iv. WILLIAM ALMER BALLARD, b. 30 May 1880, Ohio, Hamilton Co., TX; d. 1946, FT Worth, Tarrant Co., TX.

v. MARY ELMA BALLARD, b. 30 May 1880, Ohio, Hamilton Co., TX; d. 14 Dec 1973, Hico, Hamilton Co., TX.

Notes for MARY ELMA BALLARD:
Source: Evelyn Ballard

vi. THOMAS ASHLEY BALLARD, b. 28 May 1882, Ohio, Hamilton Co., TX; d. OR.

vii. FLORENCE ANN BALLARD, b. 15 Feb 1884, Ohio, Hamilton Co., TX; d. Aug 1940, CA; m. SILAS JACKSON.

viii. SAMUEL LEWIS BALLARD, b. 06 Feb 1886, Ohio, Hamilton Co., TX; d. 18 Nov 1973, Houston, Harris Co., TX; m. MOLLIE ANN LECROY, 12 Aug 1906; b. 11 Nov 1886; d. 09 Jan 1971.

More About SAMUEL LEWIS BALLARD:
Burial: Live Oak Cemetery. Hamilton TX

More About MOLLIE ANN LECROY:
Burial: Live Oak Cemetery, Ohio, Hamilton Co., TX

ix. MARTIN LUTHER BALLARD, b. 19 Aug 1887, Ohio, Hamilton Co., TX; m. STELLA JONES, 1910.

Notes for MARTIN LUTHER BALLARD:
Source: Evelyn Ballard

x. ETTA JANE BALLARD, b. 27 Mar 1889, Ohio, Hamilton Co., TX; m. HENRY GREEN, 1910.

xi. ORA EDNA BALLARD, b. 02 Jan 1891, Ohio, Hamilton Co., TX; d. 22 May 1891, Ohio, Hamilton Co., TX.

Notes for ORA EDNA BALLARD:
Source: Evelyn Ballard Family Group Sheets

More About ORA EDNA BALLARD:
Burial: Live Oak Cemetery, Ohio, Hamilton Co., TX

xii. OLA ETHEL BALLARD, b. 03 Jan 1891, Ohio, Hamilton Co., TX; d. 06 Nov 1977, Hamilton Co., OH; m. MORRIS PAUL DITTRICH, 14 May 1911; b. 08 Aug 1889, Bosque Co., TX; d. 15 Jan 1970, Eastland Co., TX.

More About OLA ETHEL BALLARD:
Burial: Live Oak Cemetery, Ohio, Hamilton Co., TX

More About MORRIS PAUL DITTRICH:
Burial: DeLeon, Comanche Co., TX

56. CLAIBORNE "DUTCH" LORENZO[8] BALLARD (WILLIAM MOSES[7], JESSE[6], WHORTON[5], JESSE[4], JOHN[3], JOSEPH[2], JOHN[1]) was born 05 May 1856 in Red Oak, Campbell Co., GA, and died 26 Apr 1937 in Clayton Co., GA. He married *SARAH CATHERINE "KATE" LEE* 21 Nov 1879 in Fayette Co., GA, daughter of *SEABORN LEE* and *ELIZABETH THAMES*. She was born 23 Dec 1859 in Fayette Co., GA, and died 03 Nov 1928 in Clayton Co., GA.

Notes for CLAIBORNE "DUTCH" LORENZO BALLARD:
Source: Hollis and Oliver Ballard notes, Lloyd Russ Ballard, Evelyn Ballard, Chris Gardner (grasp1@bellsouth.net)

More About CLAIBORNE "DUTCH" LORENZO BALLARD:
Burial: Forest Grove Baptist Cemetery, Forest Park, Clayton Co., GA

More About SARAH CATHERINE "KATE" LEE:
Burial: Forest Grove Baptist Cemetery, Clayton Co., GA

Children of CLAIBORNE BALLARD and SARAH LEE are:

    i.   WILLIAM KIMSEY "KIM"[9] BALLARD, b. 01 Nov 1880, Kimsey Station Clayton Co., GA; d. 17 Jul 1969, Hapeville, Fulton Co. GA; m. (1) FLORA R. D. C. DANIEL, 12 Nov 1902, Atlanta, Fulton Co., GA; b. 30 Oct 1882, Atlanta, Fulton Co., GA; d. 1957; m. (2) EMMA JONES, 15 Nov 1959, Hapeville, Fulton Co., GA; b. Abt. 1880.

        Notes for WILLIAM KIMSEY "KIM" BALLARD:
        Source: Oliver and Hollis Ballard notes, Chris Gardner (grasp1@bellsouth.net)

        More About WILLIAM KIMSEY "KIM" BALLARD:
        Burial: Forest Grove Baptist Cemetery., Forest Park, GA

    ii.   HORACE GREELEY BALLARD, b. 03 Dec 1882, Forest Park, Clayton Co. GA; d. 07 Nov 1967, Moultrie, Colquitt Co., GA; m. MAYME ALMA TONEY, 24 Dec 1906, Clayton Co., GA; b. 30 Sep 1887; d. 25 Apr 1960, Moultrie, Colquitt Co., GA.

        Notes for HORACE GREELEY BALLARD:
        Source: Chris Gardner (grasp1@bellsouth.net)

        More About HORACE GREELEY BALLARD:
        Burial: Westview Cemetery Moultrie

    iii.   ROBERT LEE BALLARD, b. 19 Jan 1885, Forest Park, Clayton Co., GA; d. 16 Jan 1971, Clayton Co., GA; m. LILLIAN SCHANTZ, 26 Dec 1926, Louisville, KY; b. Abt. 1885.

        More About ROBERT LEE BALLARD:
        Burial: Glenwood Cemetery.

    iv.   ANNIE BALLARD, b. 19 Mar 1887, Forest Park, Clayton Co., GA; d. 28 May 1962, Atlanta, Fulton Co., GA; m. WARD BEECHER DUVALL, DR., 24 Sep 1913, Clayton Co., GA; b. Abt. 1887.

        More About ANNIE BALLARD:
        Burial: Westview Cemetery Moultrie GA

    v.   MATTIE LOIS BALLARD, b. 07 Mar 1889, Forest Park, Clayton Co, GA; d. 02 Feb 1983, Sandersville Washington Co., GA; m. FRED BELL, 08 Nov 1916, Clayton Co., GA; b. Abt. 1889.

        More About MATTIE LOIS BALLARD:
        Burial: Oak Ridge Cemetery.

    vi.   IRBY SEABORN BALLARD, b. 03 Jun 1892, Forest Park, Clayton Co., GA; d. 06 Feb 1967, Akron OH;

m. SARAH IRWIN MCCORMICK, 03 Jun 1920, Gary IN; b. Abt. 1892.

More About IRBY SEABORN BALLARD:
Burial: Mt. Peace Cemetery.

More About SARAH IRWIN MCCORMICK:
Burial: Mt. Peace Cemetery.

vii.   RUCKER OLIVIA BALLARD, b. 01 Dec 1894, Forest Park, Clayton Co., GA; d. 22 Sep 1984, Atlanta, Fulton Co., GA; m. WILLIAM CHARLES MASON, 18 Jun 1920, Clayton Co., GA.

More About RUCKER OLIVIA BALLARD:
Burial: Forest Park Baptist Cemetery

More About WILLIAM CHARLES MASON:
Burial: Forest Park Baptist Cemetery

viii.   MARTIS OLIVER BALLARD, b. 30 Oct 1896, Forest Park, Clayton Co. GA; d. 08 Dec 1979, East Point Fulton Co., GA; m. CHRISTINE OMEGA BROWN, 26 Dec 1922, Gay, Meriwether Co., GA; b. 04 Dec 1900.

More About MARTIS OLIVER BALLARD:
Burial: Hillcrest Cemetery

ix.   JAMES PEBBLE "JIMMY" BALLARD, b. 30 Apr 1900, Forest Park, Clayton Co. GA; d. 01 Apr 1950, Akron Summit Co., OH; m. MARY DELORES COX, 02 Jun 1928, Akron Summit Co., OH; b. Abt. 1900.

More About JAMES PEBBLE "JIMMY" BALLARD:
Burial: Rose Hill Cemetery

x.   MARY ELIZABETH BALLARD, b. 19 Feb 1902, Forest Park, Clayton Co., GA; d. 25 Nov 1983, Columbus GA; m. ALVIN FRANKIN BRADFIELD/BRADFORD, 26 Nov 1926, Fairfax AL; b. Abt. 1900.

More About MARY ELIZABETH BALLARD:
Burial: City Cemetery West Point GA

xi.   KATHLEEN BALLARD, b. 04 Mar 1904, Forest Park, Clayton Co., GA; d. 07 Jan 1993; m. ALBERT MASON, 17 Jun 1927, Clayton Co., GA; b. 1895; d. 1990.

More About KATHLEEN BALLARD:
Burial: Restland Memorial. Park

More About ALBERT MASON:
Burial: Restland Memorial. Park

57. MATILDA "MATTIE" LOU EMMA[8] BALLARD (WILLIAM MOSES[7], JESSE[6], WHORTON[5], JESSE[4], JOHN[3], JOSEPH[2], JOHN[1]) was born 20 Aug 1863 in Red Oak Coweta Co., GA, and died 1930 in Americus Sumter Co., GA. She married JAMES LEWIS CROW 05 Nov 1881 in Clayton Co., GA, son of WILLIAM CROW and ELIZABETH STOVALL. He was born 04 Apr 1860 in Forsyth Co., GA, and died 1931 in Americus Sumter Co., GA.

Notes for MATILDA "MATTIE" LOU EMMA BALLARD:

Source: Frances Puckett
* Went by Mattie, could be Martha

Notes for JAMES LEWIS CROW:
Source: Frances Puckett
Buried in the Oak Grove Cemetery Americus, Sumter Co., GA

Children of MATILDA BALLARD and JAMES CROW are:

  i. CLINTON MOSES[9] CROW, b. 05 May 1883, Forsythe Co., GA; d. 16 Apr 1947, Macon, Bibb Co., GA; m. ADA FRANCES "FANNIE" MERK, 09 Aug 1903; b. 04 Sep 1887, Jackson Co., GA; d. 19 Feb 1983, Macon, Bibb Co., GA.

   Notes for CLINTON MOSES CROW:
   Source: Frances Puckett

  ii. BRICE LOFTON CROW, b. 24 Jun 1886, Forsyth Co., GA; d. 11 Nov 1945, Americus, Sumter Co., GA; m. ANNIE E. MCCARTNEY, 14 Apr 1907, Wilcox Co., GA; b. 21 Dec 1877, Wilcox Co., GA; d. 29 Oct 1948, Americus, Sumter Co., GA.

   Notes for BRICE LOFTON CROW:
   Source: Frances Puckett

  iii. CLARA CROW, b. 13 Nov 1890; d. 07 Aug 1974, Macon Bibb Co., GA; m. ERNEST VIRGIL BROGDON, 07 Aug 1910, Amboy Turner Co., GA; b. 03 Nov 1884; d. 04 Aug 1971, Macon Bibb Co., GA.

58. MARY FRANCES[8] BALLARD (WHORTON FLETCHER[7], JESSE[6], WHORTON[5], JESSE[4], JOHN[3], JOSEPH[2], JOHN[1]) was born 22 Mar 1850 in GA, and died 22 Oct 1930 in GA. She married HENRY L. SAMPLES OR SAMPLER 27 Sep 1868 in GA.

Child of MARY BALLARD and HENRY SAMPLER is:

  i. WILLIAM MAEHEL[9] SAMPLER, b. 16 Jan 1872, Coweta Co., GA.

59. JAMES MADISON[8] BALLARD (WHORTON FLETCHER[7], JESSE[6], WHORTON[5], JESSE[4], JOHN[3], JOSEPH[2], JOHN[1]) was born 03 Aug 1852 in Coweta Co, GA, and died 09 Dec 1916 in Wood Co. TX. He married LAURA WESTON MCKOY 20 Apr 1879 in Campbell Co., GA, daughter of BENJAMIN MCKOY and MARY NEAL. She was born 28 Nov 1859 in Campbell Co., GA, and died 18 Apr 1940 in Wood Co TX.

Notes for JAMES MADISON BALLARD:
Source: Evelyn Johnson Ballard, Kathren (KKarnes867@aol.com), Joe LaRue (jolaru@eastex.net)
* Moved from GA to Wood Co., TX

Children of JAMES BALLARD and LAURA MCKOY are:

  i. SARAH SELENA "SALLIE"[9] BALLARD, b. 04 Feb 1880, GA; d. 24 Jan 1935, Wood Co., TX.
  ii. WILLIAM FRANKLIN BALLARD, b. 06 Jun 1881, Wood Co., TX; d. 13 Jul 1881, TX.
  iii. JAMES THOMAS BALLARD, b. 01 Nov 1882, Camp Co., TX; d. 03 Nov 1935, TX.
  iv. ROBERT LEONIDAS BALLARD, b. 30 Sep 1884, Wood Co., TX; d. 22 Nov 1889, TX.
  v. AARON CORNELIUS BALLARD, b. 17 Oct 1886, Wood Co., TX; m. (1) MYRITE MCLARTY; m. (2) DONA BOLES, 1907.
  vi. CHARLES COLUMBUS BALLARD, b. 09 Jan 1889, Hopkins Co., TX; d. 06 Oct 1971, Denver Co., CO; m. ALICE VIRGINIA WILSHIRE, 06 Jul 1916.
  vii. ALBERT BENJAMIN BALLARD, b. 27 Jan 1891, Hopkins Co., TX; d. 07 Oct 1971, TX; m. JULIA ALICE FLORENCE ROBISON, 14 Nov 1915.
  viii. JESSIE MAE BALLARD, b. 16 Oct 1893, TX; d. 05 Jan 1973, Pittsburg, Camp Co., TX; m. JOHN HOUSTON BOYD, 16 Dec 1908.
  ix. NEPPIE HOWINGTON BALLARD, b. 14 Jan 1896, Wood Co., TX; d. 19 May 1978, Gilmer, Upshur Co., TX; m. CHARLES ADAM BLUNDELL, 02 Feb 1913.

     x.   *FLETCHER MCKOY "PETE" BALLARD, b. 25 Aug 1899, Hopkins Co., TX; d. 06 Dec 1978, Wink TX; m. ALICE EVELYN JONSON, 18 Mar 1932.*

        Notes for FLETCHER MCKOY "PETE" BALLARD:
        Living as of 1970 in Wink, Winkler Co, TX

60. *THOMAS PARKS[8] BALLARD (WHORTON FLETCHER[7], JESSE[6], WHORTON[5], JESSE[4], JOHN[3], JOSEPH[2], JOHN[1]) was born 02 Nov 1853 in Coweta Co., GA, and died 07 Sep 1929 in Tyus, Carroll Co., GA. He married MARY ELIZABETH MCCAW 09 Nov 1876 in GA. She was born 01 Aug 1860, and died 02 Feb 1922 in Centralatchie, Hearde Co., GA.*

Children of THOMAS BALLARD and MARY MCCAW are:
     i.   *WILLIAM FLETCHER[9] BALLARD, b. 06 Feb 1878.*
     ii. *ROBERT S. BALLARD, b. 26 Jan 1880.*
     iii. *THOMAS ISOM BALLARD, b. 05 Dec 1881; m. LULU, 17 May 1905.*
     iv. *HOWARD VOLLEY BALLARD, b. 14 Apr 1884.*
     v.   *MAGGIE BEATRICE BALLARD, b. 10 Sep 1886.*
     vi. *JESSIE OWEN BALLARD, b. 24 Jan 1889.*
     vii. *JOSEY ANN BALLARD, b. 20 Jan 1893.*
     viii. *MARION HUBERT BALLARD, b. 28 Dec 1906.*

61. *MARTHA ADELINE[8] BALLARD (WHORTON FLETCHER[7], JESSE[6], WHORTON[5], JESSE[4], JOHN[3], JOSEPH[2], JOHN[1]) was born 06 Feb 1856 in Coweta Co., GA, and died 02 Mar 1939 in Carroll Co., GA. She married OSCAR G. ENTREKIN 1879 in GA, son of ELIJAH ENTREKIN and ELIZABETH SHAW. He was born 26 Dec 1860, and died 19 Aug 1939 in Carroll Co., GA.*

Notes for MARTHA ADELINE BALLARD:
Source: Philip Entrekin (pentrekin@sprintmail.com)

More About MARTHA ADELINE BALLARD:
Burial: Pleasant View Baptist Church Cemetery, Carrollton, Carroll Co., GA

Notes for OSCAR G. ENTREKIN:
source: Phillip Entrekin (pentrekin@sprintmail.com)

More About OSCAR G. ENTREKIN:
Burial: Pleasant View Baptist Church Cemetery Carrollton, Carroll Co., GA

Children of MARTHA BALLARD and OSCAR ENTREKIN are:
     i.   *FLETCHER E.[9] ENTREKIN, b. 1881.*
     ii. *LOYD ENTREKIN, b. 23 Mar 1884; m. BEATRICE WALLS.*
     iii. *WALTER WILLIAM ENTREKIN, b. 1887; d. 1960; m. EFFIE SHIREY.*

62. *LORANAH ALICE[8] BALLARD (THOMAS SANFORD[7], JESSE[6], WHORTON[5], JESSE[4], JOHN[3], JOSEPH[2], JOHN[1]) was born 20 Dec 1856 in Campbell Co., GA, and died 02 May 1930 in Temple TX. She married JAMES EVANS HARRIS 08 Nov 1874 in TX. He was born Abt. 1855, and died 1915.*

Notes for LORANAH ALICE BALLARD:
Source: Mike Montgomery

Children of LORANAH BALLARD and JAMES HARRIS are:
     i.   *ELIZABETH GERTRUDE[9] HARRIS, b. Oct 1875; m. ROBERT CARDWELL.*
     ii. *LENNETTE HARRIS, b. 26 Jul 1877, Belton TX; m. JOHN T. PARKER; b. Abt. 1855.*
     iii. *THOMAS HENRY HARRIS, b. Feb 1880, Wilson Co TX; m. ELLA QUINN; b. Abt. 1880.*

iv. *ABNER HARRIS, b. 1882, Caldwell Co TX; m. LUDIE SIMMS.*
v. *KITTY ETHEL HARRIS, b. 30 Dec 1884, Caldwell Co., TX; m. CHARLES F. PARKER; b. Abt. 1880.*

63. JOHN COLEMAN[8] BALLARD (THOMAS SANFORD[7], JESSE[6], WHORTON[5], JESSE[4], JOHN[3], JOSEPH[2], JOHN[1]) *was born 28 Sep 1858 in Campbell Co., GA, and died 25 Aug 1894. He married EPSIE DUNCAN 04 Jan 1881 in Caldwell Co., TX. She was born Abt. 1860.*

Notes for JOHN COLEMAN BALLARD:
Source: Mike Montgomery, Dean Moore (dean@telemail.com.py)

Children of JOHN BALLARD and EPSIE DUNCAN are:
i. *LUKE LINNIS[9] BALLARD, b. 24 Sep 1883, Caldwell Co., TX; d. 08 Dec 1945, Bentonville, Benton Co., AR; m. MAUDE KENNEDY, 1907.*

More About LUKE LINNIS BALLARD:
Burial: San Marcos TX

ii. *JESSE BALLARD, b. 1886; d. 1888.*

More About JESSE BALLARD:
Burial: Clear Fork Cemetery. near Lockhart TX

iii. *FRANCES ELIZABETH BALLARD, b. 30 Sep 1890, Caldwell Co., TX; m. JAPHET JACKSON BAKER, 13 Sep 1903.*
iv. *ANNIE LAURIE BALLARD, b. 15 Aug 1893, TX; d. 16 May 1916; m. FRANK GROWE.*

64. THOMAS SANFORD[8] BALLARD, JR. (THOMAS SANFORD[7], JESSE[6], WHORTON[5], JESSE[4], JOHN[3], JOSEPH[2], JOHN[1]) *was born 25 Sep 1862 in Hopkins TX, and died Abt. 1891 in Dripping Springs, Hays Co., TX. He married HARRIETT MCCARLEY 09 Jan 1886 in Caldwell Co., TX. She was born 20 Jan 1862 in TX, and died Aft. 1891 in Luling, Caldwell Co., TX.*

Notes for THOMAS SANFORD BALLARD, JR.:
Source: Mike Montgomery

Children of THOMAS BALLARD and HARRIETT MCCARLEY are:
i. *CHARLES EDWARD[9] BALLARD, b. 16 Jan 1887, Caldwell Co., TX; d. 29 Jul 1950, Luling, Caldwell Co., TX; m. MINNIE THOMPSON.*
ii. *WILLIAM HUGH BALLARD, b. 10 Dec 1887, Caldwell Co., TX; d. 08 Feb 1967, Luling, Caldwell Co., TX; m. (1) CLEMA ALLEN, 10 Dec 1913, Luling, Caldwell Co., TX; m. (2) PEARL BIGGS, 1947; b. Luling, Caldwell Co., TX.*
More About WILLIAM HUGH BALLARD:
Burial: McNeill Cemetery

iii. *HENRY OSCAR BALLARD, b. 26 Dec 1889, Caldwell Co., TX; d. Luling, Caldwell Co., TX; m. THELMA PRIRKING, 19 Nov 1921.*
iv. *MARTHA ELIZABETH BALLARD, b. 06 Jun 1891, TX; m. (1) JOHN PATTON, 1906; m. (2) WILLIAM WILLINGHAM, 1911.*

65. WILLIAM MARVIN[8] BALLARD (THOMAS SANFORD[7], JESSE[6], WHORTON[5], JESSE[4], JOHN[3], JOSEPH[2], JOHN[1]) *was born 1866 in Hopkins Co., TX, and died Nov 1886 in Caldwell Co., TX. He married MATTIE B. FULLER 26 Oct 1885 in Lockhart, Caldwell Co., TX. She was born 12 Jul 1868 in Caldwell Co., TX.*

Child of WILLIAM BALLARD and MATTIE FULLER is:
i. *WILLIAM MARVIN[9] BALLARD, b. 31 Jul 1886, Caldwell Co., TX; d. 05 Jan 1962, Prairie Grove, Washington*

Co., AR; m. LILLIE ELIZABETH THURMAN; b. 20 Dec 1890, Farmington AR; d. 15 Jun 1969, bur. Summers Cemetery. Summers AR.

Notes for WILLIAM MARVIN BALLARD:
Source: 1920 Washington County Arkansas Federal Census Records, 1930 Clay County Texas Federal Census Records, Mike Montgomery
* 1920 - Living in Washington Co., AR - Ballard, William M 34 TX TX TX, Lily 29 AR AR AR, Jessie 9 AR, Clarence 6 AR, Ellis 3 3/12 OK
* 1930 - Living in Clay Co., TX - Ballard, William M 45 TX US TX, Lilly E 39 AR AR AR, Jessie W 17 AR, Lester C 16 AR, Ellis A 14 OK, Elzie G 8 AR, Evi I 5 TX, Neva L 2 11/12 TX, Juanita 0/12

66. EMILY DONA[8] BALLARD (THOMAS SANFORD[7], JESSE[6], WHORTON[5], JESSE[4], JOHN[3], JOSEPH[2], JOHN[1]) was born 24 Nov 1869 in Hopkins Co., TX, and died 20 Mar 1921 in San Antonio, Bexar Co., TX. She married GEORGE WASHINGTON HILLIS 17 Jul 1889 in TX. He was born Jul 1862 in MS, and died 20 Mar 1921 in San Angelo, Tom Green Co., TX.

Children of EMILY BALLARD and GEORGE HILLIS are:
    i.   CARRIE ELIZABETH[9] HILLIS, b. 16 May 1890, Caldwell Co., TX; d. 29 Jan 1963, Martindale, Caldwell Co., TX; m. WILLIAM DONATHAN WILLIAMSON; b. 12 Nov 1881; d. 1935, Martindale, Caldwell Co., TX.
    ii. BENNIE OLA HILLIS, b. 16 Mar 1892.
    iii. NOLAN C. HILLIS, b. 04 Nov 1894.
    iv. VERNON JAMES HILLIS, b. 19 Jul 1898.

67. JAMES MONROE[8] BALLARD (THOMAS SANFORD[7], JESSE[6], WHORTON[5], JESSE[4], JOHN[3], JOSEPH[2], JOHN[1]) was born 24 Jan 1870 in 3/24/1871 Hopkins Co., TX, and died 21 Nov 1932 in Graham, Carter Co., OK. He married CORA ELVA RATLIFF 27 Dec 1893 in Caldwell Co., TX. She was born 27 Aug 1878 in Caldwell Co., TX, and died 15 Apr 1961 in Oklahoma City, Oklahoma Co., OK.

Children of JAMES BALLARD and CORA RATLIFF are:
    i.   HOWARD CHARLES[9] BALLARD, b. 10 Feb 1895, Gonzales Co., TX; m. (1) DOROTHY O'BRYAN; m. (2) TINSIE O'BRYAN.
    ii. CORINE ELIZABETH BALLARD, b. 12 Feb 1900, Gonzales Co., TX; m. R. B. "BUCK" CREW.
    iii. GENEVA PERNICE BALLARD, b. 14 Jan 1908, Graham, Carter Co., OK; m. PETE WELLS.
    iv. LEE BALLARD, b. 02 Mar 1910; m. MAY LEAVIER.
    v. ALICE REIDA BALLARD, b. 09 Nov 1911, Graham, Carter Co., OK; m. ADRIAN L. McGOODWIN.
    vi. Q. B. BALLARD, b. 11 Jun 1913, Graham OK.
    vii. WOODROW SUNDAY BALLARD, b. 05 Jun 1916, Graham, Carter Co., OK; m. NORMA JEAN BAKER.
    viii. ROY McADOO BALLARD, b. 24 Jul 1918, Graham, Carter Co., OK; m. GERALDINE HALL.

68. WESLEY CHAPIEL[8] BALLARD (THOMAS SANFORD[7], JESSE[6], WHORTON[5], JESSE[4], JOHN[3], JOSEPH[2], JOHN[1]) was born 19 Jan 1873 in Hopkins Co., TX, and died 03 May 1930 in Gonzales TX. He married MOLLIE ELIZABETH BERRY 12 Aug 1897 in Fayette Co TX. She was born 29 Oct 1877 in La Grange Fayette TX, and died 12 Apr 1904 in Gonzales TX.

Notes for WESLEY CHAPIEL BALLARD:
Source: Mike Montgomery

Children of WESLEY BALLARD and MOLLIE BERRY are:
    i.   JENNIE LEE[9] BALLARD, b. 08 Jun 1898, TX; m. H. FLOYD TAYLOR.
    ii. OSCAR WESLEY BALLARD, b. 21 Aug 1902, TX; m. DELLA JEWEL BEAVER; b. 30 Jul 1910.
9. CHARLES BEAMON[8] BALLARD (THOMAS SANFORD[7], JESSE[6], WHORTON[5], JESSE[4], JOHN[3], JOSEPH[2], JOHN[1]) was born

11 Jun 1875 in Hopkins Co., TX, and died 24 Oct 1920 in Ardmore OK. He married JENNIE ELLEN BERRY 1898 in Fayette Co., TX. She was born 12 Oct 1879 in La Grange, Fayette C., TX, and died 27 May 1904 in Dallas, Dallas Co., TX.

Children of CHARLES BALLARD and JENNIE BERRY are:
    i.   MAE ELIZABETH[9] BALLARD, b. 06 May 1899.
    ii. BELLA LUSINDA BALLARD, b. 06 May 1901.

70. ARTHUR ELMER[8] BALLARD (*THOMAS SANFORD[7], JESSE[6], WHORTON[5], JESSE[4], JOHN[3], JOSEPH[2], JOHN[1]*) was born 20 Aug 1877 in Caldwell Co., TX, and died 30 Dec 1944 in Belton, Bee Co., TX. He married (1) MINNIE MAE MCNATT 05 Oct 1897 in Muldoon TX. She was born 30 Jul 1883 in Fayette Co., TX, and died 30 May 1907. He married (2) MYRTLE IVY HILLIS 20 Jul 1903 in Lone Grove OK. She was born in TX, and died Aft. 1930.

Notes for ARTHUR ELMER BALLARD:
Source: 1900 Fayette County Texas Federal Census Records, 1920 Marshall County Oklahoma Federal Census Records, 1930 Bell County Texas Federal Census Records
* 1910 - Living in Fayette Co., TX - Ballard, Arthur - Aug 1877 TX GA GA, Minnie - July 1883 TX TX TX
* 1920 - Living in Marshall Co., OK - Ballard, Arthur 42 TX GA GA, Myrtle 42 TX TX TX, Dow 10 OK, Jessie Mae 15 TX
* 1930 - Living in Belton, Bell Co., TX - Ballard, Arthur E 52 TX GA GA, Myrtle 2 TX, Dow A 20 OK, Arthur E Jr 12 TX

Children of ARTHUR BALLARD and MYRTLE HILLIS are:
    i.   JESSIE MAE[9] BALLARD, b. 19 Dec 1904, TX; d. Aft. 1920.
    ii. ALONZO DOW BALLARD, b. 06 Apr 1909, Marshall Co., TX; d. Aft. 1930.
    iii. ARTHUR ELMER BALLARD, JR., b. 20 Jun 1926, Bell Co., TX; d. Aft. 1930.

71. WALTER HOUSTON[8] BALLARD (*THOMAS SANFORD[7], JESSE[6], WHORTON[5], JESSE[4], JOHN[3], JOSEPH[2], JOHN[1]*) was born 29 Jan 1881 in Caldwell Co., TX, and died 12 Aug 1944 in Caldwell Co., TX. He married ANNIE ISABEL JONES 22 Jul 1903 in Fayette Co., TX. She was born 09 Jan 1884 in Fayette Co., TX, and died 25 Dec 1970 in Austin, Travis Co., TX.

Child of WALTER BALLARD and ANNIE JONES is:
    i.   ROBERT LESTER[9] BALLARD, b. 22 Dec 1906, Waelder, Gonzales Co., TX; m. ZULA MAE HIGGINBOTHAM.

72. ROXANNA J.[8] BALLARD (*THOMAS SANFORD[7], JESSE[6], WHORTON[5], JESSE[4], JOHN[3], JOSEPH[2], JOHN[1]*) was born 01 Sep 1882 in Lockhart, Caldwell Co., TX, and died 17 Mar 1952 in San Angelo, Tom Green Co., TX. She married (1) WILLIE S. POLLARD. He was born 26 Aug 1876 in TX, and died 19 Jan 1900. She married (2) ARTHUR WILLIAM MONTGOMERY 18 Oct 1903 in Florence, Williamson Co., TX, son of JOHN MONTGOMERY and MARY MORRISON. He was born 26 Mar 1885 in Florence, Williamson Co., TX, and died 12 Nov 1962 in San Angelo, Tom Green Co., TX.

Notes for ROXANNA J. BALLARD:
Source: Mike Montgomery (michael@princeton.edu), Dean Moore (dean@telemail.com.py)

Notes for ARTHUR WILLIAM MONTGOMERY:
Source: Mike Montgomery

Child of ROXANNA BALLARD and WILLIE POLLARD is:
    i.   WILLIAM MARSHALL[9] POLLARD, b. 24 Sep 1900.

Children of ROXANNA BALLARD and ARTHUR MONTGOMERY are:
    ii. ARTHUR VERNON[9] MONTGOMERY, b. 08 Sep 1904, Florence, Williamson Co., TX; d. 05 Oct 1977,

Sinton, San Patricio Co., TX; m. (1) MATTIE MOZELLE LEVERETT; b. 06 Oct 1909, Birdston, Navarro Co., TX; d. 13 Feb 1989, Corpus Christi, Nueces Co., TX; m. (2) IRBY ALILEEN SHARP, 02 Sep 1921, Sinton, San Patricio Co., TX; b. 16 Oct 1904, Gatesville, Coryell Co., TX; d. 09 Aug 1979, Tucson, Pima Co., AZ.

    iii.   *BERTHOLD LAMARR MONTGOMERY, b. 12 May 1908, Florence, Williamson Co., TX; d. Jun 1962; m. KATHRYN.*

    iv.   *BALLARD U. MONTGOMERY, b. 28 Nov 1912, Taft, San Patricio Co., TX; d. 05 Aug 1988, Corpus Christi Nueces TX; m. ADELE DODSON, 26 Jun 1935, Sinton, San Patricio Co., TX; b. 07 Apr 1914, TX.*

    v.   *ERNEST EDWIN MONTGOMERY, b. 06 Oct 1914, Taft, San Patricio Co., TX; m. WILLA KATHLYNE FRENCH, 29 May 1936, Sinton San Patricio TX; b. 21 Jan 1918.*

    vi.   *WESTON WENDELL MONTGOMERY, b. 12 Jan 1919, Sinton, San Patricio Co., TX; d. Feb 1978, Biloxi Harrison MS; m. FELICIA HEYMIGO; b. 03 Nov 1925, Puerto Rico.*

    vii.   *ROY GLENN MONTGOMERY, b. 20 Feb 1921, Sinton, San Patricio Co., TX; d. 11 May 1954, Big Spring, Howard Co., TX; m. LETA FAYE JENKINS, Abt. 1946; b. Abt. 1925.*

73. JAMES WILLIAM[8] BALLARD (*LEWIS J.*[7], *JAMES*[6], *WHORTON*[5], *JESSE*[4], *JOHN*[3], *JOSEPH*[2], *JOHN*[1]) was born 20 Feb 1845 in GA, and died 07 Aug 1906 in Henderson Co., TX. He married MARTHA JANE COWEN 10 Dec 1864 in Blount Co., AL, daughter of DAVID COWAN and ELIZABETH. She was born 18 Nov 1843, and died 29 Mar 1916.

Notes for JAMES WILLIAM BALLARD:
Source: 1870 Blount County Alabama Federal Census Records, 1880 Fayette County Alabama Federal Census Records, 1900 Henderson County Texas Federal Census Records, Kenneth Cook (Kcook@peoplescom.net)
* 1870 - Living in East Half, Blount Co., AL - Ballard, J W 25 blacksmith GA, Martha 26 AL, Mary 4 AL, S. E 2 AL, A D 1 AL
* 1880 - Living in Fayette Co., AL - Ballard, James W 35 farmer GA GA GA, Martha J 36 AL SC SC, Mary E 14 AL, Sarah E 12 AL, Toby A 10 AL, Piety 8 AL, William L 6 AL, Deller E 5 AL, George E 1 AL, Martha E 3/12 AL
* 1900 - Living in Henderson Co., TX - Ballard, J. W. - Feb 1845 GA GA GA, Martha J - Nov 1853 - 11 children 10 living, AL SC SC, Dora B - Dec 1881 AL, Lee - Nov 1883 AL and many boarders

More About JAMES WILLIAM BALLARD:
Burial: Cottonwood Cemetery, Eustace, Henderson Co., TX

Notes for MARTHA JANE COWEN:
Source: 1910 Henderson County Texas Federal Census Records
* 1910 - Living in Henderson Co., TX with daughter Mary E Bynum

More About MARTHA JANE COWEN:
Burial: Cottonwood Cemetery, Eustace, Henderson Co., TX

Children of JAMES BALLARD and MARTHA COWEN are:

    i.   *MARY ELIZABETH[9] BALLARD, b. 12 Mar 1866, Blount Co., AL; d. 23 Sep 1945, Eustace, Henderson Co. TX; m. ELIJAH COLUMBUS BYNUM, 25 Dec 1881, Fayette Co., AL; b. 16 Jan 1856, Blount Co., AL; d. 13 Apr 1947, Eustace, Henderson Co., TX.*

        More About MARY ELIZABETH BALLARD:
        Burial: Moorehead - Melton Cemetery, Eustace, Henderson Co., TX

        Notes for ELIJAH COLUMBUS BYNUM:
        Source: 1900- 1930 Henderson County Texas Federal Census Records
        * 1900 - Living in Henderson Co., TX - Bynum, Elijah C - Jan 1856 AL AL AL, Mary E - Mar 1866 - 6 children, 4 living AL AL AL, Benelly R - Nov 1885 AL, James E - Aug 1886 AL, Cordia M - May 1892 AL, Daniel B - June 1895 TX
        * 1910 - Living in Henderson Co., TX - Bynum, Elijah C 54 AL, Mary E 44 - 39 children 5 living AL, Carrie M 17 AL, Daniel B 14 TX, Quincia W 6 TX, Marthy M Ballard mother 66 - 11 children 9 living AL
        * 1920 - Living in Henderson Co., TX - Bynum, Elijah C 64 AL AL AL farmer, Mary E 53 AL,

Ruth Killingsworth 13 niece TX, Grace Bynum 8 TX, Quincy 16 TX, Bruce D 24 TX
* 1930 - Living in Henderson Co., TX - Bynum, Elijah H 74, Mary E 64, Grace 19, Charley B. Thornton 21

More About ELIJAH COLUMBUS BYNUM:
Burial: Moorehead-Melton Cemetery, Eustace, Henderson Co., TX

ii.   SARAH E. BALLARD, *b. 18 Aug 1868, Blount Co., AL; d. 25 Dec 1953; m.* ROSCOE S. WHEELER, *15 Nov 1888, Fayette Co., AL; b. 20 Feb 1867; d. 23 Jun 1943.*

More About SARAH E. BALLARD:
Burial: Moorehead-Melton Cemetery, Eustace, Henderson Co., TX

Notes for ROSCOE S. WHEELER:
Source: 1900 Henderson County Texas Federal Census Records
* 1900 - Living in Henderson Co., TX - Wheeler, R S - Sep 1866 AL, Sarah E - Aug 1867 2 children 2 living AL, Wm H - Sep 1889 AL, Rudolphus P - Apr 1897

More About ROSCOE S. WHEELER:
Burial: Moorehead-Melton Cemetery, Eustace, Henderson Co., TX

iii.   TOBY ARA D. BALLARD, *b. 02 Nov 1869, Blount Co., AL; d. 05 Jul 1926; m.* ELIJAH DANIEL COPPRELL, *08 Dec 1897, Henderson Co., TX; b. 30 Sep 1867; d. 13 Jan 1917.*

More About TOBY ARA D. BALLARD:
Burial: Moorehead-Melton Cemetery, Eustace, Henderson Co., TX

More About ELIJAH DANIEL COPPRELL:
Burial: Moorehead-Melton Cemetery, Eustace, Henderson Co., TX

iv.   PIETY E. BALLARD, *b. 13 Aug 1871, AL; d. 02 Nov 1915, Jones Co., TX; m.* WILLIAM DAYTON KILLINGSWORTH, *08 Dec 1887, Fayette Co., AL; b. 1867, Fayette Co., AL; d. 1933, Wortham, Freestone Co., TX.*

More About WILLIAM DAYTON KILLINGSWORTH:
Burial: Wortham Cemetery, Wortham, Freestone Co., TX

v.   WILLIAM LEWIS BALLARD, *b. 23 Aug 1873, Winfield AL; d. 10 May 1928, Denton Co., TX; m.* EULA GRAHAM, *04 Mar 1894, Henderson Co., TX; b. 12 May 1878; d. 20 May 1950, Eustace, Henderson Co. TX.*

Notes for WILLIAM LEWIS BALLARD:
Source: 1900-1930 Henderson County Texas Federal Census Records
* 1900 - Living in Henderson Co., TX - Ballard, William L Aug 1873 AL GA AL, Eula (married 6 yrs, 2 children 2 living) May 1878 TX MS TX, Aurthur Sep 1897 TX AL TX, Lockey (f) Aug 1899 TX AL TX
* 1910- Living in Henderson Co., TX - Ballard, Wm L - Aug 1873 36 AL GA AL, Eula - May 1878 32 TX 4 children 2 living, Arthur - Sept 1897 TX, Locky - Aug 1899 TX
* 1920 - Living in Henderson Co., TX - Ballard, William L 46 AL GA AL, Eula 41 TX MS TX, Arthur J 22 TX, Woodrow M 7 TX
* 1930 - Living in Henderson Co., TX - Ballard, William L 56 AL GA AL, Eula 51 TX MS TX, Woodrow 17 TX AL TX

More About WILLIAM LEWIS BALLARD:
Burial: Morehead-Milton Cemetery, Eustace, Henderson Co., TX

More About EULA GRAHAM:
Burial: Morehead-Milton Cemetery, Eustace, Henderson Co., TX

vi. DELLA E. BALLARD, *b. 15 Jan 1875, Fayette Co., AL; d. 14 Jul 1965, McKinney, Collin Co., TX; m.* MURRAY HEBRON WHEELER; *b. 06 Aug 1873, AL; d. 07 Oct 1959, Celina, Collin Co., TX.*

Notes for DELLA E. BALLARD:
Source: Collin County Texas Certificate of Death

More About DELLA E. BALLARD:
Burial: Pecan Grove Cemetery, McKinney, Collin Co., TX

More About MURRAY HEBRON WHEELER:
Burial: Pecan Grove Cemetery, McKinney, Collin Co., TX

vii. J. D. BALLARD, *b. 09 Dec 1876, Fayette Co., AL; d. 15 Jan 1879.*

More About J. D. BALLARD:
Burial: Ballard Family Cemetery, Stewart, Fayette Co., AL

viii. GEORGE E. BALLARD, *b. 14 Sep 1878, Fayette Co., AL; d. 05 Oct 1910; m.* JESSIE GRAHAM, *24 Dec 1902, Henderson Co., TX; b. 29 Jan 1882; d. 09 Sep 1954.*

Notes for GEORGE E. BALLARD:
Source: Kenneth Cook (Kcook@peoplescom.net), 1910 Henderson County Texas Federal Census Records
* 1910 - Living in Henderson Co., TX - Ballard, George E. 31 AL, Jesse (f) 28 TX, Verdie B 6 TX, Audie 5 TX, Buford 2 TX, William G 6/12 TX, Lee C. 6/12 TX

More About GEORGE E. BALLARD:
Burial: Cottonwood Cemetery, Eustace, Henderson Co., TX

Notes for JESSIE GRAHAM:
Source: 1930 Henderson County Texas Federal Census Records
* 1930 - Living in Henderson Co., TX - Ballard, Jessie 48 TX AL AL farmer, Verdie 26 TX, Ottie 25 TX, Buford 22 TX, Crayford? 20 TX

More About JESSIE GRAHAM:
Burial: Cottonwood Cemetery, Eustace, Henderson Co., TX

ix. MARTHA E. BALLARD, *b. 30 Mar 1880, Fayette Co., AL; d. 25 Nov 1921; m.* ROBERT H. WHITE, *1898, Henderson Co., TX; b. 28 Oct 1875; d. 26 Dec 1966.*

More About MARTHA E. BALLARD:
Burial: Morehead-Milton Cemetery, Eustace, Henderson Co., TX

More About ROBERT H. WHITE:
Burial: Morehead-Milton Cemetery, Eustace, Henderson Co., TX

x. DORA BELLE BALLARD, *b. 07 Dec 1881, Fayette Co., AL; d. 31 Oct 1905.*

More About DORA BELLE BALLARD:
Burial: Cottonwood Cemetery, Eustace, Henderson Co., TX

xi. LEE BALLARD, *b. 20 Nov 1883, Fayette Co., AL; d. 19 Dec 1956, Athens, Henderson Co., TX; m.* TRUDIE GREEN; *b. 25 Jan 1885; d. 24 Jul 1973.*

Notes for LEE BALLARD:
Source: WWII Registration Card, Henderson County Texas Certificate of Death

More About LEE BALLARD:
Burial: Morehead-Milton Cemetery, Eustace, Henderson Co., TX

More About TRUDIE GREEN:
Burial: Morehead-Milton Cemetery, Eustace, Henderson Co., TX

74. ELIZABETH[8] BALLARD (LEWIS J.[7], JAMES[6], WHORTON[5], JESSE[4], JOHN[3], JOSEPH[2], JOHN[1]) was born 1847 in GA, and died Aft. 1870. She married JAMES E. COWEN 09 Jul 1866 in Blount Co., AL. He was born Abt. 1840 in AL, and died Aft. 1870.

Notes for JAMES E. COWEN:
Source: 1870-1880 Marshall County Alabama Federal Census Records
* 1870 - Living in Marshall Co., AL - Cowan, James E 30 Farmer AL, Elizabeth 23 GA, Joan M 3 AL, William H 1
* 1880 - Living in Marshall Co., AL - Cowan, James 41, Elizabeth 33, Joann 13, William 11, Nichlas 10, James 8, Pinkney 5, Lewis 3, John 4/12

Children of ELIZABETH BALLARD and JAMES COWEN are:
  i.   JOAN M.[9] COWEN, b. Abt. 1867, AL; d. Aft. 1880.
  ii. WILLIAM H. COWEN, b. Abt. 1869, AL; d. Aft. 1880.
  iii. NICHOLAS COWEN, b. Abt. 1870, Marshall Co., AL; d. Aft. 1880.
  iv. JAMES COWEN, b. Abt. 1872, Marshall Co., AL; d. Aft. 1880.
  v.   PINKNEY COWEN, b. Abt. 1875, Marshall Co., AL; d. Aft. 1880.
  vi. LEWIS COWEN, b. Abt. 1877, Marshall Co., AL; d. Aft. 1880.
  vii. JOHN COWEN, b. Abt. 1880, Marshall Co., AL; d. Aft. 1880.

75. WILLIS ASBURY[8] BALLARD (LEWIS J.[7], JAMES[6], WHORTON[5], JESSE[4], JOHN[3], JOSEPH[2], JOHN[1]) was born 29 Jun 1848 in GA, and died 10 Sep 1923 in Collin Co., TX. He married (1) SARAH ANN BYNUM 17 Jan 1870 in Blount Co., AL. She was born 30 Mar 1847 in DeKalb Co., AL, and died 02 Dec 1881 in Fayette Co., AL. He married (2) LOUISA J. WHITE 19 Mar 1882 in Fayette Co., AL. He married (3) MARY ANN COWEN CHAFFIN 26 Oct 1888 in Fayette Co., AL. She was born 08 Aug 1841 in AL, and died 31 Aug 1928 in Collin Co., TX.

Notes for WILLIS ASBURY BALLARD:
Source: 1870 Blount County Alabama Federal Census Records, 1880 Fayette County Alabama Federal Census Soundex Records, 1900-1910 Kaufman County Texas Federal Census Records, LDS-IGI, Blount County Alabama Marriage Records

* 1870 - Living in Blount Co., AL next door to his father - Ballard, W. A. 22 farmer GA, S. A. 23 GA
* 1880 - Living in Fayette Co., AL - Ballard, Willis 32 farmer GA GA GA, Sarah A. 33 AL, Martha E. 8 AL, Margaret E. 7, Lewis J. 5, Sarah R. 3, Mary E. 1
* 1900 - Living in Kaufman Co., TX - Ballard, Willis A - June 1848 - 51 post master & farmer GA GA GA, Mary 51 - Aug 1841 SC SC SC, Timi - Apr 1883 17 AL, Willis - Aug 1885 14 AL
* 1910 - Living in Mabank, Kaufman Co., TX - Ballard, Willis 61, Mary A 68

More About WILLIS ASBURY BALLARD:
Burial: Ridgeview West Memorial Park, Frisco, Collin Co., TX

More About SARAH ANN BYNUM:
Burial: Ballard Family Cemetery, Stewart, Fayette Co., Al

More About MARY ANN COWEN CHAFFIN:

Burial: Ridgeview West Memorial Park, Frisco, Collin Co., TX

Children of WILLIS BALLARD and SARAH BYNUM are:

i. LOTTIE ADELINE[9] BALLARD, b. 04 Dec 1870, Fayette Co., AL; d. 11 Oct 1872, Fayette Co., AL.

More About LOTTIE ADELINE BALLARD:
Burial: Stewart Cemetery, Fayette Co., AL

ii. MARTHA ESTELLE BALLARD, b. 30 Apr 1872, Fayette Co., AL; d. 22 Sep 1933, Dallas Co., TX; m. WASHINGTON N. FOSTER; b. 1854.

More About MARTHA ESTELLE BALLARD:
Burial: Ridgeview West Memorial Park, Frisco, Collin Co., TX

iii. MARGARET BALLARD, b. 04 May 1872, Fayette Co., AL; d. 02 Dec 1960, Dallas Co., TX; m. JOSHUA ROBERSON; b. 1871.

iv. LOUIS JESSE BALLARD, b. 19 Mar 1873, Fayette Co., AL; d. 23 Jan 1938, Hale Co., TX; m. SOPHRONIA ELIZABETH COWAN, 16 Dec 1894, Henderson TX; b. 1876, AL; d. 1955.

Notes for LOUIS JESSE BALLARD:
Source: 1900 Van Zandt County Texas Federal Census Records, 1910 Haskell County Texas Federal Census Records, 1920 Denton County Texas Federal Census Records, Hale County Texas Federal Census Records, WWI Draft Registration Card
* 1900 - Living in Van Zandt Co., TX - Ballard, Jesse L - Mar 1875 AL, Fronie - Sept 1876 AL, Houston - Nov 1895 TX, Louis - Aug 1898 TX, Cowen, Amazone mother on law - Feb 1856 wd GA
* 1910 - Living in Weinert, Haskell Co., TX - Ballard, Jessie L 34, Sophronia E 33, Huston W 14, Louis W 11, Lonie C 9, Luther J 6
* 1920 - Living in Denton Co., TX - Ballard, Lewis J 45, Sapronie E 43, William L 21, Lontie C. 18, Jessie L 15
* 1930 - Living in Hale Co., TX - Ballard, Lewis J 54, Sophronia E 53

More About SOPHRONIA ELIZABETH COWAN:
Burial: Pecan Grove Cemetery, McKinney, Collin Co., TX

v. SARAH A. BALLARD, b. 14 Dec 1875, Fayette Co., AL; d. 29 Jul 1925, McKinney, Collin Co., TX; m. DAVID E. HARRIS; b. 1868.

vi. MARY ELIZABETH BALLARD, b. 28 Feb 1879, Talladega Co., AL; d. 22 Jul 1952, Childress Co., TX; m. WALTER M. SELF; b. 01 Apr 1874, AL; d. 22 Aug 1950, Childress Co., TX.

More About WALTER M. SELF:
Burial: Childress Cemetery, Childress Co., TX

Child of WILLIS BALLARD and LOUISA WHITE is:

vii. TINA M.[9] BALLARD, b. 22 Apr 1883, AL; d. 24 Feb 1962, Dallas Co., TX; m. J. E. RAMSEY, 15 Aug 1909, Henderson TX; b. 29 Jul 1885; d. 18 May 1948.

Notes for TINA M. BALLARD:
Source: Dallas County Texas Certificate of Death

More About TINA M. BALLARD:
Burial: Little Elm Cemetery, Denton, TX

Notes for J. E. RAMSEY:
Source: 1920-1930 Denton County Texas Federal Census Records

* 1920 - Living in Denton Co., TX - Ramsey, JE 34, Lina 36, James 0, G. S Price
* 1930 - Living in Denton Co., TX - Ramsey, J E 44, Lina 47, J. A 11

Child of WILLIS BALLARD and MARY CHAFFIN is:
 viii. WILLIAM ASBURY[9] BALLARD, *b. 19 Sep 1892; d. 16 Jul 1934.*

  More About WILLIAM ASBURY BALLARD:
  Burial: Ridgeview West Memorial Park, Frisco, Collin Co., TX

76. GEORGE W.[8] BALLARD (*LEWIS J.*[7], *JAMES*[6], *WHORTON*[5], *JESSE*[4], *JOHN*[3], *JOSEPH*[2], *JOHN*[1]) *was born 25 Nov 1854 in GA, and died 07 Jun 1918 in Coryell Co., TX. He married (1) MARTHA WORTHEY. She was born 05 Apr 1855, and died 20 Nov 1931. He married (2) CELIA ADALINE BYNUM 27 Dec 1879 in Fayette Co., AL. She was born 02 Apr 1862 in Blount Co., AL, and died 28 May 1948.*

Notes for GEORGE W. BALLARD:
Source: 1880 Fayette County Alabama Federal Census Records
* 1880 - Living in Fayette Co., AL - Ballard, George W. 25 GA GA GA, Adeline C. 18 AL AL AL, James H. 9/12 AL

More About GEORGE W. BALLARD:
Burial: Bee House Cemetery, Bee House, Coryell Co., TX

More About CELIA ADALINE BYNUM:
Burial: Bee House Cemetery Bee House, Coryell Co. TX

Children of GEORGE BALLARD and CELIA BYNUM are:
 i. JAMES HARRISON[9] BALLARD, *b. 30 Oct 1879, AL; d. 19 Jun 1959, Gatesville, Coryell Co., TX; m. MYRTLE LENA CONNOR; b. 12 Oct 1882, TX; d. 18 Oct 1958.*

  Notes for JAMES HARRISON BALLARD:
  Source: Coryell County Texas Certificate of Death

  More About JAMES HARRISON BALLARD:
  Burial: Pearl Cemetery, Coryell Co., TX

  More About MYRTLE LENA CONNOR:
  Burial: Pearl Cemetery, Coryell Co., TX

 ii. PINK ELSBERY BALLARD, *b. 17 May 1882, Winfield, Marion Co., AL; d. 14 Nov 1968, Gatesville, Coryell Co., TX; m. EMMA OLIVIA HUFF; b. 17 May 1886, Bee House, Coryell Co., TX; d. 12 Dec 1984, Gatesville, Coryell Co., TX.*

  Notes for PINK ELSBERY BALLARD:
  Source: Coryell County Texas Certificate of Death

  More About EMMA OLIVIA HUFF:
  Burial: Restland Cemetery, Gatesville, Coryell Co., TX

 iii. MYRTLE B. BALLARD, *b. Jul 1885.*
 iv. ELLIE MAE BALLARD, *b. 13 May 1891; m. EARNEST BARRINGTON; b. 24 Dec 1887, TX; d. 15 Apr 1963, Gatesville, Coryell Co., TX.*

  More About EARNEST BARRINGTON:
  Burial: Restland Cemetery, Gatesville, Coryell Co., TX

    v.   WILLIAM PARKER BALLARD, b. 27 Apr 1895; d. 01 Aug 1965, Taylor Co., TX; m. DEMBY C. PAPASAN; b. 17 Sep 1898; d. 31 Jan 1957.

        More About DEMBY C. PAPASAN:
        Burial: McBee Cemetery, Ovalo, Taylor Co., TX

    vi. GEORGE LEE BALLARD, b. 19 Mar 1898, TX; d. 17 May 1976, Amarillo, Potter Co., TX.

        Notes for GEORGE LEE BALLARD:
        Source: Potter Count Texas Certificate of Death

77. FLETCHER ELSBURY[8] BALLARD (LEWIS J.[7], JAMES[6], WHORTON[5], JESSE[4], JOHN[3], JOSEPH[2], JOHN[1]) was born 04 Mar 1859 in Blount Co., AL, and died 16 Sep 1914 in Haskell Co., TX. He married FRANCES C. LAWRENCE. She was born 13 Sep 1858, and died 02 Jul 1941.

Notes for FLETCHER ELSBURY BALLARD:
Source: 1880 Fayette County Alabama Federal Census Records, 1900 Coryell County Texas Federal Census Records, 1910 Haskell County Texas Federal Census Records
* 1880 - Living in Fayette Co., FL - Ballard, Fletcher 21 farmer AL GA GA, Frances C. 22 AL AL AL
* 1900 - Living in Coryell Co., TX - Ballard, FE - Mar 1859 AL GA GA 41 farmer, FC - Sep 1858 41 - 6 children 4 living, Mary - Nov 1880 19 AL, J M - Dec 1882 17 AL, J O - Oct 1886 AL 13, William - May 1891 9 AL
* 1910 - Living in Haskell Co., TX - Ballard, Fletcher 51 AL GA GA, Francis 51 AL AL VA, William 19 TX, Dilmus 9 TX

More About FLETCHER ELSBURY BALLARD:
Burial: Rochester Cemetery, Haskell Co., TX

More About FRANCES C. LAWRENCE:
Burial: Rochester Cemetery, Haskell Co., TX

Children of FLETCHER BALLARD and FRANCES LAWRENCE are:
    i.   MARY EMMALINE[9] BALLARD, b. 27 Nov 1880, Fayette Co., AL; d. 04 Jun 1957, Chaves Co., NM; m. LEONARD DECATUR FOSTER; b. 1877.

        More About MARY EMMALINE BALLARD:
        Burial: Hagerman Cemetery, Chaves Co., NM

    ii. J. M. BALLARD, b. Dec 1882, AL; d. Aft. 1900.
    iii. GEORGE OSCAR BALLARD, b. 03 Oct 1886, Marion Co., AL; d. 04 Sep 1944, Haskell Co., TX; m. LILLIE D. SPECK; b. 08 Oct 1889; d. 10 Jun 1977, Haskell Co., TX.

        More About LILLIE D. SPECK:
        Burial: Rochester Cemetery, Haskell Co., TX

    iv. WILLIAM ELSBURY BALLARD, b. 30 May 1891, Coryell Co., TX; d. 07 Dec 1946, Dickens Co., TX; m. ETHEL ALBIN, 25 Dec 1913, Haskell Co., TX; b. 21 Jan 1894, Haskell Co., TX; d. 31 Mar 1974, Knox Co., TX.

        Notes for WILLIAM ELSBURY BALLARD:
        Source: 1930 - 1940 Dickens County Texas Federal Census Records
        * 1930 - Living in Dickens Co., TX - Ballard, William E 38, Ethel 36, Hollis R 14, William P 11, John F 10, James M 5
        * 1940 - Living in Dickens Co., TX - Ballard, W E 49, Ethel 46, Preston 21, Marvin 15, Billie Ray 10, LeNey 8

More About WILLIAM ELSBURY BALLARD:
Burial: Rochester Cemetery, Haskell Co., TX

More About ETHEL ALBIN:
Burial: Rochester Cemetery, Haskell Co., TX

v.   MALE BALLARD, b. 20 Dec 1893, Coryell Co., TX; d. 10 Jan 1894, Coryell Co., TX.

More About MALE BALLARD:
Burial: Bee House Cemetery, Coryell Co., TX

vi.   DILMUS CLIFTON "PAT" BALLARD, b. 22 Apr 1901, Coryell Co., TX; d. 24 Feb 1960, Knox Co., TX; m. SUDIE MAE MITCHELL, 14 Jan 1923, Haskell Co., TX; b. 30 Oct 1900, Jones Co., TX; d. 18 Mar 1984, Rochester, Haskell Co., TX.

Notes for DILMUS CLIFTON "PAT" BALLARD:
Source: WWII Draft Card, 1940 Haskell County Texas Federal Census Records
* 1940 - Living in Haskell Co., TX - Ballard, Pat 39 TX, Susie Mae 39 TX

More About DILMUS CLIFTON "PAT" BALLARD:
Burial: Rochester Cemetery, Haskell Co., TX

More About SUDIE MAE MITCHELL:
Burial: Rochester Cemetery, Haskell Co., TX

78.   FRANCES MINERVA[8] BALLARD (LEWIS J.[7], JAMES[6], WHORTON[5], JESSE[4], JOHN[3], JOSEPH[2], JOHN[1]) was born 09 Jun 1868 in AL, and died 02 Feb 1945 in Austin, Travis Co., TX.   She married JAMES CICERO LONG 22 Jan 1883 in Fayette Co., AL.   He was born 20 May 1860 in AL, and died 1907 in Huntsville, Walker Co., TX.

Notes for FRANCES MINERVA BALLARD:
Source: 1910 - 1920 Erath County Texas Federal Census Records, Travis County Texas Standard Certificate of Death
* 1910 - Living in Erath Co., TX - Long, Francis 42 wd 12 children 9 living AL GA GA farmer, Halie 21 AL, Wylie 17 TX, Clara 13 TX, Sallie 11 TX, Huston 9 TX, David 8 TX, Louella 4 TX
* 1920 - Living in Alexander, Erath Co., TX - Long, Francis M 51, Dora B 22, David M 18, Susie 20, Lue E 13

Notes for JAMES CICERO LONG:
Source: 1900 Erath County Texas Federal Census Records
* 1900 - Living in Erath Co., TX - Long, J. C - May 1860 AL NC GA, F M wife - June 1868 AL GA GA, 8 children 7 living, William J - Jan 1882 MS, LA fe - July 1888 AL, JC - Apr 1889 AL, MB fe - June 1891 TX, W. E - Feb 1893 TX, J. T - Jan 1895 TX, D. B fe - May 1897 TX, S E fe Jan 1899 TX
* listed as a Convict in Huntsville, Walker Co., TX Convict Record Ledger for 2nd Degree Murder shows died Mar 25, 1907. Was scheduled for release in 1910

Children of FRANCES BALLARD and JAMES LONG are:

i.   WILLIAM J.[9] LONG, b. 04 Jan 1886, MS; d. Aft. 1900.
ii.   LUCY ANN LONG, b. 10 Jul 1887, AL; d. Aft. 1900.
iii.   HOLLIE C. LONG, b. 27 Apr 1889, AL; d. 11 Sep 1967.
iv.   MINNIE BELL LONG, b. 07 Jun 1891, TX; d. Aft. 1900.
v.   WYLIE ERASTUS LONG, b. 24 Feb 1893, Coryell Co., TX; d. 29 Sep 1975, Bell Co., TX; m. MAEBELLE GILLITAN.
vi.   J. T. LONG, b. 25 Jan 1895, TX.
vii.   DORA BEATRICE LONG, b. 10 May 1897, Hamilton Co., TX; d. 12 Apr 1993, Erath Co., TX;

m. *ALGERNON SIDNEY FARRAR; b. 04 Aug 1882, Ellis Co., TX; d. 10 Apr 1971.*

> *More About DORA BEATRICE LONG:*
> Burial: East Memorial Cemetery, Stephenville, Erath Co., TX
>
> *More About ALGERNON SIDNEY FARRAR:*
> Burial: East Memorial Cemetery, Stephenville, Erath Co., TX

> viii. SUSIE ELIZABETH LONG, b. 15 Jan 1899, TX; d. 13 Oct 1974, Ballinger, Runnels Co., TX; m. ROY D. JACKSON.
>
> > *Notes for SUSIE ELIZABETH LONG:*
> > Source: Runnels County Texas Certificate of Death
> >
> > *More About SUSIE ELIZABETH LONG:*
> > Burial: Garden of Memories Cemetery, Runnels Co., TX

> ix. WADE HOUSTON LONG, b. 02 Oct 1900, TX; d. 20 May 1969; m. ALBERTA ALICE; b. 1902.
>
> > *More About WADE HOUSTON LONG:*
> > Burial: Crutsinger Cemetery, Hickory Co., MO

> x. DAVID MONROE LONG, b. 01 Jan 1902, TX; d. 1971; m. NAOMI LORENE KELSAY.
>
> > *More About DAVID MONROE LONG:*
> > Burial: Tulocay Cemetery, Napa Co. CA

> xi. F. M. LONG, b. 09 Dec 1903, TX.
> xii. LOU ELLA LONG, b. 24 Jan 1906, TX; d. Aft. 1920.

79. ANDREW JACKSON[8] BALLARD (LEWIS J.[7], JAMES[6], WHORTON[5], JESSE[4], JOHN[3], JOSEPH[2], JOHN[1]) was born 01 Aug 1870 in AL, and died 01 Oct 1900. He married CLARA EUGENIA WHITE 22 Jan 1889 in Fayette Co., AL. She was born 11 Oct 1871 in AL, and died 07 Aug 1931.

Notes for ANDREW JACKSON BALLARD:
Source: 1900 Henderson County Texas Federal Census Records, Debra Tucker (Keep On Tuckin@aol.com)
* 1900 - Living in Henderson Co., TX - Ballard, A J - Aug 1870 AL GA AL, Eugenia - Oct 1871 AL GA AL (5 children - 5 living), Lewis A - June 1890 AL, Chester N - July 1890 AL, Minnie O - Oct 1894 TX, Lester M - Nov 1895 TX, Pervy A - Sept 1899 TX and several boarders

More About ANDREW JACKSON BALLARD:
Burial: Cottonwood Cemetery, Eustace, Henderson Co., TX

Notes for CLARA EUGENIA WHITE:
Source: 1910 Henderson County Texas Federal Census Records
* 1910 - Living in Henderson Co., TX - Gunter, Eugenia is 38 md to Manual W. Gunter step children & her children by Andrew J. - Ballard, Chester 18 AL, Minnie O 16 AL, Lester M 14 TX, Pervy A 11 TX, Perry R 10 TX

More About CLARA EUGENIA WHITE:
Burial: Cottonwood Cemetery, Eustace, Henderson Co., TX

Children of ANDREW BALLARD and CLARA WHITE are:
> i. LEWIS ADOLPHUS[9] BALLARD, b. Jan 1890, AL; d. Aft. 1900.
> ii. CHESTER NEWTON BALLARD, b. 23 Jul 1891, Fayetteville, Talladega Co., AL; d. 15 Dec 1944, Coleman Co., TX; m. ETTA ANNA FRAZIER, 1913, Anthens, Henderson Co., TX; b. 12 Apr 1896, Eustace, Henderson Co., TX; d. 01 Mar 1991, Coleman Co., TX.

Notes for CHESTER NEWTON BALLARD:
Source: 1920 Henderson County Texas Federal Census Records, 1930 - 1940 Coleman County Texas Federal Census Records, WWI Draft Registration Card, WWII Draft Registration Card, Coleman County Texas Standard Certificate of Death

* 1920 - Living in Henderson Co., TX - Ballard, Chester 28 AL, Etta 23 TX, Rosa L 2 2/10 TX, Courtney 1 5/12 TX
* 1930 - Living in Coleman Co., TX - Ballard, Chester N 37 AL AL AL, Etta 34 TX LA AL, Roseleen 13 TX, Courtney 11 TX, Mary M 9 TX, James 7 TX, Melba 5 TX, Alene 3 11/12 TX, Billie 2 2/12 TX, Aleta 5/12 TX
* 1940 - Living in Coleman Co. TX - Ballard, C N 48 AL, Etta 43 TX, Mary 19 TX, Jesse? 17 TX, Melba 15 TX, Alene 14 TX, Billy 12 TX, Alsta 9 TX, Clara Belle 8 TX, Jean 6 TX Joan 4 TX, C. N Jr 2 TX

More About CHESTER NEWTON BALLARD:
Burial: Brown Ranch Cemetery, Coleman, Coleman Co., TX

More About ETTA ANNA FRAZIER:
Burial: Brown Ranch Cemetery, Coleman, Coleman Co., TX

iii.   *MINNIE ONNIE BALLARD, b. 05 Oct 1893, AL; d. 04 Apr 1971, Collin Co., TX; m. GUNTER.*

More About MINNIE ONNIE BALLARD:
Burial: Chambersville Cemetery, Collin Co., TX

iv.   *LESTER MEDIE BALLARD, b. 20 Nov 1895, Lampasas Co., TX; d. 06 Jan 1982, McKinney, Collin Co., TX; m. JEWEL FRANCIS LOVELADY; b. 29 Dec 1899, Collin Co., TX; d. 15 Nov 1986, McKinney, Collin Co., TX.*

Notes for LESTER MEDIE BALLARD:
Source: 1920 Van Zandt County TX Federal Census Records
* 1920 - Living in Van Zandt Co., TX - Ballard, Lester M 24 TX, Eugena Gunter (Mother) 48, Uola Gunter, Ballard Ballard (bro) 19, Ranie 18 sister in law

More About LESTER MEDIE BALLARD:
Burial: Ridgeview Memorial Park, Allen, Collin Co., TX

More About JEWEL FRANCIS LOVELADY:
Burial: Ridgeview Memorial Park, Allen, Collin Co., TX

v.   *JEROLD "PURVEY" ANDREW BALLARD, b. 02 Sep 1899, TX; d. 1969; m. DELLA MAE KANADAY; b. 22 Jan 1906, Hanceville, Cullman Co., AL; d. 25 Jan 1991, McKinney, Collin Co., TX.*

Notes for JEROLD "PURVEY" ANDREW BALLARD:
Source: 1930 - 1940 Coleman County Texas Federal Census Records
* 1930 - Living in Coleman Co., TX - Ballard, Pervie A 30, Della 24, Letrise 4, Lois R 2
* 1940 - Living in Coleman Co., TX - Ballard, P A 40, Della 34, Letris 14, Fredia 12, Joyce 9, Tony Joe 4

More About JEROLD "PURVEY" ANDREW BALLARD:
Burial: Ridgeview Memorial Park, Allen, Collin Co., TX

More About DELLA MAE KANADAY:
Burial: Ridgeview Memorial Park, Allen, Collin Co., TX

    vi.   PERRY ROSCOE BALLARD, b. 28 Nov 1900, TX; d. 12 Dec 1968; m. MARY RNNIE LAMBRIGHT; b. 21 Sep 1900, TX; d. 30 Nov 1994, Coleman Co., TX.

More About PERRY ROSCOE BALLARD:
Burial: Brown Ranch Cemetery, Coleman, Coleman Co., TX

More About MARY RNNIE LAMBRIGHT:
Burial: Brown Ranch Cemetery, Coleman, Coleman Co., TX

80. AMAZONIA ANNETTE[8] BALLARD (WILLIS ASBERRY[7], JAMES[6], WHORTON[5], JESSE[4], JOHN[3], JOSEPH[2], JOHN[1]) was born 26 Feb 1856 in Cobb Co., GA, and died 04 Apr 1938 in Collin Co., TX. She married JAMES WILLIAM COWEN 17 Aug 1875 in Blount Co., AL. He was born 22 Aug 1850 in AL, and died 23 Feb 1900 in TX.

More About AMAZONIA ANNETTE BALLARD:
Burial: Little Elm Cemetery, Denton Co., TX

Notes for JAMES WILLIAM COWEN:
Source: 1880 Blount County Alabama Federal Census Records
* 1880 - Living in Blount Co., AL - Cowen, James 30 farmer AL SC SC, Amizonia 25 AL MS GA GA, Suffrona 3 AL, Cora 1 AL

Children of AMAZONIA BALLARD and JAMES COWEN are:
    i.   CORA[9] COWEN, b. 16 Jun 1879, AL; d. 03 May 1909, TX.
    ii.   MARY MAUD COWEN, b. 28 Feb 1881, AL; d. 09 May 1912, TX.
    iii.   DAISY ETHEL COWEN, b. 22 Aug 1885, AL; d. 07 Apr 1979.
    iv.   PINKIE AURELLA COWEN, b. 17 Apr 1887, AL; d. 16 Jul 1982, TX.
    v.   WILLIAM ELMER COWEN, b. 12 Dec 1889, AL; d. 28 Dec 1958, TX.
    vi.   CHARLES CLAUDINS COWEN, b. 19 Jun 1892, AL; d. 28 Jul 1893, AL.
    vii.   CARRIE AMAZONIA COWEN, b. 22 Aug 1895, TX; d. 18 Jun 1931, TX.
    viii.   FLOY ESTELENA COWEN, b. 30 Aug 1896, TX; d. 27 Oct 1897, TX.
    ix.   SOPHRONIA ELIZABETH COWAN, b. 1876, AL; d. 1955; m. LOUIS JESSE BALLARD, 16 Dec 1894, Henderson TX; b. 19 Mar 1873, Fayette Co., AL; d. 23 Jan 1938, Hale Co., TX.

       More About SOPHRONIA ELIZABETH COWAN:
       Burial: Pecan Grove Cemetery, McKinney, Collin Co., TX

       Notes for LOUIS JESSE BALLARD:
       Source: 1900 Van Zandt County Texas Federal Census Records, 1910 Haskell County Texas Federal Census Records, 1920 Denton County Texas Federal Census Records, Hale County Texas Federal Census Records, WWI Draft Registration Card

       * 1900 - Living in Van Zandt Co., TX - Ballard, Jesse L - Mar 1875 AL, Fronie - Sept 1876 AL, Houston - Nov 1895 TX, Louis - Aug 1898 TX, Cowen, Amazone mother on law - Feb 1856 wd GA
       * 1910 - Living in Weinert, Haskell Co., TX - Ballard, Jessie L 34, Sophronia E 33, Huston W 14, Louis W 11, Lonie C 9, Luther J 6
       * 1920 - Living in Denton Co., TX - Ballard, Lewis J 45, Sapronie E 43, William L 21, Lontie C. 18, Jessie L 15
       * 1930 - Living in Hale Co., TX - Ballard, Lewis J 54, Sophronia E 53

81. A. HARRISON "HARRIS"[8] BALLARD (WILLIS ASBERRY[7], JAMES[6], WHORTON[5], JESSE[4], JOHN[3], JOSEPH[2], JOHN[1]) was born 10 Aug 1858 in MS, and died 02 Nov 1898 in Blount Co., AL. He married (1) ALICE G. BALLARD. She was born 1868. He married (2) HETTIE ANN JACKSON 02 Dec 1894 in Blount Co., AL. She was born 26 Nov 1868, and died 24 Apr 1945.

More About A. HARRISON "HARRIS" BALLARD:
Burial: Ebenezer Methodist Cemetery, Snead, Blount Co., AL

More About HETTIE ANN JACKSON:
Burial: Ebenezer Methodist Cemetery, Snead, Blount Co., AL

Children of A. BALLARD and ALICE BALLARD are:
    i.   ELBERT V.^{9} BALLARD, b. 1888.
   ii.   OLLIE BALLARD, b. 1895.

82.   WILLIAM FLETCHER^8 BALLARD (WILLIAM REDWINE^7, JAMES^6, WHORTON^5, JESSE^4, JOHN^3, JOSEPH^2, JOHN^1) *was born 13 Nov 1860 in MS, and died 24 Jul 1950 in Fayette Co., AL. He married ANNIE INDIANA MORTON 04 Dec 1879 in Fayette Co., Al. She was born 30 Jan 1860, and died 06 Oct 1936.*

Notes for WILLIAM FLETCHER BALLARD:
Source: 1880-1910 Fayette County Alabama Federal Census Records
* 1880 - Living in Fayette Co., AL - Ballard, William 19 farmer, Indiana E 19
* 1900 - Living in Russell, Fayette Co., AL - Ballard, William F 40 - Nov 1859 MS GA GA, Indiana 40 - Jan 1860 - 9 children 8 living AL AL AL, Dosa 18 - June 1881 AL, Jas W 11 - Sep 1883 AL, Della 14 - 1885 AL, Locky 12 - Mar 1888 AL, Lela 9 - Nov 1890 AL, Lee 6 - Dec 1893 AL, Claude 1 - Oct 1898 AL, Antie 1 - Oct 1898 AL
* 1910 - Living in Russell, Fayette Co., AL - Ballard Fletcher 49 MS GA GA, Isabel I 50 AL AL AL, Lelar I 18 Al, Robert L 16 AL, Claudie F 11 AL, Ethel A 11 AL

More About WILLIAM FLETCHER BALLARD:
Burial: Ballard Cemetery, Fayette Co., AL

More About ANNIE INDIANA MORTON:
Burial: Ballard Cemetery, Fayette Co., AL

Children of WILLIAM BALLARD and ANNIE MORTON are:

    i.   DOSHIA^9 BALLARD, b. 23 Jun 1880, Fayette Co., AL; d. 18 Oct 1949.

        More About DOSHIA BALLARD:
        Burial: Ballard Cemetery, Fayette Co., AL

   ii.   JAMES WILLIAM BALLARD, b. 1884, Fayette Co., AL; d. 15 Oct 1958; m. SULTIE OWENS; b. 1885; d. 1949.

        More About JAMES WILLIAM BALLARD:
        Burial: Winfield City Cemetery, Marion Co., AL

        More About SULTIE OWENS:
        Burial: Winfield City Cemetery, Marion Co., AL

  iii.   DELIA BALLARD, b. 14 Nov 1885, Fayette Co., AL; d. 29 Nov 1921.

        More About DELIA BALLARD:
        Burial: Ballard Cemetery, Fayette Co., AL

  iv.   LOCK BALLARD, b. 07 Mar 1888, Fayette Co., AL; d. 25 Sep 1938, Fayette Co., AL.

        More About LOCK BALLARD:
        Burial: Ballard Cemetery, Fayette Co., AL

     v.   LELA BALLARD, b. 16 Jun 1890, Fayette Co., AL; d. 23 Nov 1970; m. THOMAS MCARTHUR.

         More About LELA BALLARD:
         Burial: Hubbertville Church of Christ Cemetery, Fayette Co., Al

    vi.   ROBERT LEE BALLARD, b. 16 Dec 1892, Fayette Co., AL; d. 02 Jan 1967; m. AUTIE BELL TRIMM; b. 1899.

         More About ROBERT LEE BALLARD:
         Burial: White Springs Cemetery, Hubbertville, Fayette Co., AL

    vii.   CLAUDE F. BALLARD, b. 04 Oct 1898, Fayette Co., AL; d. 29 Jul 1949; m. MAUDIE A. TRIMM; b. 18 Aug 1901; d. 11 May 1981.

         More About CLAUDE F. BALLARD:
         Burial: Winfield City Cemetery, Marion Co., AL

         More About MAUDIE A. TRIMM:
         Burial: Winfield City Cemetery, Marion Co., AL

    viii.   ETHEL ANTIE BALLARD, b. 04 Oct 1898, Fayette Co., AL; d. Aft. 1910.

83. JOHN WESLEY[8] BALLARD (WILLIAM REDWINE[7], JAMES[6], WHORTON[5], JESSE[4], JOHN[3], JOSEPH[2], JOHN[1]) *was born 17 Nov 1865 in MS, and died 23 Jul 1944 in Okaloosa Co., FL. He married HARRIET JOSEPHINE SULLIVAN 27 Dec 1886 in Fayette Co., AL. She was born 17 Apr 1865 in Blount Co., AL, and died 22 Sep 1927 in Florala, Covington Co., AL.*

Notes for JOHN WESLEY BALLARD:
Source: Fayette County Alabama Marriage Records, 1900 Fayette County Alabama Federal Census Records, 1910 Neshoba County Mississippi Federal Census Records, 1920 Walton County Florida Federal Census Records, 1930 Okaloosa County Florida Federal Census Records
* 1900 - Living in Russell, Fayette Co., AL - Ballard, Jno W 34 MS GA GA, Harit 28 AL AL AL, Rosa 11 AL, Sorona 10 AL, Dora 8 AL, Lucy 5 TX, Florence 4 TX, Julia 2 (hard to read) TX
* 1910 - Living in Neshoba Co., MS - Ballard John W 45 MS AL GA, Harriet 45 AL AL AL, Rosie 21 AL, Lucy 15 TX, Florance 14 TX, Julia 12 TX, Claudie 10 AL, Johnie 1 MS
* 1920 - Living in Paxton, Walton Co., FL - Ballard, John 53 MS GA AL, Harett 53 AL AL AL, John C 10 MS
* 1930 - Living in Niceville, Okaloosa Co., FL - Ballard, John W 62 MS, Jonnie S 20 MS

More About JOHN WESLEY BALLARD:
Burial: Almarante Cemetery, Laurel Hill, Okaloosa Co., FL

More About HARRIET JOSEPHINE SULLIVAN:
Burial: Almarante Cemetery, Laurel Hill, Okaloosa Co., FL

Children of JOHN BALLARD and HARRIET SULLIVAN are:
    i.   ROSA[9] BALLARD, b. Abt. 1889, AL; d. Aft. 1910.
    ii.   SOFRONA BALLARD, b. Abt. 1890, AL; d. Aft. 1900.
    iii.   DORA BALLARD, b. Abt. 1891, AL; d. Aft. 1900.
    iv.   LUCY BALLARD, b. Abt. 1895, TX; d. 22 Aug 1966; m. BRYAN M. SULLIVAN; b. 01 Nov 1897, FL; d. 14 Feb 1988, AL.

         More About LUCY BALLARD:
         Burial: Almarante Cemetery, Laurel Hill, Okaloosa Co., FL

         More About BRYAN M. SULLIVAN:

Burial: *Greenwood Memorial Cemetery, Covington Co., Al*

  v. FLORENCE BALLARD, b. Abt. 1896, TX; d. Aft. 1910.
  vi. JULIA BALLARD, b. 24 Dec 1897, Philadelphia, Neshoba Co., MS; d. 28 Jan 1927; m. ALLEN MONROE SANDERS; b. 23 Apr 1892; d. 04 Apr 1981.

More About JULIA BALLARD:
Burial: *Almarante Cemetery, Laurel Hill, Okaloosa Co., FL*

More About ALLEN MONROE SANDERS:
Burial: *Almarante Cemetery, Laurel Hill, Okaloosa Co., FL*

  vii. CLAUDIE BALLARD, b. 1900, AL; d. Aft. 1910.
  viii. JOHNIE BALLARD, b. 1909, MS; d. Aft. 1930.

84. ARYARIA C. L.[8] BALLARD (WILLIAM REDWINE[7], JAMES[6], WHORTON[5], JESSE[4], JOHN[3], JOSEPH[2], JOHN[1]) was born 24 Apr 1870 in AL, and died 03 Dec 1913. She married JAMES F. FREDERICK 05 Jun 1887 in Marion Co., AL. He was born 30 Jul 1866 in AL, and died 25 Aug 1939.

Notes for ARYARIA C. L. BALLARD:
Source: Walt (walt@chesapeake.net), Alabama Marriage Records

More About ARYARIA C. L. BALLARD:
Burial: *Mountain Home Cemetery, Bear Creek, Marion Co., AL*

Notes for JAMES F. FREDERICK:
Source: * 1900 -1910 Marion County Alabama Federal Census Records
* 1900 - Living in Goddard, Marion Co., AL - Fredrick, James F - July 1866 AL AL AL, Ary C - Apr 1870 AL, William - Oct 1888, Walter G - March 1890 AL, Luther L - Feb 1893, Albert E - Feb 1899 AL
* 1910 - Living in Goddard, Marion Co., AL - Frederick, James F 43 AL, Ara C 41 AL, William A 21 AL, Luther L 17 AL, Albert H 11 AL, Robert N 5 AL, Arrda 3/12 AL

More About JAMES F. FREDERICK:
Burial: *Mountain Home Cemetery, Bear Creek, Marion Co., AL*

Children of ARYARIA BALLARD and JAMES FREDERICK are:
  i. WILLIAM A.[9] FREDERICK, b. 20 Oct 1888, AL; d. 28 Sep 1962; m. MARCIA D.; b. 16 Jun 1888; d. 22 Apr 1962.

More About MARCIA D.:
Burial: *Mountain Home Cemetery, Bear Creek, Marion Co., AL*

  ii. WALTER G. FREDERICK, b. 03 Mar 1889, AL; d. 23 Jun 1967; m. NELLIE MAE; b. 17 Jan 1891; d. 08 Jan 1979.

More About WALTER G. FREDERICK:
Burial: *Mountain Home Cemetery, Bear Creek, Marion Co., AL*

More About NELLIE MAE:
Burial: *Mountain Home Cemetery, Bear Creek, Marion Co., AL*

  iii. LUTHER LEE FREDERICK, b. 15 Feb 1893, AL; d. 17 Jul 1958; m. CARRIE ELIZABETH CRITTENDEN; b. 19 Nov 1899; d. 19 Jan 1994.

More About LUTHER LEE FREDERICK:

Burial: Pleasant View Cemetery, Graysville, Rhea Co., TN

More About CARRIE ELIZABETH CRITTENDEN:
Burial: Pleasant View Cemetery, Graysville, Rhea Co., TN

    iv.   ALBERT FREDERICK, b. 15 Feb 1899, AL; d. 13 Nov 1944.

        More About ALBERT FREDERICK:
        Burial: Mountain Home Cemetery, Bear Creek, Marion Co., AL

    v.   ROBERT N. FREDERICK, b. Abt. 1905, AL; d. Aft. 1910.
    vi.   ARYARIA FREDERICK, b. Abt. 1910, AL; d. Aft. 1910.

85. HENRY ALEXANDER[8] BALLARD (WILLIAM REDWINE[7], JAMES[6], WHORTON[5], JESSE[4], JOHN[3], JOSEPH[2], JOHN[1]) was born 13 Nov 1872 in AL, and died 17 Jan 1953 in Coryell Co., TX. He married MARTHA ELIZABETH WHITE. She was born 17 Aug 1873 in AL, and died 10 Sep 1954 in Coryell Co., TX.

Notes for HENRY ALEXANDER BALLARD:
Source: 1900 Fayette County Alabama Federal Census Records, Coryell County Texas Certificate of Death
* 1900 - Living in Fayette Co., AL - Ballard, Henry - Nov 1871, (with siblings) Elizabeth - Aug 1873, Beldes - Oct 1892, Vester - Sept 1894, Turley - July 1899

More About HENRY ALEXANDER BALLARD:
Burial: Pearl Cemetery, Coryell Co., TX

More About MARTHA ELIZABETH WHITE:
Burial: Pearl Cemetery, Coryell Co., TX

Children of HENRY BALLARD and MARTHA WHITE are:
    i.   BELDER C.[9] BALLARD, b. 18 Oct 1892, Winfield, Marion Co., AL; d. 02 Jan 1963, Tarrant co., TX.

        More About BELDER C. BALLARD:
        Burial: Moore Memorial Gardens Cemetery, Arlington, Tarrant Co., TX

    ii.   VESTER BALLARD, b. 19 Sep 1895; d. 26 Jul 1982; m. FRANKIE BELLE MURRAH; b. 1902.

        More About VESTER BALLARD:
        Burial: Pearl Cemetery, Coryell Co., TX

    iii.   WILLIAM TULLY BALLARD, b. 07 Jul 1898; d. 20 Jul 1983; m. LILLIE M. MURRAH; b. 1899.

        More About WILLIAM TULLY BALLARD:
        Burial: Pearl Cemetery, Coryell Co., TX

86. FANNIE E.[8] BALLARD (WESTLEY H.[7], JAMES[6], WHORTON[5], JESSE[4], JOHN[3], JOSEPH[2], JOHN[1]) was born 28 Jun 1869 in TX, and died 19 Nov 1948 in Hunt Co., TX. She married WILLIAM D. HODGE 29 Jun 1899 in Hunt Co., TX. He was born 25 May 1845 in GA, and died 16 Jul 1933.

Notes for WILLIAM D. HODGE:
Source: 1900 Hunt County Texas Federal Census Records
* 1900 - Living in Hunt Co., TX - Hodge, W. D. - May 1850 GA A VA, FE - June 1869 TX MS AL, Izora - Aug 1883 TX , Elvira - June 1886, Minnie Ballard sister in law - Feb 1888 TX MS AL
* 1910 - Living in Hunt Co., TX - Hodge, William D 64 md 2x GA GA VA, Fannie 38 - 3 children 3 living TX AL AL, Grayden 6 TX, William W 4 TX, Bard 11/12 TX

Children of FANNIE BALLARD and WILLIAM HODGE are:

    i.   GRAYDEN[9] HODGE, b. 01 Mar 1904, Hunt Co., TX; d. 08 Oct 2001, TX.

   ii.   WILLIAM WESLEY HODGE, b. 24 Aug 1906, Hunt Co., TX; d. 03 Oct 1920, Hunt Co., TX.

  iii.   JAMES BASEL HODGE, b. 03 Jun 1909, Hunt Co., TX; d. 29 Oct 1997, Hunt Co., TX.

87. JOHN LEVI[8] BALLARD (ROBERT COLEMAN[7], JAMES[6], WHORTON[5], JESSE[4], JOHN[3], JOSEPH[2], JOHN[1]) was born 14 Jun 1858 in Dalton Whitfield Co., GA, and died 24 Feb 1918 in Sacul, Nacogdoches Co., TX. He married MARY FRANCES HANCOCK 28 Dec 1879 in Chattooga Co., GA, daughter of PASCAL HANCOCK and LUCRETIA FOSTER. She was born 18 Feb 1862 in Chattooga Co., GA, and died 29 Feb 1920 in Sacul, Nacogdoches Co., TX.

Notes for JOHN LEVI BALLARD:
Source: 1880 Cherokee County Alabama Federal Census Records, Mildred Sparks, Kathy Ballard
* 1880 - Living in Cherokee Co., AL - Ballard, John L 22, Mary F 18

More About JOHN LEVI BALLARD:
Burial: Sacul Cemetery, Nacogdoches Co., TX

Notes for MARY FRANCES HANCOCK:
Source: Mildred Sparks

More About MARY FRANCES HANCOCK:
Burial: Sacul Cemetery, Nacogdoches Co., TX

Children of JOHN BALLARD and MARY HANCOCK are:

    i.   CHARLES COLEMAN[9] BALLARD, b. 18 Jul 1881, Cherokee Co., AL; d. 21 May 1938, Nacogdoches Co., TX; m. SALLY.

        More About CHARLES COLEMAN BALLARD:
        Burial: Old North Church Cemetery, Nacogdoches Co., TX

   ii.   OSKER PASCAL BALLARD, b. 12 Feb 1883, Cherokee Co., AL; d. 12 Apr 1900, Sacul, Nacogdoches Co., TX.

        More About OSKER PASCAL BALLARD:
        Burial: Edmonson Cemetery, Mt. Enterprise, Rusk Co., TX

  iii.   JOSEPH LEVI BALLARD, b. 08 Sep 1885, Cherokee Co., AL; d. 24 Apr 1957, Cushing Nacogdoches Co TX; m. EUNA C. KING.

  iv.   ELA MAUDE BALLARD, b. 08 Jan 1888, Stockdale, Wilson Co., TX; m. SELDON BURTON SMALL, 19 Mar 1907.

   v.   CHELI DEFOREST BALLARD, b. 07 Apr 1890, Stockdale, Wilson Co., TX; d. 02 Jul 1969, Jacksonville TX; m. (1) ETHER GRESHAM; m. (2) MOLLIE PARKER; m. (3) HATTIE HILL; b. Abt. 1890.

  vi.   ROBERT LEROY BALLARD, b. 06 Apr 1892, Stockdale, Wilson Co., TX; d. 26 Apr 1943, Orange Co., TX; m. IVA GARNER, 03 Dec 1917.

        More About ROBERT LEROY BALLARD:
        Burial: Rocky Springs Cemetery, Dialville, Cherokee Co., TX

  vii.   MATTIE MAYE BALLARD, b. 17 Apr 1894, Stockdale, Wilson Co., TX; d. 04 Feb 1973, Jacksonville TX; m. LEWIS GRESHAM, 28 Dec 1911.

 viii.   NORA ETHEL BALLARD, b. 30 Nov 1896, Stockdale, Wilson Co., TX; d. 10 Aug 1970, Lufkin Angelina CO TX; m. CARLTON EARL BUCKNER, 25 Nov 1917; b. 23 Sep 1894, Melrose, Nacogdoches Co., TX; d. 16 Aug 1954, Lufkin, Angelina Co., TX.

Notes for NORA ETHEL BALLARD:
Source: Mildred Sparks

Notes for CARLTON EARL BUCKNER:
Source: Mildred Sparks

88. MILLARD FILLMORE *"MID"*[8] BALLARD (ROBERT COLEMAN[7], JAMES[6], WHORTON[5], JESSE[4], JOHN[3], JOSEPH[2], JOHN[1])
*was born 20 May 1860 in Chattooga Co., GA, and died 14 Oct 1927 in Menlo, Chattooga Co., GA. He married
SUSAN ADALINE WHITTEN 07 Aug 1879 in Chattooga Co., GA. She was born Feb 1858 in AL, and died 24 Feb 1927
in Chattooga Co., GA.*

Notes for MILLARD FILLMORE "MID" BALLARD:
*Source: Death Certificate, 1870 Cherokee County Alabama Federal Census Records, 1900-1920 Chattooga County
Georgia Federal Census Records*

* 1870 - Living in Cherokee Co., AL - Ballard, Millard 21, Susan A 22, Haltz 1/12
** 1900 - Living in Alpine, Chattooga Co., GA - Ballard, Millard F - May 1860 GA, Susan A - Feb 1858 GA, Felton -
Aug 1881 AL, Robert - Mar 1884 GA, John S - Dec 1886 GA, Carie C - June 1890 GA, Chelie H - Dec 1892 GA,
Chelie H - Dec 1892 GA, Millard C - Jan 1895, Ella May - July 1881, Norra - Apr 1896 GA, Annie L - Apr 1898 GA*
** 1910 - Living in Alpine, Chattooga Co., GA - Ballard, Millard F 40 GA, Addie 54 AL, Staton J 26 GA, Chalia 17
GA, Ella M 16 GA, Millard C 15, Narra L 12, Anna L 10, Carrie Reid 19*
* 1920 - Living in Menlo, Chattooga Co., GA - Ballard, Millard F 59 GA CA GA, Addie S 62 GA GA GA

More About MILLARD FILLMORE "MID" BALLARD:
Burial: Menlo Cemetery Menlo, Chattooga Co., GA

Children of MILLARD BALLARD and SUSAN WHITTEN are:

    i.   ELLA M.[9] BALLARD, b. Jul 1881, GA; d. Aft. 1910; m. BEN HARDIN.
    ii.   LATIMER FELTON BALLARD, b. 08 Aug 1881, Jamestown Cherokee Co., AL; d. 04 Dec 1942, Menlo
        Chattooga Co., GA; m. LULA HOLBROOK, 16 Jun 1907, Chattooga Co., GA; b. 1883; d. 1956,
        Chattooga Co., GA.

        Notes for LATIMER FELTON BALLARD:
        Source: 1910 Chattooga County Georgia Federal Census Records, Kathy Ballard
        * 1910 - Living in Alpine, Chattooga County GA - Ballard, L Felton 27, Lula 26

        More About LATIMER FELTON BALLARD:
        Burial: Alpine Community Church Cemetery, Menlo, Chattooga Co., GA

        Notes for LULA HOLBROOK:
        Source: Missy Mayne

        More About LULA HOLBROOK:
        Burial: Alpine Community Church Cemetery, Menlo, Chattooga Co., GA

    iii.   ROBERT LEE BALLARD, b. 24 Mar 1884, GA; d. 15 Aug 1930, Menlo Chattooga Co., GA; m. DOVIE;
        b. 1887; d. Aft. 1920.

        More About ROBERT LEE BALLARD:
        Burial: Alpine Community Church Cemetery, Chattooga Co., GA

    iv.   JOHN S. BALLARD, b. Dec 1886, GA; d. Aft. 1900.
    v.   STATEN BALLARD, b. Abt. 1887, GA; d. Aft. 1920; m. EMMA; b. 1897, GA; d. Aft. 1920.

Notes for STATEN BALLARD:
Source: 1920 Walker County Georgia Federal Census Records
* 1920 - Living in 1920 Walker Co., GA - Ballard, Staton 32 GA, Emma 23 GA

vi.   NARRA BALLARD, *b. 05 Apr 1888, GA; d. 26 May 1926, Menlo Chattooga Co., GA; m. (1) J. D. LOGAN; m. (2) F. LEE JOINES; b. 30 Nov 1885; d. 12 Jul 1964, Menlo Chattooga Co., GA.*
vii. CARRIE C. BALLARD, *b. 05 Jun 1891, GA; d. 23 Apr 1911, Menlo, Chattooga Co., GA; m. MR. REID, Bef. 1910.*

More About CARRIE C. BALLARD:
Burial: Alpine Community Church Cemetery, Menlo, Chattooga Co., GA

viii. CHELIE N. BALLARD, *b. 05 Jan 1893, GA; d. 17 Mar 1919, Chattooga Co., GA.*

Notes for CHELIE N. BALLARD:
Source: Chattooga County Georgia Certificate of Death

ix.   MILLARD COLEMAN BALLARD, *b. Jan 1895, GA; d. Aft. 1920; m. LILLIAN HAMMOND, 27 Dec 1916; b. Abt. 1897; d. Aft. 1920.*

Notes for MILLARD COLEMAN BALLARD:
Source: 1920 Chattooga County Georgia Federal Census Records
* 1920 - Living in Menlo, Chattooga Co., GA - Ballard, Millard C 23, Lillian L 23, Frances E 2 2/12

x.   ANNIE LOIS BALLARD, *b. 03 Apr 1899, Menlo Chattooga GA; d. 30 Nov 1971; m. IZEY OTTO HUCKS, 18 Oct 1919.*

89.   ROBERT CHAPMAN[8] BALLARD, JR. (ROBERT COLEMAN[7], JAMES[6], WHORTON[5], JESSE[4], JOHN[3], JOSEPH[2], JOHN[1]) *was born 25 Apr 1862 in GA, and died Aft. 1910. He married MARY ANN RUTLEDGE 14 Feb 1886 in Chattooga Co., GA, daughter of GEORGE RUTLEDGE and MARY HALL. She was born 10 Jun 1861 in Trion GA, and died 17 Apr 1920 in Pauls Valley, Garvin Co., OK.*

Notes for ROBERT CHAPMAN BALLARD, JR.:
Source: Automated Marriage CD, 1900 Walker County Georgia Federal Census Records, 1910 Garvin County Oklahoma Federal Census Records
* 1900 - Living in Cane Creek, Walker Co., GA - Ballard, Robert C - Apr 1862, Mary A - June 1862, Carl B - Nov 1886, George - March 1889, Annie Lee - March 1892, B....? - June 1894, Vada - March 1898
* 1910 - Living in Pauls Valley, Garvin Co., OK - Ballard, Robert C 48 GA GA GA, Mary A 48 GA GA GA, Carl V 23 GA, George C 21 GA, Annie L 17 GA, Vada V 11 GA, Clint H 9 GA

Children of ROBERT BALLARD and MARY RUTLEDGE are:

i.   VADA VIOLA[9] BALLARD, *b. Mar 1898, GA; d. Aft. 1910; m. JACK BELL.*
ii.   CARL VAN BALLARD, *b. Nov 1886, GA; d. Aft. 1910; m. MARY DUNN.*
iii. CLINT HOBSON BALLARD, *b. 1901, GA; d. Aft. 1910; m. SYBIL LONON LILLARD.*
iv.   GEORGE COLEMAN BALLARD, *b. 15 Mar 1889, GA; d. 09 Aug 1974; m. ETHEL LAUDON.*
v.   ANNA LEE BALLARD, *b. 24 Mar 1892, GA; d. 29 May 1978, Pauls Valley, Garvin Co., OK; m. ROY GILBERT MILLER, 04 Aug 1915, Pauls Valley OK.*
vi.   BOWIE CHADICK BALLARD, *b. 10 Jun 1895, GA; d. 11 Mar 1957; m. LONA FLEET.*

90.   MARTHA M. "MATTIE"[8] BALLARD (ROBERT COLEMAN[7], JAMES[6], WHORTON[5], JESSE[4], JOHN[3], JOSEPH[2], JOHN[1]) *was born 17 Apr 1867 in Walker Co., GA, and died 1949 in Armuchee, Walker Co., GA. She married SEABORN B. HOWARD. He was born Abt. Oct 1862 in AL.*

More About MARTHA M. "MATTIE" BALLARD:
Burial: Walnut Grove Cemetery, Lafayette, Walker Co., GA

Children of MARTHA BALLARD and SEABORN HOWARD are:
    i.   LASSIE M.[9] HOWARD, b. Abt. May 1892, AL.
    ii. WINFORD B. HOWARD, b. Abt. Jul 1893, AL.
    iii. DAYTON C. HOWARD, b. Abt. Mar 1889, AL.
    iv. FLOSSIE C. HOWARD, b. Abt. Jul 1898, AL.

91. IRA CHELEOUS[8] BALLARD (ROBERT COLEMAN[7], JAMES[6], WHORTON[5], JESSE[4], JOHN[3], JOSEPH[2], JOHN[1]) was born 03 Dec 1868 in Trion, Chattooga, GA, and died 04 Oct 1937 in Gadsden, Etowah AL (bur. Forrest Cemetery. Gadsden.. He married PLUMA ANNIE CUNNINGHAM 07 May 1899 in Ringgold, Cherokee Co., AL. She was born 21 Aug 1872 in Gaylesville, Cherokee Co., AL, and died 07 Jun 1963 in Gadsden, Etowah AL.

Notes for IRA CHELEOUS BALLARD:
Source: Kathy Ballard (grits111@hotmail.com), 1910 Etowah County Alabama Federal Census Records
* 1910 - Living in Gadsden, Etowah Co., AL - Ballard, Ira C 40, Annie 37 AL, Ira C Jr 5 AL

Child of IRA BALLARD and PLUMA CUNNINGHAM is:
    i.   IRA CUNNINGHAM[9] BALLARD, JR., b. Leesburg, Cherokee Co., AL; d. 01 Jun 1949, Gadsden Etowah Co., AL; m. NELL ELVIRA BANVILLE, 04 Apr 1931, Chicago, Cooke Co., IL; b. 18 Feb 1910, Chicago, Cooke Co., IL; d. For lower levels, look at Kathy Ballard file.

       Notes for IRA CUNNINGHAM BALLARD, JR.:
       Source: Kathy Ballard (grits111@hotmail.com)

92. TENNIE[8] BALLARD (ROBERT COLEMAN[7], JAMES[6], WHORTON[5], JESSE[4], JOHN[3], JOSEPH[2], JOHN[1]) was born 06 Jan 1871 in GA, and died 1961 in AL. She married MADISON HOOKS 24 Dec 1891 in Cherokee Co., AL. He was born 1866, and died 01 Feb 1936.

Notes for TENNIE BALLARD:
Source: Kathy Ballard

Children of TENNIE BALLARD and MADISON HOOKS are:
    i.   CARL[9] HOOKS, b. 09 Sep 1892; m. GLADYS JONES, 1942, Reno, Washoe Co., NV.
    ii. JEWELL HOOKS, b. Abt. Sep 1893; m. MR. GREET OR GREER.
    iii. MYRTLE MAY HOOKS, b. 03 May 1896; d. 11 Dec 1975; m. HOWARD TOLBERT.
    iv. DAISY BELL HOOKS, b. Abt. May 1898; d. 05 Jun 1932, Gadsden, Etowah Co., AL; m. WILLIAM CHESTNUT; b. Abt. 1890.
    v. CORA HILL HOOKS, b. Abt. May 1900; d. 09 Sep 1969; m. WARREN CANDLER HUNT.
    vi. PAUL MADISON HOOKS, b. 09 Sep 1903; d. 09 Oct 1953.

93. EULA LEE[8] BALLARD (ROBERT COLEMAN[7], JAMES[6], WHORTON[5], JESSE[4], JOHN[3], JOSEPH[2], JOHN[1]) was born 28 Dec 1874 in Chattooga Co., GA, and died Aft. 1910 in OK. She married FORREST JACKSON KENNEDY 17 Dec 1893 in Chesterfield Cherokee Co., AL. He was born Abt. Aug 1862 in AL, and died Aft. 1910.

Notes for FORREST JACKSON KENNEDY:
Source: 1900 Cherokee County Alabama Federal Census Records, 1910 Chattooga County Georgia Federal Census Records
* 1900 - Living in Waterloo, Cherokee Co., AL - Ballard, Forest J - Aug 1862 AL TN SC, Eula L - Dec 1876 AL AL GA
* 1910 - Living in Alpine, Chattooga Co., GA - Ballard, Forrest 47, Eula L 26, Claude T 15, Annie F 12, Henry L 11, Frances M 5, Loraine E 4

Children of EULA BALLARD and FORREST KENNEDY are:
    i.   DON RAY[9] KENNEDY.
    ii. RUTH NORVELLE KENNEDY, m. ROSS S. CARNES.
    iii. CLAUDE TIMOTHY KENNEDY, b. Abt. Jan 1895, AL; d. Aft. 1910; m. ANNIE F.; b. Jan 1897; d. Aft. 1900.

        Notes for CLAUDE TIMOTHY KENNEDY:
        Source: 1900 Cherokee County Alabama Federal Census Records
        * 1900 - Living in Waterloo, Cherokee Co., AL - Ballard, Claude T - Jan 1895 AL, Annie F - Jan 1897 AL, Harves L - Apr 1899 AL

    iv. ANNIE FAYE KENNEDY, b. 26 Jan 1897, AL; d. 09 Apr 1981; m. JOHN SANFORD LUCAS, 26 Sep 1923.
    v. HARNER L. HARVEY KENNEDY, b. Abt. Apr 1899, AL; d. Aft. 1910; m. AENESEA.
    vi. MARTHA FRANCES KENNEDY, b. 1905; d. Aft. 1910; m. MARVIN L. EATON.
    vii. EREATH LORRINE KENNEDY, b. 1906; d. Aft. 1910; m. EUGENE DIEHR.

94. PAUL CEPHUS[8] BALLARD (ROBERT COLEMAN[7], JAMES[6], WHORTON[5], JESSE[4], JOHN[3], JOSEPH[2], JOHN[1]) was born 20 May 1876 in GA or AL, and died 26 Jul 1964 in Stockdale, Wilson Co., TX. He married BETTIE AKIN. She was born 24 Aug 1877 in TX, and died 25 Jul 1948.

Notes for PAUL CEPHUS BALLARD:
Source: 1910 -1920 Wilson County Texas Federal Census Records, 1930-1940 Bexar County Texas Federal Census Records
* 1910 - Living in Wilson Co., TX - Ballard, Paul C 33 GA Scotland Ireland (? was he adopted), Bettie A 32 TX AR AR, William F 12 TX, Flora B 7 TX, Clara L 5, King C 3/12
* 1920 - Living in Wilson Co., TX - Ballard, Paul C 44 GA Scotland GA (?), Bettie A 33, Flora B 19 TX, Clara L 14 TX, King C 10 TX, John K 8 TX, Winston 3, John N Akin 70 AR father in law
* 1930 - Living in San Antonio, Bexar Co., TX - Ballard, Paul C 53 AL, Bettie A 52, Clara L 25 TX, John C 18 TX, Winston P 14 TX, Geraldine 9 TX, Clyde Akin 22 nephew TX
* 1940 - Living in San Antonio, Bexar Co., TX - Ballard Paul C 63, Bettie 62

More About PAUL CEPHUS BALLARD:
Burial: Stockdale Cemetery, Stockdale, Wilson Co., TX

More About BETTIE AKIN:
Burial: Stockdale Cemetery, Stockdale, Wilson Co., TX

Children of PAUL BALLARD and BETTIE AKIN are:
    i. JERRY LEE[9] BALLARD, b. Bet. 1896 - 1930.
    ii. FRED WILLIAM BALLARD, b. 29 Jul 1897, Stockdale, Wilson Co., TX; d. 03 Mar 1960, Houston, Harris Co., TX; m. FERN ANN MARKHAM; b. 07 Apr 1909, IL; d. 19 Nov 1986, Houston, Harris Co., TX.

        More About FRED WILLIAM BALLARD:
        Burial: Memorial Oaks Cemetery, Houston, Harris Co., TX

    iii. FLORA BALLARD, b. 21 Apr 1900, Stockdale, Wilson Co., TX; d. 07 Jan 1981, Bexar Co., TX; m. ALBERT CHESTER HASTINGS; b. 22 Oct 1899, Wilson Co., TX; d. 30 Nov 1977, McLennan Co., TX.

        Notes for ALBERT CHESTER HASTINGS:
        Source: 1930 Bexar County Texas Federal Census Records

        * 1930 - Living in Bexar Co., TX - Hastings, Albert 30 TX TX TX, Flora 29 TX TX TX, Chester 1 11/12 TX, Annie Frick 20 lodger, Eloise Dawson 26 lodger, Cora Collins 27 lodger

More About ALBERT CHESTER HASTINGS:
Burial: Stockdale Cemetery, Stockdale, Wilson Co., TX

 iv. CLARA LOU BALLARD, b. 13 Mar 1905, Wilson Co., TX; d. 25 Sep 1978, San Antonio, Bexar Co., TX; m. BILL R. RIEMENSCHEIDER; b. 1895.

  More About CLARA LOU BALLARD:
  Burial: Stockdale Cemetery, Stockdale, Wilson Co., TX

 v. KING C. BALLARD, b. 01 Jan 1910, TX; d. 05 Jan 1934.

  More About KING C. BALLARD:
  Burial: Stockdale Cemetery, Stockdale, Wilson Co., TX

 vi. JOHN C. BALLARD, b. 08 Nov 1911, TX; d. 17 Mar 1982, Bexar Co., TX.

  More About JOHN C. BALLARD:
  Burial: Ft. Sam Houston National Cemetery, San Antonio, Bexar Co., TX

 vii. WINSTON PAUL BALLARD, b. 1917, TX; d. Aft. 1930.
 viii. GERALDINE BALLARD, b. 13 Mar 1921, TX; d. 02 Dec 1999.

  More About GERALDINE BALLARD:
  Burial: Stockdale Cemetery, Stockdale, Wilson Co., TX

95. ROBERT ALONZO[8] BALLARD, DR. (WILLIAM R.[7], WILLIAM ROBERT[6], WHORTON[5], JESSE[4], JOHN[3], JOSEPH[2], JOHN[1]) was born 01 Jun 1857 in GA, and died 01 Sep 1897. He married MARY JEMIMA ROACH. She was born 09 Apr 1858, and died 07 Mar 1940.

Notes for ROBERT ALONZO BALLARD, DR.:
Source: 1880 Coweta County Georgia Federal Census Records
* 1880 - Living in Coweta Co., GA - Ballard, Robert A 22 GA, Mary I 21 Ireland, Ossie T 1 GA, Robert P 3/12 Feb GA

More About ROBERT ALONZO BALLARD, DR.:
Burial: May Cemetery, Brown Co., TX

More About MARY JEMIMA ROACH:
Burial: Sardis Baptist Church Cemetery, Palmetto, Fulton Co., GA

Children of ROBERT BALLARD and MARY ROACH are:
 i. OSSIE T.[9] BALLARD, b. 07 Aug 1878; d. 07 Jul 1896.

  More About OSSIE T. BALLARD:
  Burial: May Cemetery, Brown Co., TX

 ii. ROBERT P. BALLARD, b. 29 Feb 1880; d. Aft. 1880.
 iii. LAVENDER RAY BALLARD, b. 29 Feb 1880, GA; d. 03 Dec 1931, Campbell Co., GA; m. ETHEL D. STAMPS, 18 Jun 1918, Fulton Co., GA; b. 10 Sep 1881, Fulton Co., GA; d. 11 Dec 1949, Coweta Co., GA.

  Notes for LAVENDER RAY BALLARD:
  Source: Campbell County Georgia Local Registrars Record of Death, 1920 Coweta County Georgia Federal Census Records, 1930 Campbell County Georgia Federal Census Records

* 1920 - Living in Cedar Creek, Coweta Co., GA - Ballard, Lavender 39, Ethel 38, Ethel
* 1930 - Living in Goodes, Campbell Co., GA - Ballard, Luvender R 50, Ethel D 36, Ethel R 10

Notes for ETHEL D. STAMPS:
Source: 1940 Coweta County Georgia Federal Census Records
* 1940 - Living in Coweta Co., GA with her mother Dora A Stamps

More About ETHEL D. STAMPS:
Burial: Sardis Baptist Church Cemetery, Palmetto, Fulton Co., GA

96. JOHN FRANKLIN[8] CARROLL (HULDA SMITH[7] HEARN, JANE[6] BALLARD, WHORTON[5], JESSE[4], JOHN[3], JOSEPH[2], JOHN[1]) *was born 27 Nov 1839 in Coweta Co., GA, and died 26 Aug 1910 in Jackson Parish, LA. He married* MARY ELIZABETH JORDAN. *She was born 29 Mar 1841 in Cobb Co., GA, and died 12 Sep 1903 in Oswego Co., NY.*

Notes for JOHN FRANKLIN CARROLL:
Source: Valerie Austin (va5303@nersp.nerdc.ufl.edu)

More About JOHN FRANKLIN CARROLL:
Burial: Mt. Pleasant Cemetery, Jackson Parish, LA

More About MARY ELIZABETH JORDAN:
Burial: Mt. Pleasant Cemetery, Jackson Parish, LA

Children of JOHN CARROLL and MARY JORDAN are:
    i.   MARY IDELLA[9] CARROLL, b. 03 Mar 1866; d. 12 Feb 1926; m. PERNAL ASHBURY SMART; b. 1866.
   ii.   WILLIAM REDWINE CARROLL, b. 25 Sep 1867; d. 22 Dec 1951; m. MARY CATHERINE; b. 11 Nov 1866; d. 21 Feb 1951.

       More About WILLIAM REDWINE CARROLL:
       Burial: Mt. Pleasant Cemetery, Jackson Parish, LA

       More About MARY CATHERINE:
       Burial: Mt. Pleasant Cemetery, Jackson Parish, LA

  iii.   EMMA LOU CARROLL, b. 02 Jan 1873; d. 06 Oct 1918; m. WALTER H. HEARNE; b. 12 Apr 1873; d. 16 Feb 1930.

       More About WALTER H. HEARNE:
       Burial: Mt. Pleasant Cemetery, Jackson Parish, LA

  iv.   THOMAS HARDY CARROLL, b. 07 Jul 1875; d. 22 Feb 1949; m. NETTIE JOHNSTON STEGALL; b. 26 Mar 1880, LA; d. 20 Nov 1971.

       Notes for THOMAS HARDY CARROLL:
       Source: Valerie Austin (va5303@nersp.nerdc.ufl.edu)

       More About THOMAS HARDY CARROLL:
       Burial: Oakwood Annex Cemetery, Montgomery Co., AL

       More About NETTIE JOHNSTON STEGALL:
       Burial: Oakwood Annex Cemetery, Montgomery Co., AL

97. ALFRED O.[8] BALLARD (EDMOND S.[7], WESLEY[6], WHORTON[5], JESSE[4], JOHN[3], JOSEPH[2], JOHN[1]) *was born 1859 in AL,* *and died Aft. 1887. He married CALLIE BOWMAN. She was born 28 Feb 1861.*

Notes for ALFRED O. BALLARD:
Source: Rick Green (rickgreen@ibm.net)

Child of ALFRED BALLARD and CALLIE BOWMAN is:

     i.   ALVIN FREEMAN[9] BALLARD, b. 06 Mar 1887, AL; d. 1959, AL; m. LENA EDNA COOPER; b. 20 May 1885.

          Notes for ALVIN FREEMAN BALLARD:
          Source: 1920-1930 Talladega County Alabama Federal Census Records, Rick Green
          (rickgreen@ibm.net), Donna Carpenter (dcvegas@psn.net)
          * 1920 - Living in Fayetteville, Talladega Co., AL - Ballard, Alvin F 32, Lena E 33, Celey 6, Chester
          M 2 6/12
          * 1930 - Living in Hackneyville, Tallapoosa Co., AL - Ballard, Alvin F 43, Lena E 45, Celia Mae 16,
          Chester 12, Lester B 6

          More About ALVIN FREEMAN BALLARD:
          Burial: Sunny Level Cemetery, Alexander City, Tallapoosa Co., AL

98. JOHN EDMOND "DOC"[8] BALLARD (THOMAS W.[7], WESLEY[6], WHORTON[5], JESSE[4], JOHN[3], JOSEPH[2], JOHN[1]) *was born 1848 in AL, and died 04 Jan 1909 in Dadeville, Tallapoosa Co., AL. He married ANN SUSAN DEAN 07 Dec 1870 in Tallapoosa Co., AL. She was born 05 Aug 1853 in Dadeville, Tallapoosa AL, and died 19 Jun 1930 in Macon Co., AL .*

Notes for JOHN EDMOND "DOC" BALLARD:
Source: 1880 Tallapoosa County Alabama Federal Census Records, 1900 Comanche County Texas Federal Census Records, John Robertson
* 1880 - Living in Tallapoosa Co., AL - Ballard, John E 28, Susan 24, John H 8, Thomas O 7, William R 4, Lara B 2
* 1900 - Living in Comanche Co., TX - Ballard, J E 49 - Feb 1851 AL Al AL, Susan 46 - Aug 1852 - 10 children 9 living AL AL AL , Ida 17 - Dec 1882 AL, Green 15 - Apr 1885 AL, Olive 12 - Apr 1888 AL, Minnie 9 - Nov 1890 AL, Jackson 7 - June 1892 AL

More About ANN SUSAN DEAN:
Burial: Antioch Methodist Church Cemetery, Macon Co., AL

Children of JOHN BALLARD and ANN DEAN are:

     i.   JOHN HENRY[9] BALLARD, b. 16 Nov 1871, Tallapoosa Co., AL; d. 17 Apr 1957, Colorado City Mitchell Co., TX; m. CORDELIA LATROBE WILSON, 10 Dec 1896; b. 1880.
     ii.   THOMAS ONZIALO BALLARD, b. 17 Sep 1873, Tallapoosa Co., AL; d. 22 Feb 1950, Port Arthur, Jefferson Co, TX; m. BERTHA M. STRONG, 16 Jan 1901; b. 27 Mar 1884; d. 19 Aug 1950.

          Notes for THOMAS ONZIALO BALLARD:
          Source: 1900 Comanche County Texas Federal Census Records
          * 1900 - Living in Comanche Co., TX - Ballard, TO - Sept 1873 AL AL AL farmer, living next door to his parents

     iii. WILLIAM "WILL" RUFUS BALLARD, b. 03 Feb 1874, Tallapoosa Co., AL; d. 28 Sep 1956, Dadeville, Tallapoosa Co., AL; m. CLEOPATRA DUFFEY, 27 Sep 1894.
     iv. BARBARA ELIZABETH "LAURA" BALLARD, b. 27 Mar 1880, Tallapoosa Co., AL.
     v.   IDA SUSAN BALLARD, b. 10 Dec 1883, Talladega Co., AL; d. 08 Jan 1971; m. JOHN ROBERT BRASELL.
     vi. GREEN HENRY BALLARD, b. Apr 1885, Talladega Co., AL; d. 1963; m. ALICE ELLEN OLIVER.
     vii. OLIVE "OLLIE" VESTER BALLARD, b. 03 Apr 1888, Talladega Co., AL; d. 24 May 1954; m. BERTHA M. STRONG, 16 Feb 1905; b. 27 Mar 1884; d. 19 Aug 1950.

viii. MINNIE MARY BALLARD, b. 24 Nov 1890, Dadeville, Tallapoosa Co., AL; d. 26 Feb 1970, Loraine, Mitchell Co., TX; m. JAMES FRANKLIN "JIMMIE" OLIVER, 18 Feb 1906, Tallassee AL; b. 01 Oct 1885, AL; d. 15 May 1969, Loraine, Mitchell Co., TX.

More About MINNIE MARY BALLARD:
Burial: Colorado City Cemetery, Mitchell Co., TX

More About JAMES FRANKLIN "JIMMIE" OLIVER:
Burial: Colorado City Cemetery, Mitchell Co., TX

ix. ANDREW JACKSON "JACK" BALLARD, b. Jun 1892, Talladega Co., AL; d. 1913; m. LAVADA CARLISLE, 13 Jan 1912.

99. ENOCH BURTON[8] BALLARD (THOMAS W.[7], WESLEY[6], WHORTON[5], JESSE[4], JOHN[3], JOSEPH[2], JOHN[1]) was born 19 Jun 1855 in Tallapoosa Co., AL, and died 04 Mar 1914. He married MARY H. ISABELLA DEAN. She was born 03 May 1858, and died 06 Mar 1910 in Tallapoosa Co., AL.

Notes for ENOCH BURTON BALLARD:
Source: 1880-1900 Tallapoosa County Alabama Federal Census Record , 1910 Elmore County Alabama Federal Census Records, John Robertson
* 1880 - Living in Tallapoosa Co., AL - Ballard, Enoch B 25 Farmer AL NC NC, Mary Belle 22 AL GA GA, Susan B 1 AL
* 1900 - Living in Alexander, Tallapoosa Co., AL - Ballard, Enoch - June 1855 AL, Mary - May 1858 - 8 children 7 living, Rite - Feb. 1884 AL, Rufus - Aug 1886 AL, Archie - Feb 1890 AL, Henry - Oct 1891 AL, Lamend - Oct 1894 AL, Susie B. Langley dau - July 1878 AL, Jola grand dau - July 1896 AL, Willie - grandson - Oct 1897 AL, Oct grandson - Mar 1899 AL
* 1910 - Living in Elmore Co., AL - Ballard, Enoch B 55, Mary I 53, Henry A 17, Loman A 15, Dettie A 10, Zalon C Langley 13, Henry W Langley 12

More About ENOCH BURTON BALLARD:
Burial: Pleasant Grove Cemetery, Eclectic, Elmore Co., AL

More About MARY H. ISABELLA DEAN:
Burial: Pleasant Grove Cemetery, Eclectic, Elmore Co., AL

Children of ENOCH BALLARD and MARY DEAN are:
i. SUSAN ISABELLE "BELL"[9] BALLARD, b. 29 Jul 1879, AL; d. 17 Oct 1901; m. C. C. "BUD" LANGLEY, 08 Nov 1895; b. Abt. 1870; d. 1900.
ii. IDA FLORENCE BALLARD, b. 28 Dec 1881, AL; d. 19 May 1960; m. WALTER LAFAYETT COLLUM; b. 13 Jan 1880; d. 09 Nov 1942.

More About IDA FLORENCE BALLARD:
Burial: Rose Hill Cemetery, Tallassee, Elmore Co., AL

More About WALTER LAFAYETT COLLUM:
Burial: Rose Hill Cemetery, Tallassee, Elmore Co., AL

iii. M. M. L. BALLARD, b. 07 Jun 1883, AL.
iv. LAURA REEDIA BALLARD, b. 18 Feb 1884, AL; d. Aft. 1900; m. THOMPSON.
v. RUFUS WASHINGTON BALLARD, b. 28 Aug 1886, AL; d. Aft. 1900; m. TALITHA LAMBERT.
vi. ARCHIE DEAN DUPRIEST BALLARD, b. 06 Feb 1889, AL; d. 27 Jan 1957; m. EULA COTTON; b. 23 Aug 1891; d. 20 Nov 1937.

More About ARCHIE DEAN DUPRIEST BALLARD:

Burial: Rose Hill Cemetery, Tallassee, Elmore Co., AL

More About EULA COTTON:
Burial: Rose Hill Cemetery, Tallassee, Elmore Co., AL

vii. *HENRY GRADY BALLARD, b. 06 Oct 1892, Tallapoosa Co., AL; d. 15 Sep 1971, Tallassee, Elmore Co., AL; m. MARY PIERCE; b. 10 Dec 1891, Elmore Co., AL; d. 09 Feb 1961, Tallassee, Elmore Co., AL.*

More About HENRY GRADY BALLARD:
Burial: Rose Hill Cemetery, Tallassee, Elmore Co., AL

viii. *LOMAN ARTHUR BALLARD, b. 07 Nov 1894, AL; d. 22 Dec 1982; m. (1) EULA SMITH; b. 22 Dec 1901; d. 18 May 1995; m. (2) IDA PEARL CADE, 01 Jan 1922.*

More About LOMAN ARTHUR BALLARD:
Burial: Rose Hill Cemetery, Tallassee, Elmore Co., AL

More About EULA SMITH:
Burial: Sharon Cemetery, Reeltown, Tallapoosa Co., AL

ix. *CARRIE BALLARD, b. 19 Jul 1897, AL; d. 01 Mar 1898.*
x. *DETTIE "BETTY" ALBERTA BALLARD, b. 27 Jul 1900, AL; d. 27 Jun 1980; m. DANIEL JOSEPH NEIGHBORS; b. 07 Mar 1891, Tallassee, Elmore Co., AL; d. 03 Sep 1986, DeKalb Co., GA.*

More About DETTIE "BETTY" ALBERTA BALLARD:
Burial: Garden Hills Cemetery, Opelika, Lee Co., AL

More About DANIEL JOSEPH NEIGHBORS:
Burial: Garden Hills Cemetery, Opelika, Lee Co., AL

100. JAMES T.[8] BALLARD (THOMAS W.[7], WESLEY[6], WHORTON[5], JESSE[4], JOHN[3], JOSEPH[2], JOHN[1]) *was born 1849 in Meriwether GA, and died Aft. 1880. He married SARAH L.. She was born 1853 in AL, and died Aft. 1880.*

Notes for JAMES T. BALLARD:
Source: 1870-1880 Tallapoosa County Alabama Federal Census Records
* 1870 - Living in Tallapoosa Co., AL - Ballard, James 21 AL, Sarah 20 AL
* 1880 - The family is listed two different times. In one census, they are surrounded by Ballards but not the other
* 1880 - June 19th Living in Tallapoosa Co., AL - Ballard James F 30, Sarah 27, Mary Ann 10, Lucinda 8, Thomas 7, James A 5, Enoch A 4, Olin A 3
* 1880 - June 5th Living in Tallapoosa Co., AL - Ballard, James F 30 farm laborer GA NC SC, Sarah 21 AL SC AL, Mary Ann 10 AL, Lucinda 8 AL, William T 6 AL, James A 4 AL, Enoch A 3 AL, Roland A 1A AL

Children of JAMES BALLARD and SARAH L. are:
  i. *MARY ANN[9] BALLARD, b. 1870, AL; d. Aft. 1880.*
  ii. *LUCINDA BALLARD, b. 1872, AL; d. Aft. 1880.*
  iii. *THOMAS BALLARD, b. 1873, AL; d. Aft. 1880.*
  iv. *WILLIAM BALLARD, b. 1874.*
  v. *JAMES A. BALLARD, b. 1875, AL; d. Aft. 1880.*
  vi. *ENOCH A. BALLARD, b. 1876, AL; d. Aft. 1880.*
  vii. *ROLAND ASHTON BALLARD, b. 28 Oct 1878, AL; d. 1947; m. MARY ABBIE JENKINS; b. 1890, TX; d. 1985.*

Notes for ROLAND ASHTON BALLARD:
Source: WWI Draft Registration, 1910 Comanche County Texas Federal Census Records,

1920 Kent County Texas Federal Census Records, Lubbock County Texas Federal Census Records
* 1910 - Living in Comanche Co., TX - Ballard, Roland A 30 AL AL AL, Mary A 19 TX AR AR, Rubie M 5/12 TX AL TX
* 1920 - Living in Kent Co., TX - Ballard, Roland A. 40 AL AL AL, Mary A. 29 TX US US, Rubie M. 10 TX, Talor B. 7 TX, Jay 5 TX (hard to read)
* 1930 - Living in Lubbock Co., TX - Ballard, Roland A 51, Mary 38 Taylor 17, T. J 14
* 1940 - Living in Lubbock Co., TX - Ballard, Roland 61, Mary 19, Taylor 28

More About ROLAND ASHTON BALLARD:
Burial: City of Lubbock Cemetery, Lubbock Co., TX

More About MARY ABBIE JENKINS:
Burial: City of Lubbock Cemetery, Lubbock Co., TX

101. JOHN WESLEY[8] BALLARD (JOHN WESLEY[7], WESLEY[6], WHORTON[5], JESSE[4], JOHN[3], JOSEPH[2], JOHN[1]) *was born 23 Dec 1875 in GA, and died 25 Aug 1932. He married CARRIE BEATRICE LANCASTER. She was born 1884, and died 1954.*

Notes for JOHN WESLEY BALLARD:
Source: WWI Draft Registration Card, 1920 Carroll County Georgia Federal Census Records, Kelly Hartley (willow1@yahoo.com)
* 1910 - Living in Carrollton, Carroll Co., GA - Ballard, J Wesley Jr. 34 wd living with parents
* 1918 - Living in Carrollton, Carroll Co., GA
* 1920 - Living in Carrollton, Carroll Co., GA - Ballard, Wesley 44 GA, Carrie 33 GA, Millie 14 GA, Brewer 13 GA, Hambrick 11 GA, Merrell 6 GA, Reese 4 GA, Hardwick 2 GA
* 1930 - Living in Curroll County GA - Ballard, Wesley 54 GA, Carrie 45 GA, Thomas H 12, Mary 8

More About JOHN WESLEY BALLARD:
Burial: New Hope Methodist Church Cemetery, Carroll Co., GA

More About CARRIE BEATRICE LANCASTER:
Burial: New Hope Methodist Church Cemetery, Carroll Co., GA

Children of JOHN BALLARD and CARRIE LANCASTER are:
      i.   MILLIE[9] BALLARD, *b. 1905, Carroll Co., GA; d. 04 May 1982, Carroll Co., GA; m. VERNER E. PHILLIPS; b. 26 Feb 1902, Carroll Co., GA; d. 20 Feb 1973, Carrollton, Carroll Co., GA.*

           More About MILLIE BALLARD:
           Burial: Carroll Memory Gardens, Carrollton, Carroll Co., GA

           More About VERNER E. PHILLIPS:
           Burial: Carroll Memory Gardens, Carrollton, Carroll Co., GA

     ii.   BREWER BERNARD BALLARD, *b. 28 Dec 1906, Carroll Co., GA; d. 06 Mar 1937, Honolulu Co, HI.*

           More About BREWER BERNARD BALLARD:
           Burial: New Hope Methodist Church Cemetery, Carroll Co., GA

    iii.   JOE BROWN HAMBRICK BALLARD, *b. 27 Nov 1909, Carroll Co., GA; d. Aft. 1940; m. INEZ WEAVER, 12 Jun 1937, Cherokee AL.*
    iv.   MERRELL BALLARD, *b. 1914, Carroll Co., GA.*
     v.   REESE BALLARD, *b. 12 Nov 1915, Carroll Co., GA; d. 26 Dec 1989, Floyd Co., GA; m. MARY H.; b. 03 Jan 1914, Carroll Co., GA; d. 1971.*

           More About REESE BALLARD:

Burial: Oaknoll Memorial Gardens Cemetery, Rome, Floyd Co., GA

More About MARY H.:
Burial: Oaknoll Memorial Gardens Cemetery, Rome, Floyd Co., GA

    vi.   THOMAS HARDWICK BALLARD, b. 1918, Carroll Co., GA; d. Aft. 1930.
   vii.   MARY BALLARD, b. 1922, Carroll Co., GA; d. Aft. 1930.

102. ISAAC NEWTON[8] BALLARD (JOHN WESLEY[7], WESLEY[6], WHORTON[5], JESSE[4], JOHN[3], JOSEPH[2], JOHN[1]) was born 26 Sep 1889. He married F. VIRGINIA YOUNG 30 Jun 1912. She was born Abt. 1889.

Notes for ISAAC NEWTON BALLARD:
Source: Kelly Hartley (willow1@yahoo.com)

Children of ISAAC BALLARD and F. YOUNG are:
    i.   JAMES WOODWARD[9] BALLARD, b. Aft. 1912.
   ii.   WILLIAM NEWTON BALLARD, b. Aft. 1912.

103. MARY JANE[8] OTWELL (HESTER ANN[7] SAMPLER, ELIZABETH[6] BALLARD, WHORTON[5], JESSE[4], JOHN[3], JOSEPH[2], JOHN[1]) was born Mar 1857 in Cobb Co., GA, and died Aft. 1900 in GA. She married JOHN IDUS FINLEY 25 Apr 1875 in Cobb Co., GA. He was born 1853 in GA, and died Abt. 1900 in AL.

Notes for MARY JANE OTWELL:
Source: Tex Dick, Marriage Records from Book B, pg 121 Cobb County Georgia
* Textile Porterdale Spooler. Could not read or write

Notes for JOHN IDUS FINLEY:
Source: Source: 1880 Blount County Alabama Federal Census Records, Tex Dick, Shelea McLaughlin (shelea3@juno.com)
* 1880 - Living in Blount Co., AL - Findley, John I 27, Mary 23, Rebeca M 5, Matta H 3, Samuel G 4/12

Children of MARY OTWELL and JOHN FINLEY are:
    i.   REBECCA MAE[9] FINLEY, b. 11 Aug 1876; d. 17 Nov 1951, Newton Co., GA; m. JOHN H. ARNOLD, SR..

        Notes for REBECCA MAE FINLEY:
        Source: Shelea McLaughlin (shelea3@juno.com)

   ii.   MARTHA FINLEY, b. Nov 1877.
  iii.   SAMUEL LITTLETON FINLEY, b. 11 Mar 1880, Antantio Blu, Cobb Co., GA; d. 20 Jul 1943, Newton Co., GA; m. CELIA JAY WYLEY, 07 Feb 1904, Newton Co., GA; b. 09 Jan 1884, GA; d. 15 Sep 1967.

        Notes for SAMUEL LITTLETON FINLEY:
        Source: 1910-1940 Newton County Georgia Federal Census Records

        * 1910 - Living in Cedar Shoals, Newton Co., GA - Finley, Sam 27 AL GA GA, Wylder 25 - 3 children 3 living GA GA GA, Robbie fe 5 GA, Fay 3 GA, Mary 1 2/12 GA, Mary mother 53 wd GA GA GA
        * 1920 - Living in Porterdale, Newton Co., GA - Finley, Sam L 38, Wylder 35, Robbie 14, Faye 12, Mary 10, Forrest 8, Ralph 5, Inez 1
        * 1930 - Living in Porterdale, Newton Co., GA - Finley, Sam 50, Sylda 45, Roby 24 Fay 22, Mary 19, Forest 17, Ralph 16, Inez 12, Willie 11, Celia K 84
        * 1940 - Living in Porterdale, Newton Co., GA - Findley, Sam 59, Wylder 55, Robbie 35, Forrest 28, Ralph 26, Willie Carrol 17, Earl Moore 28 Fay 32

More About SAMUEL LITTLETON FINLEY:
Burial: Southview Cemetery, Covington Newton Co., GA

More About CELIA JAY WYLEY:
Burial: Southview Cemetery, Covington Newton Co., GA

iv. LEILA ANN FINLEY, b. 10 Aug 1882, Blount Co., AL; d. 10 Nov 1966, Conyers, Rockdale Co., GA; m. (1) W. A. TERRY; m. (2) JOHN WASHINGTON KIRKES, 01 Apr 1899, Newton Co., GA; b. Apr 1882, DeKalb Co., GA; d. 17 Dec 1918, Newton Co., GA.

Notes for LEILA ANN FINLEY:
Source: Tex Dick
* Spooler Tender Textile Bibb Manufacturer

Notes for JOHN WASHINGTON KIRKES:
Source: Tex Dick

v. OLLIE SMITH FINLEY, b. 25 Dec 1884, Blount Co., AL; d. 01 Aug 1955, GA; m. MAMIE EMILY ?, Abt. 1912; b. 13 Aug 1888; d. 19 Mar 1977, Newton, GA.

104. CHARLES "CHARLIE"[8] OTWELL (HESTER ANN[7] SAMPLER, ELIZABETH[6] BALLARD, WHORTON[5], JESSE[4], JOHN[3], JOSEPH[2], JOHN[1]) was born Apr 1866 in Cobb Co., GA, and died 1936 in Cobb Co., GA. He married CLIFTON MAY FARR 1891. She was born Jun 1874 in GA, and died 1955.

Notes for CHARLES "CHARLIE" OTWELL:
Source: 1900 - 1910 Cobb County Georgia Federal Census Records
* 1900 - Living in Roswell, Cobb Co., GA - Otwell, Charles 34, Clifton M 25, Lena M 7, Forice R 4, Louie G 1, Irene C 2, Lucy Elliot 40
* 1910 - Living in Roswell, Cobb Co., GA - Otwell, Cherlie C 44 GA GA GA Cliffton M 36 - 6 children 6 living GA , Lena M 17 GA, Forrest R. 15 GA, Lore G 13 GA, Charlotte I 11 GA, Hester R 7 GA, Charlie C Jr 2 GA, Lucy Elliont 55 boarder

More About CLIFTON MAY FARR:
Burial: Old Roswell Cemetery, Fulton Co., GA

Children of CHARLES OTWELL and CLIFTON FARR are:

i. LENA M.[9] OTWELL, b. 21 Oct 1892, GA; d. 10 Dec 1980, Fulton Co., GA; m. O. J. COWART, DR.; b. 23 Apr 1887; d. 16 Dec 1930.

More About LENA M. OTWELL:
Burial: Old Roswell Cemetery, Fulton Co., GA

More About O. J. COWART, DR.:
Burial: Old Roswell Cemetery, Fulton Co., GA

ii. FORREST R. OTWELL, b. 03 Sep 1894, Cobb Co., GA; d. 30 Oct 1953, Jefferson Co., AL; m. LEE BYRON PLANT; b. 18 Dec 1889, Meriwether Co., GA; d. 14 Oct 1931, Jefferson Co., AL.

More About FORREST R. OTWELL:
Burial: Old Roswell Cemetery, Fulton Co., GA

More About LEE BYRON PLANT:
Burial: Old Roswell Cemetery, Fulton Co., GA

> iii. LOUIE G. OTWELL, b. Jun 1896, GA; d. Aft. 1920.
> iv. IRENE CHARLOTTE OTWELL, b. Mar 1898, GA; d. Aft. 1920.
> v. HESTER R. OTWELL, b. Abt. 1903, GA; d. Aft. 1920.
> vi. CHARLES C. OTWELL, b. 09 Jan 1908, GA; d. 22 Apr 1918.
>
> More About CHARLES C. OTWELL:
> Burial: Old Roswell Cemetery, Fulton Co., GA
>
> vii. PAUL LAMAR OTWELL, b. 07 Apr 1918, GA; d. 18 Sep 1972.
>
> More About PAUL LAMAR OTWELL:
> Burial: Old Roswell Cemetery, Fulton Co., GA

105. EMMA LEE[8] SAMPLER (WILLIAM WESLEY[7], ELIZABETH[6] BALLARD, WHORTON[5], JESSE[4], JOHN[3], JOSEPH[2], JOHN[1]) was born 11 May 1873 in Murray Co., GA, and died 11 Apr 1946 in Glendale, Los Angeles Co., CA. She married MICHAEL FRANCIS CROSS Jun 1900. He was born 27 May 1860 in England, and died 31 Jul 1931 in Glendale, Los Angeles Co., CA.

More About EMMA LEE SAMPLER:
Burial: Forest Lawn Memorial Park, Glendale, Los Angeles Co., CA

Notes for MICHAEL FRANCIS CROSS:
Source: 1910 Oklahoma Federal Census Records
* 1910 - Living in Oklahoma City, Oklahoma Co., OK - Gross, Michael 49 England, Emma 35 - 4 children 3 living GA, Alta 7 NE, Thelma 5 GA, Audrey 1 NE

More About MICHAEL FRANCIS CROSS:
Burial: Los Angeles National Cemetery, Los Angeles Co., CA

Children of EMMA SAMPLER and MICHAEL CROSS are:
> i. RICHARD[9] CROSS, b. Apr 1901; d. Apr 1903.
> ii. ALTA LOUISE CROSS, b. 10 Feb 1903, Omaha, NE; d. Aft. 1920; m. EMMETT A. VICKERS, 30 Apr 1932, Yuma Co., AZ; b. 19 May 1902.
> iii. THELMA CROSS, b. Abt. 1905, GA; d. Aft. 1920.
> iv. AUDREY SUE CROSS, b. Abt. 1909, NE; d. Aft. 1910.
> v. MARY JANE CROSS, b. 01 Jan 1911, OK; d. 04 Mar 1985, Los Angeles Co., CA.

106. WILLIAM WALDEN[8] SAMPLER (WILLIAM WESLEY[7], ELIZABETH[6] BALLARD, WHORTON[5], JESSE[4], JOHN[3], JOSEPH[2], JOHN[1]) was born 19 Feb 1872 in Tunnel Hill, Whitfield Co., GA, and died 10 May 1951 in Murray Co., GA. He married NORA EMMA HUMPHREYS 25 Dec 1898 in Murray Co., GA. She was born 30 Aug 1877 in GA, and died 19 May 1952 in Murray Co., GA.

Notes for WILLIAM WALDEN SAMPLER:
Source: 1910 Murray County Georgia Federal Census Records, 1920 McCurtain County Oklahoma Federal Census Record, 1930 Fulton County Georgia Federal Census Records, 1940 Murray County Georgia Federal Census Records
* 1910 - Living in Murray Co., GA - Sampler, William W 38 GA GA GA, Nora E 32 GA GA GA 5 children 5 living, Martha A 8 GA, Charles H 6 GA, Lara L 5 GA, Edna J 2 GA, William 1/12 GA
* 1920 - Living in Fowler, McCurtain Co., OK - Sampler, William W 47 GA, Nora E 42 GA, Martha R 18 GA, Charles H 16 GA, Laura Lee 15 GA, Edna Jane 12 GA, Clyde 10 GA, Louis B 7 GA, Myra Joe 1 GA
* 1930 - Living in Fulton Co., GA - Sampler, William W 26 AL, Nora E 52 GA, Martha R 28, Laura L 25 GA, Edna J 23 GA, Louis B 16 GA, Myra Joe 11 GA, Francis E 9 GA
* 1940 - Living in Doolittle, Murray Co., GA - Sampler, William 69, Nora 63, Annie Humphries 56, Mary Waldon 72

More About WILLIAM WALDEN SAMPLER:
Burial: Mt. Zion Cemetery, Chatworth, Murray Co., GA

More About NORA EMMA HUMPHREYS:
Burial: Mt Zion Cemetery, Murray Co., GA

Children of WILLIAM SAMPLER and NORA HUMPHREYS are:

i. MARTHA REBECCA[9] SAMPLER, b. 10 May 1901, Murray Co., GA; d. 27 Oct 1998, GA; m. WILLIAM HOWARD MCLEROY; b. 10 May 1901, Banks Co., GA; d. 28 Jan 1983, Fulton Co., GA.

   More About MARTHA REBECCA SAMPLER:
   Burial: Westview Cemetery, Atlanta, Fulton Co., GA

   More About WILLIAM HOWARD MCLEROY:
   Burial: Westview Cemetery, Atlanta, Fulton Co., GA

ii. CHARLES HUMPHREYS SAMPLER, b. 02 May 1903, Cobb Co., GA; d. 23 Jan 1974, Grundy Co., TN.

iii. LAURA LEE SAMPLER, b. 28 Nov 1904, Murray Co., GA; d. 19 Mar 1984, Fulton Co., GA.

iv. EDNA JANE SAMPLER, b. 22 Jul 1907, Murray Co., GA; d. 14 Jul 1981, Whitfield Co., GA; m. MALVERN DUNFORD; b. Abt. 1900.

v. WILLIAM CLYDE SAMPLER, b. 06 Mar 1910, Murray Co., GA; d. 10 Oct 1973, Fulton Co., GA.

vi. LEWIS BERTRAND SAMPLER, b. 21 Sep 1912, Murray Co., GA; d. 21 Aug 1977, Murray Co., GA.

vii. JUIAN RANDALL SAMPLER, b. 28 Jun 1915, Murray Co., GA; d. 30 Jun 1915, Murray Co., GA.

viii. MYRA JO SAMPLER, b. 28 Jul 1918, McCurtain Co., OK; d. 15 Jul 1996, GA; m. EUGENE E. MURPHY, 30 Nov 1937, College Park, Clayton Co., GA; b. 25 Feb 1913.

ix. FRANCIS EUGENE SAMPLER, b. 05 Nov 1920, Murray Co., GA; d. 17 Aug 1943, Hall Co., NE.

William L. Ballard

Generation No. 1

1. WILLIAM L.[1] BALLARD *was born 1813 in GA, and died Aft. 1870. He married* SARAH ANN HUNTER *23 Jan 1836 in Stewart Co., GA. She was born 1816 in GA, and died Aft. 1870.*

Notes for WILLIAM L. BALLARD:
Source: 1850 Randolph County Georgia Federal Census Records, 1860 Barbour County Alabama Federal Census Records, 1870 Montgomery County Alabama Federal Census Records

* 1850 - Living in Randolph Co., GA - Ballard, Wm. L. 37 GA Hotel Keeper, S. A. 25 GA, Wm. L. 6 GA, SJ 3 GA
* 1860 - Living in Barbour Co., GA - Ballard, Wm. L. 47 GA City Marshall, Sarah W 44 GA, Wm L GA apprentice mechanic GA, Joseph W. 13, Julian P. 11 GA, Amelia 8 GA, Eugene M 6 GA, Edgar E. 4 GA, Gertrude 1 GA
* 1870 - Living in Montgomery Co., AL - Ballard, Wm. L 57 GA, S.A. 48 GA, E.M 17 GA, E.E. 15 GA, R. R. 10 AL, Fletcher 6 AL, C. G 12 AL (next door) C.C. Curry 20 (fe) GA, Willie Ballard 6 AL, W. L. 26 (ma) GA, J. W. 23 (fe) AL

Children of WILLIAM BALLARD *and* SARAH HUNTER *are:*

2.	i.	WILLIAM L.[2] BALLARD, b. 1845, GA; d. Aft. 1880.
	ii.	JOSEPH W. BALLARD, b. 1847, GA; d. Aft. 1870.
	iii.	JULIAN BALLARD, b. 1849, GA; d. Aft. 1860.
	iv.	AMELIA BALLARD, b. 1852, GA; d. Aft. 1860.
3.	v.	EUGENE M. BALLARD, b. 17 Oct 1849, GA; d. 22 Feb 1932, Childress Co., TX.
	vi.	CLARA GERTRUDE BALLARD, b. 1859, GA; d. Aft. 1860; m. THOMAS BRACEY, 1877, TX; b. 1850, TX.
4.	vii.	ROBERT REEVES BALLARD, b. 24 Jan 1861, AL; d. 03 Apr 1917.
	viii.	FLETCHER BALLARD, b. 1863; d. Aft. 1870.

Generation No. 2

2. WILLIAM L.[2] BALLARD (WILLIAM L.[1]) *was born 1845 in GA, and died Aft. 1880. He married* M. A. SPEAR *20 Oct 1869 in Montgomery Co., AL. She was born Abt. 1847 in AL.*

Notes for WILLIAM L. BALLARD:
Source: 1870 Montgomery County Alabama Federal Census Records, 1880 Austin County Texas Federal Census Records

* 1870 - Living in Montgomery Co., AL - Ballard, Wm L Jr. 26 farmer (m), M. A 23 (f), J. W 23 (m)
* 1880 - Living in Austin Co., TX - Living with his brother Eugene

Children of WILLIAM BALLARD *and* M. SPEAR *are:*

	i.	ARTHUR[3] BALLARD, b. 1873, TX; d. Aft. 1880.
	ii.	ELLA BALLARD, b. Abt. 1875, TX; d. Aft. 1880.

3. EUGENE M.[2] BALLARD (WILLIAM L.[1]) *was born 17 Oct 1849 in GA, and died 22 Feb 1932 in Childress Co., TX. He married* LILLY HARVEY *Bef. 1880, daughter of* RICHARD HARVEY *and* ELIZA BIGNELL. *She was born 21 Aug 1861 in London Lambert Dist. England, and died 06 Dec 1901 in Santa Anna, Coleman Co. TX.*

Notes for EUGENE M. BALLARD:
Source:1880 Austin County Texas Federal Census Records, 1900 Palo Pinto County Texas Federal Census

Records, *1910 Ellis County Texas Federal Census Records, Childress County Texas Standard Certificate of Death, Johnnie Gilbreath*
* *1880 - Living in Austin Co., TX - Ballard Eugene M 25 GA KY TN, Elizabeth 18 Eng, Eng Eng, W L 35 farmer GA KY TN, Arthur 5 TX GA AL, Ella 5 AL*
* *1900 - Living in Mineral Wells, Palo Pinto Co., TX - Ballard, E M - Oct 1855 GA GA VA, Lillie - Aug 1861 Eng Eng Eng, Birdie - May 1886, Fred - Aug 1896 TX, Pearl Bracey niece - Mar 1887 TX*
* *1910 - Living in Ellis Co., TX - Ballard, Eugene M 56, Joe Griffin, 26, Birdie 27, Couter 5, Ella W.2*

Children of EUGENE BALLARD and LILLY HARVEY are:

5.   i.   BIRTIE EUGENE[3] BALLARD, b. May 1886, Austin Co., TX; d. 20 May 1941.
        ii.   RAY BALLARD, b. Abt. 1890.
      iii.   FRED BALLARD, b. 31 Aug 1896, TX; d. 16 Mar 1973, Paducah, TX; m. LUCILLE STILLWELL, Abt. 1934; b. Abt. 1896.

4. ROBERT REEVES[2] BALLARD (WILLIAM L.[1]) was born 24 Jan 1861 in AL, and died 03 Apr 1917. He married (1) 1ST WIFE Bef. 1893. He married (2) IDA Bet. 1900 - 1910.

Notes for ROBERT REEVES BALLARD:
Source: *1900-1910 Austin County Texas Federal Census Records*
* *1900 - Living in Austin Co., TX - Ballard, Robert - Jan 1861 wd Al AL AL, Mildred - Apr 1893 TX AL TX 7, Effie Aug 1895 TX,, D - Jan 1896 TX4, Hilda - Mar 1897 TX 3, Robert - May 1898 2 TX*
* *1910 - Living in Austin Co., TX - Ballard, Robert R 49 AL AL AL md 2x, Ida 36 1 zero children MS AL MS, Mildred 17 TX, Effey 15 TX, Dee (m) 14 TX, Robert 12 TX, Annis Brock sister in law 26 MS, Marshall Brock brother in law 24 MS, Bell 19 sister in law MS, Jody brother in law 15 MS, and a boarder*

More About ROBERT REEVES BALLARD:
Burial: Sealy Cemetery, Austin Co., TX

Children of ROBERT BALLARD and 1ST WIFE are:
        i.   MILDRED[3] BALLARD, b. Apr 1893, TX; d. Aft. 1910.
      ii.   EFFEY BALLARD, b. Aug 1895, TX; d. Aft. 1910.
    iii.   DEE BALLARD, b. Jan 1896, TX; d. Aft. 1910.
    iv.   HILDA BALLARD, b. Mar 1897, TX; d. Aft. 1910.
     v.   ROBERT BALLARD, b. May 1898, TX; d. Aft. 1910.

Generation No. 3

5. BIRTIE EUGENE[3] BALLARD (EUGENE M.[2], WILLIAM L.[1]) was born May 1886 in Austin Co., TX, and died 20 May 1941. She married THOMAS JEFFERSON GILBREATH Abt. 1900. He was born 21 Dec 1884 in Hunt Co TX.

Notes for THOMAS JEFFERSON GILBREATH:
Source: *1930 Cottle County Texas Federal Census Records, Johnnie Gilbreath*

* *1930 - Living in Cottle Co., TX - Gilbreath, Thomas F 44 TX, Bertie E 43 TX, John W 0/12 TX, Ballard, Eugene father 77 wd GA US US*

Child of BIRTIE BALLARD and THOMAS GILBREATH is:
        i.   JOHNNIE W.[4] GILBREATH, b. 06 May 1930, Paducah, Cottle Co., TX; m. MURIEL ELIZABETH ROSS; b. 08 Oct 1830, Wichita Falls TX.

William Orby Ballard

Generation No. 1

1. WILLIAM ORBY[1] BALLARD *was born 1874 in Morgan Co., GA, and died Aft. 1930. He married* MINNIE ELIZABETH JENKINS *29 Jul 1902 in Morgan Co., GA. She was born 05 Jun 1876 in GA, and died 05 Aug 1937.*

Notes for WILLIAM ORBY BALLARD:
Source: 1910-1930 Morgan County Georgia Federal Census Records, Morgan County Georgia Marriage License, Light238@aol.com

* 1910 - Living in Fairplay, Morgan Co., GA - Ballard, WO 36 GA GA GA, Minnie 32 4 children 4 living, GA, George 18, Mary 12, Edward 7, Albert 11/12
* 1920 - Living in Adsboro, Morgan Co., GA - Ballard, William O 45, Minnie 43 GA GA GA, May 18 GA, Edward 17 GA, Albert 9 GA, Joe 5 GA
* 1930 - Living in Harris, Morgan Co., GA - Ballard, W. Orby 56 GA GA GA, Minnie 53 GA GA GA, Edgar 26 GA, Albert 20 GA, Joe 16 GA, Bertie 10 GA

Children of WILLIAM BALLARD *and* MINNIE JENKINS *are:*

	i.	GEORGE HENRY[2] BALLARD, b. 1892, Union Co., GA; d. Aft. 1910.
2.	ii.	MARY BALLARD, b. 1898, Union Co., GA; d. 08 Feb 1978, Morgan Co., GA.
	iii.	EDWARD BALLARD, b. 1903, Union Co., GA; d. Aft. 1920.
	iv.	ALBERT BALLARD, b. 1911, Union Co., GA; d. Aft. 1920.
	v.	JOE BALLARD, b. 1915, Union Co., GA; d. Aft. 1920.
	vi.	BERTIE BALLARD, b. 1920, Union Co., GA; d. Aft. 1930.

Generation No. 2

2. MARY[2] BALLARD (WILLIAM ORBY[1]) *was born 1898 in Union Co., GA, and died 08 Feb 1978 in Morgan Co., GA. She married* FLOYD HANSON. *He was born Abt. 1896 in GA, and died Aft. 1940.*

Notes for FLOYD HANSON:
Source: 1940 Morgan County Georgia Federal Census Records

* 1940 - Living in Askew, Morgan Co. GA - Hanson, Floyd 44 GA, Mary B 39 GA, Lillian 7 GA, Joe 5 GA, Chas H Sullivan 18 GA

Children of MARY BALLARD *and* FLOYD HANSON *are:*

	i.	LILLIAN[3] HANSON, b. Abt. 1933, Morgan Co., GA; d. Aft. 1940.
	ii.	JOE FLOYD HANSON, b. Abt. 1935, Morgan Co., GA; d. Aft. 1940.

Index of Individuals

Ballard, Adella: 34
Ballard, Adolphus Greene: 13
Ballard, Adolphus W.: 26, 27
Ballard, Aford: 223
Ballard, Agnes: 217
Ballard, Al: 224
Ballard, Albert: 111
Ballard, Albert: 114
Ballard, Albert: 265
Ballard, Albert "Bert": 120, 131, 136
Ballard, Albert Benjamin: 228
Ballard, Albert C.: 12, 25
Ballard, Albert James: 118, 129, 130, 136
Ballard, Albert Sidney: 25
Ballard, Albert Wright: 60
Ballard, Alene: 172
Ballard, Alexander: 48, 49, 51
Ballard, Alexander Henry: 125, 134, 135
Ballard, Alexis: 51
Ballard, Alfred: 111
Ballard, Alfred: 154
Ballard, Alfred A.: 223
Ballard, Alfred O.: 212, 254, 255
Ballard, Alice Arvella: 87
Ballard, Alice Bell: 85, 106
Ballard, Alice G.: 243, 244
Ballard, Alice H.: 118
Ballard, Alice Mabel: 26
Ballard, Alice Maude: 22
Ballard, Alice Reida: 231
Ballard, Allander B.: 89
Ballard, Alleck: 211
Ballard, Allene Clay: 27
Ballard, Alma: 42
Ballard, Alma E.: 138
Ballard, Alma Judy: 176
Ballard, Almeta: 217
Ballard, Alonzo: 119, 131
Ballard, Alonzo Dow: 232
Ballard, Alphonso: 38
Ballard, Alton Eugene "Gene": 176
Ballard, Alton Powerll: 178
Ballard, Alva R.: 178
Ballard, Alvan: 44
Ballard, Alvey Scott: 166
Ballard, Alvin: 114
Ballard, Alvin Freeman: 255
Ballard, Alvin Monroe: 192, 200, 221-223
Ballard, Amanda: 17
Ballard, Amanda Jane: 9, 22
Ballard, Amanda Sarah: 157
Ballard, Amazonia Annette: 207, 243
Ballard, Ambrose B.: 182, 184, 185
Ballard, Amelia: 263
Ballard, America M.: 117, 129
Ballard, Andar: 222

Ballard, Andie: 40
Ballard, Andrew: 109
Ballard, Andrew "Drew": 131
Ballard, Andrew Jackson: 207, 241
Ballard, Andrew Jackson: 77
Ballard, Andrew Jackson "Jack": 256
Ballard, Andrew Sherman: 146, 148, 149
Ballard, Ann: 209
Ballard, Ann E.: 17
Ballard, Ann Francis: 194
Ballard, Ann Ophelia: 127
Ballard, Anna: 43
Ballard, Anna: 30
Ballard, Anna: 20, 41
Ballard, Anna: 84
Ballard, Anna Bang: 42
Ballard, Anna Cordelia Camak: 13
Ballard, Anna E.: 47
Ballard, Anna Laurie: 85, 106, 107
Ballard, Anna Lee: 73
Ballard, Anna Lee: 250
Ballard, Anne Elizabeth: 65-67
Ballard, Annie: 211
Ballard, Annie: 118
Ballard, Annie: 28
Ballard, Annie: 226
Ballard, Annie: 164
Ballard, Annie: 184, 187
Ballard, Annie A.: 80
Ballard, Annie Elizabeth "Bessie": 92
Ballard, Annie Ghneva: 175
Ballard, Annie Isabella: 118
Ballard, Annie Kate: 94
Ballard, Annie Laurie: 230
Ballard, Annie Lois: 250
Ballard, Annie Lou Frances: 185
Ballard, Annie Reah: 130
Ballard, Annie Z.: 118
Ballard, Anthony: 115
Ballard, Archie Clayton: 71
Ballard, Archie Dean Dupriest: 256
Ballard, Ardelia "Delia": 163, 171
Ballard, Arma: 143
Ballard, Armistead: 9, 19, 20, 40, 41
Ballard, Arthur: 17
Ballard, Arthur: 263
Ballard, Arthur Elmer: 205, 232
Ballard, Arthur Elmer , Jr.: 232
Ballard, Arthur Roland: 168
Ballard, Artie Ida V.: 125, 134
Ballard, Artimissa: 109, 115, 125, 126, 135
Ballard, Aryaria C. L.: 209, 246
Ballard, Asa T.: 212
Ballard, Asberry Newton: 207
Ballard, Augustus: 189
Ballard, Aurelia A.: 212

Ballard, Austin: 129
Ballard, Avery: 161
Ballard, Axie Ellen: 71
Ballard, B. V.: 35
Ballard, Barbara Elizabeth "Laura": 255
Ballard, Baxter Jones: 210
Ballard, Beatrice: 40
Ballard, Beatrice D.: 87, 88
Ballard, Belder C.: 247
Ballard, Bella Lusinda: 232
Ballard, Belle: 120
Ballard, Ben Graden: 71
Ballard, Bena A.: 178
Ballard, Benjamin: 7-10, 12, 14-27, 29, 32-43
Ballard, Benjamin: 56
Ballard, Benjamin: 11
Ballard, Benjamin: 14
Ballard, Benjamin "Benj": 17
Ballard, Benjamin "Bennie": 23
Ballard, Benjamin "Randall": 30, 31
Ballard, Benjamin Cumble: 33
Ballard, Benjamin Frank: 19, 37, 38
Ballard, Benjamin Franklin: 135, 137
Ballard, Benjamin Franklin "Frank": 165
Ballard, Benjamin O.: 196
Ballard, Benjamin Randal "Butler": 16, 33
Ballard, Benjamin Randall: 8, 15, 29, 32-34
Ballard, Benjamin Walter: 13, 27
Ballard, Benjamin Walter: 27
Ballard, Bennetta: 88
Ballard, Benniola "Bennie": 89
Ballard, Berlon: 133
Ballard, Bernice: 107
Ballard, Berta: 29
Ballard, Bertie: 265
Ballard, Bessie: 50
Ballard, Bessie: 121
Ballard, Bessie: 88
Ballard, Bessie: 154, 156
Ballard, Bettie: 21
Ballard, Betty Jo: 173, 174
Ballard, Bibb Hunter: 29
Ballard, Biddie: 212
Ballard, Birtie Eugene: 264
Ballard, Blueford Harold: 107
Ballard, Bob: 223
Ballard, Bob: 51
Ballard, Booker E.: 129
Ballard, Bowie Chadick: 250
Ballard, Brents Larrimore: 29
Ballard, Brewer Bernard: 258
Ballard, Bryant: 154
Ballard, Buna M.: 140
Ballard, Burse Lasting Gale: 16, 34
Ballard, Burton: 87
Ballard, Byron: 137

Ballard, Caledonia: 146
Ballard, Calvin M.: 34
Ballard, Calvin M.: 34
Ballard, Cara B.: 208
Ballard, Cardie: 40
Ballard, Carl: 130
Ballard, Carl Bethel: 171
Ballard, Carl Cecil: 187
Ballard, Carl Edison: 69
Ballard, Carl Thomas: 51
Ballard, Carmella: 212
Ballard, Caroline: 199
Ballard, Carrie: 25
Ballard, Carrie: 257
Ballard, Carrie C.: 250
Ballard, Carrie Mae: 214
Ballard, Carrie S.: 81, 98, 99
Ballard, Cartie: 130
Ballard, Cassandra Cassidy: 19, 39
Ballard, Catherine: 19
Ballard, Catherine: 105
Ballard, Catherine "Kate": 152
Ballard, Catherine "Katie": 181
Ballard, Cecil Franklin: 178
Ballard, Cecil M.: 189
Ballard, Cecile: 156
Ballard, Cena: 38
Ballard, Charles: 18
Ballard, Charles: 182
Ballard, Charles Beamon: 205, 231, 232
Ballard, Charles Coleman: 248
Ballard, Charles Columbus: 228
Ballard, Charles Edward: 230
Ballard, Charles H.: 26, 42
Ballard, Charles Henry: 153, 155
Ballard, Charles Herman: 54
Ballard, Charles Hudson: 13
Ballard, Charles Levens: 36
Ballard, Charles Wesley: 218, 219
Ballard, Charles Wesley: 79
Ballard, Charles Young: 94
Ballard, Charlie Monroe: 31
Ballard, Charlotte Alberta: 131, 136
Ballard, Charlotte Dena: 87
Ballard, Cheli Deforest: 248
Ballard, Chelie N.: 250
Ballard, Chester Newton: 241, 242
Ballard, child: 20
Ballard, Chloe: 132
Ballard, Christopher Wren: 28
Ballard, Cicero: 116, 128
Ballard, Cicero B.: 128
Ballard, Claiborne "Dutch" Lorenzo: 203, 225, 226
Ballard, Clara: 211
Ballard, Clara: 49
Ballard, Clara Ann: 114

Ballard, Elijah Jasper: 139, 141
Ballard, Elijah Maddox: 80, 97
Ballard, Elijah W.: 75-77, 79-93, 95-108
Ballard, Elijah W.: 75-77, 84-88, 106-108
Ballard, Eliza: 21
Ballard, Eliza: 199
Ballard, Eliza Jane: 157-159
Ballard, Eliza Jane: 150
Ballard, Eliza Ophelia: 81
Ballard, Elizabeth: 192, 197, 214, 215, 259-261
Ballard, Elizabeth: 58
Ballard, Elizabeth: 9
Ballard, Elizabeth: 109, 112
Ballard, Elizabeth: 14
Ballard, Elizabeth: 111, 117
Ballard, Elizabeth: 80
Ballard, Elizabeth: 116
Ballard, Elizabeth: 19
Ballard, Elizabeth: 206, 236
Ballard, Elizabeth: 11, 24
Ballard, Elizabeth: 20
Ballard, Elizabeth: 19
Ballard, Elizabeth: 27
Ballard, Elizabeth: 184
Ballard, Elizabeth "Bessie": 24
Ballard, Elizabeth "Bessy" Tinsley: 13
Ballard, Elizabeth "Eliza Sue" Ann: 9
Ballard, Elizabeth "Lizzie": 152
Ballard, Elizabeth "Lizzy": 26
Ballard, Elizabeth A.: 75
Ballard, Elizabeth A.: 78, 90, 91
Ballard, Elizabeth Ann: 194
Ballard, Elizabeth Ann "Betsey": 15
Ballard, Elizabeth Bussey: 161
Ballard, Elizabeth G.: 212
Ballard, Elizabeth Lanie: 15
Ballard, Elizabeth Pearl: 120, 131, 132
Ballard, Elizabeth Rebecca: 80
Ballard, Elizabeth Rebecca: 97
Ballard, Elizaeth Jane: 155
Ballard, Ella: 263
Ballard, Ella: 219
Ballard, Ella: 34
Ballard, Ella: 34
Ballard, Ella Lydia: 198, 215, 216
Ballard, Ella M.: 249
Ballard, Ella May: 140
Ballard, Ellen: 211
Ballard, Ellen: 65, 71, 72
Ballard, Ellen Orey: 114
Ballard, Ellie Mae: 238
Ballard, Elmer Gerald: 137
Ballard, Elmira I.: 120
Ballard, Elmo Marion: 217
Ballard, Elton Kelly: 169
Ballard, Emaline "Emily": 181, 182, 184

Ballard, Emily: 62
Ballard, Emily Dona: 205, 231
Ballard, Emily F.: 65
Ballard, Emily J.: 211
Ballard, Emma: 150
Ballard, Emma: 162
Ballard, Emma: 183
Ballard, Emma Clara: 104
Ballard, Emma Gerina: 31, 32
Ballard, Emma Lene: 133
Ballard, Emma Rebecca: 61
Ballard, Emma Swanson: 153
Ballard, Ennes Wendell: 169
Ballard, Enoch A.: 257
Ballard, Enoch Burton: 213, 256
Ballard, Erasmus: 114
Ballard, Erin: 29
Ballard, Ernest: 164
Ballard, Ernest D.: 84
Ballard, Esma: 29
Ballard, Essie: 162
Ballard, Estelle: 93
Ballard, Ethel Antie: 245
Ballard, Ethel Lee: 52
Ballard, Etta: 167
Ballard, Etta Jane: 225
Ballard, Eugene "Dollie": 164
Ballard, Eugene M.: 263, 264
Ballard, Eula Lee: 210, 251, 252
Ballard, Eula Mae: 164, 175
Ballard, Eula Ywachette: 175
Ballard, Eulah L.: 143
Ballard, Eunice: 154
Ballard, Eunice Cooper: 90
Ballard, Euphronias Franklin: 10, 23
Ballard, Eva: 161
Ballard, Eva: 217
Ballard, Evah E.: 122
Ballard, Evaline " Evie": 49
Ballard, Evan Adolphus: 43
Ballard, Evan Coleman: 30
Ballard, Evan Frank: 42
Ballard, Evan Joshua: 8
Ballard, Evan Powell: 13, 25, 26, 42
Ballard, Evans Coleman: 16, 29-31
Ballard, Evans Coleman: 31
Ballard, Eveline: 53
Ballard, Evelyn: 166
Ballard, Evelyn Aileen: 155
Ballard, Everett LeRoy: 69
Ballard, Evlenor O.: 86, 107
Ballard, Ewell Francis: 103
Ballard, Excy R.: 199
Ballard, F. Rutha: 12
Ballard, Fait B.: 222
Ballard, Fannie: 21

Ballard, Guy Edward: 45, 46
Ballard, Guy Edward , Jr.: 46
Ballard, H. W.: 113
Ballard, Hardy: 166
Ballard, Hardy Sellers: 33
Ballard, Hariette E.: 208
Ballard, Harold B.: 164
Ballard, Harriet "Hattie": 183, 185, 186
Ballard, Harriet M.: 80
Ballard, Harriet Margaret: 200
Ballard, Harrietta: 12
Ballard, Harrison Monroe: 218
Ballard, Harrison Taylor: 200
Ballard, Harry: 120
Ballard, Harvey E.: 86, 108
Ballard, Harvey Morris: 142-144
Ballard, Hasting Uriah Gilchrist: 16, 33, 34
Ballard, Hattie: 178
Ballard, Hattie O.: 129
Ballard, Hector: 133
Ballard, Helen G.: 131, 136, 137
Ballard, Helen L.: 47
Ballard, Hendris: 29
Ballard, Henrietta A: 12
Ballard, Henry: 157
Ballard, Henry Alexander: 209, 247
Ballard, Henry C.: 77
Ballard, Henry Cleburn: 130
Ballard, Henry David: 139, 143
Ballard, Henry Grady: 257
Ballard, Henry J.: 160
Ballard, Henry Lewis: 199, 216
Ballard, Henry Oscar: 230
Ballard, Henry R.: 149
Ballard, Henry Savage: 36
Ballard, Henry T.: 129
Ballard, Henry Tomas: 142
Ballard, Herbert Gilson: 216
Ballard, Herbert Weldon: 83, 104, 105
Ballard, Herman Brown: 51, 53, 54
Ballard, Herman Leverette: 11
Ballard, Herman O. Geissler: 42
Ballard, Hilda: 264
Ballard, Hilson L.: 73
Ballard, Hiram: 48-53
Ballard, Hiram: 48, 50, 53
Ballard, Hiram D.: 199
Ballard, Hiram Eassy: 216
Ballard, Hiram Hillary: 217
Ballard, Hiram Rhodes: 221
Ballard, Hiram Thomas: 212
Ballard, Homer: 184
Ballard, Horace Greeley: 226
Ballard, Horace Weldon: 164
Ballard, Hortense: 217
Ballard, Howard Bennett: 103

Ballard, Howard Charles: 231
Ballard, Howard Clay: 169
Ballard, Howard Roy: 53
Ballard, Howard Volley: 229
Ballard, Hoyt: 40
Ballard, Hugh Dent: 29
Ballard, Humphrey: 55, 56, 58-66, 68-72
Ballard, Ida: 44
Ballard, Ida: 11
Ballard, Ida Belll: 114
Ballard, Ida Florence: 256
Ballard, Ida Susan: 255
Ballard, Ike Vale: 44
Ballard, Ila: 143
Ballard, Ima Lee: 165, 177
Ballard, Ima Ruth: 164
Ballard, Imogene: 173
Ballard, Indiana Elizabeth: 203
Ballard, Inez Ella: 173
Ballard, Infant: 221
Ballard, Iona: 199
Ballard, Ira: 223
Ballard, Ira Cheleous: 210, 251
Ballard, Ira Cunningham , Jr.: 251
Ballard, Ira Mason: 24
Ballard, Irby Seaborn: 226, 227
Ballard, Irene: 25
Ballard, Irene: 132
Ballard, Irene: 108
Ballard, Irene O.: 165
Ballard, Irma L.: 84
Ballard, Isaac: 89
Ballard, Isaac Asberry: 111, 117, 118, 129, 130, 136, 138
Ballard, Isaac Asbury: 109, 112, 113, 120, 122, 131-133
Ballard, Isaac Edward.: 116, 128, 129
Ballard, Isaac Faust: 121
Ballard, Isaac Lonnie: 88
Ballard, Isaac Newton: 214, 259
Ballard, Isaac Tinsley: 114, 124
Ballard, Isaac Vinson: 77, 88
Ballard, Iva: 166
Ballard, Iva Jewell: 168, 180
Ballard, J. Alvin "Al": 201, 223, 224
Ballard, J. D.: 235
Ballard, J. H.: 211
Ballard, J. M.: 239
Ballard, J. S.: 113
Ballard, J. W.: 177
Ballard, J. Walker: 68, 69
Ballard, Jack: 152
Ballard, Jackson: 76
Ballard, Jacob "Jake": 32
Ballard, Jacob Howard: 22
Ballard, James: 75-77, 79-93, 95-108

Ballard, Lucy: 90
Ballard, Lucy: 245
Ballard, Lucy "Mae" Gray: 163, 172
Ballard, Lucy A.: 157, 159, 167
Ballard, Lucy A.: 16
Ballard, Lucy Ann: 157, 163, 170
Ballard, Lucy K.: 92
Ballard, Luke Linnis: 230
Ballard, Lula Catherine: 83, 104
Ballard, Lula Evelina: 118
Ballard, Lula Katherine: 103
Ballard, Lum: 79
Ballard, Lumsden: 96
Ballard, Luna: 122
Ballard, Lural Jettra: 136
Ballard, Luther Andrew: 142, 144, 145
Ballard, Lydia Ioma: 71
Ballard, Lyman: 133
Ballard, M. A. H.: 14
Ballard, M. M. L.: 256
Ballard, Mabel Elizabeth: 22
Ballard, Mabel Wilder: 92, 108
Ballard, Mable Grace: 46
Ballard, Mae Elizabeth: 232
Ballard, Maggie: 25
Ballard, Maggie: 50
Ballard, Maggie: 149
Ballard, Maggie Beatrice: 229
Ballard, Magnolia E.: 118
Ballard, Mahala Jane: 116
Ballard, Malachi C.: 34
Ballard, male: 59
Ballard, male: 60
Ballard, male: 240
Ballard, Malinda: 150, 151
Ballard, Malinda: 21
Ballard, Malinda: 21
Ballard, Malinda: 152
Ballard, Malissa: 20
Ballard, Mamie: 177
Ballard, Mamie Susan: 50
Ballard, Margaret: 206
Ballard, Margaret: 22
Ballard, Margaret: 237
Ballard, Margaret: 124
Ballard, Margaret "Mattie": 181
Ballard, Margaret A.: 16
Ballard, Margaret Adele: 105
Ballard, Margaret Adeline: 203
Ballard, Margaret Hill: 42
Ballard, Margaret Katherine: 76
Ballard, Maria: 19
Ballard, Mariah I.: 77
Ballard, Mariam Mary: 65, 70
Ballard, Marian Benton: 45
Ballard, Marian Ernest: 13

Ballard, Marion Ernest: 26, 42, 43
Ballard, Marion Hubert: 229
Ballard, Marion M.: 113
Ballard, Marjorie: 172
Ballard, Marshall: 40
Ballard, Martha: 61, 64, 65
Ballard, Martha: 15
Ballard, Martha: 115
Ballard, Martha: 112
Ballard, Martha: 36
Ballard, Martha: 46
Ballard, Martha A.: 200
Ballard, Martha A.: 80
Ballard, Martha A.: 182
Ballard, Martha Adeline: 204, 229
Ballard, Martha Ann: 18
Ballard, Martha Bellah: 76
Ballard, Martha C.: 192
Ballard, Martha E.: 235
Ballard, Martha Elizabeth: 230
Ballard, Martha Elizabeth "Lissie": 65, 69
Ballard, Martha Emma Lou: 224
Ballard, Martha Estelle: 237
Ballard, Martha F. " Mattie": 60
Ballard, Martha Frances: 194
Ballard, Martha J.: 200
Ballard, Martha J.: 38
Ballard, Martha Jane: 75
Ballard, Martha Jane: 19
Ballard, Martha Jane: 117
Ballard, Martha Jane: 113
Ballard, Martha Jane: 104
Ballard, Martha Jane: 125
Ballard, Martha M.: 116
Ballard, Martha M. "Mattie": 210, 250, 251
Ballard, Martha Nancy: 79, 80
Ballard, Martha S.: 81
Ballard, Martha Vollie: 222
Ballard, Martin: 76
Ballard, Martin: 153
Ballard, Martin Luther: 225
Ballard, Martis Oliver: 227
Ballard, Marvin: 93
Ballard, Marvin Conrad: 169
Ballard, Mary: 7
Ballard, Mary: 58
Ballard, Mary: 192, 196, 214
Ballard, Mary: 193
Ballard, Mary: 200
Ballard, Mary: 38
Ballard, Mary: 38
Ballard, Mary: 201
Ballard, Mary: 92
Ballard, Mary: 98
Ballard, Mary: 183
Ballard, Mary: 265

Ballard, Mary: 259
Ballard, Mary A.: 58
Ballard, Mary A.: 150
Ballard, Mary A.: 80
Ballard, Mary A. E.: 61
Ballard, Mary Adelia: 85
Ballard, Mary Alice: 114, 123, 124
Ballard, Mary Alice: 172
Ballard, Mary Ann: 8, 16
Ballard, Mary Ann: 195
Ballard, Mary Ann: 15
Ballard, Mary Ann: 257
Ballard, Mary Ann Elizabeth: 60
Ballard, Mary B.: 147
Ballard, Mary Caldonia "Donnie": 142
Ballard, Mary Catherine: 192, 201
Ballard, Mary Catherine: 199, 217
Ballard, Mary D.: 212
Ballard, Mary Dene: 133
Ballard, Mary E.: 117
Ballard, Mary E.: 112
Ballard, Mary E.: 77, 85, 86
Ballard, Mary E.: 209
Ballard, Mary E.: 129
Ballard, Mary Elizabeth: 76
Ballard, Mary Elizabeth: 233
Ballard, Mary Elizabeth: 237
Ballard, Mary Elizabeth: 227
Ballard, Mary Elizabeth: 177, 178
Ballard, Mary Elizabeth "Libba": 105
Ballard, Mary Elizabeth "Lizzie": 171
Ballard, Mary Ella: 92
Ballard, Mary Ellen: 216
Ballard, Mary Elma: 225
Ballard, Mary Emmaline: 239
Ballard, Mary Ethel: 180
Ballard, Mary Etta: 19
Ballard, Mary Etta "Mollie": 82, 101, 102
Ballard, Mary Evelyn: 160
Ballard, Mary F.: 128
Ballard, Mary Frances: 204, 228
Ballard, Mary J.: 60, 63
Ballard, Mary J.: 218
Ballard, Mary Jane: 116, 127
Ballard, Mary Jane: 158
Ballard, Mary Lena: 108
Ballard, Mary Louella: 118
Ballard, Mary Ollie: 140
Ballard, Mary Orzilla: 144
Ballard, Mary S.: 94
Ballard, Mary S.: 138
Ballard, Mary Sue: 53
Ballard, Mary Sue: 52
Ballard, Mary Susanne: 17
Ballard, Mary Weldon: 79, 96, 97
Ballard, Mary Willie: 161

Ballard, Matilda "Mattie" Lou Emma: 203, 227, 228
Ballard, Matilda Caroline: 17, 35
Ballard, Mattie: 23
Ballard, Mattie: 84
Ballard, Mattie: 166
Ballard, Mattie: 88
Ballard, Mattie Lois: 226
Ballard, Mattie Maye: 248
Ballard, Maud: 121
Ballard, Maude: 182
Ballard, Maude: 149
Ballard, Maude: 42
Ballard, Maude C.: 163
Ballard, Maude Victoria: 82, 100, 101
Ballard, Maudie Jane: 130, 136, 138
Ballard, May: 93
Ballard, Meeky: 199, 217
Ballard, Melvena: 113
Ballard, Melverdia: 125, 134
Ballard, Melvil: 179
Ballard, Merrell: 258
Ballard, Mickey: 223
Ballard, Mildred: 264
Ballard, Mildred E.: 173
Ballard, Mildred Frances: 179
Ballard, Miles: 157-159, 161-172, 174-177, 179, 180
Ballard, Miles Lafayette: 157
Ballard, Millard Coleman: 250
Ballard, Millard Fillmore "Mid": 210, 249
Ballard, Milledge: 183
Ballard, Miller Calton: 93
Ballard, Millie: 221
Ballard, Millie: 258
Ballard, Milton Mae: 49
Ballard, Minerva Lorena: 172
Ballard, Minnie: 211
Ballard, Minnie: 183
Ballard, Minnie: 31
Ballard, Minnie: 36
Ballard, Minnie: 144
Ballard, Minnie L.: 129
Ballard, Minnie Mary: 256
Ballard, Minnie Onnie: 242
Ballard, Minnie R.: 34
Ballard, Minnie Swanson: 153
Ballard, Miriam: 62
Ballard, Miron Job: 73
Ballard, Monna: 50, 51
Ballard, Monroe: 152
Ballard, Morgan L.: 182
Ballard, Morris Eugene: 144
Ballard, Morris R.: 192, 199, 200, 217-219, 221
Ballard, Morton: 9, 20
Ballard, Moses: 222
Ballard, Mr.: 188, 189
Ballard, Myrlte: 165

Ballard, Myrtle: 86, 87
Ballard, Myrtle: 52
Ballard, Myrtle: 171
Ballard, Myrtle Annie: 140, 141
Ballard, Myrtle B.: 238
Ballard, Myrtle Lee: 68
Ballard, Myrus Cecil "Toby": 103
Ballard, N. A.: 14
Ballard, Nadene Margarette: 173
Ballard, Nancy: 58
Ballard, Nancy: 112
Ballard, Nancy: 212
Ballard, Nancy: 211
Ballard, Nancy "Nannie" Elizabeth: 165
Ballard, Nancy "Nannie" Jane: 81
Ballard, Nancy Adeline: 193
Ballard, Nancy Ann: 199, 216
Ballard, Nancy Ann: 16
Ballard, Nancy Ann: 43
Ballard, Nancy Caroline: 216
Ballard, Nancy Henrietta: 31
Ballard, Nancy Jane: 16, 32
Ballard, Nancy Stella: 141
Ballard, Naoma: 165
Ballard, Naomi Elizabeth: 172, 173
Ballard, Narcissus C. "Narra": 210
Ballard, Narra: 250
Ballard, Nathan: 56, 58, 61, 64-66, 68-72
Ballard, Nathan: 135
Ballard, Nathaniel Harrison: 22, 42
Ballard, Nathaniel Joshua: 42
Ballard, Neal: 41
Ballard, Nell: 26, 27
Ballard, Nellie: 171
Ballard, Nellie Blanche: 73
Ballard, Neppie Howington: 228
Ballard, Nettie Marcelle: 118
Ballard, Ninnie Mae: 121
Ballard, Noah G.: 225
Ballard, Nora Ethel: 248, 249
Ballard, Obediah: 9, 20, 21
Ballard, Odis Nelson: 71
Ballard, Ola Ethel: 225
Ballard, Olin Wellborne: 143
Ballard, Olive "Ollie" Vester: 255
Ballard, Olive Jenetta: 85
Ballard, Oliver: 11
Ballard, Oliver Levi: 41
Ballard, Oliver Louie: 144
Ballard, Olivia: 209
Ballard, Ollie: 211
Ballard, Ollie: 244
Ballard, Ollie James: 168
Ballard, Ollie W.: 130
Ballard, Ora Edna: 225
Ballard, Orbie James: 88

Ballard, Oressa: 178
Ballard, Orvel Otto: 71
Ballard, Osborn S.: 12, 25
Ballard, Osborn S.: 25
Ballard, Oscar: 23
Ballard, Oscar Lee: 71
Ballard, Oscar Wesley: 231
Ballard, Osker Pascal: 248
Ballard, Ossie T.: 253
Ballard, Owen R.: 196
Ballard, Pascal: 145
Ballard, Patsy: 177
Ballard, Paul: 184
Ballard, Paul: 27
Ballard, Paul: 121
Ballard, Paul Cephus: 210, 252
Ballard, Pearl: 42
Ballard, Pearl Emma Jane: 142
Ballard, Permelia: 15
Ballard, Permelia Ann: 8
Ballard, Permilia "Pam" M.: 77
Ballard, Perry Marvin: 201, 221
Ballard, Perry Roscoe: 243
Ballard, Phillip: 56-60, 62, 63
Ballard, Phillip: 58, 60, 63
Ballard, Piety: 206
Ballard, Piety "Phida" Wright: 194, 207, 208
Ballard, Piety E.: 234
Ballard, Pink Elsbery: 238
Ballard, Polly: 86
Ballard, Polly C.: 9
Ballard, Polly Susana: 16
Ballard, Porter: 27
Ballard, Powell F.: 157, 159, 160, 167-169, 177, 179, 180
Ballard, Presley Preston: 16
Ballard, Preston Greenberry: 33
Ballard, Preston Hallman: 28
Ballard, Priscilla: 192, 198
Ballard, Q. B.: 231
Ballard, Rachel: 19, 39
Ballard, Rachel Mae: 173
Ballard, Ralph: 29
Ballard, Ralph: 223
Ballard, Ralph Lee: 154-156
Ballard, Randolph: 27
Ballard, Randolph Malone: 43
Ballard, Ray: 29
Ballard, Ray: 264
Ballard, Raymond W.: 74
Ballard, Rebecca: 8
Ballard, Rebecca: 14
Ballard, Rebecca: 62
Ballard, Rebecca: 160
Ballard, Rebecca: 98
Ballard, Reese: 258

Ballard, Sera Armeta Magodlen: 142
Ballard, Sherry: 185
Ballard, Shirley F.: 136
Ballard, Silas H.: 8, 18
Ballard, Silas Joseph Hardy: 7, 8, 14-18, 27, 29, 32-37
Ballard, Silas S.: 14
Ballard, Simeon Edward: 26
Ballard, Simeon L.: 181, 182, 184, 185
Ballard, Smith: 137
Ballard, Smyley D.: 155
Ballard, Sofrona: 245
Ballard, Soloma: 195
Ballard, Solomon R.: 192
Ballard, Sophronia: 10
Ballard, Stanley: 155
Ballard, Stark Rives: 36
Ballard, Staten: 249, 250
Ballard, Stella Elizabeth: 164
Ballard, Stephen B.: 65, 69
Ballard, Stephen Lafayette: 48, 49, 51, 52
Ballard, Susan: 113
Ballard, Susan: 128
Ballard, Susan: 93
Ballard, Susan Evelina: 157, 162
Ballard, Susan Isabelle "Bell": 256
Ballard, Susannah E.: 146
Ballard, Tabitha A.: 111, 118
Ballard, Tallulia "Talley": 209
Ballard, Talton: 136
Ballard, Tellie: 50
Ballard, Temore: 40
Ballard, Temperance Tabitha: 8, 17, 36, 37
Ballard, Tennie: 210, 251
Ballard, Thad C.: 108
Ballard, Thedar Jackson: 142
Ballard, Thelma: 51
Ballard, Thelma: 74
Ballard, Thirston: 88
Ballard, Thomas: 176
Ballard, Thomas: 203
Ballard, Thomas: 150, 155
Ballard, Thomas: 257
Ballard, Thomas: 82
Ballard, Thomas: 209
Ballard, Thomas: 104
Ballard, Thomas Ashley: 225
Ballard, Thomas B.: 92
Ballard, Thomas Cleamon: 147
Ballard, Thomas Daniel: 139, 140
Ballard, Thomas Edward: 15, 29
Ballard, Thomas F.: 206
Ballard, Thomas Hardwick: 259
Ballard, Thomas Isom: 229
Ballard, Thomas Jefferson: 30
Ballard, Thomas Jefferson: 69

Ballard, Thomas Kelly: 154
Ballard, Thomas Lon: 140
Ballard, Thomas M.: 200, 219, 220
Ballard, Thomas Onzialo: 255
Ballard, Thomas P.: 221
Ballard, Thomas Parks: 204, 229
Ballard, Thomas Sanford: 194, 204, 205, 229-232
Ballard, Thomas Sanford , Jr.: 205, 230
Ballard, Thomas Victor "Vic": 83, 104
Ballard, Thomas W.: 196, 213, 255-257
Ballard, Thomas W.: 78, 91, 108
Ballard, Thomas Weir: 220
Ballard, Thomas Weldon: 75, 79, 95-97
Ballard, Thomas Weldon: 76, 82, 83, 104, 105
Ballard, Thomas William: 49
Ballard, Thomas Winfield: 48-53
Ballard, Thomas Winston: 118, 130, 136, 138
Ballard, Timothy C.: 77, 84, 85, 106
Ballard, Timothy S.: 17
Ballard, Tina M.: 237
Ballard, Tinnie: 130
Ballard, Tipson: 111
Ballard, Toby: 129
Ballard, Toby Ara D.: 234
Ballard, Tom: 10
Ballard, Troy: 132
Ballard, Troy: 177, 178
Ballard, Ursley O.: 86
Ballard, Ursula M.: 109, 110, 116
Ballard, Vada Viola: 250
Ballard, Valeta: 40
Ballard, Valton D.: 171, 180
Ballard, Van Buren: 130
Ballard, Vera: 143
Ballard, Vera M.: 74
Ballard, Vernie: 121
Ballard, Vester: 247
Ballard, Veto: 124
Ballard, Victor Herbert: 106
Ballard, Victor Hollis: 125
Ballard, Vienna Lucinda: 146
Ballard, Vila J.: 220
Ballard, Villeta Adelaide: 22
Ballard, Vinie Caroline: 165, 166
Ballard, Vinnie: 149
Ballard, Vinson: 223
Ballard, Viola Delula: 31
Ballard, Virginia "Jennie": 128
Ballard, Vivian Goodloe: 36
Ballard, Vollie M.: 40
Ballard, W. Frank: 218
Ballard, Walter Eugene: 83, 105
Ballard, Walter Eugene "Gene": 105
Ballard, Walter Houston: 205, 232
Ballard, Walter S.: 189
Ballard, Walter Scott: 158, 166, 167, 177

Montgomery, Arthur William: 232
Montgomery, Ballard U.: 233
Montgomery, Berthold Lamarr: 233
Montgomery, Ernest Edwin: 233
Montgomery, John Matthew: 232
Montgomery, Roy Glenn: 233
Montgomery, Weston Wendell: 233
Moore, Asa: 29
Moore, Gerina Caroline: 29-31
Moore, Jane: 79
Moore, Mary Amy: 129, 130
Moore, T B: 216
Morgan, Annie Mae: 32
Morgan, Effie Belle: 63, 64
Morgan, Frances: 28
Morgan, Sophia: 200
Morris, Tommie Lee: 93
Morrison, Mary Magdeline: 232
Morton, Annie Indiana: 244
Morton, Rosie Helen: 71
Moseby, Charles B.: 22
Mote, Felix: 215
Murdock, Ola Eller: 144, 145
Murphy, Emeline D.: 16
Murphy, Eugene E.: 262
Murrah, Frankie Belle: 247
Murrah, Lillie M.: 247
Murray, Maude: 114
Murrey, Elizabeth: 37
Murry, Lucy E.: 209
Myrtle, Unnamed: 96
Nance, Mona: 175
Nancy, Unnamed: 199
Nancy, Unnamed: 34
Neal, Mary Elizabeth: 228
Neighbors, Daniel Joseph: 257
Nelson, Harris: 12
Nelson, Kathleen: 42
Nester, Lurta: 87
Nichols, Andrew: 119
Nichols, David W. "Dave": 118
Nichols, Laura B.: 118
Nichols, Lauretta: 118
Nichols, Leo: 119
Nixon, Joseph J.: 45
Nixon, Lauren Tina "Tinnie" E.: 83, 84
Noeth, Mr.: 164
Noles, Effie Mae: 24
Noles, John T.: 24
Norris, Gilbert: 172
Norris, Janell: 172
Norris, Marie: 172
Northington, Mary: 124
Northington, William: 124
Norton, Betty Jane: 136, 138
Norton, Mary Lou: 137

Norton, Willie Renon: 136
Oaks, Unnamed: 185
O'Bryan, Dorothy: 231
O'Bryan, Tinsie: 231
O'Dell, Mr.: 183
Olds, John W.: 22
Oliver, Alice Ellen: 255
Oliver, Docia: 221
Oliver, James Franklin "Jimmie": 256
One, Wife Number: 109
Ophelia, Mary: 98
Orr, George Smith: 119
Osborn, Green B.: 57
Ottwell, William S.: 215
Otwell, Benjamin F.: 215
Otwell, Charles "Charlie": 215, 260
Otwell, Charles C.: 261
Otwell, Forrest R.: 260
Otwell, Hester R.: 261
Otwell, Irene Charlotte: 261
Otwell, John M.: 215
Otwell, Lena M.: 260
Otwell, Littlenton M.: 215
Otwell, Louie G.: 261
Otwell, Mary Jane: 215, 259
Otwell, Paul Lamar: 261
Otwell, Robert Joseph: 215
Owen, Tabitha: 30, 31
Owens, Emily: 31
Owens, Julliett Jetta Catherine: 120, 121
Owens, Sultie: 244
Oxford, Charles Evan: 92
P., Syble: 120
Padgette, Lemuel A.: 155
Palmer, Curtis: 50
Palmer, Martha Jane: 124, 125
Pannell, Daniel M.: 112
Pannell, George Potter: 112
Pannell, James Riley: 112
Pannell, Jeremiah J.: 112
Pannell, Levi Garrison: 112
Pannell, Lucretia: 112
Pannell, Martha Ann: 112
Pannell, Mary: 112
Pannell, Nancy: 112
Pannell, Ursley Matilda: 112
Pannell, William: 112
Papasan, Demby C.: 239
Parker, Unnamed: 182
Parker, Annie Bertha: 218
Parker, Charles F.: 230
Parker, Forrest: 182, 184
Parker, Forrest: 184
Parker, Grace: 184
Parker, John T.: 229
Parker, Margaret: 184

www.ingramcontent.com/pod-product-compliance
Lightning Source LLC
Chambersburg PA
CBHW060438110626
46523CB00042B/588